Deep Education

Across the Disciplines and Beyond

A 21st Century Transdisciplinary Breakthrough

Dr. François Victor Tochon
University of Wisconsin—Madison, USA

and

Dr. Daniela F. Busciglio
University of Oklahoma, USA

Editors

Deep University Press

Blue Mounds, Wisconsin, USA

Deep University Online!

For updates and more resources
Visit the Deep University Website:
www.deepuniversity.net

Copyright © 2017 by *Deep University Press*, Poiesis Creations LLC
Member of Independent Book Publishers Association (IBPA)

All rights reserved. Permission is granted to copy or reprint portions up to 5% of the book for noncommercial, educational use, except they may not be posted online without written permission from the publisher.

For permissions, contact: publisher@deepuniversity.net

ISBN 978-1-939755-32-2 (pb)

Library of Congress Cataloging-in-Publication Data

1. Deep Education. 2. Early Childhood Education. 3. Second Language Acquisition—Study and teaching. 4. Language Education. 5. Tochon, Francois Victor

Keywords: Deep Education, early childhood education, intercultural competence, multilingual education, peace education

Target audience: Collegiate language instructors – language education instructors – second language acquisition – field researchers – cultural studies students –graduate students - university researchers

Topics:, Deep Education, Deep Turn, deeper learning, identity engagement, multi-literacies, Deep Approach

Version 1

Cover photo: Ryan McGuire
Proofreading: Dr. Kristine M. Harrison, Dr. Daniela F. Busciglio
Translation of Chapter 10 from French: Sunny Schomaker

Deep Education® is a trademark that is licensed for high quality standards.

The publication of this research work was supported by funds provided by Poiesis Creations LLC with which Professor Tochon has financial interests and by Deep University International, a Section 509(a)(2) tax-exempt Charity of which he is the President.

Deep Education
Across the Disciplines and Beyond
A 21st Century Transdiciplinary Breakthrough

Authors

Jambul Akkaziev, University of Wisconsin-Madison, USA
Phil Bostic, University of Wisconsin–Madison
Daniela F. Busciglio, University of Oklahoma, USA
Manuel Fernández Cruz University of Granada, Spain
José Gijón Puerta, University of Granada, Spain
Merrie Koester, University of South Carolina, USA
Alexandra Lakind, University of Wisconsin–Madison
Connie Lent, University of Wisconsin–Madison, USA
Gizem Girgin, Gedik University, Istanbul, Turkey
Xiang Long, Guilin University of Electronic Technology, China
Kate MacCrimmon, University of Wisconsin–Madison
Amos Margulies, Bronx, New York, USA
Anna Nesterchouk, University of Wisconsin-Madison, USA
Shirley O'Neill, University of Southern Queensland, Australia
Harun Serpil, Anadolu Open University, Turkey
Mary Alice Sicard, University of Wisconsin–Madison, USA
Francois Victor Tochon, University of Wisconsin–Madison, USA
Tomoko Wakana, University of Wisconsin–Madison
Jianfang Xiao, Guangdong University of Foreign Studies, China.
Snezhana Zheltoukhova, University of Wisconsin-Madison, USA
Mary Zuidema, University of Wisconsin–Madison, USA

Contents

Foreword 7
Daniela F. Busciglio, University of Oklahoma

Book Highlights 11

PART I INTRODUCTION TO DEEP EDUCATION 19

1. Deep Education. 21
   Francois Victor Tochon, University of Wisconsin–Madison

2. (Auto) Biographical-Narrative Approach for a Deep Professional Development. 45
   Manuel Fernández Cruz and José Gijón Puerta, University of Granada, Spain

3. Educational Growth and the Semiotics of the Tree: Exploring the OAK as a Framework for Deep Learning. 69
   Shirley O'Neill, University of Southern Queensland

4. Foreign Language General Education and Deep Approach in China. 97
   Xiang Long, College of Foreign Studies, Guilin University of Electronic Technology, Guangxi, China

5. From Integrated English to the Deep Approach to World Languages and Cultures. 135
   Jianfang Xiao, School of English and Education, Guangdong University of Foreign Studies, Canton, China.

PART II THEORETICAL ASPECTS OF DEEP EDUCATION 167

6. Reimagining Soul Work in Deep Education within Multicultural Community-Based Educational Spaces. 169
   Phil Bostic, University of Wisconsin–Madison

7. The Parlance of Professionalism in Family Child Care: Toward a Deeper Approach in Early Childhood Care and Education. 195
   Kate MacCrimmon, University of Wisconsin–Madison

8. Mere Child's Play or Creation of Coherence? Conceptualizing Children's Dramatic Play as Life Sustaining Deep Education. 221
Connie Lent, University of Wisconsin–Madison

9. Using Freirean Ideology to Overcome a Zombie School of Thought 243
Alexandra Lakind, University of Wisconsin–Madison; Amos Margulies, Public school teacher in the Bronx, NY

10. Deep Learning in Science: An Argument for an Aesthetic Paradigm of Science Education 275
Merrie Koester, University of South Carolina

11. Toward Deep Evaluation 301
Francois Victor Tochon, University of Wisconsin–Madison

12. Application of the Deep Culture Model to the U.S. Context. 327
Tomoko Wakana, University of Wisconsin–Madison

13. Deep Symbolic Interactionism as a New Analytical Lens for Transdisciplinary Education. 357
Harun Serpil, Anadolu University and University of Wisconsin–Madison

PART III PRACTICAL APPLICATIONS OF DEEP EDUCATION 381

14. Developing Intercultural Competence at Novice Level: Deep Approach to Russian. 383
Anna Nesterchouk, Jambul Akkaziev, and Snezhana Zheltoukhova, University of Wisconsin-Madison

15. Using Web 2.0 "Deeply": Implementing Internet Technologies for Deep Language Learning. 403
Snezhana Zheltoukhova, University of Wisconsin-Madison

16. Branching Out Beyond the Standards: A Multiliteracies Framework for Deep Higher Education. 427
Mary Zuidema, University of Wisconsin–Madison

17. A Deep Approach to an Instructional Unit on Africa. 455
Mary Alice Sicard, University of Wisconsin–Madison

18. The Impact of Intrinsic Motivation through Tochon's Deep Approach: 'An Avant Garde Way of Teaching.' 477
Gizem Girgin, Gedik University, Istanbul, Turkey

19. Enhancing Agency and Autonomy through the Deep Approach in a Foreign Language Writing Classroom. 501
    Daniela F. Busciglio, University of Oklahoma, USA

20. Conclusion: Authority as the Problem and the Solution. 521
    Francois Victor Tochon, University of Wisconsin - Madison

    Contributors 539

    Glossary 546

    Deep University Press: Scientific Board Members 569

    Guide to Authors 579

    Correspondence 580

Foreword

Daniela F. Busciglio
University of Oklahoma

Upon first glance, it is evident Deep Education in the Disciplines and Beyond represents a rich tapestry of knowledge from teachers and education scholars from around the world and from different backgrounds and nationalities, races, ethnicities, all of whom are grounded in the same theoretical framework of *Deep Education* by François Victor Tochon. The Deep Education theory is the foundation of a new educational movement based on a unified, progressive framework of education and society that fundamentally believes in and supports unwaveringly the capacity, autonomy, creativity and emotional lives of the student to be nourished and flourished in inherently collaborative, social settings for pedagogical purposes. This framework moreover establishes the rationale for a revisioning of not only our students and our pedagogy but even our current and future selves. Because life itself is both process and project-oriented, the authors of this volume understand that these same principles and approaches are applied beyond disciplines and educational contexts, and are necessarily transdisciplinary. Thus it is critical that we make available our principles beliefs and values now more than ever, to instantiate critical pedagogy across and beyond disciplines, as we strive to leave the world a better place than we find it for our future and the futures of our students. The singular, most effective way to do this is, of course, through education.

As societies and technologies evolve, so must education. Yet, many, if not most education systems around the world adhere to a rigid, assembly line, reproductive, banking model of education that singularly relies on standardized testing under the assumption that all students should be learning the same types of information and that they should be able to reproduce such information lest be assumed to possess a "gap" or deficit. The very notion of our conception of students entering the classroom from a deficit prospective is not only wrong but dangerous for all involved. How can we know what students bring to the classroom and how can we build on those funds of knowledge if we do not allow for the incorporation of this and develop roles for students as curriculum builders? This suggests a fundamental and very profoundly disturbing crag in many educational systems that rely on constant testing, control, and measurement when even in the so-called "best" education systems in the world, these arbitrary and dualistic divisions of subjects and disciplines-- not to mention the arbitrary binning of students along lines of ages, sex, and abilities, to name a few categories—serve to further splinter and isolate systems of knowledge and limit ways of knowing. Furthermore, reproductive, transaction-style models of learning that overuse rote processes of learning can pin students against one another in a competitive, neoliberal style of learning that disenfranchises some and favors others. It certainly does not offer a level playing field for learners. Instead, this promotes transactional learning for the short-term, the opposite of education and learning for depth and sustainability.

Under the current waves of global orders and disorders, external "expertise" or non-expertise confirmed as sources and forces outside the realm of our control that impose a destructive will of conformity and uniformity, our responsibility lies within the capacity of our own voices to contribute to global, publicly available knowledge. It is now perhaps more so than ever a moral imperative that we use our authority with social responsibility, just as teachers do each and everyday, caring for and nurturing future members of the planet. Over these 19 chapters, researchers and teachers profoundly examine the paradoxical nature of freedom and control, authority and agency, and neoliberal classroom curriculum and pursuing healing educational ecosystems as they reflect on the dynamic, complex nature of socio-historically-situated bodies in learning environments. Within neoliberal societies that perpetuate heteronormative policies and behaviors which privilege arbitrary notions of customs (be they practices, perspectives, or products) lies the oppressing of marginalized peoples, ideas and behaviors as well as the celebration of the norm. This focus on victors and meaningful standards are inherent qualities of capitalistic systems where competition is a tool for power and control, as it pits person(s) against person(s) as an order of control and the gaining and maintaining of power. In school curriculum, this translates to standardized curricula across the school systems, districts, states and countries. This type of educational system does not promote sustainable, lifelong learning that corresponds with the unfolding of life itself.

Deep Education and the Deep Approach strive to liberate or emancipate the learner from various forms of control and effectively place ownership in the hands of the student, trusting that the student knows what is best for herself and himself. Recognizing that this requires exploration and entails "speed bumps" to realize a goal, it asks teachers to radically reconsider the type of authority they wield in the classroom by the virtue of the curriculum they design and implement as well as their own character attributes and reservoir of compassion and empathy. When discussing this type of student-centered learning, it is pertinent to note the attributes of both deep and shallow learning in order to understand the processes of mimesis and reproduction in education to poiesis. Shallow learners are characterized by their storing, memorizing and reproducing of information, of forms and signs, producing a fragmented mimesis of realities without relation to deeper theoretical constructs and paradigms manifested in and through experience. Mimesis also takes place (and arguably, it's the overall goal, intended or not) when students are seen as not thinking critically but instead using rote processes with information on language that they are required to reproduce on various assessments and checks. Deep Education and the Deep Approach always has its gaze towards self-actualization through auto-poiesis of the student, recognizing all the while the perpetual changing nature of being and becoming.

Thus, considering recent trends in the way students are being educated around the world, we understand that something has gone terribly awry and that something is missing. This book delves into the missing dimensions in order to introduce applicable approaches in forthcoming educational endeavors and applicable life experiences that resonate with educators and students in a deep way. That said, depth cannot be reified as a form of change that could simply be brought into the current system or replace our current fragmented system. Depth is not a substance, nor a "thing," and as a concept it is purposefully devoid of a particular direction, because that would defeat the purpose of such a notion in and of itself. Rather it is a form of access to the higher, sounder, more meaningful and sustainable dimensions to the status quo that fails so many students, and leaves so many educators feeling empty and unfulfilled. Thus, it is all the more difficult to introduce this notion of depth since a "deep curriculum" does not exist. But instead, there is an approach to curriculum that makes the curriculum more relevant, dynamic, authentic, and humane, and where models of authority and equity position students in control as curriculum builders.

As such, this exciting tome celebrates the scholarly work of more than 20 researcher's deep and varied interests and efforts, covering a wide range of local and global contexts consummately unified under the Deep Education theory and Deep Approach created and developed by François Victor Tochon. Reflecting their concerns for a better tomorrow, the authors of this book present a critical commentary, urging a necessary and pivotal cultural turn and integration of the physiological, the brain with the mind, the mind with the heart and body. It is not interdisciplinary that is the key to solving education's problems—it is beyond disciplines and thus it must be transdisciplinary. It is not simply developing links between other subjects or disciplines but making it mimic life around us since life is education and education is life.

Book Highlights

PART I GENERAL EDUCATION

Highlight 1

Deep Education

In his theoretical essay, Dr. Francois Victor Tochon clarifies what could be a deeper approach to education and its characteristics. The Deep Approach is a broad phenomenon that encompasses several domains. It manifests a turning point in the way we reflect on a variety of disciplines such as ecology, economy, engineering, mathematics, cross-cultural communication, psychology, and languages. The trend is influenced by semiotics–the science of meaningful signs–as an overarching discipline, process philosophy and complexity theory to address ontological dualism. The Deep Approach is an applied trend that is revolutionizing the ways we think about what should be accomplished in Education and Teacher Education, and how it should be done. It defines a move towards deeper conceptions of curricula in any disciplines and towards curriculum interconnectedness.

Highlight 2

(Auto) Biographical-Narrative Approach for a Deep Professional Development

Dr. Fernandez Cruz and Dr. Gijon Puerta's chapter develops Tochon's concept of deep approach in the field of professional development, to emphasize the need to overcome a reductive vision of training and open it to the complexity of personal situations and social interactions that allows the versatility of stories. Deep professionalism is characterized by responsibility and accountability within the dimensions of cognitive, social, moral and ethical development. The focus is placed in a situation of emancipation that overcomes other most common situation: disability and dependence in professional action, of which drift lack of social responsibility. The focus of teacher professionalization is thus extended from knowledge for intervention (practical order), to the knowledge for the analysis of the intervention (of a higher order), which makes it possible for teacher training to enable teachers to provisionally build and rebuild in a deliberative way the concepts of education and curriculum, experimenting alternatives to improve them and analysing their impact in practice. The essence of deep approach on training and professional development lies in the ability of the model to perform good practices and establish the conditions for transferring them to new professional situations of genuine, uncertain and singular quality.

Highlight 3

Educational Growth and the Semiotics of the Tree: Exploring the OAK as a Framework for Deep Learning

In her chapter, Dr. Shirley O'Neill explores the OAK tree in its ability to provide a framework for deep learning applicable to democratic learning environments. The acronym of OAK is seen as representing the values of Optimism, Affability and Knowledge and the tree is considered as a metaphor and educational semiotic for deep learning. After considering how educational semiotics is currently exerting an influence on pedagogical change the applicability of OAK to deep learning is considered on the basis of the importance of building students' capacity and the accommodation of O'Neill's (2015a) six principles of GAMMA pedagogy seen as necessary for effective learning. These are seen as operating in the context of students engaging in project-based and problem-based learning and having the opportunity and autonomy to construct their own learning pathways, a feature of Tochon's (2014) deep approach. A synthesis of the results provides a basis for the validity of OAK and suggests a framework for deep learning that interprets the oak tree and fosters educational growth within and across tailored and dynamic communities of practice.

Highlight 4

Foreign Language General Education and Deep Approach in China

In his chapter, Xiang Long articulates the concepts, development of Liberal Education, General Education, Foreign Language General Education (FLGE) and Deep Education or Deep Approach to world languages and cultures, and examines their relationships. The chapter also proposes six characters of foreign languages, and it shows how they are being applied and developed in China in the fields of foreign language education and teaching. The author points out that CAI's Academic English framework for Shanghai belongs to the domain of FLGE. Finally, Xiang Long summarizes the similarities and differences between concepts and puts forward the hope and outlook of the application to the educational approaches to foreign languages or world languages in future classrooms.

Highlight 5

From Integrated English to the Deep Approach to World Languages and Cultures

Jianfang Xiao explores integrated English (hereafter IE), an international program conducted collaboratively by some international educators. IE abides by three rationales, proposes seven teaching principles and is characterized by six beliefs in bilingual education. IE has five changes from shallow teaching to deep teaching, aiming to accelerate the developments of children's intelligence, thinking ability, and language competence. Over the past 15 years, IE has been adopted in more than fifty experimental schools and it has proved very effective. However, IE needs to develop in a deeper approach to foster learners' foreign language proficiency and increase their sensitivity to and understanding of other cultures. Furthermore, a deep approach with IAPI Model and seven instructional principles to world language education is greatly needed (Tochon, 2012), in which the teacher personalizes instructional processes in reference to a changing context and the relevance and meaningfulness of the contents and tasks chosen and developed by the students are emphasized so that learning becomes a form of engagement.

Highlight 6

Reimagining Soul Work in Deep Education within Multicultural Community-Based Educational Spaces

In this chapter, Philip Bostic argues for a re-conceptualization of the soul within community-based educational spaces; coupled with a moral obligation to initiate a work toward healing the soul by employing a deeper approach to what it means to be human. Thus, by acknowledging the manifested soul as a political entity that is invariably interconnected and sacred, this chapter proposes a human-centered ontological-epistemic framework that foregrounds the manifested soul through a curriculum that employs deep education as way to develop a way in which we are able to see ourselves in the eyes of others, regardless of our socially-constructed identities.

Highlight 7

The Parlance of Professionalism in Family Child Care: Toward a Deeper Approach in Early Childhood Care and Education

With the voices of family childcare providers noticeably absent from scholarly discussions on this topic, Kate MacCrimmon turns to her experience as a family childcare provider to critically reflect: What does it mean to be a professional family child care provider? From a poststructural perspective, she employs autoethnography to reflect upon the roles she performed including family child care practitioner, second mother, social worker, administrator, and Jill-of-all-Trades. By recounting anecdotes in each of these roles she works to uncover a deeper approach to professionalism by using a caring reflective practitioner framework. Her main finding is that by attempting to meet state requirements and her own ethics of care, she was unable to sustain high quality child care. Additionally, she argues for the primacy of professional criteria that include emotion, complexity and relationships. Finally, she found that a separate but equal professional identity and pedagogy is critical for the future of family child care.

Highlight 8

Mere Child's Play or Creation of Coherence? Conceptualizing Children's Dramatic Play as Life Sustaining Deep Education

Connie Lent explores the emergence of systems of narrative coherence and the creation of life stories through informal discourse analysis of written observations of children's dramatic play at 2, 3, and 4 years of age. She discusses select observations as examples of the early age at which children use narrative to create coherence; to mediate between reflection and action and to generate master narratives and counter-stories in the construction and co-construction of life-story narratives. The discussion aims to extend conceptualization of the value of play beyond developmental psychology understanding of play as practiced representation of symbols to achieve academic proficiency, to consider children's play through the lens of life sustaining practices and Deep Education. Implications are considered in relation to early care and education practice.

Highlight 9

Using Freirean Ideology to Overcome a Zombie School of Thought

In this chapter, Alexandra Lakind and Amos Margulies propose that the work of Freire can be an integral part of early childhood educational theory, but is often forgotten due to a prominence of a simplistic version of developmental psychology overshadowing critical pedagogy. This chapter contextualizes the work of Freire and explores the main concepts of Freirean ideology: freedom and love through dialogue and praxis. We take our inquiry across disciplinary and linguistic territories to see Freire as a leader in critical psychology, allied with influential psychological theory towards critical consciousness. Educational theory must validate the teachable heart and teachable mind through a unity based in plurality and diversity, not separateness. It is about respecting children for what they are and not for what they will be. It is committing to early childhood education as a space not to 'help' children, but to love them. Depth, to the authors, is asking questions, exploring concepts, making connections, and rooting ourselves in love.

Highlight 10

Deep Learning in Science: An Argument for an Aesthetic Paradigm of Science Education

In her chapter, Merrie Koester considers the intersections of creativity, deep learning, and ways of being science teachers and learners and proposes a model of teaching science as aesthetic inquiry. Such pedagogy is characterized by arts-infused teaching/learning performances which are metasemiotic, participatory, meaningful, and adaptive, rather than prescriptive. Today, the system of semiotic sign systems I have proposed most closely fits what is now being called STEAM education. Regardless, the metasemiotic process begins with teachers formatively diagnosing their own subject matter content knowledge, lest misconceptions be delivered in the teaching/learning performance.

Highlight 11

Toward Deep Evaluation

In American schools, the humane dimension of evaluation by the teacher has been replaced by quantitative performance assessment, which plays a political function as well in a number of countries. From a critical perspective, the validity of standardized performance testing does not deserve the place it takes in school debates. Standardized measures re-shape teaching to match the demand of the lawmakers and push instrumental reason to its extreme, as if computers could replace human agents. Standardized assessment as it is currently practiced may contribute to artificial segregation and the genocide of linguistic minorities. Standardized assessment is against everyone: it is an instrument of control at state level, an instrument of pressure against schools and school districts, an instrument propagating fear among teachers, students, and their parents. And the whole enterprise of assessment is fabricated of faulty assumptions that have migrated from the field of business and economy to the field of education. Tochon proposes a more humane and deeper approach to assessment.

Highlight 12

Application of the Deep Culture Model to the U.S. Context

What does it mean to develop intercultural understanding? Intercultural learning is often noted as a goal and a benefit of study abroad, yet defining this term can be difficult. In this chapter, Tomoko Wakana focuses on the presence of fellow international students, deep culture learning through English, and the culture of origin. She proposes that a socio-psychological school of thought, symbolic interactionism, could theoretically frame the Deep Culture Model. She does so in presenting ideas associated with international students' deep intercultural learning during their study abroad in the U.S.

Highlight 13

Deep Symbolic Interactionism as a New Analytical Lens for Transdisciplinary Education

Rejecting the shallow, inequitable, self-serving and competitive view of education, Harun Serpil calls for a deeper, more equitable, holistic and cosmopolitan perspective to analyze and improve educational phenomena. "Deep Symbolic Interactionism" (DSI) is the new perspective. The bewildering speed of information production, and the overwhelming amount of easily-accessible but "meaningless" data has made educators and learners around the globe confused and lost, aching for meaning. Wherever you go, you hear teachers complain about distracted and unmotivated students, with no real sense of direction or life-purpose. Information has become pitifully cheap and omnipresent, but wisdom has become hard to come by. DSI attempts to bridge this gap between information and wisdom in an effort to make sense of the educational phenomena we daily experience. It aims to bring some higher meaning to the conceptualization and practices of education instead of the ultimate goal of achieving personal prosperity, by drawing attention to the fact that prosperity depends on living in harmony with other world-citizens, or "cosmopolitans." Everybody seems to be aware of globalization, but yet they still seem to live as if they were above the consequences (and responsibilities) of being a global inhabitant. There seems to be an increasingly concerted effort to "remove" the human element from the educational equation. Whereas the human element might be perceived by the elites as a threat that needs to be monitored and controlled, from the DSI lens, sustainability requires serving and collaborating with others with fairness. DSI is about providing educational, holistic and humanistic tools that enable citizens to see the broader picture.

PART II WORLD LANGUAGE EDUCATION

Highlight 14

Developing Intercultural Competence at Novice Level: Deep Approach to Russian.

This chapter by Anya Nesterchouk, Jambul Akkaziev and Snezhana Zheltoukhova introduces a new approach to developing intercultural competence at the novice level of linguistic proficiency. The Deep Approach was successfully implemented in the eight-week project aiming to encourage deep cultural understanding and develop intercultural competence via self-directed project work in adult L2 Russian learners. It is argued that the Deep Approach offers an optimal framework for integrating cultural knowledge at any proficiency level and can be effectively employed by educators in a novice level classroom. By designing individualized curricula and establishing linguistic, cultural, and personal achievement goals, project participants were in charge of their learning and the process of self-actualization. The IAPI model was used as a curriculum building tool that enabled meaningful project work and facilitated autonomous linguistic and cultural exploration. This study demonstrates a successful acquisition of skills, knowledge, and attitudes essential for effective intercultural communication by novice level Russian learners.

Highlight 15

Using Web 2.0 "Deeply": Implementing Internet Technologies for Deep Language Learning

This chapter by Snezhana Zheltoukhova offers an overview of current IT trends that aim to increase the productivity and autonomy of L2 learners, while affording educators the necessary teaching support. The first part of the chapter provides an insight to the major principles of Deep Approach and the way the newest educational technologies available for foreign language learners might be applied within Deep Approach. The second part examines several experimental technology-enhanced Deep Approach teaching modules implemented in the Russian Flagship Program setting. The chapter aims to help learners and teachers alike to purposefully incorporate technology in the learning process in and out of foreign language classrooms.

Highlight 16

Branching Out Beyond the Standards: A Multiliteracies Framework for Deep Higher Education

When teaching a foreign language, a contemporary teacher might say that he or she has developed a pedagogy that follows the "communicative language teaching" method or a National Standards-based method. However, researchers recognize the limitations of these methods and have emphasized the Multiliteracies framework as a way to bring World Language Education into the 21st century. Mary Zuidema, the researcher, took a course on Multiliteracies and was intrigued by the possible practical applications of this framework to World Language Education as well as how this framework differs from instructional models taught in contemporary World Language Teacher Education programs. By attending a French 101 course that utilized the Multiliteracies framework, this researcher could see how Multiliteracies worked in practice and its translingual and transcultural applications. This researcher gained insight on how Multiliteracies differs from CLT, how Multiliteracies bridges the language-literature-culture gap, and how it aligns with the teachings of the Deep Approach.

Highlight 17

A Deep Approach to an Instructional Unit on Africa

Mary Alice Sicard's chapter outlines the plans, procedures, strategies and results of Projet : Afrique. Inasmuch as language is inextricable from its culture, deep learning is particularly appropriate in acquisition of any second language. Projet : Afrique was a class-based project whose purpose was to employ Deep Education theory in the French language classroom in order to 1) have more holistic insight into the culture of Africa, the Ivory Coast in particular, and 2) to increase acquisition of academic language in French. The project involved groups of students in a level 3 high school French class at LaFollette High School in Madison, Wisconsin choosing to investigate one of the following aspects of the Ivory Coast: geography, history, art, music, politics or linguistics. They did this through group research and also through a visit from two Ivorians, the latter of which added clarification and meaning to their learning. Through this experience, they were to demonstrate deeper understanding of West Africa and presented their findings in French to the entire group and to the African visitors. The students showed evidence of increasing in knowledge not only of their group's area of research, but that of the interconnectedness of all the groups' findings as well. Students also demonstrated increased used of French by the time the unit was finished.

Highlight 18

The Impact of Intrinsic Motivation through Tochon's Deep Approach: 'An Avant Garde Way of Teaching'

Gizem Girgin's study attempted to examine the impact of Tochon's Deep Approach on students' motivation. It involved 10 prep school students who participated in interviews. There was also a questionnaire given to 50 students who were learning English through Deep Approach for data collection. Motivation has been widely regarded as one of the most pivotal corner stones in language achievement. However, this valuable idea has not been put into practice in Turkey because external factor driven systems do not take it into consideration. Tochon's Deep Approach which puts great emphasis on intrinsic motivation can be a good means to achieve motivation in language learning. His teaching method is now being adapted and applied to native Turkish students in Turkey who want to learn English as a foreign language in prep-school before college. During this period of time, there has been an educational paradigm shift from teacher-centered to student-centered classrooms through activities including pair work, group work and role playing. Students are encouraged for self-regulation which includes metacognitive and motivational development in their learning. The result showed the relationship between teachings through Tochon's Deep Approach in TEFL and an increase in student's motivation.

Highlight 19

Enhancing Agency and Autonomy through the Deep Approach in a Foreign Language Writing Classroom

In this chapter, Daniela Busciglio discusses how teachers can use the Deep Approach (DA) in an advanced, thematic foreign language writing classroom in a study abroad setting using a democratically-negotiated curriculum and place-based research. The framework of the Deep Approach affords a consistent and paced growth of co-constructed learner autonomy and social agency that empowers students while increasing teacher autonomy, allowing students to not only choose to pursue and design writing and projects that are aligned with their own interests but also foster more accountability through peer editing and self-editing evaluation measures. Through a series of gradual, scaffolded sequences of self-reflection and review before, during, and after each writing assignment, students become better equipped to identify and correct their own errors and those of their peers without initial feedback from the teacher. Peer editing and peer meta-talk throughout the writing and editing process empowers students, permitting them the authority to micro-teach to their peers, further refining and amplifying their linguistic know-how.

Highlight 20

Conclusion. An Approach to Firstness - Authority as the Problem and the Solution

Considering recent trends in the way people are being educated around the world suggests that something has been terribly missing. The present book was to define the missing dimension and analyze means to introduce to introduce it in forthcoming educational endeavors. Depth can't be easily reified as a form of change that could simply be brought into the current system, and that would not be our intent. Depth is not a substance, it is not a "thing." Rather it is a form of access to the higher, sounder, more meaningful dimension of what is usually being done. This makes it all the more difficult to introduce as there is not really a "deep curriculum." There is an approach to curriculum that makes the curriculum more relevant, lively, authentic, and humane. In this approach, the students are the curriculum builders. The opposite of authority is agency. In Education, agency transfers authorship.

Part I

Introduction to Deep Education

1.

Deep Education

Francois Victor Tochon
University of Wisconsin-Madison
ftochon@education.wisc.edu

This theoretical essay[1] is to clarify what could be a deeper approach to education and its characteristics. The deep approach is a broad phenomenon that encompasses several domains. It manifests a turning point in the way we reflect on a variety of disciplines such as ecology, economy, engineering, cross-cultural communication, health, mathematics, medicine, physics, politics, psychology, and languages. The trend is influenced by semiotics–the science of meaningful signs–as an overarching discipline, process philosophy and complexity theory to address ontological dualism. The deep approach is an applied trend that is revolutionizing the ways we think about what should be accomplished in Education and Teacher Education, and how it should be done. It defines a move towards deeper conceptions of curricula in any disciplines and towards curriculum interconnectedness.

The concept of "depth" in education emerged from a variety of disciplines, with the recognition that continuing business as usual didn't make sense within the current state of affairs in Education. Current shallow teaching and learning practices need to be interrupted. New formats should be explored for Education at large. There are certainly new, more profound ways of understanding each discipline, and teaching and learning them. Disciplinary fields such as philosophy (Naess, 1989) and educational philosophy (Ryan & Louie,

---

[1] An earlier version of this chapter has been published in the *Journal for Educators, Teachers and Trainers (JETT)*, *1*, 1-12, 2010.

2007), ecology (Salleh, 2000), computational cognition (Ohlsson, 2011), economy (McKibben, 2007), investment (Carlisle, 2014), human resources (Newport, 2016), cultural studies (Shaules, 2007), psychology (Sternberg, 2007), ecopsychology (Roszak, 2001) and educational psychology (Berliner et al., 2007) have gone through a drastic revision of their curriculum approaches—not to speak of various other disciplines—in terms of depth of knowledge and deep reading (Roberts & Roberts, 2008). The time is ripe to introduce a new approach to Education. For a number of reasons that I explain in this theoretical essay, the new educational concept is being defined in terms of depth.

Deeper Rationale for Education: End Collective Self-Destructive Behavior

As I developed in Tochon (2010 and 2014), the rationale for the deep approach of Education is transdisciplinary. The Trandisciplinary Charter addresses the need for a global view of the human being due to the constant growth of knowledge (de Freitas, Morin & Nicolescu, 1994). The transdisciplinary project challenges "the spiritual and material self-destruction of the human species" (*Charter,* online). It considers that "life on earth is seriously threatened by the triumph of a techno-science that obeys only the terrible logic of productivity for productivity's sake". Consequently, increasing quantitative knowledge and increasingly impoverished inner identity lead to the rise of obscurantism with huge personal and social consequences. Specifically, the exponential growth of knowledge and access to it increases inequalities between the haves and have nots. "Transdisciplinarity concerns that which is at once between the disciplines, across the different disciplines, and beyond all disciplines. Its goal is the understanding of the present world, of which one of the imperatives is the unity of knowledge" (Nicolescu, 2005, p. 2). Speaking of collective self-destructive behavior and sustainability of the species may sound shocking and possibly ungrounded. It does not mean that deep education could be a salvation technique, but it posits teachers in the quest for a deeper sense of humanity and humaneness. A brief reminder of some elements that define the current world situation may explain the need to change the current ways people are being educated. There might be numerous other sound rationales, and readers might not all agree on some details of the rationale proposed. The proposal can be considered food for thought as there is not space here to fully develop the arguments and evidence.

Modern science has been developed from the understanding that objective knowledge (or the knowledge of objects) should be distinct from subjective knowledge (or the knowledge of the subject); therefore the impacts of scientific developments on the human subjects have not been considered. Material conceptions of development impoverish the planet of its resources. Such conceptions of development have generated climatic conditions that are increasingly catastrophic. The environment is destroyed in ways that places the survival of numerous species at stake. Overpopulation reaches such a point that extreme poverty and mal-nutrition affects one third of the world population. Hunger accounted for 58% of the world's mortality in 2006 (Ziegler, 2007). Malnutrition of the mother or the child is the biggest cause of child mortality, accounting for 12,600 deaths per day. Eight children die per minute from under-nutrition according to conservative measures. Instead of reducing population at the entry in educating people to reduce the number of births, so far it was deemed more profitable to operate on accelerating the exit. Wars have become a major means of feeding predatory corporations. The barrier to improvement often appears to be the economic system that focuses on the biggest and quickest profits. Because of lobbyism and the way laws and decrees are set in place, the balance between law makers, justice, and the executive has been broken. As corporate power can't be held accountable for its unethical actions, business can go on as usual for a long time until a significant number of citizens realize that the situation is insane. Such awareness raising and requirement for power-down is not 'antimodern'; it adds an integrative wisdom to both modernity and postmodernity (Gare, 2000).

We live in a world that has lost its deep values. Shallow education, misinformation, intensified work and entertainment play a key role in disabling large parts of the population from even reflecting on the situation. Interpretations of the situation vary from the metaphor of the airplane that has lost its pilot to the image of the gloomy deportation trains inexorably driven to their end by fascist regimes, which metaphors obviously refer to possible and outrageous ways of <u>not</u> coping with the immense problem of overpopulation management. Sociologists such as Beck (2006) suggest that globalization can't be democratic. Elites are preparing the shift towards a post-nuclear society in a way that may appear to many as preferable to the mess resulting from the potential of annihilation. These issues provoke deep questions (Morin & Kern, 1999). Humans don't seem to have learned how to organize themselves with harmony. Their survival, as well as the survival of their environment, is at risk.

A narrow definition of economy restricts the vision of people to material goals. It can be considered the worst possible definition of economy as it is being developed at the cost of the lives of its supposed beneficiaries. Economy has become a deadly science as it provides power and tools to the most destructive, unregulated agents on the planet (Latouche, 2005). It is time that education be recognized as the primary applied science, that is science with conscience (Morin, 1964). For that purpose, education has to go deep and be allowed to address the real issues. This survey was not meant to be scary but to indicate that it is a good time to re-think the way curricula are organized as well as their contents: we can't continue business as usual. The philosophy of curriculum must change. In the following pages, we will explore depth in education from the perspective of deep politics, deep ecology, deep economy, deep culture, and deep language.

Deep Politics

'Deep politics within schools', as Andrew Gitlin (2005) puts it, could challenge the status quo. Examining everyday politics and reconceptualizing the position of the inquirer, he was looking for means that would challenge the status quo, considering that acting on social representations might help the change process to address social hierarchies and inequalities. He found that a large part of education is assertive, in the sense that it does not tolerate critical examination but rather supports conformity, norms, standards and obedience. The goal of a deep politics of schooling would be "removing ourselves from mental slavery…and enter into a humanist inquiry project that employs imagination to foster change" (p.22). Everyday politic is grounded in ruled relations, it shapes "how we see people, our relations with those different from ourselves, and the conclusions that we draw about those relationships" (p.15). It should become the object of a constant inquiry. Some aspects of "politics of resistance" (Freire, 1970) are relevant here. However deep politics, rather than focusing on resisting the reproduction of hierarchies, centers on a freedom quest. It uses "imagination to redefine normative categories" (p.16), thereby initiating a process that can create a new terrain for equality. Thus deep politics link aesthetics with inquiry as a living process. Its commitment to social justice manifests through aesthetics to envision and create alternative imaginaries. Moral imagination provides the mythic ferment of the future, its inquiry process paints the new possibilities. Dream/critique forms political humanism and stimulates "our ethical potential to separate ourselves from the seduction of everyday politics" (p.17). It moves in the direction described by Marcuse to create "a revolutionary language that can break the spell of the established and the establishment of everyday politics" (p.18). In this process, what appears crucial is to step for a while outside one's culture to establish an ethical distance vis-à-vis everyday judgment, as conformism is imposed by a culture that uses the instruments of assertiveness to make its claim and produce authority, social hierarchies, power centralization, and delineate the margins of cultural acceptability. Deep inquiry, then, fits with "the effort to break the power of facts over the world, and to speak the language of those who establish, enforce and benefit from the facts" (Marcuse, 1960, p.x, in Gitlin, p. 18). It defines a new relationship with the world. It goes together with new, more interactional and open ways of expression. In this process, hope and love constitute non-foundational (i.e. non-universalist) foundations "at the heart and soul of humanness" (p.23).

Deep Education as a Philosophy

A philosopher named Arne Naess (1989) has developed the concept of deep ecology. Although his propositions apply closely to ecology, there is a clear connection between deep education and ecological goals. Therefore the principles of deep ecology deserve consideration here. Arne Naess was unhappy with shallow reforms. He proposed a deeper critique of human institutions and a "substantial reorientation of our whole civilization" (p. 45). The economic crisis might give us the opportunity to consider his reflections seriously. The philosophy of the deep approach is to seek "a fundamental change in the dominant worldview and social structure of modernity" (Katz, Light & Rothenberg, 2000, p. ix). It brings humanity to hard sciences and a new sense of their pragmatic potential to human sciences. Deep education concerns the whole person, it implies a sense of purpose and deep, transformational learning (O'Sullivan, 1999). Deep identity affects personal and professional decisions and choices as well as ideals and action. It is connected with environmental identity which influences decisions throughout life and is itself related to cultural identity (Sessions, 1993; Fisher, 2002). Environmental problems can be considered cultural phenomena and expressions of the consumer culture (French, 2000; Jacoby, 2003). Thus deep education involves a sense of one's deep identity (Jardine, 2004). The deep sense of human identity refers to who we are and how we see our role in relation to the world, the biosphere and the semiosphere, which is the world of meaningful acts. Deep education transforms the biosphere into 'semiosphere'—a world of meaningful signs—and creates a meaning-making environment for action. This transformation entails a sense of connection that manifests in values and actions (Thomashow, 1995). The transformation inherent with deep education supports a healthy environment "through an identification so deep that one's own self is no longer delimited by the personal ego or the organism. One experiences oneself to be a genuine part of all life" (Naess, 1989, p. 20). One consequence of this inclusive understanding is that people start perceiving the environmental damage, wars and destruction as if they were done to themselves (Macy, 1991). The sense of connection to the world and the earth precludes the behaviors and decision making that impact the environment (Berry, 1999). The sense of separation from the world and the earth is related to the harm we do to the social and physical environment. It is part of the consequences of the subject/object split. The barriers that consumer culture erects between us and the natural world is one major cause of environmental destruction (Merchant, 1992). This is an aspect to which teachers must be made sensitive (Kentel, & Karrow, 2007). Deep Education promotes a philosophy of curriculum that explains and addresses the current stakes and that requires a deep transformation of humans and human society in the direction of greater harmony.

Deep Learning

Harmony defines a homeostatic goal that defines personal and social balance. It emerges from individual and collective efforts. Deep education is significantly related to an intention to understand deeply. Deep understanding characterizes deep learning (Akbar Hessami & Sillitoe, 1990). The focus is on what is signified, and the arguments proposed, with a linking process to prior information and to everyday experience (Morgan, 1993). Studies in higher education defined a deeper way of reading texts for learning (Marton and Säljö, 1976; Biggs, 1993; Entwistle, 2000). Research on learning styles deciphered deep differences in the way learners approach texts. Ramsden (1992) contrasted the Deep and Surface approaches. Surface learning focuses on forms and signs, while deep learning focuses on meaning. Deep learning links new knowledge to prior knowledge across various fields while surface learning memorizes unrelated parts. Surface learning associates facts and concepts without reflection while deep learning relates theoretical concepts to daily experience. The emphasis is external and fragmented for the surface learners as it relates to the demands of assessment, while it is internal and holistic for the deep learner.

Deep knowledge has different dimensions (Sandberg & Barnard, 1997): it is good to know multiple models and multiple viewpoints in the domain of study; to know about the relations between models and viewpoints; and in the reasoning procedures to solve problems; and the principles to solve new, unfamiliar issues. But there is much more. Nowadays educational psychology has a hard time imagining depth. The reason is that researchers probably want to avoid falling in the trap of deep psychology, which has been associated with psychoanalysis. It overinterpretive insights were either sexually oriented or based on mythic grounds that are in disagreement with current trends, based on the cognitive transformation of the behavioral stimulus-response into if-then procedural connections across mental models. Thus psychology should reinvent depth. Sociocultural, socioaffective, ecological and philosophical understandings allow deep learners to connect the dots and transcend the limited framework of cognitive psychology. Deep processing involves a re-conceptualizing of how reality is viewed (Bradford, 2001). In contrast, surface learning is task-oriented and is based upon extrinsic motivation. Surface learners store and reproduce information while deep learners attempt to grasp meaning with the aim of transforming the material provided (Säljö, 2003). Among the factors that contribute to a deep approach, the philosophy of learning has a tremendous importance. You learn best what you feel you need to know and what you learn is life-supporting and may enhance society and the world at large. Striving for knowledge is a major characteristic of deep learners (Atherton, 2005). It determines the way of perceiving new knowledge. Therefore theorizing plays a key role in a deep approach to learning. As well, deep learning defines a situation in which the teacher is not the only source of inspiration and knowledge (Rhem, 1995).

Deep Teaching

Deep learning is sustainable and requires a different style of teaching. Some researchers have started working on the transfer from a deep conception of learning towards a deep approach to teaching (Tochon & Hanson, 2003; Wilson Smith & Colby, 2007). This transfer defines sustainable education (Warburton, 2003). Indeed deep education requires self-sustainable learning. Hargreave & Fink (2006) define its dimensions: learning has to matter for deep understanding to happen; the deep learning system must last and spread across disciplinary domains; deep learning is energizing and doesn't burn out teachers, it doesn't harm the environment; quality is linked to variety rather than standardized forms of expression; deep teaching honors the past and develops wisdom for the future. These elements are key to active participation, capacity building and accountability within learning communities (Halbert & Kaser, 2006). Deep learning "engages students intellectually, socially, and emotionally" (…); it "goes beyond temporary gains in achievement scores to create lasting, meaningful improvements in learning" (ibid, p. 8). Therefore, suggest Hargreaves and Fink, if standards are considered normative, they may be the enemies of sustainability. In deep education, standards define processes rather than products.

Deep teaching is learner-centered. It builds on the intrinsic motivation of the learner, authentic documents, and new information technologies when appropriate, conditional to integrating philosophical depth in their processing. Deep teaching is based on meaningfulness for the learner and is project-based. To teach life-meaningful contents to students, the teacher needs to know what is meaningful to them and discuss meaningfulness in life. Learning and teaching have to meet life-goals. The approach is contextualized and situated. Meanings are embodied in action. Deep education supports alternative conceptions of development such as subjective development. Indeed the concept of development in modern society can lead to a regression in human potential and values, as we are witnessing today.

No significant change can occur in education unless we confront the conception that supports the current shallow practices. Parroting information is not equivalent to acquiring knowledge and proficiency. Teachers who adopt shallow teaching cover the program, even though they realize that students do not understand and not much will remain of it. Low educational practices rest upon assumptions that Paul (1995, p.276-277) has refuted: "shallow" teachers assume that "students learn how to think when they know what to think". They believe "that knowledge can be given directly to students without their having to think it through for themselves". The storage metaphor prevails, as if the head was a computer they fill with data. Other assumptions of teachers that Paul characterizes as "shallow" include the beliefs that "quiet classes with little student talk are evidence of student learning" and "students gain significant knowledge without seeking or valuing it". Such teachers think that "material should be presented from the point of view of the one who knows". For them, program coverage is the most important, as they believe that "superficial learning can later be deepened". Shallow teachers share the assumptions on which shallow testing is based, that "students who correctly answer questions, provide definitions, and apply formulae demonstrate substantial understanding".

In contrast, those who would qualify as "deep teachers" understand and value higher order education. They hold a very different set of assumptions (Paul, 1995, p. 277):

- depth is more important than coverage: students learn what to think as they learn how to think;
- knowledge is gained through reflective engagement in action;
- education is the process of gathering, analyzing, synthesizing, applying, and assessing value-laden information;

- classes with student talk focused on life issues, is a better sign of learning than quiet classes focused on a passive acceptance of what the teacher says; students gain significant knowledge only when they value it;
- subject-matters should be related to experiences, life values, and viewpoints; students may give correct answers, memorize definitions and apply rules while not understanding the materials.
- shallow learning can be an obstacle to deep understanding.

Sustainable education is transdisciplinary (Nicolescu, 2008). Such a reflective approach characterizes transformative education in contrast to transmissive education. Transmissive education is instructive and instrumental; its information-focused training is oriented on products and based upon facts, small tasks and skills. In contrast, transformative education builds concepts and capacity: it is energized by intrinsic motivation and is grounded in ownership of action. Being process-oriented, it involves responsive world-view reframing (Sterling, 2001). It promotes individual and group work on actual, real-life situations and real-world problems. Deep teaching as well as deep learning involves reflective practices and theory-driven considerations. It integrates ethics, is politically active and aims toward social justice. It proposes non-obtrusive collaborations, working across cultural communities.

Deep Linguistics

Noam Chomsky (1965) has become famous for proposing that language and meaning processes are directed by a deep structure that generates surface expressions through a number of transformations. Lakoff (1973) mentioned that in a number of cases, Chomsky's grammar missed its goal for a 'deep reason': it didn't take into account that language is used by humans to communicate in a social context. Pragmatics was not part of the vision. Syntax is dependent on reasoning and the social and cultural assumptions of the speakers. Therefore depth should be understood as "rooted in the study of human thought and culture" (p. 3). It relates to applied semiotics rather than the abstraction of permanent and immovable universals with absolute, decontextualized rules of transformation. The clash between meaning and form only exists in dualistic ontology. Meaning and form are integrated in daily use within communicative situations.

The idea that there is depth in language that may cause transformations in behavioral rules has been transferred to psychotherapy. We have to question whether such dimensions of deep linguistics should—or not—be integrated into deep education. Deep linguistics or transformational linguistics uses language powerfully to change learners at the deepest level through suggestion and altered states of consciousness. It is being used by therapists to help patients modify their deepest passions, emotions and drives in a conversational way while they are unaware of it happening. Patients agree to the process and thus informed consent is ensured. Politicians use deep linguistics and suggestion to create mindless adherence. The topic deserves attention only insofar as it serves the autonomous purposes of the learner, and the instruments used are clearly described for what they are. Such motivational instruments must not be used unless the approach also includes critical thinking. Critical awareness will analyze logically and filter information. In this respect, the issue for the teacher and the educator is very similar to issues raised by taxonomies of socio-affective goals: as long as the learners are free to choose their own goals and are made aware of the approach, they can keep their autonomy. Critical distance is welcome in a deep approach as what is underlying it is the concept of empowerment. Teachers and educators must keep on questioning their own practices to assess in what way they are supporting or, to the contrary, restricting the freedom of the learner in the long run. The long term is what counts in the deep approach. This is not to say that anything could go in the short term if long term goals are reached. Educators must keep with the principle, dear to Gandhi, that the means used influence the attainment of the goal. The conversational suggestions induced by educators can only be ethical if it is genuine and helps consenting students to eliminate the inner constraints that would otherwise prevent successful learning, not in the terms of the teacher's goal but in terms of their own goals.

Deep Principles

In Education, one can have the feeling that one lacks specific materials for dealing with many problems; such as teaching for a specialty, internationalizing education, or being effective in foreign language teaching. Little by little, one comes to realize that the problems cannot be solved on a merely technical and disciplinary level exclusively. A holistic, human approach must be taken. Here are some principles for action that characterize deep education (Tochon & Hanson, 2003, p.31):

- Action is taken with the persons involved; they participate voluntarily and freely. The approach has an eco-cultural, philosophical dimension. It is based upon projects.
- The action is not focused on a theory or on the transmission of knowledge, but rather on resolving day-to-day problems.
- The approach is thematic and bottom-up: the themes are chosen by the participants as time goes on.
- One does not begin with the presupposition that any one environment is superior to any other: what is at issue is the relationship between people concerned with education.
- Lessons are organized on the principles of meaningful conversations (Bruner, 1990; Walsh, 1997), moderated by people with knowledge of the context. Conversations relate to real-life cases and are semi-structured around a theme.
- Participants are conducting reflective research on their own actions. The action includes regular formative evaluations intended to improve its relevance and better meet participants' needs.
- To achieve deep, lasting learning, students are engaged on many levels-emotional, physical, spiritual, and cognitive (McLeod, 1996).

For example, the taxonomy of Krathwohl, Bloom and Masia (1964) is one of the known classifications of affective goals for the purpose of instruction. It could guide some aspects of deep education as long as the learners are free to choose the instructional contents and themes within an ethical framework. This taxonomy is linked with the psychological principle of internalization that is, "the process whereby a person's affect toward an object passes from a general awareness level to a point where the affect is internalized and consistently guides ... the person's behavior" (Seels & Glasgow, 1990, p. 28). There have been initiatives to create a deeper sense of what teaching should be. For Giuliano (2008), deep teaching takes learners on "a journey from recognition and responsibility to reassessment and the creation of profound change in one's daily life". It is based on critical thinking and "non-patriarchal approaches reasoning". The "learner is challenged to think and to understand diverse cultural, social, and intellectual perspectives and to perceive the natural world as an intimate and integral part of our lives". Here are other aspects of deep teaching:

a) It resolves the performance-competence dilemma and is transformational.

b) It is built on life grammars, crosscultural pragmatics, and cultural 'beams of meaning' (Tochon, 2002).

c) It implies a deep understanding of what it means to be a learner and take responsibility for one's learning.

Deep teaching implies "deep professionalism" (Ulrich, 2000, p. 18). It is characterized by

- Awareness of the judgments on which positions rely, limiting claims accordingly.
- Responsibility, enabling the professional to deal with the consequences that are imposed on third parties; when it comes to assessing boundary judgments; no one can claim a special advantage of competence over all others concerned.
- Ethical competence and self-questioning.

- Responsible citizenship, following one's conscience rather than group pressures toward conformity.
- Emancipating ordinary people from the situation of incompetence and dependency in which professional action frequently puts them.
- Clarification that what counts as knowledge is a question of what we want to count as knowledge.

Professional competence has to do with competent citizenship; it depends on it.

The Deep Turning

In this essay, sources from different fields helped establish a new concept for education, highlighted in the title of the article. This is not to say that 'depth' has the same characteristics in politics, economy, philosophy, ecology, sciences, and educational psychology. The interpretive frameworks may have differed in various disciplines. What is being proposed here is to consider the common ground that characterizes depth as a new field of investigation for education and curriculum theory. It is the philosophy that is crucial and will inform the new curricula. Here are a few principles that stimulate, support and explain the deep turning in Education. They are derived from Naess's principles (Devall & Sessions, 1985):

- The well-being and flourishing of life on Earth, both human and non-human, have value in themselves. Such values are independent of the usefulness of the non-human world for human purposes.
- Richness and diversity of life forms, languages and cultures contribute to the realization of these values and are also values in themselves.
- Humans have no right to reduce this richness and diversity except to satisfy vital needs.
- The flourishing of human life, life forms, languages and cultures is compatible with a voluntary, substantial and harmonious decrease

of the human population for the purpose of preserving our limited resources. The flourishing of non-human life requires such a decrease. Voluntary power-down will help creating sustainable living conditions.

- Present human interference with the non-human world is excessive, and the situation is rapidly worsening and must be taken care of by international regulations, that should translate into educational policies and curricula.

- Policies must therefore be changed. These policies affect deep economic, technological, and ideological structures. The resulting state of affairs will be deeply different from the present. Peoples need to be educated to accomplish the expected result.

- The ideological change is mainly that of appreciating life quality (dwelling in situations of inherent value) rather than adhering to an increasingly higher standard of living. There is a difference between big and great.

- Those who subscribe to this philosophy have a moral obligation directly or indirectly to work in the direction of implementing the necessary changes. The disciplines taught in schools must integrate these principles in their curricula and pedagogy.

Applying deep principles aims at raising the level of consciousness of peoples and bringing forth different kinds of governments. Humans are confronted with a choice that Korten (2006) described as, on one hand, the Unraveling with a collapsing environment, violent competition for limited resources, a dieback of the population with a takeover of those who remain by local warlords or, on the other hand, the Turning from imperialism to Earth community, a possibility if we move to a 'politics of consciousness' (p. 43). It consists in moving up from the *magical consciousness* of people living in dream-like state directed by emotional impulse. Moving out of self-referential and narcissic *imperial consciousness*, with its primitive sense of justice based on enforcement and retaliation, conforming to the will of authority figures. *Socializing consciousness* to share ethical rules of conduct in society, we can internalize cultural norms as well as a sense of community. A sense is developed that security depends upon mutual loyalty. Caring individuals realize what the group interests are and collaborate in this direction. *Cultural consciousness* then emerges, when the rationales of others can be appreciated in their difference, with the understanding that cultures are social constructs and represents different 'truths'. It constitutes the moral ground for cultural change. The highest expression of this quest for humanity would define *spiritual consciousness*, which "manifests the awakening to Creation as a complex, multidimensional, interconnected, continuously unfolding whole" (p.47). The transition from cultural consciousness to spirituality would come from the search for deeper, original meanings related to profound encounters with others, each meeting with otherness representing a thorough lesson that gradually increases the awareness that we are connected. Cultural consciousness as well as spiritual consciousness act in favor of a society that is more just, peaceful and mature.

There are some risks at using such heavily connoted wording as 'spiritual consciousness raising' in the context of education (Crossman, 2003). One risk is a return to dualistic stands proper to Platonism; another risk is the resurrection of such elevated educational ideals within obedience networks, which would be just at the opposite of the goal of the present demonstration. Speaking of mindfulness and depth—and meaning it—sound appropriate wording. The word 'depth' should be understood as a continuum rather than an opposition to what 'light' or 'surface' curricula may have been. The directions taken by many disciplines so far have been led by a superficial view of their responsibility towards the world at large and the planet, the humans and the various species who live on it. The deep approach implies a change in scientific ontology. Its integrative ontology does not split the subject from its objects. It takes into account the impacts of the development of objective results on the human subjects, as both subjects and objects are one with their ecosystem. Second, it implies that science and education must shift from a view that is in the main quantitative to creating a world in which quality prevails as evaluated on the scale of deep human values such as social justice, ecological respect, fair information and communication, truthfulness, care for others, intrinsically motivated effort towards improvement, non-interference unless requested. Krathwhol et al.'s (1964) taxonomy provides a valuable orientation if the learners are free of their choices. It reminds social actors (teacher may not always remember that they *are* social actors) that the character of the means determines the character of the results. This rule applies to teaching as well: surface strategies to maintain extrinsic motivation in the learners do not do good in respect to the deeper goals of education.

Caveat

In this introduction to Deep Education, a few words of caution are necessary. The deep approach is not a 'method'. It is all about mindset and action. When human situations are reshaped into words, categories and classifications, a dimension is being lost that readers must recreate through their own experiences. Deep education is defined within the dynamics of living while this essay is in static wording. Concepts imply reductions, reifications and contradictions. Conceptual constructions have flaws, and often lack coherence whatever the efforts made to present a clear, logical line of arguments. Deep education is something people want to live and work for. It is never fully achieved, it is always in the making, and depends upon situations.

Another warning relates to methodological language. Such language gives an appearance of neutrality and objectivity but should not hide that methods are framed within philosophies. Teaching methods have been compelling in making teachers believe that they could apply certain methods to reach certain goals, and the framework was supposed to be neutral. Actually specifying goals for schools and for classroom learning implies value choices. Evaluating results is all about valuing certain tasks and devaluing others. Many teachers have become 'instrumentalists' in the sense that they never question the underlying framework for the methods they enact. They just have to apply the 'right' methods to reach the 'right' results, they were told. This was a wonderful way to maintain the status quo and perpetuate a society that may now appear as self-destructive. Nobody questioned the philosophy behind assessments. However, since Aristotle humans have been warned by numerous philosophers that restricting the motives of action to technical rationality is unrooted thinking, which may have devastating side-effects. Instruments, methods, strategies do not suffice to reach higher humane goals. Philosophy and theoretical wisdom must guide reflective practice, and only then should we start thinking about what instruments might be appropriate. Many methods of teaching seem backward in this respect, if only they would aim at certain wisdom of action. Here we will start from the philosophical rationale, to which the deep approach is subordinated. There won't be many *do*s and *don't*s here, but a philosophy with a duty tempered by reflection to enact it in the schools for the sake of working in the direction of our sustainability and fulfillment as a species.

References

Akbar Hessami, M., and Sillitoe, J. (1990) Deep vs. Surface Teaching and Learning in Engineering and Applied Sciences. Victoria University of Technology, Footscray.

Atherton, J. S. (2005). Learning and Teaching: Deep and Surface learning. UK. Retrieved on September 6, 2007 from
http://www.learningandteaching.info/learning/deepsurf.htm

Beck, U. (2006). *Power in the global age*. Malden, MA: Polity Press.

Berliner, D., Senemoglu, N., Yildiz, G., Dogan, E., Celik, K., & Savas, B. (2007, August). Approaches to learning and study skills of Turkish and American students in colleges of education. Paper presented at the EARLI Conference. Budapest, Hungary, August 31st, 2007.

Berry, T. (1999). The great work: Our way into the future. Bell Tower, New York: Random House.

Biggs, J. (1993). What do inventories of students' learning process really measure? A theoretical review and clarification. *British Journal of Educational Psychology, 83*, 3-19.

Bradford, K. (2001). Deep and Surface Approaches to Learning and the Strategic Approach to Study in Higher Education; Based on Phenomenographic Research. Retrieved on September 6, 2007 from http://www.arasite.org/guestkb.htm

Bruner, J. (1990). *Acts of meaning*. Cambridge, MA: Harvard University Press.

Carlisle, T. E. (2014). *Deep Value. Why Activist Investors and Other Contrarians Battle for Control of Loosing Corporations*. Hoboken, NJ: John Wiley and sons.

Chomsky, N. (1965). *Aspects of the Theory of Syntax*. Cambridge: The MIT Press.

Crossman, J. (2003). Secular Spiritual Development in Education from International and Global Perspectives. *Oxford Review of Education, 29*(4), 503-520.

Freitas (de), L., Morin, E., & Nicolescu, B. (1994). *Charter of Transdisciplinarity*. Adopted at the First World Congress of Trandisciplinarity, Convento da Arrábida, Portugal, November 2-6, 1994. Retrieved from: http://basarab.nicolescu.perso.sfr.fr/ciret/english/charten.htm

Devall, B., & Sessions, G. (1985). *Deep Ecology*. Salt Lake City, UT: Peregrine Smith.

Entwistle, N. (2000, November). *Promoting deep learning through teaching and assessment: conceptual frameworks and educational contexts*. Paper presented at TLRP Conference, Leicester, Great Britain.

Fisher, A. (2002). *Radical ecopsychology: Psychology in the service of life.* New York: SUNY Press.
Freire, P. (1970). *Pedagogy of the oppressed.* New York: Seabury Press.
French, H. (2000). Vanishing Borders: Protecting the Planet in the Age of Globalization. Available for download at: http://www.worldwatch.org/pubs/books/15/
Gare, A. (2000). The postmodernism of deep ecology, the deep ecology of postmodernism, and Grand Narratives. In Eric Katz, Andrew Light and David Rothenberg (Eds.), *Beneath the Surface: Critical Essays on Deep Ecology* (pp. 195-214). Cambridge, Massachusetts: MIT Press.
Gitlin, A. (2005). Inquiry, Imagination, and the search for a deep politic. *Educational Researcher, 34*(3), 15-24.
Giuliano, J. A. (2008). *Deep teaching.* Retrieved on January 15, 2008 from: http://drjackie.freeservers.com/deepteach%20workshop.html
Jacoby, K. (2003). Crimes Against Nature: Squatters, Poachers, Thieves, and the Hidden History of American Conservation. Berkeley, CA: University of California Press.
Jardine, E. A. (2004). Narrative Inquiry into the Formative Aspects of Ecological Identity. Antigonish, Nova Scotia: St. Francis Xavier University.
Halbert, J., & Kaser, L. (2006). Deep Learning: Inquiring Communities of Practice. *Education Canada, 46*(3), 43-45.
Hargreaves, A., & Fink, D. (2006). *Sustainable leadership.* San Fancisco: Jossey Bass.
Katz, E., Light, A., & Rothenberg, D. (2000). *Beneath the Surface. Critical Essays in the Philosophy of Deep Ecology.* Cambridge, MA: MIT Press.
Kentel, J. A., & Karrow, D. (2007). Mystery and the Body: Provoking a Deep Ecology through the Situated Bodies of Teacher Candidates. *Complicity: An International Journal of Complexity and Education, 4*(1), 85-100.
Korten, D., C. (2006). *The great turning. From Empire to Earth community.* San Francisco: Berrett-Koehler, Kumarian.
Krathwohl, D., Bloom, B. & Masia, B. (1964). *Taxonomy of educational objectives. Handbook II: Affective Domain.* New York: McKay Company.
Lakoff, G. (1973). Deep Language. *The New York Review of Books, 20*(1), February 8, 1973. Retrieved on October 18, 2008 from nybooks.com/articles/9956
Latouche, S. (2005). *L'invention de l'économie (The Fabrication of Economy).* Paris: Albin Michel.
Macy, J. (1991). *World as lover, world as self.* Berkley, California: Paralax.
Marcuse, H. (1960). A note of the dialectic (Preface). *Reason and Revolution.* Boston: Beacon Press.
Marton, F., & Säljö, R. (1976). On qualitative differences in learning. I. Outcome and process. *British Journal of Educational* Psychology, 46, 4-11.
McKibben, B. (2007). *Deep economy. The wealth of communities and the durable future.* New York: Times Books, Henry Holt.

McLeod, A. (1996). Discovering and facilitating deep learning states. *The National Teaching and Learning Forum, 5*, 1-7.

Merchant, C. (1992). *Radical Ecology: The Search for a Livable World*. New York: Routledge.

Miyao, Y., Sagae, K., & Tsujii, J. (2007). Towards framework-independent evaluation of deep linguistic parsers. In Proceedings of GEAF, pages 238-258.

Morgan, A. (1993) Improving Your Students' Learning. London and Philadelphia: Kogan Page.

Morin, Edgar (1964). *Science avec conscience* (Science with Consciousness). Paris: Seuil.

Morin, E., & Kern, A. B. (1999). *Homeland Earth*. Cresskill, NJ: Hampton.

Naess, A. (1989). *Ecology, community and lifestyle*. New York: Cambridge University Press.

Newport, C. (2016). *Deep Work. Rules for Focused Success in a Distracted World*. New York: Grand Central.

Nicolescu, Basarab (2005). *Towards Transdisciplinary Education and Learning*. Paper presented at the Metanexus Institute for the 'Science and Religion: Global Perspectives' Conference. Philadelphia, PA, June 4-8, 2005.

Nicolescu, B. (2008). *Transdisciplinarity: theory and practice*. Cresskill, NJ: Hampton Press.

Ohlsson, S. (2011). *Deep Learning. How the Mind Overrides Experience*. New York: Cambridge University Press.

O'Sullivan, E. (1999). *Transformative learning: Educational vision for the 21st century*. New York: University of Toronto Press.

Paul, R. (1995). The critical connection: Higher order thinking that unifies curriculum, instruction, and learning. In Jane Willsen & A. J. A. Binker (Eds), *Critical thinking: How to prepare students for a rapidly changing world* (pp. 276-277). Santa Rosa, CA: Foundation for Critical Thinking.

Ramsden, P. (1992). *Learning to teach in higher education*. New York: Routledge.

Rhem, J. (1995). Deep/surface approaches to learning: An introduction. *The National Teaching & Learning Forum, 5*(1), 1-4.

Roberts, J., & Roberts, K. (2008). Deep reading, cost-benefit, and the construction of meaning: enhancing reading comprehension and deep learning in sociology courses. *Teaching Sociology, 36*, 125-140.

Roszak, T. (2001). *The voice of the earth, an exploration of ecopsychology*. Grand Rapids, MI: Phanes Press.

Ryan, J., & Louie, K. (2007). False dichotomy? 'Western' and 'Confucian' concepts of scholarship and learning. *Educational Philosophy and Theory, 39*(4), 404-417.

Säljö, R. (2003). *Laering i praksis - et sociokulturelt perspektiv (Learning and praxis: a sociocultural perspective)*. Götenburg, Sweden: Hans Reitzels Forlag.

Salleh, A. (2000). In defense of deep ecology: An ecofeminist response to a liberal critique. In Eric Katz, Andrew Light and David Rothenberg (Eds.), *Beneath the Surface: Critical Essays on Deep Ecology* (pp. 107-121). Cambridge, Massachusetts: MIT Press.

Sandberg, J., & Barnard, Y. (1997). Deep learning is difficult. *Instructional Science, 25*, 15-36.

Seels, B., & Glasgow Z. (1990). *Exercises in instructional design*. Columbus OH: Merrill.

Sessions, G. (1993). Deep Ecology as Worldview. The Bucknell Review, 37.

Shaules, J. (2007). *Deep culture. The hidden challenges of global living*. Buffalo, NY: Multilingual Matters.

Sterling, S. (2001) Sustainable Education: re-visioning learning and change. *Schumacher Briefing No.6*. Dartington: Schumacher Society, Green Books.

Sternberg, R. J. (2007). *Wisdom, Intelligence, and Creativity Synthesized*. New York: Cambridge University Press.

Tochon, F. V. (2002). *Tropics of teaching*. Toronto: University of Toronto Press.

Tochon, F. V. (2010). Deep Education. *Journal for Educators, Teachers and Trainers (JETT), 1*, 1-12. http://jett.labosfor.com/index.php/jett/article/view/6

Tochon, F. V. (2010). A Deep Approach to Language Multimedia and Evaluation: For a more Colorful Future. Invited Keynote Speech. *Proceedings of the Fourteenth international conference of APAMALL and ROCMELIA* (pp.73-92). Kaohsiung, Taiwan: National Kaohsiung Normal University.

Tochon, F. V. (2011). Deep Education: Assigning a Moral Role to Academic Work. *Educaçao, Sociedade & Culturas* (Education, Society and Cultures - University of Porto, Portugal), *33*, 17-35.

Tochon, F. V. & Hanson, D. (2003). *The Deep Approach: World Language Teaching for Community Building*. Madison, WI: Atwood Publishing.

Thomashow, M. (1995). *Ecological Identity*. Cambridge, MA: MIT Press.

Ulrich, W. (2000). Reflective practice in the civil society: the contribution of critically systemic thinking. *Reflective Practice, 1*(2), 247-268.

Walsh, D. J. (1997). Educateurs et parents: un point de vue personnel (Educators and parents: a personal viewpoint). In F. V. Tochon (Ed.), *Eduquer avant l'école. L'intervention préscolaire en milieux défavorisés et pluriethniques* (Educating before school: Early intervention in multiethnic, poverty settings, pp.151-166). Montreal, Paris & Bruxelles: Montreal University Press and DeBoeck University.

Warburton, K. (2003). Deep learning and education for sustainability. *International Journal of Sustainability in Higher Education*, 4(1), 44-56.

Wilson Smith, T., & Colby, S. A. (2007). Teaching for Deep Learning. *The Clearing House, 80*(5), 205-210.

Ziegler, J. (2007). *L'Empire de la honte* (The Empire of Shame). Paris: Fayard.

2.

(Auto) Biographical-Narrative Approach for a Deep Professional Development

Dr. Manuel Fernández Cruz
Dr. José Gijón Puerta
University of Granada, Spain

Tochon (2010) has developed the concept of deep approach of the educational processes convinced, like us, that human situations are formed and transformed into words and stories rather than categories and classifications. We apply this concept to the field of training and professional development, to emphasize the need to overcome a reductive vision of training and open it to the complexity of personal situations and social interactions that allows the versatility of stories.

From the perspective of Ulrich (2000), the "deep professionalism" is characterized by responsibility, allowing the professional to face the consequences of their actions, to the extent that has been confronted with his personal vision of performance, and with their dimensions cognitive, social, moral and ethical. Therefore, the focus is placed in a situation of emancipation that overcomes other most common situation: disability and dependence in professional action, of which drift lack of social responsibility.

If the focus of teacher professionalization is extended from knowledge for intervention (practical order), to the knowledge for the analysis of the intervention (of a higher order), then is possible that teacher training take like backbone, the depth of analysis of the own professional action, enabling teachers to appropriate the necessary theoretical elements to provisionally build and rebuild in a deliberative way the concepts of education and curriculum, experimenting alternatives to improve them and analysing their impact in practice. The essence of deep approach on training and professional development lies in the ability of the model to the performance of good practices and to establish the conditions for transferring them to new professional situations of genuine, uncertain and singular quality.

New Directions in the Training of Education Professionals

The important social, political, economic and educational changes in the last 15 years have affected the trend of training and development internships of professionals of education and the subsequent research approaches in this area. Some of the main changes concern to the demographic structure of developed societies and their impact on national policies, the rise of the global economy and the subsequent economic crisis and the emergence of new political movements, including social and educational policies. Among these new educational guidelines we find the emergence of standards for evaluation, conducting international comparative reports, policies of privatization of public services, which have severely affected the educational service, the markets pressure on education systems to generate new curriculum reforms and the spreading of the culture of quality in social organizations.

Along with these changes of social order, the support to reflection and educational research has generated new approaches that have greatly influenced the trends of the training of the professionals of education.

For us, it was heartening to know the perspective of deep education that Tochon (2010) has reconceptualized for two reasons. First, by the closeness we have with Professor Tochon, who in 2010 was invited as scholar in the Erasmus Mundus Master Program – Mundusfor- coordinated by the University of Granada and it was in our city where he drafted the manuscript of his article and it was published in the first issue of our Journal for Educators, Teachers and Trainers. Second, because his reconceptualization of this deep approach largely connects with the (auto) biographical-narrative approximation in which we have been working for over twenty years.

In an effort to upgrade our own vision of professional development and to complete it with the deep approach, we wrote this article, which collects previous ideas, we order our discussions and talks on the matter, and reorganize information and we facilitate it to our postgraduate students interested on it, like us, to grant an added value -which exceeds the idea of technical professionalization-to the concept of professional development. It's what we call Deep Professional Development.

We have understood the deep professional development from the integration of three educational trends emerging at this time: the concern for quality, sustainability and deep education. We have considered whether to reconcile these three trends, with our (auto) biographical-narrative approach to describe professional development as an approximation of quality, sustainable and deep. Finally, we have recovered the characteristics that Hopkins and Sterns (1996) already anticipated about the meaning of educational professionalism, to widen them with the essence of what we consider to be deep professional development.

Concern for Quality

After years of implementation of the quality culture, it seems that we have reached an agreement that teacher quality is an essential element for the educational systems but are still at odds over what teachers' quality is and what are the teaching features related to the desirable educational results. Regarding the quality of education, the present-day scene seems marked by five major trends: increased attention to teacher quality; change in the demographic profile of the school population and the lack of criteria for allocating educational funding to address the growing diversity; criticism of traditional teacher education programs with increasing pressure to demonstrate their impact on students' learning; the multiplicity of agendas to focus the reform of initial teachers' training programs; and discussed predominance of the sciences of education as a presumed solution to educational problems.

Moreover, there is consensus to consider that the quality of teachers is a significant difference in students' learning and overall school effectiveness. Politicians, administrators and researchers use the term "teacher quality" to refer to the critical influence of teachers on the students' learning (Rose and Gallup, 2003). The belief that the demand for high educational standards to the system and the existence of measurable goals can improve individual educational outcomes; this led the United States Senate to the approval of the proposal No Child Left Behind Act under which teachers' quality could reach all students demanding a high school teacher qualification that should be achieved by highly qualified training and professional development programs. However, the proposal has failed to unequivocally define what teaching quality is.

For the scientific community the concept of teacher quality is becoming operational in two possible ways: measured in terms of academic achievement of the students or measured in terms of professional qualifications attained by teachers themselves. Both ways are not mutually exclusive but obviously are not similar.

For those placed in the first approximation to the concept, as Hanushek (2002, p.3), "good teachers are those that improve the academic performance of students in their classes" and bad teachers those who get the opposite results. For Rivers and Sanders (2002), a good teacher is the single factor that provides added value to the students learning from its previous performance and considering contextual factors such as class size, cultural background or socioeconomic status. As we see, both definitions materialize the concept of teacher quality in terms of students´ performance.

The second conceptual approach refers to clearly to the professional qualification of teachers-even so it is expected that this professional qualification influences on the improvement of the students' performance-. That is, students learn more with teachers who have certain professional features: aptitudes, knowledge, skills, competences, etc. The problem is to determine and measure clearly what are those characteristics that are on the basis of teachers' quality, although there are many suggestions that venture to offer the keys of this quality. It is the example of Kosnick and Beck (2009) who found the key to educational success in mastering the seven principles considered necessary for the success of educational programs: proper planning, formative assessment, careful class management, strengthening of inclusive education, attention to the discipline subject and pedagogical knowledge, professional support to the process of identifying and facilitating a broad view of education.

In parallel to the development of the culture of evaluation by standards, it has been growing dissatisfaction with the results of traditional teacher's training programs. This widespread dissatisfaction has a historical origin in the lack of consensus on key issues about the school itself and the role of education. Education authorities are suspicious about the processes of initial certification of teachers and demand changes in the curricular structure of their academic programs and its contents, leaving those curriculum components that are not based on scientific evidence and require higher levels of certification.

This represents a significant pressure for teachers' educators and a demand to conduct an investigation of the impact on the validity of teachers' education programs and their effectiveness in improving the academic performance of the students.

While the inclusion of initial training programs for teachers in the university systems led us to speak of an age (80's and 90's) of marginalization of the sciences of education within universities and, therefore, scientific research. The truth is that, in the last 20 years, we have seen that with the access of a new generation of teachers of higher education in educational studies and teachers' training programs, submitted to assessment practices and standard professional accreditation processes among university instructors and the need to focus their professional growth on peer review scientific research, the sciences of education have started to abandon their extreme marginalization within the social sciences.

It is true that educational research has had to acquire a conceptual framework that has nurtured of theoretical formative references of teacher's training programs at the expense of contents more related to professional skills and competences. Progress has been remarkable and now we are in a position to require the research on sciences of education to create a methodological apparatus which allows establishing causal correlations between training and professionals' development and students' academic results and the educational system. That's our concern for quality.

Sustainability Perspective as a Trend

Sustainability in training and professional development is revealed as one of the major emerging educational trends. The interest of bringing the new sustainability trends emerging in the field of environment and in the field of the economy to the field of training, are not alien to the boom in the studies of economic and political nature in education.

We, present, summarize and recreated based on Hargreaves and Fink (2006) proposals this new trend based on the following principles:

(a) Depth. In training and development we must preserve, protect and promote the fundamental purpose of deep learning for the development of a profession beyond the immediate assessments that do not measure the real impact in practice.

(b) Length. Change and sustainable improvement in training and development have continuity in time beyond the succession of agents and training leaders.

(c) Width. Change and sustainable improvement in training and development require leadership to be distributed in the school both to know precisely the extent and form of leadership itself that is already exercising, and to determine, intentionally, the form and degree of leadership that can be achieved.

(d) Justice. The training activities that produce sustainable development will not cause any harm or damage to persons or institutions and improve in a short time the nearest environment; they have no meaning by themselves, but in their achievements. They are socially fair.

(e) Diversity. Training and sustainable development promote cohesive diversity in teaching and learning while it creates a network of connections among its components.

(f) Resources. Formative and sustainable change and improvement increase human and material resources, they never reduced them. They recognize and reward the talent of organizations since its inception. They concern about their professionals making them look after themselves and their colleagues. They renew the energy of the people. They do not exhaust their professionals fussing them with continuous implementation of innovative methods or setting unrealistic dates for achieving a change or improvement. Sustainable change and improvement are achieved by acting prudently and providing adequate resources; never wasting resources and wearing people out.

(g) Conservation. Sustainable training and development are based in the past and try to preserve the best of it in order to create a better future situation.

This being so, the role of professional development models is to support and provide resources to institutions, provide support to achieve the objectives and foster adequate social environments as well as to ensure effective monitoring and launch it with responsibility.

Deep Education

Convinced, like us, that human situations are formed and transformed into words and stories rather than into categories and classifications, Tochon (2010) has developed the concept of deep education that we apply to professional development, to put the emphasis on the need to overcome a reductive vision of training and open it to the complexity of personal situations and social interactions that allows the versatility of the stories. The application of the deep education to professional development should, in principle, allow to:

(a) Adopt a philosophical and eco-cultural, project-based dimension, where professionals integrate voluntarily to pursue goals freely chosen and who motivated by improving their professional performance, as they conceive it.

(b) Adopt a practical dimension so that the training focuses not on theory or in the transmission of knowledge, but rather in solving everyday life problems.

(c) Admitting that the approach is thematic and bottom-up, admitting also that topics are chosen by the trainees as they progress in their development process to address their particular performance in the unique conditions in which it occurs.

(d) Advance from the assumption that there is not professional intervention strategy morally superior to any other, because what is in question in education is the relationship between the people concerned and, at most, of what can speak is of honest and effective professional performance of the people involved in certain contexts.

(e) Recognize that training and development are organized under the principles of the development of stories, the questioning and the exercise of meaningful conversations moderated by facilitators who know the context. The stories, inquiries and discussions refer to real life cases and professional practice.

(f) Encourage participants so they can make a reflective inquiry about their own actions.

(g) Ensure deep training and sustainable development, causing the participants to be involved in activities that stir them emotional, physical, moral and cognitively.

(h) Include regular formative assessments to improve the relevance of the processes and meet the needs of professionals better.

Ulrich (2000) anticipated that "deep professionalism" is characterized by responsibility, which allows professional to face the consequences of their actions, since they are confronted with his personal vision of the performance and its cognitive, social, moral and ethical dimensions. Therefore, the focus is placed in a situation of emancipation that overcomes more frequent situations of disability and dependence on the professional action, from which the lack of social responsibility drifts.

The essence of Deep Approach on training and professional development lies in the ability of the model to perform good practices and to set transfer conditions thereof.

The study of good educational practices and its transfer problems are at the forefront of efforts to improve education. Benavente and Panchaud (2008) analyze the minimum conditions necessary for a good practice to have an effect and transfer on educational policies. In their study, the authors set questions like: How can you learn from good practices? How its transfer can become the strength of the plans to improve educational organizations and academic results? Under what conditions? Can good practices really influence educational policies to administrative and educational levels? And a central problem of teaching practices is its availability in formats that can be coded, recognized, revised, distributed and subsequently transferred.

But this problem in the chain of coding-recognition-review-dissemination and transfer, had already been addressed (although it is true that from other research interests) from those studies on the metaphor of the teacher as the builder of curricula in the 90's in which it was intended to find the missing link in the chain that gears educational research and teaching improvement. The problem of the spread of this knowledge, derived from the educational research and its use in practice to improve the teaching has been tried to be resolved in several ways, aware that only an increase in quantity and quality improvement of the possible dissemination channels that have not solved the problem. Moreover, most of the experiences of incorporation of faculty to collaborative research networks, comprising both specialist and teachers themselves, have opened a good and efficient way of transfer of knowledge generated in research to the practice but this has not been enough. The problem, then, would not reside on the difficulty to transfer knowledge about teaching, but in the separation between practical thinking and formal or higher thinking that the tradition accumulated in teacher' s training and curriculum development has kept.

Therefore advocating for a new stage of educational professionalization around training for the construction of the curriculum is to admit that professionals should not give up in maintaining a higher-order knowledge about his professional activity, and therefore the inquiry into their practice is an effective way of building higher-order knowledge that allows professionals reaching a unique position to be the architect of the improvement of their teaching. It is about defending a more global concept of teachers' professionalism involves mastering a reflective competence for teaching related to skills of inquiry, self-assessment, systematic observation, simulation and collaboration to practice improvement contrasting with other technical, dominant, and certainly more limited vision, focused exclusively in the domain of knowledge for the intervention.

If the focus of teachers' professionalization is extended from knowledge for practical intervention to knowledge for the analysis of the intervention of a higher order, just then it is possible that teacher s' training adopts curriculum development at schools as the core itself facilitating teachers to take ownership of the theoretical elements necessary to build provisionally and rebuild deliberative the curriculum, experiencing improvement alternatives and analyzing their impact in practice. As a field of professionalization, curriculum development requires a reorientation -contextualized, flexible, dynamic of the underlying assumptions that animate the curriculum- of educational, psychological, epistemological and social character in teaching practices, that being consistent with the general educational objectives should materialize reflexively in the best possible proposals for action at all times and in every context.

The consideration of the teacher as a professional, as a person and as an adult, makes its education in regards with professional development to be understood as a personal appeal from his teaching experience, which is able to follow a process of appropriation and integration of this experience, his practical knowledge of the elements of the institutional context in which it operates and its universe of meanings, consistent with his life story and as a projection of their improvement. Our thesis is that the stories about the school and the teachers are narrative images of the teaching-learning relationships that act as privileged platforms to facilitate teachers understanding of classroom situations at the same time that reveal understanding to those with access the story. For them, the curriculum is nothing but the experience in the classroom and its narrative reconstruction- that is the story. The cognitive power of narrative gives stories such a force that puts them in an intermediate position between personal development and practical knowledge and that other higher-order knowledge which gives the status of teachers' professionalism.

Moreover, studies on professional knowledge and teachers teaching skills have allowed generalizing a number of topics that affect the conceptual structure of the teaching profession itself. The evidence does not allow keeping a steady sense of professionalism over the time. The idea that the initial training does not end with the aim of having taught the basic tools of the profession is validated, but they are acquired during the period of education in the context of practice. The schemes of professional performance do not appear out of nowhere with the start of the teaching, but are shaped through the pre training experience and initial training and are affected by a process of teaching socialization understood as the social conditioning of professional performance patterns.

The (re) construction of professional performance schemes is a situational process in which the interpretation of each unique situation, in the light of performance schemes formed beforehand, creates new modes of action valid in the practical context of reference. The development model could follow a cycle in which understanding, interpreting, teaching, evaluating, reflecting and new understanding, are the cognitive processes that enable the emergence of a new structure of knowledge adapted to the social conditions of practice which include "objective" aspects -fines immediate goals, long-term goals, contextually relevant values, social responsibility and "subjective" aspects of teacher identity–self-perception, need for acceptance in the group, need for success with the students, security, etc.. Thus the new action scheme replaces the previous one.

(Auto)Biographical Narrative Approximation as a Sustainable and Deep Model of Quality

The approach (auto) biographical narrative, we have extensively described in various publications, has been revealed as an approach to combining the new trends of quality, sustainability and depth of the training and development of the professionals of education.

Depth and Legitimacy

Previously we have stated (Fernandez Cruz, 2010) five issues that act as organizers the of the approach and that in one way or another have been present in most of the studies reviewed about the biographical method (Roberts, 2002; Miller, 2005): (1) What is the state of development of the research on teachers' education and what can the biographical approach provide? (2) Is it useful and legitimate to access to teachers' life introspectively? (3) Does the personal casuistry emphasized from the biographical-narrative approach help or hinder the process of professionalization of the teaching community? (4) Does the understanding of professional motivations of the education professionals provide criteria to refocus educational policies? (5) Do experience stories are an adequate support for the transfer of good teaching practices? (6) What are the immediate challenges of the approach?

The first one is a prior question whose answer must justify the use of the (auto) biographical narrative approach. The second of the issues raised can be considered "classical" in the discussion, argument and conceptual construction of the (auto) biographical narrative approach on which we do not expect a clear and definitive answer, however we consider appropriate to start reflecting on the approach providing the vision we have generated in these twenty years of experience. The following two questions also refer to key aspects always latent among those who use the approach and critically review it. The proper correspondence between the individual and the collective, self-interest and community interest, the particular and the social, will be behind the answers that we are able to offer. Reflection on the fifth question forces us to focus the debate on the use of the approach beyond mere intellectual exercise to connect to the uses and benefits it may have for improving education. The discussion on the final question should lead us to suggest a development agenda of the (auto) biographical narrative approach in the specific area of training and development of professionals of education.

The biographical approach of teachers' professional development tried to join the proposed conceptual apparatus of the biographical method with the interest for studies on the professional lives of teachers, which has gained strength in the field of sociology and has been used by scholars of teaching.

The problem of interfering in the private lives of teachers is served from the beginning. And the moral problem of this interference is also linked from the origin, the use and the legitimacy of the biographical approach as it has been widely connected to studies on school change management. We use the grouping made by Butt and Raymond (1989) of three blocks of questions to be answered from the research on teachers' professional life: (a) Substantial requirements-What are the key aspects of teachers' knowledge interpreted at this stage of his/her professional and personal life and in the current context? What forms do they take? What are the main elements of the current personal and professional context of teachers? What are the main elements of the past professional and personal lives of teachers that are relevant to their professional knowledge? (B) Training Issues -How do the elements of the current context modeling the knowledge of teachers and their expressions interact among them? What are the major sources of influence on the teaching knowledge of past experience? How are the elements of the past perceived by teachers and how do they influence the formation of their professional knowledge? How are the backgrounds of the current situation narrated? What are the crucial episodes of life, in which new lines of activity are based and which new aspects of him/herself were provided? How and why? And (c) issues related to the context -What interactions with the context are problematic? How is the life of a teacher with them? Which interactions have issues that require continued resolution? Are they of a dialogic or dialectic nature? In which interactions is there a significant degree of congruence between person and context?

Research accumulated over the past twenty years has been offering contextualized answers –never general but contextualized never definitive but provisional- to many of the questions asked. We have desired with our research to provide answers to some of the questions raised and we considered useful the results obtained and disseminated. Still, we always left the question of the legitimacy of certain practices of biographical research that are never to be defended by their usefulness. All this despite of always taking into consideration the three ethical principles of the procedure prescribed for making life stories: the principle of respect for personal autonomy; the principle of confidentiality; and the principle of justice.

Improving teaching as the last orientation of educational research does not justify, by itself, the use of biographical approach. The legitimacy of the approach must be sought for in the specific and contextualized consideration of the specific interests of the teacher who provides evidence of his professional and personal life, so as a first source of authorization. The overall legitimacy is reached when the focus is based on the level of connection between the individual professional interests and common professional interest of improving teaching. Understanding they are not matching fields we do expect to have a good intersection space in which researcher and teacher can move comfortably using the biographical approach to provide useful knowledge for the individual and the collective.

Basis and Assumptions

The basis of the approach links with the auto ethnography because although it focuses preferably on the narrative production of professional experience as an essential technique, it refers to its relevant issues according to Hughes, Pennintgton and Makris (2012):

(a) The autobiography allows reformulate relevant social problems as referred to meanings that people give to events that may influence the development of training problems, or how the vision of a problem or phenomenon of interest evolves over the time; or how multiple qualitative standards may support or constrain opportunities to articulate and reformulate the root of the problems and the distribution of resources or the symbols and the language of training speeches, or how various aspects of the formulation of research problems allow researchers specify and become familiar with the circumstances of a given context.

(b) The autobiography facilitates informed discussion and elaboration of criticism from the evidence shown or technique or techniques used.

(c) The autobiography provides multiple levels of critical analysis, including self-criticism, pointing out privileges or penalties, and allows selection of schemes and classifications of units for analysis.

(d) The autobiography provides opportunities for analysis and interpretation of evidence from credible narratives and is connected with the investigation of the self and of course, the professional him/herself.

In short autobiography joins the epistemological and methodological history of interpretive research as a political act, socially fair and socially aware in which a researcher as well as a trainer or a recipient subject and protagonist of the self-training uses narrative principles to make and write stories as a method and as a product.

The basic assumptions upon which the approach is based are the following (Fernandez Cruz, 2006):

(1) Since their initial training and throughout his entire career, changes in knowledge and identity of professionals are produced. They appear not only in response to critical incidents in the area of his/her personal life strictly private, or in his professional life, which brings together private and public interests, but also

changes that are the result of experience, the cumulative effect of training activities and the evolutionary development itself, or all integrated into a whole. We can call it changes due to progressive maturity.

(2) Changes in maturity affect professionals with whom they interact regularly and with whom a professional niche, in a reciprocal effect, is shared so we can assume that there is a social dimension of maturational change that allows us to understand the why professionals working together generate, also together, a language and a cultural interpretation code of professional purposes, the validity of the practices, the processes of interaction with the public and other processes relevant to the exercise of profession.

(3) Thirdly, one can speak of a universal dimension of change promoted by the personal appropriation of the historical events that affect the professional group and the social progress interpreted from the own keys of the life cycle in which they are installed and which allow us to establish common phases in professional development that affect universal and generationally to successive cohorts of professionals from the different groups.

Based on these basic assumptions that inform of an individual dimension, a social dimension and a universal-generational dimension of professional growth and maturity, the (auto) biographical-narrative approach is revealed as one of the most desirable methods of intervention in the training and continuous development of professional.

Immediate Challenges

The agenda of the development of the (auto) biographical-narrative approach for the training and development of education professionals should allow arguing and nurturing a new discourse that does not reduce the findings of the investigation to a sort of subsidiary academic knowledge of the advances of the professional learning in competences -and that can be tendency-. Against that, we must assume the complexity of the processes of professionalization as an educational problem requiring its own agenda and autonomous research and best practices; the biographical approach gives us possibilities, supplemented with other research models, should facilitate key tasks for the construction of the field of study as we have discussed here and have recently argued (Fernandez Cruz, 2007):

(a) It is necessary to further advance in the research on professional identification processes, both in the individual aspects of identification and in the collective aspects.

(b) We must generate more powerful models for assessing the professionalization to ensure social control of public education services through of teachers' training and professional development improvement process

(c) Similarly, to collect and disseminate examples of good training practices deepening on the mechanisms of innovation, adoption, contextualization and internalization of external proposals.

(d) It will be important to settle a teaching language as a vehicle of professional communication for the teaching community to help the transfer of good practice.

(e) Boundaries between the speech of higher education and practical training of professionals must be removed, transferring to the University all the knowledge and effective training models in vocational training accumulated.

(f) With the biographical approach we will continue to study the social and working conditions of the teaching practice in all areas, levels, subjects and contexts.

(g) It is required to improve ties with the social, cultural and institutional agents that will use the available knowledge generated by this research.

After twenty years of experience in the application of the approach with speculative approximations in most cases, we are now opening a new era to create a dual research / intervention practice to facilitate the improvement of education from the preferable angle of improving the training and development of professionals.

The (auto) biographical narrative approach gives us an effective method of diagnosis including personal situations in their socio-professionals contexts, which can become illustrative of collective behaviors and ways of understanding and engaging with the teaching profession contexts. All data that guide the implementation of political objectives established arise from periodic evaluations of statistical character through comparative reports carried out by international agencies. But clearly, these reports lack the necessary illuminating aspects for understanding what will be the interaction of teachers with the measures applied, their degree of compliance with them and their acceptance and collaboration, the degree of internalization and cultural appropriation.

The (auto) biographical narrative approach (and we have experience of it), it is valid not only as a diagnostic method, but also it becomes an effective method of training intervention because it has the ability to reveal,, the actors themselves and for actors themselves the essential core of training based on experience, the building of the teaching knowledge, the objectification of personal practice and its contribution to the consolidation of a collective professional knowledge which is what is demanded from the research on teachers' training and the necessary guidelines on training policies.

Characteristics of Deep Professional Development

The study of quality standards, its evaluation and certification in the practice of a profession, has been studied under the concept of professionalism. There are any studies appearing in recent years about the professionalism in education trying to offer a set of features from which address the training and development of teachers to help them achieve higher levels of professionalism.

In this sense, and based on a classic study of Hopkins and Sterns (1996), we have been developing a catalog of features with which now we want to characterize what we call deep professional development. These features, which are the basis for achieving a genuine educational professionalism, are: true educational commitment with students; domain of instructional knowledge; reflective capacity; and teamwork competence.

Real Educational Commitment

Professional commitment is based on the attitude of the educator that allows him/her to direct the work towards a valuable social and educational achievement of which is responsible. A goal beyond the specific objectives pursued when teaching a particular topic of the program or when delivering a training unit.

On the one hand, the educational commitment is manifested in concern for the student. The commitment exceeds the learning objectives of the material itself and is in the orbit of the sense that school or training experience has to student development, for future, for life beyond the training period. It is a commitment to the educational impact of the training experience makes each student. A commitment that individually, from the standpoint of matter and from the perspective of human relationships in the classroom, teachers must acquire, but obviously you overcome and must be accompanied by a collective commitment that the educational impact is the result of entire school experience and responsibility of the whole educational team. But watch out, the joint responsibility should not mask the personal responsibility that each teacher has with each of the students who share precious time educational relationship (Fernandez Cruz, 2006).

Studies on the evolution of professional concerns of teachers report, persistently, that the concern guiding teaching activities during their first years of teaching is the class management command. Unless there is an effective training action, only among expert teachers emerges what the critical professional concern should be: the impact of educational activities. It is for this reason that these teachers confess that one of the greatest rewards of their work lies in the realization of how and how much they have contributed to the formation of young or adult people who had as a students at school. The existence of this educational commitment improves the vision that teachers support about what is good teaching and even the kindness criteria of certain teaching practices, such as adaptation to diversity or evaluation.

But commitment is not only with the student. It is also a commitment of social nature leading to expert teacher to consider not only the impact of their teaching in private lives of their students, but in improving somehow future society, despite all the difficulties and contradictions, he is helping to build. From this commitment, the subordination of the learning objectives of the subject to the general objectives of education, or the introduction of cross-cutting themes in their own educational discipline are therefore deep professionalism criteria.

Instructional Knowledge

The mastery of the subject in the classroom not only requires understanding the discipline it also requires good education professionals to develop their own instructional knowledge of the discipline they teach. A instructional knowledge, characterized by Shulman (1986), which is not acquired during initial training but in theoretical contact practice and therefore should be taught in the training and development plans. This instructional knowledge of the content is the most genuinely kind of knowledge for teachers in the sense that it incorporates a professional skill- the transformation of academic knowledge into teachable content-, which may characterize the professional work of the teacher. It is composed of four essential elements: the understanding of the subject, learning to think about the subject matter from the perspective of the student, learning to represent the content of the subject and, finally, learning to organize students for learning the subject.

Therefore, the instructional knowledge of the content requires a deep knowledge of how students learn; knowledge of aids and teaching resources; knowledge of instructional strategies and processes in relation to the discipline; and knowledge of the final goals of the teaching the subject. In short, this is a knowledge, which enables the teacher to organize the academic content in a comprehensive education speech for the students.

The whole process described has three basic implications to establish professionalism criteria. First, not just the mastery of the subject but also good teachers develop a instructional knowledge of the content of the subject matter that allows them to offer an education of quality. Second, there is not a unique method for teaching the subject. So we understand that good professionals flexibly use diverse and varied methodologies to mediate between students and knowledge, adapting its intervention to contextual peculiarities and specific educational needs of students and group of student. Third, mastery of the instructional knowledge enhances teaching and its flexibility; it develops with experience in practice although not only practice guaranties its development.

Reflexivity

Quality educators should be, cooperatively, involved in reflexive actions to address the possible change in training from alternative perspectives that the current ideological, legislative and administrative conditions, towards improving education. This is the capacity for reflection or reflexivity that should be promoted in the training action and professional development (Villar, 1995).

The assumptions underlying the promotion of reflexivity are, first, that adults learn more effectively when they feel a need to solve a particular problem. Moreover, people understand better what is required to improve a job when it is closely linked to that work. Their experiences provide instructors teaching guides to solve problems. Finally, teachers acquire important knowledge and skills in their involvement in the process of school improvement and curriculum development.

The strongest reconceptualization platform of reflection is well reflected in Kemmis (1999) set of propositions, which articulated a transformative vision of the reflective process: (1) the reflection is not determined neither biologically nor psychologically, nor is "pure thought"; reflection is action-oriented and deals with the relationship between thought and action in the real historical situations in which we find ourselves; (2) reflection is not the individualistic mind work like a mechanism or speculation, is and prefigures social relations; (3) reflection is not value less nor value-neutral, and is expressed in the service of human, social, cultural and political interests; (4) reflection is not indifferent or passive to social order, or stretches agreed social values, it actively reproduces or transforms practical ideologies that are the basis of social order; (5) reflection is not a mechanical product, nor a purely creative exercise for building new ideas, is a practice that expresses our power to rebuild the social life participating in communication, decision making and social action.

But critical thinking involves more than an activity of logical reasoning or depth examination of certain arguments. Critical thinking involves the recognition of the assumptions underlying our own beliefs and behaviors. It means we can justify our ideas and actions, justifications whose rationality we try to judge. It means we can think, plan and anticipate the consequences of those actions. And it means that we can test whether these justifications are appropriate or not. In short, critical thinking has a reflexive dimension. The idea of reflective learning is therefore related to critical thinking.

Teamwork Skills

It seems that the above features of professionalism would dissolve in relative futility if we do not recuperate one of the essential ideas of educational quality. The educational commitment with the student, with the mastery of the subject, with the flexibility and reflexivity that make sense when it is extended from the individual to the collective level of the institution and the team work, with its difficulties and conflicts, from the conviction that you cannot give up to achieve quality.

We have seen how most of the training and research efforts are devoted to the professional development of teachers, seeking as final goal to improve their professional knowledge, skills and attitudes in the management of teaching in a particular school. But besides the necessary teacher preparation for professional practice, it is also needed a continuous training in the workplace that empowers professors and teaching staff to offer institutionally the educational answers expected from the institution. For the history of research in education and teachers´ development this represents to admit a supra-individual dimension of educational professionalization whose substantive area is the institutional organization itself and its ultimate goal is the training of the teaching staff to lead and manage the continuous improvement of the training center. We call this "organizational development" (Fernández Cruz, 2002).

From a vision of educational innovation focused on the substantive aspects of the school curriculum for what organizational changes are needed to facilitate or hinder making curricular decisions and the adoption of significant changes, and from the consideration of the educational organization as a cultural reality rather than as a structural unit of the educational system, the central idea is that organizational development is that educational change is, itself, an organizational change because it always involves a reconstruction of the organizational culture.

Therefore, it is not possible to achieve school improvement through the coordinated sum of individualities no matter how exceptional they may be. This does not mean that teaching uniqueness of teachers, as individuals, are not the best starting point for the staff training. The educational team is not a collection of individuals but an organizational reality constructed in the professional interactions among its members. The training action is guided to this built reality. Needless to say that staff training becomes a privileged stage for the professional development of individual teachers.

Bibliography

Benavente, A. & Panchaud, C. (2008). Good practices for transforming education. *Quarterly Review of Comparative Education, 38* (2), 161-170.
Butt, R. L. & Raymond, D. (1989). Studying the nature and development of teachers' knowledge using collaborative autobiography. *International Journal*

of Educational Research, 13, 403-419.

Fernández Cruz, M. (2002). El cambio educativo. *Profesorado, Revista de currículum y formación del profesorado, 6,* 1-3.

Fernández Cruz, M. (2006). *Desarrollo profesional docente.* Granada: GEU.

Fernández Cruz, M. (2007). Claves de la formación de postgrado de los profesionales de la formación. Propuesta curricular de un Master Erasmus Mundus. *Formación XXI. Revista de Formación y Empleo, 6.*

Fernández Cruz, M. (2010). Aproximación biográfico-narrativo a la investigación sobre formación docente. *Profesorado. Revista de currículum y formación de profesorado, 14* (3), 17-32.

Hanushek, E. (2002). Teacher quality. In Izumi y Evers (eds.): *Teachers quality* (1-12). Palo Alto: Hoover Institution.

Hargreaves, A. & Fink, D. (2006). Estrategias de cambio y mejora en educación caracterizadas por su relevancia, difusión y continuidad en el tiempo. *Revista de Educación, 339,* 43-58.

Hopkins, D. & Stern, D. (1996). Quality teachers, quality schools: international perspectives and policy implications. *Teaching and Teacher Education, 12* (5), 501-517.

Hughes, S. A., Pennington, J. L., & Makris, S. (2012). Translating autoethnography across the AERA standards: Toward understanding autoethnographic scholarship as empirical research. *Educational Researcher.* August/September. 41(6).

Kemmis, S. (1999). La investigación-acción y la política de la reflexión. En Angulo, J.F. Barquín, J. y Pérez Gómez, A.I. (eds.). *Desarrollo profesional del docente: política, investigación y práctica.* Madrid: Akal, 95-118.

Kosnick, C. & Beck, C. (2009). *Priorities in teacher education.* New York: Routledge.

Miller, R. (2005). *Biographical research methods.* London: Sage.

Rivers, J. & Sanders, W. (2002). Teacher quality and equity in educational opportunity: findings and policy implications. In Izumi y Evers (eds.): *Teachers quality* (13-23). Palo Alto: Hoover Institution.

Roberts, B. (2002). *Biographical research.* Philadelphia: Open University Press.

Rose, L. & Gallup, A. (2003). The 35th Annual Phi Delta Kappa / Gallup Pollo f the public's attitudes Howard the public schools. *Phi Delta Kappan,* 41-56.

Shulman, L. S. (1986). Those who understand: Knowledge growth in teaching. *Educational Researcher, 15* (2), 4-14.

Tochon, F. V. (2010). Deep Education. *Journal for Educators, Teachers and Trainers, Vol. 1,* pp. 1-12.

Ulrich, W. (2000). Reflective practice in the civil society: the contribution of critically systemic thinking. *Reflective Practice, 1*(2), 247-268.

Villar, L. M. (dir.) (1995). *Un ciclo de enseñanza reflexiva. Estrategia para el diseño curricular.* Bilbao: Mensajero.

3.

Educational Growth and the Semiotics of the Tree: Exploring the OAK as a Framework for Deep Learning

Shirley O'Neill
University of Southern Queensland
Shirley.ONeill@usq.edu.au

This chapter explores the OAK tree in its ability to provide a framework for deep pedagogy that is applicable to democratic learning environments and the concept of Deep University. Although deep learning, as opposed to surface learning, is not new (Entwistle & Entwistle, 1991; Ramsden, 1988), it has taken on a new meaning and emphasis through the impact of the Internet on learning opportunities (Akyoi & Garrison, 2011), knowledge economies (OECD, 1996), and most recently its application to advances in computer science (LeCun, Bengio & Hinton, 2015). Nelson-Laird and Garver (2010, p. 250) state that deep learning is "characterized by a personal commitment to understanding . . . [where students] integrate and synthesize information with prior learning and draw on multiple perspectives (Ramsden, 2003; Tagg, 2003)". This is borne out in Tochon's (2014, p. 129) deep approach to languages learning that advocates for a "deep apprenticeship [that] encompasses both cognitive and social aspects within a content-based, transdisciplinary perspective . . . [to fulfil] disciplinary, interdisciplinary and transdisciplinary goals". The chapter uses the OAK metaphor as a threshold in the discussion of metaphor as a pedagogical principle for deep learning. It also explores the role of applied semiotics in stimulating deep engagement, rather than limiting the perspective to Applied Linguistics. In doing so it demonstrates the relevance of the OAK metaphor to deep learning and to the principles of GAMMA pedagogy and the relevance of this to deep learning, besides their mutual compatibility, as well as the legitimacy of using metaphors to stimulate deep learning and the relevance of semiotics for such open, authoritative and autonomous approaches.

Tochon (2013) adds to the exploration of contemporary pedagogy and learning in his demonstration of how educational semiotics applies to the deepening of learning. As Bankov comments: "Educational Semiotics goes beyond conventional reflections on the optimization of learning, demonstrating the power and capacity of applied semiotics to reveal the deep transformative nature of education, Education itself is the most intensive process of semiosis." (p. 8).

With this in mind the acronym OAK may represent the values of Deep University with the oak tree acting as a metaphor and educational semiotic that can provide a basis for the development of a culture of democratic practice and deep learning. In current times the valuing of Optimism, represented by 'O', in being confident about success and the future is vital for students embarking on both their university studies and later as graduates beginning their careers. In choosing a value to represent 'A' there are several possibilities. For instance, an important outcome for students is to be Active and Autonomous in their learning, and to be Authentic as people and in their practice. Similarly, one might argue for students' Affability in being sociable/civil and courteous. This is a value that underpins quality communication, collaboration and negotiation without which little can be achieved. However, it is suggested here that the value of Altruism, in being concerned with the good of others also encompasses affability but suggests a deeper quality that is more enduring and able to relate to students ultimately seeing themselves as problem solvers and able to make a contribution to improving the world we live in in some way. This relates well to the need for transformative practice and in doing so the valuing of Knowledge for 'K', as in students having a thirst for learning and acquisition of theoretical and practical understandings, and their application, to make a positive contribution to society. These values emanating from OAK can assist in transcending the limitations of traditional epistemology and the industrial model of learning (Chandler, 2001; May, 2011) that continues to permeate educational institutions. In spite of the fact that we are in the second decade of the new millennium, which was purported to be a milestone in foreshadowing educational change and hopefully consolidation of the shift towards constructivist learning environments, research shows that the challenge continues. As might be expected it varies across contexts and sectors (Gopnik & Wellman, 2012; Le Cornu & Peters, 2005; Ultanir, 2012). Thus, this exploration is timely in advocating for deep learning and recognition of educational semiotics as essential to contemporary debate on pedagogy and learning. It acknowledges the need to embrace learning in the context of an ever challenging digital-native student population that thrives on the use of tools of digital communication technologies (DCTs) (Edwards-Groves, 2012; Macpherson, 2013), whilst providing for students' voice and agency in relation to their personal learning (Rector-Aranda & Raider-Roth, 2015). However, educators may not have a contemporary view of pedagogy and the student's and teacher's role or their responsibilities applicable to 21st century flexible democratic learning spaces (Mayer, 2014). Such learning spaces have expanded as technology has progressed, although many countries still cannot provide every citizen with the resources to engage in learning through DCTs and the Internet. Nevertheless, learning spaces today are diverse and much more likely to include students and teachers who are multilingual. The context for learning may also be virtual and synchronous or asynchronous, where members of learning communities bring different educational experiences, cultural backgrounds, and values and beliefs about pedagogy and learning. While this typically implies the sharing of a common language to be able to communicate for the purposes of instruction, Abawi's (2013a; Abawi2013b) research shows that this is not enough if students are to be deeply engaged in learning. She points out that teachers and students need to have a shared understanding of the pedagogical philosophy and practices in place in the learning environment that draw upon a shared meaning making system. O'Neill (2013, p. 115) adds to this in identifying how such effective learning environments create 'a language for learning', which involves the explicit teaching of the metalanguage and metacognitive skills required to learn. In generic form this is defined as:

> The system of communication and shared meaning-making created through the collaborative development and implementation of a group of educators' and their students' explicit shared pedagogical philosophy and practice that includes the concepts, language and metalanguage in common use by teachers and students in the process of learning, teaching and assessment.

Thus, for the case of Deep University, OAK is explored as a metaphor that is able to be used to facilitate and scaffold the building of students' and teachers' capacity to think and dialogue for deep learning. After considering semiotics and its relevance to learning and pedagogical change the applicability of OAK to deep learning is considered on the basis of the importance of building students' capacity and the accommodation of O'Neill's (2015a) six principles of GAMMA pedagogy seen as necessary for effective learning. These are seen as operating in the context of students engaging in project-based- and problem-based-learning and having the opportunity and autonomy to construct their own learning pathways (Tochon, 2014). A synthesis of the results provides a basis for the validity of OAK and suggests a framework for deep learning that interprets the oak tree in a way that can foster educational growth within and across dynamic communities of practice where students and teachers are supported by common language and culture, and meaning systems (Abawi, 2013a) and hallmark pedagogies (O'Neill, 2015a).

Educational Semiotics and Argument for Learner Autonomy

The application of semiotics to educational theory and practice has become a new dynamic in recent times. In relation to this Pikkarainen (2010) distinguishes between Anglo-American philosophy of education and the Scandinavian-Continental European pedagogical tradition, acknowledging her preference for Greimas' theory of the semiotic square (Greimas & Courtés, 1982). While she notes Stables and Gough's (2005) work on semiotic engagement as a new theory of education, which mixes both Saussurean and post-structuralistic concepts, she points out the paradox in education that continues to influence possibilities of improvement today. She attributes the identification of the essence of this paradox to Kant (1992, p. 27) in his questioning of how the learners' freedom to learn is compromised by the seemingly coercion created by formal education environments. However, she notes:

> "[T]his paradox can, to some extent, be resolved by recognizing that learning takes place only through the subject's own action, and that the educator can influence the learner's action mainly through meaning effects. Thus, it can be derived that educational coercion is not physical determination, which Kant considers as the opposite of human freedom" (2010, pp.1141-1142).

She also draws attention to a second aspect of this paradox as cited in Mielityinen (2009) that further impacts on understanding education philosophy in terms of teaching and learning. This paradox in education remains ubiquitous today, being reflected in the contrasts between education policy, societal and intergenerational expectations, cultural expectations, government economic rationalism, and traditional assessment systems (O'Neill, 2015b) and pedagogical practices to name a few. At the heart of this is the need for learners to adapt to society and interact with their learning community to create their own identity (Benson, 2013; McCaleb, 1997; Neisser & Jopling, 1997). The apparent parallel between this pedagogical paradox and Greimas' semiotic theory, relates to his identification of two conflicting categories of meaningful sign structures or discourses. These are (1) the collective of society and (2) the individual (cited in Pikkarainen, 2010, p. 1142.) The former reflects the basic values of Culture and Nature and the latter basic values of Life and Death. The making of meaning emerges from learners needing to interact and deal with the tensions within these relationships. These dynamics are represented in Greimas' semiotic square of education in Figure 1.

Chandler (2001) outlines the advantages of the semiotic square, citing Fredric Jameson's point that compared with thinking in terms of binaries " 'the entire mechanism . . . is capable of generating at least ten conceivable positions out of a rudimentary binary opposition' (cited in Greimas 1987, p. xiv). Whilst this suggests that the possibilities for signification in a semiotic system are richer than the either/or of binary logic . . . they are nevertheless subject to 'semiotic constraints' - 'deep structures' providing basic axes of signification".

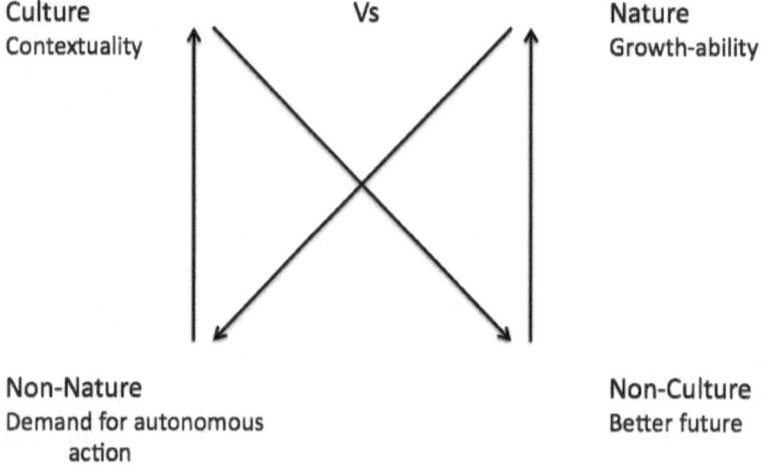

Figure 1: Semiotics square of education
(Pikkarainen, 2010, p.1142)

Pikkarainen (2010) argues that "the essence of modern education is precisely based on the dynamic contradictions between between Culture and Nature; [where] individual growth ability (the presupposed competencies) represents Nature; the demand for autonomous action (teaching) represents Non-Nature; contextuality represents the prevailing Culture; and a better future represents Non-Culture" (p.10). He notes, Greimas developed a multi-layered theory of discourse referred to as Generative trajectory that relates partly to Chomsky's concept of deep and surface levels of language. The fundamental value structure is identified at the deepest level with the basic abstract action structures and actant roles placed at the narrative level. Time, place and actor structures and their detailed features are perceived to be at the surface level (cited in Greimas & Courtés, 1982, pp. 132-134).

On this basis it is understandable that teachers' values and beliefs about learning will influence their practice. This paradox is evident in the current contrast between those educators who take a traditional view of learning as information transmission compared with those who follow a social constructivist view where meaning is believed to be constructed. A sole emphasis on rote learning and memorization where learners' recognition and recall of information is seen as learning can only be superficial, compared with the depth involved for engaged members of learning communities that work together to problem solve and think critically, and where their learning and thinking is scaffolded to construct new knowledge (See Lee, Lim, & Grabowski, 2008 for further information on generative learning). Table 1 (cited in O'Neill, 2015a, p. 112; after Thirteen, 2014) compares the key features of the traditional and constructivist classrooms.

We have seen that contemporary learning environments need to deal with student diversity, and changed roles and responsibilities in making the shift towards a democratic pedagogy where learners have greater autonomy and are able to negotiate their learning pathways. Notwithstanding the discussion so far an additional example of this paradox is evident in the continued lack of uptake of digital communication technologies in pedagogy to the point where learners as 'digital natives' could be described as already absorbed in pedagogical semiosis outside of formal education compared with their 'digital immigrant' teachers (and education authorities and curriculum and assessment decision makers).

Table 1: Comparison of key features of the traditional and constructivist classrooms

Traditional classrooms	Constructivist classrooms
Curriculum begins with the parts of the whole. Emphasizes basic skills.	Pursuit of student questions and interests is valued.
Materials are primarily textbooks and workbooks	Materials include primary sources of material and manipulative materials.
Learning is based on repetition.	Learning is interactive, building on what the student already knows.
Teachers disseminate information to students; students are recipients of knowledge.	Teachers have a dialogue with students, helping students construct their own knowledge.
Teacher's role is directive, rooted in authority.	Teacher's role is interactive, rooted in negotiation.
Assessment is through testing, correct answers.	Assessment includes student works, observations, and points of view, as well as tests. Process is as important as product.
Knowledge is seen as inert.	Knowledge is seen as dynamic, ever changing with our experiences.
Students work primarily alone.	Students work primarily in groups.

(After Thirteen, 2014)

It would seem that the established narrative on improving teaching and learning (i.e. interventionism, economic rationalism) needs to recognize the widening gap between the status quo and the need for this paradigm shift towards deep learning, student capacity building and learner autonomy. It is deduced here that such learner engagement in contemporary democratic communities co-insides with the:

1. global virtual learning space and myriad of resources and tools to support both collaborative and autonomous, personalised meaning making;

2. harnessing of contemporary 'digital native' learners 'natural skills' and 24/7 access to the Internet and mobile technology;

3. need to raise awareness and teach the skills associated with digital communication technologies for learning to the general community, government and employers as well as

teachers/educators as digital immigrants becoming 'integrated' to ensure learners and their teachers are party to the same conversation and understandings of pedagogy; and

4. building of collaborative learning communities, democratic pedagogies and mutual learning spaces.

When the constructivist, learning environment is considered (Table 1) the contrast between the traditional teacher-centred, authoritarian classroom, compared with that described by O'Neill (2015b), Mayer (2014) and Tochon (2014), becomes evident. For example, traditionally, the teacher's role is directive and rooted in authority compared with the deep approach where it is perceived as interactive, and rooted in negotiation. Mayer (2014) makes an important contribution by unpacking the vision for democratic pedagogies and democratic learning spaces, explaining how learners' voice and agency is at the core, and how they build their capacity as learners and collaborators to develop their social, intellectual, emotional and identity capital. Reiterating Tochon (2014), the deep approach demonstrates the need to develop learners' autonomy through their engagement in a cognitive apprenticeship that facilitates deeper learning in the context of project-based- and problem-based-learning with the teacher as facilitator. This recognition of the need for depth in learning and its relationship to language and semiotics as a catalyst may be argued as the essence of the paradigm shift required to transform pedagogy for the 21st century context.

The Influence of Semiotics in Pedagogy and Practice

Semiotics is defined as the study of signs and symbols and how they are used (Merriam-Webster, 2016). Floch (2001) notes it is concerned with the signs and meanings that are attached to linguistic and non-linguistic things and events and it has a broad, cross-disciplinary application. While typically applied in consumerism it has been increasingly acknowledged as a new dynamic in the ongoing search for improving pedagogy and learning. This includes the role of semiotics and semiosis in changing and strengthening the culture of learning communities in creating and sustaining shared meaning (Abawi, 2013a, 2013b; O'Neill, 2013). Queiroz and Merrell (2006, p. 41) discuss Pierce's (1998) theory of signs, noting "one of the most remarkable characteristics . . . is its dynamical nature" where the triad sign-object-interpretant (S-O-I) is the focal factor. They specify:

> it was quite natural that Peirce conceived semiosis as basically a process in which triads are systematically linked to one another so as to form a web. Sign processes are inter-relatedly extended within the spatiotemporal dimension, so that something physical has to instantiate or realize them. This means that signs cannot act unless they are spatiotemporally realized (see Deacon, 1999; Emmeche, 2003). If a sign is to have any active mode of being, it must be materially embodied . . . [concluding] that semiosis is a triadic process of communication of a form from the object to the interpretant by the sign mediation (p.42).

Through this process Pierce's theory, which identified ten classes of signs, is used to explain how meaning is made and shared through making sense of signs. Signs are the medium of communication of 'a form or a habit embodied in the object' given to the interpretant, which allows one to determine the interpreter's behaviour through inter-related inter-action with the sign. Merrell (n.d., p. 3) deduces: "[I]if semiosis is the process of signs becoming other signs, and if we as sign makers and takers are within this process, then we must try to understand how it is that we interact with signs and how they interact with us". Tochon (2013, pp. 30-31) draws attention to the kinds of interactions involved. He cites Shank and Cunningham's (1996) work, where they derived ten modes of meaning making or reasoning based on Pierce's taxonomy. These include (a) six ways of inferring the best explanation (abductive thinking) (hunch, symptoms, metaphor or analogy, clue, and diagnosis); (b) three ways of inductive reasoning (explaining, identifying, and predicting) and (c) two ways of deductive reasoning (model building and application of formal rules/logic).

Thus, the need for a mutual shared understanding at the sign level and meaning making level, as opposed to only the language level, would seem necessary for both practice and philosophy. For instance, Tochon (2013) describes how preservice teachers participated in a semiotic curriculum mapping process and collaborative discussions, which involved inductive reasoning based on various forms of feedback. This was seen as stimulating their 'transformative semiosis' as they discovered their own identity traits. Importantly, this process led them to reframe, reconstruct or reinterpret their knowledge, demonstrate their personal teaching philosophy as well as revise their belief system. On the basis of changes in their belief system it would be expected that changes in practice would follow. From this study and three others involving semiotics and semiosis he concluded: "semiotic diagrams allow the students to review their personal reflections, expectations, past goals and criticisms. The whole process was deep enough that it not only aimed at teaching and learning but gave them a taste for meaningful and deep education (Tochon, 2009; 2010)" (p. 113).

Application of Metaphor in Pedagogical Improvement

So far, we have seen how the application of semiotics in education can transform pre-service teachers' learning through the design of deeper meaning making opportunities in tertiary pedagogy. In this section we focus on how metaphor as a semiotic has been used to make deeper meaning in the design of school pedagogies. As hallmark pedagogies (O'Neill, 2015a) they are actively designed to address the specific needs of the students and have been shown to significantly improve learning outcomes (Crowther, Andrews, Morgan & O'Neill, 2012). Metaphor is increasingly being recognized as a major bridge to making meaning or a way of expanding thinking or extrapolating from the known to move between different domains of knowledge. It is well established as having underpinned scientific invention, such as the design of the syringe based on the snake's ability to inject venom or the move from the spatial domain to the temporal (O'Neill, 2009). It is already recognized as a valuable tool in teacher education (Nikitina & Furuoka, 2008; Saban, 2006; Simon, 2013; Zheng & Song, 2010).

As Lakoff and Johnson (1999, p. 3) state: "the mind is inherently embodied . . . Metaphor is the main mechanism through which we comprehend abstract concepts and perform abstract reasoning". Lakoff (1994, p. 43) notes: "the locus of metaphor is not in language at all, but in the way we conceptualise one mental domain in terms of another . . . [such that] the word metaphor has come to mean 'a cross domain mapping in the conceptual system . . . And in the process, everyday abstract concepts like time, states, change, causation, and purpose also turn out to be metaphorical". He also makes the important point that it is the mappings "'that are primary and that state the generalizations' that are our principal concern, we have reserved the term 'metaphor' for the mappings, rather than for the linguistic expression."

Such use of metaphor and semiotics applied in learning environments is exemplified in the research of Abawi (2013a, 2013b). She reports on how a school community may engage in the collaborative development of a vision for their school and an accompanying set of values designed to suit their particular context and needs. She explains how they developed pedagogical principles in accord with their values, and supporting theoretical underpinnings, as well as teasing out the implications for classroom practices. Their approach is designed to assure the school's chosen pedagogy is implemented consistently across all classrooms so it is 'schoolwide' (SWP). This addresses the well-known issue that inconsistency in pedagogical practices across classrooms within a school is a major limiting factor in attempts to improve learning (Hargreaves & Fullen, 2012).

In the projects to which Abawi (2013b) refers, the schools' visions were typically metaphorical. She reports: "metaphor- enriched artifacts of Vision and SWP within each of the participant schools convey cultural and pedagogical messages to those new to the school and help to align and sustain shared understandings focused on the achievement of shared goals". She describes how one school chose the local Jacaranda tree to represent their vision and develop their pedagogical principles. As a semiotic this metaphor provided the following mapping to pedagogical principles – (1) the trunk - Growing together; (2) the leaves, flowers and pods - Learning forever; and (3) the roots - Supporting each other. She shares the school's elaboration on their practice:

> Our Jacaranda Tree is the metaphor for the sense of purpose we feel . . . as we develop a root system embedded strongly in values education, a solid trunk built on celebrating difference in learning styles, cultures and backgrounds and producing flowers, seeds and leaves representing achievements for all to see in social skills displayed and through academic and cultural achievements . . . The staff, students and parents . . . are proud of our wonderful school and visitors are always welcome (pp. 97-98).

The fostering of 'transformative semiosis' (Tochon, 2013) through this metaphor was evident in the new meaning created from conceptualizing the Jacaranda tree's large long seedpods in terms of behavioural expectations. The acronym translated to Practicing safety, Overall respect, Demonstrating learning and Showing responsibility. Abawi (2013a, p. 90) explains how this led to "students receiving special PODS awards on parade and celebratory postcards were sent home to parents sharing their child's achievements . . . [and] a PODS day was organized as a day of fun and celebration." Another example included a school situated on a hill that selected a kite to represent their vision and SWP. Used as an acronym, KITE - Knowledge, Innovation, Taking Risks, Empowerment, Success impacted on the conceptualization of pedagogy and learning, generating a shared conversation using the attributes of the kite, for example, with respect to 'soaring' – "to be able to soar, reach our potential and to be successful as learners of the twenty-first century" (p. 99). She concludes:

As in the PODS and KITES exemplars, it appears that the use of metaphor in such context-specific meaning systems may enable students to transfer their school specific cognitive understandings wider afield. In addition, it suggests the vocabulary of a context specific meaning system carries its own messages about culture and identity to those unfamiliar with the context. Cultural metaphors (Marshak, 1996; Morgan, 1980), both visual and verbal, help to reinforce ways of working within a school enabling shared understandings to be strengthened and built upon" (p. 105).

Thus, as O'Neill (2015a, p. 120) notes in such learning communities: "[T]he expert practitioner . . . is able to draw upon metaphorical thinking to engage in their school's visioning processes, move between different cognitive domains in making pedagogical connections, and enriching and deepening their practice". She argues teachers' use of metaphor allows them to make cognitive connections between vision, values and pedagogical theory and practice, and extrapolate its meaning for themselves and students' learning. This is seen as heightening their pedagogical awareness, their conscious use of metalanguage in both their professional and teaching dialogue, and metacognitive processes. O'Neill (2013, 2015a) found that they used a range of semiotics by design as part of their schoolwide pedagogy. These included various graphic organizers, mind mapping and other visual and thinking tools to support students in making connections and constructing knowledge. For example, these included: De Bono's six thinking hats (de Bono, 1995); Gardner's multiple intelligences (Gardner, 2006; Hatch & Gardner, 1993); and Habits of Mind (Costa & Kallick, 2000). Similarly, Abawi (2013a) concluded that:

> Metaphors, images, structures and processes unique to each context appear integral to the creation of meaning within each school, and how staff and students make sense of their 'life-world'. Each meaning system works at the level of establishing and reinforcing basic norms, assumptions and ways of working. The creation of such a meaning system does not happen by accident but requires nurturing. This research suggests that over time, shared understandings appear to become intuitive to some

extent, and accepted ways of thinking and working become firmly embedded as school culture. (Abstract).

This body of research into the use of semiotics in schools and particularly metaphor as a starting point, as part of facilitating improvement, has been argued to achieve transformative semiosis, where both teachers and students engage in the making of meaning through their conscious use (Abawi, 2013a), and to also facilitate a shared 'language for learning' that marks their common pedagogical approach (O'Neill, 2013). O'Neill (2013; 2015a) reports a statistically significant improvement in students' reading and numeracy achievement over a three-year period for the same cohort moving from Year 3 to Year 5 in her case study. While the research cannot claim any direct causative relationship, the results suggest that the coordinated collaborative effort, and consistent implementation across the school of their agreed/mutually understood SWP was accumulative. It was able to facilitate the building of teachers' and students' capacity through the design of what she terms a 'hallmark pedagogy' that was best suited to the particular school's constituency.

GAMMA Pedagogy, OAK, and Deep Learning

This takes us one step further, which is to explore how the notion of a hallmark pedagogy may inform the development of OAK as a framework for deep learning. O'Neill (2015a) extrapolates from her research to argue that from such deep engagement of teachers and students in the development and implementation of their hallmark pedagogy certain principles may be derived. She uses these principles to reconceptualise pedagogy and learning through the acronym of 'GAMMA'. In applying the notion of "a third space" (Moje et al., 2004), she argues that the design of such hallmark pedagogies are necessary for 21st. century contexts for learning and that they need to be underpinned by the principles of Generative practice, Active design, Mutuality, Metaphor and Authority.

In GAMMA pedagogy students and teachers are in a new third space so to speak, where pedagogical practices and cognitive resources operate in concert, in use in a mutually agreed and understood way, in keeping with the [Hallmark] pedagogy in place. It is hypothesized that this capacity for learning provides an essential internalized generative disposition that has the potential to be the driver of lifelong learning. As students are actively engaged in their learning their capacity is self-regulating and provides an element of independence as opposed to conceptualising their learning as completed when a task is done (p.121).

These principles of GAMMA pedagogy are applied here to explore a pedagogical framework for OAK to better understand deep learning. If practice is to be *generative* and pedagogical knowledge co-constructed then educators and students of Deep University need to collaborate as a learning community to make explicit and share the theoretical base and pedagogical practices that reflect the values of OAK. Through professional dialogue and the emergent shared pedagogical language a hallmark pedagogy for deep learning should be established that is research based, achieving an *active design*. This involves the collaborative engagement of educators in a process that provides opportunity to identify their personal pedagogical beliefs and relate them and their practice to authoritative pedagogical theories. This is also a deep process in that participants need to make explicit how their OAK pedagogy will be recognizable in practice. As noted earlier, as opposed to learning contexts spawned through traditional pedagogical practices, educators infused with GAMMA pedagogy can be expected to bring in-depth knowledge to their practice. This would be evident in the learning experiences they design and their accompanying pedagogical dialogue and educational conversations, thus reflecting van Lier's (2003, p. 94) thesis that: "our dealings with the world, our meaning making (semiosis) are essentially dialogical and interactional in nature". Thus, in turn their design of learning experiences would be expected to be valid for their hallmark pedagogy across learning contexts/ institutionally.

The principle of *mutuality* acknowledges that in constructivist learning environments students' voice and agency are respected and both teachers and students are involved in a context for learning where there is a mutual awareness, understanding and use of an explicit meaning-making system (Abawi, 2013a) and language for learning (O'Neill, 2013). This is explicated through the use of shared metalanguage and metacognitive processes tied to the collaborative construction of a hallmark pedagogy. It is supported through the use of transformative semiosis in an inquiry-based approach involving personalized learning and critical reflection. This mutuality extends to students contributing to the discussion and design of the way teaching and learning relates to their goals and through this the mutual building of capacity.

Metaphor is a powerful pedagogical principle as it is well recognized as central to the role of thought and language in learning, Abductive thinking through use of metaphor (Ovchinnikova, et al., 2014; Shank & Cunningham, 1996; Tochon, 2013) can be used to facilitate a shift in educators' cognition through professional learning that is stimulated through transformative semiosis, and similarly in keeping with the principle of mutuality, students' learning as well. This pedagogical approach recognizes the need for both educators and students to build their identity capital through their engagement in ongoing personal learning (and in this case using the meanings of the oak tree as a lens). Thus, those aspiring to deploy the metaphor of the oak tree to envision their hallmark pedagogy, in collaboration with their learning community, can stimulate a journey of self-development and learning autonomy. In Tochon's (2013) terms this facilitates a transformative semiosis that creates a cognitive shift to equip them with the cognitive, executive skills to conceptualize and implement their hallmark pedagogy in practice. As experts in their field they draw upon metaphorical thinking to move between different cognitive domains in making pedagogical connections, thus enriching and deepening their practice to foster students' learning.

The principle of *Authority* in GAMMA pedagogy refers to creation of a hallmark pedagogy that is collaboratively developed through the involvement of all stakeholders, including students. It is a pedagogy that those involved have a sense of ownership of because of their input, stake in the developmental process and authorship. Educators are able to see how their own their personal philosophy of learning and pedagogy fits in relation to authoritative educational theories and the resultant authoritative hallmark pedagogy. The need for consistency in approach across learning spaces is recognized, as is the need to build in systematic feedback mechanisms/formative assessment to support an evidence-based decision-making. This is a pedagogy that is capable of being authentic and setting high aspirations and expectations of both students and teachers and imbuing the ability to take control of their ongoing learning. In a supportive context, educators would collaborate and conduct action research, and interrogate assessment and evaluative data, sharing their knowledge and pedagogy to continue to improve and sustain the authority of their hallmark practices. As O'Neill (2015a, p.121) notes, her research suggests that in the context of GAMMA pedagogy, Generative practice, involves "the Active design of a hallmark pedagogy to meet students' needs and empower them as learners . . . [reflecting] a strong Mutuality in the use of a common, pedagogical metalanguage, critical reflective practice, and consideration of interests and needs and provision of support". Teachers' and students' "use of Metaphor and metaphorical thinking is embedded in practice and used as a tool to achieve a new level of intellectual stimulation, and adoption of strategies for engagement in learning . . . the pedagogy they have created is Authoritative in its own right and becomes the hallmark of their practice" (see also Geoghegan, O'Neill & Petersen, 2013).

Students as Empowered Learners and Deepening Learning

In GAMMA pedagogy students are not passive receivers of information in contexts where the main focus is on rote learning and memorization and its reproduction. On the contrary, it is a capacity-building process that equips students with the knowledge, skills and strategies to enable their learning. The way students make meaning within the context for learning or the need for transformative semiosis is recognized. This applies to the need for students to be party to the language of learning, that includes the metalanguage, metacognitive processes and thinking tools/semiotics that are explicit to the hallmark pedagogy. Teachers are aware of their cognitive moves and language use in order to manage learning dialogue and to best scaffold students' learning. "In GAMMA pedagogy students and teachers are in a *new third space* so to speak, where pedagogical practices and cognitive resources operate in concert, in use in a mutually agreed and understood way, in keeping with the [Hallmark pedagogy] . . . in place" (O'Neill, 2015a, p. 121). In advocating GAMMA pedagogy it is hypothesized also that this should provide more opportunity for students to continue to be intrinsically motivated, self-sustaining and resilient in their learning, and ideally reach the point of 'flow' in generating a sense of self-efficacy and accomplishment. Csikszentimihalyi's (1991) concept of flow would seem an essential consideration in any model of learning that aspires to be generative since "flow may be described as a period of optimal performance that is both fulfilling and engaging. It most often occurs 'when a person's body and mind is stretched to its limits in a voluntary effort to accomplish something difficult and worthwhile' (p. 3). When one is *in the flow*, work can seem like play in that 'people are so involved in an activity that nothing else seems to matter; the experience itself is so enjoyable that people will do it at great cost, for the sheer sake of doing it (p. 4)" (cited in Huitt, 2007, p. 6).

In summary, while the concept of GAMMA pedagogy was conceived on the basis of the results of O'Neill's (2013, 2015a) research in schools that engaged in developing a schoolwide pedagogy the principles outlined may be applied in any contemporary democratic pedagogical context. This reconceptualisation of pedagogy argues that learners that acquire an internalized generative disposition and are involved in using a semiotic lens for making meaning are better equipped to engage and drive their personal/lifelong learning. This is what was qualified as deep learning in the present demonstration and thus is central to the development of the framework for the OAK.

The OAK as an Educational Semiotic and Implications for a Hallmark Pedagogy

This chapter concurs to the demonstration that Gamma is a pedagogy for deep learning which is compatible with OAK Principles and Tochon's Deep Approach. Moreover, in the field of language learning, it suggests that applied semiotics offers a more comprehensive perspective than Applied Linguistics alone in the perspective of meeting 21st Century pedagogical challenges.

Mariotti (2012, p. 27) states that "[T]aking a semiotic perspective means to acknowledge the central role of signs in the teaching-learning activity". Figure 2 shows an exploratory mapping of some meanings that may relate to the oak tree. While by no means exhaustive it provides a basis to consider the oak as a semiotic lens.

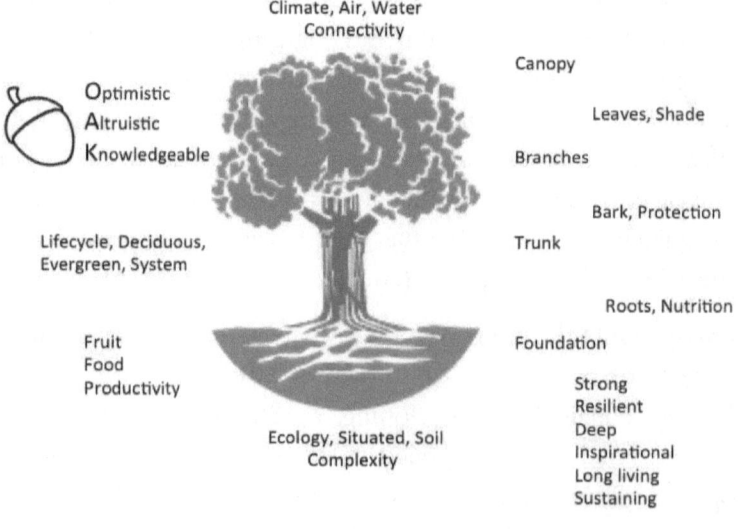

Figure 2: Exploration of the semiotics of the oak tree
(Image courtesy of https://pixabay.com)

Making meaning from the oak tree and from the concept of the tree in general may also be drawn from its cultural status and use in religion worldwide. Hamilton (2002) specifies:

> The cosmology of many early cultures involved a mythical tree which was the axis of the world, with branches reaching far into the heavens and roots penetrating into the underworld. An excellent discussion of this topic, with examples from Norse, Russian, Babylonian, Indian, Aztec, Mayan, Egyptian, Greek, Chinese, and many other cultures has been presented by Altman (1994) in a book entitled *Sacred Trees*. He classifies cosmic trees into three groups: world trees, trees of life, and trees of knowledge (p.59).

In relation to the oak, its nobleness and synonymity with strength and productivity is well established in Western cultural traditions and evident today. The "sowing of seeds" in students embarking on a pathway to success through growth in learning is embedded in the adage "Mighty oaks from little acorns grow" and the song "From little things big things grow". Its symbolism is also evident in songs such as "Heart of oak", the official march of the British Royal Navy, that signifies the strength of their navy through their oak ships. The significance of the tree, including the oak, also dates back to the Old Testament. Nielsen (1989, p. 73) specifies the tree has both material and idealogical status, and cites Gilbert Duran as identifying "the tree [as] . . . one of the archetypal images". She explains that it is symbolic of life in marking fertile ground, giving hope, and points out its imagery is extensively used to make meaning in Isaiah, since "we all have an elementary understanding of the tree as a living organism that grows and becomes old, that can renew itself by producing shoots even if a woodcutter or drought arrests growth for a time".

Similarly, Elevitch (2004, p. 34), notes "[T]the oak was worshipped by the Romans, Druids, Greeks and Celts . . . [and] in Turkish culture through attitudes to plants in general and trees in particular [and in Islam for example] planting a tree was accepted as a substitute for alms". Hamilton (2002, p. 60) also notes "oaks were the tree of life for the Greeks and the early northern Europeans. This was the symbol of Thor, Jupiter, and Zeus. It was believed that Zeus could communicate with mortals through the oak tree." Similarly, he points out that the tree is also revered in Buddhism (Buddha received enlightenment under the bo tree) and the banyan tree in Hinduism (which was protection for Lord Krishna). In addition, Allen, McClure and Allen (2013) refer to meetings "under the oak tree" when they draw a parallel with Genesis 18:1-15 to highlight the importance of community conversations for learning and for the church in providing pastoral care. In taking their "dialogical perspective" this may be seen as analogous to social constructivism and in their reference to being "open to fresh formulations of . . . doctrine and practice" suggests transformative learning. While much more can be said about the oak tree as having global applicability as a metaphor and educational semiotic for deep learning this brief insight establishes the breadth and depth of its imagery and relevance to issues related to pedagogy, learning and life.

Together with the mapping in Figure 2, the oak tree suggests a hallmark pedagogy of deep learning for Deep University would provide a strong foundation with deep roots and broad base that is is able to build the social, intellectual and identity capital of both educators and students alike (mutuality), involving them in deep learning for educational and career success. For its survival and longevity the oak can be thought of as creating an extensive dynamic networked system, branching widely, with deep connectivity, and the building of a verdant environment for deepening learning, the building of resilience and longevity. Importantly, also derived from the semiotics of the oak tree in this respect is the ecology and diversity of the learning environment; the trees cyclic response to the seasons suggests an appreciation of alternative views of learning cultures compared with the typical idea of learning as a linear process.

In this sense it reflects the internationalization of deep university and appreciation of the deep commitment and cross-cultural collaboration involved. Similarly, it reflects a balance between base and canopy, a sense of harmony, creating a fertile context for learning, that is nurturing and able to foster innovation, and generate new knowledge and productivity. The many uses of its timbers adds to the scope of meaning making, reflecting the many possibilities for the generation of new knowledge and creativity through analogy. Reiterating Kant's (2010) view of learning as dependent on the learners' own actions, and their need to deal with the tensions between *Culture and Nature* versus *Life and Death* (Greimas' semiotic theory) to make meaning, the oak tree has the potential to provide a comprehensive framework for both educational philosophy and, policy and practice.

The principles of GAMMA pedagogy assist in the mapping of the metaphor and its applicability across the many different contexts for learning, and recognizing that within these there are learning spaces that will develop their hallmark pedagogy in keeping with deep education and deep learning. Through this demonstration they should be better equipped to create and recognize their third space in which the making of meaning that takes account of the semiotics of the OAK and the language for learning, including the modes of reasoning, is explicit and in mutual use. As Tochon and Shank (2014) state:

> Semiotics is relevant to Education in two respects: it first can be crucial for a better understanding and exploration of education practices, which may lead to deeper and more meaningful practices; second it can inform deeper ways of researching education as a field for which signs and sign processes are crucial.

Where stands a silent grove black with the shade of oaks; at the sight of it, anyone could say, "There is a spirit here!" — Ovid (Fasti 3. 295-296) (cited in Hamilton, 2002, p. 57).

References

Abawi, L. (2013a). School meaning systems: The symbiotic nature of culture and 'language-in-use'. *Improving Schools, 16*(2), 89-106.

Abawi, L (2013b). Metaphor: Powerful imagery bringing learning and teaching to life. *Improving Schools, 16*(2) 130-147.

Akyoi, Z., & Garrison, D. R. (2011). Understanding cognitive presence in an online and blended community of inquiry: Assessing outcomes and processes for deep approaches to learning. *British Journal of Educational Technology, 42*(2), 233-250.

Allen, R. J., McClure, J. S., & Allen, O. W. (Eds.). (2013). *Under the oak tree: The church as community of conversation in a conflicted and pluralistic world.* Eugene, OR: Wipf and Stock.

Benson, P. (2013). *Teaching and researching: Autonomy in language learning.* New York, NY: Routledge

Chandler, D. (2001): *Semiotics: The Basics.* London: Routledge.

Chomsky, N. (1969). Deep structure surface structure and semantic interpretation. In D. D. Steingberg & L. A. Jakobovits (Eds.), *Semantics: An interdisciplinary reader in philosophy, linguistics and psychology.* (1971, pp. 183-216). Cambridge: Cambridge University Press.

Costa, A. L., & Kallick, B. (Eds.) (2000). *Discovering and exploring Habits of Mind. Habits of Mind: A developmental series.* Alexandria, VA: Association for Supervision and Curriculum Development.

Csikszentimihalyi, M. (1991). Flow: The psychology of optimal experience. New York: Harper Collins.

Crowther, F., Andrews, D., Morgan, A., & O'Neill, S. (2012). Hitting the bull's eye of school improvement: The IDEAS arrow. Leading and Managing, Summer. 1-31.

de Bono, E. (1995). Mind power: Discover the secrets of creative thinking. Crows Nest, NSW: Allen & Unwin.

Edwards-Groves, C. (2012). Interactive Creative Technologies: Changing learning practices and pedagogies in the writing classroom. *Australian Journal of Language and Literacy. 35*(1), 99-113.

Elevitch, C. R. (2004). *The overstory book: Cultivating connections with trees* (2nd. ed.). Holualoa, HI: Permanent Agriculture Resources (PAR).

Entwistle, N.J., & Entwistle, A.C. (1991). Forms of understanding for degree examinations: the pupil experience and its implications, *Higher Education, 22*, 205-227.

Floch, J. (2001) *Semiotics, marketing and communication: beneath the signs, the strategies.* Basingstoke: Palgrave.

Geoghegan, D., O'Neill, S., & Petersen, S. (2013). Metalanguage: The 'teacher talk' of explicit literacy teaching in practice. *Improving Schools, 12*(2), 119-129.

Gopnik, A., & Wellman, H. M. (2012). Reconstructing constructivism: Causal models, Bayesian learning mechanisms, and the theory of theory. *Psychol. Bull., 138*(6), 1085-108.

Greimas, A. J., & Courtés, J. (1982) *Semiotics and language: An analytical dictionary*. Bloomington: Indiana University Press.

Hargreaves, A., & Fullen, M. (2012). *Professional capital: Transforming teaching in every school*. New York: Routledge.

Hamilton, L. S. (2002). Forest and tree conservation through metaphysical constraints, *The George Wright Forum, 19*(3), 57-78.

Hatch, T., & Gardner, H. (1993). 'Finding cognition in the classroom: an expanded view of human intelligence'. In G. Salomon (ed.) *Distributed cognitions: Psychological and educational considerations*. Cambridge: Cambridge University Press.

Huitt, W. (2007). *Success in the conceptual age: Another paradigm shift*. Paper delivered at the 32nd Annual Meeting of the Georgia Educational Research Association, Savannah, GA, October 26. Retrieved from http://www.edpsycinteractive.org/papers/conceptual-age.pdf

Kant, I. (1992). *Kant on education*. Bristol: Thoemmes Press.

Lakoff, G. (1994). What is Metaphor? *Advances in connectionist theory. Analogical Connections, 3*.

Lakoff, G., & Johnson, M. (1999). *Philosophy in the flesh: The embodied mind and its challenge to western thought*. New York, NY:Basic Books.

LeCun, Y., Bengio, Y., & Hinton, G. (2015). Deep learning. *Nature, 521*, 436-444.

Lee, H. W., Lim, K. Y., & Grabowski, B. L. (2008). Generative learning: principles and implications for making meaning. In J. M. Spector (Ed.), *Handbook of research on educational communications and technology* (pp. 111-124). New York: Lawrence Erlbaum.

Macpherson, K. (2013). *Digitel technology and Australian teenagers: Consumption, study and careers*. University of Canberra: The Education Institute.

McCaleb, S. P. (1997). *Building communities of learners: A collaboration among teachers, students, families, and communities*. Mahwah, NJ: Laurence Erlbaum.

Mariotti, M. A. (2012). ICT as opportunities for teaching-learning in a mathematics classroom: The semiotic potential of artefacts. In T. Y. Tso (Ed)., Proceedings of the 36[th]Conference of the International Group for the Psychology of Mathematics Education, Vol. 1. (pp. 25-40). Taipei, Taiwan: PME.

May, G. H. (2011). Education: Time to rethink the industrial model? *Journal of Future Studies, Essay*, 101-107.

Mayer, S. J. (2012). *Classroom discourse and democracy: Making meanings* together. *Critical pedagogical perspectives.* New York: Peter Lang.

Moje, E. B., Ciechanowski, K. M., Kramer, K., Ellis, L., Carrillo, R., & Collazo, T. (2004). Working toward third space in content area literacy: An examination of everyday funds of knowledge and discourse. *Reading Research Quarterly, 39*(1), 38-70. doi:10.1598/RRQ.39.1.4.

Merrell, F. (n.d.) *Semiology meets semiotics: A case of lingering linguicentrism?* Retrieved from http://web.ics.purdue.edu/~fmerrell/linguicentrism.htm

Merriam-Webster (2016). Merriam-Webster Dictionary Online. Retrieved from http://www.merriam-webster.com/dictionary/semiotics

Mielityinen, M. (2009) Das Ästhetische in Schleiermachers Bildungstheorie. Theorie einesindividuellen Weltbezuges unter Einbeziehung der Theorie des Ästhetischen bei Schiller. Würzburg: Ergon-Verlag.

Nielsen, K. (1989). There is hope for a tree: The tree as metaphor in Isaiah. *Journal for the Study of the Old Testament*, Supplement Series. Sheffield, UK: JSOT Press, Sheffield Academic Press.

Neisser, U., & Jopling, D. (Eds.). (1997). The conceptual self in context, culture, experience, self-understanding, Cambridge: Cambridge University Press. From http://www.ncte.org/library/NCTEFiles/About/NCLE/NCLEshortlitreview.pdf

Nelson Laird, T.F., & Garver, A.K. (2010). The effect of teaching general education courses on deep approaches to learning: How disciplinary context matters, *Research in Higher Education,* 51, 248. doi:10.1007/s11162-009-9154-7

OECD (1996). *The knowledge-based economy.* General Distribution, (96)02. Paris: Organisation for Economic Cooperation and Development (OECD). Retrieved from https://www.oecd.org/sti/sci-tech/1913021.pdf

Nikitina, L., & Furuoka, F. (2008). Measuring metaphor: A factor analysis of students' conceptions of language teachers. *Metaphoik.de, 15*, 161-179.

O'Neill, S. (2009). *Relational concepts: Language, thinking and pedagogy and the spatial metaphor of time.* Brisbane: PostPressed.

O'Neill, S. (2013). Activating the *"language for learning"* through Schoolwide pedagogy: The case of MacKillop school. *Improving Schools, 12*(2), 107-118. doi:10.1177/1365480213492408

O'Neill, S. (2015a). School leadership and pedagogical reform: Building student capacity. In K. Beycioglu & P. Pashiardis (Eds.), *Multidimensional perspectives on principal leadership effectiveness* (pp. 103-131). Hershey, PA: IGI Global. http://www.igi-global.com/book/multidimensional-perspectives-principal-leadership-effectiveness/110019

O'Neill, S. (2015b). *EFL teachers' professional learning needs: Working with multimedia and the CLOUD. In L. T. Wong, & A. Dubey-Jhaveri (EDs.),* English language education in a global world: Practices, issues and challenges. New York: Nova Science Publishers, Inc.

Ovchinnikova, E., Israel, R., Wertheim, S., Zaytsev, V., Montazeri, N., & Hobbs, J. (2014). Abductive inference for interpretation of metaphors, *Proceedings of the Second Workshop in NLP*, 33-41. MD: Baltimore: Association for Computational Linguistics.

Pierce, C. S. (1998). *The essential Peirce: Selected philosophical writings. Vol. II. Peirce Edition Project*. Indiana: Indiana University.

Pikkarainen, E. (2010). The semiotics of education: A new vision in an old landscape. *Educational Philosophy and Theory, 43*(10), 1135-1144. DOI: 10.1111/j.1469-5812.2009.00632.x

Queiroz, J., & Merrell, F. (2006). Semiosis and pragmatism: Toward a dynamic concept of meaning. *Sign Systems Studies, 44*(1), 37-65.

Ramsden, (1988). Studying learning: Improving teaching. In P. Ramsden (Ed.), *Improving learning: New perspectives* (pp.268-286). London: Kogan Page.

Rector-Aranda, R., & Raider-Roth, M. (2015). 'I finally felt like I had power': Student agency and voice in an online and classroom-based role-play simulation. *Research in Learning Technology, 23*.

Saban, A. (2006). Functions of metaphor in teaching and teacher education: A review essay, *Teaching Education, 17*(4), 299-315. DOI:10.1080/10476210601017386

Shank, G., & Cunningham, D.J. (1996). *Modeling the six modes of Peircean abduction for educational purposes*. Paper presented at the annual meeting of the Midwest A1 and Cognitive Science Conference, Bloomington, IN.

Simon, S. E. (2013). The weaving of a tapestry: A metaphor for teacher education curriculum development. *Australian Journal of Teacher Education, 38*(8), 73-91.

Stables A., & Gough S. (2006). Toward a semiotic theory of choice and of learning. *Educational Theory, 56*(3), 271-285.

Thirteen. (2014). *Workshop: Constructivism as a paradigm for teaching and learning*. Retrieved from http://www.thirteen.org/edonline/concept2class/constructivism/index.html

Tochon, F. V. (2013). *Signs and symbols in education: Educational semiotics*. Blue Mounds, WI: Deep University Press.

Tochon, F. V. (2014). *Help them learn a language deeply - Francois Victor Tochon's Deep Approach to world languages and cultures*. Blue Mounds, WI: Deep University Press.

Tochon, F. V., & Shanks, G. (2014). New semiotics - Between tradition and innovation: Research methods for educational semiotics symposium. Presentation at the 12th. World Congress of Semiotics, Sofia 2014, 18-20 September, New Bulgarian University. Retrieved from http://semio2014.org/en/research-methods-for-educational-semiotics-symposium

Van Lier, L. (2003). The semiotics and ecology of language learning: Perception, voice, identity and democracy. *Utbildning & Demokrati, 13*(3), 79-103.

Ultanir, E. (2012). An epistemological glance at the constructivist approach: Constructivist learning in Dewey, Piaget, and Montessori. *International Journal of instruction*, 5(2), 195-212.

Zheng, H-B., & Song, W-J., (2010). Metaphor analysis in the educational discourse: A critical review. *8*(9), 84, 42-49.

4.

Foreign Language General Education and Deep Approach in China[1]

Xiang LONG

College of Foreign Studies, Guilin University of Electronic Technology, China, and University of Wisconsin-Madison

This chapter articulates the concepts, development and their relationship of Liberal Education (LE), General Education (GE), Foreign Language General Education (FLGE) and Deep Education (DE)or Deep Approach (DA) to world languages and cultures, the paper also proposes six characteristics of foreign language and how they are applied and developed in foreign language education and teaching and their status in China. The author points out that Cai's proposal on ESP（English for Specific Purpose）or Academic English framework for Shanghai just belongs to the domain of FLGE actually. Finally, the author summarizes the similarities and differences between GE & DE or DA and puts forward the possible applications of the educational approaches to foreign/world languages in future classrooms.

Liberal Education(LE) and General Education(GE)

The development and integration

While "LE" in Chinese "Boya Jiaoyu," "Ziyou Jiaoyu," or "Tongshi Jiaoyu," means the same as "GE" (Tongshi Jiaoyu in Mandarin), I prefer the latter, which is based on the medieval concept of liberal

---

[1] The article was presented at the 2015 International Conference on Deep Education, Wisconsin USA. The present report was achieved under the program GXSK201438 from the Guangxi Federation of Social Sciences & the 2015 Higher Education Teaching Reform Programs under the Project NO. 2015JGA206 from Education Department of Guangxi Zhuang Autonomous Region, P. R. China.

arts or, more commonly now known as the liberalism of the Age of Enlightenment in Western Europe, also known as Liberal Arts Education. The liberal art college at its inception and during its subsequent evolution, first in Europe and later in the United States, was essentially an upper-class institution, catering to the landed gentry and wealthy upper-middle class, from whose ranks were recruited the leaders of society. Certainly these people did not need a B. A. degree to obtain a job. Theirs was an education calculated that prepared the student to enjoy leisure profitably (Lipp, 1952, p.204). The middle class tried to imitate its "Upper Class;" hence the predominance in the liberal art college of a mixture of upper- and middle-class cultural values (ibid). It has been described as a philosophy of education that empowers individuals with broad knowledge and transferable skills, and a stronger sense of values, ethics, and civic engagement.

During 17th -18th century, as for the western knowledge system, the courses from arts and sciences were both very important and developed harmoniously. Early in the 19th century the scientific enlightenment was undertaking a prosperous stage and the USA was beginning to develop the west of the country and required quite a lot of talents who knew natural science and technology. Many so-called "educators" advocated practical disciplines not classic ones, so liberal arts education was questioned, that is to say, the liberal education met a big challenge at the time. To maintain the tradition of liberal arts education, the professors from Yale University came forward bravely and published the famous "The Yale's Report of 1828", in which the professors stated that "the course of instruction which is given to the undergraduates in the college, is not designed to include professional studies. Our object is not to teach that which is peculiar to any one of professions; but to lay the foundation which is common to them all (FC, 1828, p. 14). Furthermore, the report states:

> "an LE, it is believed, has been generally understood, such a course of discipline in arts and sciences, as is best calculated, at the same time, both to strengthen and enlarge the faculties of

mind and to familiarize it with the leading principles of the great objects of human investigation and knowledge. A liberal, is obviously distinct from a professional education. The former is conversant with those topics, an acquaintance with which is necessary or convenient in any situation of life, the latter, with those which qualify the individual for a particular station, business or employment. The former is antecedent in time, ... (ibid, p. 30)."

Regarding other universities' responses to this type of education,there appeared different voices. Under the strong conflict background of humanism and scientism, rationalism and utilitarianism, in 1829 Professor A. S. Packard from Bowdoin College issued a relevant article supporting the Yale Report and first proposed the concept "GE" in it. Packard pointed out American universities supported GE for students, which included the related courses about classics, literature and sciences. This was the first time the word "GE" was used in higher education (cited in Wang , 2002).

In any case, GE program always emphasizes what is commonly referred to as the "wholeness" of knowledge, as it stresses large, meaningful, related units or "wholes" rather than so-called "fragmented" and "specialized" knowledge (Lipp, 1952, p. 203). Not everything always goes smoothly. In the movement of GE, it experienced many setbacks and difficulties as LE did. Taking the courses of liberal arts as an example, with the development of society and economy, many Americans needed a B.A. degree, but then the question remained as to how to make the large number of new college students happy in a new environment; or, in "class" terms, how to make many lower- and middle-class students comfortable and well-adjusted in a socially and culturally traditionally "upper"-class atmospheres. In other words, how would it be possible to make our cultural heritage available to these students and optimized for them, without having them get lost in a welter of diverse subject matter, without causing them to suffer from a lack of wholesome educational balance ? Hence the term "GE" and opposition of some educators to what they considered premature specialized education. Hence the unhealthy antagonism which has crept into some quarters between the faculties of GE and liberal arts and thus, the unwelcome deduction and the unwholesome distinction was created: LE for "classes" and GE for "masses" (Lipp, 1952, p. 204). Apparently, "GE" is supposed to be "integrated" and to cross subject matter lines and "liberal arts education" is "fragmented" and too "specialized." As a matter of fact, "fragmentation" need not characterize LE. It is merely an unfortunate development in an age of specialization, which has resulted in oft-quoted "counter cafeteria" style of "shopping" for credits (ibid).

This is a weakness which GE has been quick to seize upon and exploit for its advantage. All the elements necessary for GE can be found in liberal arts curriculum. If liberal education were to undergo currricular reform, it is quite possible that the "heavy guns" of the "separatist" general educationist would be spiked. For the objectives of both general ad liberal education are so close as to be able to be merged. One of the things needed is the will and the interest so to organize the courses make broader offerings possible. Moreover, GE should not necessarily be limited to the freshmen and sophomore years; it can go on continually, in varying proportions during other years, side by side with "specialized" education (Lipp, p. 205). GE in the terminal, two-year college can stand by itself, although such programs also need to be liberalized to withstand vocational pushes. .

Actually the Association of American Colleges & Universities (AAC&U) was found in 1915 in the USA and this year 2015, AAC&U is celebrating its 100th birthday for the leadership of liberal education. Anyway the first real journal about "GE" was pressed in 1946 while the first journal about "LE" was issued in 1959 in the United States. For more than 200 years, liberal education and general education have experienced conflicts and mixture of ideas but eventually harmonized. Here is a reasonable interpretation about the changing nature of liberal education, which represents a new developmental stage of higher education in the USA.

Table 1. The Changing Nature of **Liberal** Education (adapted from College Learning for the New Global Century, AAC&U (2007, 18, 5)

	Liberal Education in the Twentieth Century	Liberal Education in the Twenty-First Century
What	- intellectual and personal development - an option for the fortunate viewed as non-vocational	- intellectual and personal development - a necessity for all students - essential for success in a global economy and for informed citizenship
How	- through studies in arts and sciences disciplines ("the major") and/or through **general education** in the initial years of college	- through studies that emphasize the essential learning outcomes across the **entire** educational continuum—from school through college—at progressively higher levels of achievement (recommended)
Where	- liberal arts colleges or colleges of arts and sciences in larger institutions	- all schools, community colleges, colleges, and universities, as well as across all fields of study (recommended)

What is GE or LE?

So far, it seems that there is not an exact definition about what GE is and different history scholars have various understandings of it. As mentioned above, general educationists often stress its "wholeness" of knowledge, that is, large, meaningful, related units or "wholes". Here is a committee of the American Council on Education, which defined that GE should be the common possession, the common denominator, so to speak, of educated persons as individuals and as citizens in a free society. It also included a list of objectives of GE, stated as follows:

... In the committee's judgment, GE should lead the student;

(1) To improve and maintain his own health and take his share of responsibility for protecting the health of others

(2) To communicate through his own language in writing and speaking at the level of expression adequate to the needs of educated people

(3) To attain a sound emotional and social adjustment through the enjoyment of a wide range of social relationships and experience of working cooperatively with others.

(4) To think through the problems and to gain the basic orientation that will

better enable him to make a satisfactory family and marital adjustment

(5) To do his part as an active and intelligent citizen in dealing with the interrelated social, economic, and political problems of American life and in solving the problems of postwar international reconstruction

(6) To act in the light of his human society and human welfare, to use scientific methods in the solution of his problems, and to employ useful nonverbal methods of thought and communication

(7) To find self-expression in literature and to share through literature man's experience and his motivating ideas and ideals

(8) To find a means of self-expression in music and in the various visual arts and crafts, and to understand and appreciate art and music as reflections both of individual experience and of social patterns and movements

(9) To practice clear and integrated thinking about the meaning value of life

(10) To choose a vocation that will make optimum use of his talents
    a. and enable him make an appropriate contribution the need of
    b. society

From a survey of the general outcomes, it may seem that the committee omitted one of the most important aims of GE: the ability to think rigorously and critically. The committee took the position, however, that this ability should be developed and applied as an integral aspect of the learning process throughout the educational program. The knowledge, skills, abilities, and attitudes involved in critical and reflective thinking should be emphasized as the necessary tools for the analysis and solution of problems in all fields (cited in Bigelow, 1947, p. 258).

What Is a 21st Century LE or GE?

In this following section I will elaborate on specific working definitions to categorize the various iterations of general and liberation education frameworks and institutions:

LE: An approach to college learning that empowers individuals and prepares them to deal with complexity, diversity, and change. This approach emphasizes broad knowledge of the wider world (e.g., science, culture, and society) as well as in-depth achievement in a specific field of interest. It helps students develop a sense of social responsibility; strong intellectual and practical skills that span all major fields of study, such as communication, analytical, and problem-solving skills, and the demonstrated ability to apply knowledge and skills in real-world settings. The broad goals of LE have been enduring even as the courses and requirements that comprise a liberal education have changed over the years. Today, an LE usually includes a general education curriculum that provides broad learning in multiple disciplines and ways of knowing, along with more in-depth study in a major.

- Liberal Arts: Specific disciplines (i.e., the humanities, sciences, and social sciences).

- Liberal Arts College: A particular type of institution—often small, often residential—that facilitates close interaction between faculty and students, and whose curriculum is grounded in the liberal arts disciplines.

- Artes Liberales: The historical basis for the modern liberal arts, consisting of the trivium (grammar, logic, and rhetoric) and the quadrivium (arithmetic, geometry, astronomy, and music).

- GE: That part of an LE curriculum that is shared by all students. It provides broad exposure to multiple disciplines and forms the basis for developing essential intellectual, civic, and practical capacities. GE can take many forms, and increasingly includes introductory, advanced, and integrative forms of learning[2].

Here are some universities' GE objectives excerpted from their website:

Complementing the rest of the curriculum, this program aims to achieve four goals that link the undergraduate experience to the lives students will lead after Harvard:

(1) to prepare students for civic engagement;

(2) to teach students to understand themselves as products of, and participants in, traditions of art, ideas, and values;

(3) to enable students to respond critically and constructively to

---

[2] Retrieved from http://www.aacu.org/leap/what-is-a-liberal-education

change;

(4) and to develop students' understanding of the ethical dimensions of what they say and do[3].

Why Study the Liberal Arts at University of Wisconsin?

Liberal arts is a cornerstone of the American higher education system. A liberal arts degree focuses on interdisciplinary learning that connects math to literature, language to science. A liberal arts education provides breadth and scope and gives students the tools to make a good living and live a good life.

A liberal arts degree is increasingly met with derision and even skepticism. Who hasn't heard this before: "How will that degree help you get a job?" More than half of all living UW-Madison alumni are graduates of the College of Letters & Science. The College teaches the skills students need to make a good living and lead a good life[4].

An LE at Bowdoin College

"The offer of Bowdoin College" written by the seventh president William DeWitt Hyde spelled out a vision of the aspirations of a liberal education appropriate to the early twentieth century. Many of its elements still have value one hundred years later. At the beginning of the twenty-first century, a vastly changed College in a dramatically altered world provided a related but expanded offering of intellectual challenge and personal growth in the context of an active and engaged learning community closely linked to the social and natural worlds.

An LE cultivates the mind and the imagination, encourages seeking after truth, meaning, and beauty, awakens an appreciation of past traditions and present challenges, fosters joy in learning and sharing that learning with others, supports taking the intellectual risks required to explore the unknown, test new ideas and enter into

---

[3] Harvard University Retrieved from: http://isites.harvard.edu/icb/icb.do?keyword=k69286&pageid=icb.page343093

[4] Retrieved from http://www.ls.wisc.edu/whystudy.html

constructive debate, and builds the foundation for making principled judgments. It hones the capacity for critical and open intellectual inquiry; that is, the interest in asking questions, challenging assumptions, seeking answers, and reaching conclusions supported by logic and evidence. An LE rests fundamentally on the free exchange of ideas — on conversation and questioning — that thrives in classrooms, lecture halls, laboratories, studios, dining halls, playing fields, and dormitory rooms. Ultimately, an LE promotes independent thinking, individual action, and social responsibility[5].

Nearly all the American higher education institutions focus on the GE program.

Deep Approach (DA) and Deep Education (DE)

The Deep Turn

"Deep" structure may seem to be inspired by N. Chomsky's transformational-generative grammar. For Chomsky, a grammar is "a finite system of rules that generate infinitely many deep and surface structure appropriately related." The surface structure of a sentence contains within it the output of its semantic and phonological components; it is "that aspect of syntactic description that determines its phonetic form. "Deep structure," on the other hand, is the formal structure, which relates directly, not to the sound but to the syntactic description interpretation of the sentence" (Chomsky, 1955/1975, quoted from Vaugh, 1968, p. 14).

Deep Learning: As devoted educators, we place helping students achieve deep learning, as opposed to superficial learning, among our highest goals. Miller (1999, p. 46) describes such learning as "transformational," in which the point is not simply intellectual development but also "physical, emotional, aesthetic, moral, and spiritual growth." Similarly, Bentz (1992) suggests that a "deep learning experience" is one that "is at once emotional and intellectual,

---

[5] http://www.bowdoin.edu/academics/curriculum/liberal-education-statement.shtml

mental and physical, social and personal, totally unique yet freely shared" (p.72).

Deep learning is a branch of machine learning based on a set of algorithms that attempt to model high-level abstractions in data by using model architectures, with complex structures or otherwise, composed of multiple non-linear transformations (Deng, & Yu, 2013; LeCun, Bengio, Hinton, 2015, pp. 436-444). The theory is widely used in computer, neurology, cognitive science and education etc. Eric Jensen's (2008) book *Deeper learning: 7 powerful strategies for in-depth and longer-lasting learning* was translated in Chinese in 2009, in which the author proposed theory of Deep Learning Cycle (DeLC).

The term of Deep Reflection was first used in earthquake survey (ECORS Pyrenees Team, 1988). Some scholar sees it Deep Thinking (Healy, 1996; Nadelson, 1996; Gentner & Rattman, 1998) or Thinking Deep (Fox, 1992). People call it "Shendu Fansi" in Chinese.

The term of DA was used in Chemistry education in 1980s (Vickers, 1986), and in 1990s it occurred in the assessment of law program (Marchetti, 1997) and the science learning (Chin & Brown, 2000). Entering the 21th century, some scholar views the term as Deep Teaching (Miller, 2009). Tochon (2002, 2003a, 2003b, 2009, 2011) sees it as DA or Deep Methodologies or DE. Recently Tochon (2014) proposed the deep turn toward wisdom and autonomy, which is meant "the cosmopolitan turn" in language education going with the move toward 6Cs standards with the overarching C of Cosmopolitanism as the key to value creation (pp.291-324), which stands for the coming of a real "deep" educational era.

The concepts of DA and DE

The DA or DE were first proposed by Tochon (2002, 2003a, 2003b, 2014) for world language teaching and second language community building through a deep rethinking about other scholars' ideas, i.e., outcome-based teaching model by Bobbit (1918); taxonomy of educational objectives by Benjamin Bloom (1956); active learning by Jean Piaget (1960); instructional outcome in curriculum by Robert Mager (1975); Zone of Proximal Development by Vygostky (1934/1986); "i+1" input hypothesis by Krashen(1985); output hypothesis by Merrill Swain(1985); cognitive learning theory by Bruner (1986, 1990); task-based teaching and learning by Prabhu (1987), Nunan (1989), J. Willis (1996), Skehan (1996) , Ellis (2003), Willis & Willis (2007); the ATCFL National Standards (2006). Later Tochon's studies (2014) in elementary schools and higher institutions and improved its theory and operational contents.

What is the DA or DE? Simply speaking, it is an education that is counter to a superficial education. It is "deep, reflective language learning stressing reading and writing before listening and speaking, promoting open project-based activities such team and peer work, placing the student as curriculum builders on the basic of intrinsic motivation; code-switching and scaffolding among peers is concerned a natural part of deep second and third language development, which results not from automatism but from reflexive output in writing accompanied with extensive reading and listening or watching, and then in speaking" (Tochon, 2014, p. 359). Its most systematic theory can be found in the book *Help Them Learn A Language Deeply: Francois Victor Tochon's DA to World Languages and Cultures* (Tochon, 2014). As Macedo stated, "Tochon's book is more than a treatise on language pedagogy. It presents a grammar and [plans] the strategy of [their] action for deep instructional planning, a grammar for action [which implies understanding] of adaptive and complex cross-cultural situations [that should] be the prime focus of such a hermeneutic inquiry" (cited from Tochon, 2014, p. 351). Donaldo Macedo is a Cape Verdean- American critical theorist, linguist, and expert on literacy and education studies, and he is professor of English and a Distinguished Professor of Liberal Arts and Education at the University of Massachusetts Boston. He was the Graduate Program Director of the Applied Linguistics Master of Arts Program at the University of Massachusetts Boston.

The IAPI model

The IAPI model is one of the key contents in the monograph *Help Them Learn A Language Deeply: Francois Victor Tochon's DA to World Languages and Cultures* by Tochon (2014) and one of the most interesting parts to me. The model's name, IAPI, comes from the acronym of its tasks domains; I for Interpret, A for Analyze, P for Present, I for Interact. While the IAPI was conceptualized years before the ACTFL model and derives from ethnographic research on how genuinely experienced teachers organized their language classes, the IAPI model is clearly an enhancement of the ACTFL (2006) model. It takes into account years of research on seasoned language teachers' practices. This model, based on the classroom observations and interview of teachers on their classroom planning not only makes more sense, but it also works in practice (Tochon, p. 77). The model is mainly used to guide the instructor to realize the curriculum goals and each part plays a different role and focuses on different tasks. As Tochon (2014) proposes, "Interpret" focuses on "Read, Watch, Listen", "Analyze" focuses on "Language", "Present" focuses on "Write, Speak, Record," and "Interact" focuses on "Exchange and Act with people"(p.77). Each part of the model is in charge of the different task domains as follow (pp. 225-226):

- INTERPRET: Film viewing, readings and discussion, answering questions
- ANALYZE: Integrating grammar in texts and discussion, language awareness activities in the accomplishment of projects, homework.
- PRESENT: Report on authentic, continuing project tasks (blog, e-mail, ipod, portfolio, PowerPoint, Skype…)
- INTERACT: Quality participation in small group projects; regularity, motivation and empathy

The major components of this model are Access and Voice. Both are needed to develop proficiency. Access includes tasks related to Interpretation and Analysis. Voice includes Presentation and Interaction. Access and Voice tasks unite in identity-building. Thus, this model is clear and maneuverable in language and culture learning.

GE & DE in China

GE

In China, GE (Tongshi Jiaoyu in Mandarin) originated from Europe and the United States. Among the outstanding scholars returning from the oversea in 1910s, two of them who strongly influenced the GE in China were Cai Yuanpei and Mei Yiqi. In 1910s-20s, Cai Yuanpei, a German-educated Chinese scholar and President of Peking University, advocated the philosophy of "integration of arts and science", which was an idea of LE or GE from Europe. In 1920s-30s, MEI Yiqi, an American-educated Chinese scholar and President of Tsinghua University, proposed the instructional idea that "GE is a root while specialized education is a terminal (Tongshi Weiben, Zhuanshi Weimo)" (cited in Long, 2010, p.103). Tsinghua University offered an American-style GE program to all its freshmen in the faculties of arts, science and law, which was composed of Chinese, English, Mathematics or Logic, History of China or Western History, and at least one subject of natural sciences, viz., Physics, Chemistry, Geology or biology (TDXY, 1991, pp. 170-171, Chen, 2004, p. 2).

After the establishment of the People's Republic of China in 1949, Chinese higher education was "converted into a new specialized education from an old liberal education" by the Soviet-derived reform in the early 1950s summarized under the term "the reordering of colleges and departments" (Chen, 2004, p.2). Since then, GE had been neglected in China and many specialized universities or institutes were set up in accordance with particular governmental sectors or product areas such as mechanical engineering, iron and steel engineering, aeronautics and astronautics, metallurgy, geology, and textiles, etc. Each specialized institution mainly offered programs in their own field. Higher education institutions almost had no connections with one other because of the rigid barriers among them. Even the so-called comprehensive universities, i.e., Peking University, could only offer a general education with just a few credits and GE owned various definitions. From this perspective till the early 1990s, Chinese higher education could be seen as being completely opposite to GE. Comparatively, GE has been widely executed in Taiwan and Hong Kong, China.

With the development of Chinese economy and the deepening of Chinese reform and open policy, Chinese higher education was dramatically reformed in the middle and late 1990s. The most obvious change was mainly to increase the number of humanities and decrease that of specialization. Thus, GE has been strengthened since the middle and late 1990s in China. For instance, in 1998, the year of its one hundredth anniversary, Peking University put forward the strategy to construct a world-class university, and formulated the following idea of an undergraduate program (BDNB, 2000):

"To empower the students to have broad basic knowledge, to cultivate strong creative consciousness, to master the scientific methods, to develop rich humanistic qualities, and to develop practical and adaptable capabilities" (ibid, p. 16)

Based on the above idea, the university sets up the directions for undergraduate curriculum reform:

(1) To offer LE in the lower years of undergraduate programs;

(2) To offer a broadly-definite specialized education in the upper years of undergraduate program;

(3) To establish a complete credit system gradually, under the guidance of syllabus and advisors (BDJ, 2000, p. 2)

From then on, the GE curriculum gradually offers 150-200 courses and updates 10-15% each year. Meanwhile, Peking University set up the following principles for the offering of courses in GE curriculum. The "Notice on Offering GE Curriculum," states that the courses should:

(1) enable students to learn the arts of thinking and methods of understanding and transforming the world through the basic fields of knowledge;

(2) enable students strengthen the development of personal qualities and creativity;

(3) enable students to understand the connections between disciplines and to improve interdisciplinary learning;

(4) enable students to develop critical thinking skills and analytic ability;

(5) enable students to understand new developments, new tendencies, and new information in certain disciplines;

(6) enable students to master the fundamental spirit of classic works and to enlighten their thoughts;

(7) enable students to take courses offered by distinguished professors;

(8) enable students to better understand the fields of study (ibid, pp.6-7).

While there has been an argument about the classification of fields in GE curriculum (ibid, p. 3) Peking University offers GE curriculum in the following five fields (Table 2):

    A. Mathematics and natural sciences;
    B. Social science;
    C. Philosophy and psychology;
    D. History;
    E. Language, literature and fine arts.

Table 2. Undergraduate Curriculum Structure at Peking University, 2001-2002

Undergraduate Curriculum	credits	proportion
Required courses	60	15%
Common courses	34	
Required specialized courses	55	
Required electives	18	24%
Computer	3	
Specialized theoretical courses	16-22	
Specialized courses	6	
Readings of physics literatures	2	
Free electives	6	4. 05%
GE curriculum	16	10. 81%
Graduation thesis	10	6. 75%
Total requirement	148	100%

Source: BDJ, 2000, pp.16-18, from Chen (2004)

Peking University is a flagship higher education institution in China. Entering into a new century, GE has been widely used in China, for instance, Guilin University of Electronic Technology (GUET), where I am teaching, can offer the undergraduate program 40-50 credits related to required and elective GE courses. In some universities, such as Fudan in Shanghai, Hubei in Wuhan, especially build Liberal Arts Education Colleges and develop GE in Mainland China.

With regard to the status of GE in high school in China, the definitive answer is not optimistic nor satisfactory at this time. Historically speaking, the national examination of the entrance to higher institution has been divided into art papers and science papers in China. A potential change will take place in 2017, in which the national examination will cancel the division of art and science papers and GE will be taken seriously in high schools. Thus, some progress is certainly being made in terms of embracing GE in secondary schools in China.

DE in China

"Deep learning" ("Shendu Xuexi" in Chinese), originated from deep machine learning, is widely used in computer science and artificial intelligence especially with the advent of the 21st century in China and several scholars have finished their Ph.D. dissertations in this field (Chen, 2014; Zou, 2014). "Deep teaching" or "In-depth teaching" ("Shendu Jiaoxue" in Chinese) was first proposed by Guo Yuanxiang (2009), an educator from Central China Normal University (CCNU), which is a core university in China. What is Shendu Jiaoxu (deep teaching)? Guo (2009) states:

> "the nature and internal structure of knowledge to decide that sufficient teaching must be complete or holistic teaching, and sufficient teaching must transcend semiotic teaching in surface. I call the unity from semiotic teaching to logic teaching and sense teaching, deep teaching". He further explains: "Deep teaching doesn't mean the depth and difficulty of the teaching contents and doesn't mean the teaching contents the deeper the better, either, but relative to the constructional components of knowledge, its teaching doesn't stay at the level of signs or semiotics" (ibid,p.22).

This explanation is akin to Tochon's idea (2003) about DA or DE. What are the basic strategies of deep teaching? Guo Yuanxiang (ibid) summarizes 4Rs, viz, Richness teaching (Fengfuxing Jiaoxue), Recursion teaching (Huiguixing Jiaoxue), Relation teaching (Guanlianxing Jiaoxue), and Rigor teaching (Yanmixing Jiaoxue) (pp.22-23). Compared with Tochon's Hol-acts in the DA (Tochon, 2014, pp. 196-224), it seems that Guo's strategies are not specific and difficult to operate in practice. Tochon (2010) gave the first lecture about DA (Shendu Jiaoyufa) or Deep Education (Shendu Jiaoyu) in Taiwan, China and he (2011) began to disseminate his theory about DA or DE in Mainland China, but fewer scholars prefer to the term "Shendu Jiaoyu" (DE), or "Shendu Jiaoyufa"(DA) in their studies in China. It is difficult to find research related to DA or DE in China since the practice is not common, as LI Ping (2014) states that the related research on deep teaching or deep learning is not much and over 20 articles are found and most of which stay in a descriptive level in her MA thesis(p.11). Deep teaching is also proposed under the background of educational theory to the large-scale development. It plays an important role in actual classroom teaching, and plays a huge role in promoting deep learning for students. But the theoretical researches are still at the initial stage, there are little theory researches, and practical understanding is insufficient(ibid, p.I).

With the rapid development of teaching and education reform in China, scholars get to learn that the current core problem is a lack of deep teaching, as a Ph.D. scholar in education, LI Songlin (2014) points out "… the problem in the current situation is the lacking of depth, which presents itself the fact that students' experience is not profound, their thinking is not penetrating, and their understanding is not deep. Instruction lacking depth can't exert a far-reaching influence on students' learning and development, but in-depth teaching is the nature and direction of promoting classroom teaching reform in depth and breadth"(pp.53-56). Thus, the question remains as to how teachers manage and cope and, additionally, defining what deep education is exactly. Li, S. (ibid) proposes four suggestions for instructors' practice:

(1) to go deep into students' feelings and thinking,

(2) to touch the nature of subjects and the core of the knowledge,

(3) to expose the internal transformation of students' learning and development,

(4) to promote students' autonomous discovery and real understanding.

Generally speaking, the theory of DA or DE is quite fragmented, not systematical and the related practice is lacking in China.

Foreign Language General Education (FLGE) in China

The stages of foreign language development

As shown in 3. 1, GE was neglected after the establishment of new China in 1949 and so-called foreign language teaching was mainly Russian language because China followed its brother socialist country, the Soviet Union, at that time. Without any doubts, Russian became nearly an arbitrarily taught foreign language in the classrooms in China. From 1958 to the beginning of 1960s, the reform of specialized foreign languages was put on the agenda and eight higher institutions held language teaching movements. College foreign language education had been in a neglected state since this reform of specialized foreign languages was only for Chinese officials who traveled to the Soviet Union or for foreign trade affairs, in order to finish interpreting or translating work (Wang & Li, 2010, p. 4).

From 1966 to 1976, the period of *the Great Proletarian Cultural Revolution*. During the period, many teachers or intellectuals were regarded as capitalists and criticized or fought by the Red Guards or the young students. Most of the high school students were forced to work in the countryside and the annual National Examination was quitted and the workers with good family background were directly recommended to the universities. Actually foreign language education was laid aside and all learning of foreign language was solely for political propaganda and facilitation(Wang & Li, 2010). During this period, no student needed learning knowledge and foreign language in high schools, and a student named ZHANG Tiesheng, who handed in an empty paper in the examination, was seen as a hero by "the Gang of Four" at the Cutlural Revolution Period, during which a more knowledgeable person was regarded as a more reactionary one. What does "the Gang of Four" mean?

"The Gang of Four (simplified Chinese: 四人帮; traditional Chinese: 四人幫; pinyin: Sìrén bāng) was a political faction composed of four Chinese Communist Party officials. They came to prominence during the Cultural Revolution (1966–76) and were later charged with a series of treasonous crimes. The gang's leading figure was MAO Zedong's last wife JIANG Qing. The other members were ZHANG Chunqiao, YAO Wenyuan, and WANG Hongwen (https://en.wikipedia.org/wiki/Gang_of_Four)".

For the reason above, that might present a prohibition stage of foreign language in China.

The reform and open policy of China began in the late 1970s: the national entrance examination for higher education institutions was reinstated in 1977, and the first freshmen came into universities or colleges in the spring of 1978. Many kinds of foreign languages were taught in higher institutions, i.e. English, Russian, Japanese, Spanish, French, German, etc., and while all the middle school and high school students began to learn English, English was also offered as a college course with the end of the Cold War and the falling down of Berlin Wall . As a course of general education, English became the top priority in foreign language education. Anyway the main objectives of college English courses were to develop reading and writing ability but most students couldn't listen or speak. Subsequently, in the late 1990s, the head of Gaojiaosi of Chinese Ministry of Education Cen Jianjun called the college English teaching "Dumb English"(Huang, 1999, p.20) and pointed out that kind of foreign language education didn't meet the needs of development of the national reform and open policy, and emphasized that foreign language education must reinforce the fostering of "communicative competence"(Bachman,1990), especially the abilities in listening and speaking. Then we could say this period is a "dumb" foreign language stage.

Entering the 21st century, foreign language education began to enter a flourishing stage in China. Pupils began to learn English all over the country and the comprehensive abilities of students' foreign language, especially English, developed much more before going into higher institutions. In *College English Curriculum Requirements* (CECR) (JG, 2007), three levels of college English development are demonstrated and the three levels are Basic requirements, Intermediate requirements, and Higher requirements. Different institutions can make a suitable teaching syllabus according to the students' English proficiency under the guise of CECR. Prestigious universities then initiated their College English education from Higher requirements while lower tier institutions began their College English education for Basic requirements and most intermediate-level universities began their College English education from Intermediate requirements for some students and began their College English education from Basic requirements for others. Meanwhile three-year institutions execute different requirements for their College English education.

While the CECR structure is decent and flexible, choosing content and teaching material for students in college English courses really leads to a variety of proposals in China. A known scholar Cai (2004) proposed that ESP (English for Specific Purposes) should be the developmental orientation for College English, and this idea has been supported by some language teachers in China. Cai (2007) further called for scholars of English language teaching to transition general English (Chinese College English) into ESP, then in 2012 stated EAP (English for Academic Purposes) is one part of ESP, citing the achievements accomplished of EAP students at Fudan University in Shanghai. As the Dean of the Shanghai Higher Education College English Teaching & Guiding Committee, Cai (2013) developed *A Framework of Reference for EFL Teaching at Tertiary Level for Shanghai* and this framework officially decides ESP as a guideline and that EAP is a required course for freshmen. Recently Cai (2014, 2015) has consistently called for all the national higher institutions to substitute College English with EAP. However, China is a very large nation with

1.4 billion people, including more than 24 million college students (excluding postgraduates) , so if all college students are required to take EAP courses, this proposal is not necessary and inadvisable and we propose foreign language education should be polynary or multiple-level, i.e., DE for world languages and cultures, FLGE may be good perspectives. During foreign language education the curriculum should NOT be unified/standardized.

FLGE

Why propose FLGE

First, entering a new century with the rapid development of elementary education in China, in the last decade pupils have begun to learn English from Grade 3, and some began to learn English from Grade 1, and some from kindergarten. The students have attained intermediate language proficiencies before enrolling in university. If the English faculty members just teach form-focused grammar and based-on analyzing grammatical forms and not the actual production of communication in colleges, students may typically be bored in the classroom, even play hooky, since students are boring of language form, Instead, students should be able to choose the contents they are interested in to be taught or transcend the contents which make students the center of learning.

Second, following the national general education program in order to reach the empowerment education proposed by the Minister of P. R. China (Jiaoyubu, 1999).

Third, we must find a way to help reconnect and harmonize the discord between English and non-English major faculties. For example, Proposing Foreign Language General Education (FLGE) and reconstructing Department of English GE can make much sense and the faculties from non-major English can develop their own major and research orientations, which will foment mutual respect among English teachers and other departments(Long, 2014a).

The traits or nature of foreign language

A foreign language mainly has six traits as any language has:

(1) Instrument (Gongjuxing)

Language as an instrument relates to its communicative function, because it can communicate via tone, pronunciation, sign, carrier of history. An instrument is the basic of a language or a foreign language and language is an instrument of thinking, an instrument of human communication, an instrument of other disciplines as the linguistics reach a common sense.

(2) Humanity (Renwenxing)

Briefly, language humanity means language itself contains humanistic spirits and cultural heritages. Language humanity means its ideology, wihich includes man and culture.Humanity is a distillation of language.Instrument and humnaity are two characteristics of a language, and they are highly unified.However we must see other straits of a language as follows.

(3) Scientificity (Kexuexing)

Scientificity and humanity of languages have a relation of opposition and unification. Language has both its humanity and scientificity. Mark Pagel, a professor of Evolutionary Biology in Reading University in the UK, said in a TED(technology, entertainment and design) lecture about how language changes human: he can observe Homo erectus, Zax (stone axe) 2 million years ago and the shape of the Homo erectus did not change and our close relative, the Neanderthal, did not change the design of Zax among 300, 000 years ago because they had no language.Pagel(2012) further proposed a capacity for culture also makes human unique, why? Because human can speak language (pp.297-299).

Named as a pioneer in science and technology, Kelly (2010) stated in his book *What Technology Wants*, that the most important technological inventor in the history of human civilization. His view is very similar to Mark Pagel's idea. The basic of information technology is language.No language , no Scientificity. So, when we use language to research or teach, we should pay much attention to its scientificity, which will bring us a better outcome.

(4) Ethnicity & Cosmopolitanism or Publicity (Minzuxing & Shijiexing or Gonggongxing)

Usually language reveals a person's identity, since people can judge who he is and where he is from through his language. From this perspective we purport that language has its own ethnicity, but language is also public and necessary , just like the air around us and everybody in the world can use it free of charge, from this perspective we can say language also contains cosmopolitanism or publicity and it is a public resource(Long, 2014).

(5) Generality (Tongshixing)

Generality means the most common or basic knowledge in human life. Once a person can own this kind of common knowledge, he will be able to study and gain more in-depth knowledge. We say that foreign language has its generality relative to language 1, language 2, etc., as Liu, S (2012) states "Foreign language is general" , while Hanstedt(2012) points out an integrative approach to an interdisciplinarity is the trend of general education, he also teaches an integrative course on science and literature (pp.13-17), I proposed the integrated content in various courses is general in language taeching, seen from this inspective, language or foreign language owns its generality.

(6) Education (Jiaoyuxing)

Different nationalities have different cultures or customs and some learners have difficulty accepting a foreign language or culture and they may not accept the people from this kind of language or culture or they will be hostile, or vice versa. In the history of human development many wars or conflicts have erupted because of misunderstandings or no way to understand another people's tongue. The tale of The Tower of Babel gives us humans a deep implication, the tale tells people that there was only one language in the world at the beginning, and people's pwower was so indefinite that, some day the people with the same language decided to build a tower to heaven.When the god got to know this, he made people speak different languages, then people could not know each other and began to fight each other (Chapter 11, in *Bible*). Because language is educative, all foreign language educators or instructors should be teaching for world peace and manage to exert and use well all the characters of a language to be an excellent educator, giving back greatly to the educational cause of world languages and cultures.

FLGE and its current status

In China, there is no exact definition of it. In brief, foreign language general education is an approach to a GE program where learners can achieve through foreign language-- or it is a type of GE that realizes its own functions and characters through foreign language learning. It should be part of GE in the reform of Chinese empowerment education. Only a few scholars, Zhang (2007), Wu (2003, 2005) Wu & Han(2010), Wang & Li(2010), Huang (2011), Cai(2011), Feng(2012), Wang(2013), Long(2010, 2012, 2013a, 2013b, 2014a, 2014b, 2014c, 2014d, 2015a, 2015b, 2015c), Liu (2012, 2014, 2015), Zeng (2015), Liu, X. (2015), Shao(2015), Huang, J.(2015), Huang,L.(2015) among others, advocate for FLGE in foreign language teaching and research. Nevertheless, this idea is questioned by some scholars such as Cai (2010, 2013). Cai (2013) manages to substitute ESP or EAP for overall Chinese College English education. As I mentioned previously, however, foreign language education should not be standardized across the nation and I propose foreign language education should instead be personalized and diversified.

I propose College English should follow a GE approach speaking briefly about the currently status of Chinese College English GE in mainland China. Coming from College of Foreign Languages, Nanjing University of Aeronautics and Astronautics, Wu (2003) first proposed College English GE aiming at pushing forward "quality-oriented education" and upgrading College English teaching and learning in China. "Quality-oriented education" means "empowerment education" (Liu & Liao, 2002). In 2005 he further proposed the idea of "Three-strand framework" as the content of College English GE courses, that includes "English language, Chinese and foreign cultures, multidisciplinary knowledge " (Wu, 2005, p. 65). Wang & Li (2010), comes also from Faculty of English Education, Sun Yat-sen University, which is one of the top universities in China, expounds the concept and basic content of general education, and introduces several successful GE colleges, i.e. Class Yuanpei from Peking University, Class Zhu Kezhen from Zhejiang University, Class Jidi from Nanjing University, Fudan GE College from Fudan University, and presents the achievements of GE practice in the university (pp. 3-8).

Here I introduce the deepest reform of English GE from College of Foreign Studies (CoFS), Guilin University of Electronic Technology (GUET), which represents one of most general higher institutions in China. LIU Shaozhong, coming from USA with two Ph.D.s, one from North Carolina State University in 2011, the other in Foreign language linguistics and applied linguistics from Guangdong University of Foreign Studies in 1997, became dean of CoFS in in November 2012. Liu (2012) began to reform the organizational institutions according to American models: the original Office of College English Teaching & Research was renamed Department of English General Education; Office of English Major Teaching & Research was renamed the Department of English Education for professionals; Office of Postgraduate Teaching & Research was renamed the Department of Postgraduate Education. Changing the name from "Office" into a department and "Teaching & Research" into "Education," he restructured six research entities, one of which is the Institution of Foreign Language General Education Research (IoFLGER). I am the Chair of IoFLGER, GUET and Dr. Joy Zeng is Vice Chair. Our CoFS' GE program met much difficulty at its incipit and some faculties were not willing to accept the program changes because they were content with things as they were. In 2013, Liu proposed the related theory research as a priority and so far the CoFS has gained over 10 relevant projects and published a book series entitled *Contemporary International Studies*, including a series of article about the FLGE program(Long, 2015). From 2014, our CoFS launched the program in several majors in GUET and our accomplishments are welcomed by the enrolled students as well as from faculty members both coming from CoFS of GUET and several other higher education institutions in China.

The relation of foreign language and GE

Usually where there is GE, there is foreign language and the two camps can't depart from each other. As Lipp (1952, p. 202) points out: "if foreign language teachers and general educationists are to learn from each other, GE will be enriched by offerings in foreign languages and foreign language teachers will have their intellectual horizons broadened as a result of new experience with wider and interrelated fields of study." Furthermore, "a language year would benefit enormously both GE and study in the major" (Sudermann, 1993, p.161). Obviously one's foreign language learning can promote GE as well as major study. In other words, foreign language learning or teaching is not contradictory to GE and both are fully integrated. We have more evidences that show they are harmonious, in fact, and this paper will use ESP as an example of this.

Cates (1987), coming from the Faculty of GE of Japanese Universities, proposed a very good design for ESP and the GE program according to a needs analysis approach. Cates (1987, p. 233) called this term a GEFL (general education foreign language) program, which is analogous to the FLGE program this paper proposes. Do FLGE learners have specific needs for learning a foreign language? This is a valid question. For many years the answer was assumed to be "No" in Japan. The standard joke about general education English, for example, was instead of using the term TEFL, it would be better to use the term TENOR (Teaching English for No Obvious Reason). As Hutchinson and Waters (1987) point out, all language teaching must be based on some needs, otherwise there would be no language teaching. Cates (ibid) modified Hutchinson and Waters 1987's ESP model and applied it in ESP for FLGE programs and analyzed the needs and wants in detail from present to future, potential vs. actual, needs vs. wants, target vs. learning for students' ESP learning and from present and future education, future occupation, present and future travel, and present and future social for students' GE. He lists at least four parties involved in university foreign language teaching: the students, the teachers, the university and community (pp. 239-240).

Cates believes ESP should be part of FLGE, and through a modified version of curriculum models proposed by Valette (1971) and Stern (1983) he produces the new framework for ESP for FLGE program, which includes two parts: content and communication. Content includes academic disciplines, ESP, and culture, while the communication component includes language and culture. Finally, the program will realize five objectives: proficiency, knowledge, affect, social reform, and transfer (Cates, 1987, p. 247). From this perspective, academic English is separate from ESP, Cai (2005, 2007, 2010, 2011, 2012, 2013, 2014, 2015) sees it as part of ESP, and ESP belongs to one of the main contents in the framework. In 2014 while working in Youjiang Medical University for Nationalities as a supporting teacher, I gave lectures to non-English major students (mainly), English major students, and teachers about FLGE including *Academic English*, *ESP* (i.e., *Socialist Core Values*, *Vocabulary*) which were warmly welcomed by the audience. Any discipline may have its own GE contents.

The Similarities & Differences Between GE and DE

The similarities

(1) Both are new approaches to such an education which overall empowers students. GE was proposed in 1920, neglected or stopped after 1949 in China, and recovered in the middle or the late 1990s, while deep learning was proposed at the beginning of

the 21st century, and deep teaching was first put forward by Xie in 2009 and DE or DA was introduced by Tochon in 2010 in Taiwan and in 2011 in Mainland China. It seems that the former began at first and in fact both of their histories are quite short. Both approaches to languages and cultures began in the 21st century.

(2) Both have many same objectives, i.e., cultivating citizens of the world who are responsible for the peace of the world, the whole-person education, proficiency, knowledge, affect, social reform, and transfer, etc.

(3) Both teach disciplinary knowledge and focus on teaching contents or materials that transcend the contents and underlying skills.

(4) Both can be applied in all types of disciplines including languages and cultures.

(5) Both take into account students' interests and needs.

(6) Both are sensible for faculty members and may widen their perspective.

(7) Both concern educational depth.

(8) Both concern critical thinking.

(9) Both have intradisciplinary, interdisciplinary, and transdisciplinary contents and knowledge to teach (Tochon, p. 142).

(10) Both concern students' future life.

The differences

GE is different from DA or DE, as follows (Table 3).

Table 3. The differences between GE & DE

Items	GE	DE
Emphasis	Generality, breadth, though concern depth as well	Depth, thoroughness
Learning strategy	Student-and learning-centered	student-and learning-centered, also project-centered
Curriculum-builder	Made by educators according to students' needs	Made by educators and learners
Current status in USA	Very Mature	New
Language skills' focus	Listening, speaking, reading, and speaking nearly simultaneous	Text is given priority

It seems that Foreign Language GE and the DE to world languages and cultures have something different in teaching models. The former does not have a definitive teaching model, and the later has an interesting model "IAPI" (interpret, analyze, present, and interact) (Tochon, 2014, pp. 77-79). The latter contains a systematic pedagogical holistic action (ibid, pp. 197-224) and the former does not, but has a distinct curriculum framework (Cates, 1987, pp. 233-258).

Conclusion and Outlook

The chapter stated the general historical overview and relation of LE, GE and DE, language characters, the relation between language and GE, and also presented the practice and use of FLGE and DA in China. Meanwhile it points out that any learning approach, i.e. the ESP approach Cai (2004, 2007, 2012, 2013, 2014, 2015) proposed in College English course, must not be standardized.

Through research and deep understanding, we argue that both the GE and the DA are sound theories to current Chinese education. We emphasize that FLGE and the DA bring language faculty members and educators innovative ideas for language teaching, learning and research. Though these two approaches are still facing difficulties in China, we do believe they will continue to reach their own objectives and significance.

Since these two approaches are so well-conceptualized, a final idea: In figure 1, the AACU states that America reaches LE before the 21st century, and that the answer is "through GE." So then how about in the 21st century? The recommended answer is "across the entire educational continuum." We believe that "entire" should be "general" and "deep".

References

ACTFL - American Council on the Teaching of Foreign Languages (2006). *Standards for foreign language learning in the 21st century.* Lawrence, KS: Allen Press.

Bachman, L. (1990). *Fundamental considerations in language testing.* Oxford: Oxford University Press.

BDJ - Beijing Daxue Jiaowubu (2000). Tongshi kecheng shouce (Handbook of GE curriculum). Beijing: Office of Academic Affairs of Peking University.

BDNB - Beijing Daxue Nianjian Bianweihui (2000). *Beijing daxue nianjian 1999 [Peking University Yearbook 1999].* Beijing: Peking University Press.

Bentz, V. M. (1992). Deep Learning groups: Combining emotional and intellectual learning. *Clinical Sociology Review, 10,* 71-89.

Bigelow, K. (1947). Review of education research. *Education for Citizenship, 17*(4), 258-265.

Bloom, B. S. (1956). *Taxonomy of educational objectives, handbook I: the cognitive domain* (2nd Ed). New York: Wesley.

Bobbit, F. (1918). *The curriculum.* New York: Houghton.

Bruner, J. (1986). *Actual minds, possible worlds.* Cambridge, MA: Harvard University Press.

Bruner, J. (1990). *Acts of meaning.* Cambridge, MA: Harvard University Press.

Cai, G. (2010). Creativity-oriented General Education reform. *Computer-aided Foreign Language Education (CAFLE), 135,* 14-19.

Cai, J. (2004). ESP yu woguo daxueyingyu jiaoxue fazhan fangxiang (ESP & the direction of Chinese College English) *Waiyujie (World of Foreign Language),* (2), 22-28.

Cai, J. (2007). Characteristics and solutions of college English teaching in transition. *Foreign Language Teaching and Research* (bimonthly), *39* (1), 27-32.

Cai, J. (2012). Academic English:Needs analysis and teaching methods. *Foreign Language Learning Teaching & Practice (FLLTP),* (2), 30-35.

Cai, J. (2013). Daxueyingyu shengcun weiji jiqi xueke diwei yanjiu(On the crisis of College English & Its discipline position) . *Zhongguo Daxue Jiaoxue. (Chinese Colleges & Universities Teaching),* (2), 10-14.

Cai, J. (2014). Four major innovations of a framework of reference for EFL teaching at tertiary Level (Shanghai implementation). *Zhongguo ESP Yanjiu(Chinese ESP Studies),* 4(1), 1-12.

Cai, J. (2015). Development review, problems and tasks of ESP teaching in mainland China. *Journal of Xi'an International Studies of University, 23*(1), 68-72.

Cates, K. A. (1987). ESP and the General Education Foreign Language program. A needs analysis approach to program design. 鳥取大学教養部紀要, 21, 233-258.

Chen, X. (2004). Social changes and the revival of Liberal Education in China since the 1990s. *Asia Pacific Education Review, 5*(1), 1-13.

Chen, Y. (2014). *Research on Chinese information extraction based on Deep Belief Nets* . Harbin Institute of Technology Dissertation for the Doctoral Degree in Engineering.

Chomsky, N. (1955/1975). *Logical structure of linguistic theory*. MIT Humanities Library. Microfilm/ Chicago, IL: University of Chicago Press.

Chin, C., & Brown, E. D. (2000). Learning in science: A comparison of Deep and Surface Approaches. *Journal of Research in Science Teaching, 37*(2), 109-138.

Deng, L. & Yu, D. (2013). Deep Learning methods and applications. *Foundations and trends in signal processing,* 7(3-4)/*The Essence of Knowledge* (2014).

ECORS Pyrenees Team. (1988). The ECORS deep reflection seismic survey across the Pyrenees. *Nature,* (331), Feb. 11, 508 - 511.

Ellis, R. (2003). *Task-based language learning and teaching*. Oxford, UK: Oxford University Press.

Feng, X. (2012). *College English teacher personal belief in General Education :An action research*. Shanghai International Studies University Doctorate Dissertation.

FC - Faculty Committee.(1828).Report on the course of instruction in Yale College. New Haven: Printed by Hezekiah Howe.

Fox, J. (1992). Thinking deep. *Nature, 351*, 462-463.

Gagne, R. M., & Briggs, L. J. (1974). *Principles of instructional design* (2nd Ed.). New York: Holt, Rinehart, and Winston.

Gentner, D., & Rattermann, J. M. (1998). Deep thinking in children:The case for knowledge change in analogical development. *Behavioral and Brain Sciences, 21*(6), 837-838.

Guo, Y. (2009). The nature and structure of knowledge and Deep Teaching. *Curriculum, Teaching Material and Method, 29*(11), 17-23.

Hanstedt, P. (2012).General Education Essentials: A guide for College Faculty. San Fransisco, CA: Jossey Bass/A Willey Imprint.

Healy, B. J. (1996). Deep thinking. *Outdoor life. 197*(3), 66.

Huang, F. (2011). College English teaching innovation for cultivating excellent engineering talents. *Computer-aided Foreign Language education (CAFLE),* 137, 15-19.

Huang, H. (1999). Probe in "Dumb English." *Journal of Xiamen Education College,* 4, 20-23.

Huang, L. (2015a). An analysis of College English teaching in the science and technology university and literary General Education. *Contemporary International Studies, 1*(1), 11-18.

Huang, J. (2015b). On College English textbook development and application from the perspective of general education. *Contemporary International Studies, 1*(1), 34-44.

Hutchinson T., & Water, A. (1987). *English for specific purpose.* Cambridge: Cambridge University Press.

Jessen, E. (2008). *Deeper learning:7 powerful strategies for in-depth and longer-lasting learning.* Thousand Oaks, CA : Corwin Press.

Jiaoyubu. (1999). *The laws on education of People's Republic of China.* Beijing: Foreign Language Press.

JG-Jiaoyubu Gaojiaosi (2007). *College English Curriculum Requirements.* Shanghai: Shanghai Foreign Language Education Press.

Fox, J. (1992). Thinking deep. *Nature, 351,* 462-463.

Krashen, S. D. (1985). *The input hypothesis: issues and implications.* London: Longman.

Kelly, K. (2010). *What technology wants.* New York: Penguin.

LeCun, Y., Bengio, Y. and Hinton, G. E. (2015). Deep Learning. *Nature,* 521, 436-444.

Li, P. (2014). *Teaching for Deep Learning: Rational seeking and strategic practice of Deep Teaching theory.* Najing Normal University MA dissertation.

Li, S. (2014). The four points for the in-depth teaching: Also on the nature and direction of promoting classroom teaching in depth and breadth. *Theory and Practice of Education, 34*(32), 53-56.

Lipp, S. (1952). Foreign language and General Education. *The Journal of General Education, 6*(3), 202-208 .

Liu, S.,& Liao,F.(2002).Translating"Su Zhi Jiao Yu" into English: An Email Survey. *Shanghai Journal of Translators for Science and Technology,* 2，55-57.

Liu, S. (Reporter) (2012, Dec. 17/28). *Organizational restructuring & COFS' development.* Guilin, GX: College of Foreign Studies, Guilin University of Electronic Technology.

Liu, S. (Reporter)(2014, Dec. 27). *Jutongshiqi zoutongshilu, yutongshicai: Yingyu zhuanye jianshe Zaisikao (Raise the GE flag, take the GE road, foster the liberal talents: Rethinking of the English major construction)*:Hezhou, GX: An Invited Lecture for the 18th Annual Conference of Guangxi Higher Institutions English Major Teaching & Research. Retrieved from http://www.hzu. gx. cn/fsc/?p=1408

Liu, S. (2015). Preface. In Long, X. (Ed.). *Contemporary International Studies 1*(1). Beijing: Guangming Daily Press.

Liu, X. (2015). On construction of eco-class for English GE. *Contemporary verbal communication.* Shanghai: Shanghai International Studies *International Studies, 1*(1), 9-27.

Long, X. (2010). *A study on Chinese EFL learners' pragmatic failure in* University Doctorate Dissertation.

Long, X. (2012, Jun. 18). *FLGE series(1): English learning and life orientation*. Zhangjiang, GD: Guangdoong Ocean University. Retrieved from: http://News.Gdou.Edu.cn/show. php?contentid=12049

Long, X. (2014a, Mar. 30). *FLGE series(1): On FLGE*. Handan, HB: Handan University. Retrieved from:
   http://www.Hdc.Edu.cn/News_View. asp?NewsID=5651

Long, X. (2014b, Mar. 30). *FLGE series(2): General knowledge transfer between English IPA and Chinese Pingyin*. Handan, HB:Handan University. Retrieved from: http://www. hdc.edu.cn/News_View.asp?NewsID=5651

Long, X. (2014c, Dec. 3). *FLGE series(1): Four-yin Approach to English vocabulary learning*. Baise, GX: Youjiang Medical University for Nationalities. Retrieved from:
   http://dxwyb.ymcn.gx. cn/info/1030/1671.htm

Long, X. (2014d, Nov. 30). *FLGE series(2):Foreign language learning & the development of patriotism spirits*. Baise, GX: Youjiang Medical University for Nationalities. Retrieved from: http://dxwyb. ymcn. gx. cn/info/1005/1116. htm

Long, X. (Reporter)(2014e, Dec. 15). *FLGE series(1): Four-yin Approach to English vocabulary learning*. Guilin, GX: Guilin Tourism University Retrieved from: http://www.glit.Edu.cn/glitxw. asp?id=1249

Long, X. (2014f, Dec. 29). *FLGE series(3):Foreign language learning & the development of patriotism spirits - A perspective of scientific research*. Baise, GX:Youjiang Medical   University for Nationalities. Retrieve from: http://dxwyb. ymcn. gx. cn/info/1009/1011. htm

Long, X.(2015a, Jan. 21). *FLGE series (4): Academic English general education*. Baise, GX: Youjiang Medical University for Nationalities .
   Retrieved from: http://dxwyb.ymcn.   gx.cn/info/1003/1185.htm

Long, X. (Reporter)(2015b, Jan. 19). *FLGE series(1):New horizon for College English teaching reform: Theory and practice of foreign language general Education*. Baise, GX: Baise University. From:
   http://www.bsuccn/department/wyx/wyxw/2015012043006.html

Long, X. (2015c, Jan. 19). *FLGE series(2): Four-yin Approach to English vocabulary Learning - Taking Long's PSSA for example*. Baise, GX: Baise University. Retrieved from:
   http://www.bsuc.cn/department/wyx/wyxw/2015012043006.html

Mager, R. (1962/1975). *Preparing instructional objectives* (2nd ed.). Belmont, CA: Lake.

Marchetti, E. (1997). The influence of assessment in a law program on the adoption of a Deep Approach to learning. *Journal of Professional Legal Education* . *15* (2), 203-226.

Miller, J. P. (1999). Making connections through holistic learning. *Educational Leadership, 56*, 46-48.

Miller, L. (2009). Present to possibility: Spiritual awareness and Deep Teaching. *Teachers College Record, 111*(12), 2705-2712.

Nadelson, T. (1996). Psychotherapy, revelation, science, and deep thinking. *The American Journal of Psychiatry. 153*(7) (Suppl.)

Nunan, D. (1989). *Designing tasks for communicative classroom*. New York: Cambridge University Press.

Pagel, M. (2012).Evolution: Adapted to culture. *Nature, 482* (7385), 297-299.

Piaget, J . (1960). *The child's conception of the world*. Paterson, NJ : Littlefield, Adams.

Prabhu, N. S. (1987). *Second Language Pedagogy*. New York: Oxford University Press

Shao, H. (2015). On College English teaching from the perspective of GE. *Contemporary International Studies, 1*(1), 28-33.

Skehan, P. (1996). A framework for the implementation of task-based instruction. *Applied Linguistics. 17*(1). Oxford: Oxford University Press.

Stern, H. H. (1983). *Fundamental concept of language teaching*. Oxford, UK: Oxford University Press.

Sudermmann, P. S. (1993). The role of foreign language in general education. *Journal of General Education, 42*(3), 149-163.

Swain, M. (1985). Communicative competence: Some roles of comprehensible input and comprehensible output in its development. In S. Gass & C. Madden (Eds.), Input in Second Language Acquisition. Cambridge, MA: Newbury House.

TDXY - Tsinghua Daxue Xiaoshi Yanjiushi (1991). Tsinghuadaxue shiliao xuanbian [History of Qinhua University :Selected documents]. Beijing: Tsinghua University Press.

Tochon, F. V. (2002, Nov.). *The Deep Approach to world language teaching*. Paper presented at the Wisconsin Association of Foreign Language Teachers(WAFLT). Appleton, WI.

Tochon, F. V. (2003a). Student's assessment. In F. V. Tochon & D. Hanson (Eds.), *The Deep Approach: Second languages for community building* (pp. 225-230). Madison, WI: Atwood.

Tochon, F. V. (2003b). The Deep Approach: World Language Teaching for Bilingual Education. In F. V. Tochon & D. Hanson (Eds.), *The Deep Approach: Second languages for community building* (pp. 11-28). Madison, WI: Atwood.

Tochon, F. V. (2009). Semiotic inquiry or the advent of Deep Methodologies. *International Applied Semiotics Journal*, special issue on "Semiotics and Educational Inquiry." Online journal: http://academicepublishing.com/iasj_special_2009.pdf

Tochon, F. V. (2011). Deep Education: Assigning a moral role to academic work. *Educaçao, Sociedade & Culturas* (Education, Society and Cultures - University of Porto, Portugal), *33*, 17-35.

Tochon, F. V. (2014). *Help them learn a language deeply - Francois Victor Tochon's Deep Approach to world languages and cultures*. Blue Mounds, WI: Deep University Press.

Vallette, R. (1971). Evaluation of learning in a Second Language in Bloom, B. (Ed.), *Handbook formative and summative evaluation of student learning.* NY: McGraw Hill.

Vaugh, B. (1968). Deep and surface structure in traditional and sophisticated literature: Faust. *South Atlantic Bulletin, 33*(3), 14-17.

Vickers, T. (1986). A Deep Approach to teaching the tricarboxylic acid cycle. *Biochemical Education, 14*(4), 172-173.

Vygostky, L. (1934/1986). *Thought and language* (newly revised). Cambridge, MA: MIT Press.

Wang, L. (2013). General Education of foreign language majors: History, status and outlook. *Foreign Language Teaching and Research (bimonthly), 45*(6), 922-932.

Wang, Y. (2002). Tongshi weiben zhuanshi weimo. *Exploring Education Development*, (3), 59-62.

Wang, Z., & Li, J. (2010) A study of General Education with English medium instruction in Tertiary Education. *Computer-aided Foreign Language Education(CAFLE)*, (135), 3-8.

Willis, J. (1996). *A framework for task-based learning.* Harlow, UK: Longman.

Willis, D. S. & Willis, J. (2007). *Doing task-based teaching.* Oxford, UK: Oxford University Press.

Wu, D. (2003). College English and GE. *Journal of Zhenjiang College, 16*(4), 10-12.

Wu, D. (2005). A three-strand framework of College English teaching and fostering of high empowerment talents. *Jiangsu Gaojiao (Jiangsu Higher Education), 4*, 65-67.

Wu, D., Han, Y. (2010). Building up a new framework of ELT under the guidance of GE. *Computer-aided Foreign Language Education (CAFLE), 135*, 9-13.

Zeng, Z. (2015). On English for GE purpose instruction, its goal and features. *Contemporary International Studies, 1*(1), 1-10.

Zhang, H. (2007). *Reseach on the General Education -based innovation of the teaching of College English in China.* Shanghai Jiaotong University, Unpublished Master Thesis.

Zhou, P. (2014). *Research on acoustic modeling for speech recognition based on Deep Neural Networks.* University of Science and Technology of China. Unpublished Doctoral Dissertation.

5.

From Integrated English to the Deep Approach to World Languages & Cultures

Jianfang Xiao

Guangdong University of Foreign Studies, Canton, China
University of Wisconsin, Madison, WI, USA
Email: xiao3296888@aliyun.com

Integrated English (hereafter IE) is an international program conducted collaboratively by some international educators. IE abides by three rationales, proposes seven teaching principles and is characterized by six beliefs in bilingual education. IE has five changes from shallow teaching to deep teaching, aiming to accelerate the developments of children's intelligence, thinking ability, and language competence. Over the past 15 years, IE has been adopted in more than fifty experimental schools and it has proved very effective. However, IE needs to develop in a deeper approach to foster learners' foreign language proficiency and increase their sensitivity to and understanding of other cultures. Furthermore, a deep approach with IAPI Model and seven instructional principles to world language education is greatly needed (Tochon, 2012), in which the teacher personalizes instructional processes in reference to a changing context and the relevance and meaningfulness of the contents and tasks chosen and developed by the students are emphasized so that learning becomes a form of engagement.

Integrated English as an Experimental Program of Bilingual Education in Mainland China

On account of a rapid process of globalization and internationalization, bilingual or multilingual human resources are in great demand. This is the most important reason why bilingual education is booming in many countries nowadays.

As Tucker and Richard (1999) point out that there are many more bilingual or multilingual individuals today in the world than there are monolinguals, and there are many more children who have been and continue to be educated through a second or a later-acquired language, at least for some portion of their formal education, than there are children educated exclusively via the first language. In many places, English is widely chosen as the additional language.

Asia has the largest number of English speakers in the world. The sustainability of bilingual education in this region, where in most cases English is the 'additional language', may shed light on the development of this potentially 'very effective' ELT approach (Lasagabaster & Sierra, 2010: 374) (cf. Baetens Beardsmore, 2009) in EFL context. Mainland China is among many places, in which the development of bilingual or multiple language proficiency is regarded as favorable and desirable by policy makers, educators and parents. While mainly focusing on Mainland China as a case study example in this article, we suggest that analogous processes may be observed in other Asian countries where a foreign language (usually English) serves as an additional language in Deep Education.

Prior to the reform and opening-up policy, bilingual education in Mainland China mainly referred to helping minority people master both Chinese and their minority languages. However, primary English education in Mainland China has developed rapidly and achieved a qualitative leap since the issue of Mainland China's foreign language policy on primary English education in 2001 and bilingual education has nowadays extended to refer to using a foreign language (often English) as a target language for the teaching of content subjects in feature schools. As Wang Xudong (Wang, 2003: 77) points out that, within fundamental education, especially within the area of compulsory education, this kind of bilingual education experiments are mainly being made available in Beijing, Shanghai, Tianjin, Dalian, Guangzhou, Shenzhen, and Qingdao. Most of these experiments take the teaching of content subjects in English as their ultimate aim (Liu, 2002). For instance, the education department in Liaoning province proposed to make bilingual experiments in such content subjects as math, science, arts, and selective objects in elementary schools (Wang, 2003: 393). Up till now, People's Education Press have published some bilingual textbooks such as physics, chemistry, geometry, and algebra for junior high schools, and physics, chemistry, history, and biology for senior high schools (Wang, 2003: 400). Of course, bilingual education varies in Mainland China. There are different models. In Tianjin, Zhang Qian (2002) advocates to take "bilingual, bicultural, and bi-competence" as the Tianjin model, but in Shanghai things are quite different. According to Wang Liying (2003), in Shanghai "immersion program" is adopted at lower grades in elementary schools, and then "additive bilingualism" will be adopted at higher grades. In Guangdong province there are a few different bilingual models, one of which is Integrated English (IE). Taking the advancement of international bilingual education and the advent of China's reform and opening-up policies as the background, combining international experiences of bilingual education with the context of Mainland China's foreign language teaching, IE has been developing as a new and effective bilingual education model in Mainland China.

IE and Bilingual Education in Mainland China

Although disagreement still exists about what bilingual education is, many people agree to a working definition given in Longman Dictionary of Applied Linguistics (Richards, et al., 1985). It takes bilingual education as the use of a second or foreign language in school for the teaching of content subjects. There are also different ideas about what bilingualism is. At one extreme end of the definition, Bloomfield (1933) specifies "native-like control of two languages" as the criterion for bilingualism, while Haugen (1953) draws attention to the other extreme end, when he observes that bilingualism begins when the speaker of one language can produce complete meaningful utterances in the other language (cited by Romaine, 1995: 11). Therefore, any person may be bilingual to some degree, and bilingualism is a continuum. In Mainland China, as Zhu Pu (2004) says that "for Chinese students bilingualism refers to the ability to use English to satisfy the basic need of English for future study, work and life."

Different ideas about bilingual education result in different bilingual education models such as immersion program, maintenance bilingual education, transitional bilingual education, and etc. According to Tucker (1999), the use of multiple languages in education may be attributed to numerous factors, such as the linguistic heterogeneity of a country or region, specific social or religious attitudes, the desire to promote national identity, or innovative language education programs implemented to promote proficiency in international language(s) of wider communication together with proficiency in national and regional languages. Take immersion program, which originated in Canada, as an example. Around 1975 Canada's first French immersion programs arose, because Canadians realized English-speaking students were not acquiring enough French to attain satisfactory grades in school and to find jobs in French speaking parts of Canada (Martineau, 2002). However, in Finland, languages involved in bilingual education include French, German, and Swedish besides Finnish and English because of its favorable bilingual environment and government's encouragement (Feng, 2003: 64).

Mainland China has witnessed some new development in bilingual education in recent years. Some local governments encourage high schools, elementary schools, and kindergartens to make bilingual education experiments, which take English as the instruction language to teach content subjects. There seem to be three main driving forces behind this. First, it results from the aspiration of internationalization of education. All learners in the experimental schools are majority language (Mandarin) speakers, who do not need to "cross the bridge that helps them be proficient in their native language and in English" (José, 2004) in order to succeed in academic skills. That's to say, English is just a foreign language in Mainland China. However, it is the most widely used language in the world. In China no one doubts English is a world language and is a bridge to the world. Second, the ultimate target of bilingual education in Mainland China is to improve the effect of English learning. Many people complain about the deficiency of EFL teaching. They want to find an alternative which is more effective to substitute for EFL. Third, bilingual education in Mainland China is believed to be a kind of additive bilingual education, because it aims "to develop first and foreign language proficiency fully" (Andrew, 1998), not to thwart in any way the development of the first language.

As mentioned above, many people in Mainland China accept the definition of bilingual education given by Richards & et al. (1985) and therefore Canada's French Immersion Program is always taken as the most effective model (Wang, 2003: 82; Lu, 2005:190). Yang Sigen (cited in Huang, 2004:5) concludes that international tendency of bilingual education is to teach math, physics, chemistry, biology, and computer first in foreign language, and bilingual education should co-exist with EFL teaching. However, does this model suit the context of Mainland China? To answer this question, the status quo of Mainland China's education, especially that of Mainland China's foreign language teaching must be investigated. First, it is clear that the National College Entrance Examination is the supreme target of Mainland China's basic education. Examination-oriented education and testing have been the main characteristic of Mainland China's compulsory education. Bilingual education in Mainland China must take this factor into consideration while trying to improve the pupils' English levels. Second, much more importance is attached to EFL in Mainland China. English is one of the core subjects whether in elementary schools, high schools, or universities. However, many university students who have learned English over 10 years can not speak English fluently. This kind of phenomenon declares itself as the failure of traditional EFL teaching in Mainland China. Third, China is a developing country which lacks educational resources, including financial support and qualified teachers. Furthermore, China is a developing country which runs the largest-scale education in the world. Therefore, bilingual education in Mainland China must take cost-effectiveness into consideration. Fourth, China is a developing country with a vast territory. A deep gap exists between Mainland China's eastern areas and the western areas. Immersion programs mean a high requirement for financial and human resources such as equipment, authentic textbooks, and qualified teachers (Wang, 2003: 87) and a breakaway from an examination-oriented curriculum. It is obvious that the traditional EFL or immersion programs can not solve these problems and therefore can not suit the context of Mainland China. Hence, a new model to teach English must be established in Mainland China to address the contextual factor listed above. Under this condition, IE was established on the basis of careful studies and has enjoyed experimental experiences of twelve years. It absorbed the successful experiences of a wide range of bilingual education, and abandoned traditional EFL teaching methods such as learning by rote and grammar translation approach.

IE stresses taking English as a communication tool, and integrating the target language with content. It integrates English learning with subject learning and it is a new development model of European Content and Language Integrated Learning (hereafter CLIL) in Mainland China. As a typical language-driven program, IE advocates teaching contents in English to enrich or reinforce instruction in the student's native language, but not substituting for it. In fact, the responsibility for content learning lies with other content subject teachers. English teachers may, but unnecessarily, consult with colleagues in other disciplines to determine which, when and how content will be integrated with language. Topics and tasks for language practice may be drawn from many disciplines in a single lesson or unit. IE belongs to theme-based courses, which are language-driven: the goal of these courses is to help students develop English skills and proficiency and cross-cultural understanding as well. Themes are selected based on their potential to contribute to the learner's language growth in specific topical or functional domains. What is taught in English classes is not only the language itself. It includes all kinds of knowledge, such as knowledge of language, math, geography, history, literary, civic virtues, music, art, science, society, culture, and etc.

CLIL integrates content with language, but IE integrates more. Integration of IE consists of five aspects. First, it is an integration of content with language. IE aims to enable learners to gain more knowledge and to improve language competence. It gives prominence to the practice of language through learning knowledge of content subjects. The goal of English learning is not to be grammarians but to communicate freely in English. Second, it stresses integration of interdisciplinary theories. IE intends to incorporate contemporary psychological and pedagogical developments or achievements into bilingual education. For this reason, as Feng (2003) points out that IE concerns about the development of such theories as Lozanov's suggestopedia, Howard Gadner's Multiple Intelligences, and etc. A group of experts from different research fields often work together to analyze characteristics of language learning, and psychological and cognitive characteristics of learners. Fourth, it incorporates contents into language teaching. Knowledge about history, geography, physics, chemistry, math, literature, PE, music, art, civil virtues, etc. are all integrated and taught in English in IE classes, but these classes will never substitute for the above content subjects, which will continue to be taught in Chinese, the students' first language.

There are some similarities between IE and CLIL, which has an important role to play in ensuring the attainment of EU objectives in the area of language learning. Both integrate content with language. Nevertheless, there is a big difference. CLIL enables pupils to study a non-language related subject in a foreign language, while in IE there is no specific content subject taught in English. Only a small part of the non-language related subjects will be taught in English, often through the cooperation of bilingual teachers and non-language teachers. For example, an English teacher may cooperate with a PE teacher to give a PE class in English, but such bilingual classes only occupy a small part of PE classes.

The main purpose of IE is to develop learners' communicative competence in their foreign language in addition to their native language. It fosters bilingualism, sensitivity to other cultures and an opening to the perception of being a world citizen. Additional goals are the cognitive advantages to bilingualism and increased sensitivity to and understanding of other cultures.

Theory of Integrated English

Three rationales of IE

IE emphasizes that bilingual education must abide by three rationales: the rationale of children's development of cognition, the logic of children's development of language competence, and the principle of foreign language teaching.

Bilingual education involves not only linguistics, but also psychology and pedagogy. For this reason, IE stresses interdisciplinary insights from pedagogy, psychology, and linguistics. A group of experts in these three fields often work together to analyze psychological and cognitive characteristics of learners, and characteristics of language learning. When making a decision, IE experts will consider from three aspects: linguistics, cognition, and intelligence. For example, when allotting unit topics to textbooks for different grades, the cognitive ability of pupils in each grade must be considered. Such topics as Body Parts, Family Members, can be taught in grade one, but such topics as States of Matter must be taught after grade three. Another example is whether phonetic symbols should be taught at the beginning period. The teaching of them will enhance the learning of English, especially be useful to look up new words in dictionary. However, pupils are very young, and they are not good at abstract thinking. The phonetic symbols will aggravate the pupils' cognitive burdens, and may make them lose interest in English learning. Therefore, IE doesn't encourage teachers to teach pupils phonetic symbols at the beginning period.

IE stresses the role of acquisition in language learning, and never takes bilingual education as a castle in the air. Bilingual education should be based on children's mother language, cognitive ability, and comprehension ability. According to Vygotsky (1978), there exists a "zone of proximal development" (ZPD) between what a child can do with help and what he or she can do without guidance. Therefore, in bilingual education, the research team must consider what children have already learned, and expand what they have known. For instance, pupils in grade one (about six years old) have known such simple shapes as triangle, circle, and rectangle, but they know little about the features of them and find it difficult to differ square and rectangle from trapezoid. Then the unit about shapes in IE textbook begins with familiar shapes like circle and triangle, and expands children's knowledge to some new shapes such as oval and trapezoid, and helps them to distinguish one kind of shape from another.

IE does not exclude any useful teaching approaches. It stresses the integration of various teaching approaches. It advocates abiding by principles of foreign language teaching in bilingual education. Therefore, role playing, project-based learning, student-centered learning activities are often found in IE classes. At the same time, IE stresses that English must be taught early in order to develop children's language ability and thinking ability, because "the development of children's intelligence mainly exists in the development of language" (Feng, 2003). Therefore, the learning of a foreign language at an early age will not impede the acquisition of first langue. Instead, it will enhance the development of first language and intelligence.

Seven Teaching Principles in IE

There are seven teaching principles in IE: the principle of theme and activity-based learning, the principle of listening and speaking first, supplemented by reading and writing, the principle of operant reinforcement, the principle of direct learning and spontaneous acquisition, the principle of interest orientation and active participation, the principle of focusing on practical use of English and the principle of quick pace and high intensity in classroom teaching (Yuan, 2005).

Six Beliefs in IE

There are six beliefs in IE. They are integrating content with language, learning English at an early age; using English as the medium of instruction;, focusing on listening and speaking first; learning English subconsciously, developing fully the abilities of English learners.

Integrating content with language

As Met (1999) points out that the integration of language and content has been a growing phenomenon in language teaching since the early 1980s and continues to be a tendency of bilingual education in the world. As mentioned above, IE is a new development model of CLIL in Mainland China, but how to integrate content with language? In IE emphasis is laid on both native language learning and foreign language learning. IE opposes to postponing any specific content subject taught in native language. As Flood (1996) states that the "failure to realize the potential benefits of native language instruction has kept us from focusing on the most effective ways to teach children". Cummins (1989), Krashen and Biber (1988) also insist that instruction in the students' native language simultaneously promotes the development of literacy skills in both the native language and a foreign language. The use of the native language to develop the academic skills of students acquiring English appears beneficial for helping students avoid cognitive confusion and achievement lags in their school performance (Hakuta & Diaz, 1984; Krashen & Biber, 1988; Thomas & Collier, 1995). Thomas and Collier (1995) found that postponing the teaching of academics until students develop the academic proficiency in English they need to learn subject content does not appear educationally worthwhile. It takes students longer to acquire English when there is less native language support. Individuals most easily develop cognitive skills and master content material when they are taught in a familiar language. Cognitive or academic language skills, once developed and content subject material, once acquired, transfer readily from one language to another (Tucker, 1999). Therefore, in IE experimental schools, the integration of content and language is limited in English classes. The

English classes do not substitute for any content subjects. However, these English classes are quite different from traditional EFL classes. First, topics in IE textbooks come from content subjects. For example, there is a topic, Good Habits, which comes from the subject of social virtues; a topic titled Math in Daily Life from math ; and a unit Seeds which is about biology. Second, only a small part of such content subjects as arts, music, PE, math, and social virtues will be taught in English. Third, English is taken as a medium of instruction in classes. Pupils learn English through the process of learning knowledge in English. In the integration of contents, IE does not stress learning new knowledge of a discipline but requires pupils to know the general knowledge in the discipline and know how to express them in English.

The ultimate goal of IE is to speak English freely like native speakers and to talk about non-language topics freely. However, many English learners in Mainland China cannot achieve this target. The most important reasons may not be due to poor pronunciation or lack of grammatical knowledge but to lack of basic words and expressions used in content subjects. On the contrary to EFL teaching, IE provides many chances in English classes to contact math, physics, chemistry, arts, geography, music, PE, and so on. Pupils are expected to communicate freely about the general matters related to these subjects. Thus, in IE experimental textbooks, there are many topics from different content subjects, and even under a topic there is much knowledge concerned. For example, there is a unit entitled Wood and Iron, a topic from physics about matters in the world. But in this unit some knowledge about chemistry (e.g. corrosion) can also be learned besides some physical knowledge such as properties of wood and iron. At the same time, pupils learn how to protect our environment, why to keep world peace, and so on. Consequently, pupils in IE experimental schools can freely talk in English about knowledge of both humanities and science.

Learning English at an early age

According to popular belief young children are faster and better foreign language learners than adults, children seem to acquire a foreign language more or less without any effort and they generally attain high levels of proficiency. It is therefore often recommended that children start learning a foreign language as soon as possible. As they grow older they will gradually lose this unique capability. Then the concept of "critical period" was proposed by Lenneberg (1967) for first and foreign language acquisition. Lenneberg assumed that there is a lateralization of the brain for anyone which is finished at about puberty. Although there are doubts on this assumption, many people believe that there is a sensitive or optimal period for the acquisition of certain foreign language skills, especially pronunciation, and the social and psychological distance between the learner and the target community may be smaller for younger learners (Appel & Muysken, 1987: 94-95). For the above reasons, IE advocates starting to learn English in one's critical period.

Using English as the medium of instruction

Mackey (1978) mentions in his classic work Language teaching analysis that the estimated time in school for foreign language teaching is about 250 hours per year, while the total time for a baby to learn his or her first language during the first five years at home is about 25,000 hours. This indicates that a certain amount of time is the prerequisite to mastering a language. In Mainland China, it's hard to find a favorable bilingual environment for students to learn English. If an English teacher taught English in Chinese, his or her pupils would have less time to contact with English. For this reason, an IE teacher is required to teach his or her pupils totally in English in class, and even talk with the pupils in English after class. Sometimes it is quite difficult to explain something in English but quite easy to explain it in Chinese. When this occurs, an IE teacher is not suggested to explain it in Chinese but to explain it in English with the help of body language, pictures, or material objects. For instance, pupils in grade one find it hard to understand the meaning of "same" and "different". Then an IE teacher may draw two pictures of ducks and two pictures of rabbits. Then he will classify them into two groups, and help students understand that one duck is the same with the other and one rabbit is the same with the other, but the two ducks are different from the two rabbits. At last the teacher may draw a quite different rabbit (e.g. with very long ears) to contrast with another rabbit (e.g. with short ears), and tells his pupils that the two rabbits are the same animal but they are quite different. This will help pupils understand the meaning of "same" and "different". What the pupils learn in the process of explanation is much more that the meaning of the two words. This provides more opportunities for students to contact with English, especially the English out of textbooks.

IE objects to teaching grammatical rules directly. It stresses the internalization of language rules, and regards it as an effective way to get language sense and form a habit to think in English. It is known to all that a man can not really master what you teach without internalization. Only through internalization can the newly learned knowledge be conversed from explicit knowledge into the organization's tacit knowledge. This requires explicit knowledge be embodied in action and practice through simulations or experiments to trigger learning by doing processes. Therefore, in IE there is a well-known saying "language can not be mastered through teaching but learning". To master a language, the pupils must throw themselves into English practice to get more chances to contact with English. According to traditional grammatical approach, teachers may teach students English grammatical rules in Chinese. This may cause a ridiculous result that one can explain grammatical rules of English clearly in Chinese but cannot speak English freely.

Focusing on listening and speaking first

The acquisition of one's first language tells us that listening and speaking are earlier to happen than reading and writing. One's oral vocabulary is usually larger than his or her reading vocabulary. Thus, IE regards listening and speaking as the first step in bilingual education. It takes listening and speaking as manifest instruction and takes reading and writing as hidden instruction at lower grades, and gradually takes reading and writing as manifest instruction in higher grades.

Then how to focus on listening and speaking first? Some researches on first language learning have found that how often and how well parents communicate with their children is a strong predictor of how rapidly children expand their language learning (Cuevas, 1996). As Slobin (1977) points out that parental speech to young children is so redundant with its context that a person with no knowledge of the order in which parents' words are spoken, only the words themselves, can infer from transcripts, with high accuracy, what was being said. For this reason the research team encourages teachers to speak as much English as possible in their classes and even after class even if the pupils can not understand them completely. Pupils may not understand all you say, but gradually they will understand more and more with the help of gestures and language context. But keeping on talking does not only mean repetition. Besides some necessary repetitions, a bilingual teacher in IE experimental schools is expected to speak English centering on a topic rather than on a few words or sentence models. For instance, a teacher can talk about spring outing, the trees, flowers, water, sky, kite, dressing, food, weather, activities, animals, the color of a flower, the width of a river, the price of a skirt, or even the number of swallows when he or she is teaching a unit about spring. He or she should never limit his or her lecture within a few words (e.g. season, spring, rain, swallow) and expressions (e.g. Spring is coming.) about spring. What's more, IE encourages teachers to talk about episodes or incidents in classes in English. For example, a butterfly flew into the classroom when a teacher was giving her lesson. It attracted the attention of all pupils. The teacher took the opportunity and said to her pupils, "Look, boys and girls! My lesson is so interesting. It attracted the attention of a butterfly! Who can tell me the color of this butterfly?" In this way, she kept on speaking English and made good use of the opportunity to teach students the authentic language. Pupils thus acquired English rather than learned English. This helps them speak English naturally in their daily life.

Learning English subconsciously

You may feel confused when you find pupils in IE classes making a kite after the bilingual teacher tells them the steps to do it in English. Is this a bilingual class or a hands-on activity class? You can often find such cases in IE classes. Pupils are more interested in hands-on activities than in learning English words, sentences, and grammatical rules. What the research team advocate is not to teach English directly but to teach English subconsciously through some activities or tasks. This is why IE stresses language acquisition and task oriented learning.

Language learning and language acquisition are different. The learning of one's first language is a kind of acquisition. It's something every child does successfully, in a matter of a few years and without the need for formal lessons. Nevertheless, the learning of one's foreign language is so hard even with the help of textbooks and teachers. Language is a tool and is different from other content subjects like math or history. A man can not master a language through learning the language itself but through using a language to do something. For instance, when teaching something about "poster", the traditional grammatical approach will ask students to learn by heart a few words about poster and some so called typical sentence models in the textbook. What the students can learn is only a few words and sentences. However, in IE classes, pupils will be encouraged to make some English posters. In the process of making them, pupils can learn much more than a few words and sentences about poster.

Hidden curriculum is an important part of a school's curricula today. It is also called implicit curriculum, and "is taught by the school, not by any teacher...something is coming across to the pupils which may never be spoken in the English lesson or prayed about in assembly. They are picking-up an approach to living and an attitude to learning" (Meighan, 1981). IE stresses the mutual complement of manifest curriculum and hidden curriculum in order to increase the effect of English learning. On the campus of an IE experimental school, you can find many English posters, slogans, and signs. Pupils and teachers including the school master like to greet each other in English and speak some daily English. There are many kinds of English activities including English salons and English corners. All this can help the pupils feel like studying in a favorable environment of English, and exert a subtle influence on pupils' acquisition of English.

Developing fully the abilities of English learners

IE opposes teaching English in Chinese or dismembering English into pieces and then feeding learners with them. It focuses on the full development of a learner's language abilities, and stresses language teaching satisfying the requirements of children's language development. It advocates taking English as an entire system instead of a collection of vocabulary and grammar that can be dissected and then individually taught. This can liberate foreign language teaching from the teaching method of rote learning, and then teach more for meaning and less for forms. This is the essence of the communicative language teaching (CLT) approach developed by scholars such as Hymes (1972), Canale (1983), and Beale (2002). IE stresses the full development of language skills, especially the communicative competence of pupils, which lacks in traditional language teaching.

IE highlights thematic activities (teaching activities must center on a topic), the interest of learners, and the characteristics of life. Teachers adopting the IE approach must try their best to create an authentic setting for pupils to contact English. To create a vivid and natural environment of English learning, such teaching methods as Total Physical Response (TPR), Communicative Language Teaching (CLT) Approach, Audio-lingual Method, Community Language Learning, and Natural Approach are often used in IE classes. For example, IE advocates the use of Natural Approach in classes, and admits a "silent period" which could last a few months, because pupils "are overwhelmed and scared when introduced to a foreign language" (Watson, 1995). During this silent period, output of language is not required. Therefore, students "absorb language without the stress of audio-lingual-type listen and repeat drills" (Oebel, 2001). For TPR approach, it combines information and skills through the use of the kinesthetic sensory system. This combination of skills allows the student to assimilate information and skills at a rapid rate. As a result, this success leads to a high degree of motivation. In short, different teaching methods are integrated in IE classes. The purpose of such integration is to achieve the best teaching effect, and develop fully the language competence of English learners.

Five Changes in IE, from Shallow Teaching to Deep Teaching

IE encourages deep teaching and has five changes: the teaching language changes from the students' first language into their target language, the teaching model changes from reading new words first into doing activity first; the teaching unit changes from single words into full sentences; the teaching priority changes from knowledge into ability; the learning system changes from separated learning into integrated learning.

Three Aspects of Development Accelerations

According to IE, bilingual education must meet the requirements of both bilingual education and developmental psychology. Most researchers believe that knowing two languages and perspectives gives bilingual children a more diversified and flexible basis for cognition than their monolingual peers have, and provide an "excellent tool" that can help students of all language backgrounds fulfill their academic and intellectual potential (Appel & Muysken, 1987). This was confirmed in IE experiments. As mentioned above, the development of pupils' intelligence mainly exists in the development of language, and a pupil in an IE experiment can talk freely in English to a level analogous to his native language (Chinese) because he can express everything in his life in English, and IE applies theories of ZPD and i+1 into bilingual education experiment. For these reasons, pupils in IE experimental schools can accelerate their intelligence, thinking ability and language competence. For example, a common pupil in grade one may only know the names of a few kinds of flowers, but an IE pupil in grade one can not only tell you the names of many flowers in English but also tell you the flower meanings and even how to raise a flower in English.

Effectiveness of IE

Achievements by pupils

Krashen & Biber (1988) reported that children who participate in properly designed bilingual programs reach satisfactory levels of competence in all academic areas. Genesee, Saunders, and Christian (2003) found that students in bilingual programs can develop academic skills on a par with, or superior to, the skills of comparison groups of their peers educated in English-only classrooms. August & Hakuta (1997) have also found that highly bilingual students reach higher levels of academic and cognitive functioning than do monolingual students or students with poor bilingual skills. How about IE? Can IE enhance pupils' learning of English? Does it have negative effects on the learning of content subjects? Ma Cuiwei, an IE bilingual teacher, made a statistical research on the effect of IE on the development of academic skills (2003). Analyses of collected data show that IE can greatly improve English levels of pupils, and enhance the development of pupil's academic skills simultaneously(See Table 1 and Table 2). Bilingual teachers from Huiyang Experimental Primary School report (Feng, 2003:257) that "evaluation indicates that pupils have improved their English levels greatly and become more active and creative...some pupils even became the interpreters when their parents communicate with foreigners." In April 2006, the improvisational performances of pupils from Boluo Experimental Primary School were live broadcast by local municipal TV station in Huizhou city. In the municipal park, these pupils debated with some foreigners in English, and did their oral compositions as soon as they got the topics from the audiences. More than ten thousand audiences in the park watched the performance and were shocked by the amazing performance of the pupils.

Table 1.

Assessment on Grade 2 students' Oral English Proficiency Level (2003.5)

	Sum	Accuracy	Fluency
Experimental	138	96.7%	93.4%
Control	128	88.6%	77.5%
Z		2.54*	2.72**
P		P<0.05	P<0.01

Table 2.

Excellence rate of Grade 3 students' Subject Learning (2004.5)

	Sum	Chinese	Math	Science
Experimental	138	92.6%	94.5%	95.6%
Control	128	85.8%	89.4%	91.2%
Z		3.28**	2.45*	2.13*
p		p<0.01	p<0.05	p<0.05

Popularity of Experimental chools

Guangdong is one of the most developed provinces in Mainland China. Now in Guangdong there are many foreign-funded enterprises and Sino-foreign cooperative enterprises. In recent years, teaching English as a foreign language in Guangdong is of great importance for many parents. They think that their children can benefit a lot from learning English as early as possible. Parents in Guangdong could not agree more with Barratt-Pugh and Rohl (2001, p.664) that learning two languages seems to be most beneficial to anyone's future. Many parents therefore send their children to bilingual schools. A famous bilingual school can always attract a crowd of parents and pupils. The number of experimental schools has increased rapidly in recent years, because IE is widely seen as an approach based on educational theories, coordinates bilingual education with full development of experimental schools, and meets the need of schools. Almost every IE experimental school or kindergarten is famous and popular in their respective communities now. For instance, Jiangmen Second Education Kindergarten in Jiangmen City has become one of the most famous kindergartens in Mainland China, and now it is planning to run a chain of kindergartens. Media School in Foshan City has become one of the top-class schools in Guangdong province because of practice of IE for more than 12 years. Guancheng English Experimental School in Dongguan City enrolled more than 1,700 students only one year after it was built and half a year after it participated in IE experiment. Jiamei School in Zhaoqing city was about to close down before it decided to join in IE experiment. However, only one year after it had joined in IE experiment, it became a very popular school in Zhaoqing city. There are also experimental schools or kindergartens in other provinces beyond Guangdong, such as Anhui, Hunan, Guizhou and Qinghai (Xiao, 2011).

Raised Quality of Teaching Resources

IE has a one-week teacher training program every year, which aims at changing IE teachers' philosophy of language education and improving their teaching skills. In the past 15 years, more than 1,000 bilingual teachers took this training and became qualified IE teachers. This has accelerated the professional development of English teachers. Their qualities are obviously improved in a relatively short period, and most of them could voluntarily lay more emphases on the development of students' language abilities while teaching for examination and improve their theoretical levels through reading some books about pedagogy and linguistics. Many of them applied IE experimental theories to the analyses of their teaching activities. Some of them have become outstanding English teachers, and got many prizes in various English teaching competitions.

IE experiment has not only improved the quality of English teaching of experimental schools, but also pushed ahead English teaching levels of non-experimental elementary schools. Almost every experimental school has held some large scale English teaching forums in the city or county where it is located. For instance, in 2002 Boluo Experimental School held an English teaching forum in Boluo county. In 2003 and 2010, the 3rd and 10th International Symposia of IE were also held in this school. Jianghua Primary School held an English teaching forum in Jiangmen city every year. The other experimental schools such as Jiaxin School in Foshan city, Huiyang Experimental School in Huizhou city, Longmen Primary School in Longmen County, Media Experimental Primary School in Foshan city, and Jiamei school in Zhaoqing city introduced and extended the IE experiment to local societies. Over 15 years, 14 symposia on bilingual instruction reform have been held. All these helped IE experiment exert great influence on local societies, and also pushed ahead the English teaching levels of local schools and kindergartens.

A Deeper Approach To World Languages And Cultures

There is a deeper approach, the Deep Approach (hereafter DA) to foreign language teaching than IE, put forward by Tochon (2002). It is an approach to world languages and cultures and aims to stimulate action projects in language and culture learning that are in touch with real life, culture, and society. This approach moves holistically towards language integration into world-or life-related thematic projects and requires contextualized, holistic experiences in which the personal identity narrative can expand with new life meanings. The focus is on the process rather than the outcomes and emphasizes quality, relevance, and purposefulness rather than rote learning. Learning a new language is understood as a process of cultural accommodation and abstraction, which is tied to a variety of subtle pragmatic meanings and situational elements that need to be related to perceive the whole.

DA to Foreign Language Education and its Characteristics

DA is a transdisciplinary approach. Transdisciplinarity concerns that which is at once between the disciplines, across the different disciplines, and beyond all disciplines. The goal of the approach is the understanding of the present world, of which one of the imperatives is the unity of knowledge. It promotes a philosophy of curriculum that explains and addresses the current stakes and that requires a deep transformation of humans and human society in the direction of greater harmony, which defines a homeostatic goal that defines personal and social balance. It emerges from individual and collective efforts.

DA may represent the next mainstream in language learning methods. The test of deep learning in the intermediate and advanced courses of foreign language with undergraduate students shows convincing results, such as a reduction of shallow learning, an increase in strategic learning, an evidence of a higher degree of deep learning than in the control group. It can now serve as a model for its implementation in other language programs, and in language programs for beginners (Tochon, 2013).

DA emphasizes deep teaching and encourages deep learning. Deep teaching is learner-centered. It honors the past and develops wisdom for the future. These elements are key to active participation, capacity building and accountability within learning communities (Halbert & Kaser, 2006). It builds on the intrinsic motivation of the learner, authentic documents, and new information technologies when appropriate, conditional to integrating philosophical depth in their processing. Deep teaching is based on meaningfulness for the learner and is project-based. To teach life-meaningful contents to students, the teacher needs to know what is meaningful to them and discuss meaningfulness in life. Teaching and learning have to meet life goals.

Deep teaching understands and values higher order education. In DA, classes with much student talk focused on life issues, is a better sign of learning than quiet classes focused on a passive acceptance of what the teacher says; students gain significant knowledge only when they value it; subject-matters should be continually related to the learner's experiences, life values, and viewpoints.

Deep teaching is not prescriptive. The teacher personalizes instructional processes in reference to a changing context. Deep language pedagogy emphasizes the relevance and meaningfulness of the contents and tasks chosen and developed by the students. Project-based units are viewed flexibly and respond to students' own impulses to learn.

Deep learning system must last and spread across disciplinary domains; it is energizing and doesn't burn out teachers, it doesn't harm the environment; quality is linked to variety rather than standardized forms of expression; it engages students intellectually, socially, and emotionally; it goes beyond temporary gains in achievement scores to create lasting, meaningful improvements in learning; it requires personal engagement: being in charge of one's own learning (Tochon, 2010). If the teacher provides adequate resources, the students can create their own projects. The project of the Self of the student is included in educative projects. Students can work at their own pace on topics of their own interest.

Seven Instructional Principles of DA

In DA, the conception of a self-determined apprenticeship in languages is a revolution against traditional language teaching methodology. Self-determination and the awareness of one's own way of knowing and learning is the cornerstone for the possibility of deep apprenticeship. When students are allowed to plan their own productions, they organize their knowledge autonomously and develop their reflectiveness. In an educative production, the students are brought to evaluate themselves. The path to self-evaluation is acquired gradually, by experience. Studying the directives develops a working methodology as well as reflexive aptitudes. In the final learning phase, evaluative metacognition becomes a fundamental competence.

There are seven instructional principles for teachers in DA (citation from Tochon, 2014, p. 26-27):

"1) Go by the results of motivation research, and provide incentives for self-directed learning and self-determination.

2) Help students build their curriculum through their own literacy-based thematic units, indexing all language modalities to each other. As an instructor, merely scaffold possibilities; make your landscape as flexible as possible for the student to choose, select, and frame on his or her own. Use online modules rather than a textbook or supplement with a large variety of multimedia resources for blended learning.

3) Emphasize process rather than outcomes; refer to instructional organizers in forward planning rather than goals or outcomes in a backward planning.

4) Encourage individualized, peer-oriented, and small group project-based learning, focusing on cultural content and social action.

5) Give primacy to text. Consider grammar as storytelling about language; target extensive reading/viewing and intensive writing/recording.

6) Use deep formative feedback and empowerment evaluation; integrate self-evaluations and peer-evaluations.

7) Focus on value creation: highlight critical issues related to the respect of other languages and cultures, language status and invisible or open discrimination, the colonial mindset versus principles of social justice, and linguistic human rights for peace building." (Tochon, 2014)

Tochon's IAPI Model in DA

Identity-Building depends on Access to knowledge through deep interpretation and critical analysis, and Voice which allows persons of all genders, races, classes, social conditions and statutes to present their thoughts and who they are, and have free interpersonal relations that lead to social action and accomplishments. Tochon proposed a Model of the means available to Access and Voice in the different task domains as follows (Figure 1).

Interpret: The interpretation task domain implies tasks that encourage students to read, watch and listen. Tasks could be film viewing, readings and discussion, answering questions, etc.

Analyze: The analysis task domain implies tasks, which encourages students to focus on language in an autonomous way, using all the resources of language techniques available in the program and on the internet. Such tasks need to be integrated within other task domains, and it needs to be self-directed to become operational. This was presented in the action grammar.

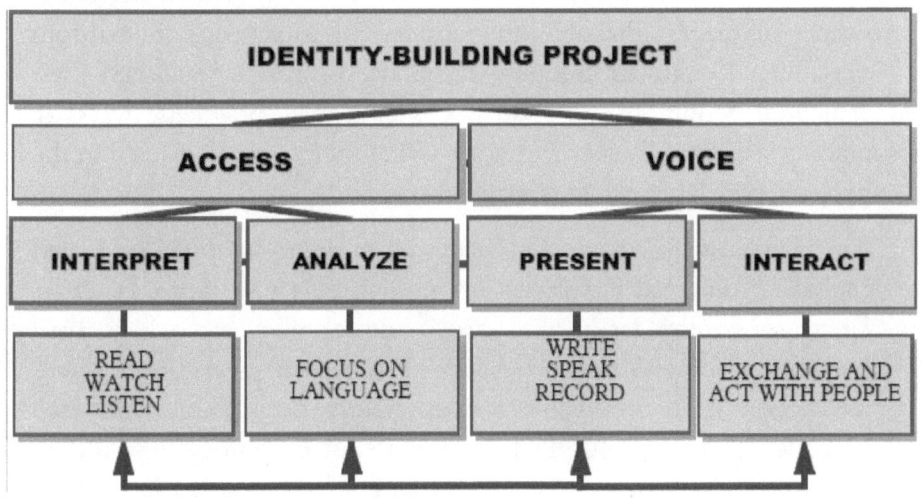

Figure 1.
Tochon's IAPI Model and the Educative Projects' Task Domains
(Tochon, 2014, copyrighted figure published with the author's authorization)

Present: The presentation task domain implies tasks that encourage students to write, speak, audio and video record and report, and create their own PowerPoints, films, personal learning environments or multimedia such as blog, email, ipod, protofolio and Skype, etc.

Interact: It implies interaction across cultures. The interaction task domain integrates tasks that encourage students to exchange and interact among themselves and with other people in the target language. (Tochon, 2014, pp. 226-244)

Students use thematic organizers to guide their projects. A thematic organizer is a specific subject-matter focus that matches students' self project and interest and will serve as a pivot to build self-determined, educative actions.

What is new here is the emphasis on the deep transformational dynamics of learning—in which learners become social activists for other languages through the interactive practices of wisdom pertaining to various cultures. Thematic organizers transcend their structural definition and soon become flexible, pragmatic ways of guiding students' choices without reifying the concepts enacted in the projects, which are like personalized standards.

The dynamism of human exchange is meaning-producing through multiple connected intentions among language task domains. Here, language-learning tasks have cross-cultural purposes which then become meaningful within broader projects that meet higher values and aims such as deep ecology, deep culture, deep politics and deep humane economics. Applied semiotics will be a tool beyond the linguistic in favor of value-loaded projects that are chosen in order to revolutionize the current state of affairs, in increasing our sense of responsibility for our actions as human's vis-à-vis our fellow humans and our home planet.

Five Distinctions of DA

Compared with IE and other foreign language teaching approaches, there are at least five points that make deep approach distinct.

1) The students are placed in charge of building their own curriculum and projects to achieve their own desired expertise, using accountability measures through instructional agreements.

2) The basis of the students' curriculum building is the teacher's provision of literary and multimedia resources organized adaptively. The teacher becomes expert in scaffolding and facilitating feedback.

3) Knowledge is not a 'thing' that can be taught as an object: it is understood as deep, subjective and inter-subjective, inseparable from the identity process. Depth is defined in opposition to the commodification and commoditization of knowledge. Educative projects are open and become ways of preventing knowledge crystallization and sedimentation. Rather, it is about situated knowledge in action.

4) The focus is on deep processing, not standardized outcomes similar for all. There is room for diversity and flexibility, non-native speaker comfort, code-switching, and unique perspectives.

5) It targets transdisciplinary values for a more sensible and wiser world—this way language learning becomes the means toward conflict resolution, ending war and poverty, re-greening the planet, and turning to politics for the human. Yet, rather than a dualistic view, the principle of the included middle (or third space) is applied, through which two apparently opposed elements can be integrated at a higher (still relative) level.

Eight Advantages of Learning a Foreign Language in DA
(citation from Tochon, 2014, p.17):

- "Learning a foreign language in the DA to world languages and cultures will help you to:
- Understand how self-motivation could be the best incentive for deep language learning,
- Provide themes, motives, templates and incentives for self-directed learning and self-determination,
- Empower the student to be the curriculum builder by scaffolding possibilities and making the instruction flexible,
- Emphasize the learning process rather than predetermined outcomes,
- Encourage individualized, peer-oriented, and project-based learning by focusing on cultural contents, value creation and social action,
- Consider grammar as story-telling about language, and
- Use formative, deep evaluation of integrated skills.
- Focus on value creation: highlight critical issues related to the respect of cultures, language status and discrimination, the colonial mindset and social justice, and linguistic human rights for peace building."

"The Deep Approach establishes a link between language education policies and an open curriculum design focusing on values and creative proficiency in action rather than imposed outcomes. It places the learner as the curriculum builder" (Tochon, 2014, p.17).

Conclusion

IE is a fruitful 15-year-long experimental bilingual education program for teaching English as a foreign language in China. IE is an international program conducted collaboratively by educators from different countries and it abides by three rationales, proposes seven teaching principles and is characterized by six beliefs in bilingual teaching. IE has five changes from shallow teaching to deep teaching, aiming to accelerate the developments of students' intelligence, thinking ability, and language competence. Over the past 15 years, it has been proved effective in students' achievements and development and teacher development as well. However, IE needs to develop in a deeper approach to foster learners' communicative competence or language proficiency in their English (L2) in addition to their native language (L1) and increase their sensitivity to and understanding of other cultures, because deep intercultural development requires a dialogical, reflective, and non-intrusive approach. The integration of language and culture in education settings should accompany the experience of other cultures (Tochon and Karaman, 2009). Furthermore, the Deep Approach (DA) with IAPI Model to world language education is greatly needed (Tochon, 2012), in which the teacher personalizes instructional processes in reference to a changing context and the relevance and meaningfulness of the contents and tasks chosen and developed by the students are emphasized so that learning becomes a form of engagement.

DA fosters a critical attitude in learners that has been consigned to oblivion for many years and that will provoke a change in the vision of key aspects such as culture, human rights or social justice. It is a broad phenomenon that manifests a turning point in the way we reflect on a variety of disciplines. DA has seven instructional principles, at least five distinctions and eight advantages. Deep learning is sustainable and requires deep teaching. Deep teaching is learner-centered. It builds on the intrinsic motivation of the learner, authentic documents, and new information technologies when appropriate, conditional to integrating philosophical depth in their processing. Deep teaching is based on meaningfulness for the learner and is project-based. To teach life meaningful contents to students, the teacher needs to know what is meaningful to them and discuss meaningfulness in life. Learning and teaching have to meet life-goals.

References

Akbar Hessami, M., and Sillitoe, J. (1990) Deep vs. Surface Teaching and Learning in Engineering and Applied Sciences. Victoria University of Technology, Footscray

Appel, René, & Muysken P. (1987). Language Contact and Bilingualism. London: Edward Arnold.

Andrew S. L. Ed. (1998) The Advantages of Bilingualism. Educational Leadership, Nov. 1998.

August, D., & Hakuta, K. (1997). Improving schooling for language-minority children: A research agenda. Washington, DC: National Academy Press.

Baetens Beardsmore, H. 2009. 'Bilingual education: Factors and variables.' In O. García (ed.), Bilingual Education in the 21st Century: A Global Perspective. Malden, MA: Wiley-Blackwell, pp. 137-58.

Beale J. (2002) Is communicative language teaching a thing of the past? Online documents. http://www.jasonbeale.com/essaypages/clt_essay.html

Beverly A. C. (2002) First- and Second-Language Acquisition in Early Childhood. Online documents.
http://ceep.crc.uiuc.edu/pubs/katzsym/clark-b.html

Conway, G.R. (1997). *The Doubly Green Revolution*. London: Penguin.

Cummins, J. (1989). Empothe research teamring minority students. Sacramento, CA: California Association for Bilingual Education.

Duncan, C. M. and Lamborghini, N. (1994). Poverty and social context in remote rural communities. *Rural Sociology, 59*(3), 437-461.

Feng Z. J. & et al. (2006) Zong He Ying Yu Jiao Xue Mo Shi Gai Lun (An Introduction of Integrated English Teaching Model). Guangzhou: Guang Dong Ren Min Chu Ban She (Guangdong People's Press).

Feng Z.J. (2003). Shuang Yu Jiao Yu Yu Zong He Ying Yu (Bilingual education and Integrated English). Guangzhou: Zhong San Da Xue Chu Ban She (Sun Yat Sen University Press).

Flood J. et al. (1996). Literacy instruction for students acquiring English: Moving beyond the immersion debate. *The Reading Teacher. 50*(4).

Genesee, F., et al. (2003). Educating English language learners: A synthesis of *empirical evidence*. New York: Cambridge University Press.

Hakuta, K., & Diaz, R.M. (1984). The relationship between research degree of bilingualism and cognitive ability. A critical discussion and some new longitudinal data. In K. E. Nelson (Ed.), Children's language (Vol. 5, pp. 319-344). Hillsdale, NJ: Erlbaum.

Halbert, J., & Kaser, L. (2006). Deep Learning: Inquiring Communities of Practice. *Education Canada*, 46(3), 43-45.

Hargreaves, A., & Fink, D. (2006). *Sustainable leadership*. San Francisco: Jossey Bass.

Huang L. N. (2004) Xue Xiao Shuang Yu Ke Cheng (School Based Bilingual Curriculum). Nanning: Guangxi Jiao Yu Chu Ban She (Guangxi Education

Press).

José L. R. (2004). Defining Our Transitional Bilingual Program. *IDRA Newsletter*, Jan. 2004.

Krashen, S., & Biber, D. (1988). *Online course: Bilingual education's success in California.* Sacramento, CA: California Association for Bilingual Education

Lasagabaster, D., & Sierra, J. M. (2010). Immersion and CLIL in English: More differences than similarities. *ELT Journal, 64*(4), 367-75.

Liu H. R. (2002). Shuang Yu Jiao Xue Yao Shen Zhong (Be Cautious in Bilingual education). *Mainland China Education Daily*, Sept. 3, 2002.

Lu Danhuai (2005). *Xiang Gang Shuang Yu Xian Xiang Tan Suo* (An Exploration of the Bilingual Phenomenon in Hong Kong). Hong Kong: Joint Publishing.

Luo D (2002). *Xiao Xue Zong He Ying Yu Jiao Shi Shou Ce* (A Handbook for IE Primary School Teachers). Guangzhou: Zhong San Da Xue Chu Ban She (Sun Yat Sen University Press).

Ma, C. W. (2003). Xiao Xue Zong He Ying Yu Jiao Xue Shi Yan Yan Jiu Bao Gao (A Report on Primary Integrated English Experiment). Online document. http://www.integratedenglish.com/teachersforum/teachersforum22.asp

Mackey, W. F. (1978) Language teaching analysis. London: Longman Group.

Marien, C. and Pizam, A. (1997) Implementing sustainable tourism development through citizen participation in the planning process. In S. Wahab and J. Pigram (eds) Tourism, Development and Growth (pp. 164-78). London: Routledge.

Met, M. (1999). Content-based instruction: Defining terms, making decisions. NFLC Reports. Washington, DC: The National Foreign Language Center.

Morgan, A. (1993) Improving Your Students' Learning. London and Philadelphia: Kogan Page.

Oebel, G. (2001). *So-called Alternative FLL Approaches.* Online document. http://www.hausarbeiten.de/faecher/hausarbeit/paq/20953.html.

Richards, J., J. Platt, & associated research team. (1985). *Longman Dictionary of Applied Linguistics.* London: Longman.

Romaine, S. (1995). *Bilingualism* (2nd edition). Oxford, UK, & Cambridge. USA: Blach research team.

Meighan, R. (1981). *A sociology of educating.* London: Cassel.

Ryan, T. (2002) Using Information Effectively in Education. Bilingual Education. Rachel Cargas's Online Research Portfolio. May 7, 2002

Tochon, F. V. (2002, November). The Deep Approach to World Language Teaching. Paper presented at the Wisconsin Association of Foreign Language Teachers (WAFLT). Appleton, WI.

Tochon, F. V. & Hanson, D. (2003). *The Deep Approach: World Language Teaching for Community Building.* Madison, WI: Atwood Publishing.

Tochon, F. V. and Karaman, A. C. (2009). Critical reasoning for social justice: moral encounters with the paradoxes of intercultural education. *Intercultural Education, 20*(2),135 –149.

Tochon, F. V. (2010). Deep Education. *Journal for Educators, Teachers and*

Trainers JETT, 1(1), 1-12.

Tochon, F. V. (2012, April). Instructional Organizers to Stimulate Deep Learning of World Languages and Cross-Cultural Pragmatics. Paper presented at the annual meeting of the American Educational Research Association (AERA). Special Interest Group in Foreign language Learning Research. Vancouver, BC, Canada. April 15, 2012.

Tochon, F.V. (2013). Effectiveness of deep, blended language learning as measured by oral proficiency and course evaluation. *Journal of the National Council of Less Commonly Taught Languages, 14,* 53-88.

Tochon, F. V. (2014). *Help them learn a language deeply: the deep approach to world languages and cultures.* Blue Mounds, WI: Deep University Press.

Tucker G. R. (1999) A Global Perspective on Bilingualism and Bilingual Education. *ERIC Digest.* ERIC RIEO, 19990801.

Wang B. H. (2003). *Shuang Yu Jiao Xue Lun Cong* (Collection of Papers on Bilingual education). Beijing: Ren Ming Jiao Yu Chu Ban She (People's Education Press).

Wang, J. J., et al. (2005). Primary Integrated English. Guangzhou: Guangdong Ren Ming Jiao Yu Chu Ban She (Guangdong Education Publishing House).

Wang L. Y. (2003). *You Nan Du Dan Bu Zhi Bu, Tian Liang Dian Rang Xue Zi Shou Hui* (Continue in spite of difficulty, and stand out to benefit the students). Shanghai Jiao Yu (Shanghai Education). 2003 (2).

Warburton, K. (2003). Deep learning and education for sustainability. *International Journal of Sustainability in Higher Education, 4*(1), 44-56.

Wilson Smith, T., & Colby, S. A. (2007). Teaching for Deep Learning. *The Clearing House, 80*(5),205-210.

Xiao, J. F. (2011). *Dang Dai Guo Ji Shunag Yu Jiao Xue Mo Shi Gai Lun* (On the Contemporary International Bilingual Instruction Models). Guangzhou: Guang Dong Ren Min Chu Ban She (Guangdong People's Press).

Yuan, C. Y. (2005). *Zong He Ying Yu Jiao Xue Lun* (Teaching Methods of Integrated English). Guangzhou: Zhong San Da Xue Chu Ban She (Sun Yat Sen University Press).

Zhang, Q. (2002). *Zhong Xiao Xue Jiao Xue Yun Zuo Mo Shi De Jian Gou Fang Shi Yu Ban Kuai Lei Xin* (The constructional orientation and plate types of operational bilingual models in primary and high schools), Tianjin Shi Jiao Ke Yuan Xue Bao (Journal of Tianjin Institute of Educational Science), 2002 (5).

Zhu, P. (2004). *Shuang Yu Jiao Xue Jiang Zuo (I): Shuang Yu Jiao Xue De Ding xing, Fen Lei, Ren Wu He Mo Shi* (A Course of Lectures about Bilingual education (I): The Orientation, Classification, Mission, and Model of Bilingual education), Ji Suan Ji Jiao Yu Xue (Computer Teaching and Learning), 2004 (3).

---. The European Council gives its support to CLIL/EMILE. Online document. http://www.euroclic.net/index.php?inhoud=inhoud/news/main.inc

Part II

Theoretical Aspects of Deep Education

6.

Reimagining Soul Work in Deep Education within Multicultural Community-Based Educational Spaces

Phil Bostic
University of Wisconsin-Madison

When examining the history of the African American struggle in the United States, one quickly finds that they are a people that have been historically minoritized by a system that to the present day continues to deny their humanity. The notion of freedom legally sanctioned for the political majority has, for example, been structurally repressed from African Americans and "other" similarly minoritized groups throughout United States history. Legitimate spaces such as jobs, housing, and schooling have continued to be a struggle to obtain for many people of color. However, if made fairly and appropriately available, these resources provide opportunities for psychological and spiritual development (Hillard, 1992; Hooks, 2010; Ladson-Billings, 2009; Tate, 1997). Indeed, since the arrival of the African on American shores, the struggle has been for more than just material and legal legitimacy, and in fact a battle over the soul.

In his book, *The Education of the Negro*, historian Carter G. Woodson (1919) wrote:

> We were not brought to the United States to be educated. Rather, we were brought over as part of a massive labor force. Since then, the African soul has been a political liability for the White race in the United States. In order to continue slavery with a clear conscience, a rationale was developed to help argue that the slave had no soul. (p.2)

It is this particular historical "rationale" toward the African American soul that this chapter seeks to interrogate and interrupt by examining the ways in which it continues to negatively influence the souls of African Americans and other historically minoritized people in educational research and everyday schooling practices (Dillard, 2012; Grant, 2012; King, 2005). To address these issues, this chapter will examine the following questions:

1. How do we create a worldview that consciously opposes dehumanization, and moves in ways that enable creative, expansive self-actualization in educational research and everyday schooling practices?
2. How might teachers conceptualize a deeper work for the soul that focuses on connecting to their students; in order that their teaching practices may embrace the full humanity of all people?
3. What is the role of soul work and deep education in this process?
4. How can this re-conceptualization be applied to historically-minoritized populations?
5. How do these translate into multicultural community-based educational spaces?

This chapter argues for a re-conceptualization of the soul within community-based educational spaces; coupled with a moral obligation to initiate a work toward healing the soul by employing a deeper approach to what it means to be human. Thus, by acknowledging the manifested soul as a political entity that is invariably interconnected and sacred, this chapter proposes a human-centered ontological-epistemic framework that foregrounds the manifested soul through a curriculum that employs deep education as way to develop a way in which we are able to see ourselves in the eyes of others, regardless of our socially-constructed identities.

Toward A Humanizing Turn in Education

Most recently, as an attempt to push the boundaries of the *Western scientific imagination* in educational research, a number of scholars have called for the humanization of educational reform, thus foregrounding "human interests" as a priority in theory and practice (Brown, 2013; De Lissovoy & Brown, 2013; Kraehe, 2013; Warren,

2012). For instance, Tuck (2009) called for the suspension of what she refers to as "damaged-centered" research, including frameworks suggesting that historically minoritized populations are "lacking to explain underachievement or contemporary brokenness, such as poverty, poor health, and low literacy" (p. 413). For Tuck (2009), the contemporary notion of change theory is built on a "common sense that tells us this is a good thing, but the danger in damage-centered research is that it is a pathologizing approach in which the oppression singularly defines a community" (p. 413). An alternative worldview that is more "concerned with understanding complexity, contradiction, and the self-determination of lived lives," and that documents "not only the painful elements of social realities but also the wisdom and hope of the people" is recommended (Tuck, 2009, p. 417).

De Lissovoy and Brown (2013) emphasize the importance of "finding a new form of coexistence and shared-humanity as an ethical imperative against a form of political being founded on partition and exclusion" (p. 2). When examining the fundamental aspects of racism as a "global ordering of social life", the authors argue that many White social justice advocates and critical educators have lacked the critical attentiveness necessary to effectively confront the social-political-economic entanglements of selfhood in relation to Whiteness, as well as the scientific-reasoning that permeates educational research and practice as harmful barriers to genuine antiracist solidarity in education. As a result, the authors propose that White advocates who seek to work in solidarity with the historically minoritized must "reorient their purposes and identities" and reframe the idea of solidarity as a progressive action in U.S. politics, and educational research (p. 9).

In addition to reframing the idea of antiracist solidarity as a liberal approach, De Lissovoy and Brown (2013) argue that our ability to rebuild our relationships and willingness to reimagine our humanity as one of a collective is vital to real social change. The critical scholars insist that relationships of solidarity need to be reframed and rebuilt on the recognition of and respect for difference, and the radical autonomy that exists within our historically minoritized communities. Henceforth, coupled with the task of rebuilding meaningful relationships with one another, we are also charged with the responsibility of reimagining our personal senses of humanity. Said another way, the authors contend that in order to reconstruct our relationships in a more meaningful way, it is imperative that we also rethink our shared-place of interconnectedness:

> If whiteness is as much an ontological and epistemological ordering of human being as it is a system of material and cultural oppression, then antiracist solidarity projects have to contemplate a basic reorganization of being and knowing, and not merely a critique of ideology. (ibid, p. 2)

The re-articulation of what it means to "know" and "be known" as a human is paramount. Moreover, by "refusing the category of the human as it is given in Western traditions" (Lissovoy & Brown, 2013, p.13), we are then able to move past the discursive limits of the Western Scientific notion of humanity (Brown, 2013), and begin to strategically identify more clearly the problems that exist because of the convergence of epistemic limits that continue to frame, sustain and make the troubles of the historically minoritized possible (Brown, 2013; Dillard, 2006). As an attempt to disrupt this negative pattern of thinking of the historically minoritized in education, the following section will explore the recent call by scholars to commit to a work for human freedom in educational practices as well as in research that also embraces the notion of teaching as a sacred practice as work for the soul.

The Universal Call for Human Freedom in Educational Research and Practice

Although tremendously persuasive work has been done to show how the uncontested ontological rules of representation in educational research, and the discursive limits of Western humanity generally converge into epistemic limitations, we continue to see the same dilemmas that frame, sustain and re-inscribe the dehumanization of historically minoritized students as the negative ontological other in the classroom (Bostic & Manning, 2013; Brown, 2013; King, 2005; Tuck, 2009; Ullucci & Battey, 2011; Popkewitz, 1998; Wynter, 2004; 1987). For this reason, it is important to briefly outline recent calls by various multicultural and critical scholars to commit to more humanizing approaches to research and practice (Dillard, 2013; King, 2005; Tuck, 2009).

Paris and Winn (2014), have called for the illumination of the need for a humanizing turn in research and practice specifically in relation to the well-being of historically minoritized youth:

> We are especially concerned that continued and long-standing efforts to make the process and product of qualitative inquiry fit in positivist notions of what research is and how it should look often silence and minimize what it is we actually do in coming to know about the youth we spend months and years with. (p. xix)

Paris and Winn (2014) add:

> We can be a part of solutions that support equality within our research practices and in the lives of the young people and communities we learn from…To understand what it means to humanize research, it is important to consider the ways in which people and more specifically youth, are often dehumanized. (Paris and Winn, 2014, p.1)

Cultural critic bell hooks (1990) has added that instead of relying on the familiar ways of being and knowing to confront the struggle for freedom in research, we should consider a deeper question:

> How do we create an oppositional worldview, a consciousness, an identity, a standpoint that exists not only as that struggle which also opposes dehumanization, but as that movement which enables creative, expansive self-actualization? (p.15)

For hooks (1990), opposition is simply not enough; there remains the necessity for the historically minoritized "to make one self-anew" (hooks, 1990, p.15). hooks (1990) argues that we must return to identity and culture for relocation, linked to political practice, that leads to a more humanizing outcome. If we are to be truly free, we have to accept the realization that "racism is perpetuated when blackness is associated solely with concrete gut level experience conceived as either opposing or having no connection to abstract thinking" p.23). She argues for a new identity that welcomes the complexity and variety of Black subjectivity and moves toward a deeper struggle on a new ground (hooks, 1990). Moreover, this renewed ontological grounding must allow us to work toward deconstructing our notions of race and detangling our commitments to limiting ways of seeing human possibilities (Crawford, 2011; hooks, 2013). Hillard (2001) similarly insists: "We must clear our thinking of gross error. We must apply ourselves to correct our systems of reasoning and structures" (Watkins, 2001, p. 34).

The self-identified endarkened feminist Cynthia Dillard (2000) reasoned that in developing this new way of being and seeing:

> We must begin to move beyond race, ethnicity and gender as biological constructions of being human, when we seek to examine the origins of such knowledge constructions as to the very nature of how reality is known, we will find that what constitutes knowledge depends profoundly on the consensus of those in the community in which it is grounded. (p. 662)

Dillard (2000) invites researchers to become more aware of the multiple ways of knowing and doing research while continuing to interrogate the epistemological, political, and ethical level of their work. We must continue to investigate the notion of teaching as a moral and intellectual practice; working toward a praxis that examines the function as well as the purpose of education in every sector of society (Banks, 1996; Hansen, 2001; Popkewitz, 1998; Gordon, 1993).

In Joyce E. King's (2005) seminal book, *Black Education*, the prolific scholar offers a collective work with a transformative research and action agenda that explores the fundamental roots of the crisis in contemporary Black education. In an attempt to unveil "the entrenched system of thought that justifies our current predicament" (King, 2005, p. xxii), she argues that we are called to "a specific task:

to understand the cause of the cause of the common problems, to think out solutions and organize ways to apply them" (King, 2005, p. xxiv).

In order to decipher the core issues pertaining to Black education within this Western civilization, Sylvia Wynter's culture-systemic theoretical analysis informs King's work (Banks, 1996; Wynter, 1987; 2001; 2003). Throughout her career, Wynter (2001) has contended the difficult task of dismantling the disciplinary boundaries in academia to work toward re-envisioning our idea of the human being in its totality (Wynter, 2003). According to Wynter's analysis, scholars in any society reproduce knowledge to sustain the prevailing belief system. Hence, within our current Western Scientific paradigm, "the notion of being human has been biologically defined and embedded with a flawed belief in the construction of racial categories that serves the purpose of a few, above the general well-being of all people" (as cited by King, 2005, p. xxv). Wynter proposes that, at least one way out of this self-destructive system of reasoning is to "decipher rather than be controlled by the limited conceptions of what it means to be human within the terms of this belief system" (as cited by King, 2005, p. xxv).

The initiative that undergirds King's (2005) vision of transformative Black education is the fundamental belief that,

> Human freedom in this millennium remains inextricably bound up with the life chances and therefore the education of African people. Thus, the theoretical underpinning of this understanding of Black education and the possibilities for human freedom depends upon ending our dispossession. (p. 4)

King (2005) points out that although multicultural education advocates have worked hard to address the crisis in Black education, unfortunately, they too have missed the mark regarding this concern. With that said, Wynter (1987) argued for an explicitly new role for historically minoritized scholars and educators to allow their inherently liminal position in society and in the academy to bring about the ending of this dispossession of humanity. The postcolonial scholar calls for a "new science of the human" that seeks to liberate thought and social action from the distorted vision of the Western Scientific notion of what it means to be human (Wynter, 1987, p. 241).

To confront this dilemma in education, Dillard (2012) adds another dimension to the concept of working toward a new human science for the soul. In addition to working toward human freedom in research and practice directly for students, she argues that research and teaching needs to also work toward healing the souls of *educators*. For Dillard (2012), this implies that teaching and research must be seen as a "sacred practice" that promotes scholarship as a means to heal the soul through the proper use of wisdom, history, and cultural production as tools that inform academic research and pedagogical practices in the classroom. In other words, "It's seeing research and teaching as a responsibility for (re) membering our ability to recognize ourselves in the gaze of another and not looking away, but instead looking deeper... We must (re) member in order to be whole" (Dillard, 2012, p.4).

In synthesizing the main themes regarding the call for universal human freedom in multicultural education with those centered on connecting with and teaching to the soul, this chapter is informed by four key concerns highlighted in Dillard's (2013) Endarkened Feminist theory:

1) A calling to heal the soul of humanity through new eyes,

2) Acceptance of the responsibility to unlearn the past,

3) Mastery over the seductions to remain critically conscious of one's own being, and,

4) Transformation of the ontological rules representing research by an embracing of research and teaching as sacred.

The following section will explore the origins of soul work in education, and the historical contextualization of the academy in relation to the well-being of society.

Origins of Soul Work in the Academy

The soul is an ancient concept, central to traditions in both the East and the West. The earliest history of the soul in higher education finds its origins in Ancient Egypt (Martin, 2013; Asante, 2005; Furst, 1997; Moore, 1963). The philosopher, Georg Hegel (2006) shared in a lecture that, "For the history of the Greek life, we must go back further. In dealing with great art and life, we are led to Asia and Egypt" (p. 10). As such, many of the earliest ancient Greek philosophers such as Pythagoras, Thales, Socrates, Plato and Aristotle traveled to the "*Black Land*" (Rosalie, 1997, p.18), which was at the time called by its people *Kemet*, to be educated primarily for the purpose of enhancing and liberating one's soul (Hegel, 2006; Asante, 1992; James, 1954); a metaphysical tradition rooted in ancient alchemy. Ancient African historian, Dr. George James (1954) describes the requirements of a new initiated graduate of the ancient Egyptian university system as such: "The neophyte was required to manifest the following soul attributes: (1) Control of thought (2) Control of action, and (3) the steadfastness of purpose" (p. 30). Essentially, the enlightenment of one's soul was paramount in order to accomplish deliberate praxis of thought and action in ancient traditions (Asante, 1992).

For the ancient Egyptian, Greek, and other spiritual, metaphysical, and psychological practitioners, soul itself appears to connect three seemingly different aspects of our being—*the mind, the will and the emotional state of the individual* (Asante, 1992). The ancient Egyptians believed that the heart of alchemy is spiritual. Moreover, the notion of transmuting lead into gold, for example, served as an analogy for personal transmutation, purification, and perfection of the soul; thus obtaining what is known as the "Philosopher's stone", being the knowledge of one's self (Linden, 2003; Foucault, 1997).

Views of the Soul in Contemporary Educational Research

Unlike ancient times, and as a result of the Western Scientific imagination and the aims of modernity, the soulful pursuit in academia has been replaced with a fragmented approach to learning for material gain; consequently, neglecting the soul for the sake of certitude and efficiency (Dirkx, 2001; Jung, 1933; Tochon, 2010). As a result, Sardello (1992) contends:

> Education instead has become an institution whose purpose in the modern world is not to make culture, not to serve the living cosmos, but to harness humankind to the dead forces of materialism. Education as we know it, from preschool through graduate school, damages the soul. (p. 50)

In attempts to reclaim the soulful connection in academia, scholars and practitioners have conceptualized the soul in multiple ways. Some scholars have framed the soul as a "perspective" or as an elusive source of energy driven by "a deep connection between people" that can be emotionally "felt" by connected-participants in the classroom (Kessler, 2002, p. 5). In such cases, the notion of "reclaiming our souls" has often been reduced to an overarching agreement set by teachers or school administrators alike, to lead students to their own celebratory experience through some sort of relationship in the classroom that, too often, has little to do with personal growth or collective well-being.

Unfortunately, in educational research, the soul has been often viewed as an afterthought or otherwise assumed as some mystic and elusive force that best serves as a metaphor for community building or improving self-efficacy among students in the classroom (Miller, 2000; Miller and Drake, 1997). As a result, work for the soul in education in contemporary times lacks substantial theoretical grounding and conceptual clarity and prevents research from fully extending its reach beyond a simple motivational schema in the classroom and toward praxis by the best of our educators in multicultural education spaces (Lewis, 2006; Dalton, & Crosby, P, 2006; Palmer, 1999; Tisdell, 2008).

A Definition of the Manifested Soul in Education

In attempt to address the apparent lack of theoretical grounding in contemporary educational thought and practice, I offer a re-conceptualization of the soul within an educational context that embodies one's mind, will and emotional state for the activation of enlightened personal agency within the educator for him- or herself and his or her classroom and community (Asante, 2005). According to Asante (1998),

> There are three fundamental existential postures that one can take with respect to the human condition: *feeling, knowing,* and *acting,* which are sometimes known as the *affective, cognitive,* and *conative* positions...I am most free when I am most active on the basis of my own volition. Even if I am active and believe myself to be free under the will of another, I am not truly liberated. (p. 20-21).

I agree with Asante (1998; 2005) who maintains that personal agency that liberates one's mind and moves the person closer to self-actualization can only occur through an understanding and acceptance of that which inspires one's soul, such as his or her culture. Foucault (1997) further illuminated this point when he said,

> These practices of freedom [for the soul] are nevertheless not something invented by the individual himself, but rather they are habits of being and knowing that he finds in his culture and are therefore proposed, suggested, imposed upon him by his culture, his society, and his social group. (p. 229)

Lastly, womanist scholar, Barley-Brown (1989) also influences this working definition of soul for soul work in the classroom. I find the following statement on her conceptualization of polyrhythmic realities to be especially poignant:

> [Polyrhythmic realities] reflects the belief that individuals do not just have multiple realities and distinct understandings of them. Instead, individuals experience intersecting realities simultaneously—thus the realities are polyrhythmic. (as cited by Phillips, 2006, p. 270)

Hence, informed by Foucault (1997) and Woodson's (1919) notion of the soul, as a political entity, which Foucault points out functions through multiple formations of the self (e.g. Woman; Mother; Daughter; Graduate Student; African American; Christian), as well as the womanist scholar, Barley-Brown's (1989) concept of polyrhthmic realities, I theorize the soul to be a constitution of multiple regimes of self-identified truths each manifested and governed at once separately and together as they are imposed on the mind, will and emotional state of the individual by society and its power relations over the individual; and thus balanced and responded to through one's own consciousness and actions for the purposes of, as Asante (1998; 2005) explains one's own liberation in each contextualized setting. This altogether constitutes the manifested soul, and all its parts that should be of central concern in soul work in education. This definition of the soul both acknowledges and embraces the multiple complexities of what it means to be human.

Perhaps most importantly, this notion of the polyrhythms of the soul is a deliberate departure from the Western Scientific idea of the world and reality. As a result, I recognize as Rose (1998) did that, "The self should not be investigated in the terms in which it has historically come to relate to itself" (p. 171). And as Barkley-Brown (1989) cautions us:

> People and actions do move in multiple directions at once, if we analyze these people in actions by linear models, we will continue to create dichotomies, ambiguities, cognitive dissonance, disorientation, and confusion in places where none exists. (p. 17-18)

From this frame of thought, I seek to scaffold the soul in education through a *socially oriented ontologic-epistemic praxis* that strives to serve the soul for the sake of the soul. By recognizing the soul as a socially, culturally and historically influenced entity that manifests itself through multiple-formations of the self (Foucault, 1997), I argue in this chapter that the soul is also culpable of being politicized and therefore has the potential to reveal our inherent interconnectedness as fellow humans. It has long been accepted in contemporary academia that our own thoughts, words and actions are interwoven on multiple levels and thus directly influences the way we come to see and know ourselves. It should therefore require no stretch of the imagination to also view our manifested souls as important to our social interactions and ourselves, especially in relation to educational research and our everyday schooling practices. Hence it is maintained throughout this study that the soul and its various manifestations is sacred and deserves to be valued and protected at all costs.

As Foucault (1997) has asserted,

> ...taking care of the soul is always a real activity and not just an attitude. We have to worry about our souls. That is a principal activity of caring for ourselves. The care of the self is the care of the activity and not the care of the soul as substance. (p. 230)

In other words, the ethical practice of caring for the soul emphasizes an all-encompassing worldview that requires us to embrace the conscious practices of freedom as a vital means of cultivating one's true self on an ongoing basis. The current shift in education toward a more humanizing approach to educational research in connection to historically minoritized populations in traditional and non-traditional spaces seems to provide for fertile ground for the re-commitment to the soul in education (Paris & Winn, 2014; Tuck, 2009; King, 2005). Peace studies are an inspiration for more depth in the classroom. The next section will examine a similar charge by leading scholars in the field of peace studies to move away from focusing solely on issues pertaining to global violence and nation rebuilding and seek to cultivate more viable spaces for self-care and social change by developing new forms of communication and practices in the classroom that embraces the human as a key priority (Mahiri, 2004).

Work for the Soul in Deep Education

It has been widely argued that deep education, aimed at promoting critical consciousness among students in the classroom, is one of the most well developed curricula in the last half century (Crawford, 2011). Many peace educators believe that it provides students with a deeper contextual understanding of the social and political issues surrounding their everyday lives while at the same time identifying potential spaces for activism and change (Freire, 1993). In addition to commitment to social change, it has also been argued by peace educators in recent times that "peace must first start from within each individual person and then spread outwardly" (Barash and Webel, 2014, p. 534). In order to address both the social and holistic dynamics of deep, peace education, specific ways of teaching and communicating the various aspects of our reality is required. Moreover, it is believed that such deep education requires a language of conviction that is, contrary to indicative language, concerned with the totality of reality (King, 2005).

In other words, deep education in the classroom must incorporate a language and pedagogical practice imbued with love for self and others, in intent and in action. In turn, to confront the multiple challenges that continue to plague our world and within ourselves, deep teaching practices must further examine the interconnectedness between the past, present and future in relation to the individual. We must seek to acknowledge and cultivate viable spaces of growth and awareness that promote solidarity and wholeness among all learners (Tochon, 2011). This implies not only exploring our own life and making changes that seem congruent with our beliefs, but also identifying those personal patterns that continue to reinforce the various systems of oppression toward others. Based on the notion that all humans are sacred, I argue that a deliberate effort must be made to ensure that traditional as well as non-traditional spaces of learning need to be considered when committing to work for the soul. This work must reflect a comprehensive approach to which new ways of seeing ourselves and others is paramount (Tochon, 2010).

Steps toward Soul Work in Deep Education

In this chapter, the concept of work for the soul in a peace-centered classroom is largely informed by Danesh's (2006) integrative theory of peace and Tochon's (2010) deeper approach to education. Danesh's integrative theory posits; "peace is, at once, a psychological, social, political, ethical and spiritual state with its expressions in intrapersonal, interpersonal, intergroup, international, and global areas of human life" (p.55). The theory contends that "all human states of being, including peace, are shaped by our worldview—our view of reality, human nature, purpose of life and human relationships" (Danesh, 2006, p.55). According to Danesh (2006), there are four preconditions for effectual peace education to take place in the classroom:

1) Unity-based worldview,
2) Culture of healing,
3) Culture of peace, and,
4) Peace-oriented curriculum

In similar fashion, Tochon's (2011) deeper approach to education argues for:

> A philosophy of curriculum that explains and addresses the current stakes that requires a deep transformation of humans and human society in the direction of greater harmony; it brings humanity to sciences and a new sense of their pragmatic potential to human sciences. (p. 5)

The deeper approach to education entails a sense of one's deep identity (Tochon, 2013), which signifies "who we are and how we see our role in relation to the world" (Tochon, 2010, p. 5). This deeper approach to education is concerned with breaking the barriers that prevents the human race from seeing and knowing the world in a deeper and more meaningful way that keeps people from living a life that reflects harmony in values and actions. The ontological vision inherent within deep education supports a healthy environment, "through a personal identification so deep that one's own self is no longer delimited by the personal ego or the organism. [Thus] one experiences oneself to be a genuine part of all life" (Tochon, 2010, p.7). Tochon's (2010) deeper educational framework is based on two major components, deep learning and deep teaching.

Soul Work in Education

For the sake of clarity, I have identified a two-phased, four-step socially oriented ontologic-epistemic praxis definition when referring to soul work in an educational space, which utilizes Tochon's (2010) conceptualization of deep education and deep apprenticeship in connection with my definition of the manifested soul. Dillard's (2012) Endarkened Feminist approach to analysis assists with the following methodological assumptions:

1) A calling for a healing the soul through a new worldview, where all humans are seen as sacred

2) Accepting the responsibility to unlearn the past

3) Mastery over the seductions to remain critically conscious of one's own being, and

4) Transformation of the ontological rules representing research by an embracing of research and teaching as Sacred.

In similar fashion, Tochon's (2010) deep apprenticeship pedagogical model serves as the teaching praxis for soul work in the classroom.

The Deeper Apprenticeship as Praxis for Work for the Soul

Tochon (2010) explains that in order for deep learning to take place, deep educators must provide a space and place that embraces a different style of teaching, one that encourages self-sustainable learning:

> Deep teaching is learner-centered. It builds on the intrinsic motivation of the learner. Deep teaching is based on meaningfulness. Learning and teaching have to meet life goals. The approach is contextualized and situated. Meanings are embodied in action. Deep education supports alternative conceptions of development such as subjective development. (p.6)

In relation to learning, Tochon (2010) defines deep learning in the following way:

Deep learning links new knowledge to prior knowledge across various fields. Deep processing involves a re-conceptualizing of how reality is viewed (Bradford, 2001). As well, deep learning defines a situation in which the teacher is not the only source of inspiration and knowledge (Rhem, 1995). Deep learning "engages" students intellectually, socially, and emotionally" (...); it "goes beyond temporary gains. (p. 6)

For Tochon (2010) a deep educator proposes an interactional dynamic where students organize and pursue meaningful tasks clustered within educative projects that focus on meaningful results and operational knowledge that is beneficial and historically aligned with their present state of affairs. The deep educator would be available for increased dialogue in the target aims; showing the resources, and provide extensive feedback on students' writing for their projects. The sense of feedback means much more interaction than usual in our text than usual. Thus, what articulates learning is a sense of unity, in conversation feedback on a sense of waiting, a sense of expression workshops, as well as individual and group projects. During project-driven learning, the deep educator monitors students' chosen actions, helping the students frame structure meaningful projects and facilitate resources for particular projects. In other words, students learn best through experience (Tochon, 2010; Tochon and Karaman, 2009).

The Disposition of Soul Work Educator

Due to the humanistic aims in this chapter, I agree with Brown & De Lissovoy (2013) that in order to effectively to work for social justice, it is imperative that educators must be willing to find:

> A new form of coexistence and shared humanity against and beyond whiteness is an ethical imperative against a form of political being founded on partition and exclusion...[thus recognizing] whiteness is as much an ontological and epistemological ordering of human being as it is a system of material and cultural oppression (p. 13).

It is reasoned that White teachers must be able to disentangle themselves from the enchantment of Whiteness on their soul and be willing to consider a basic reorganization of being and knowing, and not merely a critique of ideology. (Brown & De Lissovoy, 2013; Dillard, 2012; King, 2005; Wynter, 1987)

Another important aspect of being a deep soul work educator is to be willing to commit to an ethical role to the educational profession (Bostic and Manning, 2013; Dillard, 2006). Tochon (2011) contends researchers and educators must be willing to embrace:

> The process of rethinking our connection to earth and to the world and revisit our relation to and with otherness...This dimension of caring constitutes one value of education to the world, since bridging the perceptual and conceptual distance that separates us from others is one major step towards world reconstruction...The recognition of the humanness of science is the ground for compelling claims on the resistance of normal science to scientific revolutions. (p. 21-22)

In short, soul work educators must be willing to make significant effort to value the lives of others and come to a better understanding through an academic mindset that is engaged and creative, instead of detached and reactive. They must be willing to embody the work and practice and this new proposed notion of seeing and knowing themselves and others as sacred in their everyday lives. In the next section, I will discuss the rationale for conducting research or focusing on a community-based educational space and the potential benefits.

Rationale for Conducting Deep Soul Work in Community-Based Educational Spaces

Statistically, children from historically minoritized communities continue to be over-represented in prisons and under-represented in the nation's workforce and colleges, coupled with increasingly enforced neoliberal ideas that act through educational policies that continue to normalize standardization, privatization and the de-professionalization of teachers and the continued disfranchization of targeted students of color (Giroux, 2003), schools are becoming more and more inflexible, often denying second or third chances for students who need the help, who are often denied the opportunity to regain a solid footing in the classroom (Baldridge et al., 2011). For example, literature has revealed how this inflexibility has aided to the ever-increasing dehumanization of African American males and other historically minoritized children as threatening and menacing presence within the classroom (Ginwright, 2009; Noguera, 1996). As a result of this mindset, these students are often regarded as malefactors within the classroom (Darling-Hammond, 2000) and more susceptible to be suspended from school more than any other racial group for the same behaviors (Gregory, Skiba, and Noguera, 2010; Giroux, 2009). Another severe consequence of negative mindset toward historically minoritized children in inflexible school settings is the children's over-representation in special education programs, especially African American males (Noguera, 1996; Giroux, 2003). Nonetheless, the educational performance of historically minoritized children is greatly challenged by negative interactions with the everyday schooling practices in the classroom. As a consequence, Baldridge (2011) and Davis (2006) have explained how these children's presence within school settings are often disregarded or by devalued as problematic liability that needs to be resolved.

The significance of Community-based Spaces for Deep Soul Work

As a result of the continuous dehumanization of historically minoritized children in traditional school settings, an increasing body of work has emerged, examining the importance of community-based spaces in relation to academic lives of these underserved students (Baldridge 2011; Ginwright 2009; Woodland 2008). Furthermore, Baldrige (2011) points out the advantages of community-based educational spaces as places to circumvent the negative consequences of viewing historically minoritized children as less than human:

> They [community-based educational spaces] are regularly situated both within and outside of traditional school buildings. While often situated within the same social, political, and economic contexts as traditional schools, community-based educational spaces are typically not held to the same type of bureaucratic constraints that schools are forced to negotiate...Consequently, they are able to function with greater curricular and programmatic flexibility. (Baldrige, 2011, p.125)

Consequently, community-based educational spaces are "in a critical position to increase the level of support available" for students from historically minoritized communities with specific needs. Further research has shown the benefits of community-based educational spaces. For example, students are more likely to increase the social and cultural capital and trust in the educational process and develop a better understanding of the social and political dynamics that impact their everyday lives (Baldridge, 2011; Ginwright 2007; Mahoney, Larson, Eccles and Lord, 2005). Lastly, Baldridge (2011) highlights the fact that community-based educational spaces have shown to help improve "students' academic achievement, build meaningful relationships between peers and adults, develop resistance skills against risky behaviors, and develop youth capacities and transferable skill sets...[and] provide crucial 'second chances' for youth" (Baldridge, 2011, p. 127). As a result of the needed flexibility and opportunity to employ a variety non-traditional teaching practices, I argue that community-based educational spaces are favorable places for this kind of research, soul work, and deep education.

Conclusion

Due to its ontological and epistemological nature, a large part of research in education has positioned historically minoritized populations as less than equal in the classroom. In response to this deficit in educational reform, multicultural scholars have been calling for a humanizing turn in research and in everyday schooling practices. The thesis proposed here is to create an oppositional worldview, a stream of consciousness that exists not only to confront the struggle which also opposes dehumanization, but as that undertaking which empowers creativity and self-actualization.

This chapter has demonstrated that deep education that includes the notion of soul work within community-based educational spaces provides the best opportunity for educators to address both the social and holistic dynamics that influence work for the soul in education. It is here that that peace education can help to cultivate a language of conviction (Dillard, 2006; Tuck, 2009) that positions all as sacred beings worthy of respect and love at all times regardless of one's social construction. Moreover, by replacing the "damaged-centered" approach to teaching with a deeper approach toward work for the soul where research and everyday schooling practices in the classroom seeks to engage all members of a learning community intellectually, socially, and emotionally and moves past materialistic rewards and unnecessary competition.

References

Asante, M. K. (2005). Race, rhetoric, and identity: The architecton of soul. Amherst, NY: Humanity Books.

Asante, M.K. (1998). The Afrocentric idea. (Revised and Expanded ed.). Philadelphia, PA: Temple University Press.

Asante, M. K. (1992). Kemet, Afrocentricity and knowledge. Africa World Press.

Baldridge, B. J., Lamont Hill, M., & Davis, J. E. (2011). New possibilities :(re) engaging Black male youth within community-based educational spaces. Race Ethnicity and Education, 14(1), 121-136.

Banks, J. A. (Ed.). (1996). Multicultural education, transformative knowledge, and action: Historical and contemporary perspectives. New York: Teachers College Press.

Barkley-Brown, (1989). African-American women's quilting. Signs, 14(4), 921-929.

Bostic, P., & Manning, K. (2013). Learning to (re) member the things we've learned to forget: endarkened feminisms, spirituality, & the sacred nature of research & teaching. International Journal of Qualitative Studies in Education, 1-6.

Brown, K. (2013) Trouble on my mind: toward a framework of humanizing critical sociocultural knowledge for teaching and teacher education. Race Ethnicity and Education, 16:3, 316-338.

Dalton, J., & Crosby, P. (2006). The neglected inner lives of college students. Journal of College and Character, 7(8).

Danesh, H. B. (2006). Towards an integrative theory of peace education. Journal of peace education, 3(1), 55-78.

Darling-Hammond, L. (2000). How teacher education matters. Journal of teacher education, 51(3), 166-173.

David P. Barash, & Charles P. Webel. (2014). Peace and Conflict Studies.

Davis, J.E. 2006. Research at the margins: Dropping out of high school and mobility among African American males. International Journal of Qualitative Studies in Education 19: 289-304.

De Lissovoy, N., & Brown, A. L. (2013). Antiracist Solidarity in Critical Education: Contemporary Problems and Possibilities. The Urban Review, 45(5), 539-560.

Dillard, C. B. (2000). The substance of things hoped for, the evidence of things not seen: Examining an endarkened feminist epistemology in educational research and leadership. International Journal of Qualitative Studies in Education, 13(6), 661-681.

Dillard, C. B. (2006). On spiritual strivings: Transforming an African American woman's academic life. SUNY press.

Dillard, C. B. (2012). Learning to (Re) member the Things We've Learned to Forget: Endarkened Feminisms, Spirituality, and the Sacred Nature of Research and Teaching. Black Studies and Critical Thinking. Volume 18. Peter Lang New York. 29 Broadway 18th Floor, New York, NY 10006.

Dirkx, J. M. (1997). Nurturing soul in adult learning. New directions for adult and continuing education, 1997(74), 79-88.

Dirkx, J. M. (2001). Images, transformative learning and the work of soul. Adult learning, 12(3), 15.

Foucault, M. (1997). Ethics, Subjectivity and Truth: Essential Works of Foucault 1954-1984 (Vol. 1). New York: The New Press.

Freire, P. (1993). Pedagogy of the oppressed (Rev. ed.). New York: Continuum, 1970.

Furst, J. L. M. (1997). The natural history of the soul in ancient Mexico. New Haven: Yale University Press.

Ginwright, S. 2007. Black youth activism and the role of critical social capital in black community organizations. American Behavioral Scientist 51, no. 3: 403-18.

Ginwright, S. (2009). Black youth rising: Activism and radical healing in urban America. New York: Teachers College Press.

Giroux, H. A. (2003). The abandoned generation: Democracy beyond the culture of fear. New: Palgrave Macmillan.

Giroux, H.A. 2009. Youth in a suspect society: Democracy or disposability? New York: Palgrave MacMillan.

Grant, C. A. (2012). Cultivating flourishing lives a robust social justice vision of education. American Educational Research Journal, 0002831212447977.

Gregory, A., R. Skiba, and P. Noguera. 2010. The achievement gap and the discipline gap: Two sides of the same coin? Educational Researcher 39, no. 1.

Hansen, D. T. (2001). Exploring the moral heart of teaching: Toward a teacher's creed. New York: Teachers College Press.

Hegel, G. W. F. (2006). Lectures on the History of Philosophy: Greek philosophy. II (Vol. 2). London: Oxford University Press

Hillard, A. (1992). "Behavioral style, culture, and teaching and learning." The Journal of Negro Education 61, 3, 370-377.

Hillard. A. (2001). A race, identity, hegemony, and education: What do we need to know now? In Watkins, W. H., Lewis, J. H., & Chou, V. (Eds.). Race and education: The roles of history and society in educating African American students. Boston, MA: Allyn and Bacon.

Hooks, B. (1990). Yearning: Race, gender, and cultural politics. Boston: South End Press.

Hooks, B. (2010). Writing beyond race: living theory and practice. New York: Routledge.

James, G. G. (1954). Stolen legacy: Greek philosophy is stolen Egyptian philosophy. Trenton. NJ: Africa World.

Jung, C. G. (1933). Modem man in search of a soul. New York: Hartcourt, Brace and World.

Kessler, R. (2002). Nurturing deep connections: Five principles for welcoming soul into school leadership. School administrator, 59(8), 22-26.

King, J. E. (1991). Dysconscious racism: Ideology, identity, and the miseducation of teachers. The Journal of Negro Education, 60(2), 133-146.

King, J. E. (Ed.). (2005). Black education: A transformative research and action agenda for the new century. Routledge.

Kraehe, A. M., & Acuff, J. B. (2013). Theoretical Considerations for Art Education Research with and about" Underserved Populations". Studies in Art Education, 54(4), 294.

Ladson-Billings, G. (1995). But that's just good teaching! The case for culturally relevant pedagogy. Theory into practice, 34(3), 159-165.

Ladson-Billings, G. (2000). Fighting for our lives preparing teachers to teach African American students. Journal of teacher education, 51(3), 206-214.

Ladson-Billings, G. (2001). The power of pedagogy: Does teaching matter. Race and education: The roles of history and society in educating African American students, 73-88.

Ladson-Billings, G. (2003). It's your world, I'm just trying to explain it: Understanding our epistemological and methodological challenges. Qualitative Inquiry, 9(1), 5-12.

Ladson-Billings, G. (2009). Critical Race Theory in Education. Routledge International Handbook of Critical Education, 110.

Lewis, H. R. (2006). Excellence without a soul: How a great university forgot education. Boston: Public Affairs.

Linden, S. J. (Ed.). (2003). The Alchemy Reader: From Hermes Trismegistus to Isaac Newton. Cambridge: Cambridge University Press.

Martin, T. R. (2013). Ancient Greece: from prehistoric to Hellenistic times. New Haven: Yale University Press.

Miller, J. and Drake, S. (1997). Toward a spiritual curriculum. Curriculum Inquiry, 27(2), 239-245.

Miller, J. P. (2000). Education and the soul: Toward a spiritual curriculum. New York: Suny Press.

Moore, C. H. (1963). Ancient Beliefs in the Immortality of the Soul: With Some Account of Their Influence on Later Views. Boston: Rowman and Littlefield.

Noguera, P. 1996. Responding to the crisis confronting California's Black male youth without
furthering marginalization. The Journal of Negro Education 65, no. 2: 219-36.

Nicolescu, B. (2007). Transdisciplinarity as methodological framework for going beyond the science-religion debate. The Global Spiral, 9(4).

Palmer, P. J. (1999). Evoking the spirit in public education. Educational leadership, 56, 6-11.

Paris, D., & Winn, M. T. (Eds.). (2014). Humanizing research: Decolonizing qualitative inquiry with youth and communities. New York: SAGE Publications.

Phillips, L. (Ed.). (2006). The womanist reader. New York: CRC Press.

Popkewitz, T. S. (1998). Struggling for the Soul. The Politics of Schooling and the Construction of the Teacher. New York: Teachers College Press.

Rosalie, David (1997). Pyramid Builders of Ancient Egypt: A Modern Investigation of Pharaoh's Workforce. New York: Routledge.

Rose, N. (1998). Inventing our selves: Psychology, power, and personhood. Cambridge: Cambridge University Press.

Sardello, R. J. (1992). Facing the world with soul. Lindisfarne Books.

Tate, W. F. (1997). Critical race theory and education: History, theory, and implications. Review of research in education, 22, 195-247.

Tisdell, E. J. (2008). Spirituality and adult learning. New Directions for Adult and Continuing Education, 2008(119), 27-36.

Tochon, F. V., & Hanson, D. (2003). The deep approach: World language teaching for community building. Madison, WI: Atwood Publishing.

Tochon, F. V., & Karaman, A. C. (2009). Critical reasoning for social justice: Moral encounters with the paradoxes of intercultural education. Intercultural education, 20(2), 135-149.

Tochon, F. V. (2010). Deep Education. Journal for Educators, Teachers and Trainers (JETT), 1, 1-12.
http://jett.labosfor.com/index.php/jett/article/view/6.

Tochon, F. V. (2011). Deep education: Assigning a moral role to academic work. Educação, Sociedade & Culturas, 33, 17-35.

Tochon, F. V. (2013). Signs and Symbols in Education: Educational Semiotics. Deep University Press.

Tuck, E. (2009). Suspending damage: A letter to communities. Harvard Educational Review, 79(3), 409-428.

Tuck, E., & Yang, K. W. (2012). Decolonization is not a metaphor. Decolonization: Indigeneity, Education & Society, 1(1).

Ullucci, K., & Battey, D. (2011). Exposing Color Blindness/Grounding Color Consciousness Challenges for Teacher Education. Urban Education, 46(6), 1195-1225.

Woodland, M. (2008). Whatcha doin' after school? A review of the literature on the influence of after school programs on young Black males. Urban Education 43: 537-60.

Woodson, C. G. (1919). The Education of the Negro Prior to 1861: A History of the Education of the Colored People of the United States from the Beginning of Slavery to the Civil War. Association for the Study of Negro Life and History.

Woodson, C. G. (1933). The mis-education of the Negro. New York. Book Tree.

Wynter, S. (1987). On Disenchanting Discourse:" Minority" Literary Criticism and beyond. Cultural Critique, (7), 207-244.

Wynter, S. (2001). Towards the Sociogenic Principle: Fanon, Identity, the Puzzle of Conscious Experience, and What It Is Like to Be" Black". HISPANIC ISSUES, 23, 30-66.

Wynter, S. (2003). Unsettling the coloniality of being/power/truth/freedom: Towards the human, after man, its overrepresentation--An argument. CR: The New Centennial Review, 3(3), 257-337

7.

The Parlance of Professionalism in Family Child Care: Toward a Deeper Approach in Early Childhood Care and Education

Kate MacCrimmon
University of Madison – Wisconsin
maccrimmon@wisc.edu

Scholars, experts, and stakeholders from around the world purport to know what makes a family child care provider professional, yet no consensus exists on what it means to be a professional family child care provider. Furthermore, many of these sources contradict each other. Areas such as business versus relational models are particularly contested. Providers who attempt to meet all the standards required of them become too absorbed and distracted to nurture authentic connections among children and families, and feelings of ambivalence lead to disillusionment and burnout.

With the voices of family childcare providers noticeably absent from scholarly discussions on this topic, I turn to my experience as a family childcare provider to critically reflect: What does it mean to be a professional family child care provider? From a poststructural perspective, I employ authoethnography to reflect upon the roles I performed including family child care practitioner, second mother, social worker, administrator, and Jill-of-all-Trades. By recounting anecdotes in each of these roles I work to uncover a deeper approach to professionalism by using a caring reflective practitioner framework. My main finding is that by attempting to meet state requirements and my own ethics of care, I was unable to sustain high quality child care. Additionally, I argue for the primacy of professional criteria that include emotion, complexity and relationships. Finally, I found that a separate but equal professional identity and pedagogy is critical for the future of family child care.

What is professionalism in family child care (FCC)? Scholars, experts, and stakeholders from around the world purport to know what makes a FCC provider professional, yet no consensus exists on what it means to be a professional FCC provider. Furthermore, many of the criteria and characteristics from various sources contradict each other. This is highly problematic given that in 2013 the U.S. Census Bureau issued a report by Laughlin, which states that 16.3% of *all* infants in the U.S. under one year of age are cared for by non-relatives in a provider's home. Some experts (Edie, Adams, Riley, & Roach, 2003) claim that the numbers are actually much greater due to the fact that FCC is "hidden" because it takes place in a private home (p. 1). Additionally, the Bureau of Labor Statistics predicts a higher than expected increase in the demand for child care – 14% over the average 11% between the years of 2012 and 2022, positioning FCC as a significant component of the child care workforce.

Family child care, a form of child care around the world, is commonly described as a single provider being paid to care for mixed ages of children under five years of age in a private home. There are always exceptions to this generalization because some providers hire assistants, chose to care for one age grouping, and/or have afterschool programs for older children, but the overall idea is that child care provided to children in a private home is less institutional and more personal. Families looking for care often seek out providers who are similar to them culturally and economically and hence make FCC a very diverse form of child care.

FCC providers who attempt to follow contradictory criteria and to live up to contradictory expectations can end up feeling ambivalent and burned-out, causing withdrawal followed by career change. Yet the voices of FCC providers, who should be at the forefront of determining their own professional status, are noticeably absent from the professional literature. Indeed, most of the recent measures of professionalization appear to be mandated from officials who have little knowledge or experience of FCC. If attrition continues among FCC providers due to the impossible task of meeting contradictory professional criteria, the increasing demand for child care will not be met.

The consequences of these contradictions need to be widely discussed for two reasons. Firstly, contradictions have negative consequences for FCC providers, which impact children and families with whom they work. Secondly, if FCC providers stake their claim in determining the competencies that represent professionalism from *their* perspective, not only can a more authentic, less contradictory construction of the FCC profession be built, but also the desperate shortage of child care now and in the future can be more coherently addressed.

It was during my experience as a FCC provider from 2002 to 2010 that I came face to face with contradictory measures of what it means to be a professional in the field. I was pressured to attain the standards of an early childhood teacher and all its accoutrements, while my heart remained rooted in prioritizing relational care with children and families, an aspect that was highly prized by the vast majority of my child care parents. This ambivalence about what it meant to be a professional FCC provider permeated all corners of my professional experience and detracted from the importance of cultivating deep relationships and connections among my child care children and families.

Deep Education, or the deep approach to education is in response to the need to raise our collective awareness around critical issues such as those FCC providers experience (Tochon, 2010). Not a method, it is an ongoing dynamic process, somewhat like the opt quoted phrase in early childhood, "it's the process not the product". Never fully achieved, the deep approach offers the opportunity to reflect upon the question of why particular knowledge is privileged in a specific discipline. Importantly, this approach supports that you "learn best what you feel you need to know and what you learn is life-supporting and may enhance society and the world at large" (p. 5). It is this integrated approach that I employ in my investigation.

The current literature broadly illustrates the schism between prominent models of professionalization. For example, scholars have examined contrasting forms of professionalization such as quality assurance systems as well as professional FCC accreditation. Quality assurance systems, similar to quality rating and improvement systems (QRIS), are systems that have sets of criteria and qualifications mandated from outside the field, whereas U.S. accreditation is a system that formed in collaboration from within the field. In all cases, it is glaringly apparent from the existing literature that research on FCC is outdated, inadequate, and notably meager in the U.S.

The intention of this chapter is to add an autoethnographic perspective to existing literature that gives voice to the FCC providers who up until now have been underrepresented in scholarly debates on topics that directly affect their work. As a FCC provider, I participated in and was considered successful with state licensing regulations *and* city accreditation. State licensing, although prescribing important health and safety regulations, applied these rules in a punitive, suspicious, and one-size-fits-all manner, similar to the qualities of a quality assurance system. City accreditation, a system that provided critical support for me and which I loved and depended upon enormously, was limited in its ability to support providers outside of the mainstream or to challenge state or local regulation. Thus, my sense of what was truly important as a professional FCC provider was sometimes ignored, minimized, unsupported, or even looked at askance. This sense of what was most important in my professional work was what I came to understand as an internal set of competencies based on a feminist ethics of care. That is, competencies that include of emotion, complexity, and relationships. I argue that these beliefs and practices deserve to be regarded as central tenets of what it means to be a professional FCC provider. These competencies fall within the deep approach, or revitalizing and meaningful practices based on deep reflection and active engagement in an ongoing transformative process. Therefore, the purpose of this narrative study is to critically reflect on my FCC experience in the form of an autoethnography and to explore what it means to be a professional FCC provider. Accordingly, my overarching research question asks: What does it mean to be a professional FCC provider?

This poststructural qualitative inquiry employs a caring reflective practitioner framework, and uses autoethnography as the methodological tool to explore what it means to be a professional FCC provider. In addition, a feminist approach allows a retrospective, reflective, and critical analysis of my work as a professional FCC provider in a field where the overwhelming majority of people who do carework are women.

In the next section, I broadly explore the societal and academic context in which FCC manifests to situate this problem in more depth, surveying several examples of professionalization. The investigation of these themes is linked to the problem of contradictory notions of professionalism that I have encountered.

Being a Professional

Scholars, policymakers, and FCC providers alike hotly debate what it means to be a professional FCC provider. In this section, I probe the meaning of professionalism in FCC more deeply by examining contemporary perspectives that focus on these debates. For example, I will examine interventionist forms of professionalization in the U.K. and Australia and contrast those with relationship-based accreditation in the U.S. After appraising these forms of professionalization, I will review an international study that reveals the overall lack of consistency in FCC.

To begin the investigation into what it means to be a professional FCC provider, it is important to look at recent and contested forms of professionalization: quality assurance systems. O'Connell (2011) describes this as an interventionist form of professionalization based on her research of providers in London, England. She describes the imposed agenda as one that providers are required to go through as a rite of passage, trading in their mothering traits, seen as *the* greatest barrier to professionalization, for more masculine ones.

O'Connell states that audit culture, technology, performativity, and fabrication are employed to ensure conformity to standards across FCC environments and to control the movements of women and children (2011, p. 792). She describes audit culture as prescribing childminder's language, and as requiring artifacts such as policy handbooks, training certificates, posters, business cards, and glossy brochures that distinguish the work of child care practitioners from anything resembling mothering. Additionally, providers are required to post schedules, timetables, and menus. O'Connell defines technology as instruments such as regulations, inspections, and pamphlets aimed at having providers perform this type of professionalization. Fabrication requires using what she terms paperwork, posters, words, and activity plans, otherwise known as "rotas" among providers and is central to the notion of performing professionalism (p. 792). O'Connell suggests that these mechanisms of professionalism serve to enforce and reproduce hegemonic conceptions of worth and that buying in as authentic members of the club requires childminders to relinquish and devalue the care aspect of their work, making their work less meaningful.

Although providers valued some of the skills they acquired and took advantage of these as needed, they did not welcome surrendering their ethic of care. O'Connell reports that experts and provider's mismatching definitions of quality create tension and play into the disillusionment of providers, leading to diminishing numbers of childminders. O'Connell suggests that providers need to challenge neo-liberal definitions of "quality" and "status" and to conceptualize alternative but authentic definitions of quality and professional identity based on their ethic of care.

Cook et al (2013) explore a similar type of quality assurance standardization in Australia, and discuss three discourses of professionalism that emerged in their analysis on a study of FCC providers. Also recognized as part of the reform movement, this hegemonic version of professionalization marginalizes and delegitimizes the care aspect of FCC providers by deploying a binary argument. Education is presented as rational while care is portrayed as emotional and therefore in need of surveillance and management. By characterizing FCC providers as inept and deficient, policymakers have justified a model that is competition-based, hierarchical, and rife with managerial terminology and traits.

The three discourses the authors identified from this study are "They are educators", "It's the job", and "I am a carer", (p. 115). The educator discourse distinguishes between formal (educators) and informal (mothers) providers so as to prescribe qualifications and the need for credentials, assessment, and culpability. Therefore, traditional methods such as intuition and experience become invalid.

The second discourse is the job discourse, taken up by providers in an attempt to reconcile their partial appropriation of the educator discourse and which focused on the contents of the job as opposed to the traits of providers. These providers bore an asymmetrical burden because of the difficulty of both fulfilling the demands of the system and bearing the emotional labor of their work in isolation.

Lastly is the carer's discourse wherein providers acted as second mothers and nurtured long lasting and enduring relationships, emphasizing deep connections using intuition to guide their decisions with children and families.

These two previous examples of professionalization that use quality assurance standards have been criticized for homogenizing providers, decreasing the unique aspects that reflect the diversity of FCC, silencing and pathologizing the voices and values of providers. This form of professionalization contrasts sharply with accreditation, or one of the most widely accepted forms of professionalism in the U.S. Accreditation is both a process and a status and is granted only when a program meets the exemplary standards set forth by an accrediting agency. Modigliani (2011) describes the innovative collaboration that brought accreditation into being, which is noteworthy because it *included* FCC providers and families, as well as experts and stakeholders. In addition to this inclusive approach, cultural differences were carefully considered and embraced so as not to automatically privilege mainstream values. According to Modigliani, "FCC is our nation's most culturally diverse form of early education and care" because a large percentage of minority women perform this work (p. 14). FCC accreditation standards also needed to acknowledge the unique aspects of FCC, which include mixed age groupings of children, the challenges of blending a business with a home, and the fact that FCC providers often work alone.

Modigliani states that the demanding four-year construction of FCC accreditation in 1999 resulted in the adoption of these standards by all 50 states in the U.S., the District of Columbia, and parts of the military. This working group labored to establish the formal goals of national accreditation from the ground-up. One area that diverse respondents in the working group agreed upon immediately was that the most important characteristic of a top quality FCC program was "a warm, loving, nurturing provider" (p. 16). Also noteworthy because of the effort put forth to include all voices was that when faced with an impasse on a particular standard, the working group yielded to the "many right ways" of providing diverse quality care (p. 19).

Investigating two similar forms of quality assurance systems in the U.K. and Australia, as well as accreditation in the U.S. brings into question what the guidelines are, cohesive or otherwise, from an international perspective. The work of Davis et al (2012) broaden the picture with their international comparison of regulated FCC based on data from ten countries: Australia, Canada, England and Wales, Germany, Ireland, Japan, Norway, New Zealand, Sweden, and the U.S.A.

In their analysis, the authors cite the ample research demonstrating elements that are necessary for the growth and sustainability of FCC but that are not always being incorporated. They included increased and targeted education, fewer children in care, and the provider's use of staffed support organizations. Their analysis also reported that structural characteristics as being far from universal. Some countries subsidize low-income families, some countries employ their providers through local associations, some countries offer union membership, and some offer start-up assistance. In the U.S.A., these factors vary state by state, but *all* providers are self-employed.

These examples of FCC illuminate not only a lack of consistency, but offer a distinctly mercurial picture of FCC and one that is mired in inertia. From quality assurance systems to accreditation there is wide variance on what it means to be a professional FCC provider. As a state licensed and city accredited provider I worked hard to meet what Osgood (2010) calls the regulatory gaze, as well as to authentically meet the needs of children and families. The ambivalence that resulted is what I will discuss in my autoethnography after briefly describing the theoretical framework.

A Caring Reflective Practitioner Framework

In this section I assemble carework theory amassed by England (2005) with reflective practitioner theory proposed by Schön (1983) to examine my experience as an FCC provider. This built-from-scratch blend of frameworks provides the necessary mechanism to dive more deeply into the overall question of what it means to be a professional FCC provider.

The first component of this compound framework is carework theory, proposed by England (2005). Carework theory is comprised of five sub-theories: devaluation, public good, prisoner of love, commodification of emotion, and lastly, the love and money theory.

Devaluation theory is based on the lower overall cultural worth of women as compared to men, and by association, the lower value of the worth accorded to the work women do. Researchers found that work that interfaces with the public and requires workers to nurture others – suffers from what they term a "pay penalty", which ends up being equivalent to 5-10% less income than otherwise comparable workers (p. 383).

The public good theory is focused on the benefits of carework to society rather than to the recipients of care or to caregivers. Public good theory defines carework as work that has both direct and indirect social beneficiaries. Recognized by conservatives as well as liberals as work that will yield public as well as private returns, it is best exemplified by education and parenting.

The prisoner of love theory takes into account how caring motivations and altruism impact careworkers, and why low pay for carework persists. England observes that intrinsic gratification is often counted as partial compensation for careworkers, which perpetuates the status quo. Due to their emotional attachments, careworkers may not advocate for better pay or benefits, a condition employers and the state exploit.

The commodification of emotion theory looks at the way careworkers are required to be emotionally engaged in employment and the costs involved in doing so. One example of this theory is when affluent families hire immigrant women to do child care – what England calls the extracting of natural resources from developing countries with love as the "raw material" (p. 392). This perspective sees labors of love as intimate exploitation and as costing the seller more than if they were doing work such as cleaning or landscaping, work which does not require an emotional investment.

Lastly, the love and money theory refutes the oft-cited dichotomy between these two concepts in favor of an integrated approach. This theory contends that carework *can* align with the private sector, which has the potential to provide both fair pay *and* quality care. It also argues that research should focus on what wage structures can eliminate the pay penalty and which cultural traits of behavior have negative consequences for engagement in carework, rather than engaging in a collective wringing of hands over the impossible harmony between love *and* money.

The second component of this compound framework is the reflective practitioner theory proposed by Schön (1983). Schön proposes to invert current practices of technical rationality and to examine professional artistry via a new epistemology of practice. He argues that by examining what makes exceptional professionals through a four-part process of knowing-in-action, reflection-in-action, practice, and practicum, we can analyze their practices and learn by identifying what sets them apart.

Of this four-part process, knowing-in-action is an embodied knowledge or acting without conscious thought. For example, learning to crawl or walk - the kind of knowledge that is learned by feeling and doing rather than by teaching.

Reflection-in-action comes from experimentation, invention, and improvisation that stems from encountering something unexpected; it is meant to address a specific problem either on the spot or after some reflection. In a metaphorical sense, it's like a group dance, where one must simultaneously watch out for and respond to other dancers.

The third component, practice, is the set of criteria that contribute to professional knowledge. This is embedded in the professional context and is a pivotal point upon which Schön makes his argument. He contends that rather than constraining the complexity of reality into a static box, we must draw from a constructionist epistemology whereby new understandings are built by negotiating variables and anomalies into new frameworks of possibilities.

Lastly is the practicum, where by being immersed into a particular community as an apprentice, one learns the language, culture, and expectations of the profession. In this space, one can explore and try out ideas under the guidance of a mentor.

These two complementary theoretical frameworks will be the single lens with which I analyze my autoethnographic anecdotes. Carework theory addresses the issues of gender in FCC and helps to explain some of my experiences as a woman providing childcare. Reflective practitioner theory addresses the complexity of providing childcare, and provides tools that can be used to discern what it means to be a professional FCC provider.

Autoethnography

Autoethnography, the symbolic heart of this study and chosen method of data collection, is underpinned by a poststructuralalist epistemology. Richardson (2003) states that this perspective "directs us to understand ourselves reflexively as persons writing from particular positions at specific times; and second, it frees us from trying to write a single text in which we say everything at once to everyone" (p. 929).

A feminist approach makes an apt companion to poststructural underpinnings, because of the acknowledgment of complexity. Olesen (2011) claims that this perspective leaves interpretation open, blurred and changeable, and in a sense, allows the reader and writer to read and to be read simultaneously, making this epistemology highly compatible with autoethnography.

Ellis et al (2011) view autoethnography historically as a reaction to the crisis of confidence triggered by postmodernism and to the more canonical and traditional methods of research. Instead of depending on the dichotomous thinking exemplified by the scientific method paradigm, autoethnography adopts a both/and philosophy in search of a more multifaceted truth, deliberately moving away from the belief system in which there is one universal truth or script. The authors suggest that by situating the researcher as the researched, personal values can be fully embraced rather than denying their existence. Autoethnographers employ multiple components of storytelling such as plays, poetry, temporal variety, and character and storyline development. In the showing of inner life via thoughts and feelings, an outsider can, in a sense, experience what the researcher has experienced. This allows marginalized groups to be heard in what could be considered a reversal of the research process. As I worked on this project, my ideas about what it means to be a professional FCC provider changed. Thinking that I knew what a professional FCC provider was, it turns out that what defines a professional FCC provider is more amorphous. It's not simply an either/or definition of a "teacher" or a "caregiver," it is a blend of both. The anecdotes in the next section illustrate some of these findings. Lastly, no work on human subjects other than myself is exercised; therefore, there is no need for an institutional review board (IRB).

What Does it Mean to be a Professional FCC Provider?

FCC Practitioner

There were many areas in which I developed my expertise while working in FCC. One area was as a FCC practitioner. This encompassed being a provider, a child development expert, an "educarer," and an educator. To use medical analogy, I was a generalist. I learned to identify areas that seemed like red flags based on regular observation of a child in my care nine and a half hours a day. I participated in confidential consultations with my support group and had conversations with my local accreditation consultant. In addition, I asked questions of parents and based my appraisal on my experience with other children. These skills were not something that came naturally, but developed over time, with great effort, patience, and intense communication.

Early identification of a range of issues can have a *major* impact on a child's life, as well as on public and private resources. With one child, I identified the need to have his eyes checked, after which he received medical intervention early enough so that he can see normally. I often predicted when a child was about to be sick, shared insights about a child's emerging personality and temperament with parents, which parents seemed to appreciate very much. One family wrote in their annual review, "Our whole family has been beautifully, thoughtfully, and generously nurtured by Kate for almost seven years." Other families, though very few, made their mark with malicious comments or underhanded behavior. While polite to my face one family castigated me in their review. They said that I had "abused" and "neglected" their child, took naps during daycare, and charged too much for my child care service. Ironically, it felt like I was the one being abused. I even changed my name from "Child Care" to "Nursery School" after a couple of years in hopes of garnering more respect.

My elderly neighbor captured a different attitude. He would greet me as I wheeled a cartload of six boisterous children past his house. He would shake his head and tell me that there was a place in Heaven just for me because of the work I was doing. But how, I would wonder, am I going to pay my bills until then? Why do I need to wait for my reward? Don't I deserve to be paid now? What if I don't believe in Heaven? I was not doing this work so I could reserve a place in heaven. I was doing this work so that I could care for my own children *and* get my husband through school so that one of us could have a stable job with benefits!

Thankfully, there were many wonderful experiences, but I did finally put a name on this baffling experience - it was **visual gestalt**. I was a moving target; I had a fluid identity. People saw me as what they wanted to see. Although I was the same person, parents would perceive vastly different versions of who I was. Some parents perceived me as *She Who is Wonderful*. No matter when these parents dropped off or picked up their child, I was *always* doing something marvelous with the kids. They loved and respected me. I felt great with these parents, and their children seemed to thrive. Then there were the suspicious parents. *She Who Whenever They Pick Up or Drop Off There is Something Wrong*. Their perceptions of me affected the events that shaped their experience, and their children seemed to suffer because of it.

Second Mother

> *I'm everything I'm supposed to be so why am I still stuck back here?*
>
> *She who never fits, but sits on the benches watching others live their lives. Sacrificing everything in order to satisfy a*

> *momentary obligation/ need/ desire/ requirement that gets her no closer to a better life over and over again. Struggling in silence, not being able to share because of the shame of not fitting in. Not being able to fit in. Unable to converse in the language of success because she never made it. So tired of being perceived as unequal, as lessor, as nothing, as a service. The work is so hard, but I struggle to make it look easy.*

Being a second mother was another role I played. I loved being nurturing, providing deep and loving care, sensing what a person or child needed, and then supplying it. I cooked wonderful food and happily fed parents if they should visit at mealtime, sharing homemade food grounded in fulfilling an everyday necessity. It was lovely and delectable, seductive and alluring in all of the best ways. It was an earthy, heady feeling, providing sustenance at the most fundamental level. Giving and receiving love from children with hugs, kisses, sweet looks and touches. I loved it - there was so much joy in that aspect. Such physical closeness is essential for young children and especially babies, but that contact was healing and nourishing for me too. The intersubjectivity that I experienced with my own and other people's children was one large reason I could do care - the merging of myself with children eliminated barriers. Upon reflection, it's interesting to realize what this role actually entailed, and it took a long time to recognize that being a nurturer should not mean being a doormat.

Mothers are often taken for granted, seen as less intelligent, and told that what they are feeling is all in their heads, so my embodiment of this role did not lead me to be perceived as professional by, strangely and paradoxically enough, some of my very own acquaintances. When I began my daycare, other providers warned me to be judicious about accepting friends as clients. But being inexperienced, being afraid to set boundaries, and just wanting to be nice, as well as being constantly worried about making money, it took learning the hard way to be more cautious. I summed it up as **Acquaintances Are the Worst**. There were many examples of this. Some people asked me to put them on my waiting list but did not want to pay the nonrefundable deposit because they were "friends". That way they would have more childcare options available if a space opened up in a center and they could save money while I lost a security deposit and some of my self-worth. Other "friends" just did not bother to read my policies at all so I would then have to awkwardly explain what my policies were, sometimes in front of other parents who had taken the time to read and respect my policies.

Social Worker

Being new parents is a time in life that is oftentimes very stressful. A new baby can prompt parents to move to a better neighborhood, into a house, or to start a new job so they can have more flexibility in order to have a better future or to be with their children more. This was true in my case. I somehow found the strength to move to a new house and begin a business with my first baby. However, as a provider, I felt as if I were caught in the middle. I needed support and resources too, yet I was expected to act not only as a social worker, but also as advisor, counselor, and resource specialist for daycare parents.

In some cases, playing multiple roles involved me in situations in which daycare parents displaced their own anxieties or frustrations onto me. In one case, when I attempted to make my income more predictable by asking parents to commit for the following year with a deposit and a contract, something that made me feel more powerful and in control, one parent responded by haggling with me over fees and schedules and by lying about her income. The unhappy parent expressed her resentment and stress in a letter. In her letter, she writes that with a job prospect she might need full-time care as opposed to part-time care for the following fall, but that she didn't know whether to reserve full or part-time care because a nanny she shared with another family hadn't made up her mind to be available until June. She tells me that she is "agonizing" over what to do and presents me with four solutions, one of which asks me to make an exception for her by breaking my attendance requirement of either two or four days a week and to offer her three days instead *and* to give it to her at a discount. She then asks me if I could take our vacation when she and her husband take theirs so as to save them money, citing the fact that her husband, an employed professional at a nearby university, gets just eleven months pay, and that she only gets paid when she works as a self-employed consultant. She goes on to complain about my yearly registration fee, wondering why the entire "security deposit" fee is not given back. She then adds that "one of the hardest things about family day care is the unreliability," because she has to find someone else to cover for her child when the daycare is closed due to sickness. She proposes that I arrange to have my assistant go to their house to provide childcare on those days, since otherwise my assistant gets a "paid vacation". I responded the same day as compassionately as I could, and taking a stand for my policies. I realized later that this parent lied about her income so as to get the lowest rate on my sliding scale the following year. This was in spite of the fact that we depended greatly on my income, food stamps, and free state health insurance while I was putting my husband through school - something most the daycare parents were aware of. I was too busy and distracted to think about the veracity of her income claim until later, because I assumed people would be honest, especially in light of my circumstances. I never fully understood why this parent resented me so deeply, but dealing with her unhappiness took my focus away from providing care to children. It didn't feel good to have someone in the daycare who was clearly resenting me and my policies, and in hindsight I think her unhappiness may have undermined my authority in my daycare with my own employees and poisoned other parents' respect for me as well.

Administrator

> *filling in boxes, blanks, and forms*
> *paperwork, taxes, attendance, and norms*
> *flyers, menus, and post that certificate*
> *"This is where the money is at!"*
> *filing and recording every tiny receipt*
> *along with your time/space percentage honest to Pete*

> *they're just trying to help you can't you see?*
> *especially those "providers in Milwaukee"*
> *it's a service, it provides "choice", "It's a license to steal!"*
> *quality assurance systems, what a deal!*

One label that went along with being a paperwork minion, project engineer, performer, and technician was being an administrator. It was one of my least favorite jobs in FCC because it took such an inordinate amount of my time. I felt like I couldn't even acknowledge the children at times because I was so focused on paperwork, employee issues, training, or recording information. Along with the paperwork, however, were other administrative issues like late pick up. It was an issue that seemed to confront all FCC providers because it was talked about a lot in my support group. After providing non-stop care for nine and a half hours, the one thing I really needed was to have the evening reserved for myself or for time with my family. Most families generally arrived on time, but some were habitually late or arrived five minutes before our ending time of 5:00 p.m., only to expect a full rundown of their child's day. It was a chaotic time of day, with parents piling in all at the same time, trying to find coats, hats, mittens, belongings, dirty diapers, and shoes before leaving, as well as trying to hear about the day. Some parents didn't expect anything when they arrived late, but it was sometimes very stressful for us.

My assistant and I finally decided to impose a late fee. It made me so uncomfortable that I told her that if she collected it, she could keep the money. So we tried that for a while, and it didn't really affect parents much; they made late payments, and I still felt uncomfortable. One parent even shared about Freakanomics (2010), a study where a late fee was accepted as a license to pick up late because the fee wasn't steep enough and parents could then "buy off their guilt" (p. 20). We eventually just dropped the late fee because it felt like it didn't fit with our philosophy of kindness and understanding, and we found it more effective to share from our perspective how late pick-ups impacted us on a personal level. It felt like it broke our agreement with parents and that I was no longer on their side, because it was a business policy and it just felt mean spirited. I could imagine how frustrating it would be for a parent who, after a long workday and after fighting traffic, arrived late, only to get a late fee. So I decided that we live in an imperfect world and that I would just go about my evening, and my husband or assistant would hand over the child to their parents. I enjoyed talking with many of the parents anyway, so I adopted a both/and philosophy by the end and stopped feeling guilty if I had to leave at the specified time.

Jill-of-All-Trades

I was the person who acted as CEO, director, employer, recruiter, fixer; I was the person responsible for everything, including the very lives of all the children. I was faced with big changes in the childcare system in Wisconsin that began while I was a provider. The state created the Wisconsin Department of Children and Families (DCF) and the Youngstar system, a quality rating and improvement system (QRIS) designed to give parents "choice." This business model ranks all providers receiving state subsidies between one and five stars, as well as each provider's violations, and location on the state website. They held a "listening session" on the 29th of October 2008. I wrote a letter, intending to read it in front of the audience. But when the time came, the representatives of the newly formed department told the audience of several hundred people how the new system was going to work, speaking at such length that I felt intimidated and left before I read it. In it, I stated that I wanted to be treated like the professional I was and that the state of Wisconsin needed to be a leader in changing the status quo for hardworking providers. Five years later, with Youngstar in full swing, I am saying the same thing.

Discussion

This discussion is intended to focus on a process of analysis and to understand myself reflexively, as an FCC provider writing from a particular time and place. By analyzing these representations and by being fully rooted in my personal perspective, I will sift my reflections through the framework of a caring reflective practitioner to draw comparisons, make observations, and note themes and connections on what it means to be a professional FCC provider as it relates to the internal set of competencies; emotion, complexity, and relationships, and therefore to the deep approach in each of my roles.

As a FCC Practitioner, I honed my skills as an observer, a communicator, a synthesizer of information, a child development expert, a parent educator, and a provider of care with lots of time, practice, and support from my accreditation consultant and support group actively engaged with all four parts to Schön's reflective practice. I learned what was important to do and when to do it since I knew the children and families so intimately – it was an incredibly complex dance. I felt supported in this role through the process of accreditation, which as Modigliani (2011) asserted, is one that incorporates respect and friendliness into the process, and the process felt uplifting and affirming, unlike state licensing. With state licensing, like the quality assurance systems, I experienced many of the externally imposed sets of competencies applied with the tools of technology described by O'Connell (2011). Emotions, complexity, and relationships played a primary part in my role as FCC practitioner. Deely (2007) contends, "communication can be real only if relations are real" (p. xxv). This was very true with the families where we had an easy and trusting reciprocity. When relationships were on the surface I became the victim of the devaluation theory of carework leading me to my own theory of visual gestalt.

In my role as second mother I relied heavily upon emotion and intuition. The effect emotions had in essentially feeding my spirit was invaluable and incredibly powerful, not just for me, but for the children for whom I cared *and* their parents. The assumption that this should be part of the compensation providers can expect to receive, an assertion made by the public good theory, is untenable, as this "benefit" worked both ways. Parents appreciated the connection with me particularly with the youngest of children. I also used my intuition to guide me and made the job at times look easy and fun, and for that reason, worthless to some. The appearance of this job coming "naturally" and like the work any mother could do, unfortunately did not always work in my favor since this seemed to give permission for acquaintances in particular to take advantage of me as defined by devaluation and prisoner of love theory.

The role of social worker was aided by the fact I had my accreditation consultant and support group to turn to for difficult answers. Independently dealing with the difficulties families faced when I myself needed support, is because, as Davis et al (2012) point out, all providers in the U.S. are self-employed and therefore ultimately have only themselves to rely on. I was lucky enough to have the accreditation agency close at hand, but even so, there was only so much they could do. Again, close relationships and complexity played a primary part in determining whether this was easier or harder.

Being an administrator was generally incompatible with the more preferred roles of practitioner and second mother; however, I did, like some providers in O'Connell's (2011) appreciate some of the requirements of licensing and accreditation such as a contract and creating a philosophy statement. I even made business cards of a smaller non-standard size, which families seemed to like.

As Jill-of-All-Trades I learned on the job how to fix problems and improvise on the spot, like Schön's reflection-in-action, as well as the idea of a practicum, or being immersed in a professional environment. I liked being able to say that I owned and operated a child care business in my home. Like the love and money theory, I felt not only good about being able to earn money in exchange for loving and caring for children and their families, I felt empowered by it. Learning to speak in front of committees was nerve-wracking at the time but it was a good experience for me to advocate for FCC when I was asked to do so.

Conclusion

What we could be
a permaculture of the mind,
the borders,
the edges,
the space where life feeds,
is fed,
is a place of transition,
and most of all flourishes

As argued by many scholars in the field, FCC providers need to stake their claim on *their* version of professionalism, a claim based on concepts, characteristics, knowledge, ethics, and lived experiences that they consider vital to them. Based on my experience, I didn't know exactly where I stood on professionalization until I read deeply in the literature, and reflected upon my experience. I can see the desire I had to be perceived as professional, to have the extremely difficult work of child care seen as valuable *and* as requiring skill, as well as the desire I had for decent pay and benefits. Having to be self-employed kept me isolated and vulnerable to attack, ignorant of anything better, and sometimes feeling like I was imagining all the difficulty. Maybe it was just me, I wasn't up to snuff, couldn't handle just hanging out with kids, or was too high-strung. I also saw in myself a resistance to being "professionalized."

It was especially awkward to think of myself as a professional while working in my own home, which blends public and private spheres, a phenomenon observed by O'Connell (2011). I was expected to display certificates and flyers, as well as pictures and artifacts that weren't necessarily of my choosing in my own home, and I didn't like it. I didn't really want to display posters intended for kids in my living room, but I did it because that was part of regulation. It was always a challenge to post something at child height in a way that a child could not pull it down. My husband finally built a picture frame that we could screw to the wall and change the photos and pictures inside. It felt like I was required to display artifacts as part of a performing of professionalism as described by O'Connell (2011).

Part of the performance was that I threw around words and phrases I didn't completely understand, like "developmentally appropriate practice," and "gross" and "fine motor skills," that I felt sounded impressive. I didn't realize at the time that developmentally appropriate practice was based on the achievements of white middle class kids and that all other children were measured against it. Child development can be a valuable tool, but it isn't the only tool in assessing a child. So performing professionalism was somewhat like the word game described in Cook et al (2013), in which educational terms override care terms in an effort to separate care and education.

I resented feeling imposed upon in my own home as a FCC provider. Again, many requirements were very important because they ensured that health and safety standards were preserved, but equally important were my relationships with children and families. However, it was exhausting and draining to do both, like Cook et al (2013), to give good care and meet standards with no state support, while independently trying to keep my business alive. Having a FCC business felt kind of like being a neglected stepchild that no one really wanted.

After the deep reflection, however, I recognize that a process of professionalization is the only real possibility for the survival of FCC, since the tasks demanded of childcare workers are so great and entail such complex skill. Just as Armenia (2009) suggests, care is not natural, and care is not easy. The question of *what kind* of professionalization is really the question, *who* should define it, *how* it should be applied, and *how* it will be supported. The kind of professionalization that felt the best to me was the process of accreditation because it was similar to Lanigan's (2011) collaborative style, with friendliness and respect embedded in it. Modigliani's (2011) idea of building the accreditation process required a team effort as well; one that involved people from all parts of the field who really knew what it was like from the inside. However, Moss (2003) challenges us to imagine a new kind of professionalization that has a contextualized evaluative structure, and Osgood (2007) challenges us to imagine an emotionally appropriate practice with a movable conception of what it means to be a professional. Several scholars argue that providers should determine what professionalization might look like. I agree that provider's voices not only need to be heard but that they need to be a much larger part of the equation. Parent groups also need to be a larger part of this equation rather than continue the dynamic of providers versus parents in a cycle that never achieves resolution. If this were to happen, honest conversations about the provision and cost of care could take place and collaborative activist work could be fashioned toward initiating changes in policies and practices. In this way, the complexity and indeterminacy of providing care, and the relationships involved, would become a central consideration. Lanigan (2011) brings forth the idea of having regulation and professional development work hand in hand, in a more productive and positive process. It would certainly make the process less punitive.

In summary, what it means to be a professional FCC provider is a complex question. In my experience, it was a blending of various facets of regulation, accreditation, and my own spirit, and these were woven together with relationships in an asymmetrical tapestry reflecting real life and having no definitive ending. It is a continuous story that unfolds differently depending on who reads it and how it's read, with my self-perception colliding with that of other's perception of me along the way.

References

Armenia, A. B. (2009). More Than Motherhood Reasons for Becoming a Family Day Care Provider. *Journal of Family Issues, 30*(4), 554-574.

Cook, K., Davis, E., Williamson, L., Harrison, L. J., & Sims, M. (2013). Discourses of professionalism in family day care. *Contemporary Issues in Early Childhood, 14*(2), 112-126.

Davis, E., Freeman, R., Doherty, G., Karlsson, M., Everiss, L., Couch, J., ... & Hinke-Rahnau, J. (2012). An international perspective on regulated family day care systems. *Australasian Journal of Early Childhood,* 37(4), 127.

Deely, J. N. (2007). Intentionality and semiotics: A story of mutual fecundation.

Edie, D., Adams, D. B., Riley, D., & Roach, M. A. (2003). *Family child care*. (Public Policy Series on Alternative Policy Options Report No. 3). Madison: University of Wisconsin--Extension. Retrieved December 8, 2014, from http://www. http://sohe.wisc.edu/outreach/wccrp/pdfs/policy0903l.pdf

Ellis, C., Adams, T. E., & Bochner, A. P. (2011). Autoethnography: an overview. *Historical Social Research/Historische Sozialforschung*, 273-290.

England, P. (2005). Emerging theories of care work. *Annual review of sociology*, 381-399.

Levitt, S. D., & Dubner, S. J. (2010). *Freakonomics* (Vol. 61). Sperling & Kupfer editori.

Lanigan, J. D. (2011). Family child care providers' perspectives regarding effective professional development and their role in the child care system: A qualitative study. *Early Childhood Education Journal*, 38(6), 399-409.

Laughlin, L. (2013). Who's minding the kids? Child care arrangements: Spring 2011. Current Population Reports, P70-135. Washington, DC: US Census Bureau; 2013.

Modigliani, K. (2011). "Who Says What Is Quality?": Setting Quality Standards for Family Child Care. *Zero to Three, 31*(5), 14-21.

Moss, P. (2003). Whither Family Day Care?. Family Day Care: *International Perspectives on Policy, Practice and Quality*, 234.

O'Connell, R. (2011). Paperwork, rotas, words and posters: an anthropological account of some inner London childminders' encounters with professionalisation. *The Sociological Review, 59*(4), 779-802.

Olesen, V. (2011). Feminist qualitative research in the millennium's first decade Developments, challenges, prospects. In N.K. Denzin & Y.S. Lincoln (Eds) *The Sage handbook of qualitative research* (pp. 129-146). Thousand Oaks, CA: Sage.

Osgood, J. (2010). Reconstructing professionalism in ECEC: the case for the 'critically reflective emotional professional'. *Early Years, 30*(2), 119-133.

Richardson, L. (2003). Writing: A method of inquiry. In *Collecting & interpreting qualitative materials*. N.K. Denzin & Y.S. Lincoln (Eds) pp. 923-948.

Schön, D. A. (1983). *The reflective practitioner: how professionals think in action*. New York: Basic Books.

Tochon, F. V. (2010). Deep education. *JETT*, *1*(1), 1-12.

8.

Mere Child's Play or Creation of Coherence? Conceptualizing Children's Dramatic Play as Life Sustaining Deep Education

Connie Lent
University of Wisconsin
connie.lent@gmail.com

The emergence of systems of narrative coherence and the creation of life stories are explored through informal discourse analysis of written observations of children's dramatic play at 2, 3, and 4 years of age. Select observations are discussed as examples of the early age at which children use narrative to create coherence (Linde, 1993); to mediate between reflection and action (Rosenwald, 1992) and to generate master narratives and counter-stories in the construction and co-construction of life-story narratives (Nelson, 2001). The discussion aims to extend conceptualization of the value of play beyond developmental psychology understanding of play as practiced representation of symbols to achieve academic proficiency, to consider children's play though the lens of life sustaining practices and deep education (Tochon, 2013). Implications are considered in relation to early care and education practice.

Life Sustaining Deep Education

In this theoretical chapter, I examine human creation and co-creation of narrative identity through the lens of early childhood. I explore the developmental emergence of systems of narrative coherence for the creation of life stories (Linde, 1993), narrative mediation (Rosenwald, 1992); and the generation of counter-stories (Nelson, 2001) in children two to five years of age through analysis of written observations of children's self-initiated dramatic play. The purpose is to demonstrate the importance of the narrative process as a fundamental human skill consistently practiced in children's play that begins with the child's earliest stages of language development. I suggest that narrative theorists may be neglectful in their appreciation of the early age that narrative identity appears as demonstrated through children's dramatic play.

Further, child development theorists may neglect the importance of children's use of narrative to stimulate innovation and mediate development (Rosenwald, 1992) in favor of its use as a tool for concrete representation. Due to the common application in early childhood classrooms of Piaget's cognitive, Vygotsky's sociocultural, and Erikson's psychosocial development theories, these theories were selected to consider in relation to narrative theory. When taken together, developmental and narrative theory form an extended framework to conceptualize children's play as a transdisciplinary experience wherein children naturally use a multifaceted, deep approach to negotiate tensions in order to create coherence from their experiences and generate narrative stories and counter-stories. In this manner the seemingly innate, universal drive for children's ongoing practice of narrative story and counter-story creation during spontaneous play can be understood as a necessary, life-sustaining, deep education process.

Deep education is a holistic approach to teaching and learning that engages learners on intellectual, social, and emotional levels (Tochon 2010). It recognizes the connection among humans and all life forms that Kentel and Karrow (2007) refer to as deep ecology in which embodied, situated knowing supports deeper understanding of our connections to the earth and to each other. Rather than a sole focus on the transmission of knowledge, deep education is concerned with relationships between people engaged in learning activities to create transformational experiences (Tochon, 2010). Deely (2007) emphasizes that we cannot form a picture of the world as isolated beings and that we must form our reality within our social context. According to Deely (2007) reality is shaped by the intersubjective processes of cognition and consensus within which we co-create and interpret meanings of social and cultural life as we communicate with others. For children, this emphasizes the importance of ongoing practice to perfect co-construction of their own narrative stories within their specific social contexts such as is done during play.

The goal is not to imply one theoretical framework as more important than the other but rather to draw attention in a new way to the seemingly miraculous ability and driven need of young children to practice the art and skills of personal and socially constructed narratives. This is significant because increasingly, children are afforded fewer and fewer options to engage in spontaneous, uninterrupted play during which they can practice these skills. Increased emphasis on academic aspects of development and the promotion of global mandates for Early Education for All (UNESCO, 2006; World Bank, 2002) require increased standards and program accountability. Expectations of accountability raise questions regarding governmentally regulated, one-size-fits-all early education systems (Fuller, 2007; Bloch & Swadener, 2009). Even in classrooms for children as young as two to five years of age, these standards emphasize the use of structured lessons with didactic methods for language, math, and literacy, that align with outcomes-driven curriculum goals intended to improve test scores when children enter 'real' school (Fuller, 2007). Outcomes-based standards mandate a top-down curriculum with prescribed learning processes (Tochon, 2013) that impede children's ability to form and follow their own patterns of thinking and learning (Lent, 2004) within the natural learning flow (Danesi, 1998) that takes place during self-selected play. A better understanding of children's play may support implementation of increased opportunities for children to engage in deep education processes.

The chapter provides an overview of principles of three narrative theorists Linde (1993), Rosenwald (1992), and Nelson (2001), a brief review of the most common developmental play theories applied in early childhood settings, and a discussion of the emergence of narrative processes in children's play. A set of four observations are presented as examples of play that demonstrate children's use of narrative principles. The concluding discussion for the chapter aims to extend conceptualization of the value of play beyond developmental understandings of play as practiced representation of symbols to achieve academic proficiency, to consider children's play though the lens of life sustaining practices and deep education (Tochon, 2013). Implications are considered in relation to early care and education practice.

The Creation of Coherence, Narrative Mediation, and Counter-stories

Theorists of narrative inquiry and narrative process examine methodological as well as conceptual frameworks to understand how the stories people tell influence both individual and societal experience and development. Theoretical analysis is typically based on narratives of young adults or adults who are considered mature enough to have developed a narrative identity and the skills to express their narrative identity in writing or discourse. Yet the application of systems of narrative such as the creation of coherence, mediated negotiation and the generation of counterstories is evident in children's play. These narrative systems are described below.

The Creation of Coherence

According to Linde (1993) "in order to exist in the social world with a comfortable sense of being a good, socially proper, and stable person, an individual needs to have a coherent, acceptable, and constantly revised life story" (p. 3). Linde describes the powerful significance of the social practice of telling one's life story and emphasizes its influence on both individual and group experiential processes. She notes, "the process of creating coherence is not a light matter; it is in fact a social obligation that must be fulfilled in order for the participants to appear as competent members of their culture" (Linde, 1993, p. 16). It could be said that she is analyzing the co-creation of social norms and practices between the individual and the societal group as they strive for meaning or coherent understanding. She defines a life story as "an oral unit that is told over many occasions" (Linde, 1993, p. 11) and notes that it maintains cultural specificity in that it typically includes specific content related to landmark events such as profession, marriage, divorce, and religious experiences found in any given culture.

Linde's (1993) work to define the life story as a precise and accessible unit of analysis provides a useful foundation for this essay because it gives structure to the concept of a coherent life story and makes it possible to tease out the emergence of this structure in the development of young children. Coherence, according to Linde involves three levels of structure: Level 1) the discourse that narrates the sequence of events; Level 2) the use of coherence principles that form adequate accounts of causality and continuity; and Level 3) the use of culturally specific social assumptions in the form of coherence systems.

In her analysis, Linde (1993) contrasts her notion of the life story with that of various other disciplines including developmental psychology and argues against a rigid interpretation of fixed stages of development that result in specific personality traits in favor of a more general approach wherein developmental theory offers a guide for evaluation of more broadly conceptualized life stages. The later approach forms the basis of her idea of the life story and her view that it involves a life-long fluid process of interpretation rather than a fixed collection of facts. It is the development of the fluid process of interpretation demonstrated in children's experimentation with notions of coherence that I highlight in the observations of children's play that I present in a later section of this chapter. However, in contrast to Linde's (1993) discussion that it is "unclear at what age the life story actually begins to be developed" and her contention that "some time during early adolescence is a good candidate period" (p. 24), I suggest this process begins much sooner. While keeping with Linde's interpretation of the life story as a fluid process of interpretation rather than a fixed collection of facts I suggest that children as young as two and three years of age actively engage in the process of interpreting their life stories. I further suggest that the perfection of this skill is as fundamental and necessary to health and wellbeing as all other aspects of development.

Narrative Mediation

Rosenwald (1992) suggests that "life stories play a significant role in the formation of identity, and that these stories—and the lives to which they relate—may be liberated by critical insight and engagement" (p. 265). He conceptualizes narrative as an evolving - process in which people tell life stories based on culturally specific models and contexts to broaden understanding and action. Such models allow us to communicate and serve to socialize acceptable behaviors that are "implicated in the conventions of discourse" and are "renewed and strengthened each time they become manifest in a narrative" (p. 265). He describes the individual as undergoing a constant process of tension between these stabilizing conventions and restless desire that serves to push them towards new actions as well as new compromises. Additionally he notes his believe that there are factors present in narrative accounts that potentially "help speakers to progress beyond confining models as well as factors that inhibit such progress" (p. 266). Finally, he asserts "narratives exhibit the mediation between the person and the situation and reflect critically on both because they are not reducible to either" (p. 269).

While Rosenwald (1992) clearly acknowledges the importance of the interplay between social processes and the development of narrative identity, he also critiques social constructionist theory for its over emphasis on socialization and societies role in the formation of personality, noting that this view fails to accurately account for individual human agency. He suggests that individuals are engaged in a constant state of conforming to and then challenging narrative conventions. According to Rosenwald (1992) "social development is promoted not by the conformity of narratives to convention but by the tension between them. What presses to be said beyond the merely acceptable can become a stimulus to critique and innovation (p. 271)."

This concept validates my own assumption that the continuous generation of personal narrative and the negotiation between personal narrative and social convention is an essential life skill. Rosenwald (1992) articulates this when he states:

> It is the difference between subjectivity and its obsolescent narrative manifestations that moves life forward in a search for new more satisfying identities: the life story is always false; it contains both more and less than the subject's potential. This falseness is neither accidental nor a liability, as some critics imply; it is essential. (p. 286)

I suggest that the essential nature of this process contributes to the universal drive of young children to engage in the acting and reenacting, the telling and retelling, of their own personal narratives in the form of dramatic play.

Counterstories

As a final consideration in my discussion of the creation of narrative as a vital and necessary life skill and the early onset of this practice by children, I consider Nelson's (2001) work regarding master stories and counterstories. Nelson argues that conceptualization of the narrative act as reading, the genre as literary works, or even the more liberal interpretation of genre as theatrical works, fails to account for individuals who may not have the skills or the access necessary to participate in this view of the narrative act. Further she notes that such conceptualizations assume shared cultural interpretations and contexts. Nelson's position provides insight related to the lack of understanding and acceptance of young children as active narrators of their life stories. Each of her arguments apply to young children who are not yet readers, who are not considered educated, and who may not have fully adopted shared interpretations of their specific cultural contexts. Yet, as I hope to demonstrate children actively engage in the process of creating narrative identity.

Counterstories, according to Nelson (2001) are constructed by the narrative agent. She defines a counterstory as a "story that resists an oppressive identity and attempts to replace it with one that commands respect " (p. 6). Nelson argues that "the narrative agent who constructs, rather than reads stories to enhance her own and others' perception of herself requires no particular narrative or normative expertise (p. 66)" and that "inventing good counterstories requires only ordinary amounts of narrative and normative competence, and these may be exercised by even minimally educated people" (p. 66). I am not arguing for the position that we view children as an oppressed class but rather that we can Nelson's context because as individuals that are completely dependent on others for their survival, and as beings that are in the process of gaining both cognitive and social cultural competence regardless of what culture or community they are a part of, children must continuously act as narrative agents who invent and reinvent their personal life stories.

As children work to integrate and understand their life experiences they must draw on both master narratives of the broader culture as well as the intricacies of their family culture and even the specifics of their relationships with each family or community member. Nelson states the following.

> The teller of a counterstory is bound to draw on the moral concepts found in the master narratives of her tradition since these played a key role in her moral formation [...] but she isn't restricted to just these concepts. To the extent that her experiences of life and considered judgments make them available, she can also help herself to alternative understanding of lying, heroism, fairness, or propriety, testing her conceptions of these things for adequacy against conceptions offered both within her found communities and her communities of choice. (p. 67)

I suggest that this is what children do or at the very least are practicing continuously and learning to do as they engage in what is commonly referred to as dramatic play.

Children's Play

The purpose and reasons for children's play has been theorized in a number of ways including as a means to expend surplus energy, as recreation, as instinctual, and as recapitulation of inherited human survival behaviors (Tomlin, 2008). The most common theories of children's play applied in today's early childhood classrooms stem from the work of Piaget, Erikson, and Vygotsky. This chapter considers each of these theories briefly and builds on them to incorporate ideas from narrative theorists. Ultimately, the chapter seeks to conceptualize play as a transdisciplinary, deep education process that encompasses multiple purposes and theoretical frameworks as needed by the individual or individuals involved and supports transcendence of thought to deeper integration of concepts and ideas for communication, learning and innovation.

Play as Symbolic Representation

Piaget notes that between ages 12 and 24 months, the emergence of pretend play marks the transition from the sensorimotor stage of development to the preoperational stage in which children begin to develop symbolic representations of their world. The importance of symbolic play continues throughout early childhood. Piaget believed that children use symbolic play to build on their current knowledge and construct and refine their increasing understanding of reality (Gowen, 1995). According to Piaget, play emerges from sensorimotor schemes first as practiced repetition of actions and manipulations followed by construction of symbolism and finally the interactive and collective construction of social rules (Nicolopoulou, 1993).

Play as Co-construction of Knowledge

Vygotsky considered play between an adult and child or between two children as the catalyst that promotes learning within the "zone of proximal development." According to Vygotsky:

> Play creates a zone of proximal development in the child. In play, the child always behaves beyond his average age, above his daily behavior; in play

it is as though he were a head taller than himself. As in the focus of a magnifying glass, play contains all developmental tendencies in a condensed form and is itself a major source of development (Vygotsky quoted in Berk, 1994, p. 31).

For Vygotsky, play provides the opportunity for children to process their own inner speech as well as to support or be supported in their quest to make sense of the world through reciprocal interactions within the zone of proximal development.

Play as Psychosocial Mastery

Erikson's theory of psychosocial development notes that to gain mastery over emotional and relational experiences, children engage in play to represent relationships and feelings from their real lives (Jones & Reynolds, 1992). Erikson's theory, suggests that during play, young children practice negotiating the tensions between trust and mistrust, autonomy and doubt, initiative and guilt, and industry and inferiority. From this perspective, dramatic play for young children offers a safe place to explore boundaries, take charge, and experiment with self-directed initiative.

Play in the Early Childhood Classroom

Jones and Reynolds (1992) note the significance of interactive dramatic play as "an intermediate stage in the development of representation (p. 7). They state that Piaget and Erikson both share the view that the primary developmental task in preschool is "mastery of play" (p. 10) and emphasize that, "pretending enables children to represent problems and practice solving them, to ask questions and learn about the world in terms they can understand" (p. 10). They describe the purpose of dramatic play as a method of gaining familiarity with life's scripts so that children will be more efficient as adults. In addition, they note that given the opportunity children will engage in play with pens, crayons, markers, paint, blocks, and other items to create increasingly complex representations of the larger world (Jones and Reynolds, 1992).

Canning (2007) advocates for the importance of play as a support to children's emotional and social development. She argues that children are empowered by flexibility, freedom, and autonomy as they plan and create "meaning that is understandable to the children involved" (Canning, 2007, p. 229). Further, Canning notes that play helps children practice cultural values and understandings within a non-threatening context and supports them to develop a sense of themselves and their unique identity in relation to others. From a narrative theory perspective, the social-emotional development value of play suggests the process of generating a narrative identity. However, it does not necessarily consider the importance of maintaining the ability to be fluid with one's identity or the importance of the ability to generate counterstories and form new identities as a skill in and of itself that is required to manage the many changes encountered in life.

Most often when we read about children's play we read of its role in the formation of concrete symbolic representation or the understanding and adoption of specific culturally accepted roles and norms. This developmental perspective of the purpose of children's pretend play emphasizes the importance of children's dramatic play as a means to integrate and represent cognitive understanding of emotional or logical processes. The following section presents observations of children's play analyzed from a narrative theory perspective. The analysis extends conceptualization of the significance of children's dramatic play by emphasizing how children practice the skills to generate master narratives, negotiate the tension between master and counter narratives, and ultimately develop counterstory narratives that offer opportunities for new identities with new goals and roles.

Observation Selection and Method of Analysis

The observations of children's play used for this analysis were obtained from multiple sources. Some were conducted as formal observations as part of a thesis project for a master's degree in Human Development (Lent, 2004). Others were obtained as excerpts from publications of Elizabeth Jones and Gretchen Reynolds (1992, 1997) two early childhood researchers known specifically for their extensive work of observing and analyzing the play of children in early childhood settings. While several observations were reviewed, only those that best exemplify narrative principles were included. Informal, interpretive, discourse analysis and reflection were applied to theorize how children's play demonstrates principles of narrative theory as defined by the selected narrative theorists, Linde (1993), Rosenwald (1992), and Nelson (2001), and to consider how this information might contribute to extend developmental theories of the importance of play

Observations

What follows are observations of children at play selected as examples from several that I examined for evidence of key principles of narrative theory. The observations provide examples of children's use of narrative to create coherence as described in Linde's (1993) three levels of coherence (reviewed below), the developmental function of narrative as it supports the individual to mediate between reflection and action (Rosenwald, 1992), and the important role that master narratives and counter-stories play as individuals act with agency in the construction and co-construction of their life narratives (Nelson, 2001). I also highlight examples within the observations that demonstrate developmental principles of Piaget's cognitive, Vygotsky's sociocultural, and Erikson's psychosocial theories. The full analysis serves to highlight distinctions between the developmental emphasis of the importance in achieving concrete representation and the extended view I present of children's consistent practice with narrative processes to generate narrative identity as a vital and necessary life skill in and of itself.

Concrete Representation or Level One Creation of Coherence?

As noted previously, the creation of coherence involves three levels of structure: 1) the discourse that narrates the sequence of events; 2) the use of coherence principles that form adequate accounts of causality and continuity; and 3) the use of culturally specific social assumptions in the form of broader coherence systems (Linde, 1993). The first observation example demonstrates level one creation of coherence. Wade, 25 months, is in the play area making "wunch" (lunch). He is engaged in self-initiated, uninterrupted play that provides an example of repetition and simulation that leads towards creation of coherence.

Observation 1, age 25 months: Wade's Wunch, (adapted from Lent, 2004)

> "Wunch" said Wade as he looked at a small table set with placemats, plates, and play food. "Wunch, wunch," he repeated and he walked toward a shelf with more play food on it. "Apple, apple" he said, and he took an apple and a banana from a basket on the shelf. "Lemon, lemon, cup, cup, cup," said Wade. He pulled a lemon out of the basket and got a cup from the shelf. "Up, up," said Wade, and he put the lemon on top of the cup. Clutching the apple and banana in his left arm, and balancing the lemon on top of the cup, Wade returned and placed them on the table. He brought item after item to the table, verbally labeling each one until at last, he gently placed "bear, bear, bear," and "rabbit, rabbit," in chairs at the table. Wade wiggled his fingers as he glanced around the table and around the room. "Chair, chair, chair," he said as he picked up a chair and brought it to the table. He placed the chair near the table, turned around one time to survey the room, and sat at the table for "wunch" with bear and rabbit.

In this example, Wade is engaged in the enactment of what can be considered the master narrative of mealtime. The developmental interpretation of his play is that his primary purpose is to firm up his understanding of appropriate labels for the objects he is using and to represent the social experience of having lunch with friends. Further, he is engaged in assimilation of new ideas as he coordinates the items to develop a representation of lunchtime. According to Linde (1993), the first of the three levels of structure involved in the creation of coherence is the use of discourse that narrates the sequence of events. From a narrative theory perspective, the observation demonstrates a clear process of narrating a sequence of events. This raises the question "At what point do children begin the process of creation of coherence and is there a distinction between this process and other developmental processes?"

Creation of Coherence Levels One and Two: Causality and Narrative Mediation

The second observation can be considered an interim example that demonstrates both coherence levels one and two and also demonstrates narrative mediation (Rosenwald, 1992) as the children work to co-create the master narrative story.

Observation 2, 3-4 years old: Planning as Play (Reynolds & Jones, 1997, p. 41)

> Dennis is sitting outside the edge of the sandbox with Greg and Sean. They are using small plastic shovels to scoop sand into a paddle wheel sand toy. There are several large rubber dinosaurs scattered around them.
>
> Dennis: Big, big pile, right? Right, Greg?
>
> Greg: Right. They're goin' big hole.
>
> Sean: No, we're not doing that.
>
> Dennis: No. No.
>
> Greg: Right?
>
> Dennis: Right.
> Greg: We're playing Batman right?
>
> Sean: Right.
>
> Greg: This is our cave for the Joker. Right?
>
> Dennis: Right, Joker.
>
> Greg: I'm Batman, right? Hey, I know what. We're gonna be two Batmans. Yeah.   We're putting dirt right here, right?
>
> Dennis: Yeah, We're making a big, big pile of dirt.
>
> Greg: Yeah, right? Yeah, for our dinosaurs.

From the developmental perspective, Dennis is negotiating the tensions between autonomy and doubt as he suggests the direction of the play but constantly checks in with Greg for reassurance. The children have not quite established the narrative story in this excerpt from the full observation but seem to be engaged at practice with mediation and negotiation as described by Rosenwald, (1992). Elements of Rosenwald's notion of fluidity are present in the emerging narrative as the children explore different play options. Even as negotiation of a master narrative is underway, the children also seem to be exploring potential counterstories as they consider alternative understandings and the potential of two batmans, even though everyone knows there is only one batman.

Creation of Coherence Level Two: Causality and Narrative Mediation

The following observation example demonstrates the use of culturally specific social assumptions in the form of coherence systems to create adequate accounts of causality. As the two children play they practice narrative mediation (Rosenwald, 1993) for the development of stories and counterstories (Nelson, 2001).

Observation 3, age 3 years: Ride 'em Cowboy Girl (Lent, 2004).

> Lilly put on a swimsuit she found in the dress-up clothes. She looked at Anna and called out, "I'm ready for swimming! Will you take me there?"
>
> Anna responded, "OK, first I have to get on my horse."
>
> Lilly, "I have to get my horse too, and our hats!"
>
> Lilly grabbed a purple, broad rimmed sun hat and Anna grabbed a pink baseball cap. Lilly stopped, glanced at the pink cap and said, "Hey, I want the pink cap!"
>
> Anna responded, "Yeah, but I gotta have it because I'm the baseball cowboy girl."
>
> "Oh," said Lilly as the two scrambled to the top of the climber and each straddled a leg over the top.
>
> Anna shouted as she waved her pink cap in the air. "Yee Haw, Yee Haw, Ride 'em cowboy girl!"
>
> Lilly responded, "Yee Haw, Yee Haw! OK we are at swimming."
>
> The girls jumped from the climber, laid flat on the rug, and flailed their arms as though swimming.

"Oh wait," said Anna, "We forgot, you are sleeping over."

"Oh, that's right," responded Lilly. "But first we have to get Jordan from school."

"OK, let's get on our horses!" Anna shouted as she ran to the climber.

"Yee Haw, Yee Haw!" they shouted in unison. "Ride em, cowboy girl!"

The developmental interpretation of this observation will again emphasize Erikson's psychosocial development theory and the positive social relationships the girls are forming. Further, the girls seem to be practicing common parenting roles to get children to extra curricular events such as swimming and to pick children up from school. This provides a clear demonstration of Reynolds and Jones (1997) description of the importance of practicing for adult roles. From a cognitive development perspective applying Piaget's theory the children are engaged in logic and reasoning as they problem solve and progress through the sequence of the day. However, it can also be noted that at the same time, they are engaged in creating coherence by generating a believable sequence of a days events and also exploring stories and counterstories in a fluid manner that meets the needs of their master narrative. In addition, Linde (1993) speaks of the importance of establishing causality to the coherence of a life story by linking identity to a personal trait or interest. In this observation, when Anna wants to wear the pink cap, she successfully establishes causality for the coherence of her new identity (Linde, 1993) and uses alternative understanding and fairness to generate a counterstory (Nelson, 2001)—she must wear the hat because she is the baseball cowboy girl.

Creation of Coherence Levels Two and Three: Causality and Cultural Specificity

The fourth and final observation demonstrates Linde's (1993) creation of coherence level two: adequate accounts of causality and continuity; and level three: the use of culturally specific social assumptions in the form of coherence systems. In addition, it providers an example of narrative mediation (Rosenwald, 1992); and the generation of counterstories (Nelson, 2001).

Observation 4, 4 year olds: Mommies (Reynolds and Jones, 1997)

> Kim is pushing dolls in two strollers; now she parks the strollers next to a large block structure, built earlier in the morning by other children and sits down on it. Anna sits in front of her, conjures a steering wheel out of the air, and starts driving. Teresa arrives with her doll.
>
> "You two are daughters, OK?" says Anna.
>
> An argument follows. They're mommies, not daughters.
>
> Anna gives in. "I go get my baby." She gets another doll from the house area and lays it on the vehicle; then she drives some more, making an up-and -down motion rather than her earlier circular steering-wheel motion. She stops driving and says, "Two babies."
>
> "Drive, drive, drive!" yells the girl behind her, punching her.
>
> "I'm the mommy," says Anna.
>
> "Two mommies," says Kim, holding up two fingers.
>
> "I driving, I driving," says Teresa, establishing herself as driver. Anna leaves briefly, then returns to put her baby in the stroller, adds a telephone to the structure, and starts driving again, with vigorous arm movements and singing.

It is easy to interpret that the girls are engaged in learning about family life and social interactions as developmental theory would indicate. However, the girls also seem to be actively exploring the narrative mediation process described by Rosenwald (1992) as they navigate the tension between conforming to or challenging narrative convention? Linde (1993) describes an encounter where a friend of hers became upset when he did not agree with her account of a landmark narrative. In this observation, the landmark narrative of marriage and family life is challenged and an argument ensues. The interplay between the master narrative of one mom per family and the potential counterstory (Nelson, 2001) of two moms is evident as the girls create and co-create their narrative representations.

Mere Child's Play or the Creation of Coherence?

Each of the above observations offers insight into the world of children's play and demonstrates examples from both developmental and narrative theory that combine to form a more complex conceptualization of children's play. They point to the significance of children's play as an opportunity that goes beyond representation and includes practice of a fluid process to negotiate and create master narratives and counterstories. Linde (1993), Rosenwald (1992), and Nelson (2001) all share the view that the narrative act is an essential life skill that involves the fluid process of inventing and reinventing the self through individual, personal and interactive social processes. Each describes the powerful influence of social conventions on the formation of personal narratives, Linde (1993) with her discussion of the importance of landmark events employed to create coherence in order to establish an acceptable master narrative, Rosenwald (1992) with his position that the tension between conforming to and challenging predominant narrative conventions stimulates development and broadens understanding, and Nelson (2001) with her discussion of the power of counterstories to repair lives damaged by oppressive master narratives. During dramatic play, children draw from and build upon master narratives and include alternative understanding in order to test out new narratives in various situated contexts of their own choosing (Nelson, 2001). Children negotiate narrative do this because the human ability to form narrative stories and counterstories is a essential life sustaining process that children are driven to perfect in the same manner that they learn other skills such as speaking, writing and reading. The concluding discussion considers the implications of this for early childhood programs.

Discussion

Children are naturally transdisciplinary learners who use the deep approach during spontaneous, uninterrupted dramatic play to create coherence from their experiences and generate narrative stories and counterstories. When we are able to creatively and fluidly generate new stories for our own lives and for our local and global communities we increase our ability to adapt to our ever changing needs within an ever changing world. When children are subjected to standardized, objective-based teaching practices the missed opportunity goes beyond developmental outcomes to loss of a deeper form of self knowledge in which children are able to generate and regenerate identity through the fluid creation of coherent life stories and counterstories. When adults project their own agenda on children's play to "teach" them school readiness lessons of colors, numbers, and letters, they prevent children from engaging in essential play that supports deep integration of their sense of self and place in the world.

The dominance of standards that dictate teaching according to predetermined outcomes stifles teacher's abilities to integrate care with education (Elliot, 2006). This type of prescriptive outcomes-based lesson planning interrupts children's ability to form and follow their preferred patterns of thinking and learning (Lent, 2004). Further, it increases the potential for normative ideologies of family and culture and acts as a form of intellectual colonization (Brock-Utne, 2000; Canella & Viruru, 2004). Ultimately, the outcomes-based approach reduces, if not eliminates the potential for teachers to allow children time for sustained play that incorporates the deep education approach and supports children's full integration of knowledge (Tochon, 2013).

Many early childhood theorists including Jones and Reynolds (1992) and Canning (2007) express concern about the lack of opportunities for children to engage in sustained play experiences in early childhood programs. Jones and Reynolds (1992) comment that "many parents are skeptical if children are only playing, (p. 86) and consider teaching to be a "structured process of shaping behavior according to predetermined specifications" (p. 86). Canning (2007) states, "it is important for adults to recognize that children at play can easily achieve many of the requirements children are subjected to on their learning journey (p. 236)." This chapter extends conceptualizations of play theory to include insights derived from narrative theory that further validate the importance of play as a significant opportunity for children to engage in the life-sustaining, deep education processes of co-creation of narrative identity. By broadening understanding of the benefits of self-selected, open-ended learning processes we can create opportunities for children to engage in more holistic, deep education experiences.

References

Berk, L. E. (1994). Vygotsky's Theory: The importance of make-believe play. *Young Children.* 50(1), 30-39.

Bloch, M. N., & Swadener, B. B. (2009). " Education for All?" Social Inclusions and Exclusions-Introduction and Critical Reflections. *International Critical Childhood Policy Studies Journal,* 2(1), 1-14.

Brock-Utne, B. (2000). Whose education for all? The Recolonization of the African Mind. New York & London.

Cannella, G. S., & Viruru, R. (2004). Childhood and postcolonization: Power, education, and contemporary practice. Psychology Press.

Canning, N. (2007). Children's empowerment in play. *European Early Childhood Education Research Journal,* 15(2), 227-236.

Danesi, M. (1998). The body in the sign: Thomas A. Sebeok and semiotics. Toronto, Ontario: Legas.

Deely, J. N. (2007). Intentionality and semiotics: A story of mutual fecundation. Pennsylvania: University of Scranton Press.

Elliot, A. (2006). Early childhood education: Pathways to quality and equity for all children. Camberwell, Victoria: Australian Council for Educational Research.

Fuller, B. (2007). Standardized childhood. Palo Alto.

Gowen, J. (1995). The early development of symbolic play. *Young Children* 50(3), 75-84.

Jones, E., Reynolds, G. (1992). *The play's the thing: Teacher's role in children's play.* New York: Teachers College Press.

Kentel, J. A., & Karrow, D. (2007). Mystery and the body: Provoking a deep ecology through the situated bodies of teacher candidates. *Complicity: An International Journal of Complexity and Education,* 4(1).

Lent, C. (2004). *Understanding learning through observing children's play: Applying the perceptual thinking patterns model.* Unpublished Master's Thesis. Pacific Oaks College, Pasadena, CA.

Linde, C. (1993). Life stories: The creation of coherence. New York: Oxford University Press.

Nelson, H. L. (2001) Damaged identities: Narrative repair. Ithaca, N. Y: Cornell University Press.

Nicolopoulou, A. (1993). Play, cognitive development, and the social world: Piaget, Vygotsky, and beyond. *Human Development,* 36(1), 1-23.

Reynolds, G., Jones, E. (1997). *Master players: Learning from children at play.* New York: Teachers College Press.

Rosenwald, G. C. (1992). Conclusion: Reflections on narrative self-understanding. In G. C. Rosenwald and R. L. Ochberg (Eds.)., *Storied Lives: The cultural politics of self-understanding.* (pp. 265-289). New Haven: Yale University Press.

Tochon, F. V. (2010). Deep education. *Journal for Educators, Teachers and Trainers, 1*.

Tochon, F. V. (2013). Transcending outcomes, tasks, and standards. In F. V. Tochon, Help Them Learn a Language Deeply (pp. 43-80). Blue Mounds, WI: Deep University Press.

Tomlin, C. (2008). Play: A Historical Review. Retrieved August 8, 2015 from http://www.earlychildhoodnews.com

UNESCO. (2004). Education for all: The quality imperative (EFA global monitoring report, 2005). Paris. UNESCO Publishing.

World Bank. (2002). Retrieved March, 2015, from http://www.world.org/afr/findings/english/find200.

9.

Using Freirean Ideology to Overcome a Zombie School of Thought

Alexandra Lakind
University of Wisconsin-Madison, WI
Amos Margulies
Community School for Social Justice Bronx, NY

In this chapter, we propose that the work of Freire can be an integral part of early childhood educational theory, but is often forgotten due to a prominence of a simplistic version of developmental psychology overshadowing critical pedagogy. This chapter contextualizes the work of Freire and explores the main concepts of Freirean ideology: freedom and love through dialogue and praxis. We take our inquiry across disciplinary and linguistic territories to see Freire as a leader in critical psychology, allied with influential psychological theory towards critical consciousness. Educational theory must validate the teachable heart and teachable mind through a unity based in plurality and diversity, not separateness. It is about respecting children for what they are and not for what they will be. It is committing to early childhood education as a space not to 'help' children, but to love them. Depth, to us, is asking questions, exploring concepts, making connections, and rooting ourselves in love.

Our Deep Approach

In institutionalized North American schooling[1], learning can be dissociated from life experience outside the classroom: subject matter is fragmented; student and teacher assessments standardize and objectify those being assessed; technical/administrative knowledge supersedes civic mindedness. In François Victor Tochon's words, "Bureaucracy has created increasingly rigid institutions, to the point

---

[1] For the purposes of this chapter, 'school' refers to any institutional and organizational space designated for 'learning'. We use 'preschool' and 'school' interchangeably. School is when children are separated from their parents and wider community, and where activities are determined by adults towards specific learning goals.

of endangering the rights of citizens, freedom of thought, and the freedom to pursue knowledge" (2010, p.5). These pervasive issues are working their way, evermore, into the world of early childhood. While unintentional, the universal pre-k movement in conjunction with the accountability movement is placing more and more children into the hands of tightly managed institutional learning settings (Christakis, 2016). Once a space for play, preschool is becoming a place for future preparation, i.e. 'kindergarten readiness.'

Deep education calls for examination, considering what can be done to transform this system from root causes that instantiate these patterns of interaction. This chapter hopes to bring to the world of deep education two main points: 1) we strive to place the focus of early childhood educators' attention back to, what we believe is at the root: love (or lack thereof), and 2) we use Freirean ideology to think deeply about these 'roots' as we create a bridge between Freirean pedagogy and Educational Psychology. We have found that Freirean pedagogy illuminates the aforementioned pervasive dilemmas providing insight into possible transformations. Moreover, as we strive to uncover, or re-insert love, deep education provides the fodder to carry on – to look closely, question, and embrace that which is hard to articulate but imperative to enact.

This chapter argues that education has as much to do with the teachable heart as the teachable mind and that many prominent theories can be harnessed towards this end. We propose that the work of Paulo Freire can be an integral part of early childhood educational theory, but is often forgotten due to a prominence of developmental psychology over critical pedagogy. In seeing the connection, educators can restore heart in the way we use a myriad of educational theories. In the following pages, we will introduce our deep approach in relation to an overarching mission: to align dominant perspectives in educational psychology with the work of Paulo Freire as a means to find love. First, we will present the chapter's aims to make connections across disciplines through Transdiciplinarity, a concept explored in this opening segment. To understand the concept of love, we then turn to the metaphor of the heart. After that, we introduce the figure of Freire to contextualize his work and begin to trace his ideas from, alongside, and to psychology. From this section, we maintain that learning doesn't happen in isolation; we continue to make connections to the past, present, and future. To link this work to that of deep education, we then explore the semiotics of the OAK tree, which allows us to examine notions of how we teach and learn and which models may act as oppressive forces, restraining freedom and preventing love. Next, in order to better understand this notion of freedom, we define it in the context of its ethical component – the missing heart – before outlining the common ground between Freirean ideology and prominent theories in psychology. We culminate refining our toolkits of praxis of dialogue, and in the last section reinstating our main argument that learning has the potential to foster unification of both head and heart.

In the world of early childhood education, connections must be made on all levels. This is congruent with our belief that love is at the root of worthwhile early childhood education. As Erika Christakis, author of The Importance of Being Little: what preschoolers really need from grownups, writes: "learning and love are mutually reinforcing concepts" (2010, p.xix). Yet, Christakis goes on to say that this takes place in "the mind of a growing child" (Ibid). Like many early childhood educators, her use of the word mind is suggestive of the enormous impact of psychology in education, and the current leaning towards cognitive psychology as a staple of early childhood education. The mind, in this language, is the basis of thought, perception, emotion, and behavior.

Demonstrating that early experiences impact future years, theory from psychology empowered many who already believed that caring for the young was an incredibly important role to play. Moreover, future developmental and cognitive psychologists became the cornerstone of policy, parenting philosophy, and teacher education. However, as advanced by Tochon in "Deep Education", present day iterations of psychology can "have a hard time imagining depth" (2010, p.5). Thus, due to the fact that early childhood education is so influenced by the realm of psychology, we hope to build bridges to and from the field that encourage greater depth. Our building material is the work of Freire, offered to the reader as a theoretical framework to motivate deep education.

Before discussing Freire, we'd like to introduce Deep Education as it correlates to our work. Deep education is dependent of situation and grounded in connection and responsiveness. It is a commitment that people can live and work towards, but can never fully achieve. It is, therefore, "defined within the dynamics of living" (Tochon, 2010, p.2). Deep education, as we see it, is a response rather than a continuation of the status quo that comes from a place of interconnectedness and love. It is not a 'thing to do' rather it is a 'way to be,' performed in our relationships, animated in our activated reflections.

This can be approached in infinite ways, therefore, it doesn't hold to the bounds of an academic discipline. In fact, deep education champions *transdiciplinarity*. This holistic approach focuses less on disciplines and more on finding common ground. Various disciplines use different interpretive frameworks; however, transdiciplinarity strives towards "unity of knowledge" (Nicolescu, cited in Tochon, p.8). Unity is not to say that plurality and difference are not valued, but that finding shared language to examine core assumptions can breakdown barriers to foster in-depth, connected knowledge.

Instead of following a particular discipline, the authors of this chapter take on what Anthropologist Tim Ingold has referred to as an anti-disciplinary approach: "Instead of a territorial surface segmented into domains or *fields of study*, we have something more like a rope, wound from corresponding strands or *lines of interest*" (2013, p.12). While it may seem like we are weightily focused on the discussion of discipline in this chapter it is because: "In binding these lines together our aim has been to undo the territorialization of knowledge implied in the way disciplines are normatively understood, and to create the openness of knowing from the inside" (Ibid).

Our process examines the work of Freire, often left outside the realm of both Psychology and early childhood education, in a move towards transdiciplinarity. We seek alignment and connection, bringing together often disparate philosophies to find shared ideas in hopes that we might inspire resistance and response to the lack of love in early childhood education. Our deep approach is to embrace critical psychology. We hope to overturn the trends in early childhood towards shallow, individualistic, reductionist strategies, and find a body of interconnected knowledge, language, and values that moves us towards a better system.

Examining the theories of Paulo Freire alongside several developmental psychologists, we see that Freirean theory is compatible with scientific underpinnings, running parallel to constructivists such as Dewey, Piaget, Montessori, and Kincheloe. Furthermore, throughout Freire's work he cites Fromm. We imagine that illuminating this connection is imperative to understanding Freire in relation to his alignment with psychology. In this chapter, we suggest that, while the respective semantics of Freire and canonical educational theorists or developmental psychologists seem to speak different languages, the messages are the same: education is responsible for developing both heart and mind. Paulo Freire posits that an ideal environment is one of love, which is inextricably linked with the universal quest for human freedom, as well as the notion that schooling must actively endeavor to provide humanity. If students are denied their personal quest for freedom, they are denied their humanity and risk becoming zombies.

In this opening, we have raised concerns regarding a tendency in education to forgo love for preparedness. As we continue to discuss love as an educational agenda, the following segments will maintain our commitment to critical reflection and unity to open space for transformation in how we conceptualize and create educational environments. Before arriving at theories of the mind, we will begin with heart to metaphorically explore notions of love.

Locating the *Heart*: Psychology and Education

Our hearts weigh a measly 10 ounces, and still they supply blood and oxygen to bodies that are 248 times their mass (250 on a bad day). They may be small, but they are crucial to human existence. Understood metaphorically, a broken heart is devastating; literally, it is life ending. This chapter addresses a pervasive dilemma: early childhood education in the United States has a broken heart. And this predicament leaves us with only a small handful of possible explanations, all of them fit for a horror film: if our educational system no longer values the heart, it creates zombies – voracious, unrelenting, and heartless. Before we discuss Freire as a means to fight Zombies, we will present our conceptual groundwork. Love and freedom, explained in more detail later, become the motivation to implore unity not as a disciplinary aim, but a societal one.

The transformation needed in the system must come from the system itself. Education must reinstate itself as a rehearsal space for individuals to learn how to interact with the world and others, "to envision and create alternative Imaginaries" (Tochon, 2010, p.3). This type of engagement demands love, which unavoidably supplies heart. Erich Fromm (1900-1980), a psychoanalyst who greatly influenced the work of Freire, asserts that if education lacks love, the self remains separate, imprisoned, insular, insulated, and unaware of how to interact with others (Fromm, 2006). Thus, love is a "non-foundational (i.e. non-universalist)" core constituent of civilization, 'at the heart and soul of humanness'" (Marcuse cited in Tochon, 2010, p.3). Heart, in this sense, provides the ability to make necessary connections and paves way for "more interactional and open ways of expression" (Tochon, 2010, p.3).

Education is at the heart of society, yet in our educational system students develop without an emphasis on this external connection, the ability to act and react. In the U.S., early childhood education is overwhelmingly disconnected from the lived experiences of students and teachers. This is not conducive to the progress and growth of the individual or the community. Progress hinges on development. This transformation does not mean reproduction of the status quo; it means a continual reshaping of the educational environment to account for the personal strengths and interests of students, teachers, and society. Freire is one of many theorists that we can look to in order to restore *heart*: the development of love as a means to connect to one another and invest in the outside world. This is an alterative conception, and one that eschews 'development' as productivist and reductionist, which leads to a "regression in human potential and values" (Tochon, 2010, p.6). In *Democracy and Education* Dewy speaks of education as a means to change society. This change is possible if education does not aim to perpetuate its own customs, but rather strives towards progressive educational ideals. Thus, "when it is said that education is development, everything depends upon *how* development is conceived" (Dewey, 2008, p. 49). Freire posits that development is based on love. Far from sentimental idealism, this assertion is grounded in the field of Psychology and can be applied to early childhood education.

Influenced by Freud and Marx (Fromm, 2001), Fromm adjoins a new concept to their deterministic systems: freedom (Fromm, 1994). To be liberated, as Erich Fromm asserts, is hinged on one's deepest need: to reach out and unite with other people and the outside world (Fromm, 2006). He contends that one "would become insane could he not liberate himself from this prison (separateness) and reach out, unite himself in some form or another with men[2], with the world outside" (Ibid., p. 7). But separate is too passive a word. The reality is that separateness means being cut off, amputated, and sequestered, without any capacity to fulfill human potential. Hence, to be separate is to be helpless, unable to grasp the world actively; "it means the world can invade me without my ability to react" (Ibid). Therefore, love is essential in the pursuit of freedom. Love and freedom can be applied to all childhood learning, and educational venues that (at least nominally) promoting learning. The metaphor of the heart will aid in

---

[2] It is worth noting that we would prefer a non-gendered notion of the individual human, yet these authors use 'man' in their language.

our effort to make meaning of the system and its needs. We have just provided an analogy with heart and education as systems at the core of our bodies and societies. In the next section we will introduce Freire to better situate his theories within their socio-cultural context in relation to traditional education.

Freire and Freirean Ideals

Paulo Freire was born in 1921 in Recife, Brazil. In 1964, due to the military coup, he was imprisoned and then exiled for his radical views (Darder, 2002). When assessed discursively, Freirean methodology is not at all radical. This becomes apparent when Freire's 'radical views' are explicitly linked to established disciplines. His pedagogy presents an intuitive and incisive theoretical and practical framework that manifests as a scientific, psychological, and philosophical set of ideas: literacy, equality, dialogue, and love. However, we must examine his ideas and the research that supports them, because sound intuition does not immediately translate into lived reality. To genuinely integrate the aforementioned values, the system as it stands will not suffice – de-institutionalization, rehabilitation, or abandonment of the current system may result (Tochon, 2011, p.6). Surely, if the aforementioned ideas were incorporated into our educational system, it would, in fact, be revolutionary.

Freire is most widely known for his theory outlined in *Pedagogy of the Oppressed* (2000), which seeks to break down any power dynamic resulting in oppressive situations. In essence, oppressive situations are exemplified when individuals are objectified and dehumanized by their roles as oppressor and oppressed; in order to be free, both must be liberated from these identities. This will be explored further in this chapter when we discuss freedom. To facilitate the liberation from the parasitic dichotomy of oppressor/oppressed, and thus regain humanity, is the goal of Freire's methodology. Freire is highly value-driven, embracing a humanist mindset that knowledge emerges via people. Knowledge is horizontal and shared, and "intelligence...emerges from reciprocity and not from an external intelligence" (Tochon, 2002, p. 4). This framework encourages constant questioning. Nothing is safe from questions – not even the framework itself – nor is there one 'right' view of how this framework should manifest. While it is polemic, it is not rigid.

In deconstructing the power dynamics of education, Freire sometimes refers to the students as the oppressed. This does not, however, necessarily mean that the teachers are the oppressors. In many cases the system is the cause of oppression. Thus, teachers themselves need to enact love, interrupting "shallow teaching and learning practices" (Tochon, 2010, p.2). Moreover, the system in which educators and students find themselves needs redesign; policy must support learning environments grounded in love. Teachers need support in their practice. Yet, in the U.S., "we are witnessing an 'anti-teacher' movement, backed by a generous group of billionaires" (Tochon, 2011, p.2), saturated with punitive, oppressive policies. Thus, next, we will offer a few examples of the style of oppression taking place in and around our schools.

There are many illustrations of this in educational policy and reform and the ideological underpinnings therein. One such instance inside the classroom involves teacher portfolios. Tochon has observed that, once a tool for contemplation of "career-long evolution," portfolios have become "banal to the point where they are tools in the standardization of behavior and accountability, losing much of their meaning" (2011, p.2). Another patent example of objectification happened in New York when the city released the rankings of about 18,000 fourth-to-eighth grade teachers based on standardized Math and English test scores. This exemplifies an adherence to the simplistic notion that testing is the clearest demonstration of good teaching and learning and that technical knowledge is the sole aim of our nation's educational system. The individual assessments dehumanize and demoralize teachers who need support rather than humiliation, contributing to an environment of competition over cooperation.

This style of reform has become popular across the country, though contentious. In practice, this is indicative of problematic assumptions and goals that are not deeply thought through. These reforms lack the crucial understanding that learning cannot be measured by these tests, and that teaching is more complex than these evaluation methods. These oppressive techniques of micromanagement and oversight stimulate competition over solidarity. Rankings clearly undermine teachers, using them as scapegoats for systemic problems, pitting them against one another which breaks down their sense of unity. It promotes the de-skilling and de-valuing of teaching as a profession, and neglects the notion that students and administrators are adequate structures for teacher assessment (Harris, 2011). Freire stresses the restoration of equality and justice – which is only possible when we combat the objectification that occurs *within* the educational system. But to change the system, we must be able to *see* the system. To understand it and understand our relationship within it. This is only likely to happen if education fosters critical reflection by instantiating a process of reflection. Let's take a moment to reflect by embracing the semiotics of deep education weaving in the OAK tree to connect to our purpose and indicate methods the either stifle or foster our objectives.

OAK and the Praxis of Deep Education

Deep education employs the semiotics of the oak tree. OAK – Optimism, affability (or altruism), and knowledge - are emergent from the support of the earth. Oak is the grounding in, and cultivation of, warmth and protection (Tochon, 2015). In this way, there is a continual foundation and direction. The tree comes from the earth and the branches connect back to common ground. Yet, the symbol of the tree can often lead to a narrative of unity and progress (arborescent in a Deleuzian sense), that doesn't characterize deep education or Freire very well. While progressivism is not to be ignored, it is not unidirectional. It is more a matter of process. In this section we will employ the semiotics suggested by OAK to ask what might be preventing love and what might release love. We will review notions of how we teach and learn that act as oppressive forces, restraining freedom and preventing love. We will also suggest a convergence of ideas and actions towards liberation and love through dialogue and praxis.

The tree metaphors Tim Ingold uses to describe process seems particularly fitting. He references the adage 'they cannot tell wood for the trees,' meaning too much attention to details may hinder an understanding of what it important in a given situation. Thus, the process of 'seeing the wood' is imperative, as it is incredibly easy to get lost in countless oppressive policies and activities. To see the wood, Ingold suggests, one must get out from among the trees to take a long view (Ingold, 2013). This is both temporal as well as spatial. The Oxford English defines wood as "trees collectively growing together" (Ingold, 2013, p.87). This is no longer about the individual tree, but about the forest and all the interactions within. Ingold writes:

…in the twisting, turning, gnarling, knotting and branching of its roots, trunk and limbs, each tree bears testimony to a process of growth that is continually responsive to that of its neighbors, as well as to rainfall, wind, light and the passage of seasons. To perceive the wood from within is to become immersed in these ongoing entanglements of life. It is to see every tree not as discrete, bounded individual but as something more like a bundle of fibrous threads tightly wound along the trunk but splaying out above ground in the canopy and below in the roots. And it is to see the wood no longer as a mosaic of individual pieces but as a labyrinth of tread lines. (Ingold, 2013, p. 87)

This is the indispensable process of thinking systemically and understanding interconnectedness. In the following paragraphs we will explore notions active in our school system leading to learning as individualization and knowledge as simplistic and the means to overcome them through a labyrinth of thread lines.

The teaching model Freire refers to as 'banking' (Freire, 2000) is a major obstacle to this deeper thinking. In banking, students are merely 'piggy banks' waiting passively to be filled with information

(Ibid). This dates back to enlightenment era thinking that children can be molded into the ideal form (Cunningham, 2006). We see it in an arrangement of acquiescent students listening to teachers giving lectures, or practicing rote memorization to be parroted back (Tochon, 2010). This leaves students few options, like feigning sick days, disobedience, or passively accepting the hegemonic norms of this imposed ideology. However, Freire suggests that a dialogical method may overcome the banking model.

Dialogue requires active participation. This, to Freire, is the essence of critical reflection – reflecting on the world through rational thought and analysis. The process of reflection is situated and active. Henri Lefebvre wrote: "go deeper… be like the wind that shakes the trees" (cited in Ingold, 2004, p. 80). This suggests that to reflect is to participate. It is not about stepping back to look at the trees, but about roaming among them. Understanding reality and acting upon reality is one and the same. Critical reflection and action constitute an ideal outcome in Freirean education. He refers to this as *praxis*: the simultaneous manifestation of critical reflection and action.

Facilitating a state of praxis combats the disconnect between education and learning. It creates an environment wherein learning (the development of the individual) cannot remain separate from the development of society. In doing so, it prevents the segregation of learning from the body politic. Because critical thought is best practiced in real life dilemmas, not just conceptualization and abstraction, in Freirean pedagogy students are able to put their ideas into practice. They are able to affect their surroundings and use their abilities to further beneficial growth in society. This can be developed through a harmonization of love and learning.

As Freire writes: "Only by abolishing the situation of oppression is it possible to restore the love which that situation made impossible" (2000, p. 90). Love is an exercise of endless modeling – students must be given love in the process of learning to love. We can locate this love from an academic perspective; in doing so, we can access "the courage to love and to speak about love without fear of being called a-scientific, if not anti-scientific" (Freire, 1998, p. 3). However, before we arrive at the 'scientific' we want to examine Freirean freedom. What do we mean by freedom and how is it connected to love? What are the procedures for accomplishing or approaching this type of freedom? It is in these questions that we can address the needs of our educational system recognizing the overlooked ethical component: the missing heart. Moreover, we will finally begin connecting these concepts to influential psychologists and educational theorists, looking at freedom as antithetical to oppressive models of education, such as banking.

All for One and One for All: The Freirean notion of Freedom

According to Freire (2000), love must generate other acts of freedom; otherwise, it is not love (para. 90). And, just as with love, freedom is achieved when freedom is supplied. As Freire (2000) writes, "education must [begin]...dialogically with the people" (p. 124). Each student must be in partnership with the teacher, learning and responding together. This is crucial in early childhood, when primary caregiver relationships are central, and signs of love are vital (Zanolli et al., 1997). The authoritarian barriers found in traditional early childhood education stand as the antithesis of freedom and preclude teacher-student relationships and dialogue (Shor, 1999).

Freire grounds his notion of *freedom* in the dialectical process. As exemplified in Hegel's *Phenomenology of Spirit* (1998), the dialectic is the process of change. In its most reduced form, the Hegelian dialectic is distilled to the following equation: A (thesis) versus B (anti-thesis) equals C (synthesis) (Ibid). Those of us involved in education, including policy makers of any kind, must seek this kind of syntheses; listening and responding are inherent to the dialectical process. Indeed, many psychologists have advocated for a greater commitment towards cultivating student's freedom to make informed, ethical, and meaningful actions.

Joe Kincheloe (2008), a well-known critical pedagogue and critical psychologist, maintains: when learning and development occur through "an interacting dialectic between content and cognitive processes" (p. 163), students are able to critically perceive reality through personal development. Our human potential can only be realized, however, when freedom is regarded not as a paradigmatic model for utopia, but rather a touchstone, a prerequisite for our basic humanity. Maria Montessori (2005), prominent scientist and pedagogue, departed from the black slate model. She empirically made her way to a constructivist approach that embraced sensory exploration for early childhood learning. Throughout her writings, she was ceaselessly focused on how to enable freedom for the very young. She writes, "[F]reedom is not only an external sign of liberty, but a means of education" (p.55). As educators, we must be mindful of both an internal and external sense of liberation, which, in turn, provides the foundations for meaningful development. "Freedom," according to Freire (2000), "is not an ideal located outside of [people]; nor is it an idea, which becomes a myth. It is rather the indispensable condition for the quest for human completion" (p. 47).

Freedom is inextricably linked to autonomy, which is (at least nominally) is one of the most important goals of our educational system. In the Eriksonian psychosocial stages of development, autonomy, trust, and initiative define a basic developmental stage during preschool years (Paplia, Olds, & Feldman, 1998). Nevertheless, the building of autonomy is met with resistance in our educational system. It is thwarted by the fragmentation of both subject matter and Subjects, a quest for content over autonomy. A lack of choice in learning activities inhibits the learner from taking true ownership over their educational experience, and preschool teachers are constantly worn out prepping activates not generated from the children's interests and needs. Without autonomy for both teachers and students to follow their interests, no one will want to be there. Investment is a function of ownership. After years of observing preschools, Christakis points out: "it is not any lack of goodwill, but the absence of recognition of young children as unique people with their own ideas, their own feelings, their own thoughts and tastes and experiences" (Christakis, 2016, p.16). We do not acknowledge young people, particularly those who are too young to speak, as communicative beings. Students are simultaneously shackled to and separated from their education, and from those who facilitate that process. And the consequences are detrimental: according to Fromm (20006), the awareness of human separateness, without reunion by love, is the source of shame and guilt (para. 8). Isolation precludes freedom.

Ethicist and political philosopher Martha Nussbaum makes a similar point to Freire. Nussbaum (1995) argues that objectification occurs when people are denied autonomy or treated as if they lack agency. This is a core component of the ageism so entrenched in our system. Development is seen as linear and progressive, children are either blank and waiting to be filled, or working towards the next step on their path towards adulthood (which is often homogenized in terms of steps that all children experience). This frames adulthood as the successful outcome of childhood. It is the belief that with age, one improves. Thus older people are constantly believing that they are better or wiser and that young people will inevitably experience the same things as they have. This bias leads to a constant prejudice that children know less and are less. With the education system seeped with rampant ageism, objectification is not a byproduct of our educational system; rather, it is intrinsic to it. Following from this, freedom (the opposite of objectification) is not simply absent in our educational system, but actively denied to our children. A lack of freedom is characterized by a denial of student Subjectivity, which, in turn, leaves students unequipped to reflect on and actively participate in society. This lack of freedom is elemental in "banking" or "factory model" schooling (Lillard, 2008). Since the industrial revolution, 'mass schooling' (Lillard, 2005, p.3) has operated on the Lockean concept of the 'blank slate' (as cited in Gay, 1971), referred to earlier. Seeing students as 'empty vessels' waiting to be filled assumes no subjectivity significant enough to preserve.

The factory model of schooling promotes "a conception of mind that is archaic in light of what scholars from numerous fields have asserted over the last few decades" (Kincheloe, 2008, p. 161). In actual fact, "technical standards promote intellectual poverty in the guise of excellence" (Ibid). This is not only an intellectual poverty, but also a lack of personal desire to grow, understand, and make meaningful contributions from the self to the world. The goal in quashing subjectivity is the bureaucratization of the body and mind. Students who perform well in school settings learn how to stay quietly in their seats, sit up straight, face forward, raise hands, don't call out, hold your pencil just so, fill in the bubble completely, etc. Indeed, it is easy to lose one's self in what Dewey has called, the 'inertia of habit'– the mechanized routines of habituation that maintain the status quo. While there are many forms of rebellion and resistance, those who don't resist become susceptible to the curriculum's hidden intention: acquiesce.

The lack of transparency concerning these intentions helps to maintain the chicanery that students are blank slates and education is a neutral process. Yet, just as students are not passive by nature, there is no such thing as a neutral educational system, teachers, or curriculum. The choices we make, the phrases we use, and the content we teach will affect those around us. They are not neutral but loaded with who we are and where we have come from. Yet, this is not acknowledged in schooling; it is covered up and hidden in the guise of unbiased neutrality.

This neutrality in education is not only irrational, but impossible. As Richard Shaull, Professor of Ecumenics at Princeton Theological Seminary, writes, "There is no such thing as a *neutral* education process"; it is either an instrument to maintain systemic oppression or it is the 'practice of freedom' (as cited in Freire, 2000, p. 34). Issues of equality cannot remain outside the realm of rational thought. In the world of education, little is actually *neutral*; "indeed the impassioned spirit is never neutral" (Kincheloe, 2008, p. 5).

We must develop impassioned students by prioritizing their ideas, autonomous action, and collectivity by enabling the development of more full, free human beings; most importantly, we must attend to the implementation of love in our educational system.

So far we have covered our deep approach to examining key concepts in Freirean ideology. In the passages before this, we have noted some examples of competing frameworks in education, discussed love and freedom, and introduced praxis and dialogue. The next sections make the case that Freire fits into the world of psychology by identifying the most suitable common ground. To Freire, praxis comes from critical consciousness. It is this concept that gestures most directly to the field of psychology, that we will explore in the following section.

Freirean Psychology: What Contributes to Critical Consciousness

Following his career, Freire has been most widely applied to critical pedagogy; yet, as we have discussed in the previous section, Freire aligns with many theories. Now we will explicitly address prominent theories in psychology and the correlative relationships between the study of the mind and the Freirean mission to restore the heart.

According to Joe Kincheloe, through social, cultural, cognitive, economic, and political contexts, Critical Pedagogy understands schooling as a part of a larger social and cognitive vision in which educators explore social justice and 'human possibility' (Kincheloe, 2008). Although this is a valid categorization for Freirean ideology, it does not acknowledge that Freire's theories themselves can be seen in connection (influencing and influenced by) psychology. It gives him a title, a category, that we hope to dismantle. For early childhood educators, especially those influenced heavily by the world of psychology, we can take this deep approach to illuminate how Freire can influence notions of childhood development, learning, memory and cognition, and personality theory.

Critical Psychology – an approach that challenges earlier assumptions about psychology from the perspectives of social justice and liberation (Kincheloe, 2008) – runs parallel to Critical Pedagogy. Both recognize that questions of equality and justice cannot remain separate from the fundamental features of learning and teaching (Kincheloe, 2008; Cochran-Smith, 2006; Horton and Freire, 1990; Vavrus, 2002, para. 86). Justice is not separate as education is always participating in systems of power. Yet, when done well, "expertise in education is related to and creates peace...It is expressed through the art of building relationships and resolving conflicts" (Tochon, 2010, p.4). It is within our educational system that we need to prepare individuals to address these questions in their lives, and their societies.

In alignment with critical psychologists, Freire acknowledges that meaningful living is characterized by self-reflection, agency and mutuality (Sloan, 2001). It is important for teachers to reflect on their practice, and students to reflect on their world. Teachers, at their best, seek a "deeper sense of humanity and humaneness" (Tochon, 2010, p.3) and seek praxis to encourage deep learning through "open pedagogies" for their students (Tochon, 2014, p.4). This is arguably the antithesis of traditional schooling. As Piaget explains, the goal of education to turn children into autonomous citizens has scarcely been reached:

One knows how few autonomous adults there are, how inadequate our pedagogy is, when one contemplates life as one's criterion. When children are obliged to obey, they neglect their potential for reflection and critique, and because they have to adopt existing solutions, their creativity atrophies. A further goal must therefore be 'to create human beings, capable of achieving new things.' (as cited in Kohler, 2008)

Freirean theory provides a framework not only for how people learn, but how people *can* learn; it is this human potential that primarily captivated him. Not only is cognitive ability expressed in different ways, but also facilitated by environmental factors; it is not, therefore, predetermined (Kincheloe, 2008). Freirean ideology encourages a shift in environmental factors in order to cultivate various modes of thinking. In the paragraphs to come, we will use the Freirean notion of critical consciousness to explore common ground and alignment with the terminology of psychology.

Freire promotes a view of individuals aligned with Constructivism, an epistemological theory stating that in reflecting on personal experiences, the individual constructs an understanding of the world (Steffe & Gale, 1995). Swiss theorist Jean Piaget (1896-1980) is considered to be the founder of Constructivism (Bransford, Brown, & Cocking, 2000). In Piaget's theory of cognitive development, students reach a mode of *formal operational thinking*. This type of cognition connotes the ability to think logically, abstractly, and idealistically (Santrock, 2002).

According to Laurel Hughes, author of *Paving Pathways: Child and Adolescent Development* (2001), idealism manifests from a heightened capacity to apply reason and emerges as an interest in political and humanitarian causes. The desire for equality arises from the ability to think critically, which develops cognitively as well as psychosocially. For example, developing Hypothetical-Deductive Thought (the ability and desire to actively plan and problem solve) goes hand-in-hand with the ability to invest in humanity and desire change (Spodek & Saracho, 2006).

In an ideal Freirean education, environments facilitate formal operational thought and *critical thinking* – the ability to question aspects of one's life (Kincheloe, 2008) – in order to reach *critical consciousness*. Within deep education, critical consciousness is one of many desired learning outcomes, along with cultural and spiritual conscious (Tochon, 2010). According to Freire (2000), "Critical consciousness occurs when one has learned to perceive social, political, and economic contradictions and to take action against the oppressive elements of reality" (p. 35). However, critical consciousness is not simply the recognition of inequality, but also the action to change oppressive situations in the world. According to Freire, true action is not separate from reflection. Rather, action and reflection constitute a duplet verb. When we mint action and reflection on the same coin, we not only connect love to didactic methodology, but also reinstate love at the very core of it, obliterating the dichotomy between *self* and *world*.

Although Freire shares similarities to Piaget, the crossovers are even more prominent between Freire and the Soviet psychologist Lev Vygotsky (1896 –1934). Vygotsky, a contemporary of Skinner, Pavlov, and Freud, developed theories of Social Constructivism – a sociocultural psychological set of ideas emphasizing that individual cognition is socially and culturally mediated (Glasersfeld, 1995). Like Social Constructivism, Freirean ideology and Critical Psychology aim to "delve deeply into the concept of mind vis-à-vis sociocultural and political structures" (Kincheloe, 2008, p. 166). Freirean ideology takes into account the social and cultural aspects of development, distinctively emphasizing a mode of thinking that actively analyzes social and cultural circumstances.

Social Learning Theory is another prevailing theory, influencing the design of early childhood spaces, and the way teaching in early childhood is conceived of and approached. While Tochon reminds us of the "transformation of the behavioral stimulus-response into if-then procedural connections across mental models" (2010, p.5), both are linear and causal and need to be expanded upon. Developed by educational psychologist Albert Bandura, Social Learning Theory argues that attitudes and behaviors are learned from the surrounding environment. Personality develops as cognition mediates between stimulus and response (Bandura, 1976). We can take this theory as a point of departure and engage Freirean ideals to become more percipient, embedding more sociocultural and philosophical considerations. This deeper approach will help us "transcend the limited framework of cognitive psychology" (Tochon, 2010, p.5) and view these ideas from a different angle where this mediation is essentially the dialogue of which Freire speaks.

It seems an obvious assertion that listening and responding allow us to develop a sense of how to be active in the world. Yet, even a cursory glance at recent government initiated educational standards reveal that the aim of institutionalized education has been reduced to retaining, regurgitating, and passively assuming the role of 'student.' This role is performed by responding to planned curricula, predominately required and created by someone other than the student or teacher, often preventing teacher autonomy and creativity. These curricula explicitly describe what student responses are allowed, rewarding technical knowledge over creative reciprocity.

Unlike these types of prescribed teaching methods, to Freire, an ideal educational atmosphere rewards independence with empowerment and creativity with validation. Encouraging teachers and students to have their own interests, perspectives, and ways of interpreting the world are essential parts of the learning environment. In Vygotsky's work the social context in which learning takes place is known as the Zone of Proximal Development (ZDP) (Kincheloe, 2008). To Freire, an ideal ZPD fosters critical praxis by providing love, understanding, trust, and autonomy. It also facilitates reflection and metacognition – a central feature in independent learning.

Metacognologists, those who focus on cognition about cognition (i.e. thinking about how we think and learn), have long held that reflection is 'situated' on learners' familiarity with the task, and their investment in the development of autonomy and independence (Hacker, Dunlosky, & Graesser, 1998). Essentially, reflection is situated in ownership. As educators, one of our central goals is to ground this ownership in love, in action and reflection, such that students own this love and are able to use it as a tool for reflection and to participate in the world with a sense of love and ownership.

This ability to have one's ideas extend away from the self is at the core of critical consciousness. Students who develop critical consciousness are able to recognize inequalities and discover approaches to realize potential resolutions. In opposition to Edwin Thorndike's psychometric model – wherein an entity is a 'thing-in-itself' (Thorndike, 2009) – in the development of critical consciousness, there is a process of *decentration*, i.e., removal from the center (Spodek, B., & Saracho, O. N., 2006). A learner is not a thing-in-itself. He or she develops according to the surrounding environment as the self begins to interact with the outside world.

Like Critical Psychology, Freirean pedagogy "accounts for the interaction of self and context" (Kincheloe, 2008, 162) as inherent to one's personal relationship with reality. As Freire asserts, reality is the object of one's transforming actions. It is in knowing this that one can enter reality more critically (2000, p. 53).

Freirean ideology promotes critical thinking, or *divergent* thinking (Dacey & Travers, 2002, para. 76), where students devise solutions for problems with many possible answers. Cognitive thought, then, must reach past the realm of the *actual* and into the realm of the *possible;* critical consciousness demands reality and possibility, thus both must be developed. As Piaget contends, it is after the development of formal operational thought, "[that] the world of the possible becomes available for construction" (Piaget and Inhelder, 1972, pp 150-51). This ability to imagine the possibilities of construction evolves, in Montessorian terms, "at the end of a long process of cognitive development, which has absorption of reality as its beginning point (Lillard, 2005, p. 26). Freedom emphasizes possibility. According to Dewey (1959), freedom is 'measured' by our ability to imagine what is *possible*. This comes from reflecting on *what is*. Influenced by Marx, Hegel, and Spinoza, Freirean 'freedom' derives from a circumstantial understanding (Freire, 2000). For Freire, freedom is not merely an individual endeavor; rather, it is derived from collaboration. We have covered, albeit briefly, several theories in psychology that have potential links to Freire's ideas. Due to the influence of many of these theories, using them with Freirean intentions may bolster the restoration of heart in the thoughts, perceptions, emotions, and experiences of youth.

In meaningful interactions where the concatenation of elements forges even the first traces of freedom, both oppressor and oppressed are fundamentally transformed, and begin to function as equals, at which point they cease to be oppressor and oppressed. In order for a student to be truly free, the teacher must be free as well. In a situation where the adult has power over a child, this frees the adult from the responsibility to 'educate' as something done *to* the child, and enables them to learn *with* and *from* the child. In reaching critical consciousness, both students and teachers yearn for this transformation: "[They haven't] accepted a necessity as unavoidable; [they have] welcomed a possibility as desirability" (Dewey, 2008, p. 87).

The Unification of Head and Heart

We posit that the desire for possibility comes from both an internal and external awareness, cerebral and emotional. Praxis and dialogue animate our love. For even if we start from the head, as many psychologists believe, we have to move with the heart. Learning can foster and maintain this unification.

Critical thinking reaches critical consciousness when non-dichotomized thinking and feeling become open to the possibility of reflecting on existence itself and discovering a personal capacity for creating praxis (Freire, 2007, p. X). Linking *thinking* to *doing* resists the "modern day habit of mind which opposes fact to value, mind to body, head to heart, and knowing to feeling, in disregard of the mounting evidence that such dichotomies are not tenable philosophically" (Freire, 2007, p. XXXV). In reaching critical consciousness, one surpasses this disconnect, a disconnect mirrored in the way we fragment our subject matter and hermetically seal our school walls from the reality of the outside world, and seal ourselves from each other.

Walls, of course, are not solely built to restrict unwanted *in*trusions. To the extent that reality is anathema to our current educational system, there is an effort to lock up education in an ivory tower (and us along with it). In developing formal operational thought and critical thinking, there is an emphasis on studying parts in relation to whole, as well as whole in relation to parts. Education is not separate from our lived experience; on the contrary, it is comprised of our lives, replete with contradictions and paradoxes. As students encounter formal education, they are presented both with life itself and life as a developmental and processional undertaking. Thus, education and reality may become one as we dismantle dichotomies; when part and whole are no longer separated, head and heart follow suit.

In order to achieve this goal, education must develop both mind and heart – an informed love for humanity. To repeat our thesis: while the respective semantics of Freire and canonical education theorists or developmental psychologists seem to speak different languages, the messages are the same: "Education has as much to do with the teachable heart as it does with the mind. Love is the basis of an education that seeks justice, equality, and genius" (Kincheloe, 2008, p. 3).

Just as we must integrate both head and heart into our learning, we must also create an intimate, organic connection between the methods and materials of knowledge and moral growth. The separation of learning from action further distances learning from its moral imperative. Indeed, to differentiate and exorcise heart from mind is to eliminate both. It precludes the conscious personal factor and dichotomizes deeds as purely physical and external. The result is action motivated by interest as opposed to action inspired by principal (Dewey, 2008, para. 360). This kind of dichotomization undermines an educational scheme where learning is a collaborative element of ongoing action – action that has a socially conscious aim that is led in tandem by a confluence of head and heart.

A new kind of intelligence emerges when the head and heart collaborate, and the result is *possibility* itself. Vygotsky writes, "Learning is more than the acquisition of the ability to think; it is the acquisition of many specialized abilities for thinking about a variety of things" (Vygotsky et al., 1994, p. 83). For Freire, students must be encouraged to think about a variety of things and to understand and affect change in a variety of ways. These abilities enable genuine praxis. A key ingredient in a fully developed student is the understanding that "intelligence treats events as moving, as fraught with possibilities" (Dewey, 1959, p. 88). These possibilities can only be envisioned when a critically reflective understanding of events accompanies a desire for change: "[It is] in this use of desire, deliberation and choice, [that] freedom is actualized" (Dewey, 1959, p. 88). 'Desire, deliberation, and choice' convey the essential confluence of head and heart, when head and heart collaborate freedom manifests as a proliferation of possibilities. Next, we want to take a moment to consider what we mean by dialogue as model for learning.

Word = World Approach

Dialogue is a bit like laughter – we instinctively recognize when it is genuine. Also like laughter, there is a scarcity of dialogue in our schools. Instead, education increasingly resembles an anachronistic axiom of medicine: the worse it tastes, the better it is for you. Our collective consciousness knows that, for many if not most children, learning as it is enacted in our educational system no longer connotes a pleasurable experience.

There is a constellation of factors contributing to this unfortunate reality. With the assuredness of individuals who survived our education system and are now re-experiencing it from the researcher and teacher's perspective: schooling is anathema to children due to a fundamental lack of love, joy, and freedom in our system. In *The Art of Loving*, Fromm asserts that learning should be a pleasurable experience based in love. Furthermore, "Love is an action, the practice of a human power, which can be practiced only in freedom" (Fromm, 2006, p. 18). Genuine dialogue, invested with hope and trust, will lead to an understanding of the world both inside and outside the self. Dialogue must be chosen in lieu of monologue, which our educational system has opted for – classrooms led by a series of tasks instead of play. As the teachers are deskilled, the lessons themselves come from external sources, no longer composed of the teachers' interests or the students' needs, or the relationships that are so important in a person's early years.

This emphasis on content, skills and 'readiness,' often through direct instruction, leads to surface learning as young children try to "memorize unrelated parts" (Tochon, 2010, p.5). It forgoes connected learning, where prior knowledge, personal interest, and home life (and language) is deeply intertwined with learning in school. This fits all to well with the top-down approach to assessment that continues to standardize what each child should do and when. When language is disconnected from one's whole self, it becomes nothing more than vocal sound. In fact, in *The Elements of Style*, Strunk and White (2008) refer to certain words becoming "...detached from the language and inflated like little balloons." They describe such words that "at a first glance seem freighted with delicious meaning but soon burst into air, leaving nothing but a memory of a bright sound" (p. 119). Words may sound eloquent, but they are impotent without the substance and significance that arises from praxis. Language, instead, can be used as a tool for communication, and invitation to hear about student's lives.

Without love, dialogue devolves into utilitarianism and manipulation. Words are not something to enact on a child, but something to share and show. It is not purely cerebral intellectualism emptied of communicative impetus and removed from the context that relates to one's emotional and physical existence. Moreover, communication extends far beyond words and we must listen to one another through our bodies, observe gestures, and embrace creations. Love requires respect: listening, responding, changing, caring, and openness. Indeed, "Genuine dialogue cannot exist...in the absence of a profound love for the world and for people" (Freire, 2000, p. 89). To Freire (2000), the fundamental goal of dialogue is to enable a process of learning and knowing. Genuine dialogue connects to the world.

In genuine dialogical interactions, content is always-already a part of reflection/action. Speaking is a manifestation of the expression of thought, externalizing the internal, and universalizing (without generalizing) the personal. Genuine dialogue is expansive – promoting connections that extend as far as the mind can reach. If educational discourse is interwoven with life, it can act as bridges for people to discover reality and, therefore, possibility. To shift how we think about growth in early childhood, we need to validate new languages rooted in love. As authors we ask, can we integrate a new conception of psychology in education? Can we support dialogue with freedom, praxis with love?

A Call to Arms (or at least a call to hearts and minds)

This chapter has argued that ideal education cultivates both heart and mind and that by threading the lines between developmental psychology and critical pedagogy, we can embolden the ideas of Freire as an integral part of early childhood educational theory and practice. Freire and Fromm both recognize an over-intellectualization taking place in education and psychology. A heavy-handed and often exclusive reliance on cerebral knowledge has served to distance us from the humanitarian ends that the discourses of education and psychology originally championed. We may as well substitute 'education' where Fromm (2006) writes 'psychology', for his words still remain too true: "While the great popularity of psychology certainly indicates an interest in the knowledge of [humans], it also betrays the fundamental lack of love in human relations today…Psychological knowledge thus becomes a substitute for full knowledge in the act of love, instead of being a step towards it" (p. 26). When we forgo love, the consequences prove detrimental. Without love, humanity, and freedom, schools are attempting to transform children into objects – into inanimate, programmable beings that lack agency and vitality. In other words: zombies. Indeed, "Empty vessels are passive by nature" (Lillard, 2005, p. 9), and cannot actively seek freedom. Children, however, are not empty vessels. A deep approach respects their human identity (Tochon, 2010). Adults, who embrace this approach, seek to know the young people in their lives. They learn about and support them as they embrace new connections and invest in their relationship to the world.

Our task, therefore, is twofold: First, we must create the condition wherein transformational thinking is possible. Secondly, we must work towards Freirean love and freedom and seek to combat the downward spiral of zombies educating future zombies. We must, in other words, engender freedom: "The freedom to create and to construct, to wonder and to venture. [A freedom that] requires the individuals to be active and responsible, not a slave or a well-fed cog in the machine" (Fromm, cited in Freire, 2006, p. 68).

Freedom transforms objective reality (Hegel cited in Freire, 2000, p. 49). This kind of freedom, while fantastic, is not the vision of a fantasist. To truly live within the world is not an exorbitant vision for the future, but in early childhood education we seem to be making all attempts to accomplish its antithesis: "we have made thinkers whose tendency will be to live without the world. We have lost sight of the chief end of education, which is to put [people] in communication with the external world" (Montessori, 2005, p.114). To communicate with the world in the way Montessori suggests requires a multifaceted approach to education. But even as we enact these progressive, life-affirming pedagogical practices, we must also acknowledge the damage that has been done. We have sustained serious injuries, and zombies continue to infiltrate on every level. Indeed, the push is to reproduce heartless zombies demanding a 'freedom' that is no longer based on love and equality, but on individual entitlement. And so we must wield our love not as a weapon, but as a beacon of hope, and mend every ruptured artery and torn capillary until the broken heart of our education system is mended.

Clearly, this call to action is not aimed directly at practitioners. The educators in this system live in "an increasingly sinister environment" (Tochon, 2011, p.4) designed to obstruct those in public service from a deep commitment to "human values, secularism, and civil society" (Ibid). Policy and infrastructure need changing (Freire, 2000). Hyper-capitalism and corporatization are no stranger to these issues, for schools in the U.S. habitually aim to "homogenize scholastic achievement according to a philosophy fashioned in response to economic demands" (Tochon, 2011, p.3). Therefore, we must first grant tenure to our humanity and see education beyond workforce development.

Truly, love cannot be instilled without a Kierkegaardian leap of faith: faith in the ideas, faith in the implementation and, most of all, faith in children. Love requires faith, just as "dialogue cannot exist without hope" (Freire, 2000, p. 91). Rational faith is rooted in productive intellectual and emotional activity. "In rational thinking, where love allegedly has no place, rational faith is an essential component" (Fromm, 2006, p.102).

Our suppositions about Freirean ideology are founded upon rational faith, for it is through understanding that we have found hope. The key is to create unity based in plurality and diversity, not separateness. Unity of rationality and faith, of critical thought and love, learning and freedom, psychology and Freirean pedagogy, head and heart, reflection and action, world and word, desire and change, and with humanity's need for both progress *and* peace. It is incumbent upon us all to enact the kind of change that Freire advocates. As we learn, we are all implicated in the need for action and change. Inaction is a choice, as well, and its consequence is not the perpetuation of the status quo, but rather an exacerbation of the current dilemma. We must act on social representations that incite the process of change to address social hierarchies and inequalities (Gitlin cited in Tochon, 2010). This can begin with honing our Freirean lens and applying it to early childhood education to notice the oppression enacted on the lives of youth. It is about respecting children for what they are and not for what they will be, particularly those who are most different from us adults – often the youngest. Babies are not simply 'cute' objects with squishy knees, but lives full of experience, thought, and feeling. It is questioning everything; like what it means to be 'young' in our society. It is committing to early childhood education as a space not to 'help' children, but to love them.

At last, we will return to the trees, sites of untold possible encounters. We will enter the world of early childhood education as we would 'enter the wood,' casting aside the myth "that the world we inhabit is spread out like a mosaic beneath our feet, with its forms and patterns already impressed upon the physical substrate of nature" (Ingold, 2013, p.88). We will not stand outside the world of our students, looking in. Rather, we will "join in a dynamic world of energies, forces and flows" (Ibid). Instead of presenting ready-formed, outward surfaces for inspection, the systems, the schools, and those within, will become our forest as it is "in the depths of the woods that the world opens up most fully to our perception, by 'allowing us in' to observe what is going on" (Ibid).

To take the deep approach is to begin the ameliorative process, starting with the validation of heart and love. We do not, of course, require an entire discourse on love to prove its legitimacy. Experiential knowledge should be impetus enough to change our broken system. Deep education is not a method, but incentive to draw inspiration and make connections. This Freirean framework provides us with a toolbox of concepts to combat the ideological apparatuses that atrophy our hearts. Understanding interdependence is empowering, and it is exactly this power, this human potential, that we must locate in order to create a link between the words herein and the world of education – a world poised for genuine dialogue, on the brink of transformation.

References

Bandura, A. (1976). *Social Learning Theory*. New York: Prentice Hall.
Cochran-Smith, M. (2006). *Policy, Practice, and Politics in Teacher Education: Editorials From the Journal of Teacher Education* (1st ed.). Thousand Oaks, CA: Corwin Press.
Christakis, E. (2016). *The Importance of Being Little: what preschoolers really need from grownups*. New York: Viking of Random House Press.
Cunningham, H. (2006). *The Invention of Childhood*. New York: BBC Books.
Darder, A. (2002). *Reinventing Paulo Freire: A Pedagogy Of Love*. New York: Westview Press.
Dewey, J. (2008). *Democracy And Education: Complete And Unabridged* (p. 41). CreateSpace. Online.
Dewey, J. (1959). *Dewey on Education* (3rd ed.). New York: Teachers College.
Freire, P. (2000). *Pedagogy of the Oppressed* (30th ed.). New York: Continuum.
Freire, P. (1998). *Teachers as cultural workers* (p. 140). New York: Westview.
Fromm, E. (2001). *Beyond the chains of illusion* (p. 196). New York: Continuum International.
Fromm, E. (1994). *Escape from Freedom* (p. 324). New York: Macmillan.
Fromm, E. (2006). *The Art of Loving* (15th ed., p. 27). New York: Harper Perennial Modern Classics.
Gay, P. (1971). *John Locke on Education*. New York: Teachers College Press.
Glasersfeld, E. (1995). *Radical Constructivism*. New York: Routledge.
Harris, Douglas N. (2011). *Seven Misconceptions About Value Added Measurements*. March/April 2011 Harvard Educational Letter, 27(2).
Hacker, D. J., Dunlosky, J., & Graesser, A. C. (1998). *Metacognition in Educational Theory and Practice* (illustrated edition.). Mahwah, NJ: Lawrence Erlbaum.
Hegel, G. W. F. (1998). *Phenomenology of Spirit* (p. 648). New Delhi, India: Motilal Banarsidass.
Horton, M., & Freire, P. (1990). *We Make The Road by Walking: Conversations on Education and Social Change*. Philadelphia: Temple University Press.
Hughes, L. E. (2001). *Paving Pathways: Child and Adolescent Development* (1st ed.). Belmont, CA: Wadsworth Publishing.
Ingold, T. (2013). *Making: Anthropology, Archeology, Art and Architecture*. New York: Routledge.
Kohler, R. (2008). *Jean Piaget*. New York: Continuum.
Kincheloe, J. L. (2008). *Critical Pedagogy Primer* (2nd ed.). New York: P. Lang.
Shor, I. (1999). *"Introduction" to Critical Literacy in Action edited by Ira Shor & Caroline Pari*. New York: Heinemann Press.
Sloan, T. (2001). *Critical Psychology: Voices for Change* (1st ed.). New York: Palgrave Macmillan.
Spodek, B., & Saracho, O. N. (2006). *Handbook of research on the education of young children*. New York: Routledge

Steffe, L. P., & Gale, J. E. (1995). *Constructivism in education* (p. 598). New York: Routledge.

Strunk, W., & White, E. B. (2008). *The Elements of Style* (p. 180). London: Penguin Group.

Thorndike, E. L. (2009). *Educational Psychology.* New York: General Books LLC.

Tochon, F., Karaman, C., & Ökten, C. (2014). "Online Instructional Personal Environment for Deep Language Learning." *International Online Journal of Education and Teaching,* 1(2), 151-163

Tochon, F. (2015). "Deep Learning: The Symbolism of the Oak." International Conference on Deep Education. July 7-8, 2015.

Tochon, F. V. (in press, January 2011). Le nouveau rôle des formateurs dans une approche profonde, une interview d'Elisabetta Pagnossin. (The New Role of the Teacher Educator in the Deep Approach). *Formation et pratiques d'enseignement en question,* numéro spécial « Propos libres sur la formation des enseignants » , 12.

Tochon, F. (2010). "Deep Education." *Journal for Educators, Teachers and Trainers,* 1, 1-12.

Tochon, F. V. (2002). *Tropics of Teaching: Productivity, Warfare, and Priesthood.* Toronto, ON: University of Toronto Press.

Vavrus, M. J. (2002). *Transforming the multicultural education of teachers* (p.242). New York: Teachers College Press.

Vygotskiĭ, L. S., Vygotsky, L. S., & Cole, M. (1978). *Mind in society* (p. 180). Boston, MA: Harvard University Press.

Zanolli, K., Saudargas, R., & Twardosz, S. (1997). "The development of toddlers' responses to affectionate teacher behavior." *Early Childhood Research Quarterly, 12*(1), 99-116.

10.

Deep Learning in Science
An Argument for an Aesthetic Paradigm of Science Education

Merrie Koester
University of South Carolina

In the 1800's, Chief Seattle, chief of the Suquamish Indians, is said to have written the following statement in a letter to the American government:

Humankind has not woven the web of life.
We are but a thread within it.
Whatever we do to the web of life,
we do to ourselves.
All things are bound together.
All things connect.

For thousands of years, humans lived in harmony with nature, taking only what they needed to survive. They believed that the hurt of one is the hurt of all. In a geologic blink of the eye, however, we have overfished the oceans to the brink of disaster and burned so many fossil fuels that global warming threatens every single coastline. Floods and droughts are becoming more common planet-wide and entire ecosystems are becoming de-stabilized. This is the stuff of science and it impacts every single one of us from the moment we are conceived. And yet, we are mostly a nation of science-illiterate adults; unaware of—or, worse, not caring about— the ways in which the interconnection of biotic and abiotic factors affect us. A *deep* approach to science education can, with hope and significant effort, reverse "The Great Turn Off" to Science which science educators like James Trefil (2008) have conceptualized as a disheartening event in the lives of many adolescents that occurs sometime around middle school:

> Normal curiosity about the world seems to turn into disdain for, and perhaps even a fear of, things scientific.... In eighth grade, a student is likely to encounter more vocabulary words in his or her science class than in English.... What should have been a vital, engaging hands-on subject was turned into a dry exercise in rote memorization.... The high school years in America are a continuation of the turning away from science that starts earlier (pp. 131, 137, 145).

I have been called a dreamer by some. I imagine schools full of students who wake up in the morning thinking, "I *get* to do science today!" (vs. "I've *got* to somehow endure it"). The question of what constitutes an educative experience is an enduring philosophical and socio-political query, about which there has been (and likely never will be) any agreement. Dewey (1938) challenged us all to consider what conditions have to be satisfied in order that education become a "reality and not just a name or slogan" (p. 116). He called on educators to eradicate those experiences which were either non-educative or mis-educative. To date, hundreds of thousands of American students have been anesthetized *in vivo* in classrooms featuring mainlined, monolingual content, represented and delivered by dominant culture teachers via text-based, didactic, linear, auditory means (Koester, 2015). For those who have been cropped out of this classroom picture (think culturally and linguistically diverse students), this system is not working by any measure, qualitative or quantitative. To leave culturally and linguistically diverse students out of the learning equation by not holding them to high standards is *non-educative*, demeaning, and limits both their freedom and cultural capital (Delpit, 1988; Ladson-Billings, 1994; Lee, 2002).

From non-educative and mis-educative classrooms alike emerge human beings ill equipped to succeed in the 21st Century, where decisions based on science and technology are made on their behalf every single day. Students who are afforded only one way of experiencing and knowing science (which is traditionally taught in standard English via culturally impoverished text and lecture) are placed in positions of profound weakness, marginalization, and disconnection (Koester, 2015). Feinstein (2010) proposes a kind of science literacy that is useful and pragmatic in a Deweyan way—one that helps them lead "happier, more successful, or more politically savvy" lives (p. 169). Instead of a prescriptive form of science literacy (as determined by a checklist of requisite knowledge and skills), Feinstein calls for a kind of science literacy that applies to things students actually care about. This kind of literacy is the hallmark of the best *informal* science education settings—whose directors understand the value and power of sharing and caring. In these venues, science is cool! Students enter into the wonder that is science and come away wanting more. Even if they are struggling-readers-failing-school-science, at a "discovery" center, these same students can become science *literate* in the wow-this-might-be-useful-for me-to-know kind of way.

Dylan inwardly screams when asked to memorize yet another list of science facts he-can-not-even-read. Nor can he de-code the homework assignment (written inside the hated box in the top right corner of the blackboard). Teacher's eyes on him, he labors to copy into his notebook twenty words which have no meaning for him. In his mind, he imagines yet another Minecraft world, where he must somehow secure resources and defend his territory. He inhabits an as-if world of his own making—one where he always wins (and where he does not have dyslexia). His teacher calls him out for tapping on his desk. He puts his head down and checks out....

The advocacy group, Understood.org, reports that 1 in 5 children in the U.S. struggle with issues related to reading, writing, math, focus, and organization. Strong performance in all five areas is practically essential for success in a traditional, test-driven, didactically oriented science classroom; and yet, each can be incredibly difficult for those who cannot de-code words or who have "messy" minds and habits. Those who have dyslexia and/or attention issues are among the most creative of all human beings and include Leonardo da Vinci, Pablo

Picasso, Jørn Utzon, Agatha Christie and Albert Einstein (Peterson, 2012). Richard Hagerty, a gifted, innovative cleft palate plastic surgeon and American surrealist painter, is himself profoundly dyslexic. He defiantly pushes back against conceptualizing dyslexia, autism, or other human condition as a disorder or disability, but rather regards each one of us all as part of a spectrum where there is no such thing as *normal*. Rather, he argues, those on the edges have as much if not more to contribute to the robustness and strength of the human population. He would have us all acknowledge the need for a h-u-m-a-n language that everyone can understand (personal interview, February 19, 2016). As I conversed with this brilliant polymath, his face reddened and his fists clenched when he described the isolation experienced by the dyslexic learner. Apparently, he was also a gifted athlete and took out his frustrations as a football linebacker! He now self describes as a "poster child" for all those who have suffered as he once did from being so profoundly misunderstood. His personal get-out-of-jail moment came when he discovered that *drawing* was the only language that made sense both to him and the rest of the world, too. He quite literally drew his way through medical school and created diagrams of heretofore never imagined solutions to complex cleft palate presentations. Every year, he travels to impoverished nations to volunteer his time as a cleft palate surgeon. In that single interview, Richard Hagerty validated my lifetime of research on art as meaningful language in science education. However, this man had significant help and support along his journey. What about the other less privileged 1 in 5?

Tochon (2013), a semiotician and language specialist, has argued that the form *communication* symbols take and the way they are presented (performed) is the key to whether the educational system functions. By *functions*, he means that the sign meaning-making process (semiosis) must communicate information in such a way that it is *mutually* understood by teacher and student. Conceptualized in this manner, students may be "starved" if the meaning of signs and symbols is not made accessible to them. As a result, they will become marginalized within the ecology of the classroom and forced to develop their own entrenched niches, left to survive by their wits.

On Becoming a Science Teacher Who Draws

My worst science teachers (not very many, fortunately) used mostly esoteric vocabulary and a few randomly sprinkled mathematics symbols here and there, together with textbook diagrams that were often very confusing. Their labs were prescriptive, linear, unimaginative, and worse, graded according to one's per cent error. There is a very good reason that I became neither a pharmacist nor a nuclear engineer! Lab partners, however, always sought me out because they saw my notebooks, which were more like spiral bound science pictionaries. Shortly after beginning my undergraduate studies, I developed a reputation for being able to explain "science things" through drawing. The next thing I knew, I was leading study groups. An evolving visual artist, I had developed the habit of translating into drawings the key concepts even a boring science lecturer delivered. Drawing also helped keep me awake in such a class! As I listened to the spoken word, mind's eye images that signified the key concepts would take shape. I would then organize and layout the page, visually synthesizing what I *thought* I had heard and then later comparing what I captured to vetted (pre-internet) text and graphical resources. I was careful with my typography, white space, and placement of key images that often portrayed science "actions" and equipment being used in an experiment. Caveat: I did have some formal artist's training by the time I arrived at college. In fact, I wanted to major in art, but my practical German Lutheran parents discouraged me from doing so with the argument that I would be unlikely find gainful employment. Since I loved science, too; I became a biology major and minored in chemistry, and admit that at times, I chose playing with models of stereoisomers over going to the movies with friends. I was and will ever be a nerd.

As I honed my graphical representation skills, I came to understand that a truly effective visual composition could tell the story of what had happened during the moment of science inquiry. In short, if my drawings were successful, they could be "read." My working knowledge of biology and chemistry grew rapidly as I took more science courses. I kept drawing and learning and soon parlayed this drawing-to-learn skill into a job as a student lab teacher in the

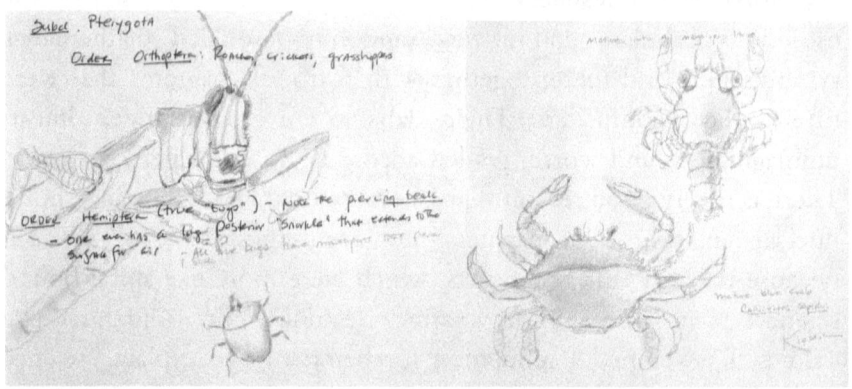

anatomy lab.

At this point in my life, I was an eager twenty-one-year-old idealist. I next earned my teacher certification in middle and secondary science with a perfect 4.0 GPA. So what! Back then, not a single one of my pre-service courses addressed the problem of being hired to teach a science subject for which you yourself had no mastery. In my case, this under-developed cognitive and intellectual territory was physics. Like most biology majors, I had taken only the required two introductory physics courses, and those I crammed into an eight week summer session. I could not properly teach force and motion to a four year old. In my first teaching job, however, I was to teach high school physics to a class of thirty held-back ninth graders, most nearly 17, who were all reading below grade level. The text the principal handed to me was over ten years old and written on the college reading level. There was no teacher induction or mentoring program at this school.

Virtually all my students (mostly boys) were from poor families. The "gifted" students, mostly middle and upper class white students down the hall, had an excellent science lab. I was horrified at the injustice of the situation and so far beyond the level of my competence that I felt almost panicky. How could I teach physics of all things to students, many of whom, through marginalization, tracking, and neglect, were functionally illiterate?

Deep education does, at the very least, require that the teacher know her stuff. Hashweh (1987) has shown that poor content knowledge significantly impacts teaching and is a source of misconceptions directly communicated to students (in Cochran et al., 1991, p. 12). I was completely on my own—the subject of my own project based learning narrative. I was immersed in a plot line I desperately wanted to steer in a different, more hopeful direction (I was too young and idealistic to know that failure was not an option.). It seemed clear to me that if they stayed their present course, my students were doomed to become science illiterate adults. Somehow, I had to get them to actually care about learning this stuff. And then I had my epiphany. Might we not, together, *draw* our way out of this black hole?

After two exasperating weeks of trying to re-learn content from my college physics text (which was still over my head), I took myself and my sons to the local library and checked out every book I could find that explained physics principles to *kids* using pictures. That night, I practiced drawing funny little cars, pulleys, and inclined planes with little cartoon people doing *physics things*. Over the weekend, I composed a *Phew Phunny Physics* poems. In the process of making this teaching art, concepts I had previously not understood myself became much clearer to me. I could not wait to try my teaching experiment the following Monday! To my delight, my students were immediately engaged and they started filling their own notebooks with science-themed drawing artifacts. Within a week, we were using physics concepts like Newton's First Law of Motion to explain the Couch Potato Phenomenon (Koester, 2015). A palpable form of aesthetic energy seemed to be transforming these students. In fact, two of these students, previously denied the privilege of playing for the school's basketball team because they had been failing science, suited up once again. How I loved cheering them on at the games.

Now, many years and a few degrees later, I now teach a graduate methods course called Teaching Science through Drawing. My master's thesis title was "Science and Art Together Again" and my doctoral thesis called "Science Teachers Who Draw: A Study of Metasemiotic Curriculum Inquiry." I have lived and breathed this stuff for most of my entire life.

What Is Happening Here?

In my journey as a teacher educator and researcher, I have kept returning to role of feelings, emotions, and empathy in the teaching/learning experience. As a former science bench researcher, I believed there must be some neurobiological explanation for why some teachers can connect with their students on deep personal levels, while other inspire their students only to bolt for the door when the bell rings. My artist self (I am also a practicing poet, painter, novelist and amateur actor) seemed to instinctively *know* when my science teaching performances fell flat (an astonishing 100% of the time whenever I resorted to lecturing). All I had to do to gauge the effectiveness of my teaching performance was "measure" the mood of my students and "read" their bodies. In an instant, I knew how they felt about what was happening in the moment of teaching and learning (or not). Our pedagogical relationship, i.e., the way they felt about me and what I was teaching, waxed and waned in direct proportion to how effectively I used specific art forms as language to communicate science concepts. A working hypothesis gradually evolved: Art truly did seem to make science matter to more of my students and was most effective when I *modeled with them* the arts practice we would be using before and during our STA (Science through Art) projects. But why and how was teaching science through the arts so engaging? Over time, it seemed that a combination of drawing, storytelling, and creative drama produced the most positive responses from my students (evidenced by parents telling me their kids wanted to work on their STA projects at the expense of their other subjects). The level of student engagement was especially high when I gave students a *choice* of what art language (poetry, music, dance, drama, drawing, etc.) to employ to re-present their learning. Whatever was happening here was a phenomenon I have sought to understand for over the last twenty-five years.

In the late 1980's, at the University of Hawaii, I researched, developed, and field tested a curriculum I called Teaching Science through the Arts (TSTA), which has continued to evolve over the last two decades. The first iteration was conceptualized before STEM (Science, Technology, Engineering, and Mathematics) was an acronym and also before our nation began to implement science teaching standards. Today, the system of sign systems I have proposed most closely fits what is now being called STEAM (An Arts-integrated approach to the teaching and learning of STEM concepts). That being said, I have never been much for semantics, especially where educational acronyms supposedly signifying some collection of agreed upon skills, knowledge sets, and practices are concerned. Whatever you want to call what it is I am trying to communicate here is fine with me. I am at your service, whether you represent an organization that labels itself as doing science, STEM, STEAM, TSTA, or something similarly catchy. We are all together in this business of educating. In my science teacher education programs, I strive to help educators learn to create teaching art so that science actually matters to their students. Otherwise, their students will resist pursuing advanced levels of study of this highly important subject. Moreover, the pathway to those STEM job positions which require *deep* learning will be closed to them.

The German language has a word, *Umwelt*, which Kull (1998), a semiotician, has described as "all the *meaningful* aspects of the world for a particular organism" (no pagination, my emphasis). I believe that deep education can be achieved only when teachers make the time to identify the *Umwelt* of each student, that is, what matters to each of them and what makes them feel important. Discovering a student's *Umwelt* includes learning what kind of language makes sense to him or her. The *Umwelt* of a student with dyslexia does not include words or text, which are cruel facts of their lives that can place them in positions of isolation and destroy their self-esteem. Deep education in science means that a teacher understands that ecology is not just something that takes place outside in nature, but instead is about the importance of diversity as well as the evolutionary survival power of adaptation and the establishment of healthy social relationships. Deep education in science is about bringing students into an awareness and appreciation that science can uniquely help them understand three things: 1) what is happening in the world, 2) how this happening affects them, and 3) how they themselves affect the happening. They cannot learn these things when they are texting.

Conceptualized as language, the arts convey meaning by what they signify and communicate. Their effectiveness depends on whether empathy is achieved and their language (words, song, movement, gestures, images, etc.) can be interpreted. Really *competent* artists are experts at figuring out the *Umwelt* of their fellow human beings and knowing what stimuli might elicit an enthusiastic response. They excel at noticing. Artists deeply understand relationships and draw their willing participants into shared community through narrative that connects them in time and space. They develop followings and fans. Through my teaching and research, I have discovered that when science teachers communicate meaning through the arts, they are much more likely to achieve semiotic lift-off. A palpable form of aesthetic energy fills the classrooms of such teachers, where students say things like the following:

> *I want to come to science every day now.*
> *I feel refreshed here.*
> *This makes me feel like I'm getting help* (Koester, 2015).

Adjibolosoo (1995) and Uhrmacher (2010) have written that affording students aesthetic capital can result in transformations that can cause them to undergo entirely new ways of being in the world. Their ways of feeling, acting, and being are different and better. They feel they are part of something bigger than themselves. It's called a *community*. Within a community, there is shared language and a sense of belonging.

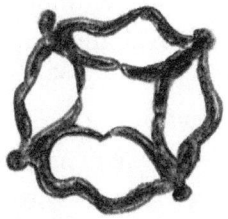

I propose that, in order to effect deep learning, science teachers be trained in methods of *aesthetic inquiry*. Aesthetic inquirers recognize that the creative process (always present at the heart of science) spirals outward through cacophony and chaos; and that neat, harmonious compositions may not always be the result, especially as new and yet unanswered questions emerge (Van Sickle and Koester, in press). Maxine Greene (2001) has described aesthetic education as "an intentional undertaking designed to nurture appreciative, reflective, cultural, participatory engagements with the arts by enabling learners to notice what there is to be noticed" (p. 6). From deep reading of other aesthetic educators like Pestalozzi (1894), Dewey (1938), Eisner (1972, 1976, 1991, 2002, 2009), Siegesmund (2010), and Latta & Baer (2013), I have developed curriculum performance goals that include the seeking of possibilities, deep personal knowing of a subject, sharing, connection with self/ideas, and "others," and the establishment of healthy relationships within a community. Rubrics of practice and performance to assess whether these goals are achieved are jointly created by teachers and students as we engaged in the process of deep curriculum inquiry.

A deep approach to science foregrounds the nature of science as being at once kinetic and still—excited and contemplative—wrong and less wrong—that is, evocatively and empathically human. In some of his early writings, scholar Michael Apple (1979) argued that most teachers fail to convey that "science is not just a group of knowledge or techniques of discovery...it is a group (or rather groups) of individuals...pursuing projects in the world" (p. 88). Apple has always reminded us that where there are people involved, there is always conflict and struggle (think drama) even and especially in the domain of science. In "real life" science, there is always a story playing out in the background; one that is full of tension and plot twists. How often in your own science classes did you learn about the competition, ethically questionable behavior, jealousy, and most of all disagreements which have spiced the ways in which science knowledge has historically been acquired? Out of conflict grow challenges, which stimulate new ideas and solutions through creative encounters (Koester, 1989). This kind of science is both interesting and engaging on a deep, human level. Some of the most important scientific discoveries have been the result of experiments "gone wrong." We instinctively want to know more about these events, as who hasn't goofed up in a big way at some time in their lives? And yet, what is presented in science textbooks is mostly always about *method* and rarely about the madness. That's a shame, because in the mess are the juicy bits of the human story.

Of course, science students need to learn how to methodically and purposefully advance from question to hypothesis, conduct experiments, gather data, draw conclusions, and suggest revisions, but they can do so in the spirit of adventure and curiosity, without having to fear that they will fail because they didn't arrive at "the right answer." They can become part of science dramas in which they are, for example, forensic experts. They can give "news reports" on their findings and humbly confess the ways in which they may have messed up. In all these ways, students imagine stories in which they themselves are "sciencing." From the time they are infants, children learn through play and through modeling, learn what specific verbs mean—to run, to sing, to jump, to skip, to laugh, to make a cool robot at a science museum. Similarly, I propose that, in *school* science settings, students need to be brought into playful, imaginative relationship with the verb, *to science*. Just this year (2016) I listened with delight when the protagonist in the movie, *The Martian*, declared that in order to survive on this desolate planet, he was going to have to "science the hell out of it." And then, we lucky viewers got to see exactly what actor Matt Damon meant by that, as he cleverly designed ways to make water, nutrient-rich soil, and a crop of potatoes, as well as repair a decrepit old spaceship and use nuclear energy to keep himself warm. Impressive stuff. In every way, our viewers' brains were performing these same actions, as we entered into the constructed as-if world so that we, too, could figure out ways to survive on Mars! Such is the power of empathy, and artists are *the* best at tapping into this reservoir of caring about something.

A couple of years ago, I finally came across a scientific explanation for empathy. It was a Eureka moment for me. As it turns out, in 1992, a team of researchers at the University of Parma, Italy, working with macaque monkeys discovered that the same brain cells fired when the monkeys performed a task (like picking up a peanut) as they did when the monkeys simply watched a person do the same task. They named these brain cells *mirror neurons* (Ehrenfeld, 2011). Neuroscientists became very excited about this discovery, and soon found that human beings also had mirror neuron systems. Were mirror neurons the scientific explanation for empathy? Was it true, as Merleau-Ponty (1962) had suggested, that the body uses its own parts "as a general system of symbols for the world, and through which we can consequently 'be at home' in that world, understand it and find significance in it?" (p. 237). Gallese (2005), an Italian neuroscientist, certainly thought so. He took a lead in the mirror neuron research and discovered that indeed, mirror neurons fire in our brains even when we just *imagine* doing a specific task. For example, we can look at a picture of a hammer, and the motor neurons that we would use to pick up a real hammer are excited. When we see another person smile, the muscles in our own face that control smiling light up on functional MRI. Gallese (2005) had determined that our brain can "model the acting body of other individuals." He called this phenomenon "embodied simulation" and conceptualized what was happening as a kind of *resonance* between bodies, which he theorized could be at the heart of all social cognition (pp. 23-48). I think the phenomenon might also help explain the addictive powers of video games, but that is for another paper.

Based on the compelling discovery of the mirror neuron phenomenon and the theory generated from it, I feel even more confident stating that if we want our students to produce excellent work, we must first model what excellent work looks like. Furthermore, when students observe teachers and those in the STEM workforce, who portray science as a highly imaginative, visual, and creative, that is, as a significantly artistic human endeavor, they will mirror that behavior in their own practice of science and quite likely, enjoy it immensely at a very deep level (Koester, 2015). Through embodied simulation, they will themselves enter as-if worlds where they, too, are sciencing in relationship with a focused visualization of themselves doing science. Achieving empathic and embodied connection with another are at the heart of creative drama and theatre practice. They are also an important part of a repertoire for effecting deep education.

Academicians have come to understand that drama, make-believe, and role-play in the science classroom (not just in the elementary school) can be a vital part of conceptualizing the nature of science (Aubusson, Fogwill, Barr, & Perkovic, 1997; Barab & Duffy 2000; Dorion, 2011). Dorion's (2011) extensive literature review has contributed greatly to the disrupting of negative stances against the use of anthropomorphic analogies to teach science. He cited the work of Taber and Watts (1996); who determined that even undergraduate level science students defaulted to anthropomorphic explanations, in which "cause is assigned to desires and perceptions (e.g., atoms *want* to form bonds) as part of their scientific reasoning" (p. 1).

Drawing to Achieve Deep Content Knowledge

I have discovered that one of the best ways for teachers to identify weaknesses in their content and procedural knowledge is what I call the "back-of-the-napkin-test." This can be a liminal experience for many teachers. What they quickly discover is that they are more than capable of making a simple explanatory drawing of a subject they know well and about which they care. However, when tasked to draw about a science subject which they understand poorly, the napkins quite often remain blank, and their faces furrow with scowls. Only a few moments later, they more or less confess that they do a terrible job of teaching about their weak areas. Then, we spend the rest of our time together (usually several months at least) drawing our way into deeper relationship with their most dreaded content area. As it turns out, many middle school science teachers have quite inadequate content knowledge about the physical sciences, and so, through community and empathy, we get the job done by creating standards-based drawing repertoires. Along the way, we work very hard to uncover the misconceptions that many science teachers commonly believe about the content they are teaching.

As part of the capacity building training to teach science through drawing and visual thinking, I teach basic drawing skills; the description of which is beyond the scope of this chapter. At the forefront of our work, however, is practice with the elements of graphic design, training I believe should become an integral element of all science teacher education. Too often, the science teacher assumes that the student can make sense of the spoken or textual language of science. This is far from being the case, as stated earlier in this chapter. If 1 in 5 of our students have some form of dyslexia or attention issue, then talking and telling (the main way science concepts are communicated in a traditional classroom) completely leaves them on the edges—isolated and dreading being outed for being "stupid" or "slow." My interviews with such learners had led me to understand that these students need teachers to use language their brains can actually de-code. Above all else, struggling readers need not to be given the job of "secretary" when put into cooperative learning groups. At this point, they are sure to resort to any number of creative (and even disruptive) means possible to avoid having to read or write. To a person, all struggling readers have reported to me that they readily understand pictorial and embodied language. They also confirm the validity of Paivio and Csapo's (1973) so called "picture superiority effect" by making statements like:

> Pictures help me think way better than just listening does.
> When I draw my notes, they just come back to me.
> They're not gone anymore!

Few science teachers with whom I have worked over the last three decades have been afforded any training in the graphic art of visually organizing text and images on a single page. Often their notes are splattered across their classroom white boards like symbolic vomitus. Student versions of these notes are often even more confusing and certainly do not invite later study. Why? Because there is no story—nothing to make the scribbles (strange symbols written in a strange language) *mean* something. The result is complete semiotic breakdown. Thus, I have sought to develop a graphic visualization instructional tool through which a teacher might use drawing to achieve epistemic clarity, especially for the struggling reader. I challenge teachers to conceptualize and design graphic compositions I call "Know"tations, one page teaching/learning artifacts which clearly communicate (by employing elements of graphic design) the narrative of situated, contextual, intellectually purposeful, inquiry-based learning. The prefix "know" is in parens to remind the designer that the very nature of science involves a constant re-testing and revision of what we *think* we "know" based on the evidence we may have at a given time.

I explain to teacher participants that while there is no one "right" way to design a "Know"tation, the composition should incorporate the elements of graphic design and include, as much as possible, all four of Lemke's (2002) *languages of science*—words, images, symbols, and actions—on one page, so that the relationship between these languages was readily apparent (that is, can be "read"). Depending on the phase of the 5E science inquiry learning cycle—Engage, Explore, Explain, Extend, or Evaluate (Bybee et al.,1989)—the balance of these languages would differ. For example, and Explore

"Know"tations (usually created during an experiment or demonstration) would include graphs, tables, charts, and equations (words and symbols) together with a central image of a lab set-up (images and actions), and an indication of the essential question (words) being investigated. An Explain "Know"tation would likely have more drawings, symbolic icons, and key vocabulary concepts (Koester, in press, in *Cases on STEAM Education in Practice*). We work hard to disrupt the tendency to march through the 5E's and then check them off as "done." By stark contrast, aesthetic inquiry (like authentic science practice, which is not static or even all that predictable at times) is recursive and reflective, always open to revision as new knowledge is constructed. Community critique is an essential component of this pedagogy. In all ways, the "Know"tation as I am developing it is to be viewed as an act of critical, creative *making*, the kind Seymour Papert (1991) had in mind when he developed his theory of constructionism. The "Know"tation is what Papert would call a "public artifact," a composition that informs and transforms learning by its being made in the first place.

I am presently engaged in dialogue with far more skilled arts educators than I am to develop a STEAM teacher education model that involves science and art educators cross-training each other. In one middle school, where I am conducting research with both the science and visual arts teacher. The sixth grade science teacher teaches science in the arts class and the arts teacher works with the science students in theirs to improve their graphic design skills. Eighth grade art students who are now three years into this cross-training program are now training sixth grade science students in the art of creating "Know"tations. Yes, this is very exciting! Just imagine the educational impact if such cross-training would become normative practice in teacher education programs.

Conclusion

I believe that deep education brings with it a sense of something new being born inside you as you become empowered to create the future you *imagine* for yourself. Eisner (2002) wrote that promoting a love affair between the student and his or her work is one of our schools' most important aims (2002). However, imagining possibilities for oneself is very difficult for a child who has found him or herself the victim of institutionalized marginalization. Eisner pronounced himself a childhood victim of norm-referenced testing and mind-numbing lectures. In a heartwarming videotaped interview with Audrey Amreim-Beardsley (2014) of Arizona State University, Eisner, the polymath, remarked with a wry smile and a twinkle in his eye that he had scored in the lowly 33rd percentile among his high school classmates. Eisner, thank goodness for all of us, found educative salvation in the arts and was magnificently restored. In his review of *The Arts and Creation of Mind*, James Haywood Rollling, Jr. (2006) paid tribute to Eisner, whom he regarded as role model. Rolling noted that like Eisner, the practice of the arts not only shaped him into a life-long learner but also provided "models of what educational aspiration and practice might be at its very best" (Eisner, 2002, p. xii, in Rolling, 2006, p. 114). All who have studied and been moved into action by Eisner stand by him to disrupt the pervasive mindset that the arts are "nice but not necessary" (Koester, 2016, paper presented at AERA, Eisner SIG, Washington, DC.).

One thing seems certain; when achieving science literacy depends primarily on reading and listening fluency, there can be profound problems. The robust correlation between reading comprehension and science achievement test scores has been well documented (Carnine & Carnine, 2004; Cromley, 2009; Lee, Fradd, & Sutman, 1995; Norris & Phillips, 2003). Even if the classes are boring and tedious, at least the proficient reader can advance to higher levels of science education and into the STEM pipeline of well-paying jobs with health insurance. NAEP test results (2009-2011) consistently show that the poorest readers and lowest achieving science students in America often come from either low income families or from culturally and linguistically diverse families. These students, far more so than dominant culture students, are often tracked into the lowest level classes with the least highly qualified teachers and with consistently low expectations made of them (Oakes, 2005). Tochon (2010) laments that "the exponential growth of knowledge and access to it increases inequalities between the haves and have nots" (p. 2).

Effecting this kind of practical science literacy can be accomplished in the school science setting, too—even in this era of testing and accountability—by *caring* science teachers. Van Sickle and Spector (1996) have determined that one of the hallmarks of the caring science teacher is that they take the time to find out what matters to their students. Another finding in this same study is that caring science teachers go to great effort to improve their own content knowledge. Thompson, Braaten, and Windschitl (2014) have developed extraordinary "tools for ambitious science teaching" (http://ambitiousscienceteaching.org/); many of which are dedicated to improving teacher content knowledge (ie., the science literacy of teachers themselves). Their Big Idea Tool requires the teacher to write out a "causal explanation" of the science phenomenon he or she is going to teach, together with an explanatory diagram, all the while grounding the content in the prior experience of the learners. This is a deep approach to lesson planning and curriculum inquiry, which I believe will significantly improve the likelihood that science teachers can deliver educative performances that don't turn off or mis-inform.

I propose that we seek to develop science curriculum (knowledge, skills, practices, and eventually habits) which foregrounds the *common* languages, habits of mind, and meaning-making practices of art and science. To do so will require high levels of imagination, which scholar Ralph Ellison (1963) wrote was one of the things most *missing* from the discussion of American education. Fifty years later, Rolling (2013) has similarly argued that schools, by design, *under-develop* creativity in favor of the "development of citizens who are easy to categorize, easy to sort into cubicles or assembly lines, and easy to manage" (p. 42, in Koester, 2015). Indeed, when science classes are structured as regimented progressions toward pre-ordained results and right answers that have little to do with students' lives, there is very little room for imagination and creativity to emerge. For the struggling reader, there is even less incentive to invite science into their lives. For them, science has little to no value, and worse, makes them feel stupid. They will invariably enroll in the fewest and "easiest" science classes they can in order to graduate from high school (if they do).

Tochon (2013) has called on educators to engage in the practice of metasemiosis, or thinking about how it is that we effect meaning-making. How we construct our symbol system (semiosphere) is crucial if we hope to accomplish deep education. I propose that this goal is hardly possible unless we learn to employ empathic, *aesthetic* forms of communication symbols.

To date, teaching in an aesthetic manner is not yet part of most science teacher education programs. I sincerely hope that those who drive policy in the emerging STEM to STEAM movement will insist on research and training that closely examines the ways in which an arts-infused pedagogy can effect deep learning in science. I repeat: In no way, however, am I seeking to displace in any way the important traditions of situated, constructivist scientific inquiry (Brown, Collins, & Duguid, 1989). I seek, instead, to convincingly argue that intrinsically *inexact*, artistic, and poetic ways of understanding and communicating the meaning, context, and processes of science phenomena can catalyze learning reactions resulting in a broad, meaningful spectrum of understanding for all students—not just dominant culture students who can read well (Koester, 2015).

When asked to describe or provide a *typology* of aesthetic edusemiotic resources, I usually push back as if I have been asked to create a paint-by-number composition. Instead, I am more likely to respond by offering examples of arts sign systems which I believe Lemke (1999) would describe as being *topological*; including embodied learning, creative drama, improvisation, musical performance, gesture, dance choreography, creative writing, and of course, drawing and visual representation. I also think it's extremely important to recognize that most science teachers have never received formal training in multimodal, arts-integrated pedagogy and may likely feel threatened on both ontological and epistemological levels at the mere suggestion of doing so. Rollo May (1975) has written that it takes *courage* to create—to "bring something new into being" (p. 37); whether it is an idea, performance, or object. Thus, my first responsibility to science teachers working with me is to call for a collective celebration of our bravery as we enter into what Peter London (1989) has called a "period of disequilibrium" (p. 79), scary territory where self-efficacy hangs in the balance and conceptual change is anything but certain. London's suggested approach is a caring one, allowing as much time as necessary for the science teacher to develop repertoires for teaching practice which are securely aligned with the new understandings they are constructing. Such practice is congruent with Huberman's (1995) model for effecting conceptual change.

Is it not true that we will nurture and protect (care *for*) that which we care *about*? At the heart of a deep education approach is a focus on value creation (Tochon, 2010, 2012). What if, through deep science education, students could be guided into states of caring for themselves, each other, and their planet through community, tolerance, and a celebration of what makes us each different from one another? I propose that a caring, project-based model of teaching science as aesthetic inquiry will lead to deep learning and an appreciation not only of how we are all connected to each other but for our responsibility to protect and preserve our environment. Such a curriculum would be transdisciplinary, the hallmark of deep education (Tochon, 2012). I envision the creation of research and education partnerships between institutes of higher education, school districts, and informal learning centers through which collaborative action research could generate findings on the interventions. Results would be compiled and shared to effect a *collective* impact not possible with isolated efforts purported to offer a "cure" for educational problems of practice and policy. Such collective and collaborative endeavors would be characterized by a belief in the transformative nature of aesthetic inquiry.

In the end, we must be leaders of our *own* learning. Humbly and determined, we must first deepen our own repertoires of content knowledge through metasemiotic curriculum inquiry; lest we inadvertently deliver misconceptions during teaching/learning performance. After that comes the hard part – that of skilfully (artfully) communicating our own understanding of the natural world in some kind of symbolic form (preferably an empathic, multimodal use of words, graphics, symbols, gestures, etc.) to the brains or our students, who must then not only decode our intended message, but also (if we have created teaching art) begin to care about what is happening in the teaching/learning context. We improve our chances of creating empathic connections with each of our students and the content if we can share stories and narratives through which they can visualize themselves "sciencing." In the physical world (as conceptualized by scientists), unless an object is moved by a force, no work is done. Moved by aesthetic energy and through participation in the arts, science students can become motivated to achieve meaningful, exciting work (learning) that is remarkable for its depth. Truly, STEAM has the *potential* to become powerful pedagogy.

References

Adjibolosoo, S. (1995). *The human factor in developing Africa.* Westport, CT: Praeger.

Amreim-Beardsley, A. (2012). *Inside the academy with Elliot Eisner* [videotaped interview]. Retrieved from http://insidetheacademy.asu.edu/elliot-eisner

Apple, M. (1979). *Ideology and Curriculum.* London, UK: Routledge and Paul.

Aubusson, P. J., Fogwill, S., Barr, R. & Perkovic, L. (1997). What happens when studentsdo simulation role play in science? *Research in Science Education, 27*(4), 565-579.

Barab, S. A., & Duffy, T. M. (2000). From practice fields to communities of practice. In D. H. Jonassen & S. M. Land (Eds.), *Theoretical foundations for learning environments* (pp. 35-56). Mahwah, NJ: Lawrence Erlbaum.

Bazler, J. & Van Sickle, M. (Eds.) (In press). *Cases in STEAM Education.* Hershey, PA: IGI Global.

Brown, J. S., Collins, A., & Duguid, P. (1989). Situated cognition and the culture of learning. *Educational researcher, 18*(1), 32-42.

Bybee, R.W. et al. (1989). *Science and technology education for the elementary years: Frameworks for curriculum and instruction.* Washington, D.C.: The National Center for Improving Instruction.

Carnine, L. & Carnine, D. (2004). The interaction of reading skills and science content knowledge when teaching struggling secondary students. *Reading and writing quarterly. 20*, 203-218.

Cochran, K. F. (1991, April). Pedagogical content knowledge: A tentative model for teacher preparation. Paper presented at the annual meeting of the American Educational Research Association, Chigago, IL.

Cromley, J. (2009). Reading achievement and science proficiency: International comparisons from the programme on international student assessment. *Reading psychology, 30*(2), 89-118.

Delpit, L. (1988). The silenced dialogue: Power and pedagogy in educating other people's children. *Harvard Educational Review, 58*, 280-298.

Dorion, K. (2011b). A Learner"s Tactic: How secondary students" anthropomorphic language may support learning of abstract science concepts. *Electronic Journal of Science Education, 15*(2).

Dewey, J. (1938). *Experience and education.* New York, NY: Kappa Delta Pi.

Eisner, E. (1972). *Educating artistic vision.* New York: Macmillan.

Eisner, E. (1976). Educational criticism and connoisseurship: Their form and function in educational evaluation. *Journal of Aesthetic Education, 10*(3/4), 135-150.

Eisner, E. (1991). *The enlightened eye: Qualitative inquiry and the enhancement of educational practice.* New York: Macmillan.

Eisner, E. (2002). *The arts and the creation of mind.* New Haven, CT: Yale University Press.

Eisner, E. (2009). What education can learn from the arts. *Art education, 62*(1), 6-9.

Ellison, R. (1963). What these children are like. September, 1963 lecture. Retrieved from http://teachingamericanhistory.org/library/ document/what-these-children-are-like/

Ehrenfeld, T. (2011). Reflections on mirror neurons. *Observer, 24*(3), March. Retrieved from http://www.psychologicalscience.org/index.php/publications/observer/2011/march-11/reflections-on-mirror-neurons.html

Feinstein, N. (2010). Salvaging science literacy. *Science Education, 95*(1), 168-185.

Gallese, V. (2005). Embodied simulation: From neurons to phenomenal experience. *Phenomenology and the Cognitive Sciences4(23),* 23-48.

Greene, M. (2001). *Variations on a blue guitar: The Lincoln Center Institute lectures on aesthetic education.* New York and London: Teachers College Press, Columbia University.

Gudmundsdottir, S. & Shulman, L. (1987). Pedagogical content knowledge in social studies. *Scandinavian Journal of Educational Research*, 31. 59-70.

Hagerty, R. (2016). Personal interview.

Hapgood, S., & Palincsar, A. S. (2006-2007). Where literacy and science intersect. *Educational Leadership, 64*(4), 56-61.

Hashweh, M. Z. (1987). Effects of subject-matter knowledge in the teaching of biology and physics. *Teaching and teacher education, 3*(2), 109-120.

Huberman, M. (1995). Networks that alter teaching: Conceptualizations, exchanges and experiments. *Teachers and Teaching: Theory and Practice,* 7(2), 193-211.

Koester, M. (1989). *Science and art together again.* Unpublished master's thesis. University of Hawaii Manoa.

Koester, M. (2015). *Science teachers who draw: The red is always there.* Blue Mounds, WI: Deep University Press.

Koester, M. (2016). Imagination and the arts as antidotes for STEM education malaise. Paper presented at the at the annual meeting of the American Educational Research Association, Washington, DC.

Koester, M. (in press). Getting to "Know" STEAM. In Bazler, J. & Van Sickle, M. (Eds.) *Cases in STEAM Education.* Hershey, PA: IGI Global.

Kull, K., Emmeche, C. & Favareau, D. (2008). Biosemiotic questions. *Biosemiotics,* 1, 41-55.

Ladson-Billings, G. (1994). *The dreamkeepers/Successful teachers of African American children.* San Francisco: Jossey-Bass.

Latta, M. & Baer, S. (2013). Aesthetic inquiry: About, within, and through repeated visits. In T. Constantion and B. White (Eds.), *Essays on aesthetic education for the 21st century* (pp. 93-107). Rotterdam: Sense Publishers.

Lee, E. (2002). Coaching for equity. *New Teacher Center Reflections*, 5(1), 1-2.

Lee, O., Fradd, S. H., & Sutman, F. X. (1995). Science knowledge and cognitive strategy use among culturally and linguistically diverse students. *Journal of Research in Science Teaching, 32*(8), 797-816.

Lemke, J. L. (1999). "Typological and Topological Meaning in Diagnostic Discourse." *Discourse Processes. 27*(2), 173-185.

Lemke, J. (2002). Enseñar todos los lenguajes de la ciencia: palabras, símbolos, imágenes y acciones. In Montse Benlloch (Ed.), *La educación en ciencias: ideas para mejorar su práctica* (pp.159-186). Barcelona, Spain: Paidos.

London, P. (1989). *No more secondhand art: Awakening the artist within*. Boston, MA: Shambhala.

May, R. (1985). *The courage to create*. Toronto, Canada: Bantam.

Merleau-Ponty, M. (1962). *Phenomenology of Perception [Phénoménologie de la Perception]*. Routledge & Kegan Paul.

Norris, S. P., & Phillips, L. M. (2003). How literacy in its fundamental sense is central to scientific literacy. *Science Education, 87*(2), 224-240.

Oakes, J. (2005). *Keeping track: How schools structure inequality*. New Haven, CT: Yale University.)

Paivio, A., & Csapo, K. (1973). Pictorial superiority in free recall: imagery or dual coding? *Cognitive Psychology 5*(2), 76-206.

Papert, S. (1991). Situating constructionism. In I. Harel & S. Papert (Eds.), *Constructionism* (pp.1-11). Norwood, NJ: Ablex.

Pestalozzi, J. (1894/1973). *How Gertrude teaches her children*. New York, NY: Gordon Press.

Peterson, S. (2012). Dyslexia and creativity. *Huffpost Education*. Retrieved from http://www.huffingtonpost.com/soren-petersen/ dyslexia-and-creativity_b_1531298.html

Rolling Jr, J. H. (2006). The arts and the creation of mind. *Journal of Curriculum Studies, 38*(1), 113-125.

Rolling, J.H. (2013). *Swarm intelligence: What nature teaches us about shaping creative leadership*. New York, NY: Palgrave MacMillan.

Siegesmund, R. (2010). Aesthetics as a curriculum of care and responsible choice. In T. Constantion and B. White (Eds.), *Essays on aesthetic education for the 21st century* (pp. 81-92). Rotterdam: Sense Publishers.

Taber, K, & Watts, M. (1996). The secret life of the chemical bond: students' anthropomorphic and animistic references to bonding. *International Journal of Science Education*, 18 (5), 557-568.

Tochon, F.V. (2010). Deep education. *Journal of Education for Teachers and Trainers, Vol. 1*. Retrieved from:
http://www.ugr.es/~jett/articulo.php?id=1

Tochon, F. V. (2012, August). *Deep Education: Transdisciplinary Pedagogy and Wisdom*. Guest Plenary Lecture given at the Conference on Leadership and Pedagogy held at University of Southern Queensland. Brisbane, Australia. August 4th, 2012.

Tochon, F.V. (2013). *Educational semiotics: Signs and symbols in education*. Blue Mounds, WI: Deep University Press.

Thompson, J., Braaten, M., & Windschitl, M. (2014). The big idea tool. Retrieved from http://ambitiousscienceteaching.org/

Trefil, J. (2008). *Why Science?* New York: Columbia University, Teacher's College Press.

Uhrmacher, P.B. (2010). The power to transform: Implementation as aesthetic awakening. In T. Constanton and B. White (Eds.), *Essays on aesthetic education for the 21st century* (pp. 183-203). Rotterdam: Sense Publishers.

U.S. Department of Education, Institute of Education Sciences, National Center for Education Statistics, National Assessment of Educational Progress (NAEP), 2009 and 2011 Science Assessments. Grade 8 State Results retrieved from http://nationsreportcard.gov/science_2011/g8_state.asp?subtab_id=Tab_4&tab_id=tab1#chart

Van Sickle, M. & Koester, M. (in press). Teaching science as aesthetic inquiry: Directing the flow of energy through the teaching/learning performance. In Bazler, J. & Van Sickle, M. (Eds.), *Cases on STEAM Education in Practice*. Hershey, PA: IGI Global.

Van Sickle, M., & Spector, B. (1996). Caring relationships in science classrooms: A symbolic interaction study. *Journal of research in science teaching*, *33*(4), 433-453.

11.

Toward Deep Evaluation[1]

François Victor Tochon
University of Wisconsin—Madison

Assessment, as it is lived in American schools, has changed its role. The humane dimension of teacher know-how in assessment has been replaced by quantitative performance assessments that play a political function in a number of countries as well. This essay discusses it from a critical perspective, considering research on the validity of standardized performance tests. Teachers' field assessments tend to integrate the human factor as a major consideration, to the contrary of standardized measures that re-shape teaching to match the demand of the lawmakers. The current totalitarian movement in the field of school assessment places instrumental reason to its extreme, as if machines and bureaucratic criteria could replace human agents. It may contribute to the genocide of linguistic minorities. Assessment is always a relative enterprise, as it depends upon a conceptual interpretation and the context of its application. A more humane and deeper approach to evaluation is proposed.

Two decades of research on teachers' professional philosophies have indicated the importance of recognizing the intricacies of their decisions regarding assessment and the humaneness of their evaluative abilities (Tochon, 2000). Despite this considerable evidence, educational assessment has been used as a weapon by aggressive politics seeking to replace teachers in the arena of educational evaluation in certain Anglo-Saxon countries, as well as in countries that have adopted their model and planned economies. Assessment entails forms and educational content, and its automatization without theoretical or practical knowledge has proven itself to be dangerous. In several nations, quantitative testing is

---

[1] English translation of an article published in French in the international journal of Measure & Evaluation (Tochon, 2011a).

mandated; the argument that the validity of standardized tests is more robust obscures other arguments, specifically economic arguments. Through this mechanism, the evaluative capacity of teachers is pushed into the background.

In this critical essay, I examine how this question of evaluation and assessment is taken up in research. I give examples of the ill effects of the generalizability of standardized testing that, despite a limited usefulness according to certain contexts and specific goals, can endanger personal freedom and the ideal of equal opportunity for all, and even contribute to linguistic genocide of minority languages. I then analyze how teachers' evaluative knowledge is unique, and how its humane quality proves to be indispensable for academic assessment. I also probe the hidden logic of the movement to remove teachers as primary evaluators, including to what extent this question has become political. Finally, I explore certain characteristics of the practical knowledge of evaluation, the models to which it corresponds; I also attempt to revalorize this capacity of evaluation within a professional development framework.

Practical prudence and theoretical wisdom in evaluative knowledge

The instruments of evaluation used in an academic context must not separate practical knowledge and the theoretical conceptualization that serve as their foundation; this will uproot both theory and practice (Tochon, 2001a). This proof had been made by Aristotle (350 BC/2004)—technique (*techne*) only has meaning if it is guided by practical knowledge and prudence (*phronesis*) for a goal of theoretical wisdom (*sophia*). Kant (1784) reexamined this proof; he deplored the absence of theoretical Reason behind technical goals that used instrumental logic, an argument taken up by Habermas (2003): instrumental thought only has meaning if it is tied to practical expertise and theoretical knowledge. Together, they permit the social critique necessary for democracy. This argument, corroborated by critical systems theory (Fuenmayor, 2006), which gives priority to human thought, contextualized in processes imposed by instrumental logic. For example, in educational assessment, this arises from privileging the relationship between student and teacher in an iterative evaluative process rather than ceding power to instruments applied independently of the context, as in the case of standardized quantitative tests.

Bain (1987), in a study of time in schools, noted that in middle school (11-15 years), 300 hours were allocated each year for evaluation; those hours were unavailable for teaching and learning. Today, these hours have multiplied due to the imposition, by political motivations, of a form of accounting influenced by economic modeling. Most notably in the US, politicians have imposed on schools a type of evaluation influenced by New Public Management.

> New Public Management promotes standardized testing as the core of institutional accountability based on four principles:
> 1) educational attainment is measurable; 2) it must be measured through scientifically valid instruments; 3) participants who are allowed autonomy must be accountable for their actions; 4) schools should be regulated by the results. From this point, the logic of evaluation and ensuing construction of tests are disconnected from the reality in the schools and the reality of the human beings who are the target of evaluation. Standardized testing, which draws on a model of industrial engineering, acquires a political standing in the macrosystemic regulation that is hardly compatible with the organic microprocesses involved with teaching and learning. (Tochon, 2017).

However, no tidy empirical consensus has been indicated regarding the value of these reforms (Mons, 2009). Additionally, the negative impact of standardization on the educational performance of students from low-income, ethnic minority, and immigrant groups, as well as students with disabilities, can be observed.

New Public Management, the dominant paradigm in the United States, particularly in the analysis of institutional management, is in response to political and economic exigencies, which are often in contradiction to the human relationships necessary in education. The connection between praxis, instrumentality, and wisdom is broken once teachers are no longer the evaluators. The forms of evaluation introduced in classrooms under the pretext of No Child Left Behind illustrate their toxic limits when these evaluations are associated to measures that create anxiety in students, school staff, and parents.

These academic tests imposed in service to administrative goals have the effect of modifying teaching so that it is stripped of a pedagogical dimension, taking considerable time away from learning. In short, it should be asked if the philosophy of evaluation, centered on expected performance, must not be reexamined to ensure that evaluation does not create abuses, especially those Edgar Morin (1982) labeled the terrorism of the state, when instrumental logic becomes totalitarian.

Standardized tests of performance: positionality of teachers

Research on evaluation practices of teachers has largely been led by research groups separated from the field of classroom practice. There has been little participant action research, thorough autoethnography or collaborative research. The social nature of testing has been analyzed from a perspective of power relations. Brookhart (2004), for example, studied the tensions arising from the application of evaluation principles by student teachers, who had been engaged in social justice and supportive learning. Sarrazin, Tessier, and Trouilloud (2006) studied the positive climate created by teachers and the ways in which they encourage student motivation. Black & William (2006) established modalities appropriate for the application of evaluation; McMillan (2007) attempted to circumscribe the concept of equity in evaluation. Harris & Brown (2008) examined accountability from the point of view of the teacher and the student; this study was rare in that it used introspection to study what teachers thought about accountability. Simon, Chitpin, & Yahya (2010) noted how the underlying theories of evaluation processes are influenced by implications that are theoretical and technical, as well as psychological and social, to the extent that the effects cannot be examined if the people who are most directly concerned (the teachers) are not consulted. In the majority of this research, the effects of these new forms of standardized evaluation on classroom life and the perceptions of students and teachers are neglected.

In her article "The end(s) of Testing", which sought to revalorize the evaluative knowledge of teachers, Eva Baker, then the president of the American Educational Research Association, noted in her 2007 presidential address that the emphasis placed on testing created a disturbance in school life. She argued that, to recalibrate the situation according to principles of equity and justice, it was necessary to overcome the institutional logic of accountability because people need a safe place to learn. Because the use of standardized tests rejects the primary research findings on learning and motivation, many students and teachers fear and loathe the tests. What arises from this lack of a conceptual link between mandated policy and educational needs is an inconvenient truth: testing does not, in general, measure what schools want to teach. This contradicts the underlying assumption behind the push for accountability. We have very little evidence which suggest that standardized assessment achieves its goals or offers useful guidelines for decision making. "Nevertheless, we act as if tests were valid, in the face of weak or limited evidence" (Baker, 2007, p. 310). Budgetary restrictions and work schedules do not allow a qualitative interpretation of student performance, even though qualitative evaluation made by the teachers themselves have more external and ecological validity.

Evidence indicates that, in principle, teachers are not a priori opposed to evaluation, if it supports and stimulates learning. Thus, productive experiments were conducted in the United Kingdom and New Zealand, where the professionalism of teachers was recognized (Annan, 2011; Timperley, 2011). When reforms are associated with professional development, when their goals are clear and the teachers participate in the reflection necessary for change, the reforms of evaluation systems can stop the appearance of marked inequality between local programs and promote collaborative reflection around the analysis of evaluations (Behrens, 2006). On the other hand, teachers often denounce plans they perceive as negative because these programs do not take into consideration the social characteristics of the community or because they lead to a shrinking of the curriculum (Jones, 2007). These plans, when they are applied without nuance, drive certain teachers and certain schools to systematically cheat to improve the results; this has been observed in Chicago, as well as in Ontario or Sweden (Bélair, 2005). It has been noted in several states that standardized testing demotivates teachers, and the perception of the profession itself becomes negative (Debard and Kubow, 2002). This phenomenon is almost as serious as that of weak results in the schools that serve students from low-income families; socioeconomic factors are not accounted for (Jones, 2007). This demotivation is explained by a feeling of deprofessionalization; the tests take from teachers a large part of their power to improve the situation of their students (Maroy and Cattonar, 2002; Osborn, 2006); standardization has thus been perceived as a demotion.

Weakened to a semi-professional position, the teacher is no longer judged capable of the job of assessment, which confers the authority to evaluate the progress of his or her students. This is likely the reason that pushes many teachers to denounce the high stakes mechanisms that have been judged, in the final analysis, to be pedagogically negative.

The pernicious effects of standardized performance tests

Regional and national standardized tests have negative side effects; for example, they modify the content actually taught and lower the overall level and interpretation of what comprises standard skills (Koretz, 2002). In the profession of teaching, they engender a hyperconsciousness of what Weinberger (2007, p. 54) called "accountabalism," a form of "evaluative cannibalism". Teachers come to "teach to the test", which is then normalized (Igen-Igaenr, 2005). However, this may have, in certain cases, an educational effect (Demailly, 2001), if the evaluation is developed in a participative manner with strong involvement with teachers, on the basis of democratic objectives (as opposed to an authoritarian evaluation), and if the conceptualization of change has a direct connection with the field, strong convictions, and vitality. This is rarely the case.

Both in the content as well as their methods of integration, tests limit the space for the freedom and abilities of the teacher, already subject to the multiple constraints of hours, programming, and verification at several levels, not including pressure from parents. Certain teachers express the opinion that the content is almost pushed to the background, as the pressure of quantitative standardized testing is strong: it seems important that the student fits into the mold of prescribed production. Creativity in students is increasingly worn down by precise goals, defined in quantitative measurements, which assures a common calibration of acquired skills. This model reassures politicians because it seems logical to think that if a student fails in academic accomplishments, measures must be put into place to determine the possible causes, with remedies for the student, workshops for the teacher, and economic sanctions if the school achieves weak output.

But the mechanization of assessment can lead to the loss of human values. Students and teachers exhibit numerous health problems linked to high-stakes testing (Gregory and Clark, 2003). In certain countries, like the United States (although the situation may vary from one state to another), these measures can be pushed to the extreme. The interpretation of results from quantitative assessment is naturalized as an objective fact that has serious consequences, from a warning to the school in the case of low achievement on official tests, to, after a period of enforcement of measures believed to be effective for low-performing schools, closing the school if it does not improve to the minimal threshold for normal performance standards. All this so that a child is not left behind; to get to a "higher performing" school in another neighborhood or even town, the daily journey by school bus will often double in length. Mechanized evaluation in a context such as this, stripped of sense and wisdom, may create a diaspora of the poorest children. The scientific reporting on these phenomena is worn away by the insistence on objectivity that prohibits the testimony of the indignities, detrimental to a large number of students, teachers, and schools, which may be caused by such measures,

School, which should be a public space, is in the process of being relieved of its non-academic goals. Standardized testing plays a major role in this operation, which, under the guise of the marketability of knowledge, could in fact result in a deliberate destabilization of the public system to hasten its privatization (Ravitch, 2010; Tochon, 2011c). This reality is disturbing for education professionals. Certainly, the analysis made here belabors the point to bring out its problematic aspects, but these problematic aspects form the substratum of contemporary problems in the educational systems of several states. The current reaction from American conservative circles, which seeks to privatize education through eradicating the power held by labor unions, takes for its pretext the forced desegregation, in public schools, of children from different social classes, and the risk of "contamination" which follows. These arguments can be found under various forms; one of these is the English Only movement made in the push for closing low-performing schools. The connection with teachers, who have an egalitarian value, is weakened when their role is confined to the management of preprogrammed content. The normalization of new practices leads to a modification in the appreciation of these values.

Limitations of construct validity in evaluation

The principle argument that justifies the integration of standardized tests in schools is its credibility regarding teacher evaluation because these tests are believed to have more internal validity and construct validity. Although the internal validity of a test supports the relationship between cause and effect to the detriment of other possible variables, the construct validity determines if what is believed to be measured is well measured, and by extension, the generalizability of the results. However, Cronbach and Meehl, in 1955 (p. 297), had specified that generalizability of tests rests in the validation of "a principle for making inferences". Alderson and Banerjee (2001), in their review of theories of test construction, demonstrated that internal validity was not as important as ecological validity of an external nature. The validity of an evaluation rests in an interpretation subject to privileged priorities, on which generalization depends. Over the course of the last few years, the research community has become more and more conscious of the consequences of tests and their use, interpretation, and even their misuse. The question now asked is if test developers should be held responsible for the impact of their tests on society, which would constitute as new form of validity, consequential validity (Alderson and Banerjee, 2001).

Researchers who put the spotlight on this new way of thinking of evaluation, and the use of tests in particular, such as Lissitz and Samuelson (2007), or McNamara and Roever (2006), have come to the conclusion that construct validity has multiple facets. There is no simple answer to the question of how to know if a test measures what it is supposed to measure. The instruments created by teachers for their use in class, to cite one example; standardized tests must be restricted to a specific context and should not be used outside of the conceptualization and the rationale, which justifies their use. This reiterates the importance of the fundamental conception of the test—the perceived sense of its utility—is more important than the construct validity. Researchers, for this reason, must investigate the interpretive modalities in context, a test's pertinence in a particular learning situation, for example, rather than fixating on the scores. There, it focuses on a more reflexive and conceptual use of evaluation. "As a result of this unified perspective, validation is now seen as ongoing, as the continuous monitoring and updating of relevant information, indeed as a process that is never complete" and, in these facts, which cannot be assumed by anyone other than the teacher (Alderson and Banerjee, 2002, p 79). The evaluation is valid IF it is practical and IF its inferences are useful in practice. The utility of the evaluation in its context is therefore the primary criterion by which a test must be judged. The consequences of the use of the test, its authenticity or adequacy to the context, its potential of interaction and communication and its practical dimension become the major qualities and the anticipated criteria of a test that contribute to its verifiability.

Thus, evaluation has for a goal to propose a constructive feedback, an empowerment of learners in the achievement of their own goals, and in those which have already taken place (Fetterman, 2001). This proposition valorizes the evaluative competences of the teacher. The teacher is, in effect, the only person at the heart of the system who knows the personal history of the child and can construct a bridge between the child's needs and the exigencies of the school system. In the evaluation process, interpersonal evaluation becomes essential (McNamara and Lumley, 1997). The choice of which person to administer the test is crucial: what are his or her perceptions of those evaluated? If the evaluation compares learners in a normative way, who will be compared, and what influence will that have on the interpretation of the results? The feeling of competence is co-constructed during a pragmatic evaluation that evolves throughout the experience (Tochon, 1991). In addition, the evaluation cannot be conceptualized as one-dimensional. Whatever the approach taken, the strengths and weaknesses of the evaluative action must aim for practical utility for the learner. This revolution in the way we conceive of evaluation has generated several major publications in the Cambridge University Press, leading to an opening towards a better understanding in a domain that has up until now perpetuated extremely limited ideas of what evaluation should represent in the classroom.

Performance tests as social and symbolic violence

Giroux (2008) critiqued educational institutional policies and indicated how economic logic, born from neoliberalism, introduced in schools and universities, through the auspices of standardized evaluation, a form of control that has implications far beyond the academic context. In his book *Against the Terrorism of Neoliberalism: Politics beyond the Age of Greed*, Giroux traced the history of neoliberalism from the heart of authoritarianism within the legacy of fascism. He estimated that neoliberalism should be understood within the circle of influence of a sociohistorical process, characterized by forms of organization divorced from any ethos of democracy and anchored in the belief in market forces and the primacy of consumption, the reduction of the public sphere, and a messianic ideology wedded to corporatism, militarism, violence, and fear. Like fascism, neoliberalism stifles the public discourse that is the essence of the culture of democracy, directs resources to private interests with a politics of intolerance—police, surveillance, ostracism, and incarceration in an educational context. The statistical manipulation of populations and the individualization of risk denotes hegemonic neoliberal pedagogies that organize socioaffective aspirations, identities and investments and make them subservient to control networks, to which the individual must consent or suffer the consequences. Standardized testing can thus be perceived as symbolic violence.

Symbolically, standardized testing, quantitative and comparative, when it is mandated by the state and when its instrumentation becomes ubiquitous, may become an expression of fascism, which is a totalitarian attempt to control every aspect of life—political, social, cultural, and economic—through the means of a government using decrees and laws to impose measures designed and supported by a powerful minority (Baker, 2006). As an evaluation that promotes uniformity, standardization may disguise values of passive obedience to the laws, with the goal that every teacher and every student must submit to authority and conform to the will of authority. Fascism creates circumstances that legitimate the perception that institutions are going through a major crisis which requires extreme measures, as traditional solutions cannot work anymore (Paxton, 2005, p.218). The current economic crisis effectively justifies evaluative measures to an unprecedented extent, without consideration of the moral implications. In certain countries, systematic evaluations that subjugate children from low-income families certainly appears to be a form of *terreur blanche* (white terror), or domestic terrorism. Particularly in the United States, as mentioned by Giroux, the debate over evaluation and accountability has become a strategy of racialization in a society where segregation in the schools has increased since the 1960s. Racial ostracization is justified by ideologically similar arguments. Consequently, a teacher's evaluative competence must be influenced by the society which imposes it. In some of my work (2004 and 2011b), I illustrate why consciousness-raising must become one of the roles of teachers and teacher educators, a point that Freire (1992) had insisted.

It is true that many ideologies can coexist in a nation, and the situation is always complex and nuanced. Rogers (1969) proposed the freedom to learn. May some of our schools become, subtly, penitentiary spaces? Evaluation obviously constitutes only one aspect of this ideological movement. Performance testing mandated for so many students, as well as teachers and school districts, is becoming a form of social violence. When, in the name of accountability, limiting freedom eliminates the chances of success of a social class or racial or ethnic group, it then becomes a form of institutional terrorism and can be classified according to the definition used by the *United Nations' Convention on the Prevention and Punishment of the Crime of Genocide* (1948) 2 and what Stavenhagen (1990) called "ethnocide".

The concept of linguistic genocide, developed by Skutnabb-Kangas (2000), designates the transfer of children from minority groups from their own culture to the dominant culture through intellectual suffering, inflicted on them through the educational system. Two articles of the Convention on Genocide reveal themselves to be pertinent in this respect. Article 7, paragraph 1, subparagraph k defines genocide as every inhuman or similar act that intentionally causes suffering or attacks the physical or mental health of a group. The generalized mental suffering engendered by standardized testing has already been raised; it affects minority groups in particular. As an

---

[2] E793, 1948; 78 U.N.T.S. 277, applied on January 12, 1951; see http://www1.umn.edu/humanrts/instree/x1cppcg.htm

example, the intentionality appears in the documentation of a lawsuit brought against the State of Pennsylvania by the National Parents' Commission, a large group led by leading figures of the right during the last administration (Luksik, 1996 and 2005). Article 7, paragraph 2, subparagraph g indicates that "persecution" is defined by a grave and intentional privation of fundamental rights, for example, the fundamental right to equal educational opportunity and the right of citizens to refuse testing and its administration. Subparagraph h covers all forms of "persecution again an identifiable or collectivity on political, racial, national, ethnic, cultural, religious, gender...or other grounds that are universally recognized as impermissible under international law". Standardized performance tests in the United States have a racial impact, as shown by official statistics from the last fifteen years. The American Federation of State, County & Municipal Employees (AFSCME) filed suit in 1999 arguing that educational policies of testing contributed, in a systematic fashion, to low student achievement, problems with depression among teachers, and disciplinary problems in schools in low-income areas.3 A systematic reduction in academic achievement levels for African-American children year after year is evident; these differences are not attributable to cognitive deficiencies but to other factors, such as experiences linked to the community within the educational system (Finch, et al., 2002; Darling-Hammond, 2007). Evoking linguistic deficits and the characteristics of Ebonics (Sarzyniak, 2009), are among the ways of masking racial prejudice (Perry and Delpit, 1998). The rare cases of (mitigated) success from the policies of No Child Left Behind is explained by the systematic holding back of children, most notably in Florida in 2003-2004 (Haney, 2006).

To summarize, in certain countries, the situation created by standardized testing is such that the necessary foundation for a class action suit at the national level and in international courts exists. In these countries, standardized tests are instruments of scientific racism

---

[3] U.S. Department of Education Quota News:
http://www.adversity.net/fedagency_news.htm#1_fed_agency

and segregation; when they render any hope impossible and lead a vast group of people of the same ethnicity or language to segregation, an unfathomable mental suffering, and prison, we can classify this as genocide (Alexander, 2010). Along these hypotheses, mandated testing according to standardized, quantitative, decontextualized norms will become a scourge. Many teachers resist the culture of testing (Behrens, 2006). Because of the power evaluation has to modify spontaneous approaches to the knowledge of children, and to put it another way, to promote or stunt certain aspirations and to steer preferred trajectories, it proves important to deeply understand and respect the ways professionals in the schools perceive and conceive of evaluative practices (Harris and Brown, 2008).

Towards a deeper and more humane conception of evaluative competence

Performance testing, as a *cause célèbre* at the core of neoliberal ideology, places students, teachers, and schools in an unhealthy competition that can poison the social environment of school districts through creating never-ending conflicts. The publicity given to these tests is often proved to be detrimental and contrary to the goals of reform. Even if the variability of accountability models is acknowledged, systematic performance testing has unintended effects that negatively influence the process of learning. Tests cannot be justified outside of the scholastic context. They can be harmful if teachers are not involved in their conception, their administration, and their use for constructive goals. The evaluative competence of teachers cannot be dismissed, which is based on reflective practice and the wisdom of contextualized action. No matter which plan of action is adopted, it must be in conjunction with professional development, financial support for struggling schools, and support for collaborative programs between schools, for example, through a network of professional exchanges. The manner in which teachers participate in these evaluations must be reviewed in depth; the more those who participate in the conception, the administration, and the analysis of results, the greater their involvement in the process develops, as does the culture of evaluation (Mons, 2009, p.36).

When perspectives are mechanistic and superficial and when education is not truly reflective, reflexive, and profound, distortions reveal themselves; each time, it is possible to locate the problem in the absence of consideration for the knowledge of teachers because they are often not engaged in the reform process or its evaluation (Stobart, 2011). Confronted with policies that are often extremist, educational practitioners must become more active. They can conduct collaborative research with teacher educators and administrators to stimulate improve continuing education (Annan, 2011). Evaluation then allows the steering of reforms, clarifying of roles, and envisioning sustainable programming to support students from disadvantaged groups. Continuing education for teachers is a proven method to improve student outcomes. Participation action research in these networks permits the analysis of student difficulties and to locate their needs (Timperley, 2011).

The conceptions that teachers have influence their practices and act on their students' results (Muijs, 2006); however, many teachers know how to weigh their evaluative rigor with humanity in authentic evaluations. These involve the observer to take note and document the child's work in order to make decisions adapted to each situation. This approach is based on everyday educational events, allowing for the construction of evolving projects where the evaluation is integrated and continuous. This evaluation is focused on real-life problems at the heart of research that is open to reflection and interchanges between activity and social learning (Rule, 2006). Authentic evaluation is an alternative to quantitative testing (Gardner, 1991). It is responsive to several functions of teachers' evaluative competence because they wish to teach and not punish (Tochon, 2010). These functions represent the heart of teaching:

- Individualization in the face of standardization;
- encouragement in the face of discouragement engendered by testing;
- dialogue in the face of administrative monologue;
- teaching personnel in the face of public measurement.

Faced with the instrumental logic mandated in certain countries, a solution is to revalorize the evaluative competences of teachers. The research indicates changes in the representation of actors in teaching profession, their social action, and their power to act, which has been largely reduced. Research on motivation on accomplishment and self-determination has demonstrated positive effects in a climate where students are in charge of their own learning, and negative effects in a climate of competition based achievement linked to standardized testing; the cultivation of a learning context that supports student autonomy has proved beneficial (Sarrazin, Tessier & Trouilloud, 2006). To attenuate negative effects associated with standardized testing, teachers can use strategies to increase students' autonomy; integrate educational evaluations, technologies or instructional materials that students enjoy and feel comfortable with; propose independent study; rotate content; establish priorities; use multiple measurements; integrate in their evaluations content and activities with a human dimension. These strategies demonstrate the aspects of teachers' evaluative competences.

For the most part, teachers have socially useful values and an ethic of life (Noddings, 2003). They contribute to an equitable evaluation that draws on their knowledge of students and their contexts, because they are experts on their professional context (Tochon, 1993; 1994). Their participation is essential to conceive a more humane society. Empowerment evaluation (Fetterman, 2001) appears to be one of the rare forms of evaluation that stimulates learning and recognizes the teacher as expert. It increases self-determination and empowerment (Fetterman, 2005). Wandersman et al. (2005) underscores the principles of this evaluation: it must bring improvements to the human dimension; the local actors must assume the responsibility of its design, administer the evaluation and bring about the necessary measures; decision-making must be shared, based on authentic communication and collaboration; goals of social equity seeks a public benefit throughout the community through increasing the power of people; the instruments are adapted to the environment, to the culture, and to the local conditions.

Such a genre of evaluation actively involves teachers who can demonstrate and render useful their local knowledge. What is notable, if we compare these principles to those of standardized quantitative achievement testing, is the intelligent implication of local participants, an engagement that fulfills the goals of organizational and professional mastery. This approach encourages an honest discussion on the strengths and weaknesses of the programs evaluated. It follows a concerted planning effort for remediation and the identification of a useful documentation of its progress. Evaluation becomes an integrated part of program administration, not from outside but on-site (Fetterman and Wandersman, 2004). When it is centered on the development of content and brings about wisdom in contextualization action, evaluation can be what I will call a "deep evaluation"—an evaluation that stimulates deep learning.

Not to throw the baby out with the bath water, some forms of standardized assessment may support deep learning, all depends how they are used. Imagine the multi literacy forms of appreciation of complex matters on the basis of problem cases, critical incidents and whole situations on video to elucidate I mean, not memory tests. Then even in the form of multiple choice questions and answers, if the tests were "owned" by the school, the teacher or even the student and were used for self-assessment, peer-assessment, team assessment, and teacher facilitation, guidance and feedback, they could support a Deep Approach to learning. The students would not be *subjected* to testing, they would not be taught-to-test. Instead they would be provided with instruments allowing them and their teacher to get a sense of where they sit within a larger population of respondents whenever they want. It would alleviate the fear of tests.

Furthermore, text, audio and video data banks could develop broad resources on many subjects taken thoroughly and not in a shallow fashion, and associate them with forms of deep inquiry. Testing needs to be *unschooled* (Gardner, 2011). Even if they were randomized for testing purpose, complex and multi-sensory test items could serve deep learning goals. They could support freedom to learn. The issue is to give agency to the learner and the teacher, and "unlink" testing and timing, and knowledge control from the government. In *Deschooling Society*, Ivan Illich (2000) demonstrated that the separation of educational evaluation from the state is as important as the split between the state and the church. Testing creates social classes artificially and is being used as a major instrument of discrimination against certain minorities, rather than being adapted to the different types of learning. Testing data banks would guide sound certification and accreditation if they could be taken as many times as the students and teacher might want, as a referential of competence. If deep learning is the goal, then deep tests should dig deep into competence and proficiency, not be the ephemeral measure of shallow rote learning. The idea is also to *deschool* the imagination, as critical thought is a necessary social practice (Weiner, 2015).

Community schools are moving in this direction, in the name of autonomous learning and agency. In these alternative models, learning is based on projects, evaluation may be based on portfolios. Schools of practical, local wisdom exchanges and generates unique and specific knowledge, know-how, and knowledge of being. Evaluation competence thus seeks integrated dimensions of personal fulfillment, love and respect. The acquisition of wisdom replaces the logic of production; there is a return to philosophy, which constitutes the first knowledge (Fuenmayor, 2006). Because of this local and autonomous knowledge and of this wisdom, every person can grow in the freedom to recognize and act according to an ethic of life in society. Toda (2000) has therefore proposed a collection of regional societies that are smaller and more humane, based on mutual caring. Korten (2006) demonstrated how these overall communities of learning can change society. Learners journey through this network of schools, established in several countries to understand other practices and other cultures. The freedom to create other ways of being could be an antidote to administrative abuses of governmental agencies. In the face of this generous utopia, we live in a bureaucratic dystopia linked, in certain countries, to the defiance of evaluative competences of teachers because in a public educational system, teachers are the principal obstacles to its privatization.

In the Guise of a Conclusion

Changing the Nature of Scholastic Evaluation and Valorizing the Evaluative Competences of Teachers as well as Students

Briefly, the beginning of this article emphasized two contradictory forces in educational evaluation: that which supports a practice of reflexive wisdom, and that in which the aims are economic and political and focuses on accountability. The problem is that the second is carried out to the detriment of the first; in addition, the first dispossesses the teacher of a crucial dimension of his or her professional competence, which allows for teaching practices, through encouraging a dialogue with the child, that respond to the student's individual needs. This human dimension risks being excluded by the measurements of standardized testing imposed in an authoritarian manner because these measurements change the nature of teaching, which loses, in large part, its educational dimension and is relegated to technical instruction.

We have seen that, among the actors implicated in the system of evaluation that has been put in place by these reforms, administrators, teachers, learners, and parents are conditioned by the social and psychological environment created by standardized tests, pitting students, teachers, schools and school districts against each other through comparison of quantitative test scores. Although the majority of participants in these changes do not see, *a priori*, much harm in generalizing what has previously been a well-accepted local practice, it can be observed that the expansion of an evaluative program, removed from the control of educational practitioners engenders systematic distortion in the perception of the work of teachers, can be harmful to learning, to the climate in the school and the classroom, and for the humane dimension to which education has previously belonged. Standardized testing has become, in certain contexts, a factor in racial segregation and linguistic genocide. Every evaluation is socially marked because the preferential value placed on certain criteria diminishes the value of others in a way that is potentially discriminatory. The underlying culture of this process of valuing and devaluing is rarely discussed, as though evaluation is always objective, as opposed to a politically subject action. It is rarely questioned what is being devalued in the process.

A critical reflection may lead to solutions and actions that are already, in fact, shared by many. In several countries, researchers adhere to certain constants. As Morrissette, Loye & Legendre (2011, p.2) state, "evaluation of learning is more than the simple administering of the instruments"; their use must be contextualized. The professional judgment of the actors on-site is essential in this respect (Bélair, 2006; Morrissette, 2010). Educational policies must integrate complex though on what is respectful of the human beings affected. We must confront the logic that transforms us into automatons for production. Standardized testing appears to have become the only educational policy in some countries. This situation, associated with several other new constraints, entails certain characteristics of bureaucratic extremism. Western societies are not prepared to adopt post-bureaucratic systems (Maroy, 2008), as recommended by Ivan Illich (1969/2000). In several countries, the ubiquity of technical measurements of quantitative evaluation tends to strip people of the power of their own actions. Their freedom to think, to believe, and to express themselves is at stake. The danger is very real; sociometric evaluation is no longer tied to an ideal of what humanity can become, but has become a method of control and manipulation of human populations for the support of economic and security imperatives. The risk born of economic evaluation—a knowledge that has nothing to do with education—is instead compensated by the recalibration of economies and their agents, in the West as in other parts of the world, who wish a bloodless negotiated peace rather than a revolution to continue their abusive practices.

The strong hypotheses proposed here merit to be further supported argued; this limited space does not allow for this. The danger of a too general discussion of evaluation is evident in the conflation of forms, levels, and goals; however, what is targeted here is the principle of attaining individual autonomy in a mass system. Nevertheless, these questions are important because they indicate *a contrario* the role of the teacher in demonstrating the reverse. Critical analysis is concerned with standardized, qualitative performance testing, imposed on a large collection of individuals, without leaving them an alternative to obedience. Nobody finds fault a priori, even teachers, until the moment when they realize the magnitude of the consequences of the modifications on the value system; this is where the challenge is found—mandated, imposed evaluation *en masse*, has altered societal values. Evaluation, which etymologically applies to valorization what is unique to each person, becomes a tool to measure and homogenize in the commodification of knowledge.

Rethinking evaluation in terms of valorization could lead us to reconceptualize its creative power. Production should target creation, the purpose of life, the sign of intelligence, the unique expression, the art of living, and innovative individual or collaborative research, instead of that which binds us to normative standards. Thus, in order to resolve, in part, certain of the problems mentioned above, we could surpass an evaluation of products, which limits the learner to a single type of result, and achieve an evaluation of process, leading to varied results. This new evaluation favors difference instead of homogeneity and normalization, which would reconnect the idea of evaluation as encouraging learning and personal development.

References

Alderson, J. C., & Banerjee, J. (2001). Language testing and assessment (Part 1). *Language Teaching, 34*(4), 213-36.

Alderson, J. C., & Banerjee, J. (2002). Language testing and assessment (Part 2). *Language Teaching, 35*(1), 79-113.

Alexander, M. (2010). *The New Jim Crow: Mass Incarceration in the Age of Colorblindness.* New York : New Press.

Annan, B. (2011). L'amélioration continue des établissements scolaires : l'ingénierie mise en place en Nouvelle-Zélande. [Continuing improvement in schools: the engineering put in place in New Zealand]. *Revue française de pédagogie, 174*, 21-30.

Aristotle (350 BC/2004). *The Nicomachean ethics* (trad. & notes de J.A.K. Thompson; éd. rév. H. Tredennick). Londres: Penguin.

Bain, D. (1987, septembre). *La formation en évaluation formative, argumentation et plaidoyer pour une entrée par la didactique. [Education in educational evaluation and pleading for a entree for the didactic].* Genève : Centre de Recherche Psycho-Pédagogique. Exposé présenté lors du congrès international de l'Association de Mesure et Évaluation en Éducation (ADMEE), Fribourg, Suisse.

Baker, D. (2006). The political economy of fascism: Myth or reality, or myth and reality? *New Political Economy, 11*(2), 227-250.

Baker, E. L. (2007). 2007 presidential address: The end(s) of testing. *Educational Researcher, 36*(6), 309-317.

Behrens M. (2006). Analyse de la littérature critique sur le développement, l'usage et l'implémentation de standards dans un système éducatif. [A critical literature review on the development, use, and implementation of standards in an educational system]. Neuchâtel: IRDP.

Bélair, L. M. (2005). Les dérives de l'obligation de résultats ou l'art de surfer sans planche. [The derivatives of obligation of results or the art of surfing without a board]. In C. Lessard et P. Meirieu (Eds), *L'obligation de résultats en éducation [Obligation of results in education].* Bruxelles: De Boeck Université.

Bélair, L. M. (2006). L'évaluation au quotidien: conjuguer processus et produit. [The everyday evaluation : Combining process and product]. *Mesure et évaluation en éducation, 29*(1), 19-30.

Black, P., & William, D. (2006). Assessment for learning in the classroom. In John Gardner (Ed.), *Assessment and Learning* (pp.9-25). Thousand Oaks, CA: Sage.

Brookhart, S. M. (2004). Classroom Assessment: Tensions and intersections in theory and practice. *Teachers College Record, 106*(3), 429-458.

Cronbach, L. J., & Meehl, P. E. (1955). Construct validity in psychological tests. *Psychological Bulletin, 52*, 281-302.

Darling-Hammond, L. (2007). Evaluating 'No Child Left Behind'. *The Nation,* 21 mai. En ligne : http://www.thenation.com/node/22962

DeBard, R., & Kubow, P. K. (2002). From compliance to commitment: The need for constituent discourse in implementing testing policy. *Educational Policy, 16*(3), 387-405.

Demailly L. (2001), Enjeux de l'évaluation et régulation des systèmes scolaires. [Issues of evaluation and regulation of school systems]. In L. Demailly (Ed), *Evaluer les politiques éducatives [Evaluating educational politics]*. Bruxelles: Editions De Boeck Université.

Fetterman, D. (2001). *Foundations of empowerment evaluation*. Thousand Oaks, CA: Sage.

Fetterman, D. (2005). Conclusion: conceptualizing empowerment evaluation in terms of sequential time and space. In D. Fetterman et A. Wandersman (Eds), *Empowerment evaluation: principles in practice* (pp.209-214). New York, NY: Guilford.

Fetterman, D.M. & Wandersman, A. (2004). *Empowerment Evaluation Principles in Practice*. New York: Guilford.

Finch, S.J., Farberman, H.A., Neus, J., Adams, R.E., & Price-Baker, D. (2002). Differential test performance in the American educational system: the impact of race and gender. Journal of Sociology and Social Welfare, Sept 2002. Online:
http://findarticles.com/p/articles/mi_m0CYZ/is_3_29/?tag=content;col1

Freire, P. (1992). *Pedagogy of the oppressed*. New York : Continuum.

Fuenmayor, R. (2006, juillet). *El camino de la sistemología interpretativa [The way to interpretive systemology]*. VI Congreso Científico de la Universidad de Oriente. Núcleo Anzoategui, 28 juillet 2006.

Gardner, H. (1991). *The Alternative to standardized testing*. New York: Basic Books.

Gardner, H. (2011). *The Unschooled Mind: How Children Think and How Schools Should Teach*. New York: Basic Books.

Giroux, H. A. (2008). *Against the Terror of Neoliberalism: Politics Beyond the Age of Greed*. Boulder: Paradigm.

Gregory, K., & Clarke, M. (2003). High-Stakes Assessment in England and Singapore. *Theory into Practice , 42*(1), 66-74.

Habermas, J. (2003). *Truth and justification* (B. Fultner, Transl.). Cambridge, MA: MIT Press.

Haney, W.M. (2006). *Evidence on Education under NCLB (and How Florida Boosted NAEP Scores and Reduced the Race Gap)*. Boston College, Center for the Study of Testing, Evaluation and Education Policy. En ligne: http://www.bc.edu/research/nbetpp/statements/nbr6.pdf

Harris, L. R., & Brown, G. T. L. (2008). *New Zealand Teachers' Conceptions of the Purpose of Assessment: Phenomenographic Analyses of Teachers' Thinking*. Paper presented at the Australian Association for Research in Education Conference. Australia: Brisbane.

Holman, S. (2006, Août). The effects of dialogue journaling on second language acquisition. Mémoire de maîtrise en Curriculum & Instruction. Madison WI : University of Wisconsin-Madison.

Igen-Igaenr (2005). *Les acquis des élèves, pierre de touche de la valeur de l'école?* Paris: IGEN-IGAENR.

Illich, I. (1969/2000). *Deschooling society*. New York: Marion Boyars.

Jones, B. (2007). The unintended outcomes of High-Stakes Testing. *Journal of Applied School psychology, 23*(2), 65-86.

Kant, I. (1784). What is enlightenment? In Noms (Eds), *Foundations of the metaphysics of morals* (pp.80-92). New York: Bobbs-Merrill.

Koretz, D. (2002, April). U*sing multiple measures to address perverse incentives and score inflation*. Communication présentée lors du symposium Multiple perspectives on Multiple Measures au congrès annuel du National Council on Measurement in Education. La Nouvelle-Orléans, Louisiane.

Korten, D., C. (2006). *The great turning. From Empire to Earth community*. San Francisco: Berrett-Koehler, Kumarian.

Lissitz, R. W., & Samuelson, K. (2007). Dialogue on validity. A suggested change in terminology and emphasis regarding validity and Education. *Educational Researcher, 36*(8), 437-448.

Luksik, P., & Hoffecker, P. H. (1996). *Outcome Based Education: The State's Assault on Our Children's Values*. Philadelphia, PA: Vital Issues.

Luksik, P. (2005). *National Parents' Commission Report*. Johnstown, PA.

Magnusson, J. L. (2001). *Mad scientists and technosavants : exploring the cultural icons of industrial capitalist science*. Article présenté lors du congrès « Teaching as if the World Mattered ». Toronto, OISE/University of Toronto.

Maroy, C. (2008). Vers une régulation post-bureaucratique des systèmes d'enseignement en Europe? [Towards a post-bureaucratic regulation of educational systems in Europe?] *Sociologie et Société , 40*(1), 31-55.

Maroy, C., & Cattonar, B. (2002). Professionnalisation ou déprofessionnalisation des enseignants? Le cas de la Communauté française de Belgique. [Professionalization or deprofessionalization of teachers? The case of the French community of Belgium]. *Cahier de recherche en Education et Formation, 18*. Louvain-la-Neuve: Université de Louvain.

McMillan, J. H. (2007). *Classroom Assessment: Principles and Practice for Effective Teaching* (4th ed.). Boston, MA: Pearson Education.

McNamara, T. F., & Lumley, T. (1997). The effect of interlocutor and assessment mode variables in overseas assessments of speaking skills in occupational settings. *Language Testing, 14*(2), 140-56.

McNamara, T. F., & Roever, C. (2006). *Language testing: the social dimension*. Malden, MA: Blackwell.

Mons, J. (2009). Les effets théoriques et réels de l'évaluation standardisée. Compléments à l'étude « Les évaluations standardisées des élèves en Europe: objectifs, organisation et utilisation des résultats EACEA ». [The theoretical and real effects of standardized evaluation : Objectives, organization, and utilization of the EACEA results]. Grenoble: l'université Pierre-Mendès-France, Grenoble 2, Eurydice.

Morin, E. (1982). *Science avec conscience. [Science with a conscience]*. Paris: Fayard.

Morrissette, J. (2010). *Manières de faire l'évaluation formative des apprentissages: analyse interactionniste du savoir-faire d'enseignantes du primaire*. [Methods of educational evaualtion of learning : Interactionist *analysis of primary school teachers' know-how].* Sarrebruck, CH: Les Éditions universitaires européennes.

Morrissette, J., Loye, N., & Legendre, M.-F. (2011, janvier). *Autour du savoir-évaluer des enseignantes et des enseignants en salle de classe. [Around the evaluative knowledge of teachers and teachers in the classroom].* Montréal, QC : Université de Montréal.

Muijs, D. (2006). Measuring teacher effectiveness: Some methodological reflections. *Educational Research and Evaluation, 12*(1), 53-74.

Noddings, N. (2003). *Caring: A feminine approach to ethics and moral education* (2d ed.). Berkeley: University of California Press.

Osborn, M. (2006). Changing the context of teachers' work and professional development: a European perspective. *International Journal of Educational Research, 45,* 242-253.

Paxton, R. O. (2005). *The Anatomy of Fascism.* New York: Knopf.

Perry, T., & Delpit, L. (1998). *The real Ebonics debate: power, language, and the education of African-American children.* Milwaukee, WI: Rethinking Schools.

Ravitch, D. (2010). *The Death and Life of the Great American School System.* New York : Basic Books.

Rogers, C. R. (1969). *Freedom to learn.* Columbus, OH : Charles E. Merrill.

Rule, A. C. (2006). The components of authentic learning. *Journal of Authentic Learning, 3*(1),1-10.

Sarrazin, Ph., Tessier, D., & Trouilloud, D. (2006). Climat motivationnel instauré par l'enseignant et implication des élèves en classe : l'état des recherche. [Motivational climate instated by the teacher and the implications for students in the class]. *Revue française de pédagogie, 157,* 147-177.

Sarzyniak, K. (2009). *Attitudes that affect the Black-White achievement gap: how do cultural identity and the use of Ebonics affect African American students' success in the classroom?* New York : Lambert Academic.

Simon, M., Chitpin, S. & Yahya, R. (2010). Pre-service Teachers' Thinking about Student Assessment Issues. *International Journal of Education, 2*(2), E5.

Skutnabb-Kangas, T. (2000). *Linguistic genocide in education – or worldwide diversity and human rights.* Mahwah, NJ : Lawrence Erlbaum.

Stavenhagen, R. (1990). *The Ethnic Question. Conflicts, Development, and Human Rights.* Tokyo: United Nations University Press.

Stobart, G. (2011). « L'évaluation pour les apprentissages » : d'une expérimentation locale à une politique nationale. [« Evaluation for learning » : For an local experiment to national politics]. *Revue française de pédagogie, 174,* 41-48.

Timperley, H. (2011). Le développement professionnel des enseignants et ses effets positifs sur les apprentissages des élèves. [Professional development of teachers and its positive effects on student learning]. *Revue française de pédagogie, 174,* 31-40.

Tochon, F. V. (1991). Evaluation pragmatique et situations spontanées: l'indexation des activités en classe. [Pragmatic evaluation and spontaneous situations : Indexicality on class activities]. *Mesure et Evaluation en Education, 14*(4), 42-47.

Tochon, F. V. (1993). *L'enseignant expert /L'enseignante experte. [The expert teacher].* Paris : Nathan.

Tochon, F. V. (2000). Recherche sur la pensée des enseignants: un paradigme à maturité. [Research on the thoughts of teachers : A maturational paradigm]. *Revue française de pédagogie, 133*, 1-23.

Tochon, F. V. (2004). Le nouveau visage de l'enseignant expert. [The new face of the expert teacher]. *Recherche et Formation, 47*, 89-103.

Tochon, F. V. (2010). Deep Education. *Journal for Educators, Teachers and Trainers, 1*, 1-12.

Tochon, F. V. (2011a). Le savoir-évaluer comme politique éducative: Vers une évaluation plus profonde (Evaluative Knowledge as Educational Politics : Towards a Deeper Evaluation). *Mesure et Évaluation en Éducation, 34*(3), 133-156.

Tochon, F. V. (2011b). Deep Education: Assigning a Moral Role to Academic Work. *Educaçao, Sociedade & Culturas, 33*, novembre.

Tochon, F. V. (2011c). Propos libres sur la formation des enseignants: Une entrevue avec François Victor Tochon. *Formations et pratiques d'enseignement en questions. Revue des Hautes écoles pédagogiques et institutions de formation de Suisse romande et du Tessin, 12.*

Tochon, F. V. (2017). The Turn Toward Deep Value. In M. Djuraeva and F. V. Tochon (Eds.), *Re-imagining the Role of Language in a Neoliberal Society.* Blue Mounds, WI : Deep University Press.

Toda, M. (2000). 1. Emotion and social interaction: A theoretical overview. In G. Hatano, N. Okada, and H. Tanabe (Eds), *Affective minds* (pp.1-17). Amsterdam: Elsevier Science & Technology.

Wandersman, A. et al. (2005). The principles of empowerment evaluation. In D. Fetterman et A. Wandersman (Eds), *Empowerment evaluation: principles in practice* (pp.27-41). New York, NY: Guilford.

Weinberger, D. (2007, February). The HBR list: Breakthrough ideas for 2007. *Harvard Business Review, 85*(2), 21-36, 44-48, 50, 52, 54.

Weiner, E. J. (2015). *Deschooling the Imagination: Critical Thought as Social Practice.* New York: Routledge.

12.

Application of the Deep Culture Model to International Students in the U.S.

Tomoko Wakana
University of Wisconsin—Madison

From the perspective of deep learning, which involves exploration of underlying meanings, learning drawn on multiple perspectives, and personal commitment (Ramsden 2003; Tagg 2003; Tochon, 2010), Joseph Shaules (2007) presented the Deep Culture Model of intercultural learning. In his book, Shaules used interview data from his own study that involved a variety of sojourners in different countries, including language teachers, students, and persons who are married to a spouse from outside their native countries and moved overseas. My goal in this chapter is to tailor the Deep Culture Model to better fit a particular group of sojourners: international students studying in the U.S. I first review the Deep Culture Model and present what I think are its strengths. Then, I present some possible concepts to enhance understanding of his model. The three major topics I focus on in this chapter are the presence of fellow international students, deep culture learning through English, and the culture of origin. Finally, I propose that a socio-psychological school of thought, symbolic interactionism, could theoretically frame the Deep Culture Model.

What is the Deep Culture Model?

Joseph Shaules (2007) defines deep culture as "the unconscious meanings, values, norms and hidden assumptions that allow us to interpret our experience as we interact with other people" (pp. 11-12). Deep culture, therefore, does not refer to specific behavior. The Deep Culture Model has three phases toward increased cultural empathy: resistance, acceptance, and adaptation. Importantly, these concepts do not demonstrate the overall intercultural development, but they are reactions toward a particular intercultural learning experience. In addition, each phase has explicit (superficial) and implicit (deep) levels of adaptation. According to Shaules, this model demonstrates an ongoing process of reacting toward the implicit adaptive demands in the new cultural environment. Below, I briefly review the three phases of deep intercultural learning presented in Shaules's model.

Phase 1: Resistance

Resistance is defined as "an unwillingness to change in response to the adaptive demands of a new cultural environment" (Shaules, 2007, p. 150). People resist changing their behaviors by using their own, previously- established standards to judge experiences in the new cultural environment. Resistance is different from dislike. According to Shaules, resistance involves negative, ethnocentric value judgment, whereas dislike is a simple negative reaction toward something unpleasant. Surface resistance is concerned with making negative judgments on explicit symbols such as food and transportation systems. On the other hand, deep resistance involves using one's cultural values as a lens to see and negatively judge the hidden assumptions in the new cultural environment such as concepts of fairness and equalities.

Phase 2: Acceptance

The next phase is acceptance. Acceptance refers to "perceiving as valid alternative interpretations of the cultural phenomenon that one experiences" (Shaules, 2007, p. 166). It requires cognitive changes in one's perception toward unfamiliar cultural values; it is the ability to recognize one's own ignorance with other cultural values. Surface acceptance is the form of accepting differences with deep resistance; sojourners at this phase accept superficial differences such as food, but are not willing to accept one's own limitation in the context or take the perspective of the people of the culture they are learning about. On the other hand, at the level of deeper acceptance, sojourners show understanding toward how implicit culture works, from the perspective of the member of that particular culture.

Phase 3: Adaptation

At the "acceptance" phase, only cognitive transformations are demanded; however, at the phase of "adaptation," individuals allow for "change in oneself as a response to adaptive demands from a different cultural environment" (Shaules, 2007, p. 180). Making changes in one's behavior with acceptance toward other cultures can enhance his or her "cognitive empathy," which is defined as "the ability to look at cultural difference on the meta-level, with a deep and conscious acceptance of the validity of different worldviews" (p. 196). At the surface level, sojourners may simply adapt their behaviors because of explicit demands such as how to use transportation or how to greet someone. Deep adaptation, on the other hand, involves understanding the meanings behind behaviors, which are implicit. Shaules emphasizes that surface adaptation does not mean that it is thoughtless; it only means that the adaptation is not based on implicit cultural patterns.

Advantages of the Deep Culture Model

Shaules (2007) took multiple culture-learning frameworks as foundations into account to build his model, in addition to findings from his own studies.

For instance, Bennett's (1993) model of six degrees of intercultural sensitivity features two phases of integration: ethnocentrism and ethnorelativism. Both of these phases contain three stages: the first phase contains denial, resistance, and minimization; and the second, acceptance, adaptation, and integration. According to Shaules, the strengths of Bennett's model are that it is free of subjective measures, such as emotions and behaviors, and it is easy to use because it has straightforward descriptions for each of the three stages therein contained. However, its one-way design with discrete stages may not capture a reality of intercultural learning experiences in which people not only "progress," but may "go back" in developmental steps. In this sense, Shaules's model captures the realistic experiences of sojourners more effectively by describing the model of intercultural learning as a non-linear development.

In addition, while Bennett's model is designed to evaluate an overall progress rather than a particular reaction, Shaules's model is capable of explaining a sojourner who is at different levels of intercultural learning for different matters (e.g., he or she might resist something while accepting another). Thus, Shaules's model seems to be more suited to studying contradictory and complex reactions to intercultural experiences.

Besides Bennett's model of intercultural sensitivity, Shaules also discusses Weaver's (1993) model of dealings with culture shock. The three processes of culture shock described by Weaver are: loss of familiar cues; communication breakdown; and identity crisis. Although this model was not developed specifically to explain intercultural learning in overseas contexts, it still provides psychological foundations for understanding how people undertake demands of intercultural learning (Shaules, 2007).

Both Weaver and Shaules use the concept of "depth" in their models. Shaules uses explicit and implicit adaptive demands to understand the "depth" of intercultural learning. He is clear about the difference between explicit and implicit demands: explicit demands often include visible or behavioral cultural cues, whereas implicit demands involve meanings and the way people think about particular things.

One weakness of Weaver's model, however, is that it does not explain the differences among people in terms of how willing and open they are toward intercultural learning demands. In Shaules's model, however, this is improved by the notions of resistance, acceptance, and adaptations, through which sojourners change themselves to meet the adaptive demands. These concepts help us understand how explicit and implicit adaptive demands are received differently by each sojourner. There are multiple paths to making progress in understanding and accepting different cultures (Shaules, 2007).

As influential as Shaules's Deep Culture Model has been, there are things that he does not mention. In what follows, I present suggestions that could enhance his model of deep intercultural learning. In particular, I would like to shed light on the intersection of English language learning and intercultural learning during study abroad. But before doing so, I briefly discuss the way I treat English in this chapter.

English and Linguistic Imperialism

The way I see English in relation to the Deep Culture Model is educational and peaceful. I focus on the way English is willingly shared among people present in the study abroad context. But from the sociopolitical point of view, English is considered a language of power. Here I attend to this view of English as a politically dominant language in contrast to the educational one.

Robert Phillipson's (1992) notion of linguistic imperialism critically examined the position of English in today's world. According to him, linguistic imperialism is "the process by which the dominance of English is asserted and maintained by the establishment and continuous reconstitution of structural and cultural inequalities between English and other languages" (p. 47). He argued that the impact of English dominance on local languages could be serious. For one, English education is sought after more enthusiastically than the local language education, by which local language(s) will be eventually lost among future generations. Moreover, because languages are closely connected to cultures, there is also the danger that, with the global dominance of English, cultures might eventually blend in and disappear (Pennycook, 2007).

Being able to use English is an asset; it could bring more job opportunities and thus more monetary gains. Such a possibility for upward mobility encourages people to learn and use English, and it further reinforces the unequal positions of English among world languages. In this way, English could, in fact, be valuable for some people even at the expense of losing resources that they would otherwise invest to learn other world languages.

Another way to view English from a sociopolitical perspective is to see it as a postcolonial language. According to Pennycook (1998), English is "a major language in which colonialism has been written" (p. 9). A case in point is India, which had been colonized by the United Kingdom for a long time. Today, English is still used widely in India along with other languages such as Hindi. In postcolonial countries, how to revive the languages that were once suppressed by the colonizers is a crucial issue.

But the sociopolitical view of English has been criticized. For instance, in his paper Schulzke (2014) has argued that English is described as being overly detrimental toward other world languages. He states that English has inarguably been powerful in the past, but just because it has always been so does not meant that it is wise to predict its political and economic strengths in the future.

One motivation for study abroad is, in the first place, to learn English, knowing and desiring the benefit of having English proficiency. As for the group of students I discuss in this chapter, it is important to emphasize that these individuals choose to come to the U.S. for study abroad. They are by no means forced to study in the U.S. and use English, after all. The use of English in this context is willingly accepted by international students. As such, I argue that the view of English as a hegemonic language does not seem to apply to the learning of English among international students. Although the high-status of English is deniable when considered from economic and political perspectives, I argue that English needs to be conceptualized more as a language of communicative means in this specific context of study abroad.

Below, I discuss the application of the Deep Culture Model for international students in the U.S. with regard to interactions among international students themselves.

The Presence of Fellow International Students

During study abroad, international students learn the differences between their own cultures and the host country's culture by interacting with host nationals. Although this is well known, my work focuses on how international students also interact with fellow international students from other countries. Living in a foreign country does not necessarily mean that international students always interact with the host nationals; there are always non-native speakers of the target language around the sojourners. In his model, Shaules (2007) does not discuss this type of interaction in detail. Thus, I am concerned with what international students gain in such multinational interactions, and how do such interactions fit with the Deep Culture Model.

Friendships of International Students

Researchers have reported the difficulty of international students in making and maintaining contact with native speakers (e.g., Byram & Feng, 2006; Wilkinson, 1998). International students often find themselves isolated, resulting in progressively fewer interactions with native speakers. Shockingly, researchers have even demonstrated that some international students made no meaningful social connections with locals during their study abroad (e.g., Meier & Daniels, 2011).

One reason for the difficulty of international students in interacting with locals includes language proficiency, particularly oral communication. International students in their co-national clique naturally speak in their native language, and can avoid the shame and anxiety that could come from using the target language, which they are still in the process of developing. But this reasoning for avoiding the use of the target language does not explain another frequently observed phenomenon regarding international students in English-speaking countries. That is, although international students often have a hard time forming close relationships or interacting with locals, they form and develop bonds relatively easily with fellow international students even from outside their own countries (e.g.,

Kobayashi, 2006; Rosenthal, Russell, & Thomson, 2007). This phenomenon is intriguing because in order to communicate with most other international students, they need to speak in their lingua franca, English, regardless of their English language proficiency. Yet interactions among international students take place as often as, or more often than, interactions between international students and locals (Constantine & Sue, 2005). The shared foreignness to the language and culture of their host community creates attachments among international students to one another.

For instance, Rosenthal et al. (2007) showed that in Australia, East Asian international students tended to develop bonds with those from similar cultural backgrounds, and this tendency was stronger for them than it was for non-East Asian international students. In one study on Japanese students studying in Canada, Kobayashi (2006) demonstrated Japanese students' comfort with Korean students. The racial, cultural, and geographic proximity could have contributed to such feelings of attachment between Japanese and Korean students. Furthermore, some Japanese and Korean international students in the study reported being discriminated against by European international students (Kobayashi, 2010). In this process, Japanese students created the sense of a "we East Asians" identity with Korean students vis-à-vis non-East Asian international student groups, such as Europeans.

The border between Asians and Europeans is observed in other studies as well. For instance, Brown (2009) demonstrated that interactions among international students took place within regional groups: the Asian "camp" and the European "camp." Each group distanced themselves from the other and strengthened their collective identities. Clearly, cross-cultural interactions were based on a choice rather than an automatic response to the culturally diverse environment in which international students lived.

Benefits of Multinational Friendships

Research on multinational friendships is scarce compared to those on co- national friendships and internationals-locals friendships (Young et al., 2002). The three types of bonds described by Bochner, Hutnik, and Furnham (1985) are the ones among co-nationals, international students and locals, and multinationals. In their work, Bochner et al. argued that multinational bonds were least valuable because such bonds provide neither a source for learning the culture of the host community (as locals would), nor emotional support (as co-nationals would). Nevertheless, it is the most commonly observed pattern of friendships experienced by international students (Bochner et al., 1985).

Multinational friendships are undeniably valuable. As Hendrickson et al. (2011) summarized, for one, they would function as a networking process, and international students can benefit from expanded friendships even after they complete the program and leave the study abroad site. Additionally, international students can create a support network by sharing linguistic and cultural difficulties.

One of the most commonly-noted advantages of multinational friendships is that international students are able to learn about each of their cultures besides that of their host community. But surprisingly few studies have investigated what is involved in such intercultural learning experiences. Some researchers have identified "product" gains as a result of intercultural learning. Learning culture as product refers to gaining concrete knowledge about cultural objects and practices in other cultures. Examples would be learning about food, languages, etiquette, and customs of a particular culture.

Another type of intercultural learning outcomes is cognitive changes. Examples of these gains include open-mindedness, empathy, and eradication of stereotypes (Lee, 2006; Schartner, 2015). International students can acquire these qualities through learning the concrete cultural objects and practices. International students compare and contrast their cultures and enjoy finding differences and similarities

(Lee, 2006), and in this process, they question and revise their knowledge about the cultures of their multinational friends (Schartner, 2015). This echoes what Shaules (2007) emphasizes in his discussions on the tenets of deep culture learning.

Intercultural Learning as a Community of Practice

The existence of multiple points of comparison and contrast in intercultural learning is one of the best benefits of multinational friendships. For instance, Lee (2006) demonstrated that international students not only discussed each other's cultures, but also engaged in intersubjective explorations of the host culture in which they lived; international students in the U.S. often had discussions not only about their own cultures but also about American culture.

This model of learning resembles what Shaules (2007) calls the "triangulation" (p. 224) model of cultural comparison. He argues that having intercultural experiences in multiple cultural settings would make it possible for learners to be aware of a range of cultural differences, whereas having experiences with only two cultural settings would merely give a binary cultural comparison. But importantly, here Shaules is talking about having experiences in multiple "settings," or locations; he is not talking about having multiple "perspectives." I argue that having access to multiple perspectives is as helpful as having physical contact with the setting in order to develop one's intercultural understanding. Interactions with others are, in fact, an important source of learning through which international students can gain input to become aware of differences and similarities between cultures.

For international students studying in the U.S., the main culture they are supposedly exposed to is American culture. However, in reality, international students often create a community of their own with those from other countries and develop their global perspectives, rather than create a community with the host nationals (e.g., Montgomery & McDowell, 2009), speaking English as a lingua franca. Such a community may be referred to as a "third culture" (Casmir,

1999) or an international "community of practice" (Lave & Wenger, 1991).

International Community of Practice

Although not many, some researchers (e.g., Baker, 2009; Montgomery & McDowell, 2009) have discussed the international community of practice model, using the community of practice model that was originally proposed by Lave and Wenger (1991). From this perspective, participation is significant to acquisition of knowledge and skills, and the critical elements to learning include: the existence of multiple groups within the community, activities that they engage in together, and shared resources. Individuals generally start with "legitimate peripheral participation," as "newcomers" to the community of practice. But with the knowledge passed on by the "old-timers" and experiences shared together, the "newcomers" eventually achieve full participation.

In a study of friendships among international students, Montgomery and McDowell (2009) demonstrated that international students created their own community for academic success and emotional support. Three elements of learning were found in an international community of practice: multiple nationalities (i.e., the existence of multiple groups within the community), studying and extracurricular activities (i.e., activities that they engage in together), and common topics of conversations and shared history as international students (i.e., shared resources). Montgomery and McDowell (2009) concluded that what they saw among their participants seemed to match the functional and supportive characteristic of the community of practice as Lave and Wenger originally proposed.

I suggest that such "learning" that takes place among international students in their community of practice can be that of intercultural learning. Through interactions, such students can learn about each others' past and present to find similarities and differences. Becoming aware of these factors can lead to the development of cognitive empathy. Moreover, by being questioned by fellow multinational friends, international students also have opportunities to reflect on their own culture. I will revisit this last point in a later section in this chapter.

Until today, few researchers have investigated intercultural learning among international students as a part of a community of practice. How such learning takes place remains topic for future research. In addition, examining the "culture" of such a learning community would be interesting. In the case of study abroad in the U.S., even though the main culture of the living environment may be "American," the particular "culture" that exists within an international student community is not necessarily so. International students may define and view the "culture" they create together in unique ways.

Why Multinational Friendships Can Be a Source of Deep Culture Learning

If we define intercultural learning as accumulating knowledge "about" a particular culture, the source of such learning seems to be limited in multinational interactions compared to interacting with host nationals "in" the host community because the context of living itself has cultural symbols that may be used as a source of cultural learning. "Cultural symbols" could be physical or non-physical objects that convey meanings in a particular society, such as buildings, food, religions, and gestures. For instance, by living in Japan, sojourners may have opportunities to eat traditional Japanese cuisine, or *washoku*. A genre of food that has been recently added to UNESCO's list of Intangible Cultural Heritage, *washoku* is characterized by freshness of ingredients (chefs often use seasonal vegetables), mild seasonings (so that people can enjoy the inherent flavor of the ingredients), and delicate arrangement when served ("Washoku," 2014). In these ways, *washoku* can be considered a cultural symbol that represents both the respect the Japanese hold for nature as well as the emphasis they place on detail and precision.

However, in the Deep Culture Model, the focus is on the learning process and on cognitive changes. In other words, the indicator of deep cultural learning is one's perspective toward different cultures rather than how much one knows about particular cultures. Therefore, what matters is the opportunities to reflect on implicit cultural differences between oneself and another, which leads to the development of cognitive empathy. An individual needs to be located in the environment to receive direct exposure to cultural symbols, but opportunities to reflect on implicit cultural differences can occur between anyone in any environment.

In this way, interacting with international students must be just as meaningful as interacting with host nationals in order to achieve deep culture learning. As a matter of fact, Shaules (2007) states that:

> The reason that short-term stays in another cultural community are not deep is not because sojourners are not exposed to objects of symbolic importance, it is because they are not required to adapt to the hidden differences implied by those objects. (p. 189)

This argument implies that exposure to cultural objects and immersion in specific cultural contexts are not necessarily significant in deep culture learning. Rather, it is the moments to reflect on cultural differences that make differences in the development of deep cultural understanding.

Deep Culture Learning through English

Many languages have relatively clear "corresponding cultures." For instance, in general, German language is associated with German culture. However, as Shaules (2007) briefly states, English does not have a particular, single corresponding culture in today's globalizing society, and English is referred to by multiple names, such as "English as a lingua franca." Intercultural learning for international students in the U.S., therefore, may mean something different from those involving other world languages and cultures that have specific correspondences. Considering the unique position of English, I present the concept of cosmopolitanism, which may help us better understand intercultural learning among international students during study abroad.

Language-Culture Connection

Researchers have discussed the importance of language-culture connections. A good command of language is considered a significant part of learning the culture of the language community (Byram et al., 2001; Damen, 1987; Kramsch, 1998; Matsumoto et al., 2001, Olson & Kroeger, 2001). On the other hand, inclusion of a cultural component has become a significant part of curricula in world language education these days. Shaules (2007) summarizes the relationship between languages and cultures: "Language is a symbolic system that represents the conceptualization of the values and worldview of its speakers and speaking a language implies membership...of a community of speakers of that language" (p. 101). According to Shaules, the concept of language-culture connection was originally presented by Edward Sapir and Benjamin Lee Whorf (Carrol, 1956; Sapir, 1921). The Sapir-Whorf hypothesis articulates that the language an individual speaks inevitably influences his or her cognition, which further affects the way he or she views the world. It happens because each language has its particular way of categorizing objects and meanings (Shaules, 2007).

Knowing and using the language is also related to forming relationships with other individuals in the community (Shaules, 2007). Through the use of language, an individual is able to interact with others in the community to learn their cultures. In this way, language use is connected with cultures. Indeed, Shaules (2007) states that relationship building and interactions are crucial meeting points for language education and intercultural education.

Language-Culture Connection for English

The connection between language and culture certainly seems self-evident. However, as Shaules notes, such a relationship is questionable for English; English has a lot of corresponding cultures and countries. English today is referred to variously as World

Englishes, a lingua franca, an international language, or an intercultural language, all of which imply the global nature of English as a communication tool across nations and cultures. English is no longer solely associated with countries traditionally known as English-speaking countries, such as the U.S., the U.K., and Australia, which are categorized in the inner circle in the model of World Englishes by Kachru (see Kachru, 1985 for details). In this sense, the notion of English-speakers and cultures associated with English-speakers are not clearly defined, which is to say that they are abstract.

English as a Bridge

English as a lingua franca is defined as "a way of referring to communication in English between speakers with different first languages" (Seidlhofer, 2005, p. 339). The definition of English as a lingua franca matches the way international students use English with other international students, as well as with native speakers of English. From this perspective, some researchers perceive speakers of English as a lingua franca as those who possess different "linguacultures" (Jenkins, 2006, p. 164), rather than categorizing these speakers according to the native or non-native status. English as a lingua franca does not have a single discrete culture that corresponds to it, because speakers bring each of their linguacultures to the moment of communication every time (Baker, 2009).

A similar perspective is found in Sifakis's (2004) presentation of English as an intercultural language. For Sifakis, English as an intercultural language has its emphasis on the occasion in which it is used, rather than the identity of its speakers. He argues that, from this perspective, English is "owned" equally by its non-native as well as its native speakers. In describing English as an intercultural language, Sifakis contrasts it with English as an international language, which tends to distinguish the variations of Englishes by the type of speakers, based on "norms." By contrast, the view of English as an intercultural language rather embraces the varieties. By using English, it becomes possible for an individual to communicate with people whose mother languages he or she does not understand. English language is a bridge between people. This view of English is compatible with cosmopolitanism. Development of cosmopolitan perspectives seems to correspond to the acquisition of cognitive empathy, which is a major part of the deep intercultural learning suggested in Shaules's model.

Cosmopolitanism

This view of English as a lingua franca and an intercultural language seems oddly similar to cosmopolitanism, a concept that can help us rethink Shaules's Deep Culture Model. Cosmopolitanism refers to the consciousness in which individuals have positive attitudes toward those who are different from others (Shueth & O'Loughlin, 2008). Under cosmopolitanism, diversity is seen as an opportunity for self-enrichment; it is the source of knowledge (Mora & Golovatina-Mora, 2011). When individuals have developed a cosmopolitan view, they have a readiness to accept differences between themselves and others. Possessing a cosmopolitan perspective is an asset because it enables individuals to navigate international spaces and be successful at negotiating transcultural exchanges. In this sense it is a form of both social and cultural capital (see Bourdieu, 1986 for details.).

Learning and using English can facilitate learners' cosmopolitan attitudes toward globalizing societies. English as a lingua franca enables people to communicate across national boundaries, cultures, ethnicities, and races. By using English, people from different linguistic and cultural backgrounds can benefit from deepening the understanding toward each other's and their own cultures, which helps individuals to acquire a cosmopolitan perspective. Use of English from this perspective matches with cosmopolitanism.

Furthermore, acquiring a cosmopolitan perspective echoes the process of deep intercultural learning presented by Shaules. In the illustration of the Deep Culture Model, Shaules emphasizes the development of cognitive empathy. Development of cognitive empathy requires deepening the understanding toward each other through interactions by following the steps of resistance, acceptance, and adjustment. On the other hand, cosmopolitan perspectives involve a willingness to accept differences, which resembles cognitive empathy. Therefore, deep intercultural learning and the development of cosmopolitan perspectives seem to follow similar processes.

Critiques of Cosmopolitanism

However, there are critiques of cosmopolitanism that should be attended to before moving onto the next part of this chapter. One critique is that, from a political perspective, creating a universal community is difficult and too idealistic given the existing boundaries between nation-states. In addition, cosmopolitanism might denigrate the group formations and their memberships (Calhoun, 2003) by favoring the world-state. Yet there is a counter-critique for this view, emphasizing the diversity within such "groups" and lack of solidarity in interests among group members (Kleingeld & Brown, 2014).

From the perspective of moral and developmental psychology, cosmopolitanism lacks an understanding of the significance of attachment to a particular nation or culture. Some researchers argue that individuals must have a solid attachment to a particular place in order to appreciate and embrace their participation in a larger moral community (Kleingeld & Brown, 2014). This seems to imply that it is not possible to maintain attachments to a specific place and culture while also having a sense of a membership in a cosmopolitan society. I revisit this dichotomy in the following section.

The Culture of Origin

Shaules's (2007) Deep Culture Model does not discuss what happens to sojourners' views of their own cultures in the process of learning the deep culture of the host community. Below, I discuss how the perceptions toward one's culture of origin might change in the process of learning, and whether it is possible for international students to develop deep intercultural understanding while retaining identification with their culture of origin.

Views toward Culture of Origin

Intercultural learning allows an individual reflect on his or her own culture because one way to learn about the new, unfamiliar culture is to compare and contrast the concepts, values, and objects of the new culture with one's own. Therefore, I argue that the Deep Culture Model could have another layer for developing awareness toward one's own culture.

In the first place, Thinking about what a deeper understanding toward one's own culture involves is crucial. This is about becoming aware of the "deep" culture of one's own. To review, deep culture refers to "unconscious meanings, values, norms, and hidden assumptions" (Shaules, 2007, p. 11). Because cultural values that individuals grow up with are so natural to themselves, and they have accepted such implicit cultural values without thinking about them, it requires some effort to become aware of what the deep culture is, moving from the state of unconsciously accepting them to consciously reflecting on them. Such learning opportunities may arise when international students ask questions to each other about unfamiliar behaviors and concepts associated with them. These questions require international students to think about what they (naturally) do, and it might lead to becoming aware of their deep culture, letting them acquire meta-level perspectives on their own cultures.

One example is the "cultural onion" (Trompenaars & Hampden-Turner, 1998) of one's own culture. In this bull's eye-shaped model, there are three "bands": (a) the outermost band represents explicit behaviors; (b) the next band represents norms and values; and (c) the center, basic assumptions. To illustrate, Shaules uses an example of bowing by the Japanese. Bowing may seem odd to those who are not used to doing so. The explicit behavior is (a) the act of bowing; and the idea behind it is (b) to show respect to people (i.e., value) or to follow others' patterns of behavior (i.e., norms). But it is difficult to answer the question of why it is important to show respect, meaning

(c) the basic assumptions (that are foundational to the (a) explicit behavior and (b) associated values and norms).

Taking Perspectives of Others

Learning about one's own culture may also involve taking the perspective of other people to look at one's culture from a different angle. "Culture" is a construct that is crafted by a number of people in different positions. In other words, there is no set definition for a particular culture, because how it is defined depends on the perspective of who defines it. For instance, the way an American defines "Japanese culture" might differ from how a Japanese person defines it. Through interactions, an international student may become aware of the existence of perspectives held by host nationals and fellow international students toward her or his culture.

A study by Dolby (2004) on American students' view of their national identities provides a hint to think about this learning process. For one, Dolby (2004) demonstrated that participants' national identity as Americans became activated through study abroad; before study abroad, they did not consciously think of their identities as Americans. Additionally, participants came to realize that their "American-ness" was constructed not only by themselves but also by individuals from outside the United States.

Attachment to the Culture of Origin

Shaules (2007) argues that one of the outcomes of deep intercultural learning was the development of an ability to recognize and accept cultural frameworks other than one's own as valid. If this is true, then is maintaining identification with one's culture of origin an indication of "superficial" cultural learning? In his book, Shaules (2007) discusses two opposing perspectives on cultural realities. On the one hand, Sparrow (2000) presented the argument that successful intercultural learners show an attachment to a particular cultural community. In her study, her participants always used a specific cultural framework relate their international experiences. On the other hand, for Bennett (1993), successful intercultural learners will not belong to any cultural community, and stand outside all cultural frameworks.

It seems like these two perspectives occupy opposite sides of a continuum. However, I would argue that it is possible to simultaneously identify with a particular cultural community while having a neutral stance toward different cultures by having no primary affiliation. That is to say, identification with a specific culture does not necessarily mean that individuals are aware of only one cultural framework; they may be aware of the existence of multiple cultural frameworks, yet choose a cultural framework that they want to use to see the world. While having no primary affiliation with a particular culture, a sojourner may adopt a specific cultural frame to see the world in a specific context.

In this sense, Sparrow's view and Bennett's view are not necessarily on a continuum.

Local Attachment and Global Embrace

Similar discussions are found in terms of national identities and cosmopolitanism.

For instance, Nussbaum (1996) has argued that it was necessary to abandon attachments to a particular country in order to nurture identities that embrace the whole global community. On the other hand, Robbins (1998) has suggested that individuals with cosmopolitan attitudes did not have to give up on having local attachments; individuals are able to cherish national loyalties as well as non-national, universal identities (see also Roudometof, 2005; Tomlinson, 1999).

However, to date, there are few studies in which researchers investigated international students' sense of attachment to both the local and global communities. One exception is a study on American students and their national identities by Dolby (2004). She found a type of identity among her participants, which was "affirming and often displaying membership in a nation and a national imaginary, while at the same time questioning the assumed equivalence of state and nation" (p. 151). She called this a "postnational" identity, which was characterized with multiplicity and openness, being simultaneously local and global.

Changes in perspectives on one's culture of origin, as well as embracing the local and global communities as a sign of deep intercultural learning with a cosmopolitan perspective, may be informed by the concept of imagined community.

Imagined Community

An imagined community refers to a group of individuals who are linked to each other through the power of imagination rather than through mere geography. Anderson (1991), who originally proposed this well-known term, argued that nations are imagined communities, "because the members of even the smallest nation will never know most of their fellow-members, meet them, or even hear of them, yet in the minds of each lives the image of their communion" (p. 6). Imagination is the strategy that individuals employ in the age of globalization in order to understand themselves (Appadurai, 1996).

International students who achieve deep intercultural learning during study abroad may come to realize that definitions of cultures and borders between nations are indeed ambiguous, or imaginary. In addition, by developing a cosmopolitan view toward cultures, cultural and national borders may become blurrier, creating an even broader imagined community of global citizens.

For example, what a Japanese student imagines to be an essential part of Japanese culture, such as an emphasis on education and family, might in fact also be found in Jewish, Iranian, and other cultures. Moreover, the same student might also realize that what is widely thought of as Japanese culture today has roots in other cultures. For instance, Japanese comics (*manga*) has been deeply influenced by Western comics, despite the fact that many people believe *manga* to be something uniquely Japanese. One of the leading scholars of Japanese *manga*, Jaqueline Berndt, writes "what is globally known today as 'manga style' is, in fact, the result of intercultural exchange" (Berndt, 2008, p. 299). When the image of one's culture of origin becomes complexified, one realizes that culture is always imagined.

Furthermore, the concept of imagined community is compatible with the view of English as a lingua franca, as mentioned earlier. In the past, the imagined community of English-speakers might have been limited to those from countries that are traditionally known as English- speaking counties, such as the U.S. and the U.K. However, in today's ever- increasingly globalizing society, the community of English speakers is so diverse and extensive that English speakers can create and retain their bonds only through imagination.

Symbolic Interactionism as a Theoretical Framework for the Deep Culture Model

In the development of his Deep Culture Model, Joseph Shaules (2007) examined many intercultural learning approaches that had been suggested by other researchers, such as Bennett (1993), Sparrow (2000), and Trompenaars and Hampden-Turner (1998). However, there is no overarching theoretical framework that can inform the Deep Culture Model. Here, I suggest that Shaules's Deep Culture Model can be theoretically framed through symbolic interactionism. Symbolic interactionism is a socio-psychological perspective that has roots in several antecedent schools of thought, such as Evolutionism, Scottish Moralists, German Idealism, and Pragmatism. Symbolic interactionism emphasizes micro-level, actual behavior and emotions experienced in everyday life. Negotiations of meaning, perspective-taking (i.e., viewing oneself from another's perspective), subjective experiences, and creations of social realities are the main principles of symbolic interactionism. Some of the key ideas related to symbolic interactionism seem to facilitate understanding of the Deep Culture Model, which "requires an ongoing interaction with [his or] her new social environment" (Shaules, 2007, p. 137).

Meanings

Deep learning focuses on meanings (Tochon, 2010). Meanings are, as a matter of fact, one of the keywords in Shaules's (2007) Deep Culture Model; he has adopted Hall's (1959) view of "culture as a system of shared meaning and expectations" (Shaules, 2007, p. 35). Therefore, in his model, the process of deep intercultural learning revolves around learning meanings of concepts and actions. Meanings are revised through intercultural interactions with others, and that is how sojourners move between levels of resistance, acceptance, and adaptation. In addition, as stated earlier, each language has its unique system for categorizing objects and their meanings (Shaules, 2007). Therefore, language learning and deep learning of meanings in a particular culture during study abroad are closely related.

These perspectives on meanings are compatible with the symbolic interactionist view of meanings. Any action a human being takes depends on the meaning or meanings that she or he attaches to the goal of that action. In symbolic interactionist views, individuals inhabit the worlds that they create by using their own interpretations; and by exercising their interpretations, they construct their behaviors actively (Denzin, 2007; Reynolds, 1993). Additionally, the meanings people associate with objects, behavior, and concepts are considered as social products, generated and learned within social interactions. Meanings are always created in interactions.

Cognitive Empathy, Role-taking, and Reflexivity

Development of cognitive empathy, or the ability to recognize multiple cultural perspectives as valid and shift between them, is a part of deep intercultural learning. Being able to stand outside one's own culture and look at it from the perspective of those who are from other cultural backgrounds requires an individual to have an ability to role-play.

The ability to role-take is foundational to human interactions (Mead, 1934). During interactions, individuals mentally place themselves in the shoes of others, and see themselves objectively from the viewpoint of others. Furthermore, individuals are able to take the perspective of not only the specific person(s) they interact with, but also of a "generalized other," or an imagined set of attitudes held by other individuals in the society (Mead, 1934). People adjust their behaviors by taking the role or the perspectives of generalized others (Turner & Stets, 2005).

In particular, an ability to role-take regarding oneself is referred to as reflexivity. Reflexivity is one's ability to reflect on what he or she does, and his or her awareness of the influence of such behavior (Frame, 2014). It involves "conversations" with oneself; it is the moment of asking oneself questions about what a particular matter means to him or her. Standing outside one's own perspectives to scrutinize his or her way of thinking can give an individual a new way of perceiving the world, and in this sense, it is similar to cognitive empathy. As Shaules (2007) has stated, having cognitive empathy is to understand "that one's point of view is a product of one's experience" (p. 140).

Conclusion

In this chapter, I presented ideas associated with international students' deep intercultural learning during their study abroad in the U.S. In doing so, I touched upon topics that were not discussed in details in Joseph Shaules's (2007) illustration of the Deep Culture Model. My intention was not to present concrete research ideas or findings from empirical research, but rather to show multiple possibilities for expanding the deep intercultural learning model that Shaules has proposed. First, I argued that multinational friendships could provide opportunities for deep intercultural learning among international students. I also presented the argument that cosmopolitanism could successfully capture the nature of English used in deep intercultural learning during study abroad. Next, I discussed that it would be possible to have a simultaneous attachment to local and global communities, and mentioned that the concept of imagined community might explain the development of such an attitude. Finally, I proposed symbolic interactionism as an overarching theoretical framework for the Deep Culture Model, emphasizing its focus on meanings and human interactions.

Given the dearth of research conducted on the topic, more studies are warranted to investigate what international students gain through interactions among their community of international students, particularly in terms of learning their own deep cultures and the culture of their host community.

Deep intercultural learning requires individuals to reflect on where they have come from, what they know, what they learn, what they believe, and what they are becoming. This they do through resisting, accepting, and adapting to implicit and explicit cultural demands of the new context. In this perspective, intercultural learning seems to deal greatly with reflecting on one's self. Studies concerning the nexus of the Deep Culture Model and identity development theories might be a direction for further exploration.

Ultimately, each context has different conditions for deep culture learning. For instance, in this chapter I focused on the fact that the U.S. attracts international students from all over the world and interactions among these students are active. I also discussed that English, through which international students engage in intercultural learning in the U.S., does not have a specifically corresponding culture the way that Chinese language and culture are profoundly associated with one another. Although the Deep Culture Model is used effectively to explain the experiences of sojourners in many countries in Shaules's (2007) work, I suggest that it is nevertheless meaningful to consider how the Deep Culture Model fits in a specific environment given its unique social, linguistic, historic, and political background.

References

Anderson, B. (1991). *Imagined communities: Reflections on the origin and spread of nationalism*. London: Verso.

Appadurai, A. (1996). *Modernity at large cultural dimensions of globalization*. Minneapolis: University of Minnesota Press.

Baker, W. (2009). The cultures of English as a lingua franca. *TESOL Quarterly, 43*(4), 567-592.

Bennett, M. J. (1993). Towards ethnorelativism: A developmental model of intercultural sensitivity. In R.M. Paige (Ed.), *Education for the intercultural experience*. Yarmouth, ME: Intercultural Press.

Berndt, J. (2008). Considering manga discourse: Location, ambiguity, historicity. In M. MacWilliams (Ed.), *Japanese visual culture: Explorations in the world of manga and anime* (pp. 295-310). Armonk, NY: M.E. Sharpe.

Bochner, S., Hutnik, N., & Furnham, A. (1985). The friendship patterns of overseas and host students in an Oxford student residence. *The Journal of Social Psychology, 125*(6), 689-694.

Bourdieu, P. (1986) The forms of capital. In J. Richardson (Ed.), *Handbook of theory and research for the sociology of education* (pp. 241-258). New York: Greenwood.

Brown, L. (2009). Worlds Apart: The Barrier Between East and West. *Journal of International and Intercultural Communication, 2*, 240-259.

Byram, M., & Feng, A. (Eds.). (2006). *Living and studying abroad: Research and practice*. Clevedon, UK: Multilingual Matters.

Byram, M., Nichols, A., & Stevens, D. (2001). *Developing intercultural competence in practice*. New York: Multilingual Matters.

Calhoun, C. (2003). "Belonging" in the cosmopolitan imaginary. *Ethnicities, 3*, 531-53.

Carroll, J. B. (Ed.). (1956). *Language, thought, and reality: Selected writings of Benjamin Lee Whorf*. Cambridge: M.I.T. Press.

Casmir, F. L. (1999). Foundations for the study of intercultural communication based o a third culture building model. *International Journal of Intercultural Relations, 23*(1), 91-116.

Constantine, M. G. & Sue, D. W. (2005). The American psychological association's guidelines on multicultural education, training, research, practice, and organizational psychology. In M.G. Constantine, D.W. Sue (Eds.), *Strategies for building multicultural competence* (pp. 3-15). Hoboken, NJ: John Wiley & Sons.

Damen, L. (1987). *Culture Learning: The Fifth Dimension on the Language Classroom*. Reading, MA: Addison-Wesley.

Denzin, N. K. (2007). *Symbolic interactionism and cultural studies: The politics of interpretation*. Wiley-Blackwell.

Dolby, N. (2004). Encountering an American self: Study abroad and national identity. *Comparative Education Review, 48*(2), 150-173.

Frame, A. (2014). Reflexivity and self-presentation in multicultural encounters: Making sense of self and other. In J. Byrd Clark, F. Dervin (Eds.), *Reflexivity in language and intercultural education: rethinking multilingualism and interculturality* (pp. 81-99). New York: Routledge.

Hall, E. T. (1959). *The silent language*. New York: Anchor Books.

Hendrickson, B., Rosen, D., & Aune, R. K. (2011). An analysis of friendship networks, social connectedness, homesickness, and satisfaction levels of international students. *International Journal of Intercultural Relations, 35*(3), 281-295.

Jenkins, J. (2007). *English as a lingua franca: Attitude and identity*. Oxford: Oxford University Press.

Kachru, B. B. (1985). Standards, codification and sociolinguistic realism: the English language in the outer circle. In R. Quirk and H.G. Widdowson (Eds.), *English in the world: Teaching and learning the language and literatures* (pp. 11-30). Cambridge: Cambridge University Press.

Kleingeld, P. & Brown, E. (2014). Cosmopolitanism. In E. N. Zalta (Ed.), *The Stanford encyclopedia of philosophy*. Retrieved from: http://plato.stanford.edu/archives/fall2014/entries/cosmopolitanism/

Kobayashi, Y. (2006). Inter-ethnic relations between ESL students. *Journal of Multilingual and Multicultural Development, 27*(3), 181- 195. Available from Iwate University Repository http://ir.iwateu.ac.jp/dspace/handle/10140/1917 [re-accessed June 30, 2014].

Kobayashi, Y. (2010). Discriminatory attitudes toward intercultural communication in domestic and overseas contexts. *Higher Education, 59*(3), 323-333.

Kramsch, C. (1998). *Language and culture*. Oxford: Oxford University Press.

Lave, J. & Wenger, E. (1991). *Situated learning: legitimate peripheral participation*. Cambridge University Press.

Lee, P. (2006). Bridging cultures: understanding the construction of relational identity in intercultural friendship. *Journal of Intercultural Communication Research, 35*(1), 3-22.

Matsumoto, D., LeRoux, J. A., Ratzlaff, C., Tatani, H., Uchida, H., Kim, C., et al. (2001). Development and validation of a measure of intercultural adjustment potential in Japanese sojourners: The Intercultural Adjustment Potential Scale (ICAPS). *International Journal of Intercultural Relations, 25*, 483-510.

Mead, G. H. (1934). *Mind, self, and society*. Chicago: University of Chicago Press.

Meier, G., & Daniels, H. (2011). "Just not being able to make friends": Social interaction during the year abroad in modern foreign language degrees. *Research Papers in Education, 28*(2), 212-238. doi:10.1080/02671522.2011.629734

Montgomery, C., & McDowell, L. (2009). Social networks and the international student experience. *Journal of Studies in International Education, 13*(4), 455-466.

Mora R. A. & Golovátina-Mora, P. (2011, August). *Bilingualism – A bridge to cosmopolitanism?* Keynote Presentation at the ELT Conference 2011, Medellín, Colombia. Retrieved from http://eric.ed.gov/?q=author%3a%22mora%22&ff1=autMora%2c+Ra%C3%BAl+A.&id=ED547646

Nussbaum, M. (1996). Patriotism and cosmopolitanism. In M. Nussbaum et al. (Eds.), *For love of country: Debating the limits of patriotism* (pp. 2-20). Boston: Beacon Press.

Olson, C. L. & Kroeger, K. R. (2001). Global competency and intercultural sensitivity. *Journal of Studies in International Education, 5*, 116-137.

Pennycook, A. (1998). *English and the discourses of colonialism*. New York: Routledge.

Pennycook, A. (2007). *Global Englishes and transcultural flows*. New York: Routledge.

Phillipson, R. (1992). *Linguistic imperialism*. Oxford: Oxford University Press.

Ramsden, P. (2003). *Learning to teach in higher education*. London: Routledge Falmer.

Reynolds, L. (1993). *Interactionism: Exposition and critique* (3rd ed.). Dix Hills, NY: General Hall.

Robbins, B. (1998). Introduction part I: Actually existing cosmopolitanism. In P. Cheah and B. Robbins (Eds.), *Cosmopolitics: Thinking and feeling beyond the nation* (pp. 1-19). Minneapolis: University of Minnesota Press.

Rosenthal, D. A., Russell, J., & Thomson, G. (2007). Social connectedness among international students at an Australian university. *Social Indicators Research, 84* (1), 71-82.

Sapir, E. (1921). *Language an introduction to the study of speech*. San Diego: Harcourt Brace & Company.

Schartner, A. (2015). 'You cannot talk with all of the strangers in a pub': a longitudinal case study of international postgraduate students' social ties at a British university. *Higher Education, 69* (2), 225-241.

Schulzke, M. (2014). The prospects of global English as an inclusive language. *Globalizations, 11*(2), 225-238. DOI: 10.1080/14747731.2014.904173

Seidlhofer, B. (2005). English as a lingua franca. *ELT Journal, 59*(4), 339-341.

Shaules, J. (2007). *Deep culture: The hidden challenges of global living*. Clevedon: Multilingual matters.

Shueth, S. & O'Loughlin, J. (2008). Belonging to the world: Cosmopolitanism in geographic context. *Geoforum, 39*, 926-941.

Sifakis, N. (2004). Teaching EIL: teaching international or intercultural English: what teachers should know. *System, 32*(2), 237-250.

Sparrow, L. (2000). Beyond multicultural man: Complexities of identity. *International Journal of Intercultural Relations, 24* (2), 173-201.

Tagg, J. (2003). *The learning paradigm college*. Boston, MA: Anker.
Tochon, F. (2010). Deep education. *Journal for Educators, Teachers and Trainers JETT, 1*, 1-12.
Trompenaars, F., & Hampden-Turner, C. (1998). *Riding the waves of culture: Understanding cultural diversity in global business*. New York: McGraw-Hill.
Turner, J. H. & Stets, J. E. (2005). *The sociology of emotions*. Cambridge: Cambridge University Press.
Washoku designated UNESCO Intangible Cultural Heritage. (2014, January 14). Retrieved from http://www.nippon.com/en/genre/culture/l00052/
Weaver, G. R. (1993). Understanding and coping with cross-cultural adjustment stress. In M. Paige (Ed.), *Education for the intercultural experience* (pp. 137-168). Yarmouth, ME: Intercultural Press.
Wilkinson, S. (1998). Study abroad from the participants' perspective: A challenge to common beliefs. *Foreign Language Annals, 31*, 28-39.
Yeh, C. J., & Inose, M. (2003). International students' reported English fluency, social support satisfaction, and social connectedness as predictors of acculturative stress. *Counseling Psychology Quarterly, 16*, 15-28.
Young, T. J., Sercombe, P. G., Sachdev, I., Naeb, R., & Schartner, A. (2012). Success factors for international postgraduate students' adjustment: Exploring the roles of intercultural competence, language proficiency, social contact and social support. *European Journal of Higher Education, 3*, 151-171.

13.

Deep Symbolic Interactionism as a New Analytical Lens for Transdisciplinary Education

Harun Serpil
Anadolu University and University of Wisconsin-Madison
hserpil@anadolu.edu.tr

Abstract
Benefiting from semiotics and drawing on both Symbolic Interactionism (SI) and Deep Approach (DA), this chapter proposes a new analytical framework labeled as *Deep Symbolic Interactionism* (DSI) to fathom educational issues, and to gain (and enable) a deeper grasp of them. SI stands at the liminal junction of individual and society, providing the micro lens of the socio-cognitivity, but the DA magnifies the scope by taking it to the macro level, with its concern and deep care for the sustainability of the Earth, aiming to achieve equity for everybody, and using education as transformatory tool with a humble worldview by embracing all cultures towards overcoming colonialism without assuming superiority. Although the DSI lens proposed here is far from complete, it is hoped to provide a more holistic and transcendent cognitive tool for all educators interested in making sense of their specific teaching contexts situated within the increasingly singular world, and looking for ways to improve them.

Predicated on meaning, language and thought, the SI theory helps explain the symbolic interplay between the self and the society. People visualize how they look to another person, and create a "generalized other" (me), by incorporating responses and expectations from other people, attaching meaning to actions through interpreting symbols. Consciousness, mind, and self emerge as a result of the mental personal conversation and taking multiple interpersonal perspectives. Shaped by inspecting oneself from the community view, the self emerges in a dual layer: the "I," as the source of social creativity and innovation, and the "me," as the adopted set of others' behaviors, enabling social mechanisms to work on the self. The proposed DSI framework further develops this basic premise by adding a "deep" perspective, with the deeper dimensions of the "deep me" and "deep I". At its innermost level, the "deep I" signifies a part of creative self that strives for the ultimate transformation towards equity for all humanity. The "deep me", on the other hand, indicates a level of awareness of the interconnectedness with all other earthlings, a broader sense of the social "me" self with an inward view from the global cosmopolitan perspective. Thus, the self is able to transcend the complexity and meaninglessness of the immediate context, and can situate itself in a global position by pursuing a transdisciplinary purpose. DSI also offers a critical lens on the "selfish" self, ideally paving the way for the recognition that the egoistic ambitions divorced from the good of global society ultimately ends up in self-destructive behavior.

Symbolic Interactionism (SI)

Rooted in pragmatism and widely used in sociological analyses, SI is the process of social/self interaction in the formation of meanings for individuals. Blumer (1969) formulates SI as:

> ...human beings interpret or "define" each other's actions instead of merely reacting to each other's actions. Their "response" is not made directly to the actions of one another but instead is based on the meaning which they attach to such actions. Thus, human interaction is mediated by the use of symbols, by interpretation, or by ascertaining the meaning of one another's actions. This mediation is equivalent to inserting a process of interpretation between stimulus and response in the case of human behavior (p. 180, italics added).

Developed at the University of Chicago in the 1920s, the SI theory consists of three core principles: meaning, language and thought, which form the basis for a person's self and socialization. People are able to change the meanings and symbols they use in their interaction depending on their interpretation of the situation partly because they can interact with themselves, allowing them to assess the potential pros and cons of certain possible courses of action and then act on their selected decision (Ritzer, 2011). Humans act toward people and things according to the meanings that they give to those people or things. Language gives humans a means by which to negotiate meaning through symbols. As a mental conversation, thought modifies each individual's interpretation of symbols, which requires different points of view. People use the looking-glass self: they take the role of the other, imagining how we look to another person. Our generalized other is the sum of responses and expectations that we pick up from the people around us. We tend to give more weight to the views of significant others, like family members. When one imaginatively rehearses the likely outcomes of various future conducts in light of previous experiences before picking a single action, then one is engaging in "minded" behavior (Reynolds, 2003). This minded behavior is where positive changes can occur towards a more equitable society; depending on how aware and open you are to others, to becoming "enminded" with others' minds (or collective minds, as in culture). SI opposes the psychological reductionism of behaviorism and the structural determinism of more macro-oriented sociological theories such as structural functionalism. Its distinctive focus is on the mental capacities of actors and their relationship to interaction as a process; actors are seen as driven neither by internal psychological states nor large-scale structural forces. SI theory accords primacy to the social world because it is where consciousness, the mind, and the self emerge. With four dialectically related stages (impulse, perception, manipulation, and consummation), "act" is the most basic unit in SI. It involves at least two persons, and its basic mechanism is the gesture. People have the unique ability to have an inner conversation with themselves in assigning meaning to their situations. "The subjection of the act to the process of self-interaction imparts a career to the act – the act may be stopped, restrained, abandoned, resurrected, postponed, intensified, concealed, transformed, or redirected (Blumer, 1975, p.60)." Mental processes including reflective intelligence, consciousness, mental images, and meaning are part of the larger social process. The self is the ability to take oneself as an object, put oneself in the place of others, and to see oneself as others see it. The self develops through the play, the game and the final "generalized other" stages of childhood, with increasing awareness of other actors.

Seeing oneself from the community point of view is essential to the emergence of the self as well as of organized group activities. The self has two components: the "I," which is the creative aspect and the source of innovation in society, and the "me," which is the organized set of attitudes of others assumed by the actor, allowing social control to operate. Lacking a macro sense of society, SI treats social institutions as collective habits (Ritzer, 2011). Mead (1934) underscores the "I" because it is the basic source of novelty and personal values. It is what enables us to develop a unique personality and the realization of the self. Mead sees an evolutionary process in which people have progressed from a mostly "me" self toward a more "I" self. "It is through the 'me' that society dominates the individual. ...The 'me' allows the individual to live comfortably in the social world, while the 'I' makes change in society possible. The 'I' and the 'me' are thus part of the whole social process and allow both individuals and society to function more effectively (Ritzer, 2011, p.363)." Helen Keller's life story illustrates all aspects of Mead's theory because after becoming "capable of symbolic interaction, she not only possessed a 'me' as well as an 'I,' but she could also 'take the role of the other' and could internalize the 'general other,' allowing her to form her social self (Wallace & Wolf, 2005, p.205).

As the founder of SI, George H. Mead explains individual behavior within the context of the collectivity, in which others are always mentally present, even if they are physically absent. Society is possible because human beings act in cooperative behavior, which is itself made possible because people have the ability to take the point of view of the other(s), mentally place themselves in the position of the other. Each acting individual ascertains the intention of the acts of others, and then makes his/her own response on the basis of that intention, and can guide his/her own behavior to fit in with those lines of action. We are more or less seeing ourselves as others see us. We are unconsciously addressing ourselves as others address us and putting ourselves in the place of others and acting as others act (Mead, 1934). This gives us the relativism of self and ethnicity; one is not necessarily superior on another. Instead of strengthening ill-conceived stereotyping and biases, understanding self-construction of prejudices is the most important step towards destroying them.

SI is also supported by phenomenological thought, asserting that the objective world has no reality for humans, only subjectively-defined objects have meaning. We respond to the world in which we live by representing it, by constantly classifying and reclassifying it. We create a world of objects with abstract individual and social goals. We are born into an existing symbol system, with seemingly fixed objects, and predetermined meanings where the responses are variable and the actions are creative. The object itself has no value; humans load it with their values. For me, understanding how this is accomplished through symbols is helpful. For example, the word "cilantro" has deep symbolic cultural connotations for a Mexican, while for most Turks it is virtually unknown. Also, "tea" and "simit" (Turkish sesame bagel) have deep connotation for Turks, while they may mean nothing special for the US citizens, for example. Likewise, religious Christians would react very differently to a necklace in the shape of a cross, due to its sacred religious value, while a devout Muslim might see it from the opposite perspective. Another example is the symbolic power of the initials "T.C." which stand for "Turkish Republic." This has recently become a huge Facebook controversy when many Turkish people began adding "T.C." in front of their Facebook names, just to protest the new government policy of removing "T.C." from the signs of official public institutions. Evidently, "T." and "C." are more than just two letters for millions of Turks; they symbolize an essential part of their Turkish identity. More recently, the initials "F.G." has become a taboo in the public sphere, because it symbolizes Fethullan Gulen, a Muslim cleric living in Pennsylvania, the suspected mastermind of the coup in Turkey that was attempted on July 15, 2016. Many Turkish people have been applying to the DMV to remove the FG letters from their license plates.

Mead (1934) and Blumer (1969) present a critical paradigm to analyze how selves and others use and manage identities, appearances, strategic forms of discourse, and anticipations to respond to various social arrangements. Society is symbolic interaction with direction, memory, and people 'committed to its endurance' (Katovich & Maines, 2003). Unfortunately, "endurance" usually translates to the reproduction of the existing injustices. Such reproduction relies on the construction of "the generalized other" by individual members of a society, but it can be resisted and challenged: "To stand up to the generalized other, the individual must construct a still larger generalized other, composed not only from the present but also from the past and the future, and then respond to it (Ritzer, 2011, p.362)."

SI tries to achieve an in-depth, contextualized understanding of human behavior, with no ambition to predict and control it. SI underscores the social, emergent, and alterable characteristics of human behavior, and thus justifies melioristic social reconstruction (just like Deep Approach). In fact, this is not a simple process of "reconstruction," but creating a unique hybrid "third space" (Bhabha, 1990, Soja, 1996, 2004) by merging deconstruction and reconstruction. Using the Heideggerian dialectical process, this third space is used to reach something more than just thesis or anti-thesis, but more of a synthesis in the Gestaltian sense. Nominalism and realism meet in the trialectics of a third space to create an ontology of complexity (Tochon, 2013, personal communication). Interactionists believe that power and politics influence whose definitions of reality are accepted. Unlike postmodernists (who accept all reality claims as equally sound), interactionists do not avoid political responsibility by taking diversity in interpretation as a basis for judgmental relativism. They are ontological realists, but at the same time aware that the world is systematically interpreted through symbols of epistemological (social) constructivism. This is a crucial point because through symbolic systems, people are connected or separated by certain interpretive practices (Soja, 1996, 2004). The symbols that people use to communicate are interpreted through the lenses of particular situated cultural lenses, "corresponding to a set of internalized representations imbued with values that make communication possible" (Tochon & Azocar, 2003, p. 219). But how can we gain a deeper understanding of these representations? The next section focuses on answering this question through Deep Approach (DA), postulated by Tochon (2003, 2010, 2012).

Deep Approach (DA) To Education:

The humankind has increasingly become an invasive species; let alone recognizing and respecting diversity among human cultures, it denies the right to live for other species, moving toward an ecological uniformity, not unity. In reverse ratio to exponentially increased quantity of knowledge, people's inner identities have become more and more deprived and out of touch with the earth society. The humankind moved from a "mother-earth" paradigm, when its sustenance was based directly on earth, to a "more-earn" paradigm, where its relationship to earth is lost or rendered insignificant. The carrots-and-sticks paradigm devalues human life if it cannot be turned into cash. Human value hinges upon its profitable value. The industrial revolution destroyed the social aspect of humanity, the very fabric of being human. So now people are richer but not necessarily happier. Humans control the machine, but the dominant profit-based paradigm stays the same. It's time to notice that there's something above information and knowledge: wisdom. It's the internal voice in all of us, it is the conscience-wisdom that is rooted in knowledge-in-action. Happiness must be (re)connected to internal reasons rather than the external.

Drawing attention to this alarming problem, Tochon (2012) makes a case for a paradigm shift, for an integrative ontology, for the need for social and ecological action, and not taking the current world for granted. Equity in the sense of raising uniform people by subjecting them to same procedures and expecting standard outcomes does not work anymore. Shallow education, misinformation, and intensified work has led to a loss of deep values and disabled majority of people from reflection.

The Deep Approach (DA) views both subjects and objects as one with their ecosystem and recognizes unique characteristics, skills and aspirations of individuals. DA is transdisciplinary (Nicolescu, 2008, 2010) and stresses curricular interconnectedness and strives to address ontological dualism by synthesizing a wide range of disciplines such as ecology, ecopsychology, economy, politics, cross-cultural communication, psychology, and languages. It is strongly informed by semiotics, process philosophy and complexity theory (Tochon, 2010, 2012; Nicolescu, 2008). "Depth is plural, multivalent, and relative to the variety of microworlds that constitute our visions of reality as a space filled by the mind" (Tochon, 2012, p.286). The current system of education serves to reproduce the "social divide" and financial interests of a few, ignoring the costs on ecological systems. To turn the tide, Tochon (2010, 2012) urges for a "deep turn" in education. This "deep turn" means that regardless of their usefulness to humans, all life forms on Earth are inherently valuable and their diversity is a value in itself, which is not to be reduced by humans. Thus, aspiring for higher "cultural and spiritual consciousness," people must be educated to become aware of their moral obligations to earth and appreciate life quality, not higher standards of living and accumulation of wealth. The biosphere must be turned into a "semiosphere," where all living systems are valued members share meaningful signs. All educational endeavors need to revise their basic underlying instrumental reasoning to complete it with practical (how to act) and theoretical (how to appreciate) reason, to gain meaningful purpose and critical reflection, otherwise instrumentality alone will lead to irrational self-destruction. In fact, theoretical wisdom (*sophia*) should be the overarching tool governing others, not the other way around. When exponential knowledge doesn't match higher virtues and morals, social inequalities, injustices and oppression deepen, with catastrophic effects for everybody (Tochon, 2010, 2012). Science and education must shift from a predominantly quantitative orientation to a quality-oriented one, in which quality "prevails as evaluated on the scale of deep human values such as social justice, ecological respect, fair information and communication, truthfulness, care for others, intrinsically motivated effort towards improvement, non-interference unless requested" (Tochon, 2010, p.9). This shift to quality also brings a better appreciation of the aesthetics of life, a deeper reading of the seemingly superficial and meaningless because DA values dynamically interconnected human experiences by unifying theory, practical reflection and instrumental operation. It can be understood as a dot-linking process, a discovery of the hidden code within inexplicable "truths." It involves emotion and reason, signs and symbols, meaningfulness and situatedness (deixis). It deciphers embodied "epistemic beams of meaning" (Tochon, 2002) embedded in cultural worlds and identities that interact with each other and explicate the complexity of agency, which is never linearly or fully directed by structures or systems. Embedded within the surface layers of worldliness are deeper connections that lead to layers of interpretation that arise from a postulated primary world, a constantly re-visited and non-foundational foundation. Its understanding is not dualistic, and it is based on an integrated semiotics with moving signifiers, signified and situated interpretants that interact symbolically.

This type of poietic semiosis collaborates with inquiry through deep politics: while it imagines moral alternatives for the future, the inquiry paves the way for new possibilities for justice (Tochon, 2010).

Instead of competing and killing for limited resources, humankind must practice ' politics of consciousness' by moving out of the emotionally-driven consumerist trance (magical consciousness) and self-centered but uncritically obedient imperial consciousness, advancing toward a caring, ethical, collaborative socializing consciousness and appreciating diversity and relative truths by cultural consciousness. The culmination of this quest would be spiritual consciousness, the realization of multidimensional interconnectedness and complexity of holistic creation. The transition from cultural consciousness to spirituality can come from deep encounters with others, eventually resulting in the awareness that we are all connected. Cultural and spiritual consciousness help build a more just and peaceful society (Korten, 2007, Tochon, 2010).

Transcending paradigmatic dualism, the DA integrates modern and postmodern approaches at a higher third space, where both construction and deconstruction dialectically engage in a new and complex dynamic of trialectics. It then resituates ontological realism in relative ontology, which necessitates a relative realism of layered and overlapping realities, thus resolving the problem of syllogism. This dialectic and dialogical process is more important than the outcomes. This conceptual third space defines a "semiotic niche" where developmental psychology and sociocultural dimension become compatible. Since no one single theory can account for the complexities of practice, their complementary features can be used to avoid linear reasoning and define a theory that is self-adaptive, blended with "learning-in-action," and rooted in "life-action." Supporting what is proposed by the DA, and underscoring the importance of diverse funds of knowledge, famous multiculturalist Sleeter (2005, p.7) urges benefiting from diverse communities in fixing some US problems like the majority of Americans' insisting on communication be done in English, prizing excess materialism rather than spiritual development, discarding past insights and human wisdom about living sustainably with the earth, and feeling powerless to change society to make it more egalitarian and democratic.

Deweyan Reconstructionism and future dreams may be utopic, but symbolic language can still be positively used to stimulate self-determination, instead of its widespread political misuse for deception. Theoretical wisdom and wisdom of action must be the basis for reflective practice, and choosing appropriate instruments for higher humane goals (Tochon, 2010).

Tochon and Karaman (2009) suggest elimination of "colonial positioning" and "sense of superiority" to be able to have a common ground with others. This sense of superiority indicates a low level of social awareness. One way resolving this is communicating with 'the foreign within.' Through mediation and symbolic action, the representation of the *Other* becomes the representation of the *Self* as *Other*. Aspects of the *Other* are perceived as aspects of *Self*. Knowing the *Other* is restricted and shaped by how the *Self* defines itself. "Humans look at others through a broken mirror. The *Self* on the other side is different. The other "Self" does not have the same cultural reactions, and may be sensitive to other things and other values. Every tiny bit of difference may be screened and judged, until the perceiver perceives that he or she is judging, and is judgmental. This awareness of the spontaneous cross-cultural screening, of this judgmental process comes only at a point when self-awareness rises in such a way that it can perceive its values and commitments as being relative. ... At that point the judgmental process may be suspended. It never fully ceases, but it can be suspended" (Tochon & Karaman, 2009, p.146). This process of slowly growing out of prejudices is an indispensable part of deep cultural learning. This requires dialogical looking at the world through another lens, from immediate experience. This way of fundamental reflective questioning of prejudices in everyday practice, language and discourse is the foundation for caring. This ongoing critique focuses on what claims to validity are, who benefits from activities, and for what reasons, who guards the 'protected' knowledge, and how knowledge is commodified and used for oppression. These elements of oppression could be imposed worldviews shaping the cultural or ideological thinking processes. When a society does not solve inequity, it becomes a polarized society with self-destructive tendencies, with fear of otherness. The discriminated people may become persuaded that the arguments of the dominant class are valid, by internalizing the imposed qualifiers and accepting the conceptual moulds created for them.

Harmony has a major role in DA, because it is the code that creates a dialogue between worlds, across events and experiences, fulfilling homeostatic balance in the end. DA tries to capture human experience at a more profound level by trying to go beyond the superficial or secondary level and connecting it to the primary level. The connection between primary (the world you read this from) and secondary world (the world you read on paper) are sought in a third space. This connection in human experience is enabled by the transformative, deep education framework offered by DA.

Rooted in DA, deep education is thematic, transformational, bottom-up and eco-conscious, which focuses on voluntary participation, responsible citizenship, tackling real life problems, organized around meaningful conversations, self-reflective, strives to engage all levels of emotion, spirit, cognition and body, and is grounded in life grammar by crosscultural ' beams of meaning,' guided by process, not products (Tochon, 2002, 2012, Tochon & Hanson, 2003).

In this sense, discourse of education can be reflectively connected to identities and subjective interpretations through DA (Tochon, 2010, 2012). This way, teachers filter the outside discourse around themselves and construct their identities and interpretations in the primary world, which provides a sense of continuity. Through disrupting of routine conceptions in the field, suspending interpretations during reflection, and knowledge reframing, educators can reach a high level of metasemiosis, and further relating the curriculum knowledge to responsible professional action, can develop semioethics (Tochon & Ökten, 2010). Acting as a resource, the deep educator has a strong commitment to educate better and stimulate deeper in this world of opposite top-down forces and structural demands, devoted to freeing others from the official chains of schooling and "institutionalized stultification," which can be achieved by "thorough training, expertise, relevance and aptness, delicacy and tact, and a new rapport with the students' lives, who must be considered as adult learners, grown-up with the potential of leading their projects, even in the K-12 grades" (Tochon, 2012, p.280). The deep educator seeks what is meaningful to the learners and situates learning within the larger context of meeting lifegoals. Forward-planning with a focus on process rather than outcome-focused backward-planning is suggested; "deep formative feedback" and empowering through self/peer assessment is essential. Value-creation through respecting other cultures is emphasized, while discrimination or colonialism are countered.

Furthermore, in DA while the educator and the apprentice can negotiate instructional arrangements, "the major agreement is to take place within the learner and his or her own self" (Tochon, 2012, p.250). Driven by independent, deliberate and intrinsic motivation, this agreement allows the apprentice to go deeper into the target culture. When students are freed from linear, surface curricula and allowed to organize their own projects and resources, they will show real interest in learning. Curriculum designers cannot initiate changes without addressing the mental models and recognizing "teachers' and students' knowledge, beliefs, values and interests in the instructional process" (Tochon, 2012, p.25). Empowerment in DA comes from a critical stance of constantly questioning self practice to see whether it is limiting or liberating the learners, whether learners' inner constraints are eliminated, keeping an eye on the long-term goals, but not for sake of short term, since "the means used influence the attainment of the goal" in Gandhi's words (Tochon, 2010). In this sense, the DA strives to achieve freedom for people who are enslaved by the normative schooling practices. However, this is quite different from the self-centered, irresponsible, destructive freedom of the cancer cell that modernism imposes. As the freest cell in the body, a cancer cell grows rapidly and freely, destroys all the other cells but dies with the dying body in the end. Modernism disrupted the balance between freedom and responsibility.

In the educational premises of DA, "teaching self and otherness is part of teaching cultures and languages. Accessing another culture is the identity building process. Interactions need to be biographically situated. Beliefs about ontology and reality as well as social positioning play a huge role in the perception and stands vis-à-vis the other language and culture" (Tochon, 2011, p.19). At this stage, three levels of interaction determine holistic learning: " the mastery of declarative knowledge, the transfer of procedural strategies, and the expression of situated understanding (a holistic action) encompassing three levels of an educative production – the discipline, the interdiscipline, and the transdiscipline" (Tochon, 2012, p.28). Evaluative metacognition is the final step in the learning process that integrates all previous levels of learning and transcending the subject area, culminating in meta-awareness.

However, the DA is not to be taken purely as a teaching method, but rather as a lens to see the world through. The official curriculum may try to bend the mind to its will, but the DA is not about "bending" minds; it's more about empowering and freeing the inner soul. Knowledge is an essential part of identity building process that is not viewed as an object, but rather an intersubjective opposition to commodization and reification. "...Both declarative and procedural knowledge are highly context-dependent and influenced by biographic (diachronic) knowledge as well as contextual knowledge present within the interactional situation. Biographic and situated knowledge together constitute the experiential knowledge proper to language apprenticeship" (Tochon, 2012, p.249). To gain knowledge, educative projects are situated in action, disallowing sedimentation. Instead of uniform, standardized outcomes, deep processing and gaining unique perspectives are targeted. Language learning serves higher ambitions toward a wiser world, where people collaborate to solve conflicts, wars, poverty, desertification, deprivation and non-humane politics. This requires viewing the curriculum as a tool to achieve democracy, civic participation, and a more equitable society, as opposed to the prevalent conceptualization of curriculum as "the development of cognitive processes" (Ladson-Billings, 2016). Language depth "relates to applied semiotics rather than the abstraction of permanent and immovable universals with absolute, decontextualized rules of transformation. The clash between meaning and form only exists in dualistic ontology. Meaning and form are integrated in daily use within communicative situations" (Tochon, 2010, p.7). Learner knowledge and reflectivity are contextualized through better attention, a positive attitude, and a personal involvement in interactions "about and in" the target language. 5 Cs standards are subsumed by the overarching C of "Cosmopolitanism," and becomes 6 Cs following Daiseku Ikeda's suggestion. Instead of aiming for "the ideal citizen," this Cosmopolitanism is reached through "politics for the human," involving micro-politics of linguistic, pragmatic and cultural value creation, "forming an interface between government policies and classroom practices" (Tochon, 2012, p.32). DA projects also stimulate a sense of soul searching and therefore identity building. Language learning is a way of this identity construction, but also paves the way for the internalization of cosmopolitanist values such as compassion, wisdom and courage (Ikeda, 2010, 2013). Integrated with cosmopolitan philosophy, critical multiculturalism undergirds the intercultural dimension of the DA. Applied semiotics is favored for hermeneutic value-laden projects to increase sensitivity and responsibility towards other people and our home planet, which involves a deep understanding of adaptive and complex cross-cultural situations. Based on an open approach to world languages and cultures, DA encourages deep reading in the form of dialogue with the *Other* as part of "transpersonal development" (Tochon, 2012).

"Global citizenship requires the development of virtues of imagination, empathy, and compassion within the acquisition of the other languages and cultures to create an antidote to collective egoism, ethnocentrism, and the pathology of divisiveness" (Tochon,

2012, p.272). Thus deep education involves a sense of one's deep identity that refers to who we are and how we see ourselves in relation to the world. Creating a sense of connection, "deep education transforms the biosphere into 'semiosphere' —a world of meaningful signs—and creates a meaning-making environment for action" (Tochon, 2010, p.4). This deep identification of self with the world frees the person from the confines of ego, the sense of separation from the earth (subject vs. object) is gone, so one begins to feel directly affected by all kinds of destructive human behavior on earth. DA values diversity of all forms of life, and diversity of cultures, no matter how small or materialistically insignificant they might be perceived. Through symbolic interaction, teachers socialize into particular shared cultural practices through their interactions with students, parents, and school staff. This shared social ground operating through symbols forms the basis of what Heidegger (1962) calls as being and what Bourdieu (1977) – based on the Aristotelian concept of hexis – calls habitus, the set of dispositions that allow novice teachers to develop their professional understanding over time. Schooling enculturates students into various discourse communities (Resnick, 1991), leading them to personalize concepts and forms of reasoning that characterize those communities. These discourse communities also shape the way teachers think and teach. "Indeed, patterns of classroom teaching and learning have historically been resistant to fundamental change, in part because schools have served as powerful discourse communities that enculturate participants (students, teachers, administrators) into traditional school activities and ways of thinking" (Putnam & Borko, 2000, p.8).

A teacher simultaneously handles two Saussurian axes of knowledge: diachronic (where prior knowledge and new knowledge co-occur), and synchronic (where present circumstances and all their ramifications are considered) (Tochon, 2000, Tochon & Munby, 1993). Tochon and Munby (1993) demostrated that teaching knowledge is a focal point merging instructional diachrony with synchrony. This concept suggests that situated in the present locales and time, teachers develop a broad knowledge of the present, comprising both in and of class rules and values.

The individual person is part of the spatial and temporal situation (Heidegger, 1962). To Heidegger (1962), all interpretation and achieving meaning begins with a shared symbol system, a Vorhabe (pre-understanding). Then the interpretation is referenced form a certain perspective and expectations about the meaning. Understanding self and others is tied directly to being-in-the-world, the Dasein, which requires constant reinterpretation of the particular situation. For teachers, this understanding is actualized in lived educational situations. When teachers participate in professional development communities, they draw on each other's unique experiences, and different strengths to gain insights and transform their teaching. Each member contributes to this collaborative discourse by making his or her knowledge available to the others. Communication of meaning depends on cultural artifacts, language being the most important of them but also other culture-specific semiotic signs and symbols, like gestures. It is through the participation in the symbolic systems of the culture that a shared background is developed enabling mutual understanding (Bruner, 1990). People find themselves in situations formed by all that has occurred in the past, from which they project themselves into the future. Tochon's (2000) model of authentic learning situations describes (pedagogical) authenticity as an intersection of the situated (lived) experience of the learners and the disciplinary mind expressed in planned and enacted pedagogical context. The mind of the discipline is historic and contained within the community of practice and it is integrated with the present locality of pedagogical experience (where the learners are guided by the more experienced members of the community of practice). Tochon (2000) further argues that planning and enacting curricula is a process of enminding classroom action with the historic mind of the discipline. He considers disciplines as school genres. This enminding becomes the particular genre and discourse of the subject matter. The learner and the mind of discipline are dialectically bound together as they shape each other. In the process of reflection on experiences, the culture, learners, and teachers become reconstructed. However, there is a further "trialectical" dimension where deep educational reflection on the symbolic interactionist experience may potentially result in personal/professional transformation. Such intersectional dimensions of the interplay between Symbolic Interactionism and Deep Approach are the focus of the following section.

Synthesis of SI and DA: Deep Symbolic Interactionism (DSI)

Mind is a symbolic process that reflects an ongoing larger social process, which ties in with the DA in that personal symbolic constructions are connected to the bigger symbolic scope of other ecological systems like schooling, in the search for meaning and purpose for actions. SI helps with the theorization of how student teachers enact imaginary scenarios in their minds and interact with the society, but building on this, the DA allows a researcher to further analyze how these teachers make meaningful bridges between their primary and secondary worlds. Both SI and DA are deeply rooted in Peircean semiotics, which focuses on how people create and interpret signs and symbols to make meanings in their lives. The signs (called "representamens" by Peirce); themselves don't have any inherent meanings in them, until people assign them those meanings. In the mind of that person, a sign creates an equivalent or even a more developed sign, which creates the interpretant of the first sign. The sign stands for its object, not in all respects, but in reference to a sort of idea, which Peirce calls the ground of the representamen. Interaction between the representamen, the object and the interpretant is referred to by Peirce as semiosis (Peirce, 1931-58, p. 484). In his model, for example, a traffic light sign for "stop" would consist of: a red light facing traffic at an intersection (the representamen); vehicles stopping (the object) and the idea that a red light indicates that vehicles must stop (the interpretant). It is the deep semiosis that SI and DA (DSI) try to explicate and understand.

Like SI, DA values the agency and autonomy of the individual rather than the structural mechanisms operating on the learning process because excessive focus on the structural constraints has the potential to stifle individual creativity. DA values each learner by allowing him/her to bring original perspectives into the educational interactions. DA helps expand SI analysis by its insights into deep individual experiences and by connecting it to the global perspective, since SI shuns the macro-structural analysis considering it inaccessible to examination. However, the global perspective of DA refers not to an attempt to lay bare the undergirding social structures at work, but to provide a higher macro purpose and direction (like social justice) for the individual micro actions and choices. Therefore, with its endeavor to reach a deep, holistic understanding of the present by honoring the past, while developing wisdom for the future, DA complements the microsocial perspective of SI. I believe that DSI provides a deeper analysis because it helps explain both the use of symbolic interaction at the symbols level and and the way it is idiosyncratically used by an educational stakeholder as part of a larger life goal. The DSI provides a lens that enables looking at phenomena through a transdisciplinary perspective (Nicolescu, 2008), but also allows for an analysis of the micro-level symbolic interactions between self and the world in the third space, as these interactions occur in a larger semiosphere of signs and symbols. DSI completes the SI framework by adding the DA framework to it, so that it helps analyze not only "how" educators and learners make sense of their experiences, but also "why" they do so in certain ways by situating and reframing their experiences in line with a certain worldview, a higher transdisciplinary purpose, and intentions guided by certain beliefs and knowledge. The graph below represents the various dimensions of the DSI model.

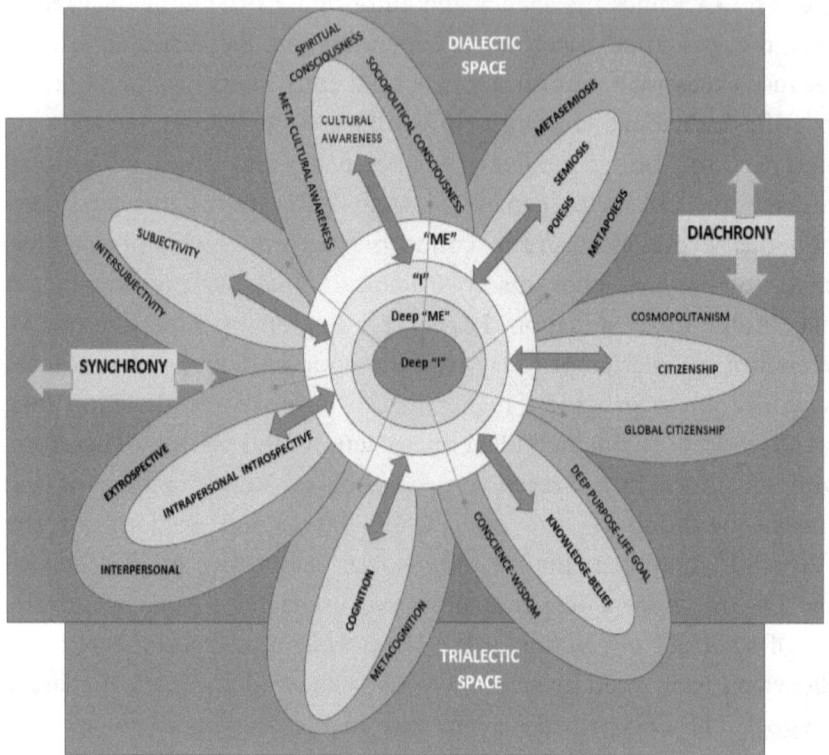

The DSI model

The blossom of the DSI Model above demonstrates the micro dimension (represented by the inner petals of light pink) of when, where, and how the SI process is enacted. The time dimension (in blue) comprises diachronic and synchronic experience, spanning across childhood, adolescence and adulthood.

The temporal context here refers to the present situated in the past (lived) and future (imagined), so the "now" is situated in the "then." The spatial dimension of the deep symbolic experience (in green) refers to the third space, whereby changes occurring in the interpersonal and intercultural contact points allow semiosis and poiesis. Thus, the deictic "here" is situated in the retrospective and prospective "there." The process dimension refers to how the symbolic interpersonal and cross-cultural dialectics and poiesis work. The blue and green dimensions together form the semiosphere. Composed of "me" and "I" at the SI level, and deep "me" and deep "I" at the DA level, the identity dimension refers to how the self and other are described and how self is related to others and how self-integrity/consistency is maintained across various educational contexts. The Deep "I" with its transformative and moral aspects is the deepest dimension of self, constituting the core self and governing the "deep me," "me" and "I". In the macro dimension of the DSI (represented in the model by the outer petals of dark pink), based on the personal worldview, life purpose and transcendental positioning of the self in the semiosphere, the dialectics of the SI becomes the trialectics of DA, semiosis turns into metasemiosis, and the poiesis transforms into meta-poiesis, resulting in the emergence of semioethics. The subjectivity of SI experience becomes related to the intersubjectivity of DA. In the trialectic third space the knowledge-belief ultimately becomes transcendental conscience-wisdom. This higher level of conscience/wisdom allows teachers develop deeper level of meta-cultural awareness and appreciation, through which then they can reframe their lived experiences from a macro perspective of (interpersonal and global) transformation.

Conclusion

The DSI lens outlined above aims to offer a fresh look into the educational problems we are suffering today and help negotiate deeper solutions to them. It asserts that at the root of many of these problems lay superficiality, selfishness, instrumentalism, colonialism, and lack of wisdom. Given the interconnectedness of everything we experience, it is evident that we need to use a more comprehensive and holistic analytical tool to make sense of phenomena and improve them accordingly. An increasing sense of being lost or feeling drowned in a ceaseless bombardment of "meaningless" information is plaguing students and teachers, causing them to give up on superficial, uncaring, and individualistic education isolated from the social issues that really matter. DSI hopes to provide this much needed meaning and depth by bringing two lenses together: SI (micro-social) and DA (macro-social). While the SI allows an insight into the socio-cognitive symbolic interpretations, the DA brings in the global, cosmopolitan, and spiritual sensitivities framing the transdisciplinary and critical educational action, hoping to ultimately bring social justice for all.

References

Bhabha, H.K. (1990). The third space. In J. Rutherford (Ed.), *Identity, community, culture, and difference* (pp. 207-221). London: Lawrence and Wishart.

Blumer, H. (1969). *Symbolic interactionism: Perspective and method.* Englewood Cliffs, NJ: Prentice Hall.

Blumer, H. (1975). Exchange on Turner 'Parsons as a Symbolic Interactionist' *Sociological Inquiry*, 45, 59-68.

Bourdieu, P. (1977). *Outline of a Theory of Practice.* Cambridge University Press.

Bruner, J. (1990). *Acts of meaning.* Cambridge, MA: Harvard University Press.

Heidegger, M. (1962). *Being and Time.* Harper & Row, New York.

Ikeda, D. (2010). *Toward a New Era of Value Creation: 2010 Peace Proposal.* Retrieved from: http://www.daisakuikeda.org/main/peacebuild/peace-proposals/pp2010.html

Ikeda, D. (2013). *Compassion, Wisdom and Courage: Building a Global Society of Peace and Creative Coexistence: 2013 Peace Proposal.* Retrieved from: http://www.daisakuikeda.org/main/peacebuild/peace-proposals/pp2013.html

Katovich, M. A., Maines, D. R. (2003). Society. In Reynolds, L. T. & Herman-Kinney, N. J. (Eds). *Handbook of Symbolic Interactionism* (pp. 289-307). Altamira Press, Rowman & Littlefield Publishers.

Korten, D. C. (2007). *The Great Turning: From Empire to Earth Community.* (2nd Ed.) Berrett-Koehler Publishers, Bloomfield, CT: Kumarian Press.

Ladson-Billings, G. (2016). And then there is this thing called the curriculum: Organization, imagination, and mind. *Educational Researcher*, 45(2), 100-104.

Mead, G. H. (1934). *Mind, self and society.* Chicago: University of Chicago Press.

Nicolescu, B. (2008). *Transdisciplinarity: Theory and practice.* Cresskill, NJ: Hampton Press.

Nicolescu, B. (2010). Methodology of transdisciplinarity—Levels of reality, logic of the included middle and complexity. *Transdisciplinary Journal of Engineering & Science, 1*(1), pp.19-38.

Peirce, C. S. (1931-58). *Collected Writings* (8 Vols.). (Ed. C. Hartshorne, P. Weiss & A. W. Burks). Cambridge, MA: Harvard University Press.

Putnam, R. T., Borko, H. (2000). What do new views of knowledge and thinking have to say about research on teacher learning? *Educational Researcher, 29*(1), 4-15.

Resnick, L. B. (1991). Shared cognition: thinking as social practice. In *Perspectives on Socially Shared Cognition* (1-20).

Reynolds, L. T. (2003). Early Representatives. In Reynolds, L. T. & Herman-Kinney, N. J. (Eds). *Handbook of Symbolic Interactionism.* (pp. 253-266). Altamira Press, Rowman & Littlefield Publishers.

Ritzer, G. (2011). *Sociological Theory.* (8th Ed). New York, NY: McGraw-Hill.

Sleeter, C. E. (2005). *Un-Standardizing Curriculum: Multicultural teaching in Standards-Based Classrooms.* Teachers College Press.

Soja, E. W. (1996). *Thirdspace.* Malden (Mass.): Blackwell.

Soja, E. (2004). *Postmodern geographies: The reassertion of space in critical social theory* (2nd Ed.). New York: Verso.

Tochon, F. V. (2000). When authentic experiences are "enminded" into disciplinary genres: Crossing biographic and situated knowledge. *Learning and Instruction, 10*(4), 331-359.

Tochon, F. V. (2002). *Tropics of Teaching: Productivity, Warfare and Priesthood.* Toronto: University of Toronto Press.a

Tochon, F.V. (2010). Deep Education. *Journal for Educators, Teachers and Trainers JETT*, Vol. 1, pp. 1-12.

Tochon, F.V. (2011). Reflecting on the paradoxes of foreign language teacher education: A Critical system analysis. *Porta Linguarum*, 15, 7-24.

Tochon, F.V. (2012). *Help them learn a language deeply: The deep approach to languages and cultures.* Deep University Press.

Tochon, F. V., Azocar, A. (2003). Conclusion: The FLES School as a linguistic and cultural community. In F. Tochon & D. M. Hanson (Eds.) *The Deep Approach: Second Languages for Community Building.* Madison, WI: Atwood Publishing, (213-224).

Tochon, F. V., Black, N. J. (2006). Psychosemiotic analysis of reflective conflict and equilibrium in a video study group. *International Journal of Applied Semiotics*, 5(1-2), 219-233.

Tochon, F. V., Hanson, D. M. (2003). *The deep approach: second languages for community building.* Madison, WI: Atwood Publishing

Tochon, F.V., Munby, H. (1993). Novice and Expert Teachers' Time Epistemology: A Wave Function From Didactics to Pedagogy. *Teacher and Teacher Education*, 9. 2: 205-218.

Tochon, F. V., Karaman, A. C. (2009). Critical reasoning for social justice: moral encounters with the paradoxes of intercultural education. *Intercultural Education, 20*(2): 135-149.

Tochon, F. V., Ökten, C. E. (2010). Curriculum mapping and instructional affordances: Sources of transformation for student teachers. *Transnational Curriculum Inquiry, 7* (1).

Wallace, R. A., Wolf, A. (2005). *Contemporary Sociological Theory: Expanding the Classical Tradition* (6th Edition). Upper Saddle River, N.J: Prentice Hall.

Part II

Practical Applications of Deep Education

14.

Developing Intercultural Competence at Novice Level: Deep Approach to Russian

Anna Nesterchouk
Jambul Akkaziev
Snezhana Zheltoukhova
University of Wisconsin-Madison

Although recent applied linguistics and education scholarship provides various instructional frameworks for intercultural competence development, the question of more effective and student-centered approaches to introduce authentic target language culture to beginner learners requires further investigation. This study aims to demonstrate a successful implementation of the Deep Approach theory in the acquisition of intercultural competence by adult novice level L2 Russian learners through autonomous project work. The project's learning outcomes, as well as the participants' feedback, encourage educators to integrate deep cultural learning into the novice-level language curriculum.

In accordance with the recent internationalization processes that affect all aspects of contemporary worldwide society, there is an increased need for higher educational institutions to prepare students to become competent speakers in more than one language. Particularly, global competence is regarded by language educators to be a critical component of 21st century higher education and plays a central role in any university curriculum (Global Competence Position Statement, 2014). Global competence is defined as profound understanding of international phenomena of all sorts including the "ability to learn and work with people from diverse linguistic and cultural backgrounds, proficiency in a foreign language, and skills to function productively in an interdependent world community" (NEA, 2010, p.1).

Intercultural competence (IC), as the ability to increase knowledge about target cultures and interact with the people of other cultures in target languages, represents an inherent component of global competence, thus inviting further investigation on the part of language educators. Our interpretation of IC is based on Byram's (1997) descriptive model of Intercultural Communicative Competence. The four main factors involved in the phenomenon construction include **skills** to interpret, evaluate, relate, discover, and interact; **knowledge** of self and other, political education, critical cultural awareness; **relativizing** one's own and **valuing** others' experience.

Within the higher educational context, the development of IC may be fostered through various curricular as well as extracurricular activities, with study abroad remaining one of the most preferable approaches to students' IC growth among post-secondary institutions (Deardorff, 2006). However, due to high costs and mixed outcomes of study abroad learner experiences, there is a need for a greater variety of innovative approaches that aim towards the development of IC among language learners. Thus, the main research objective of the present study is to evaluate the application of the Deep Approach (DA) language learning framework to the intercultural competence development by novice level L2 Russian speakers. We start the chapter with a description of our understanding of the intercultural competence as an integral aspect of *World-Readiness Standards for Learning Languages* (2015). We then provide a brief overview of major theoretical aspects of DA, as well as its practical implementation in language study through the IAPI model. Further, we describe the institutional setting of the DA experimental implementation: the Russian Flagship Program (RFP) at the University of Wisconsin-Madison, as well as the study participants' background. The chapter continues with an overview of the project participants' collaborative work throughout the eight weeks of the project timeline and concludes with the discussion of the students' feedback and facilitators' reflections on the study outcomes. The terminology we employ throughout the chapter includes the concept of DA, created by François Tochon, a leading scholar in language education at the University of Wisconsin-Madison. DA represents an interdisciplinary project-based framework aimed to foster an effective language proficiency development through increased awareness, internal motivation and autonomy of language learners. Finally, we use the terms "mentors" and "facilitators," to refer to ourselves, the three co-authors of the chapter, while the term "participants" refers to the four undergraduate students who took part in this unique language learning experience.

Framework

The development of IC is increasingly stated as one of the key goals in world language curricula all over the world. The importance of providing students with knowledge, skills, and attitudes necessary for effective cross-cultural communication is recognized by researchers, language instructors, and policy makers. In light of growing opportunities for prolonged intercultural communication both inside and outside one's home country and prospects of study/work in different cultural environments, language programs are placing increased emphasis on competencies that prepare students for global citizenship. *World-Readiness Standards for Learning Languages* (2015) stress the importance of integrating cultural knowledge into the curriculum with a focus not merely on accumulating a variety of culture-specific facts, but rather on understanding values and beliefs as a matrix for all cultural practices and products, as well as on the ability to communicate with cultural competence.

Despite the overall consensus on the importance of including cultural content in the language curriculum as a necessary prerequisite for developing intercultural competence, in reality, culture is frequently a missing or a 'bonus' part of a language classroom, textbook, or test, or a mere transaction in which the information is deposited by the teachers and stored by the students. The "banking" system of education criticized by Freire (1970) does not promote critical thinking and creativity. *Teaching* culture to students neither develops the ability to view the world and one's own culture from a different cultural perspective, nor promotes cultural empathy. This "banking" approach often distorts cultural reality and fails to foster *deep* cultural learning emerging in "the process of acquiring the ability to step into [...] new frameworks of meaning" (Shaules, 2007, p.12).

Researchers provide a number of explanations for the largely peripheral place of culture in the world language curriculum: the lack of a consensus on cultural content and methods of integrating that content into everyday lesson plans; limited instruction time in addition to overloaded syllabi; teachers' fear of cultural instruction due to self-perceived incompetence (Bennett, Bennett & Allen, 2003); the absence of clear guidelines on what intercultural skills students should master and how to assess their performance (Seelye, 1993); time and effort required on the part of teachers to stay current in the ever-changing and all-encompassing world of culture; unwillingness to deal with students' negative attitudes and controversial issues (Hadley, 2001); and a traditional lesson format that does not allow successful integration of linguistic and cultural content (Tochon, 2010).

These challenges are even more evident in beginner-level language courses. Students' cultural experience at the beginning of their language learning journey is often of a superficial nature due to the fact that traditional language instruction does not equip learners with interpretive, comparative, and communicative cultural skills essential for successful interaction, relationship building, and appreciation of diversity. Deep cultural learning and independent cultural exploration are often assumed to be too challenging for novice learners. This assumption is rooted in the idea that intercultural competence can only be developed at higher levels of proficiency when the target language is exclusively used for the input, output, and processing of culturally charged data, thus equating linguistic and cultural proficiency, and therefore ignoring the processing and analytical skills of learners, especially at the college level. However, many foreign language students do not reach intermediate and advanced levels of proficiency (Hebel, 2002, as cited in Shardakova & Pavlenko, 2004). This especially applies to slowly acquired languages, such as Russian. A typical college-level Russian language program does not have sufficient instructional hours in order to help students progress to advanced levels (Rifkin, 2005). By delaying the process of developing intercultural competence, language educators are depriving novice level students of the opportunity to develop the skills critical for effective intercultural communication.

In this project we employed a new method of achieving intercultural goals via meaningful project work based on the DA theory (Tochon, 2010). Although various frameworks exist for designing an intercultural curriculum, we were interested in an approach that does not paralyze students' intrinsic motivation and narrow their intercultural experience down to the achievement of pre-packaged goals. While DA does not focus solely on the development of IC, we believe it provides an original framework for achieving student-initiated linguistic and intercultural goals. In DA, culture is organically incorporated into the language acquisition process due to its transdisciplinary nature. It permeates the disciplinary and interdisciplinary levels of content and skills and transcends them by providing a meaningful context for "learning in action". In contrast to teacher-orchestrated cultural learning, Tochon encourages autonomous exploration of cultural complexities and stresses the importance of nurturing students' interest toward other cultures, which would guide them on their life-long journey of language and culture learning. This position is harmonious with Byram's (1997) emphasis on the process of IC development rather than a specific observable outcome and Shaule's (2007) understanding of deep cultural learning that can only occur through continuous internally driven cultural and linguistic exploration. The process of developing IC is complex and non-linear; in an educational context it requires a competent teacher and a learning environment that would embrace its dynamism and multidimensionality. The DA principles of relevance, holism, direction, and connectedness as well as the project planning concepts of ACCESS and VOICE provide ample opportunities for developing the five intercultural *savoirs* in a meaningful, individualized way.

Tochon's (2014) project planning model (IAPI) was used as a template for the student projects presented in this chapter. The IAPI model is a curriculum-building tool that incorporates four domains: Interpret, Analyze, Present, and Interact. It serves as a frame that is progressively filled with tasks designed by the students. The interpretation domain insures that students watch, listen, and read to ensure extensive input essential for developing proficiency. The analysis domain encourages students to concentrate on language, to examine and study grammar forms independently, and to practice various grammar points through active writing and speaking. This domain does not exist in a vacuum; it is treated as an integral part of Interpreting, Presenting, and Interacting. The presentation domain encourages extensive output as a prerequisite for proficiency; it ensures that students plan a variety of speaking, writing, recording, filming, and presenting tasks. The interaction domain targets successful communication within and across cultures, relationship building, and transcultural understanding. Interpersonal exchange can take place in real-life mode or on-line. This four-domain project planning model is an enhanced and expanded interpretation of the ACTFL organizing principles grounded on Interpersonal, Interpretive, and Presentational modes of communication; it enriches the ACTFL model as it encourages identity building as well as linguistic development through ACCESS and VOICE.

Our goal for the project was to provide adult novice learners of Russian with opportunities for self-actualization, to stimulate their intrinsic motivation for language learning, and to ensure a successful development of intercultural competence. Organizing learning around a particular theme chosen by the students allowed us to interweave the cultural thread into all individualized tasks and activities and encouraged students to explore the target culture on their own. Meaningful interaction was achieved through in-session and social media discussions with project teammates and online community. Pronunciation practice, listening skills, acquisition of authentic speech patterns, acquaintance with cultural norms and values, as well as the analysis and practice of grammar forms, were achieved through various activities based on the authentic materials used for the projects. Students were discovering deeper layers of culture through the analysis of Russian cartoons, folktales, and web resources. Culture was further explored through independent reading, meaningful discussions with members of Russian-speaking online communities and addressing areas of possible intercultural misunderstanding with project mentors. A cultural matrix was also discovered through humor relevant to the theme, culture-rich images, videos, and music. As the students took charge of their learning and acted as curriculum builders, the mentors provided scaffolding, suggested a variety of resources, and helped students polish their work by providing feedback. Although the teachers were an available resource, students were encouraged to overcome the anxiety triggered by linguistic and cultural challenges and engage in independent cultural exploration.

The Study Setting

The DA project took place in Spring 2015 at the University of Wisconsin-Madison. As a group of facilitators, we developed an eight-week experimental course for novice-level volunteer students from the RFP. On a practical level, the ultimate goal of the DA project was to help the novice learners to develop intercultural competence through self-directed creative work. We recruited Russian Flagship students of novice level proficiency based on their unofficial OPI assessment. The recruitment procedure was completed through e-mail correspondence. Four second-semester Russian Flagship students agreed to participate in the uniquely designed project-based course. During the weekly informal meetings, we observed how participants created and interacted with the experiential organizers, as well as how they responded to the overall approach. We evaluated participants' experiences based on our observations of student work and interactions, informal discussions with participants during the weekly meetings and the results of a written survey at the end of the project.

Who and When: Project Mentors and Project Participants

The role of a researcher is important in qualitative studies due to the fact that the data are collected, represented and triangulated through the prism of the researcher's identity. Various aspects of our respectively situated identities, as well as our assumptions and biases, affected the project outcomes and conclusions. We are native speakers of Russian and world language professionals at the University of Wisconsin-Madison. Our distinct backgrounds contributed to the variety of linguistic, cultural, and academic perspectives within the project framework. In order to present the research results from the emic perspective, we participated in each session as DA co-instructors, while facilitating the learning process at every stage of the project. The study participants were one male and three female undergraduate students enrolled in the RFP at the University of Wisconsin-Madison between the ages of 19-21. All project participants were L1 English-speaking volunteers from the pool of all students that were enrolled in the second-semester Russian language course in Spring 2015.

Where: The RFP at the University of Wisconsin-Madison

The RFP at the University of Wisconsin-Madison was established as a result of the national effort to address the need for young specialists to acquire high levels of linguistic proficiency and cultural competence in foreign languages. "Flagship programs do not adhere to any single teaching model; rather, they are firmly grounded in best pedagogical practices drawn from research in SLA" (Spring, 2012, p. 143). The program at UW-Madison is a special program designed for undergraduate students to study the Russian language and culture. The National Security Educational Program initiated four Russian

Flagship programs in the U.S.: at Bryn Mawr College, Portland State University, UCLA, and UW-Madison. The Russian Flagship programs at all four institutions share the goal of enabling students to reach the Superior level of proficiency on the ACTFL scale (IRL 3) in Russian, although their curricula are not homogeneous. The four programs share the same language proficiency requirements for the domestic part of language study: Advanced Low according to the ACTFL scale or 2 according to the ILR (Interagency Language Roundtable) scale. However, the four programs offer different curricular and extracurricular activities tailored to specific institutional environments and resources. Among its various components, including credit-based coursework, weekly Social Hours, and other initiatives. The UW-Madison RFP offers one to four hours of individual or small-group tutoring weekly for every Flagship student. Each weekly tutoring hour can be dedicated to any or a combination of the four language skills of reading, writing, listening, and speaking, but speaking is emphasized. Besides advanced coursework and tutoring as described above, UW-Madison RFP students are required to participate in a weekly Social Hour and attend special lectures and workshops in Russian with visiting scholars, film screenings in Russian, and a variety of other extra-curricular events, both on campus and in the community, dedicated to Russian language and culture. The DA project was launched in Spring 2015 as a supplement to the tutoring component of the RFP and did not exempt the participants from completing other program requirements. At the end of the eight-week course, the students presented products of their project work to the Flagship community at the end-of-semester Talent Show event.

Week-by-week Description of the Project

As indicated above, our project involved working with several undergraduate students from UW-Madison's RFP who were novice learners of Russian and who had expressed their willingness to participate in the project in addition to their regular classes and activities. We met with the participants once a week for the duration of the project (8 weeks). The first meeting was scheduled after preliminary email discussions about the participants' backgrounds and their interests in both Russian language study and other areas. We invited a total of four participants to the first meeting during which we introduced ourselves in person and discussed the project's goals and objectives, as well as the design, in more detail. The participants were encouraged to bring any questions they had about the project to the table. We spent the entire first meeting elaborating on the project specifics and inquiring about the participants' interests and themes they might explore. In addition, we emphasized the project goals of developing intercultural competence, honing participants' curriculum building and collaboration skills, fostering creativity, and achieving tangible project results in the form of final products. We also highlighted that our project was premised on participants' independent work intended to develop intercultural competence. We explained that our role, by contrast, was to facilitate their work and to provide the potential target language audience for the presentation component of the IAPI model, as well as to furnish linguistic and cultural feedback.

The participants chose three different projects to work on: writing a Russian fairy tale (Margaret)[1], creating a web-based travel guide to Moscow's clubs and bars for student visitors (Keith), and producing an animated film featuring archetypal Russian characters (Amber and Laura). First, the participants compiled tentative calendars outlining major steps in the process and projected goals for each week. The initial stage and meetings involved a significant amount of research and exploration on the part of the project participants. The participants read a number of Russian folk tales (Margaret), browsed websites of Moscow's clubs, bars, and other entertainment venues (Keith), and watched both Soviet and post-Soviet Russian cartoons and animated features (Amber and Laura). The INTERPRET component of the IAPI model was actualized at this stage in order to streamline the participants' exploratory potential in spite of their limited linguistic skills in the target language (see Figure 1). The participants were able to glean important cultural information, identified various linguistic cognates and sociocultural equivalents in their own culture, and processed a great amount of linguistic, visual, and aural information.

Naturally, the participants also obtained extensive practice in using available linguistic resources, such as online and print dictionaries, textbooks, and other reference materials. This type of hands-on experience, in turn, correlated with the ANALYZE component of the model, with the participants actively using available resources in order to decode and interpret the information they had discovered (see Figure 1). These resources were not limited to language materials, such as dictionaries (Lingvo, forvo.com, etc.) and encyclopedias (Wikipedia.ru), but instead included such cultural locales as Russian online forums, social networks (vkontakte.com), and various websites originating in the Russian sector of the Internet (Runet). In order to further facilitate cooperation among the participants and the mentors, we created a closed Facebook group featuring the following mission statement: "This is a group of Russian Flagship students and mentors, working collaboratively on creating educational materials designed to help novice Russian learners develop intercultural competence through self-directed project work." Thus, the participants had a platform where they could post their questions, reflections, and ideas, as well as share their progress with the project facilitators and with one another. It was further useful in providing and obtaining instant feedback on all aspects of the project work.

By Week 4, the participants had accumulated necessary cultural and linguistic materials and set out to create their own products. At this stage, we introduced Google Docs into the project work since this online tool allowed us to track the participants' progress and provide feedback whenever needed. During Weeks 4-6, the participants were actively working on their respective project goals and, step by step, created their own products in accordance with the PRESENT component of the IAPI model (see Figure 1). Margaret was writing a scenario for her Russian fairy tale that incorporated a number of archetypal Russian characters with their particular characteristics; Keith was working on creating a web-based travel guide for visitors who want to experience the nightlife in Moscow, Russia; finally, Amber and Laura were scripting, drawing and filming characters for their Russian cartoon. At our weekly meetings during this phase, the participants peer-reviewed each other's work through proof-reading, asking questions, and making suggestions on areas for improvement. They also used social media (our Facebook group page) to furnish real-time feedback to any urgent questions and aspects of the project work. In addition, the participants incorporated the feedback they had received and made adjustments to their projects. This latter aspect closely correlated with the INTERACT component of the IAPI model (see Table 1). Our role in this context was to provide scaffolding and to facilitate culture-focused discussions, in addition to offering feedback on the content and form of the participants' work. We also conducted several Skype conference calls during Weeks 5-6 in order to discuss the participants' progress and possible adjustments in the schedule and workflow.

Lastly, Weeks 7 and 8 were dedicated to polishing the final products and preparing for the end-of-semester talent show (Russian "Kapustnik") at which both project participants and other Russian Flagship students showcased their work. Margaret's fairy tale was not only read but also acted out on the stage with the participation of both students and the facilitators; Keith featured his web-based travel guide to Moscow and the city's nightlife. Finally, Amber and Laura debuted their animated film to the Russian Flagship audience and guests.

Table 1. Experiential organizer for the "Russian Fairytale" project.

Experiential Organizer for "Russian Fairytale" Project				
	INTERPRET	ANALYZE	PRESENT	INTERACT
	Read popular Russian fairytales from Russian storybook "Сказка" and note common literary techniques, common characters, and their traits	Analyze word forms and sentence structure in traditional fairytales	Write my own Сказка/fairytale	Create a Survey to collect TAs' input on memorable aspects of fairytales, popular fairytales, and favorite characters. Incorporate survey results into my project.
	Explore popular Russian websites for kids (fairytale sections)	Compile thematic vocabulary lists: animal names, connectors and descriptors used in storytelling, commonly used verbs	Create an illustrated book as well as powerpoint slides of the book	Visit Madison Russian School and interview Anna Krylova, a Russian illustrator and art teacher. Discuss my project and ask for help with a cover picture for my book.
	Watch some animated films based on famous Russian folktales and note common themes/storylines	Proofread peers' written materials for grammar and spelling	Present my tale at the Kapustnik in the form of a skit.	Reflect on Russian and American fairytale plots, discuss underlying cultural assumptions with mentors and peers

Students' Feedback and Our Reflections

Upon project completion, we conducted an anonymous written survey and an informal conversation with the participants with the goal of eliciting their thoughts, suggestions, and overall impressions of the project. The participants' feedback revealed a number of intriguing ideas about the project and the ways in which it succeeded in achieving the stated goals or veered off in unexpected directions.

Our survey was conducted through the Survey Monkey platform and included questions that ranged from students' expectations vis-a-vis actual results to participants' comfort level in exploring Russian language and culture, and their effort in developing intercultural competence at the novice level (see Appendix I). It is important to note that the participants' expectations before the project were very similar and reflected the conventional idea of what project work in a target language entails. One participant indicated that s/he "thought that the project would be about an hour or so of work each week, with most of the work going into researching [the] topic and summarizing [the] findings for our weekly meetings." Another participant similarly expected "to do lots of research and citations." However, as the surveyed participants point out, the actual project work as it progressed, as well as the results achieved at every step, were more exciting and rewarding. "I felt like the results were more achievable than what I had expected; we could adapt to time scarcity and it was flexible with my actual school workload," wrote one participant. Another participant noted that, even though "[it] took more time than [s/he] thought because [s/he] did the whole thing in Russian rather than English," such components as "the cultural aspects of the project" were "very enjoyable." When asked whether they felt that they had gained a deeper understanding of the Russian language and culture, the participants emphasized that their interactions with Russian speakers "in person, via the Internet or other media" during project work allowed them to gain a multitude of perspectives through an independent foray into Russian society both in the US and in Russia.

The second part of the survey asked the participants to reflect on and evaluate their learning process, as well as the performance and contributions of other project participants and the facilitators. In addition, the participants were asked if they felt in charge of their own learning and whether they felt confident enough to continue studying the target language and culture on their own. As expected, the responses to these questions were mixed. Nevertheless, all respondents were confident about being in control of their own learning. The responses indicated that, for instance, one "could always step backwards and take more baby steps forwards when the language was too hard." On a related note, another participant wrote, "We were largely responsible for finding all of our materials." However, the project participants differed in their responses on how much independent learning they felt they might be able to pursue in the future. While one participant indicated that s/he still needed to "[be] in the class[room]" to continue to learn about Russian culture and language, another participant was confident that s/he "can continue learning about Russian culture because [s/he] now has a better understanding on three topics of Russian culture that [s/he] can build upon through further research and reading."

The participants' responses obtained both through the written survey and during an informal conversation upon project completion reveal a number of particularly interesting perspectives on the role of language teachers, students, and peers. First, the participants appreciated having peers that had a similar level of proficiency in the target language ("It was nice to do it with people at the same level as me so that we could 'struggle through together'"). They also indicated that working with peers was particularly helpful in terms of providing/receiving feedback and generally "helping each other with their projects at various stages." The participants viewed their own performance largely in a positive way and were especially proud of their project results. One surveyed participant wrote: "Overall I thought I delivered a good product!" Yet, the participants also saw room for further improvement, which suggests that project work could serve as an impetus for further study and exploration: "I could've researched more than just kids' fairytales to get a better grip on the idea of Russian culture in fairytales."

Finally, the participants' feedback regarding the role of project facilitators reveals a number of challenges that conventionally trained students might encounter when immersing themselves in language study based on Deep Approach. For example, during the group conversation, the project participants, while expressing appreciation for the facilitators' work, pointed out that that they had not been provided with direct support and constant guidance. The students were thus drawing from their previous experiences in language study when the teacher served as a linguistic and cultural guru that would provide information, correct mistakes, and overall control the learning process. In other words, this comment was rooted in the fact that the participants were accustomed to traditional classroom culture in which the instructor is the leader and shapes both the curriculum and the learning experience.

Furthermore, the participants noted that constant negotiation of the Russian language and culture (what constitutes "Russianness," what language items are part of the vernacular, which grammatical form is standard, and similar questions) among the facilitators was somewhat confusing since it appeared that the facilitators were not in unison when it came to linguistic and cultural phenomena. However, it is precisely this constant (re-)negotiation of cultural and linguistic meaning, as well as the lack of a strictly controlled environment, that serve as hallmarks of Deep Approach. In our Deep Approach based project work, the students were put in charge of their own learning and at times it must have felt a bit overwhelming for individuals with a traditional background in language study. Indeed, the participants' feedback points to one of the successes of our project – creating an authentic cultural experience in which cultural meanings are constantly discussed and negotiated. It further attests to the productive nature of Deep Approach scaffolding which helps novice level language learners make decisions about pace and focus, learning strategy and cultural meanings in accordance with their interests, availability, and learning styles. This notion is succinctly presented in one participant's feedback which read, "The DA Project is a challenging commitment guaranteed to push you and better equip you with a critical, strategic approach to learning the Russian language." On a similar note, another participant summarized our project as "a great way to integrate your personal interests and Russian studies into a project that combines both to create a better understanding of both the Russian culture and language." These pithy statements call for further integration of Deep Approach into fostering intercultural and linguistic competence and present both language instructors and students alike with new, exciting avenues to explore their interests, expand their knowledge, and capitalize on their creativity.

Conclusion

In this chapter, we documented the development of intercultural competence by novice level Russian language learners within the DA framework. An outline of the study goals and main aspects of DA was followed by the description of the project setting and participants. The chapter continued with a week-by-week account of the project as it unfolded in the course of eight weeks. Furthermore, we reported the project's learning outcomes and analyzed the participants' feedback. Finally, we shared our reflections as the project facilitators on the project results and its DA core. As a result, we demonstrate how three creative small-group and individual Russian language projects (the book, the website, and the cartoon) attest to a successful implementation of the DA principles within the institutional context.

Our analysis of the project outcomes as well as the student feedback enables us to arrive at the following conclusions. First, the original instructional goal to provide students with an immersive authentic cultural experience was successfully fulfilled as reflected and documented by study participants. Second, throughout the project, the participants gradually became more comfortable and confident with autonomous exploration of authentic Russian-language materials as well as unassisted interaction with Russian native speakers in real-life situations. In other words, the study provides a practical example of highly motivated autonomous language and culture exploration by novice level speakers despite their limited linguistic skills. These results point to the overall success of implementing Deep Approach into world-language study.

Despite the encouraging project outcome and positive evaluations, the study has a few limitations, including the small number of participants and the reliance on the students' feedback and self-reflections. These concerns should be addressed by future research that might employ a larger sample and a more elaborate data collection methodology, including individual interviews with students, mentor self-reflections, and field notes of class observations.

References

Bennett, J., Bennett, M., & Allen, W. (2003). Developing intercultural competence in the language classroom. In D. Lange, & M. Paige (Eds.), *Culture as the core: Perspectives in second language learning* (pp.235-268). Greenwich, Conn.: Information Age Publishing.

Byram, M. (1997). *Teaching and assessing intercultural communicative competence*. Clevedon, England: Multilingual Matters.

Deardorff, C. (2006) Assessing intercultural competence in study abroad students. In M. Byram & A. Feng (Eds.), *Living and studying abroad: Research and practice* (pp. 232-256). Multilingual Matters.

Freire, P. (1970). *Pedagogy of the oppressed*. New York: Herder and Herder.

National Education Association (2010). Global Competence Is a 21st Century Imperative. An National Education Association Policy Brief Retrieved from http://www.nea.org/assets/docs/HE/PB28A_Global_Competence11.pdf

Hadley, A. O. (2001). Teaching language in context. Boston: Heinle & Heinle.

National Standards in Foreign Language Education Project. (2015) World-Readiness Standards for Learning Languages. Alexandria, VA: American Council on the Teaching of Foreign Languages.

ACTFL (2014, August). Reaching Global Competence Retrieved from https://www.actfl.org/sites/default/files/GlobalCompetencePositionStatement0814.pdf

Rifkin, B. (2005). A ceiling effect in traditional classroom foreign language instruction: Data from Russian. Modern Language Journal, 89(1), 3-18.

Seelye, H. (1993). Teaching culture: Strategies for intercultural communication. 3rd ed. Lincolnwood, Ill.: National Textbook Co.

Shardakova, M., & Pavlenko, A. (2004). Identity options in russian textbooks. Journal of Language, Identity, and Education, 3(1), 25

Shaules, J. (2007). Deep culture: the hidden challenges of global living. Buffalo, NY: Multilingual Matters.

Tochon, F. (2010). Deep education. Journal for Educators, Teachers and Trainers JETT, Vol. 1, 1-12

Tochon, F. (2014). Help them learn a language deeply: The deep approach to world languages and cultures. Blue Mounds, WI: Deep University Press.

---

[1] All participants' names have been changed to protect their privacy

Appendix I: Deep Approach Project Survey Questions

Q1: After you met with us, what expectations did you form about the project?
Q2: What were the actual results of your project and how did you feel about actual results vs. your expectations?
Q3: How do you feel this project allowed you to gain a deeper understanding of Russian culture?
Q4: Did you feel in charge of your learning? If yes, in what way?

Q5: Do you feel you can continue learning about Russian culture and language on your own? If yes, how?
Q6: Please evaluate the role and performance of other project participants (both students and instructors) in relation to your learning
Q7: What do you think about your own performance in the project?
Q8: What would be your elevator speech about this project?

15.

Implementing Internet Technologies for Deep Language Learning

Snezhana Zheltoukhova
University of Wisconsin-Madison

The chapter considers the possibility of application of current educational technology to additional language learning within the innovative Deep Approach. The numerous available Internet applications and web tools may either promote or restrict effectiveness and autonomy among second language learners. The chapter proposes a purposeful implementation of IT trends within Deep Approach supported by teacher training in order to maximize the learning outcomes. An overview of the major principles of Deep Approach is followed by a description of specific currently-developed open Internet resources for L2 Russian language learners. The two described modules help student to prepare for study abroad by targeting pragmatics and cultural nuances, areas that are often overlooked in language classrooms. The theoretical conclusions of the chapter are supported by two live-case projects of technology-enhanced Russian learning through Deep Approach. Russian Flagship Program students and tutors participated in both projects documenting the success of technology-enhanced Deep Approach theory application. As a result, the chapter's outcomes encourage educators to embrace technological and theoretical innovations that foster learner independence.

This chapter examines several experimental technology-enhanced Deep Approach teaching modules implemented in the Russian Flagship Program setting. I present the major current Internet technologies used to support Deep Language Learning (Tochon, 2010).

According to various estimates, the total number of hours required for reaching an advanced or superior level of proficiency in non-

Romance and less-commonly taught languages such as Arabic or Russian exceeds *by ten times* the average number of hours that students actively study foreign languages in college (Blake, 2013). On the other hand, researchers confirm that the use of technological applications might promote more enhanced and efficient contact with the target language. Due to the accelerated pace of technological development in general, it is imperative to regularly inform education policy makers of cutting-edge opportunities for foreign language learners to increase their level of productivity and autonomy. In order to support this autonomy, educators must "go beyond mere wishful thinking and create actual means for empowering learners to learn their own way and become parts of curriculum decision-making" (Tochon, 2015a, p. viii). Furthermore, I discuss a possible solution for a faster, more engaged, and more meaningful process of foreign language learning by applying the Deep Approach to technology-enhanced curriculums for languages less commonly taught.

Major Principles of Deep Approach

Recently, the field of SLA has been introduced to a revolutionary approach to general education that extends also to the foreign language learning process. The term "Deep Approach" (DA)—coined by François Tochon, researcher and leader of the World Language Education program at the University of Wisconsin-Madison—is meant to signify a multidisciplinary strategy encompassing several domains of education in general and language education in particular. The approach has been influenced by semiotics and is based in both process theory and complexity theory. Deep education and DA's principles of language learning align closely with the main conceptual principles of deep ecology (Naess, 1989, as quoted in Tochon, 2010). It is important to emphasize how DA differentiates between "shallow" surface learning and "deeper" learning. While shallow learning lacks reflection, integrating facts and concepts without grounding them in everyday practical experience, deep learning focuses on creating internal meaning rather than merely absorbing forms and signs. This "deep" learning incorporates assessment rooted in learners' internal sources of motivation, rather than simply requiring them to follow assessment rubrics without contemplating or participating in their design. The concept of "depth" requires transcending the attributive borders of various theoretical frameworks of education psychology. While "sociocultural, socioaffective, ecological and philosophical understandings allow deep learners to connect the dots and transcend the limited framework of cognitive psychology" (Tochon, 2010, p.5), the DA provides a fuller presentation of knowledge and meaning for deep learners and a more flexible instrument for deep teachers. In addition to its student-centered orientation, deep teaching requires the use of new technologies and is based on continuous collaboration between students and teachers. Facilitation of the learning process allows for the contextualizing and situating of theoretical knowledge within life-related practice. The concept of development—including subjective development—is understood in a broader sense. Below, I briefly review the main principles of DA as an educational concept (Tochon, 2010).

First and foremost, it is imperative to keep in mind that deep education is transdisciplinary; thus, the implementation of new information technologies is not only desirable but likely unavoidable in light of the current trend towards globalization. The transdisciplinary approach is associated with transformative rather than transmissive education. It aims to construct profound theoretical concepts and practical capacity. It is process- rather than form-oriented and involves real-life problem solving rather than small, artificially-created tasks. The depth of DA should not be confused with the internal deep structure proposed by Noam Chomsky, as Chomsky's Universal Grammar does not consider social context. DA, on the other hand, is rooted in applied semiotics, and therefore "depth" should be understood as both grounded in social context and in culture (Tochon, 2010). DA incorporates intercultural pragmatics, as well as deeper cultural meanings and conventions. In sum, DA is a transdisciplinary approach to teaching languages and cultures that targets linguistic proficiency and intercultural competence through self-directed learning and provides an alternative to current methodologies. DA to language education offers a framework for meaningful linguistic and cultural apprenticeship, taking place in a process-focused environment where both curriculum and subsequent knowledge are produced by the students. Oftentimes, teachers avoid responding to learner initiative because they believe that, otherwise, they will fail to dedicate the required amount of time to the curriculum. This problem occurs due to the popular belief that only directive and controlled environments are successful for language learning. Deep learning, however, offers freedom for language instructors and students alike. This opposes traditional "scripted instruction" in language classes, which constrains teachers' and students' creativity. Project-based learning prompts creation, action, and experience. The disciplinary content areas, in turn, are complemented by interdisciplinary strategies, which link each of the various disciplines to build a transdisciplinary experience.

Learners and teachers alike are active participants in DA. Teachers are facilitators rather than unquestionable experts. All learners must participate on an exclusively voluntary basis, due to the importance of intrinsic vs. external motivation. Within DA, intrinsic motivation is of ultimate importance. Extrinsic motivations, such as the reward of good grades or the fear of failure, are replaced with deeper forces: curiosity, free choice, and prior experience.

This principle allows students to participate in curriculum design while boosting motivation and creating deeper meaning from the exercise. In the context of foreign language, adherence to the principle accommodates the use of instructional technologies that leverage learners' deeper involvement in knowledge-creation from the beginning. DA is eco-cultural and is formatted as a project-based curriculum design. DA projects are constructed from converging tasks in different domains; learners choose the nature of the task according to their specific project. Thus, learners are also curriculum builders, and this planning phase is a crucial element in stimulating motivation. Students embark upon creative production processes that both encourage focus and hold real-life implications. Teachers serve as a bridge to possible resources, helping learners continue exploring interpersonally—that is, face-to-face—as well as within technology-facilitated environments.

The theoretical orientation of DA is strong, but it does not represent a goal in and of itself. Rather, the approach is focused on the practical results of problem-solving activities, being both bottom-up and thematic. All topics and themes are developed through the collaboration of students and teachers or, rather, learners and facilitators.

The lesson design is open and may be formatted according to the specific needs of the class. Most of the time, it adheres to the principles of meaningful conversations facilitated by experts who are present and ready to provide scaffolding if necessary. Importantly, the curriculum design must include a segment of self-reflection, wherein participants reflect on their own actions and achievements; however, this does not mean that more traditional and formal evaluations are necessarily excluded. During each lesson, facilitators must ensure that students are involved on multiple levels—not only cognitively, but also physically, socially, spiritually, and emotionally.

The concept of apprenticeship, or learning by doing, lies at DA's foundation. Within deep education, apprenticeship is understood as the creation of entirely new knowledge not produced by the teacher, conducive to both acquisition and proficiency. Thus, it is imperative that learners are active and teachers collaborative. In other words, learners must be made to feel "in charge" and competent. In a learning-by-doing environment, learners relate to others in their respective groups but ultimately work autonomously. Teachers do not teach; instead, they provide feedback, recommendations, and necessary facilitation. Students individually find the authentic material needed for their projects.

Within DA, tests are not encouraged. Rather, students choose their own forms of assessment, connected with their intrinsic motivations. The assessment phase includes a post-activity reflection (e.g. the amount of target language use), but there are no formal criteria that must be identical for all students. Comparison between projects is discouraged, except for the level of engagement. Instead, self- and peer-appreciation become the focus, not based solely in project observations, but also on the task's relevance to high-stakes creative action. This form of integrative assessment is governed by the principles of self-efficacy theory, promoting autonomous and motivated learning. Categories for assessment can correlate with ACTFL guidelines (5 Cs) or IAPI (interpret, analyze, present, interact), embedded in the framework of identity development (Tochon, 2014).

DA is based in project-based pedagogy (PbP), but has one crucial component that is sometimes absent in PbP: students choose their own projects and must produce their own artifacts as evidence of knowledge-creation. It involves in-depth research, ongoing teacher evaluation, frequent adaptation, and long-term achievement. It requires critical thinking and collaborative work as well as constant feedback and revision. The end result is usually presented for the evaluation of both peers and public (Tochon, 2014).

In their language and culture projects, students are highly invested in technology when creating blogs, wikis, podcasts, videos, and the like. eProjects with technological support can evolve into a new dimension, which François Tochon dubs "iDeep." It aims for real-life action and communication assisted by technology. DA supports the growth of learners' personal identities and helps them enhance society; iDeep is compatible with this notion as a form lifelong-learning, adding a time-related dimension that enhances students' use of technology.

The above introduction to the principles of DA demonstrates the importance of implementing educational technology within the second/foreign language deep learning process. Hereafter, I will review the newest IT trends, services, and tools specifically developed for language learners and will demonstrate numerous ways of applying computer-based leverage to DA in order to assist both students and teachers.

Educational technologies

The topic of current educational technologies available for language learners is broad and transdisciplinary on its own. For the purposes of this chapter, I will intentionally avoid a profound review of the academic literature available regarding certain aspects of this topic, such as MUVE (multi-user virtual environments), MOOC (massive open online courses), and open distance learning, in order to provide a more detailed analysis of current developments in computer learning environments, blogs, e-writing, virtual study abroad, social networks, and tools for teaching pragmatics.

Virtual Study Abroad

Study abroad is widely considered to be one of the most valuable college experiences for students (e.g. Kinginger, 2008; Berdan, 2015). Moreover, this way of learning a foreign language adheres to the main principles of DA, as it provides a truly transdisciplinary experience grounded in real-life problem solving and intrinsically-motivated communication with native speakers. At the same time, at many institutions of higher education, this experience is either financially unattainable or proves to be less effective than expected by its participants. Universities and colleges oftentimes fail to provide help in gaining the necessary intercultural skills for students to make the most of their time abroad. "The vast majority of students I have asked about cross-cultural preparation said they wished that they had been better prepared to deal with cultural differences when studying abroad. When I asked why, most said they felt confused by interactions with local people and didn't understand what was happening in social situations. Many of the students I interviewed said they felt so uncomfortable that they increased the amount of time they spent with fellow Americans and on social media with friends and family back home – the opposite of what they should have been doing" (Berdan, 2015, para. 11). The solution for this problem lies in strengthening global-education curriculums, as well as incorporating cutting-edge technologies and strategies into study abroad preparation programs. Tochon (2013) reports that the application of DA to blended-learning environments demonstrates that more advanced and successful students who underwent DA instruction "improved more swiftly and in more important ways with the Deep Approach, to the point of reporting results superior to study abroad programs" (Tochon, 2013, p. 73).

Luckily, more and more open Internet resources have been developed for students to have a virtual "study-abroad" experience prior to their actual trip. I will introduce two such projects that are intended for students of a less commonly-taught language: Russian. The developer of the first project, Shannon Spasova, hopes that the course will help students to be successful early on in their interactions in Russia, which in turn will boost their confidence to pursue social as well as linguistic progress during study abroad. The course exists on a Wordpress platform and consists of ten lessons. The lessons are made with Adobe Captivate and focus on helping students become comfortable with everyday situations they will most certainly encounter—for example, riding in a *marshrutnoe* taxi, a phenomenon nearly non-existent in the US but widespread in Russia. The course contains various tasks related to grammar but most of the exercises are centered around cultural specifics and practical problem-solving situations. The topics are carefully chosen to represent the unavoidable interactions with native speakers during meals, travel, shopping etc. Each lesson contains YouTube videos with short examples of described situations and a voice-over narrator in English. As a native of Russia, I am impressed by how closely these lessons recreate common tasks and how up-to-date the materials are. However, I suppose that these lessons will soon need a serious update to reflect the fast pace of Russia's two major cities. Ideally, this tool would produce the best outcomes for Russian students of at least three years. Nevertheless, anyone who is planning to go to Russia or is interested in Russian public life can benefit from the course's valuable information. This tool is perfect for Russian language learning through DA, as either a supplement or a part of instruction on culture and pragmatics.

The use of technology for pragmatics is currently increasing (Taguchi & Sykes, 2013), though historically pragmatics has presented a challenge for automated assessment due to a lack of suitable Internet platforms. Technology like this might promote the popularity of less commonly taught languages (LCTLs) among individual learners despite their lack of teaching materials. Godwin-Jones (2013) emphasized the significance of technology for LCTLs for economic reasons: because the demand for pedagogical resources is significantly smaller, there is a dearth of high-quality reference books, especially for higher-level learners.

Less Commonly Taught Languages Learning Web 2.0 Modules

Another technological application designed for teaching Russian pragmatics was developed by Edie Furniss, described in detail in her doctoral dissertation (Furniss, 2015). Her project included creating an interactive module to test during a six-week course for L1 English learners of Russian. The module takes the form of an instructional website using a Russian colloquial language corpus and other authentic resources, including recorded daily conversations and scenes from films, in order to facilitate the acquisition of formulaic expressions and their appropriate pragmatic uses. Over 100 participants were recruited to participate in quantitative as well as qualitative study, forming experimental and control groups. Results of the post-test demonstrate that the website meets the general criteria for technological applications designed for SLA. It serves the needs of intermediate-level learners who have been minimally exposed to target formulaic expressions, but it might also be successfully applied for more advanced L2 Russian speakers. The website's design corresponds to the main criteria of the Deep Approach: it uses exclusively authentic language samples drawn from corpus data of natural language, engaging learners both cognitively and affectively as their participation is driven by intrinsic motivation. The tasks are authentic and allow learners to practice newly-acquired formulas in everyday problem-solving situations. The only likely artificial component is that tasks are completed in writing rather than orally. This drawback is due to the current difficulty in assessing the spoken mode, and should be addressed in the future by CALL developers. The study concludes that, quantitatively, the experimental group demonstrated increased knowledge of the formulaic expressions included in the instructional module. Qualitatively, the study proved the website's positive impact on the learners, elicited and analyzed from participant evaluations. Moreover, the study confirmed that technological applications using corpus methodologies are useful and effective for L2 pragmatics.

As the technological application developed by E. Furniss does not require a teacher, it lacks the valuable feedback that interaction between learner and teacher can provide. Projects that provide a blend of face-to-face instruction and online activities prove to be more effective than traditional classroom language learning or online instruction alone. In his study on the effectiveness of deep, blended language learning, François Tochon demonstrates the successful integration of autonomous language learning, through online applications and materials, into a more formal classroom environment following the principles of DA (Tochon, 2013). Modules created for Turkish are specifically designed for project-based, blended learning following DA guidelines for languages and cultures (Tochon, 2013). As opposed to entirely online environments, blended learning spaces provide more opportunities for authentic collaborations and interactions, as well as a more structured feedback and self-evaluation. In its turn, a precast project-based learning (PjBL) environment is conducive to apprenticeship, learning-by-doing, and peer scaffolding. PjBL within DA is open and implies the learners' full involvement in curriculum building—with the instructors' facilitation rather than imposition. The project's experimental group consisted of forty-five students, while the control group consisted of thirty-one. The results of the study confirmed that students who underwent the experimental treatment were able to demonstrate faster progress to higher levels of OPI proficiency. While both groups were successful in improving their oral proficiency results, the more advanced students of the DA group developed their skills in significantly different ways at a more rapid pace. The analysis of student evaluations revealed that they found the DA-oriented, project-based courses with an online component to be effective, valuable, and clear. To summarize, the study proves a correlation between learning a foreign language through DA with the use of technology and higher unofficial OPI scores from two raters, as well as a greater student satisfaction and progress.

Deep Approach and Technologies in Practice: The Russian Flagship Program

The above review of the existing studies on implementing technology in DA language learning highlights possible ways of integrating such innovative approaches and tools into a more traditional, formal curriculum. The need for such integration is dictated by the current pace of Internet technology development, as well as by the call for foreign language proficiency among young specialists. Recently, changes in the global education environment have been addressed by many national governments, including in the U.S. The Flagship Program is one such federal-level initiative that focuses on fast and efficient ways of helping students acquire foreign languages, welcoming the newest approaches to language learning. With this movement in mind, I will briefly present two practical cases of implementing DA and technological applications into higher education, taken from the Russian Flagship Program at University of Wisconsin-Madison in Spring 2011 and Spring 2015.

The Russian Flagship Program at University of Wisconsin-Madison

The Language Flagship program is one of the initiatives of the U.S. National Security Education Program that is designed to implement a new paradigm for advanced language education through innovative approaches to collaboration between the federal government, international education institutions, and business. "The Language Flagship is a breakthrough in foreign language and culture instruction in the United States designed to help individuals achieve superior-level proficiency in critical languages including Arabic, Chinese, Hindi/Urdu, Korean, Persian/Farsi, and Russian" (NSEP, 2016). The program helps undergraduate students of all majors achieve ACTFL Superior-level proficiency in the target language. As the Language Flagship is receptive to new concepts and approaches in language instruction, I integrated DA for second/foreign language learning from Deep PjBL pedagogy to the curriculum of weekly "Social Hours" that I facilitated in Spring 2011. DA was a strong fit for the Russian Flagship program thanks to its methodological adaptability to the primary goal of the Language Flagship—namely, reaching proficiency standards through various curricular and extracurricular activities. Another important feature of DA that correlates with the Language Flagship initiative is its transdisciplinary treatment of education, "integrating disciplinary contents, interdisciplinary skills within experiential projects that aim at self-actualization and social action" (Tochon, 2011, p. 2). As a result, the successful integration of several aspects of DA concepts into a Social Hour context substantially improved the overall level of involvement and effectiveness.

Social Hour

The cohort of Russian Flagship students participating in the study consisted of eight students. Social Hour is a weekly event developed to carry out a rich program of events and activities for Russian Flagship students to provide opportunities for using Russian language and culture in a variety of authentic contexts. In the spring of 2011, these activities included: (a) conversations in Russian with visiting scholars and public figures, (b) a Russian film series, with introductions and discussions led in Russian by Russian Flagship students and other guest speakers, (c) cooking events, (d) community events (Russian Educational Association events, Wisconsin Film Festival Russian films, musical performances), and (e) a Russian icon exhibit tour. Students actively participated in the Social Hour curriculum design according to DA principles. Outcome-based and result-oriented teaching models were replaced by a dynamic and open-perspective DA model on an experimental basis. Bearing in mind the three levels of unified taxonomy—the discipline, interdiscipline, and transdiscipline (Tochon, 2014)—the curriculum was embedded into a particular system of instructional action, aiming to reach through to the transdisciplinary level for each project-based activity. Moreover, the integration of the four post-Cartesian precepts of teacher planning—namely, *Relevance* rather than the verification of veracity, *Holism* rather than the division of problems into segments, *Direction* rather than simple-to-complex gradation, and *Connectedness* rather than exhaustiveness (Tochon, 2014)—allowed for the students' deeper involvement in the planning stage of activities, thus increasing their overall motivation and interest in the language. Projects that were proposed by students became the course's main ingredient. Each project included the four domains, which refer to "the functional components of an individual and include perceptive, cognitive, affective, and psychomotor aspects" (Tochon, 2014, p. 140). As a result, while planning educational projects in collaboration with the students, I used the planning model proposed by Tochon (2014) called IAPI. "The model's name comes from the acronym of its tasks domains: I for Interpret, A for Analyze, P for Present, I for Interact" (p. 77). The instructional flexibility of the model, as well as its compatibility with the American Council on the Teaching of Foreign Language (ACTFL) proficiency standards that serve as a main criterion for Language Flagship development, makes this model a perfect match for the Russian Flagship. At the same time, this model integrates ACCESS (which in turn includes tasks related to extensive reading and language analysis in practice) and VOICE (which includes tasks related to writing, speaking, recording, and exchange with other people) as two major components of transdisciplinary-oriented projects (Tochon, 2014), making students and their learning processes the central focus of the classroom experience. "Deep teaching is learner-centered. It builds on the intrinsic motivation of the learner, authentic documents, and new information technologies when appropriate." (Tochon, 2010, p. 6)

The use of available open-access Internet applications was an integral part of every Social Hour theme. For example, a cooking event was preceded by autonomous research on websites dedicated to the Shrovetide, participating in Russian language interest groups on vkontakte.ru, and publishing videos of the recipes on a YouTube channel. Students were encouraged to take part in as many projects as they wanted. As a result, the students proposed and planned the following projects (some students were willingly involved in multiple): leading a tour of Russian icons at a Chazen Museum exhibit (a collaboration of two students), the GULAG Project (a collaboration of two students who took a class on GULAG in English and intended to share their knowledge in Russian through a web-platform), and the Slow Food project (an individual project of one of the students involved in the Slow Food movement, who created video-recipes in Russian). The results of the projects suggest a generally successful though mixed experience: despite the DA's perfect fit for the Flagship curriculum, its lack of assessment "leverage" made it less effective in terms of difficulty. In other words, students maintained an outcome-based mindset despite a theoretical introduction to the principles of DA in the beginning of the experiment. Such thinking interfered with the creation of their own assessment rubrics and, as a result, they refused to challenge themselves with more demanding activities, unwilling to "go the extra mile". The lack of time and the perception of Social Hour as an extracurricular, informal and not-so-important activity in comparison with the rest of the curricular workload, especially towards finals and the end of the semester, caused some students to leave their projects unfinished. On the other hand, the overarching idea of "deepness" and involvement in instructional planning, as well as the freedom of choice provided by autonomous learning through authentic material on Russian websites and social networks, increased students' interest in Russian culture and language—and, on a practical level, increased participation. For example, a student who served as a tour guide at the Chazen museum contacted me to ask if she could be excused after her presentation due to another examination the next day, which allowed me to surmise that she would have missed the whole class otherwise. However, she in fact stayed until the end of class despite her exam, as she was clearly interested in the other presentations. In summary, Social Hours created signature out-of-class contexts through a museum tour, conversations and debates, cooking, and other lively activities.

Chazen Museum Project. Further, I will present a personal case of PjBL as an illustration of the successful implementation of blended DA in the Flagship curriculum. The main feature of the 'Deep' Syllabus is its flexibility (Tochon, 2014): "since we want to keep the approach flexible, I do not propose one curriculum or one syllabus but principles (a grammar) that will allow educators to negotiate curricula with their classes" (p. 214). Consequently, project participants transformed the original, open syllabus into an individual syllabus that fit their goals. I informed students about a unique collection of Russian icons belonging to the Chazen museum, and students were invited to a series of lectures on the exhibition. They also viewed a Russian film about the most famous icon painter, *Andrey Rublev,* and actively participated in a face-to-face conversation in Russian with Alexei Lidov, the Director of Research at the Institute for World Culture of Moscow State University, who was invited as the keynote speaker for a "Russian Icons in Context" symposium. As a result, two students enthusiastically partook in a project centered on the exhibition. At the first stage of the project, each student chose one icon to focus on, out of the thirty-two on display. The three of us went to the museum in advance in order to choose an icon. Then, the students designed the assessment rubrics with my help as a facilitator. The rubrics included the clarity of the informational blurb, the involvement of the audience, and the fluent speech of accessible Russian without reading. The second piece of the project included examining related Internet sources both in Russian and in English. As the exhibition had been fully prepared by students from the Department of Art History, there was also the possibility of meeting with the individuals responsible for the icons of interest, and I encouraged both students to do so. However, due to time constraints, they did not take this opportunity. Instead, they each created a page-long description of one icon as a rough draft and sent it to me for revision. Upon approval, the three of us met on Skype, where I commented on their drafts and we rehearsed both presentations. At that stage, it became obvious that their original goal of speaking without text was a bit ambitious and would be hard to achieve, though their other goals were met perfectly. On the day of the tour, they presented both icons in the museum. As a post-activity reflection, each shared their concerns and self-assessment with me. Neither was quite satisfied with the quality of their presentations, and one enthusiastically decided to take part in another project. In total, the project encompassed three weeks. During this time, my assistance to the students' self-directed learning included providing web resources, offering feedback during their preparation, video-recording their presentation, and continuing post-activity communication and support as a follow-up to the presentations.

The results of the implementation of DA into the Flagship curriculum were analyzed through my own observations as a teacher, documented in weekly journal entries, and through student evaluations. The students evaluated Social Hours in the experimental format as productive and motivating. They shared favorable feedback and reported overall satisfaction. Thus, the main conclusions of this study align with the findings of the blended DA approach described above (Tochon, 2013). Namely, I observed that the students who become personally connected with Russian culture generally increased their overall interest in the language, progressing faster than students with a lack of initiative. For example, one of the Flagship students discovered that I play a Russian folk instrument in the University Russian Folk Orchestra, and, later in the semester, joined the orchestra herself. She also consistently read news updates about cultural, community-based events on the Flagship website. Subsequently, her end-of-semester unofficial OPI demonstrated a higher level of proficiency than most of her peers. Another DA initiative, allowing students to participate in social networks and develop their own online community, was highly evaluated by the learners. The possibility to collaborate on group projects, rather than working individually, allowed students to engage in activities that were "more fun." In conclusion, open communication among students and instructors, collaborative planning, intrinsic motivation, and a variety of activities became the four key ingredients that helped learners to succeed.

Deep Tutoring

In the spring of 2015, myself, Anna Nesterchouk, and Jambul Akkaziev developed a Russian language curriculum implementing blended DA to an experimental tutoring course for the Russian Flagship students. We initiated the project in order to create educational materials for novice learners that would help them develop their intercultural competence through self-directed project work. In order to evaluate the effectiveness of our materials, we sought out four Russian Flagship students (of novice level proficiency, according to their unofficial OPI assessments) who volunteered to participate in a six-week tutoring course. During weekly informal meetings, we observed how students created and interacted with the experiential organizers as well as how they responded to the overall approach. As a result, students completed, presented, and evaluated the following three projects: a cartoon based on major Soviet cartoon tropes (a collaboration of two students), a blog about the night life of Moscow (individual project), and a short play based on Russian fairytales (individual project). Among language-learning activities for the project, students participated in the following:

- Six weekly, one-hour meetings with mentors and other participants. During the meetings, students worked on their projects while mentors provided guidance, help, and feedback. Students provided peer reviews of the Russian language content of projects in progress.

- Interviews with native Russian speakers who could help with the project. For example, the two students who worked on creating a cartoon interviewed a famous cartoonist, Anna Krylova. The student who developed an eBlog on the Moscow night scene had several Skype sessions with a peer from Moscow.

- Autonomous work on the projects during the week.

- Sharing work-in-progress and peer evaluation using the Facebook DA project group page.

- Presentation of final projects during the end-of-semester Flagship Social Hour to the Flagship community of UW-Madison.

The main goals for DA project participants were to increase intercultural competence, to practice collaboration skills, to learn Russian grammar through content, and to present tangible project results to the public. The participants used up-to-date technologies in every stage of the project. First, all communication outside of tutoring hours was conducted on the DA project Facebook group in Russian. Moreover, students engaged in asynchronous interaction with Russian native speakers through such platforms as Italki and Vkontakte, seeking information and materials. Such participation in online social spaces might not only promote written language gains but may also trigger a significant shift of learners' social orientation towards "perceiving their L2 use as a social accomplishment" (Klimanova, 2013, p. 358), thus adhering to the main principle of authenticity in deep education. Second, all four students were involved in collaborative or individual web-based writing through Google Docs. Students shared all of their drafts and final versions of the play, cartoon, and eBlog with other participants. In-class and out-of-class time was especially devoted to peer-review and feedback. According to a recent study on the effects of web-based collaborative writing on individual L2 writing scores, these activities significantly increase learner language knowledge and writing skills (Bikowski & Vithanage, 2016).

Two students engaged in a more technologically-advanced project than the rest of the class. They explored another prosperous direction of DA by creating their cartoon with the help of a mobile application. The learners' initiative to use the mobile application Stop Motion Studio for iPad was enthusiastically supported by the project facilitators, as mobile-assisted language learning often gains more attention from educators due to the perceived advantage of easier access in comparison with computer-assisted language learning. While researchers emphasize not only gains but also potential complexities of integrating mobile games and other applications in second and foreign language learning contexts (e.g. Holden & Sykes, 2011; Tochon, 2015b), the use of the mobile application for the cartoon proved to be a useful tool for DA project participants.

The DA project outcomes supported the researchers' original belief in the possibility of successfully teaching intercultural competence to novice-level language learners (Nesterchouk *et al.*, this volume). The implementation of available Internet technologies as well as the careful guidance of DA-trained language instructors represented major factors that promoted student autonomous learning and acquisition of intercultural proficiency.

iDeep for Autonomy: Approach with Caution

While no one can deny the obvious influence of both computer and mobile technology on humans' everyday lives, there are heated discussions devoted to the benefits and disadvantages of this recent global trend. Language educators continue to promote cutting-edge technology implementation in the classroom, advertising its helpfulness and value. However, there is a need in teacher training to target particular approaches and encourage the wise use of the available continuum of web tools. Godwin-Jones (2012) examines the use of ubiquitous Learning Management Systems (LMSs) through the tension between the philosophical and cultural values of education and the existing standards of online learning. The design of most LMSs is oriented towards a particular pedagogical approach, not necessarily on par with the contemporary trends of student-oriented and autonomy-supportive learning that reign in second language acquisition and applied linguistics. "The essential model is a closed, self-contained system using cognitive-behavioral learning, with emphasis on information presentation and measureable performance assessment" (Godwin-Jones, 2012, p. 4). Moreover, the most popular LMSs, such as Moodle or Blackboard Learn, force educators as well as learners to operate within a pre-built and rather fixed online environment that imposes standard, predictable categories of curriculum and assessment, leaving little room for exploring alternative approaches and designs. In order to encourage students to critically consume the infinite information available to them on the Internet, to autonomously search for the approaches and tools that would benefit them most, educators must provide learners with the training to acquire the necessary knowledge base for using technology wisely, or "at least we need to find means to make our students informed consumers of technology" (Godwin-Jones, 2012, p. 6).

While examining the experiences of an adolescent learning Spanish through mobile applications offered by a school distance program, Tochon (2015b) noticed the alarming tendency of the participant to become "buried" by the overwhelming amount of material and assignments, and to study in an atmosphere of constant pressure and challenge. The researcher concludes with a call for more nuanced and adapted approaches to MOOC and mobile application development by instructional designers: "Face-to-face teaming in the project-based use of online resources may provide new solutions for distance language" (Tochon, 2015b, p.14). In summary, policymakers and educators might consider special training for teachers to maximize the effectiveness of independent language learning through DA using Internet technology as a tool.

Conclusion

In this chapter, I briefly review the recent academic scholarship on issues related to the development and implementation of innovative DLL approaches and educational technologies for the purpose of promoting autonomy among second language learners. The two live-case projects of technology-enhanced Russian learning through Deep Approach demonstrate the success of DA theory application as realized by teachers and students. As a result, I propose that education policymakers embrace technological and theoretical innovations that foster learner independence in and out of language classrooms.

The chapter starts with an overview of the major principles of DA. As an educational concept, DA allows for the fuller and deeper creation of meaning for teachers and learners alike. It is rooted in semiotics, process theory, and complex theory. The principle of transdisciplinarity emphasizes the depth of this approach, as it allows learners to break the artificial limits of shallow language learning and to construct knowledge within multilayered modalities of various social, psychological, and cognitive contexts. Within technology-enhanced DA, learners focus on language as a disciplinary content, implement a variety of applications and tools as interdisciplinary strategy, and connect their acquired knowledge with practical transdisciplinary experience. The principle of equality proposes that learners, like teachers, have the power to create curriculum and assessment rubrics, evaluate projects, reflect on peer work, and hold time for self-reflection. This principle allows for students' increased intrinsic motivation. The theoretical orientation within the approach aims for practice and real-life activities, which characterizes DA as a bottom-up methodology. The lesson plans are unique for each group of participants, shaped according to their specific interests and needs. The teachers serve as facilitators and provide scaffolding in the form of meaningful conversations. The formal assessment is combined with evaluation provided by the students and the public alike. The concept of apprenticeship, which lies at the heart of DA, allows for the authentic application of transdisciplinarity.

The chapter continues with a closer look at the currently-developed open Internet resources for L2 Russian language learners. The two described modules target pragmatics and cultural nuances. Those skills allow students to have virtual "study-abroad" experiences to better prepare for actual trips later on. The chapter continues with the practical implementation of DA theoretical principles and Internet/mobile technology innovations in the context of the Russian Flagship Program at the University of Wisconsin-Madison. The participant evaluations and practical outcomes of both projects demonstrated the successful integration of blended DA into the Flagship curriculum.

In conclusion, an innovative Deep Approach and new technologies have provided unlimited sources and tools for crossing traditional borders between standard disciplines, learning modalities, and genres. While there is evidence of their invaluable use and effectiveness, technologies should be embraced by learners and embedded into existing curricula with caution, due to the possible traps of an infinite and undirected online environment. At the same time, regular teacher training is required to maximize the impact of self-directed learning on students with the guidance of experienced facilitators/mentors. Oftentimes, untrained instructors of less commonly taught languages are hired by institutions due to the lack of professionals, which could slow students' learning progress (Tochon et. al, 2014). Thus, the comprehensive theoretical and practical training of teachers, which helps them develop within less-known and non-traditional domains, is one area that should not be neglected by educators and policymakers in creating deep, blended pedagogy for increased learner autonomy.

References

Berdan S. (2015). Study Abroad Could Be So Much Better. *The Chronicle of Higher Education.* Retrieved from [http://www.chronicle.com/article/Study-Abroad-Could-Be-So-Much/229273/]

Bikowski, D., & Vithanage, R. (2016). Effects of Web-based Collaborative Writing on Individual L2 Writing Development. *Language Learning & Technology, 20*(1), 79-99.

Blake, R. J. (2013). *Brave New Digital Classroom: Technology and Foreign Language Learning* (2d ed.). Washington, DC: Georgetown University Press.

Initiatives of NSEP. 2016. Retrieved from https://nsep.gov/content/language-flagship

Furniss, E. (2015). *A Web-based Instructional Module for the Teaching of Routine Formulas in Russian* (Unpublished doctoral dissertation). The Pennsylvania State University, State College, PA

Godwin-Jones, R. (2012). Emerging Technologies. Challenging Hegemonies in Online Learning. *LLT, 16*(2), 1-3.

Godwin-Jones, R. (2013). The technological imperative in teaching and learning less commonly taught languages. *Language Learning and Technology, 17*(1), 7–19.

Holden, C. L., & Sykes, J. M. (2012). Leveraging mobile games for place-based language learning. *Developments in Current Game-Based Learning Design and Deployment, 27.*

Kinginger, C. (2008). Language Learning in Study Abroad: Case Studies of Americans in France. *The Modern Language Journal, 92,* 1-124.

Klimanova, L. (2014). *Second Language Identity Building Through Participation In Internet-Mediated Environments: A Critical Perspective* (Doctoral Dissertation). Retrieved from LLBA. AAI3608306.

Nesterchouk, A., Akkaziev, J., & Zheltoukhova S. (in this volume) Intercultural competence through project work: A Practical guide to Deep Russian Learning. Blue Mounds, WI: Deep University Press.

Taguchi, N., & Sykes, J. M. (Eds.). (2013). *Technology in interlanguage pragmatics research and teaching.* Amsterdam: John Benjamins.

Tochon, F.V. (2010) Deep education. *Journal for Educators, Teachers and Trainers, 1,* 1-12.

Tochon, F. V. 2011, April 11. Questions and answers on the deep approach to education. [PowerPoint Presentation]. A Deep Approach to Foreign Language Project-Based Learning, FR 821, University of Wisconsin, Madison, WI

Tochon, F. V. (2013). Effectiveness Of Deep, Blended Language Learning As Measured By Oral Proficiency And Course Evaluation. LCTL Journal.

Tochon, F. (2014). *Help them learn a language deeply: The deep approach to world languages and cultures.* Blue Mounds, WI: Deep University Press.

Tochon, F. (2015a). A Deep Turn: Education for Autonomy at a Time Teachers Need Hope. *Enhancing Autonomy in Language Education: A Case-Based Approach to Teacher and Learner Development.* Oxford: Wiley-Blackwell.

Tochon, F. (2015b). Mobile Experiences of an Adolescent Learning Spanish Online in a 21st Century High School. *International Journal of Pedagogies and Learning*. 20(10), 1-16.

Tochon, F. V., Karaman, A. C., & Ökten, C. E. (2014). Online instructional personal environment for deep language learning. *International Online Journal of Education and Teaching/ISSN: 2148-225X, 1*(2).

16.

Branching Out Beyond the Standards: A Multiliteracies Framework for Deep Higher Education

Mary Zuidema
University of Madison – Wisconsin
mzuidema@wisc.edu

When teaching a foreign language, a contemporary teacher might say that he or she has developed a pedagogy that follows the "communicative language teaching" method or a National Standards-based method. However, researchers recognize the limitations of these methods and have emphasized the Multiliteracies framework as a way to bring World Language Education into the 21st century. This researcher took a course on Multiliteracies and was intrigued by the possible practical applications of this framework to World Language Education as well as how this framework differs from instructional models taught in contemporary World Language Teacher Education programs. By attending a French 101 course that utilized the Multiliteracies framework, this researcher could see how Multiliteracies worked in practice and its translingual and transcultural applications. This researcher gained insight on how Multiliteracies differs from CLT, how Multiliteracies bridges the language-literature-culture gap, and how it aligns with the teachings of the Deep Approach.

When teaching a foreign language, a contemporary teacher might say that he or she has developed a pedagogy which utilizes the "communicative language teaching" (CLT) method or the National Standards delegated by the American Council for the Teaching of Foreign Language (ACTFL). Both CLT and the ACTFL National Standards have taken language learning to a new level in the past twenty years with a focus on a students' ability to communicate in the target language. Moving from an era of audiolingualism allowed the language classroom to become more student-centered and less focused on rote memorization. This meaning-making experience ushered in the concept of "lifelong learning" as a process, not a product, of participating in World Language Education (WLE). However, some researchers have recognized that foreign language teaching has entered a "post-CLT" era due to certain limitations of this approach to language acquisition (Bourns & Melin, 2014). Other researchers have stated that language teaching has even entered a "post methods" era, stating that every teacher has their own methods that they follow (Kumaravadivelu 2003), which may include an amalgamation of many different pedagogical understandings.

The Nature of the Problem

For all of the contributions of CLT and the ACTFL National Standards, World Language (WL) teachers have begun to see the finite nature of this approach and are in need of a pedagogical restoration. CLT has become a blanket term for non-traditional language learning, or teachers piecemeal together a pedagogy adopting CLT in portions alongside audiolingualism, direct translation, and the natural approach. Glisan (2012) furthered this idea by arguing that this push for a Standards-based curriculum has created a phenomenon in which the Standards become over-applied. In textbooks, for example, publishers label certain activities as representative of certain Standards without an authentic connection to them (e.g., labeling an activity in which two students take turns reading words as a Communication activity). Not only does this process of simplification reveal profound misunderstandings of the pedagogical concepts of the Standards, but this also demonstrates much of what Pennycook (1994) considered to be the "empty babble of the communicative language class" (p. 311). With an emphasis on oral language production, reading and writing take secondary or supporting roles behind the speaking activities.

Curriculum development can be especially challenging if there is a lack of departmental vision or cohesion: Use of the same syllabus and

/or textbook across the 101-level courses does not necessarily correlate with a cohesive approach to teaching. Another challenge to teaching these beginning levels of language, which Byrnes, Norris, and Maxim (2010) mentioned, was the "bifurcation" between language, literature, and culture. During lesson plan formation, for example, instructors may build in activities that separate culture, language, and literature or relegate them to different days (e.g. Friday is deemed "Culture Day"). One day may be considered the reading day and another day may be designated for culture, cementing a separation of the two concepts in the students' minds. This approach tends to offer a superficial view of surface-level culture rather than an profound study of deep culture, emphasizing the four F's of culture (food, festivals, folklore, and fashion) instead of the deeper recesses of culture, which include: "rites of passage, the use of forms of discourse, the social 'pecking order,' their use of space," as well as the "intangible aspects of culture" (ACTFL, 1996) such as a culture's preferences for competition or cooperation, concepts of time and time management, or an emphasis on a collective or individualistic society.

A recent report in the Modern Language Association (2007) called for "translingual and transcultural competence" development for students of world languages, in which students can integrate knowledge about their native language and culture with developing knowledge about the second language and culture to gain a more conscious, inclusive worldview. To be translingual is not simply to be bilingual. Translingualism suggests a combination of one's knowledge of cultures and one's ability to move between the two languages, suggesting the need for a Deep Approach to cultural competence. Bilingualism does not necessarily take into account a familiarity with the commonly-held norms and values often imperceptibly encoded within discourse. A translingual and transcultural language learner can act as a mediator between his or her own culture and his or her peers who are present, constantly interpreting and re-interpreting the cultural phenomena implicit or explicit in the interaction. Kramsch

(2012) viewed translingualism to be more than exercise in "playful polyglottism or inconsequential code-switching. It is the much more risky circulation of values across historical and ideological time scales" (p. 20). Nevertheless, a translingual and transcultural curriculum that bridges the gap between culture, language, and literature is essential to continue bringing WL teaching into the 21st century! Paesani, Allen, and Dupuy (2015) recognized the possibility of the Multiliteracies framework as a way of bringing the post-CLT pedagogical methods up to date, and as a way to combat problematic understandings of "literacy." I believe that the Multiliteracies framework aligns well with the Deep Approach towards offering a more holistic language curriculum.

Background of Research Interest

As an SLA scholar, language learner, and language teacher of Spanish, I was intrigued by the promises of Multiliteracies and wanted an alternative form of professional development: I decided to attend a biweekly French 101 course that utilized the Multiliteracies framework. My objective was to see how Multiliteracies worked in practice and how it connected language, literature, and culture. Additionally, by seeing the ways in which a fellow graduate student approached the teaching of an introductory language course, I could gain some insight into the behind-the-scenes work involved in structuring lessons, units, and exams based on the Multiliteracies framework. I proposed the following questions to guide my semester's investigation in the hopes of gaining insight into an innovative pedagogical approach:

1) How does Multiliteracies differ from CLT in practice?

2) How does Multiliteracies bridge the gap between language, literature, and culture?

3) What elements of Multiliteracies align with the teachings of Deep Education?

Prior to beginning, I needed to remember a few of the lessons I learned as both an SLA scholar and a language teacher. For example, I recognized the benefits of participating as much as possible in the target language, knowing that communicating an imperfectly stated idea is better practice for language learning than staying quiet to avoid making "embarrassing" errors. I also reminded myself that I was not going to understand every text word for word, but I had to find a way to use available strategies for getting the text's general meaning (looking at the pictures, seeking out cognates, using knowledge of Spanish to guess at unfamiliar words, etc). Although I did use a dictionary on occasion, I did not allow myself to look up every single word I did not understand because I wanted to focus on the linguistic and cultural context. I also know that a dependence on the dictionary can lead to learner helplessness, which I wanted to avoid. I also did not receive any formal grades on tests, exams, homework, or in-class conversation, so I know that I did not have a "fear of the red pen" hanging over my oral and written participation.

Related Literature

Literacy

A Multiliteracies approach could offer a reinvigoration of the Standards-based or CLT classroom and address the other problem at the heart of this study: the concept of "literacy". Originally developed by the New London Group (1996), Multiliteracies is an avenue to education in which students are able to interpret texts outside the traditional view of literacy. Literacy has been viewed historically as: a process of decoding the written word and recoding into a visual form, reading as a way of recalling facts at the end of the text, reading as a receptive skill (as opposed to writing or speaking), knowing vocabulary and grammar, or even, according to Gee (2012), a way to "domesticate the savage mind" (p. 68). Gee found that due to this particular issue, literacy has been used more to create and maintain social hegemonies than to educate or develop human knowledge, which remains problematic in the world today, not just historically.

Teachers who adopt these perspectives of literacy often decide which interpretations are valid, alienating students who may not be as familiar with the academic genres as other students who have had this privilege. Those students are subsequently seen as communicatively inept for having a differing interpretation from the norm.

The Multiliteracies framework balks at these understandings of "literacy", and does not perpetuate this "banking model of education" (Freire, 1970) as an effective form of learning. The New London Group (1996) proposed Multiliteracies as a way of de-neutralizing the process to create what Freire (1970) called a more "emancipatory experience" of learning. Literacy, the New London Group (1996) proposed, is socio-culturally situated and contextualized. In order to meaningfully read a text, background knowledge or familiarity with the culture from which the author presents the text is necessary, not just an understanding of grammar or an ability to translate or decode words from one language to the other. For example, knowing that the word "cheating" has a negative connotation would not aide a listener if they hear a stage manager tell an actor to "cheat out upon entering the stage." Knowledge of the culture of theatre is required in order to understand that the stage manager has asked the actor to work on facing the audience when they are on-stage instead of presenting their back to the viewers. This supports Kern's (2000) argument that the Multiliteracy framework is a process of: interpretation, collaboration, discovering conventions of how texts are read and by whom, gaining cultural knowledge, problem solving, reflection and self-reflection, language use (p. 17).

Within WLE, therefore, both educators and researchers have discovered a potential answer for the question Byrnes, Norris, and Maxim (2010) posed to the MLA committee's report (2007); that is, how to create a more translingual and transcultural curriculum. Allen and Paesani (2010) have described Multiliteracies as one in which students discover different genres and begin to identify the characteristic features of these genres (p. 5). Such a focus could help students better understand style, register, and even some of the more implicit sociolinguistic structures while simultaneously learning about the products, practices, and perspectives of the target cultures through authentic texts.

Additionally, the use of the Multiliteracies framework brings WLE into the 21st century. With the shifting of the job market over the past ten years, for example, students are electing for occupations concerned with knowledge management through digital devices over more traditional or manual professions. The digital age alone has completely reshaped the way in which we communicate our ideas with each other. The New London Group (1996) stated "When the proximity of cultural and linguistic diversity is one of the key facts of our time, the very nature of language learning has changed" (p. 64).Our students have access to apps, vlogs, blogs, games, music and music videos, wikis, web pages, graphic novels, and so much more at their fingertips. If one expects to hold the attention of this generation of language learners, relying on classic literature alone cannot and will not suffice!

Multiliteracies Phases

There are four phases or curricular components that make up the Multiliteracies framework: Overt Instruction, Critical Framing, Situated Practice, and Transformed Practice. The New London Group (1996) described these components as necessary for the students' processes of meaning design: Situated Practice bases the activity on the experiences that a learner has designed or is designing; Overt Instruction allows learners to create an "explicit metalanguage of Design"; Critical Framing helps learners to connect meaning to existing knowledge and "social context"; and Transformed Practice allocates time for students to "transfer and re-create Designs of meaning from one context to another" (p. 83). It is through these components that an instructor can better connect literature to language. Furthermore, these components could help instructors create opportunities to gain a more profound understanding of culture instead of the instructors imparting overt factual knowledge and asking the students to parrot back the information.

In Overt Instruction, the instructor scaffolds the learning and encourages critical understanding by providing direction to the students or sources of information to aide in comprehension (Cope & Kalantzis, 2009; New London Group, 1996; Paesani, Allen, & Dupuy, 2015). The teacher aides in the construction of meaning and emphasizes the students' design of meaning instead of "transferring" knowledge to the student (Kern, 2000, p. 45) Some examples of Overt Instruction activities include: supplying background information on articles, websites, or videos prior to beginning the activity; co-constructing a concept map with students; discussing textual instances of code-switching; or asking students to write their own first and last sentence of a paragraph.

In Critical Framing, the learner analyses new information in an unfamiliar context in order to link to existing knowledge (Cope & Kalantzis, 2009; New London Group, 1996; Paesani, Allen, & Dupuy, 2015). These types of activities allow the learner to relate new understandings to social contexts or linguistic forms or to gain distance from what they have learned in order to constructively critique it and eventually innovate on their own. Learners have the ability to gain the Some examples of Critical Framing activities include: reading a sentence or phrase and asking students to select the correct image from a set of images that matches the sentence, showing the first three minutes of a movie and asking students to predict what will happen, comparing culture and language between the students' native language and culture and the target language and culture, and having learners relate an abstract topic to their everyday experiences.

In Situated Practice, students have the opportunity to experience learning without consciously reflecting on what they are reading or seeing (Cope & Kalantzis, 2009; New London Group, 1996; Paesani, Allen, & Dupuy, 2015). These types of activities allow learners to practically apply what they have learned in authentic activities. The instructor scaffolds the participatory activity as a way of guiding students towards competence and comprehension of the target structure. Some examples of Situated Practice activities include: Think-Pair-Share freewriting, playing songs to focus on the meaning instead of a grammatical form (at first), Jigsaw-type activities, acting out a text, letter writing, journal writing, and other forms of creative writing (Kern, 2000).

In Transformed Practice, students can apply what they have learned into practical situations, creating new texts on the basis of the existing text they have studied while reflecting on what they have learned from the experience (Cope & Kalantzis, 2009; New London Group, 1996; Paesani, Allen, & Dupuy, 2015). Through these activities, students can even demonstrate critical understandings at the higher levels of Bloom's Taxonomy (1956): evaluating and making judgments about textual material, comparing and contrasting, justifying, interpreting, summarizing, criticizing, composing, rewriting, or networking. Some examples of Transformed Practice activities for students include: inventing story continuations or changing the ending of an existing story, rewriting a text from another character's point of view, creating a personal dialogue between the character and the student, creating a personalized research project on a specific topic of interest, or genre reformulation.

Data Collection

> Texts are more than an ensemble of words. Texts can contain or be comprised of visual images, audio, gestural and spatial features. Taking into account the gestural resources of text, for example, exposes learners to non-verbal components of a language, as situated in a cultural context. (M. Henderson, personal communication, January 18, 2015)

This quote from a colleague in an email demonstrates the heart of a curriculum that utilizes the Multiliteracies framework: the concept of "texts." Texts can be considered a number of sources, not just the traditional written input comprehension activity. After completing the work for the French 101 course, I compiled a list of the different types of texts that we experienced within the course, making sure to include image-based texts in addition to those texts that were coded with written words.

Table 1 below indicates the title of the text, the type of genre to which the text belongs (e.g. painting, song, podcast, etc.), and the topic for which it was used. The topics include a range of vocabulary-related, grammar-related, and cultural subjects.

Not included in this list is the numerous examples of pictures used on exams or vocabulary practice that were used to help the learner "bind" the meaning of the word to the written form, that is, the relationship between the signifier and the signified (e.g. a picture of two people meeting and the concept of *faire la bise*, an aspect of French culture in which individuals exchange kisses on both cheeks upon greeting each other). Although I would certainly categorize pictures as a type of socially-contextualized text, the exclusion of these photos from the following chart is simply to reduce confusion due to their lack of titles.

Table 1. Texts used in the class

	Genre	Topic
Simple comme "bonjour"	Essay	Greetings, Introduction
"Sympathique" by Pink Martini	Song	Negation
"La trahison des images"	Painting by René Magritte	Negation
"La france vue de l'étranger"	Youtube video	Cultural Stereotypes
Numéros de Teléphone en France	Grocery receipt	Telephone numbers
Nouveau contact	Cell phone contacts	Telephone numbers, Names
Le monde à Paris	Story, Essay	Nationalities of Parisians
Let's Travel With…	Blog excerpts	Nationality, Age, Hometown
Une famille internationale	Podcast	Family, Family Tree
Chazen Art Museum	Museum Tour	Art, Paintings, Colors
Les opinions sur les Français	Online Editorials	Personal Opinions
Décrivez oú vous habitez	Apartment Ads	Lodging, Adjectives
Cherchecoloc.com, colocation.fr	Apartment Ads	Personal descriptions
Les professions	Leaflet	Professions
Langues d'Europe	Short Essay	European Union languages
Aimez-vous Picasso?	Online Comment Section	Art, Picasso, Preferences
Meetic.com / Missed Connections	Online Profile	Descriptions
Les Français préfèrent…Dr. House	Report from a National Survey	Television Preferences
"Seated Woman (Marie-Therese)"	Painting by Picasso	Body Parts, Physical Description
Les loisirs et les sports	Survey Data	Leisure Activities, Faire de
Quelle heure est'il?	Pictures of Clocks	Telling Time
Horaire des trains	Train Schedule	Telling Time, Partir vs. Arriver
L'événement	Invitations to Events	Formal vs. Informal questions
Déjeuner du Matin	Poem by Jacques Prévert, youtube video	Present perfect tense

Pour Toi, Mon Amour	Poem by Jacques Prévert	Present perfect tense
Biographie de Léopold Senghor	Biography	Present perfect tense
Les jours fériés en France	Online video	Holidays, Festivals
Pour décrire vos etudes à la fac	School Schedules	Courses, Studies
Le look qui tue	Online TV Series Clips	French Youth Culture
Une Journée Avec Alice Isaaz	Interview	Daily Life
L'Auberge Espagnole	Movie	Movies, Cinema vocabulary
Montréal Realia	Photographs, Maps	Travel vocabulary, Montreal
Du romantisme des transports	Editorial	Travel vocabulary
www.routard.com	Blogs	Travel reasons
Journée spéciale	Study Abroad Advertisement	Study abroad, Erasmus program
Choisir son hôtel	TripAdvisor, Youtube video	Hotel ammenities
La rue Cler	Map, Instagram comments	Directions, Description
Situer les endroits	Map of Paris	Directions
Trouver un hôtel à Montreal	Article by David Seyve	Montreal description
Do you speak Touriste?	Paris Regional Committee Guide	Tourism
Mademoiselle, la case en trop!	Propaganda	Madame / Mademoiselle

After compiling this list, I also decided to include the questions (Table 2) that we were given to guide our reading of the texts as a way of comparing the ways in which texts presented within the Multiliteracies framework differ from the ways in which they are analyzed or discussed in CLT:

Table 2. Authentic Text Questions

What is the main idea of the text? How could I summarize this text (in complete or incomplete sentences)?
1. Is this a formal or informal situation/text?
2. What is my personal reaction to the text?
3. Does this text come from a "genre" that I recognize?
4. Is this a text I could imitate (ex: blog post)?
5. Are there any linguistic features I recognize that connect form and meaning?

Data Analysis

How does Multiliteracies differ from CLT in practice?

As mentioned earlier, CLT emphasizes interaction and oral production as the ultimate goal and demonstration of language learning. Within the classroom, I do believe that we were given many opportunities to interact with our partners to practice our budding abilities in speaking French. A survey, for example, allowed us to ask each other about movie preferences or daily course schedules to compare and contrast our interests and lives as students. A "Jigsaw" type activity allowed individuals to become experts on holidays and festivals of different countries and present this knowledge to their group members, who then shared the information with others in the class. There were a few instances, however, in which interaction occurred without a true exchange of information, such as comparing answers on mechanical exercises. This could be an example of the over-applied Communication Standard within the textbook's activities as mentioned earlier. Nevertheless, the majority of the interactive activities allowed for creativity and a variety of responses.

I also noticed an incredibly significant emphasis on the use of texts. With only 30 classes, one can see from the chart above that there was an average of at least one text used in each class, which does not even account for the numerous photos or images used to help the process of binding the form to the meaning for vocabulary words or cultural concepts. Furthermore, when the text's topic contextualized grammar, the questions used to analyze and discuss the texts offered a mixture of an inductive and a deductive approach to grammar, which overall allowed the student and the instructor to co-construct the meaning together instead of relying on lengthy in-class grammar explanations or self-taught grammar breakthroughs at home. Despite a few moments in which the instructor's Overt Instruction stage seemed less about scaffolding knowledge and more about a clarification of the rules or a formula, I would say that grammar instruction was constantly reinforced with contextualized texts. I also believe that she used these formulas as a way to help the more Spatial-Logical learners to create links between their preferred learning styles to the grammar concepts, since there were a few classmates who appreciated the charts or rule clarifications. Furthermore, the questions found in Figure 1.2 which the instructor provided aptly exemplify many of the goals of Multiliteracies: interpretation of the main idea of the text, reflection, self-reflection, and recognition of the characteristic features of particular genres.

I noticed, however, that other techniques or features of CLT were utilized in many of the classes, which indicates that although the main framework of the class was Multiliteracies, some elements of CLT are hard to eliminate completely from the language learning process, nor should they be! For example, we worked to develop communicative and grammatical language competences in order to make meaning, demonstrated by a mixture of comprehension and grammar-based questions following our reading of different texts. I was pleased to see that many of the follow-up comprehension questions allowed for personal reflection, consideration of formal or informal register, and discussion of genre conventions as well as questions that allowed the learner to consider the grammar structures and how one might formulate the grammar in context. There were also times when fluency was held in higher esteem than accuracy, another element of CLT, which was demonstrated by an encouragement to produce with the language early on in the learning process foregoing corrections on our accuracy errors. Also, the instructor took the initiative to consider her learners' interests and needs in order to make the experience more fulfilling. For example, she organized a guided tour in French for us at the local art museum; she provided supplementary authentic texts for those students who asked for extra reading practice; and she constantly gave suggestions for podcasts, books, music, youtube videos, and television shows in order for us to find accessible French realia of interest.

The assessments seemed to offer a range of exercises that reflected different aspects of audiolingualism, CLT, and Multiliteracies. Certain mechanical fill-in-the-blank sections required the learner to have memorized the verb paradigm to write the word instead of to demonstrate a more in-depth demonstration of critical thinking. To me, these tasks align with the tenants of audiolingualism over CLT or Multiliteracies. On other quizzes, we could, for example, write a dialogue between ourselves and our host-mother in France in which we introduced a friend. In these sections, there was much more freedom for creativity and expansion, as we could use any vocabulary or grammar we had learned to write out a potential script as long as it fit the prompt. To me, this type of activity exemplifies CLT's emphasis on written presentation. Finally, in a reading section on one quiz, we were asked to choose the main idea and tone of the text. These types of questions completely diverge from the more traditional reading sections that prompt the learner to search for information mentioned in the text and "regurgitate" it back using exact quotations as a way to demonstrate reading comprehension. These particular tasks address the goal of Multiliteracies of reading "into" a text versus reading a text.

Another element of Multiliteracies that helped with our interpretation of texts is the use of the multiple readings to guide our understanding of different textual elements. One perfect example of this practice was an activity that utilized an apartment advertisement found on the website cherchecoloc.com. For our pre-reading activity, we made a list of the typical information found in an advertisement seeking a roommate. Following this activity, we "read" the ads by skimming them for specific examples of the typical information we had listed in the pre-reading activity. (For example, a typical piece of information to include in a roommate announcement would be to mention if pets are allowed to live in the apartment. One would then skim the advertisements for vocabulary such as *chien*, *chat*, or *animaux domestique* to ascertain if this information was indeed mentioned). After the pre-reading activity, we began the *lecture initiale* to write down information regarding the authors of the announcements, the descriptions of the apartment rooms, and qualities that the authors were seeking in a potential roommate. Finally, in our third reading, we noted the differences between the organization and content of these ads and ads found on colocation.fr. We then chose an apartment that we would live in and explained why we made this choice.

Overall, I would say that CLT is not in itself obsolete, but it certainly needs to adapt towards a more text-friendly pedagogy if it is to remain the cultural norm of WL teachers. With regard to assessment, however, it is hard to say if there is a best method, as the tests, quizzes, and exams did not always follow one particular pedagogical structure due to the need to conform to the program requirements. I am not aware of a school-based WL classroom that does not have to conform to such requirements, but if Deep Education is to occur, then perhaps assessments in CLT and Multiliteracies could allow for even more project-based learning or for the students to be curriculum builders alongside the instructors.

How does Multiliteracies bridge the gap between language, literature, and culture?

During the first week of class, the instructor used the painting *La trahison des images* by René Magritte and the song "Sympathique" by the musical group *Pink Martini* as two examples of authentic texts. With regard to language, the phrase at the bottom of the painting, "Ceci n'est pas une pipe" (This is not a pipe), and the refrain of the song "Je ne veux pas travailler / Je ne veux pas déjeuner / Je veux seulement oublier / Et puis je fume" (I do not want to work / I do not want to have lunch / I just want to forget / and so I smoke) utilize grammatically negative sentences using the structure "ne + verb + pas." With regard to literature, the students were able to interpret both the painting and the song in order to get at the meta-messages and meanings of the texts. The painting, for example, conveys the semiotic concept that the image of a pipe is not a pipe; it only displays a representation of a pipe. This concept is one with which students must contend: seeing a pipe, a student unfamiliar with semiotics might describe the painting as one with a pipe in it despite the sentence that states that it is not a pipe. Although this would not match the traditional view of literacy, this painting does require the viewer to read the sentence at the bottom of the text, which acts as a literary device to enhance the painting and produce the specific effect of negating the signifier being the same as the signified. The song also connects to literature as it is an authentic text. To clarify, this means that it was written by a native French speaker for an audience of fellow native French speakers. It also represents a traditional prose piece of text, allowing students to recognize that it is a song by recognizing characteristics of the genre of music: it has a melody, it is set to music, it has a recurring refrain, it has rhyming mechanisms, and it is a written work.

With regard to culture, finally, each piece represents distinct products, practices, and perspectives only available in the target culture. In the painting (a product), the author offers insight into the perspective of semiotics and brings to light the frequent misinterpretations that occur when individuals mistake the signifier for the signified (and vice versa). The song and the music video that accompanies the song (also products), also demonstrate certain practices in the French world, such as smoking cigarettes: Smoking has not been as negatively viewed and smoking laws not as widely enforced in France as it is in other cultures, which demonstrates a perspective that differs from one which dissuades cultural members from smoking.

In the final week of class, we finished watching the movie *L'Auberge Espagnole*, directed by Cédric Klapisch (which translates to "The Spanish Hostel" or "The Spanish Apartment"). From a language perspective, we were given a pre-viewing activity in which we had to find translations to some slang terms that the characters used in the movie. Although the academic classroom favors a more professional and proper register, the reality is that slang terms are prevalent in any conversation, and so gaining exposure to them is indeed gaining access to language that would otherwise not be studied. From a literary perspective, interpretation of gestures and actions was a necessary component for a non-native French 101 student. Lacking fluency, I found it difficult to understand what the characters discussed in their conversations. However, by focusing on the facial expressions, interactions, and motions, I was able to parse together the main ideas of the conversations. The characters also tended to use code-switching, as the main characters, who live in an apartment together, represent a variety of countries, including France, Italy, England, Denmark, and Belgium among others. In this particular film, then, the lingua franca to bridge all the conversations was actually a mixture of English, French, and Spanish, instead of one singular language. This kind of code-switching between languages allows the viewer to understand the process as both a literary device and as a cultural practice. Furthermore, from the cultural perspective, the film takes place in Barcelona but is seen through the eyes of a French citizen who decided to study abroad through the Erasmus program, a way for students in the European Union to study internationally. By allowing the narrator and main character to be from France, the film offers a glimpse of the Spanish lifestyle from a French perspective. Typically, in WL courses, students only learn about countries that utilize the target language. In this particular case, we were able to create a transcultural bridge by stepping into a Spanish-speaking country with a French lens as North American students, which I believe demonstrates a way to fulfill Byrnes, Maxim, and Norris' (2010) call for action for transcultural and translingual learning experiences.

These texts came from the first days and the last days of the course, which shows that even lower-level courses can include cultural texts instead of perpetuating the aforementioned bifurcation between language, literature, and culture that often distinguishes upper-level courses from lower-level courses in WL programs. Language learners at the beginning levels have an interest in culture and literature, too, not just students at the upper levels of WL education. Perhaps embracing this interconnected notion of language, literature, and culture could promote more enrollment in WL programs across the nation, as well, especially considering the drop in modern language course enrollments since the 1960's (according to the MLA Report, 2007). The MLA committee likened this drop to a "crisis," especially concerning the "nation's language deficit" (p. 2), and confirmed a need to transform current academic practices.

What elements of Multiliteracies align with the teachings of Deep Education?
Transformed Practice.

I found that many of the stages of a Multiliteracies lesson align well with the goals of Deep Education. Perhaps most intriguing to me was the "Transformed Practice" stage, as we had the opportunity to apply our knowledge of particular texts, structures, meanings, and cultural norms to different projects throughout the semester. Our main "Portfolio" projects, for example, were: an entry for an online social media site in which we described our likes, dislikes, and ideal significant others, an interview with a faux journalist about our daily lives, and a study abroad advertisement to a Francophone country including information about transportation, lodging, and other cultural activities. There were, of course, other examples of small-scale Transformed Practice activities, but these major benchmarks every few weeks can document a student's growing abilities by assessing the amount of diverse vocabulary used and the ability of the student to express himself or herself using the Available Designs. That is, each week, upon exposure to more words and input, the student has more to draw on for output.

Transformed Practice aligns with Deep Education's rationale of transdisciplinary measures for expressing a students' budding awareness of language, literature, and culture. With regard to "Transdiciplinarity," then: "Its goal is the understanding of the present world, of which one of the imperatives is the unity of knowledge" (Tochon, 2010, p. 3). By exposing students to certain texts and subsequently asking the students to rewrite the text from a different genre, to restructure a text's ending, or redesign a text, a teacher is using a transdisciplinary approach to the learning experience. Although the classroom is that of a WL classroom, a student may be asked to read national reports or surveys, political pieces, opinion editorials, medical graphs, artistic expressions, or a city map. These texts, in particular, connect to other majors offered at the college level: International Affairs, Public Relations or Political Science, Communications, Health, Advertising, Digital Media, Theatre Arts, or even Engineering, to name a few. Tochon (2010) stated that "Deep learning focuses on meaning" (p. 5), which connects to the Multiliteracies framework's concept of "reading the world and reading the word" (Gee, 2012, p. 62), which Gee described as "making sense of the text" (reading the word) being an impossible action unless one has learned how to "make sense of the world that the text is about" (reading the world). Transformed Practice, then, allows a student to demonstrate how he or she has connected these practices and to reflect on their developing abilities.

Goal creation

In Deep Education, one of the main tenants to guide the curriculum is to ask students to provide goals at the beginning of the semester and to maintain progress throughout the semester so as to complete those goals. This represents a true and pure example of student-directed learning and a student-centered classroom: Both are utilized in WL Teacher Education classrooms to contrast with the more traditional classroom in which the teacher could be described as having an "atlas complex," carrying the weight of the world (the lesson) on his or her shoulders. Although the French 101 class I took did not utilize the exact Deep Education model of student-directed learning, we were asked to provide goals at the beginning of the semester, which ranged from achieving a few higher sub-levels on the ACTFL proficiency rating scale, to reading a book in French, to subscribing to French podcasts and music websites. Although we were never assessed on our completion of these goals, the instructor did take an interest in what we wanted to accomplish and made sure to provide extra material to support us: She uploaded numerous authentic texts to the course website for those students who wanted to read more French and utilized numerous media outlets within the classroom to expose us to different musical groups, paintings, podcasts, or television shows.

Teacher as guide

Within the classroom, our teacher acted more often as a guide than a knowledge keeper or knowledge transmitter, another element that aligns with Deep Education. There were occasional grammar rules or formulas on the PowerPoints as mentioned previously, but I would say that she constantly tried to take a step back from the "center" of the classroom and allow her students to create dialogues or small role-plays. She also used metalinguistic questions orally or provided metalinguistic feedback on our writing samples to promote more uptake from her learners (ensuring that students were self-correcting their own errors through her questions or comments). She gave examples of acronyms to help us remember adjective placement (BAGS for beauty, age, goodness, and size) or irregular past tense verbs (DR. MRS. VANDERTRAMP for *devenir, revenir, monter, rentrer, sortir*, etc.), or providing us with potential websites to guide our Portfolio projects. I believe that this is another example of Deep Education alignment, as Deep Education contrasts starkly with the traditional Direct Instruction and strives for a classroom in which the instructor allows the interests or abilities of the students to flourish while enabling the students to improve on their communication skills.

Potential for social justice

A final consideration of Multiliteracies is its potential for Social Justice, a major component of Deep Education. According to Tochon (2010), the Deep Approach to Education involves "projects that aim at self-actualization and social action" as well as "an earth centered holistic approach with the objective of social justice" (Harrison, 2013). There were, for example, a few texts we viewed and interpreted that could have led to deeper discussion and insight into social justice movements or action. After reading a piece of feminist propaganda entitled <<*Mademoiselle, la case en trop!*>> about the use of Madame and Mademoiselle as the binary options available in French society, we could have had more discussion on women's rights or on the feminist movement. We had the opportunity to view the film *The Intouchables* outside of class. This film could have prompted awareness of disability discrimination, poverty, and racism in society and taking part in awareness groups on-campus. The ability to access a multitude of texts also demonstrates an ability to access the voices of the unheard through texts that originate outside of the cultural "norm." Deep Education aligns with the International Network for Language Education Policy Studies to disrupt hegemonic power relationships in traditional views of education and "schooling" and to disseminate the status quo. By offering students texts that come from a variety of cultural representatives, a teacher can show students that a country's "culture" is not found in one particular group. Furthermore, these types of texts from the unheard can provide awareness to students who operate in the ethnocentric levels of cultural competence to recognize privilege and marginalization in their own societies. Muirhead (2009) discussed this possibility by stating that "Inseparable from language, culture is also impacted by issues of power as it can be used to marginalize or privilege." These texts allow students to avoid being bound by their own cultural perspectives in order to become more ethnorelative: accepting, adaptive, and integrative (Bennett, Bennett, & Allen; 2003), which certainly demonstrate one of the objectives of Deep Education.

Limitations to the study

I do recognize that this study does have some limitations to it, and I'd like to address a few of these:

a) I recognize that as a student in the French 101 course that I attended, I represent an anomaly: I am not an undergraduate student, I was not completing a course requirement, I was not receiving a grade on my homework or projects, and I did not have to take the quizzes or exams. Without a worry for my GPA, I could fully concentrate on the experience of learning and in participating in class discussions. I recognize my privilege in this regard, as the other students in the class did have to worry about how the grades they received on homework or tests would affect their overall GPA. They were also taking other classes in addition to French, and so their focus was not solely on learning another language.

b) Grammar activities did not always fall under one of the phases of Multiliteracies. For example, to learn the *passé composé* (what I believe would be the equivalent of the present perfect tense), we were given a chart to exemplify the irregular verbs using the acronym "DR. MRS. VANDERTRAMP" to help us memorize the verbs that use etre instead of avoir ("to be" instead of "to have"). Other verbs with irregular past participles in the *passé composé* had to be learned by rote as well, so we were given another chart with the verbs in the infinitive next to the their past participles.

c) Although I did maintain personal communication with the instructor of the course throughout the semester to discuss Multiliteracies, I did not see her lesson plans, which could have better distinguished the distinct phases (Overt Instruction, Critical Framing, Situated Practice, and Transformed Practice) of Multiliteracies in practice. Although I am familiar with these phases, I cannot say for certain the particular phase for which an activity could be categorized.

d) A curriculum founded on the Multiliteracies framework is a time-consuming endeavor. I recognize the amount of hours spent searching for texts to exemplify certain grammar or vocabulary points, and I know that not every instructor has the time to overhaul the curriculum or deviate from the textbook. Furthermore, not every instructor has the luxury to build multiple readings of a singular text into the daily lesson plan.

Implications for future research or curricular design

After completing the course, I recognized a few ideas that may help future researchers who wish to investigate a curriculum based on the Multiliteracies framework:

a) Although the course was proposed to follow the Multiliteracies framework, the textbook that was used for the course aligned with an approach based on the 4-skills pedagogy: reading, writing, speaking, listening. Because the use of the Multiliteracies framework has not yet been incorporated into the ACTFL Standards or is not as well known in K-12 classroom pedagogy, I am not aware of any existing textbook that uses Multiliteracies as its foundation approach to WL Education. Many textbooks on the market, in fact, utilize a CLT or Standards-based organization for activities due to the public's knowledge of CLT and the Standards and demand for these types of pedagogical approaches. I believe it would be worthwhile for educators and SLA researchers to collaborate to create a textbook with a Multiliteracies framework as its foundation in order to better compare the types of pedagogies or to see more of Multiliteracies in practice.

b) As mentioned in the Limitations section, vocabulary and grammar within the course seemed to still grasp at the tenets of Audiolingualism: Vocabulary had to be memorized to participate in the following class's activities and the grammar rules in the textbook were presented in English as a one-size-fit-all type of learning. These part-to-whole aspects of learning reminded me of the rote-learning exercises I have tried to steer clear of in my own classrooms. I believe that overall, grammar needs to be better addressed in WL classes to utilize the Multiliteracies framework or the Deep Approach so as to better avoid the lessons utilizing the "banking model" of education discussed by Freire, but I am not aware of an example that can demonstrate this type of education with regard to grammatical undertakings.

c) As a WL instructor, I myself must consider what qualities make a text readable when designing my curriculum at all levels. According to Swaffar and Arens (2005) a readable text: is accessible to readers through illustrations, subtitles, tends to be longer, tends to be more concrete instead of abstract, translates the unfamiliar ideas through familiar references and relatable connections or comparisons, presents topics of interest to the reader, and is age-appropriate (p. 58). Typically, texts that follow a narrative stream are longer, less abstract, and can be easier to understand than short texts with numerous theoretical or conceptual ideas. "When students are oriented to the major who, what, where, and when of the text, they will be able to hypothesize more effectively" (Swaffar & Arens, p. 62). When planning a lesson, it is also important to ensure that the task matches the learning level of the students. Perhaps this could offer a good lesson to students in a WL methods course: Change the task, not the text! Swaffar and Arens (2005) reaffirmed this sentiment by stating that "the readability of a text should be judged not on the text's own terms but according to the environment of support (facilitating tasks) needed to make the text readable" (p. 63). To give an example, as a supervisor of WL Education, I have witnessed a student teacher of Spanish rewrite a poem by Pablo Neruda so as to make the text easier for students to read. Rather than changing the text, the instructor could have chosen a few pre-reading activities so as to prime the students for the text or access their Available Designs.

d) Another way that teachers can encourage a better cognitive support system in the student is if he or she emphasizes the disadvantages of translating a text word for word.

Direct translation can often promote rote memorization and learner helplessness, or it can perpetuate drills as effective strategies for language learning, which is not as successful as a circumlocution exercise, for example.

References

ACTFL. (1996). *Standards for Foreign Language Learning: Preparing for the 21st Century*. Department of Education. Washington D.C.: American Council on the Teaching of Foreign Languages. Retrieved from http://www.actfl.org/

Allen, H. & Paesani, K. (2010) Exploring the feasibility of a pedagogy of Multiliteracies in introductory foreign language courses. *L2 Journal, 2*(1), 119-142.

Bennett, J., Bennett, M., & Allen, W. (1999). Developing intercultural competence in the language classroom. In R. Paige, D. Lange, & Y. Yershova (Eds.), *Culture as the core: Integrating culture into the language curriculum* (pp.13-46). Minneapolis: University of Minnesota Press. Print.

Bloom, B., Engelhart, M., Furst, E., Hill, W, & Krathwohl, D. (1956). Taxonomy of educational objectives: The classification of educational goals. *Handbook I: Cognitive domain*. New York: David McKay Company.

Bourns, S., and Melin, C. (2014). *The FL methodology seminar: Benchmarks, perceptions, and initiatives*. ADFL Bulletin. 43(1). 91-100. Print.

Byrnes, H., Norris, J., & Maxim, H. (2010). Realizing advanced foreign language writing development in collegiate education: Curricular design, pedagogy, assessment. *The Modern Language Journal, 94*, Supplement, 1-221. DOI: 10.1111/j.1540-4781.2010.01147.x

Cope, B. & Kalantzis, M. (2009). 'Multiliteracies': New literacies, new learning. *Pedagogies* 4(3), 164-194.

Forbes, C., & Lauderdale, T. (1997). Sympathique [Recorded by Pink Martini]. On *Sympathique* [CD]. France: Heinz Records.

Freire, P. (1970). *Pedagogy of the Oppressed*. New York: Herder and Herder.

Gee, J. (2010). *An Introduction to Discourse Analysis: Theory and Method*. New York: Routledge.

Glisan, E. (2012). National Standards: Research into practice. *Language Teaching* 45(4), 515- 526. doi: 10.1017/S0261444812000249

Harrison, K. M. (2013). Deep Education. In F. V. Tochon (Ed.), Language Education Policy Studies (online). Madison, WI: University of Wisconsin–Madison. Retrieved from: http://www.languageeducationpolicy.org (July 21, 2015).

Kern, R. (2000) *Literacy and language teaching*. Oxford: Oxford University Press. Print.

Kern, R. (2002). Reconciling the language-literature split through literacy. *ADFL Bulletin*, 33(3), 20-24. Print.

Klapisch, C. (Director). (2002). L'auberge Espagnole [Motion picture]. France: Ce Qui Me Meut Motion Pictures.

Kramsch, C. (1988). The cultural discourse of foreign language textbooks. In A. Singerman (Ed.), *Towards a new integration of language and culture* (pp. 63-68). Middlebury, VT: Northeast Conference. Print.

Kramsch, C. (2012). Theorizing translingual/transcultural competence. In G. Levine & A. Phipps (Eds.), *Critical and Intercultural Theory and Language Pedagogy* (pp. 15-31). Boston: Heinle.

Kumaravadivelu, B. 2003. *Beyond methods: Macrostrategies for language teaching*. New Haven: Yale University Press.

Magritte, R. (1928). *La trahison des images* [painting]. Retrieved from http://enculturation.net.

MLA Ad Hoc Committee on Foreign Languages. (2007). Foreign Languages and Higher Education: New Structures for a Changed World. *Modern Language Association*. Retrieved from: http://www.mla.org/flreport/ (July 23, 2015)

Muirhead, P. (2009, November). Rethinking culture: Toward a pedagogy of possibility in world language education. Presentation at the annual Wisconsin Association of Foreign Language Teachers Conference in Appleton, Wisconsin. Retrieved from https://losmuirhead.wikispaces.com/

New London Group (1996). A pedagogy of multiliteracies: Designing social futures. *Harvard Educational Review, 66*(1), 60-92.

Paesani, K., Allen, H., & Dupuy, B. (2015). *A Multiliteracies Framework for Collegiate Foreign Language Teaching*. Upper Saddle River, NJ: Prentice Hall. Print.

Pennycook, A. (2001). Critical applied linguistics: A critical introduction. Mahwah, NJ: Erlbaum. Print.

Swaffar, J. & Arens, K. (2005). *Remapping the foreign language curriculum: An approach through multiple literacies*. New York: Modern Language Association of America. Print.

Tochon, F. (2010). Deep Education. *Journal for Educators, Teachers and Trainers, 1*, 1-12.

17.

A Deep Approach to an Instructional Unit on Africa

Mary Alice Sicard
University of Wisconsin-Madison
masicard@wisc.edu

Inasmuch as language is inextricable from its culture, deep learning is particularly appropriate in acquisition of any second language. Projet:Afrique was a class-based project whose purpose was to employ Deep Education theory in the French language classroom in order to 1) have more holistic insight into the culture of Africa, the Ivory Coast in particular, and 2) to increase acquisition of academic language in French. The project involved groups of students in a level 3 high school French class at LaFollette High School in Madison, Wisconsin choosing to investigate one of the following aspects of the Ivory Coast: geography, history, art, music, politics or linguistics. They did this through group research and also through a visit from two Ivorians, the latter of which added clarification and meaning to their learning. Through this experience, they were to demonstrate deeper understanding of West Africa and presented their findings in French to the entire group and to the African visitors. The students showed evidence of increasing in knowledge not only of their group's area of research, but that of the interconnectedness of all the groups' findings as well. Students also demonstrated increased used of French by the time the unit was finished. This paper outlines the plans, procedures, strategies and results of *Projet: Afrique*.

I first heard about the Deep Approach from my peers and a student teacher I had hosted in French I at LaFollette High School in Madison, Wisconsin. I learned more about it in one of my first courses in the PhD program: Applied French Language Studies. The professor was Dr. François Tochon, author of The Deep Approach to World Languages and Cultures. As we studied various methods and standards used in France, the Deep Approach was also woven into the conversation. One of the students said she was now using it in her classroom and "It works!", she expressed with enthusiasm.

The more we talked, the more I knew that the Deep Approach was well-aligned with my philosophy of second language acquisition and the approach used at UW Continuing Studies Summer French Immersion Camp for Youth. I had experientially learned both Spanish as a child and French as an adult. Yes, I had classroom background in both, but the actual living out, exploring with my senses and motivation to make myself understood were the most effective manners of learning. I knew from my own personal experience that covering textbook material was not enough to acquire a language. "Learn it", perhaps, as one may program a disk, but "acquiring it" was more like a computer disk running and working in the computer.

I also had the privilege of reviewing *Help Them Learn a Language Deeply* by Dr. Tochon and in so doing, was able to examine the finer details of what Deep Teaching entailed. I was ready to blend my instinctive knowledge of personal language acquisition with Deep Teaching principles to see if I, like my classmate, could also say "It works!"

The Process

In my French 3 class at LaFollette High School in Madison, Wisconsin, I had a unit on Africa coming up. I decided to use this theme as the basis for my initial Deep Teaching experiment. So, the students, rather than following the more rigid demands of the textbook, were to develop a collaborative learning project on Africa and more specifically the Ivory Coast.

In planning the unit, I wanted to consider process versus outcome, so I designed a roadmap (in French) to guide the students. It was intended to motivate them by seeing that 1) they were to work collaboratively in groups, 2) they were to determine their domain of study and 3) they would have time to explore and reflect with their own personal expression. They were also expected to share their findings in French, while not being graded on correct usage. Students were put in groups of four with the goal of becoming "experts" in a specific domains relating to the Ivory Coast. They were not assigned specific domains, rather, given a list of the following domains as a springboard: food, music, art, dance, fauna, geography, history, politics, linguistics or other. As a group, they took time to reflect and determine the domain of highest interest to them in order to arrive at a consensus. Also, getting to know the composition of their particular group, they could assess the possibilities of what could be done cooperatively and what level of challenge they wanted to engage. This was our initial attempt at reflection. According to Tochon, "Reflexive apprenticeship represents a dynamic process: students reflect in the moment and make decisions for projects that play a mediating role in the apprenticeship of the language. Deep pedagogy *places reflection in the foreground.*"1 (Italics mine). It had to be clear from the very beginning that the group had ownership and responsibility for their domain.

In order to have a point of focus and direction, questions about goals were listed under Day 7. There was also a rubric for guidance, as well as for those who may have wanted a more structured guide of what was expected of them. Lastly, the author felt it was necessary, given that it was her first jaunt into Deep Education waters, not expecting to execute it perfectly her first time. It is to be noted that the grading can be done entirely by the student, measuring themselves as to whether they accomplished the goals they set for themselves.

Each group evaluates itself:

1) How have we advanced our knowledge of Africa?

2) How can we apply that to becoming a global citizen?

3) How has my French improved?

4) What can we now say / do / know that we would not have done otherwise?

5) How can we apply this way of learning to the next chapter?

After the work of reflecting, adapting, and self-determining, the outcome was to be a "fair" where each group would present the culmination of their work: research, artifacts, stories, games, anything. They would also have the opportunity, after doing research and reflection, to interview a man and a woman from the Ivory Coast. The two would speak to the entire group about education in the Ivory Coast, but would then speak with each group about its domain of expertise, asking and answering questions.

Each day, there would be steps of discovery. The students were to monitor their progress by checking off necessary steps.

The Project

DAY 1 – Exploration

This was where the thematic unit was presented. Rather than just do "Africa", we concentrated more closely on one country in West Africa: the Ivory Coast. Before the students were presented with the project, they were organized into groups of four. The attempted composition of each group was to balance gender, ethnicities and abilities to bring a more global perspective to their work. I wanted a blend of attributes, so that collectively, there would be a holistic contribution to the group work. I also intended that each group could find within itself a balance of gifts, for example, was there a good artist in your group? A good secretary? A good scout? In the process of collaboration, I intended for some self-discovery and affirmation as the student could adapt the work to his/her own inclination and profitability for the group. There was excitement as the groups started to reflect on this possibility and imagine how they might use their gifts to contribute to the project.

Inasmuch as LaFollette High School uses the block system which are ninety minutes long, the students were able to take two steps that day. Step 1 was to choose a certain domain of the Ivory Coast about which they wanted to know more. Here is how it appeared on their "roadmap":

STEP 1 - Which of the following aspects of Africa do you like to learn?

• Food (food?)	• Geography
• Music	• History
• Art	• Political
• Dance	• Languages
• Animals	• Other? _____

We went to the school library so they could access books and the internet in their domains of interest. In Step 2 They were encouraged to explore possible of information sources:

STEP 2 - Choose your materials. Here are some ideas. Write other ideas that your group suggests. Collect the materials in your green folder and bag you were given.

- Newspapers
- Magazines
- Books
- Encyclopedias
- From the internet, both   visual and audio
- interviews or visits   with African people
- Some CDs / DVDs
- Food
- Text Notes
- Art
 - Interviews with "experts" of the class
 - Maps
 - Crafts
 - Fabrics
 - Musical instruments
 - Clothing

These were put into the group's folder then we returned to our classroom for group discussion. Based on their exploration, each group was to determine the domain they were going to explore. They had two present a choice of three domains in order to not overlap with another group. The purpose of the project was to be able to view the Ivory Coast in the largest possible scope, so care was taken to not have two groups examining the same domain. If a group were interested in the same domain as another group, they would still get a chance to learn and integrate that domain into their final work.

Once their domain of study was determined, each group was encouraged to continue their search going beyond printed media. Other suggestions for them were to gather physical artifacts, interviews with African schoolmates, Ivorian crafts, fabrics, musical instruments, art and even food if it was non-perishable. An array of personal African and Ivorian artifacts from two French teachers was made available to put in their bag if they would serve the purpose of the table's exploration. All artifacts from that day and any subsequent findings that night would all go into the groups' folder or bag for further reflection.

DAY 2 – Declaration

As the students grouped together, they were then encouraged to remove the contents from their folder and bag. Here is the text from their instruction packet:

> *STEP 3 - Consider all the things that are in your bag. Listen to them. Handle them. Taste them. Feel them. What interests you? What would you like to learn more? What would you like to know more? Discuss these aspects you would like to study in more depth…"*

The purpose of this was to develop depth of knowledge, as compared to, perhaps a quip or short paragraph about a cultural element like those found in textbooks while using a theme as a basis for a larger goal of learning vocabulary and grammar. This was almost the opposite: using the available vocabulary and grammar they already had for the larger goal of learning about cultural aspects of a Francophone country. I wanted this to be the springboard for their deeper learning; I wanted them to ask themselves, to articulate for themselves, to find in themselves a road of interest that would teach them how to teach themselves. I wanted them to see it was centered on them and their interests, not on that of the teacher. Yes, I did choose the theme; however, within this experiment, I also had to consider my own constraints as a teacher in a larger department, with needs for articulation and standards to be met. Part of the experiment was to see if I could implement it, the other part was how to do so harmoniously with larger external constraints.

Step 4 was, after having decided the depth to which they wanted to examine their domain, to continue to develop their stream of resources. Having refined their search, their resource stream should have then become more focused, and perhaps more creative? This could be ongoing, with constant renewing as discoveries were made:

> *STEP 4 - Make a list of resources from which you will get your information. This list may not be exhaustive.*

1. _____
2. _____
3. _____
4. _____
5. _____

6. _____
7. _____
8. _____
9. _____
10. _____

In Step 5 the group was asked them to, after research and reflection, to take one specific point to share with the class. They were given time to discuss, reflect, write and refine. The text was as follows:

> *STEP 5 - Write about a specific point. Tell why it is worth being shared with the rest of the class. What was exciting about it? What was strange? What was fascinating? What was totally new for you? Any other comments?*

Before they were to share, in Step 6, they were to review the concept they wanted to share and determine if there were any new vocabulary words they needed to learn in order to discuss their focused point from Step 5. Use of smart phones, dictionaries and the teacher as a resource were all permitted. As homework, they were asked to prepare their ability to talk about this specific point of focus in their domain.

DAY 3 – Interaction from without

This was one of our biggest and most exciting days. We had two guests from the Ivory Coast: an Ivorian woman, mother of one of the class members and Leopold, a musician from her church. There was quite a bit of excitement as they entered in the room. The students had been looking in depth at the culture and language of the Ivory Coast for two full class days (the equivalent of four days of class in most other American high schools). Emma and Leopold were able to walk in and no longer was the students' information from a book, image or artifact. These guests were the reality of the domains of their study.

As Emma shared about schooling in the Ivory Coast, I was a little apprehensive that the students may not understand her French. Between not being the careful measured and cadenced "teacher French" and having a significantly different accent, I was worried that she might not be understood. However, this was not the case. She spoke slowly, clearly and enthusiastically about her life in the Ivory Coast. There was a palpable sense of validation of this woman's life through the ability to share with an interested, young audience. Students took note as she spoke since the instructions in Step 7 were as follows:

> STEP 7 - *Listen to our guest, Emma Wawa. She will talk about the Ivory Coast. In her presentation, what might she mention that offers insight into the*

things you have discovered? How can this add to your "expertise"? Write your thoughts here:

After her presentation, we put on a time and she and Leopold took five minutes to ask and answer questions at every table. There were tables on geography, history, art, music, food and languages. The dialogue was quite dynamic, as the students had many questions and Emma and Leopold could answer them in-depth. This was a very exciting task because the interaction simulated the natural acquisition process by means of gathering enriching information to add to their knowledge of their respective domains. Every group grimaced as their five minutes were up because the conversation was so lively, informative and interactive. Afterwards, Emma commented to me, almost surprised, "*Ils avaient de bonnes questions*" or "They had good questions."

After Emma and Leopold left, in Step 8 the students were asked to, without looking at their notes or artifacts, list as many details as possible about their domain:

> *STEP 8 - Without looking at your green folder, brainstorm about all the things that you remember in your field of interest. Consider the readings, visits and discoveries. Make as long a list as possible:*

My intention was for them to see for themselves how they were becoming "experts" in their domains. My other intention was for them to use their new vocabulary in a language refining process.

DAY 4 – Interaction from within

This day was high energy. In Step 9, we did a "jigsaw" to shae and enrich. Here we had interaction to simulate the natural language acquisition process—sharing information. The directions for the next step were as such:

> *STEP 9 - JIGSAW - We will make two circles. There will be a pair of experts from your table that will be part of the inner circle; the other two will be part of the outer circle. To start, all students of the inner*

circle will move to be in front of two experts in the following table. Students will take 5 minutes to share information on their domain.

See Figure A: Diagram of this process.

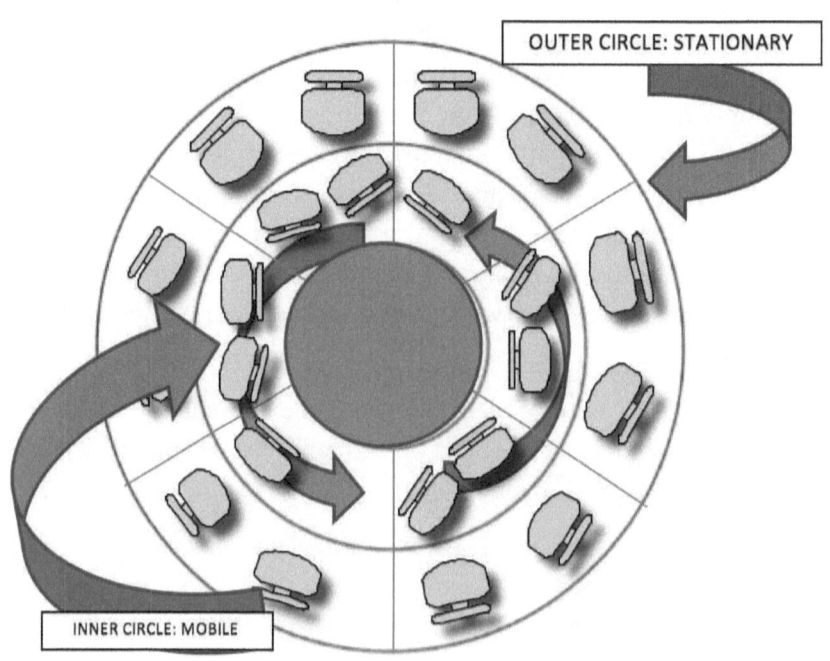

Figure A. Diagram of this process

When the students arrived back at their original group, these were their instructions:

> *Upon arrival, you will share the notes you have taken. Is there now something important to add to your own categories? Can you create a transition to the presentation of another table? What information will clarify part of your research? (For example, the story can connect with art through the theme of ivory.)*

The last step of the day, Step 10, read as such:

STEP 10 - What are your emotions? Your thoughts? At each table, as a group, write a paragraph to start preparing for us to hear all the wonderful things you've discovered.

This was the moment that the information started to culminate and synthesize. The group effort with the group knowledge was starting to work toward the group goal of "experience" for the next day.

DAY 5 – Experience

In an effort to continue to work in an adaptive and "bottom-up" way, groups had the following guidance with Step 11:

> *STEP 11 - Depending on your opening paragraph from STEP 10, organize your categories in a way that makes sense to you. Plan how your group will be presenting these aspects. Remember to use your artifacts, your knowledge, and your emotions, either negative or positive. Show us in your presentation how your group's discoveries connect with other aspects of Africa. What has it changed your mind? In your life? Your projects? Can you use the essential words mentioned in STEP 6 above?*

Having the luxury of a 90-minute class period, I as the teacher am able to afford them the time for further reflection, comfortable planning and creativity in this show of expertise in their domain. This is also a time that will be meaningful, as the other groups have grown in knowledge and curiosity about Africa. This was also a time for feedback. The student asked things such as *"Am I saying this right?"*, *"Is this how they play this instrument?"*, *"What time of day do they use this to get water?"* etc., yet they were very confident because we had explored their domains in small segments. They had been given time to reflect and refine. They had gotten their questions answered and they had been given freedom in how to present their information. The process gave them confidence. There was little angst with the outcome, because it was just seen as the end of the process, not as the crowning point or the only thing with value in the process.

The next four processes almost did not need to be delineated. It felt like a very natural "next step."

> STEP 12 - Prepare a table to share what you have learned. Put your artifacts on your table. Set up some written explanations. Remember that this may include even a craft to do, a treat to eat or an instrument to play.
>
> STEP 13 - Go around the classroom and visit other tables. Look, listen, smell, taste and touch the artifacts. Read their explanations. Write your questions and comments.
>
> STEP 14 – Return to your table. Each table will take 3 minutes to explain, demonstrate or share. Each will also respond to questions and comments.
>
> STEP 15 - Everything is open! We can dance, continue to eat or explore the exhibitions.

This may seem like the natural end of the project, but we had one two more days in "Africa".

DAY 6 - Creation

The students, now equipped with much knowledge about not only their group's domain, but other domains of Ivory Coast, the students could generate ideas and depth for a reasonably knowledgeable story. Here were their instructions:

> STEP 16 - The next day, you create a character: a child living in Africa. You will write and/or illustrate its history in your field. Make sure you use your new learning.
> - Introduction: Tell us about your character. How is he? What is their situation?
> - Development: Create a problem, a conflict.
> - Create a resolution. Make sure it is rich with information you have learned, with mentions of information from other groups
>
> STEP 17 – Recount your story orally to the class.

The main goal of this exercise was to demonstrate the inextricable connection of one domain to another: language is not apart from music, food is not apart from geography, politics are not apart from history. It was also for them to recognize that they were then a *resource*. They could draw from within to create, inform and enrich. There were varying storylines, but they all had subtle or overt references to the learning. They also participated in oral storytelling, which is another aspect of Ivorian culture.

DAY 7 – Projection

The very last day had "projection" with two meanings. The students got to review their work over the past six days through watching the videos we had made. We also danced to Ivorian music with Emma Wawa and eat Ivorian food. The students also got to "project" what the learning had done for them and would do in the future as seen in Steps 18 and 19:

> *STEP 18 – Watch the videos produced during the project.*
>
> *STEP 19 – Each group evaluates itself:*
>
> *1) How have we advanced our knowledge of Africa?*
>
> *2) How can we apply that to becoming a global citizen?*
>
> *3) How has my French improved?*
>
> *4) What can we now say / do / know that we would not have done otherwise?*
>
> *5) How can we apply this way of learning to the next chapter?*

Here are two samples of answers to these questions from students:

Jordan R.-

1) *We have advanced our knowledge of Africa by diving deep into the art, music, and culture of the continent, especially by tying it into our shared interest of the French language.*

2) *We truly are global citizens, and learning about the art, culture, and music of other places, including Africa, causes us to expand our ways of thinking, especially in regards to teamwork, education, individuality, uniqueness, and expression.*

3) *My French has improved by hearing different accents. Different accents can almost be different languages. The slightly different aural stimulation caused me to pay extra attention to my knowledge of French, especially phrases and slang.*

4) *We have compared traditional African culture to our own, and also to that of France, which has caused us to view French as a truly global way of communication, and not simply an outdated way of speaking only used by the aristocratic French. Now we can feel more at ease learning about other topics related to Africa and the French language, and we can more easily understand other accents.*

5) *We can use the openness and curiosity we gained from this chapter to dive into the next chapter unafraid, and eager to learn more about "le magnifique monde de français"!*

Jojo E. –

1) *I think that you've helped students to see Africa separately (as in the French speaking countries) rather than holistically[1] like most people do.*

2) *I think that knowing that West African, or even better Ivorian, Ghanian and other French countries have different cultures can help others become better global citizens.*

3) *(The teacher's French is) agreeable to people with different dialects which is important to people like me who have a hard time understanding European accents.*

4) *Well I think that incorporating African French rather than separating it in different units would help. And also in the past few years/decades West African music has been big for teenagers and young adults. I think using those songs and videos could be a big help.*

5) *In regards to the chapter I'd say you take the exact same approach. But I will say again that even though the countries are separate I don't believe that there is one "French" culture. Even though Africa was colonized by*

> the French these areas should be seen as an extension of the country and not necessarily France itself. In my eyes West Africa is French culture. But it's completely different from how it is in France.

[1] The student's use of "holistic" means here the idea of projecting Africa as singularly identified by one sole culture.

Conclusion

Although by no means a perfect execution of the Deep Approach, I felt from these reactions from the students, and other like it, that it was a good start. I sensed that the students were motivated from the very beginning. The energy and application with which they approached the project was palpable. They were provided with the template. The self-directed learning was launched and took on a life of its own. Choice and self-direction were granted at the very onset of the project and seemed to be appreciated by the students.

The students were the ones who built upon what they learned and became more motivated and consequentially more knowledgeable as the project progressed. They were asked to reflect, react, restate while giving them the possibility to extend and explore. Their emotions were acknowledged and they were encouraged to engage with their emotions to propagate and refine their learning.

The process was the means *and* the end. Students saw their own learning during the process and this was as important, if not more important, than the final product or presentation. The focus of their projects was determined by interest, ability and group consensus. They discovered Ivorian values seen through cultural manifestations.

The target language was used for instruction and expression. Every attempt was made to make the language level appropriate, while encouraging students to go beyond what they knew, looking for next steps in vocabulary to describe more precisely what they were learning. Guidance was given as presentations were being prepared. Value was given to new aspects of culture, race, language and politics they had theretofore not known about.

In my twenty-one years of teaching, I have no doubts that that was my best unit ever. It was high-energy, high-engagement and high-production. It may have not been textbook perfect, checking all the boxes for the correct use of the *passé compose* or the vocabulary list from Chapter 8 in our text, but the larger gains are clear. The students moved to a deeper, integrated understanding and empathy for the Ivory Coast. They understood specifics and greater implications of what it means to live in this lovely place in West Africa. The Ivory Coast became a place of value to them.

There is something that has not been mentioned about the reactions from the students above. Jordan and Jojo answered these questions after the project in 2012. However, I asked them these questions again during the writing of this paper. This unit was done two and one half years ago. They retained their gains in knowledge and empathy as if it were yesterday. I was quite overcome with the amount of what they wrote as well as depth of it. How unlike that cocktail party conversation so many of us world language teachers have with people who have studied a world language but have not retained anything: "*Oh, I took four years of French, but I don't remember a word of it!*" Something did not happen for them to make an impression or opportunity for permanent gain.

Not so with the Deep Approach. The demonstration of such a strong sense of empathy, understanding and appreciation for the Ivory Coast answered the question. Besides seeing the retaining of gains they made, I could see through walking through this process with my students that it was *the best unit I had ever experienced*. After blending my knowledge of personal language acquisition with Deep Teaching principles I can now say, along with my classmate: "*It works!*"

APPENDIX A

PROJET: AFRIQUE-IVORY COAST!

Let's discover a bit of Africa! We will do this thorough examining one African country in particular: the Ivory Coast or la *Côte d'Ivoire*. You will work in groups of 4 or "tables". You will become "experts" in a specific field. In addition, you will learn other things in general about this country thanks to the other groups. At the end, you will present your findings to the rest of the class. You will also create an "oral tradition" story based on your findings.

Each day, there will be steps of discovery. Put a cross in the box [ ] after you finish each step.

DAY 1 - Exploration

[ ] STEP 1 - Which of the following aspects of Africa do you like to learn?

_____

- Food (food?)
- Music
- Art
- Dance
- Animals
- Geography
- History
- Political
- Languages
- Other? _____

[ ] STEP 2 - Choose your materials. Here are some ideas. Write other ideas that your group suggests. Collect the materials in your green folder and bag you were given.

- Newspapers
- Magazines
- Books
- Encyclopedias
- From the internet, both visual and audio
- interviews or visits with African people
- Some CDs / DVDs
- Food
- Text Notes
- Art
- Interviews with "experts" of the class
- Maps
- Crafts
- Fabrics
- Musical instruments
- Clothing
- Other

DAY 2 - Declaration

[ ] STEP 3 - Consider all the things that are in your bag. Listen to them. Handle them. Taste them. Feel them. What interests you? What would you like to learn more? What would you like to know more? Discuss these aspects you, as a group, and write about them below and about which area you would like to study in more depth:

_____

_____

_____

[ ] STEP 4 - Make a list of resources from which you will get your information. This list may not be exhaustive.

1. _____   6. _____

2. _____   7. _____

3. _____   8. _____

4. _____   9. _____

5. _____   10. _____

[ ] STEP 5 - Write about a specific point. Tell why it is worth being shared with the rest of the class. What was exciting about it? What was strange? What was fascinating? What was totally new for you? Any other comments?

_____

_____

_____

[ ] STEP 6 - Discuss the new concepts that you have discovered. Which French words do you need to know to discuss the concept in French?

1. _____   6. _____

2. _____   7. _____

3. _____   8. _____

4. _____   9. _____

5. _____   10. _____

DAY 3 - Interaction

[ ] STEP 7 - Listen to our guest, Emma Wawa. She will talk about the Ivory Coast. In her presentation, what might she mention that offers insight into the things you have discovered? How can this add to your "expertise"? Write your thoughts here:

_____
_____
_____
_____

[ ] STEP 8 - Without looking at your green folder, brainstorm about all the things that you remember in your field of interest. Consider the readings, visits and discoveries. Make as long a list as possible.

1. _____   6. _____
2. _____   7. _____
3. _____   8. _____
4. _____   9. _____
5. _____   10. _____

• Develop categories from which one could classify these aspects.

Category #1   Category #2   Category #3

_____   _____   _____
_____   _____   _____
_____   _____   _____
_____   _____   _____

- Look in your folder. Is there anything there you may have forgotten? If there are aspects of your discovery that still are important for you, write them in their categories too.

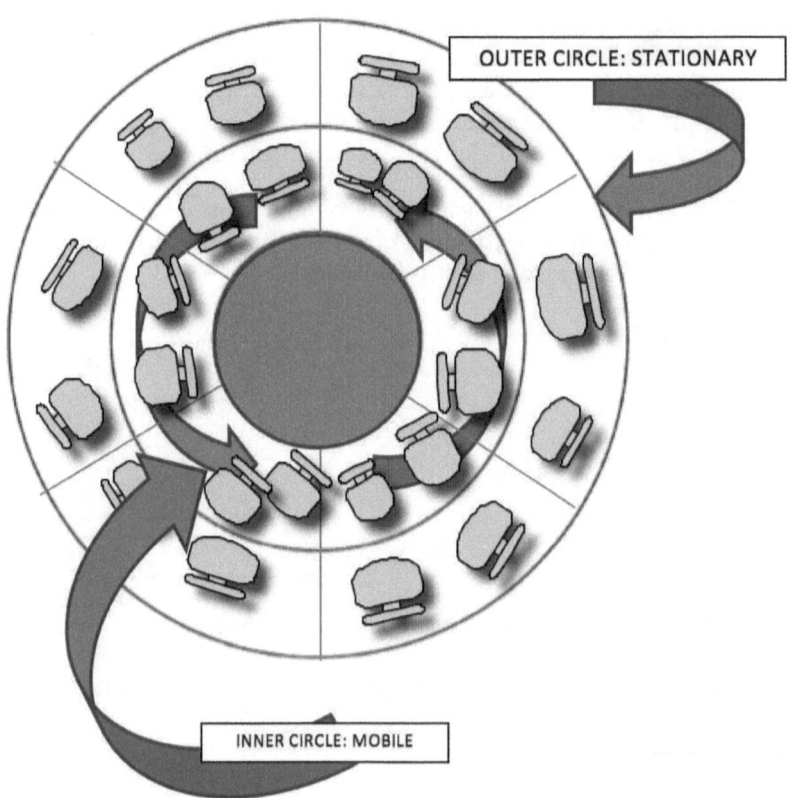

DAY 4 - Interaction

[ ] STEP 9 - JIGSAW - We will make two circles. There will be a pair of experts from your table that will be part of the inner circle; the other two will be part of the outer circle. To start, all students of the inner circle will move to be in front of two experts in the following table. Students will take 5 minutes to share information on their domain with the corresponding students. Those outside will do the same. You will take notes. The inner circle will advance to the next pair every 10 minutes. You're done when you arrive at your original table.

Upon arrival, you will share the notes you have taken. Is there now something important to add to your own categories? Can you create a transition to the presentation of another table? What information will clarify part of your research? (For example, the story can connect with art through the theme of ivory.)

_____
_____
_____
_____
_____

_____

[ ] STEP 10 - What are your emotions? Your thoughts? At each table, as a group, write a paragraph to start preparing for us to hear all the wonderful things you've discovered.

_____
_____
_____
_____

DAY 5 - Experience

[ ] STEP 11 - Depending on your opening paragraph from STEP 10, organize your categories in a way that makes sense to you. Plan how your group will be presenting these aspects. Remember to use your artifacts, your knowledge, and your emotions, either negative or positive. Show us in your presentation how your group's discoveries connect with other aspects of Africa. What has it changed your mind? In your life? Your projects? Can you use the essential words mentioned in STEP 6 above?

[ ] STEP 12 - Prepare a table to share what you have learned. Put your artifacts on your table. Set up some written explanations. Remember that this may include even a craft to do, a treat to eat or an instrument to play.

[ ] STEP 13 - Go around the classroom and visit other tables. Look, listen, smell, taste and touch the artifacts. Read their explanations. Write your questions and comments.

[ ] STEP 14 – Return to your table. Each table will take 3 minutes to explain, demonstrate or share. Each will also respond to questions and comments.

[ ] STEP 15 - Everything is open! We can dance, continue to eat or explore the exhibitions.

DAY 6 - Creation

[ ] STEP 16 - The next day, you create a character: a child living in Africa. You will write and / or illustrate its history in your field. Make sure you use your new learning.

- Introduction: Tell us about your character. How is he? What is their situation?
- Development: Create a problem, a conflict.
- Create a resolution. Make sure it is rich with information you have learned, with mentions of information from other groups

[ ] STEP 17 – Recount your story orally to the class.

DAY 7 - Projection

[ ] STEP 18 – Watch the videos produced during the project.

[ ] STEP 19 – Each group evaluates itself:

1) How have we advanced our knowledge of Africa?

2) How can we apply that to becoming a global citizen?

3) How has my French improved?

4) What can we now say / do / know that we would not have done otherwise?

5) How can we apply this way of learning to the next chapter?

References

Hamilton, H., Crane, C., Bartoshesky, A. (2005). *Doing Foreign Language, Bringing Concordia Language Villages into Classrooms.* Upper Saddle River, NJ: Pearson Education.

Tochon, François V. (2014). *Help Them Learn A Language Deeply*. Deep University Press: Blue Mounds.

Tochon, François V. (2002). *L'analyse de pratique assistée par video*. Sherbrooke, Quebec: Éditions du CRP.

Schurr, S. (2008). *Curriculum and Project Planner for Integrating Multiples Intelligences, Thinking skills and Authentic instruction*. Nashville, TN: Incentive Publications, Inc.

Sicard, M.A. (2013). *History and Development of UWCS French Camp*. Independent study.

18.

The Impact of Intrinsic Motivation through Tochon's Deep Approach: *'An Avant Garde Way of Teaching'*

Gizem Girgin Öztürk
Gedik University, Istanbul, Turkey
ggirginozturk@gmail.com

Motivation has been widely regarded as one of the most pivotal corner stones in language achievement. However, this valuable idea has not been put into practice in Turkey because external factor driven systems do not take it into consideration. Tochon's Deep Approach which puts great emphasis on intrinsic motivation can be a good means to achieve motivation in language learning. His teaching method is now being adapted and applied to native Turkish students in Turkey who want to learn English as a foreign language in prep-school before college. During this period of time, there has been an educational paradigm shift from teacher-centered to student-centered classrooms through activities including pair work, group work and role playing. Students are encouraged for self-regulation which includes metacognitive and motivational development in their learning. The present study attempted to examine the impact of Tochon's Deep Approach on students' motivation. It involved 10 prep school students who participated in interviews. There was also a questionnaire given to 50 students who were learning English through Deep Approach for data collection. The result showed the relationship between teachings through Tochon's Deep Approach in TEFL and an increase in student's motivation.

Statement of the Problem

Over the past decades, many studies have been conducted to examine the influence of motivation in language learning. However, many teaching methods have failed to provide self-directed motivation for language learning because of their overload structured systems in a controlled environment and emphasis on outcomes.

Based on interviews with students and feedbacks from the instructors, this paper examines students' motivation in language learning through deep approach, and shows that there is a noteworthy progress in terms of language learning thanks to deep approach's emphasis on self-motivation and flexibility in the curriculum. In this research, the relationship between using "deep approach" as a teaching technique in TEFL and increasing student's motivation to learn English in a prep school of a private university in Istanbul is investigated.

Justification and the Significance of the Study

A great number of research studies have been conducted regarding the issue of motivation in language achievement. Due to the fact that motivation plays a crucial role in language learning, a considerable amount of studies have investigated the relationship between the two. However, there is still a huge gap in the area. This study will be a unique one in terms of analyzing the relationship between a relatively new teaching method, The Deep Approach and motivation in a Turkish University in Istanbul.

Teaching Techniques

Changing perception in language teaching is also affecting the components of the education, such as role of the teacher and the relationship between students and the teacher. (Willis, 2007, p. 11). When teachers see their students as a whole person and they figure out the needs of their students; students feel themselves more valuable and get motivated. So it should be noted that teaching process cannot go further without motivation. Therefore, to keep students' enthusiasm about learning, teacher should consider different kinds of interest of their students. Unfortunately, traditional teaching methods are popular within teachers and because of a teacher-centered teaching process; the students are not able to be productive during the learning period. (Temiz, 2004, p. 22). Teaching process is expected to meet the needs of students and encourage them for learning. It should create a classroom environment which is more positive and cooperative (Pritchard, 2008, p. 39). However, because of lack of competence most of the teachers prefer more structured lesson plans which are dependent to course book. Deep Approach, on the other hand, provides learners to work on their own interests and this freedom increases their motivation to learn language. In fact, it is one of the essential characteristic of the Deep Approach to see students as a curriculum designer. By doing this, it aims to make students feel worthy and appreciated which will contribute to their motivation to learn the target language by their own free will.

The Deep Approach

The Deep Approach of languages and cultures were started by François Victor Tochon, Professor at the University of Wisconsin-Madison. The deep approach is a bridge between teaching language style and open curriculum focusing on values, the imaginary, and creativity in action rather than pre-determined outcomes. In this regard, the learners' role is curriculum builder. The Deep Approach aims to realize the following steps to help learners to learn the language efficiently. According to Tochon (2013), self-motivation could be the best encouragement for learning. If learners desire to learn intrinsically, they succeed it. At this point, the role of teacher is also very crucial since they are expected to help students to realize how to increase self motivation effectively. Authentic learning is another important element that the Deep Approach values since it emphasizes the learning process rather than pre-determined outcomes. Assigning the student as the curriculum builder and making the instruction flexible are different and effective ways of increasing awareness in motivation (Tochon, 2013, 173). Tochon highlights the significance of intrinsic motivation by putting emphasis on flexibility in learning which avoids predetermined outcomes and helps students to achieve self realization in motivation.

The Deep Approach uses the aforementioned techniques to build high motivation for learners. In terms of teaching techniques, some of these items make this teaching method distinctive. Flexibility, for instance, is one of the major keywords in the deep approach. Students are given a chance to build their own curriculum and projects to achieve their goals by establishing instructional agreements. And the instructor tries to broaden the landscape as much as she/he can so that students can choose and frame their work on their own. Furthermore, to energize self-directed learning and increase motivation, students are asked to share their interest in life and determine which topic would best fit their aims.

The Deep Approach comes up with a new and useful perspective to grammar. Rather than providing structured exercises in a controlled environment, it suggest to give priority to text itself and practice grammar through storytelling which will help learners to be successful in an uncontrolled environment by lowering the pressure on them. Students are motivated to learn grammar through extensive reading and intensive writing/recording not distracted with small pieces of grammar structures.

Liu states that; "Because of exam-oriented education, students have become rootless". That kind of education creates reluctant learning atmosphere that does not include any productivity and learning in the real sense. Similarly, Tochon (2010) claims that most methods and learning environments have some obstacles to learning process such as controlling and suppressing the intrinsic motivation. For instance, fear of being unsuccessful stimulates extrinsic motivation to get high grades but prevents learning. On the other hand, the deep approach incentivizes learning by putting emphasis on process not on outcomes.

Motivation

Motivation has been considered as one of most important and necessary elements of language acquisition which provide impetus to learn a foreign language. Its impact on L2 learning is so significant that many researchers consider it as an indispensable part of language acquisition. (Oxford & Shearin, 1994) Zoltan Dörnyei (2009) maintains that student achievement is not possible without satisfactory motivation even if the learner has noteworthy skills and abilities. Since language learning is a long and challenging process, achieving long term aims does not seem possible without sufficient motivation. In other words, as Brown (2007) states; "motivation is a key to learning". (As cited in Yeh's, 2010, p. 252). Due to its considerable impact on learning, motivation has been widely used in educational and research areas. Numerous researchers have tried to explain motivation in several ways. Dörnyei (2001) claims that motivation is strongly connected with learners' efforts to learn and their willingness to continue the act. Similarly McDonough (2007) considers motivation as the driving force which encourages people to move, in this case to learn a foreign language or a second language.

Two prominent researchers, Deci and Ryan (1999), have categorized motivation as intrinsic and extrinsic to give a more detailed description of motivation. Intrinsic motivation type is the one which is triggered by our internal desires. In other words, the learner participates in an activity because it is interesting and amusing to do. For this reason, personal pleasure and interest have an important place in intrinsic motivation. As for the extrinsic motivation, the situation is completely different. External factors such as academic success, parental and societal expectations or getting a well-paid job are among the vital components that motivate people (Deci, Koestner & Ryan, 1999). To conclude, reward and punishment are the two key words that characterize external driving motivation.

It is commonly believed that intrinsic motivation is more preferable to extrinsic motivation since the former provides better understanding and more satisfying results than the latter one. Dörnyei (2001) goes one step further and asserts that teachers cannot do much about extrinsic motivation so teachers' efforts, values and behaviors to increase intrinsic motivation is significantly essential to increase awareness in language learning.

This study aims to shed light on some new points of view about motivation in language learning through a new method, 'Deep

Approach'. To investigate the topic beyond, it was decided to perform the present study in Istanbul with prep school students at a university. Hence, the present study aims to provide relevant data and explore the ways to increase motivation of the students.

Research Question

The paper aims at finding answer to the following research question:

'What is the relationship between using "deep approach" as a teaching technique in TEFL and increasing student's motivation at a prep school of a university in Istanbul?'

Research Hypothesis

Considering the teachings and practices of the Deep Approach to increase motivation as a teaching method, a strong connection between the two is expected to come true.

Limitations and Delimitations

Even though this study will shed light on a number of important questions related to relationship between motivation and the Deep Approach as a teaching technique. It has still some limitations. To begin with, the participant number of the students is relatively less because of the fact that the Deep Approach is a pilot experiment. Secondly, the study is not longitudinal one. A questionnaire is used to have an idea about the relationship between the Deep Approach and motivation. Lastly, it is important to keep in mind that this study was conducted with students who are between A1 and A2 level. Therefore, the result of the study cannot be generalized to all groups.

Method

Participant

Students for Questionnaire

50 students who study English in a prep school of a University in Istanbul, Turkey were selected to join the research. 30 of the participants are female and 20 of them are male. Their ages range from 18 to 21. The Student participants were selected randomly out

of 90 students. They were selected by systematic random sampling. From the possible population, every 3rd student was selected. It was approximately a homogenous group and their English level was elementary. The student participants who took part in the questionnaire have studied English for 3 to 5 years. Participants were kept confidential and anonymous.

Students for Interviews

10 students were selected randomly from among 50 students who joined the questionnaire. 8 of them are female and 2 of them are male. Their ages range from 19 to 21. Again, they were selected by systematic random sampling. From the possible population, every 3rd student was selected. Their level was elementary. Most of them had previously experienced in learning English.

Instrumentation - *Questionnaire*

In order to elicit information on effect of teaching techniques of the Deep Approach on students' motivation for learning English or not, a 20 item questionnaire was designed. There were five-point Likert scales for each item and participants were asked to give points from 1 to 5 for each item according to their tendencies. The questionnaire items were obtained from a comprehensive literature review. The questionnaire was prepared in English and then for the sake of the participants whose L1 is Turkish, it was translated into Turkish.

Interviews

To elicit detailed opinion on the impact of the Deep Approach on students' motivation, semi-structured interview was conducted. Students' statements were grouped according to keywords which were stated by participant about their motivation.

Procedures

The questionnaires were given to the participants and the required directions were given. Conducting the questionnaire almost took 15 minutes. After the questionnaires were collected, they were numeralized to prevent any mistake or confusion.

Interviews

Interviews were conducted individually and each tone took approximately half an hour. They were recorded to provide well-developed analyze.

Data Analysis

The data collection was completed at the end of December 2014. Then the collected data were analyzed by using descriptive statistical techniques by IBM SPSS 20. In the questionnaire, frequency distributions were calculated to analyze the Likert-scale responses to figure out whether there is any effect of teaching techniques of Deep Approach on students' motivation for learning English or not.

Questionnaire

It was expected to give the questionnaire to 60 student participants; however the questionnaire was given to 50 students. There were 20 items in the questionnaire. There were five-point Likert scales for each item and participants were asked to give points from 1 to 5 for each item according to their tendencies. Question numbers 4, 9, 12, 14, and 15 were reversed coded. While analyzing the data, these five questions' scales were converted to positive scores.

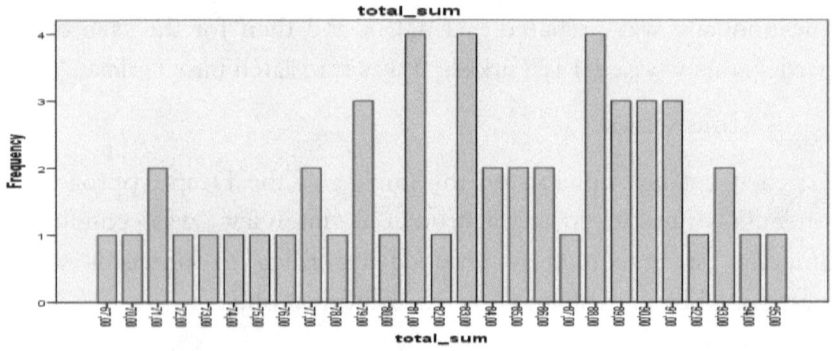

Interview

It was expected to conduct the interview with 10 participant students, but one of the participants was not able to attend the interview. Grouping technique was used to analyze interview.

Results

The following results and discussion address the research question.

What is the relationship between using "deep approach" as a teaching technique in TEFL and increasing student's motivation for learning English at a prep school of university in Istanbul?

Questionnaire

As it was indicated in the table, the minimum total score is 67 and the maximum score is 95 in the questionnaire. The mean is 83.24. The most frequent scores are 81.84 and 88 with four participants for each.

43 of the participants out of 50 strongly agree that motivation increase through encouragement, 6 of them agree and only one of them is neutral. There is no one who does not disagree with the effect of encouragement in learning environment. The mean for this question is 4.84.

The tendency of the students to work collaboratively was quite high. 34 participants had a positive attitude and 13 of them were neutral and only 3 of them had a negative aptitude for working in groups. At the same time, when they were asked about studying individually they had also high frequency of giving positive answer. While almost half of them which make 23 participants were opposed to this idea, 10 of them support the idea. The number of the students who do not want to be forced to attend class is high. The mean is 3.78/5 (Question 4). Most students (45/50) preferred to use authentic material rather than just using course book. (Question 5).

When the teacher encourages me for my achievement in class, my motivation increases

		Frequency	Percent	Valid Percent	Cumulative Percent
Valid	Neutral	1	2,0	2,0	2,0
	Agree	6	12,0	12,0	14,0
	strongly agree	43	86,0	86,0	100,0
	Total	50	100,0	100,0	

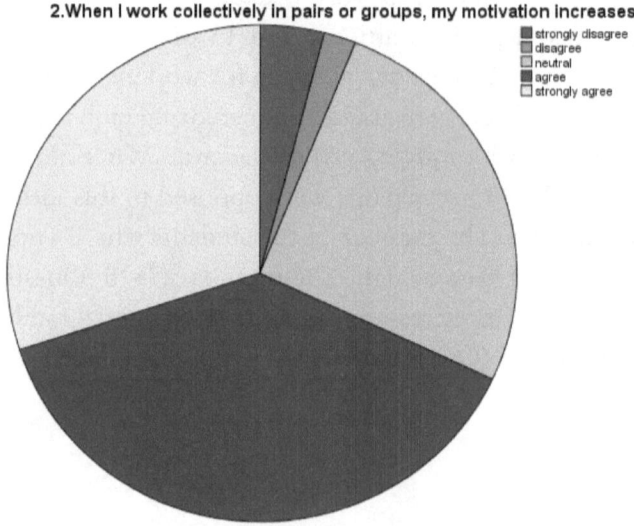

2. When I work collectively in pairs or groups, my motivation increases.
- strongly disagree
- disagree
- neutral
- agree
- strongly agree

When students were asked about the method of study, higher percentage of the students preferred to be free to choose their task and method. For Q6 while 43 of the students wanted a situation which will allow them to draw their own conclusion, 7 of them were not sure. For Q10, again more than half of the students wanted to be free in studying style.

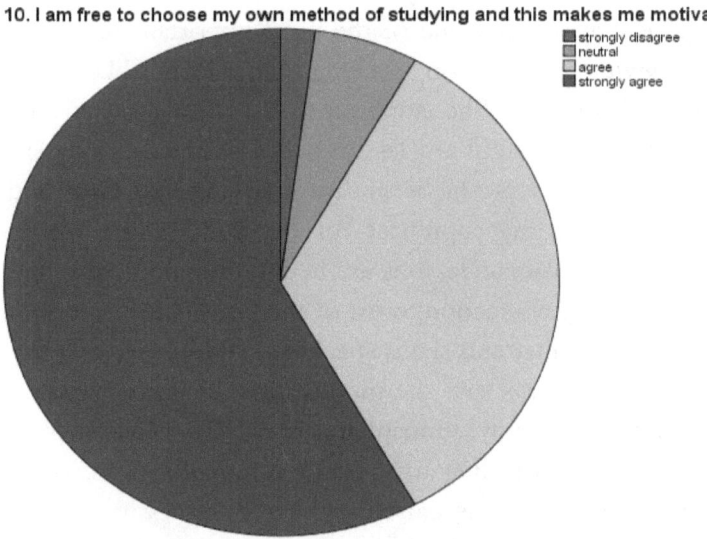

According to the participants, communicative activities in the classroom were helpful to develop abilities to communicate. While 24 out of 50 strongly agreed, 20 of them agreed and 3 of them are not certain and only 1 participant disagreed with the idea.

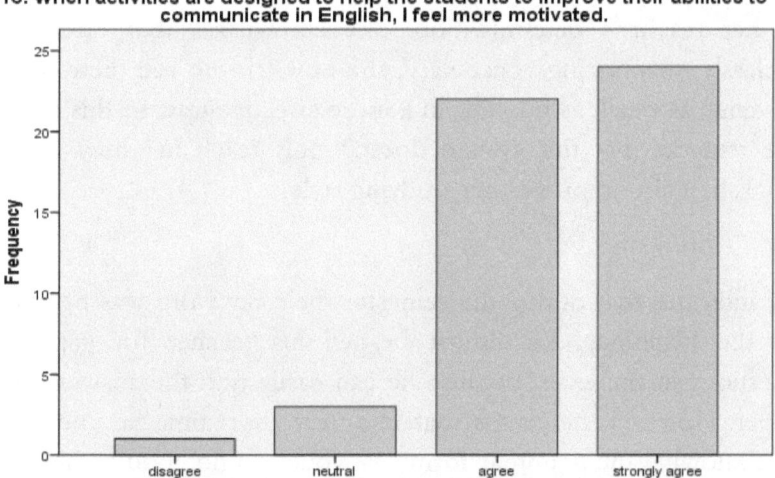

Interviews

Student 1.

She remarks that one of the most important features of this system is giving emphasis on speaking skills which is like a nightmare for almost all students. She emphasizes that throughout the semester she does not get bored in any lesson because there is no passive time for students. She says she is always active in the class and their teacher is an amazing supporter for her and for the whole class. Especially, their dialogue lessons are her favorite ones. She states that while she is acting a situation, most of the time, she imagines that she is in a foreign country and she is speaking English very well like many other people. She says that the motivation which is provided by her teacher and the friendly atmosphere in the class encourages her to speak freely without feeling any hesitation to make mistakes. Another important issue which is raised by her is excessive reading and turning their topics into discussion topics so that she can use more vocabulary while speaking. She notes that practicing the vocabulary that she learns from readings really helps her to improve not only her vocabulary but also her speaking. Lastly, she says she was always memorizing to learn because she was educated to do so.

However, she points out that she has overcome this prejudice thanks to her teacher's determination. She emphasizes that rather than uselessly memorizing vocabulary, she now tries to use them in daily speaking as much as possible in a more effective way. In this context, she remarks that this system doesn't only teach her how to learn English; it also improves her studying style.

Student 2.

He indicates that during the semester their key word was practicing. At the beginning, he almost begged his teacher for gap filling questions in the exam because he can easily find the answer on the paper. However, he claims that in a very short time he understood that knowing the grammar formulas would do no good to him since it brings no advantage if it is not used in the real sense. Therefore, he says that he decided to not to resist his teacher's instruction anymore.

Like student 1, he also says that he is very active in the lessons because the lessons require you to be so. Especially he finds grammar lessons interesting because of the fact that the only thing that came to his mind about grammar was sentence completion or gap filing beforehand. He states that previously almost in all grammar lessons, his English teachers taught the grammatical subjects and he just listened to them and did some paperwork in return. On the other hand, in the Deep Approach, he remarks that he feels quite active since he creates sentences orally which contributes to his speaking

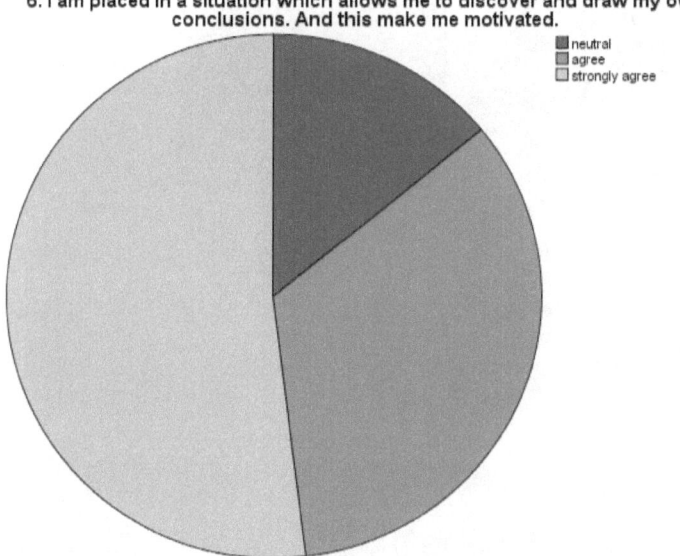

6. I am placed in a situation which allows me to discover and draw my own conclusions. And this make me motivated.
■ neutral
■ agree
□ strongly agree

ability. He also claims that they do not go much into detail in grammar lessons and that gives him a chance to practice the language rather than trying to remember all the details. He adds that he realized that he really learn it in a better way in that way. Furthermore, he emphasizes the role of the teacher by saying that his teacher's patience played a crucial role during his learning process. In addition to this, he says that his teacher was so motivated that it was impossible for him to be not motivated in the lessons.

Moreover, he puts emphasis on the fact that he feels all the activities they do are student centered and encourage students to speak any time. He insistently emphasizes that he thought he would never speak at the beginning. It was very hard for him to create long sentences since he was only familiar with doing exercises on the paper. However, he thinks that The Deep Approach provided the necessary motivation to speak and has changed his study habits significantly in a positive way.

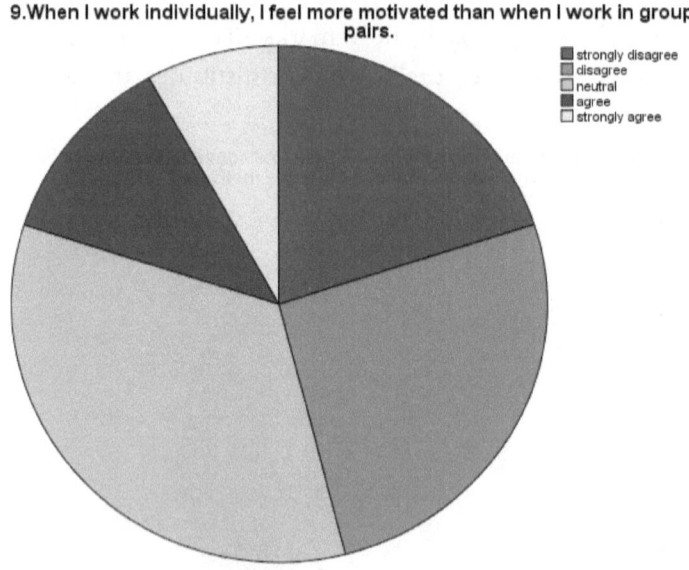

9. When I work individually, I feel more motivated than when I work in groups or pairs.

Student 3.

She indicates that the best thing about the deep approach is its focus on speaking ability. She comments that she has improved her vocabulary knowledge through speaking tasks and now she feels more confident since she has the courage to express her ideas comfortable than ever. She touches upon the issue of error correction saying that not all of her mistakes are corrected by her teacher. On the contrary, she says that her teacher lets her to speak freely and that contributes to her motivation to speak more. Furthermore, she says she feel safe when her teacher corrects her mistakes because the warm class atmosphere delivers the message that it is just for learning. She adds that students now correct the mistakes of each other and that helps them to improve their skills. According to her, through this process, they learn from each other, and also develop self-confidence for making mistakes.

She thinks that reading classes are quite different for her because in her previous attempts to learn English she was just reading the text in the class out loud. She goes on and specifies that she honestly was reading the text mechanically. She was dealing with her mobile phone or doing day dreaming in the rest of the class since she could not understand any word of it. However, she remarks that that picture changed wholly thanks to the Deep Approach. She says she is very active during the reading sessions since they come to class prepared and eager to know more through the contribution of their teacher. She highlights the fact that she has almost no chance to come to class without reading the texts since her teacher asks her to do voice recording for summary of texts before covering the texts in the class.

She asserts that after doing these individual tasks, it becomes a pleasure for her to talk about the topic and support her ideas in the class. When it comes to writing tasks, she says it was very difficult and boring at the beginning since she has not written much even in Turkish. Therefore, she finds heavy writing homework too much. However, she also admits that she has improved her writing skill significantly thanks to that horizon widening writing homework. For the listening skill, she complains that she cannot still internalize the listening sessions. She says that she feels herself unsuccessful while listening to the recordings because of the fact that she could not grasp everything.

Student 4

She remarks that she never had a chance to speak English at a desired level because traditional English classes did not offer such an opportunity. For this reason, she adds that she only studied grammar and neglected the other skills. Considering this fact, she says she almost lost her hope and motivation to speak English. However, she points out that the Deep Approach helped her to believe that she can speak from the first day of the class. She indicates that she got two crucial things from this system; one is the motivation which everyone needs to achieve and the other one is encouragement to speak in every possible situation. Even though I was thinking that I would not be able to speak English, now I feel myself very successful. The last topic that she talks about is the issue of having only one teacher during the learning process. She says that she was having difficulty in understanding and combining skills since there were four teachers for each skill and their teaching style were quite different from each other. On the other hand, she says that having only one teacher her to follow her teacher easily. In addition to that, she thinks her teacher gets the chance to know her class better since she spends more time with the class.

Student 5

She believes that English learning is a problematic issue in Turkish schools. However, after she started to learn English through the deep approach, her opinion about this situation has started to change. First of all, she emphasizes how dynamic classroom environment contributed to her motivation to learn. She really enjoys being active in the classroom. She believes that acting out situations help her to obtain knowledge in the real sense. She admits that although she hates doing homework, she knows homework is very useful for her to review all the things she learns in the class. She says that she decided to give up learning English many times, but thanks to her teachers' amazing and unending interest, she insists on learning English and now she really appreciates her teacher's efforts because she started to learn and love English.

Student 6

She believes that the Deep Approach provides the necessary independent learner atmosphere to her that's why she thinks she feel more eager to learn the English language now. She compares her previous language learning experiences with Deep Approach and she states that previously she had many books and she had to complete a lot of mechanical tasks in the books. For this reason, she finds those kinds of activities very boring and impractical. However, for her new learning experience she points out that she feels herself free because of having chance to choosing her readings, presentation topics and so on. She highlights that this experience is not just a lesson for her. It is a kind of self –development camp for her.

Student 7

She starts by sharing her previous language learning experiences and points out that her teachers were generally trying to get their attention in the class by saying that there will be questions in the exam from the covered part. She indicates that considering this fact they were trying to memorize everything that they learn and never have a look at it after the exams. She states that her classes were exam oriented and the only thing that she has cared was her grades not the learning process at that time. However, she remarks that she does not worry much about exams in the Deep Approach since the emphasis is on the learning process. She emphasizes that her teacher teaches students to use language as a tool to communicate and she strongly believes that this warm and friendly environment encourages them to learn English successfully.

Student 8

She emphasizes that she studies at home and performs in the class during the whole year. She claims that thanks to this studying style she and her friends improve themselves with each other's performance and they learn from each other a lot.

Student 9

He points out the importance of voice recording. According to him, voice recording is one of the most effective ways of evaluating students' performance because it leads to a kind of a general revision of the tasks of each day. He confesses that he does his homework to not make his teacher sad at the beginning; however, he realized that thanks to homework he started to learn very well.

Students' answers indicate that they feel more motivated to learn English thanks to the Deep Approach system. They state that especially its focus on speaking ability which they lack most provide them the belief that they can communicate with other people effectively as well. They also emphasize how it is useful to create a student centered atmosphere through much emphasis on speaking rather than submitting mechanical exercises that never end. Another important aspect of the Deep Approach which is raised by the students is the Deep Approach' less emphasis on exams. They claim that they do not much think about exams since they always deal with their projects which prepare them to learn the target language in the real sense. Students also insistently talk about the role of the teacher in the Deep Approach saying that teacher motivation and eagerness are among the key words. They point out that their teachers' motivation and eagerness to push them forward are what made them believe that they will succeed. In other words, they think teacher motivation is one of the main driving forces of their learning English. Lastly, students remark that the Deep Approach enabled them to be active almost in all activity so contributed a lot rather than being a passive listener in the class.

Discussion

In this study, the relationship between using deep approach as a teaching technique in TEFL and increasing students' motivation for learning English at a prep school of university in İstanbul were looked into. It was predicted that English language learning obtained through a new method, The Deep Approach, increases motivation of students through its teaching techniques. Our prediction was borne out by the data. This result implies that the curriculum which is designed with the Deep Approach will increase enthusiasm and eagerness of students towards the language learning. Students who participated to this research gave answers that correspond to Deep

Approach's teachings techniques to increase motivation. Student motivation increase is strongly emphasized by the Deep Approach for the achievement of the L2 proficiency. This idea is substantially supported by the students in the questionnaire. More than half of the students agreed that teacher motivation for being successful greatly motivates them.

Collaborative work is also appreciated by the students, who believe that it is an important factor to increase motivation for learning. That idea is also an important point which is emphasized by the deep approach. This result implies a consistency between the deep approach's techniques to increase motivation and students' answers. Using authentic materials in the classroom such as news, recordings and photographs is another crucial point that helps to keep students motivated in the deep approach. In the questionnaire, a great number of the students gave answers that comply with this idea which implies that the deep approach significantly successful in increasing student motivation. Student centered education is one of the core elements of the deep approach to increase motivation. When students were asked about this issue, a great number of them agreed that they feel themselves motivated if they are allowed to discover and come to conclusions by themselves. This finding suggests the effectiveness of the deep approach in terms of motivating students by its student centered techniques. Having a flexible classroom environment is also used to increase student's motivation in the deep approach. A significant number of the participant students answered this question that supports the claims of the deep approach. This shows another crucial and strong point of the deep approach to motivate students for learning. Since students are put forward in the deep approach, they feel themselves as the most important parts of the system. The questionnaire results comply with this idea. An important number of students agreed that they feel important, therefore motivated to learn. Flexibility of choosing the method of studying also was emphasized as a significant factor for motivation by the participant students. This factor which is also highlighted by the deep approach implies that student motivation can be acquired through the teaching techniques of the deep approach. The last important point to be mentioned is the issue of grammar. The deep approach, contrary to grammar and exam oriented teaching styles, encourages students to actively participate in the learning process. Similarly, more than half of the students stated that grammar is not the most important thing in an English class in the questionnaire. In conclusion, we have seen that the teaching techniques of the deep approach to motivate students to learn greatly correspond to the answers of the participant students who have stated their views about motivation in the questionnaire. The findings of the research show us that the techniques of the deep approach can be useful to increase student motivation to learn English.

Conclusion

Restatement of the problem

This study has shown that there is a strong relationship between using the Deep Approach as a teaching technique and increasing students' motivation to learn English. As mentioned in the literature review, teaching process cannot go further without motivation. The participant students tend to agree that they feel more motivated when the teaching techniques of the Deep Approach are used. As mentioned above, the present study has raised a number of issues regarding motivation. The findings may contribute to relationship between language learning and motivation.

Implication of the study to motivation of the learner

In this study, it is reported that motivation is an essential element of L2 learning which immensely contribute to learners' achievement of L2. The findings from the research have implications for the English language teachers that they should try as possible as they could to motivate their students during the teaching process by removing the exam related stress and orienting learners' to the learning process.

Implication of the study to English Language Teaching

One of the most significant roles of EFL teachers is to reveal the best ways to enhance students' self-awareness to attain the language effectively. This study will be a light to teachers and students on one of the most problematic issue regarding the L2 learning in Turkey. Moreover, institutions and teachers will have a chance to see the effect of students' motivation on language learning and develop, adopt and learn new ways to teach target L2 language efficiently.

Suggestion for Further research

There are some shortcomings that can be further explored. Participants were limited to only 50 students due to the fact that the Deep Approach was used as a pilot experiment. It would have been better to conduct questionnaires on a wide range of participants, with different English proficiency background, varying ages and different ESL learning experiences on the issue of motivation. For further studies, In addition to using a single questionnaire for the learners, additionally a questionnaire may be given out to the EFL teachers in order to bring out their observation on the relationship between using the Deep Approach and students' motivation. Moreover, interviews may be conducted to both students and teachers.

References

Deci, E. L., Koestner, R. and Ryan, R. M. (1999). A meta-analytic review of experiments examining the effects of extrinsic rewards on intrinsic motivation. *Psychological Bulletin*, 125, 627-338.

Dörnyei, Z. (2001). Motivational Strategies in the Language Classroom. Cambridge: Cambridge University Press. Bacon, S.& M. Fienmann. (1992). Sex differences in self-reported beliefs about foreign language learning and authentic oral and written input. Language Learning, 42(4), 471-95.

Dörnyei, Z. (1998). Motivation in second and foreign language learning. Language Teaching, 31, 117-135

McDonough, S. (2007). Motivation in ELT. ELT Journal. 61 (4): 369-371.

Oxford, R. & Shearin, J. (1994). Language learning motivation: Expanding the theoretical framework. The Modern Language Journal. 78(1), 12-28.

Pritchard, A. (2009). Multiple intelligences. *Ways of learning: learning theories and learning styles in the classroom* (2nd ed., pp. 34-40). Abingdon, Oxon: Routledge.

Temiz, N. (n.d.). Implications of Multiple Intelligence Theory. Middle East Technical University dissertation. *Millennium Web Catalog*. Retrieved from http://library.metu.edu.tr/search~S4?/Xnida+temiz&searchscope=4&SORT=D/Xnida+temiz&searchscope=4&SORT=D&SUBKEY=nida%20temiz/1%2C2%2C2%2CB/frameset&FF=Xnida+temiz&searchscope=4&SORT=D&2%2C2%2C

Tochon, F. V. (2010). A Deep Approach to Language Multimedia and Evaluation: For a more Colorful Future. Invited Keynote Speech. *Proceedings of the Fourteenth international conference of APAMALL and ROCMELIA* (pp.73-92). Kaohsiung, Taiwan: National Kaohsiung Normal University

Tochon, F. V. (2014). Why the Deep Approach? In F. V. Tochon, *Help Them Learn a Language Deeply* (pp.17- 29). Blue Mounds, WI: Deep University Press.

Willis, J. (2007). Success for all students in inclusion classes. *Brain-friendly strategies for the inclusion classroom insights from a neurologist and classroom teacher* (pp. 11-14). Alexandria, Va.: Association for Supervision and Curriculum Development.

Yeh, S. (2010). The international journal of learning. *Motivation in second language learning: extensive reading*, 17(4), 252. Retrieved October 31, 2014, from http://www.Learning-Journal.com

Descriptive Statistics	N	Range	Min	Max	Sum	Mean	Std. Dev.	Var.
1. When the teacher encourages me for my achievement in class, my motivation increases.	50	2	3	5	242	4.84	.42	.18
2. When I work collectively in pairs or groups, my motivation increases.	50	4	1	5	194	3.88	1.00	1.00
3. When the teacher speaks in the L2 in class (English), I feel more motivated than when (s)he speaks in Turkish.	50	4	1	5	189	3.78	1.01	1.03
4. When the teacher does not ask me in class and I do not participate, but just listen, I feel more relaxed and motivated.	50	4	1	5	189	3.78	1.21	1.48
5. When the teacher uses audiovisual and authentic aids (illustrations, photographs, recordings, news, films) I am more motivated than when (s)he only uses the textbook.	50	3	2	5	223	4.46	.73	.53
6. I am placed in a situation that allows me to discover and draw my own conclusions. And this makes me motivated.	50	2	3	5	219	4.38	.72	.53
7. Having an easygoing classroom environment makes me more motivated.	50	4	1	5	233	4.66	.77	.59
8. The purpose of my teaching environment makes me feel I am important.	50	3	2	5	226	4.52	.73	.54
9. When I work individually, I feel more motivated than when I work in groups or pairs.	50	4	1	5	131	2.62	1.17	1.38
10. I am free to choose my own method of studying and this makes me motivated	50	4	1	5	223	4.46	.78	.62
11. I have the opportunity to do what I do best every day.	50	3	2	5	197	3.94	.89	.79

Item	N	Range	Min	Max	Sum	Mean	SD	Var
12. Grammar is the most useful subject in an English class.	50	4	1	5	130	2.60	1.06	1.14
13. When I take part in class and when I participate, I feel more motivated than if I do not participate.	50	4	1	5	224	4.48	.88	.78
14. In English class, the teacher should talk more than students and the students should only answer when they are called upon.	50	4	1	5	202	4.04	1.06	1.14
15. Communication activities are a waste of time in an English class, because I only need to learn what is necessary to pass English class.	50	4	1	5	221	4.42	.94	.90
16. When activities are designed to help the students to improve their abilities to communicate in English, I feel more motivated.	50	3	2	5	219	4.38	.70	.49
17. I prefer an English class in which there are lots of activities that allow me to participate actively.	50	3	2	5	223	4.46	.84	.70
18. My relationship with the teacher in English class is important to me.	50	2	3	5	239	4.78	.55	.30
19. This English class will definitely help me improve my English.	50	4	1	5	219	4.38	.90	.81
20. Activities in this class are designed to help us to improve our abilities to communicate in English and this makes me more enthusiastic to learn English.	50	3	2	5	219	4.38	.78	.60

19.

Enhancing Agency and Autonomy through the Deep Approach in a Foreign Language Writing Classroom

Daniela Busciglio
University of Oklahoma, USA

This chapter serves as an example of how teachers can use the principles of Deep Education and the Deep Approach to enhance learner autonomy and agency in the language learning classroom through democratically negotiated curriculum. Because there is a dearth of true project-based language learning initiatives that are student-generated and student-driven, and because of my interest in innovative curricular design, my research and teaching propel one another in pursuit of higher agency and autonomy (both for student and teacher.) The experiment described in this chapter is one of my first experiences in developing and implementing a deep project-based language learning (DPBLL) in a course I had designed for intermediate level American university students of Italian studying abroad in Italy.

Autonomy and Agency

In this section it is necessary to provide working definitions for both autonomy and agency to understand the goals of this project. Language learner autonomy has gained traction in the field of language learning since the late 1970s, Holec, among the first Western scholars to instantiate claims of language learner autonomy (1979/1981), described autonomy as "capable of taking charge of his own learning...determining the objectives; defining the contents and progressions; selecting methods and techniques to be used; monitoring the procedure of acquisition properly speaking...[and] evaluating what has been acquired" (1981, p. 3). Holec's theories were mainly regarding self-access centers, an idea which would proliferate well into the 1990s, particularly with Benson and Little, two of the most renowned scholars in the field of language learner autonomy, promoting learner autonomy and social factors that might affect autonomy as distinct and separate ideas, and only as possible organizational capacities in language learning. While the research in the community of scholars who research autonomy are still rooted in and agree upon Holec's original and resilient but basic and lacking theory of autonomy as "the ability to take charge of one's learning" (1981), the field has grown substantially to encapsulate different theories. In addition, scholars call for more classroom-based practical research to demonstrate the effects of theory in practice (e.g. Vieira, 1999, 2009).

In the mid-1990s, two major shifts occur in ideas about learner autonomy: self-access (once synonymous with learner autonomy) is theorized under learner autonomy and autonomy is seen as developed from the interaction with others and therefore interdependent and multidimensional (Dam 1994, 1995; Little, 1995; van Lier, 1996, 2010; Benson & Huang 2008). At least partially as a consequence of these shifts, teachers were no longer conceptualized as a peripheral figures in the construction of autonomization (Little 1999, 2000) and teacher autonomy emerges as a notion at the heart of cultivating learner autonomy (Benson & Huang, 2008; Little, 1995; Reinders & Balcikanli; 2011, Reinders & Lamb, 2008; Smith, 2003a, 2003b; Smith & Erdoğan, 2008; Sinclair, 2009; Vieira, 2010; Ushioda, Smith, Mann & Brown, 2011; Wang & Zhang, 2014). This social turn of autonomy of both teacher and learner in a collaborative environment that benefits from the interdependence of members of the learning community is where we are currently situated in the learner autonomy literature.

One crucial way in which Little and Benson's research on learner autonomy differ from Holec's original theory on autonomy (1979/1981) is that Little and Benson's research evolved to theorize autonomy as not happening *alongside* learning, but as an integral and crucial component of the actual process of learning itself (Benson, 2012 and 2013; Benson & Huang, 2008; Little, 2007a and 2012). Thus, learner autonomy was seen as occurring alongside language learning, not as part of language learning: picture a sidecar on a motorcycle and language learning being the motorcycle: the motorcycle will run with no one in the sidecar but the sidecar cannot drive itself and the motorcycle.

Dam's (1995) watershed research study in this field allowed for the radical reframing of learner autonomy within the language learning classroom because of two main approaches she implemented: posing questions to her students that required them to think about their own learning and what would help them learn better and to subsequently choose what types of activities would help them. She also required students to keep learning journals to reflect on their learning progress. This study resulted in students who communicated more freely and authentically as compared to another class of language learners who focused exclusively on grammar and structure from a class textbook. Similarly, Nunan and Wong found in their study that the "dominant style for more effective students was 'communicative' while for less effective students it was 'authority-oriented'" (2011, p.150). Lüftenegger, Schober, van de Schoot, Wager, Finsterwald, & Spiel also found that students "are more interested, learning goal-oriented and show higher self-efficacy when they perceive themselves as more self-determined and autonomous in classroom learning activities" (2012, p. 34), a finding echoed in Yang's (1998) research. Autonomous learners are thus conceived of as motivated, successful language learners (Ushioda, 2008, 2009, 2011; Ushioda & Dörnyei, 2012; Little, 2012) and the separate views of language learning and the development of learner autonomy are now seen as integral and inseparable from the development of target language proficiency (Dam, 1995; Little, 2007b, 2009, and 2012).

As a result of the amassed learner autonomy literature, the following non-hierarchical, interacting and recursive pedagogical principles of learner autonomy were developed which are agreed upon quite unanimously across the field of learner autonomy researchers: target language usage, learner involvement in planning, monitoring and evaluating the process and content of their learning and learner reflection (Nguyen & Gu, 2013). These key pedagogical components effectively make students experimenters in their own language acquisition, and making the classroom a laboratory of discovery. This in turn suggests the emancipatory power of the autonomy classroom and points towards a pedagogy of agency. Similarly, Kumaravadivelu (2003, cited in Kumaravadivelu, 2006, p. 176), states that in post-method pedagogy, there are two views of learner autonomy, a narrow view and a broad view: a narrow view seeks to develop in the learner a capacity to learn whereas the broad view goes beyond that to include a capacity to learn and to liberate as well.

Benson & Voller's (1997) research summarizes a majority of the splintering of the concept of autonomy into at least five different uses and definitions, according to Thanasoulas (2000a): studying and learning independently; a learnable skillset which can applied in self-directed learning; an innate capacity that is suppressed by institutional/traditional education; a learner's responsibility for their own learning; and the learner's right to determine their own learning. Despite attempts to divide concepts of autonomy into various categories, by the end of the 1990s and well into the 2000s, learner autonomy has become a central axis on which the developmental learning experience may tilt. Little's research in particular positions learner autonomy as an essential element and unique universal human capacity and experience of learning (2007b). Robinson (2011), in agreement with Little's assertions to this extent, emphasizes autonomy as one of life's purposes, understanding that learner autonomy can only be actualized when teachers have autonomy as well.

A prescient scholar and leader in the field of learner autonomy, Little (2007) warned of the dilution of concept of autonomy in practice once it entered the formal discourse of language education. Since it is difficult to find common ground amongst all learner autonomy scholars in the field of language learner autonomy on what learner autonomy precisely is, there are several general principles that describe what autonomy is *not* that are agreed upon by most scholars in the language learner autonomy field concurrently. These are delineated as follows: autonomy is not a synonym for self-directed learning or self-instruction, does not "entail an abdication of responsibility on the part of the teacher," is not a "single behavior or a state that is achieved or unlocked by learners" nor is it something teachers *do* to learners, and it is not a teaching method (Little, 1995; Benson & Huang, 2008). Through this illumination, Little then stresses the three main issues that still linger in learner autonomy: the precise concept that is meant by autonomy, the pedagogical implementation and approaches to implementation of autonomy in the classroom, and finding appropriate focuses for research thereof. Pedagogical implementations and challenges thereof will be discussed in the next section of this dissertation chapter.

Despite the many and proliferating definitions of autonomy, its permanence in language education (Smith 2003b) and the research of autonomy in language education has led to several recent claims that are agreed upon regarding the realities of language learning autonomy which have yet to be repudiated by any studies. These assertions are summed up by Benson: "language learners naturally tend to take control of their learning; learners who lack autonomy are capable of developing it; and autonomous language learning is more effective than non-autonomous language learning" (2011, p. 16). That said, although the concept of learner autonomy has been around and growing for approximately 50 years, it's still regarded as a risky endeavor because of the lack (but growing fount) of practical, classroom research that involves teachers jettisoning a model of education as reproduction and instead demands the divesting of power and control over learners (Little, 2000, 2004). In addition, autonomization necessarily involves a "transformation of the learner as a social individual…autonomy not only transforms individuals, it also transforms the social situations and structures in which they are participants" (Benson, 1996, p. 34). In sum, at its very broadest, learner autonomy calls for critical reflection on society and its institutions, and to know the Other through one's self (Reinders & Balcikanli, 2011; Sameshima 2009). This idea is very similar to Apple's theories and implications for critical *repositioning* of the self for social justice in society (1982, 1983, 2013; Nicolaides, 2008). Fomenting autonomy in language learning in *deep* educational environments (Tochon, 2012) directly channels social agency as learners are presented with the opportunities to craft, monitor, and reflect upon their own learning.

Agency

However common the term agency and social agency may seem, it has been and continues to be hotly debated for hundreds of years. Acknowledging the abstract nature of the term *agency*, Ahearn suggests a "barebones definition" of agency as the "socioculturally mediated capacity to act" (2001, p. 112; 2012, p. 278). Extending this definition slightly, Taylor (1985) asserts that agency is located inside the mental processes of individuals rather than within broader social capacities. Because agency exists within autonomous agents, Ahearn and Taylor argue, within the potential of agency is the possibility to resist against existing power differentials.

Furthermore, for the purpose of this conceptual framework in this chapter, Ortner's bifurcated notion of dual agency is invoked. The first notion of agency, according to Ortner, concerns domination or resistance to dominant powers[1] in and through dominant groups, while the second kind of agency concerns

"life socially organized in terms of culturally constituted projects that infuse life with meaning and purpose" (2006, p. 147) despite often overwhelming power differentials. Additionally, the agent is always embedded in relations of (would-be) solidarity: family, friends, kin, spouses or partner, children, parents, teachers, allies, and so forth" (Ortner, 2006, p. 130-131)

yet also always "enmeshed within relations of power, inequality, and competition" (idem). This provisional but working definition of dual social agency provides a logical construct for purposes of this chapter as it concerns the well-being of the individual in social settings as well as higher purposes of the individual.

---

[1] Dominant powers can be oppressive groups at large who perpetuate, systemic hierarchical structures in society. In educational settings, these "dominant powers" may be varied. For example, an administration that enforces large enrollment classrooms for financial gains; educational policy reform that mandates standardized testing despite the fact that exams have been proven to show extensive cultural biases; or any practice that diminishes the learning capacity of an individual because of these imposed forces.

To further situate this view of social agency within educational contexts, I refer to Ladson-Billings idea of instilling agency in students in terms of academic success, a principle of culturally relevant pedagogy (CRP): "The trick of culturally relevant teaching is to get students to 'choose' academic excellence" (1995b, p.160). In this view, the teacher is positioned as a coach or guide, setting high standards for student achievement so that they must envision excellence in order to attain it. Moreover, Ayers asserts that the "ethical core of teaching toward tomorrow is necessarily designed to create hope and a sense of agency in students" (2012, p. 7) while van Lier notes that the very notion of *self* necessitates a description of agency, asserting that "person and his or her actions define each other" (van Lier, 2010, p. xi).

Consequently, in regards to language learning environments, social agency within a language learning community can be characterized by three main features, according to van Lier: "agency involves initiative or self-regulation by the learner (or group); it is interdependent, that is, it mediates and is mediated by the sociocultural context; it includes an awareness of the responsibility for one's own actions vis-à-vis the environment, including affected others" (2008). Since there is a growing field of research that utilizes language learning histories to expand our "understanding of the learner as a social actor who derives and acts upon different identity positions that are institutionally and culturally situated but that are also dynamic and individually interpreted" (Coffey & Street p. 452), my own view on social agency is viewed through the autonomous actions of the actor that is socioculturally situated based upon her life history.

This outlook on social agency and autonomy fits in well with the DA to language learning as it prefaces the learner's funds of knowledge (Amanti, Gonzalez, Moll & Neff, 1992), their already existing linguistic repertoire (Cenoz & Gorter, 2011) as well as their life histories (Mercer, 2013) as a platform for which the learner can engage in auto-poiesis (or self-organization), responding "to a need for social action" (Tochon, 2014, p. 307). Carson contends that

"[w]hen we consider autonomy from the wider perspective of ontological development, it may be understood as self-determination, self-sovereignty, or the freedom from the control of others to decide on our actions, whilst nonetheless remaining responsible for what we are or what we do" (2010, p. 2).

Similarly, with an aimed focus on action, Tochon states that transdisciplinarity "operates at the junction of ontology (what is reality) and way of knowing, and it situates the flow of knowledge in transformative *action*" (2011, p. 71, emphasis mine). Tochon moreover asserts that the importance of agency is a crucial point teachers must not neglect, and is enacted and embodied in "reflecting on the roles of identity, agency, cooperation and shared autonomy in language learning through critical discussion with the students..." (Tochon, 2014, p. 313). Creating a transdisciplinary space in which transformative *action* can occur through self-reflection and cooperative endeavors allows for students to embrace their own agency in integrating this knowledge into profound ways.

Deep Education as Framework for Autonomy and Agency

Tochon's theory of Deep Education (DE) seeks to present a model in which education can undergo a holistic and profound transformation through quality, not quantity. It is a vision of education for depth, not breadth, that is value-based and transdisciplinary in nature. DE begins as a mindset for action that is constantly developing because it is situationally contextualized and flies in the face of the status quo of standardized assessment in learning, conformity of standards, homogenization of curricula, and shallow methods of teaching and education that do not question systems of dominance and oppression that ultimately promote short-term and destructive behaviors (Tochon, 2012).

The scope of the fundamental DE philosophical objectives prompts a movement towards the transdisciplinary as an approach towards realist and realistic solutions in unity of resources, be they physical or intangible (e.g. ideas and concepts), in an effort to change power structures and policies that govern modern, techno-oriented ways of life and efficacy for efficacy's sake which inhibit profound, meaningful interactions with the self, others and with nature. This form of socialized consciousness is grounded in a unity of shared ethic of respect in and through intercultural understanding and integrity to build a core ethic of care, concern and solidarity for progress, matching Apple's (2013) core ethic of educational progress. The intention of DE within educational contexts is to facilitate the learning experiences of students so that they may go on to access their knowledge base in a way that is operational and transferrable in a multitude of circumstances and challenges they face in a globalized world where intercultural competence is a key to understanding and accessing common ground. DE is thus a framework within which students may learn to access their own skills and theories toolbox and learn how to use these strategies and frameworks in a transdisciplinary mode-- that is, within, outside, and beyond traditional learning environments-- which provides groundwork to set and achieve social as well as self-actualizing goals (Tochon, 2014, p. 127).

In concert with Tochon's DE model, Ikeda's *Soka* (literally "value-creating") education (2010, 2014) philosophy of education embraces a transdisciplinary approach that places emphasis on value creation for peace building. Soka education entails cultivating an environment where students are safe to not only express their own true selves vis-à-vis their own cultural heritages, languages, and backgrounds, but also to create the climate where students feel compelled to examine their own histories and who they desire to be and become based on what they already know are bringing into the classroom, similar to the aforementioned funds of knowledge research. In both Ikeda's and Nicolescu's research, the primacy of human dignity and happiness are emphasized, as they both express concerns over the proliferation of technologies and economies at the expensive of human integrity and dignity. Nicolescu states that "education privileges the intellect, relative to sensibility and the body...But this privileging, if it continues, sweeps us away in the mad logic of efficiency for efficiency's sake which can only end in our self-destruction" (Nicolescu, 1997). Within educational contexts, this indicates the need for learning environments that cultivate and activate the agency of the learner within strategic disciplinary, interdisciplinary and transdisciplinary configurations. The agency of the learner is necessary in order to build lifelong values in students so that they may apply these values in ways that benefit society at large.

Thus, DE is a theory that espouses the emancipation of the student from education as reproduction through learner autonomy because "autonomous, smart learners may create autonomous, smart citizens" (Tochon, 2014, p. 123) thereby seeking to cultivate a more democratic society whereby students are active agents of change from early on in their life experiences, beginning with schooling. One of the most critical aspects of deep pedagogy (DP) is to then, as previously mentioned, to create the conditions in which students are allowed to make their own learning decisions with the assistance of their teacher and classmates as guides and collaborators (Tochon, 2014). Because the deep approach (DA) in deep education is inquiry-based, the process-oriented nature of this approach allows students to not only voice their own historied stories but in doing so, the DA legitimizes their own inquiries and stories and allows them to directly and indirectly question the hierarchized structures of power (Tochon, 2014). This powerful, collective democratic stance ultimately radically recalibrates the legitimization of authority in the classroom, transforming it into an equitably distributed source amongst the teacher and learners.

Deep Education in A Study Abroad Context

For this project, the setting was a five-week intensive advanced Italian composition and culture course which took place in Florence, Italy. The first two weeks of the course (two hours per class session, four days per week), the students had a set curriculum with built-in options starting the third day of the course to familiarize themselves with the history of Florence. This allowed for students to spend time getting to know each other, myself, and for the space to be more familiar and thus become a safe space to build and share knowledge. We explored Florence together through film, non-institutional lectures, guided tours of historical sites and museum, scavenger hunts in the historic center of the city and small group discussion in and out of class, sharing our writings online on our private class blog.

This high-intermediate 300 level Italian composition and culture course, conducted completely in Italian, was designed by the author of this paper as a "travel diary" course to provide opportunities for students to heighten their oral and written language proficiency by way of meditating on and documenting their experiences in a foreign city from an anti-deficit approach to learning. One crucial aspect for me as the course teacher was to facilitate an open culture of collaboration so as to not only share in the co-construction of knowledge and feedback but also create a space where openness of writing and experiences vis-à-vis class discussions and a student-generated blog (where blog posts are "pinned" to an online canvas), created meta-awareness of the language proficiencies, shared access to personal experiences, and a collective memory of a specific shared time in space as well as an individual student and group learning portfolio, in accordance with the research of Büyükdumana & Şirin (2010), Elola (2010) and Ferrari & Zhurauskaya (2012, in press). Structuring this course in this way led to several outcomes, some planned and some spontaneous, and all rewarding.

Firstly, two short writing assignments per student per week (one "free write" and one "guided writing" prompted by several questions I would pose to the class each week based on what we learned and experienced) were always submitted to the blog and were workshopped in class on a weekly basis (two hours per week). This was a way to seek out and improve grammar weaknesses with *in situ* grammar lessons, typically provided by me. However, two weeks into the course, spontaneous student teaching began to occur, reflective especially of Dam's (1995) insights on autonomy. Students felt safe and secure enough to voluntarily (i.e., without my asking or petitioning) to explain idioms, idiomatic structures, regional pronunciations and even "text speak" syntax and grammar, orthography, and standard grammar to the class. This was an unplanned and a most welcomed outcome of learner autonomy that fostered social agency and empowerment for many of the students in the class that took this opportunity.

Another strategically planned way to foster empowerment of the students by way of autonomy involved self-regulated weekly writing and grammar workshops. Each week I disseminated written copies of their blog posts (five total weeks of writing with two assignments per student per week). Weekly writing workshops began the second week. I highlighted and wrote notes and codes about the errors in grammar, syntax and orthography on each writing assignment and then grouped the students in pairs to help each other correct the errors. Each week I lifted the bar: the third week, I simply highlighted errors and wrote codes for correction; the fourth week I simply highlighted errors; the fifth week I handed back the writing assignments without any markups, as I knew the students had the power within them to correct errors with my pointing out their errors. This was a particularly pointed strategy in letting go of control on my part and also allowing the students to see that they were indeed capable to find the errors and take learning in form of error correction and feedback into their own hands. (I was, of course, available to them as a reference during all workshops but encouraged more and more autonomy as the semester went on.)

One additional way I attempted to implement learner autonomy was during the last two weeks of the six week long semester, where the curriculum was entirely student-centered, negotiated among them and contextualized within the local Italian and classroom community, reflective of the research conducted by Brown (2011), Cormier (2008), and Cullen, Harris and Hill (2012), especially since can be static and rigid and "instructional flexibility is the basis of interactive learning" (Tochon, 2014, p. 82). Because by that point the students were familiarized with the course, the city and their fellow classmates, I petitioned students to draw up a list of possible event outings they were interested in attending (the pre-approved university budget allowed for the procurement of tickets to nearly any outing within reason, e.g. guided museum tour and similar events) and then, in class, had students vote on which one they would like to do. Acting as the class concierge and logistics coordinator, I arranged all details for the outings and then, together with the students, formulated guided writing questions for them to write on that week.

The last strategy implemented in this course to facilitate autonomy was a culmination of their experience in a final deep student-centered project. Students were given six class periods (thus, twelve hours in class) to specifically work on a project of their choice, with me available to them as an expert guide, grammarian, human dictionary, concierge of ideas, rubric co-judge, and resident techie. These projects were the culmination of their study abroad experiences, presented on the last day of classes, with each student evaluating themselves and their peers in the process.

It is important to note here that this intermediate course took place under ideal circumstances. This is because the course was located in the target language country and thus I had many resources (including financial) available to me to be able to instantiate project-based learning with the students' relative ease. In addition to this, the class was also ideal, with a total of 14 students (most in groups of twos and threes, except for one student who expressed she wanted to execute her project on her own) for the final projects. Because it was an ideal situation within the target language country, students also were able to directly observe phenomena in real-time (as opposed to watching videos or reading about their project topic) and their projects were driven by these observable phenomena around them that arose their interest. Thus, I fully recognize that socio-economic barriers of visiting the target language country was not an issue in this particular project but is a very real issue, which is why I also exemplify two other unofficial pilot studies that took place within the United States. The examples that follow will demonstrate how students responded to their curiosity and how some projects were akin to service projects that informed future students of study abroad programs.

In terms of projects, there was quite a variety in interest in topics, as to be expected with any student-directed project experience where students choose based on their own interest. I will highlight several projects and their respective formats here to demonstrate the types of projects created. One group of students created a "Study Abroad Survival Guide" video in which they demonstrated "Dos" and "Don'ts" of studying abroad in Italy, explaining cultural faux pas for Americans in Italy and how to blend into the culture and, specifically, detailing day to day life in Florence. Not only was a particularly informative video that pertained to the actions and perceptions of American college students in Italy but it also especially helped foster comparisons and connections between the two differing cultures in order for students to obtain a better sense of fostering community in a foreign place.

Another group of students examined "Calcio storico" (literally "Historical Soccer", otherwise known as Florentine soccer) in documentary style project. This group sought to this highlight local tradition of soccer and the difference of rules between traditional soccer and "Calcio Storico" – from the number of team players allowed on each team to the type of violent street-fighting allowed in the game that is not allowed in traditional soccer, for instance. The group was able to observe several games in the tournament in person during their study abroad experience and reported back on not only how the game worked but also the pre-game rituals and traditions (e.g. the special 14th-centuryesque uniforms worn to the ritualistic walk toward the stadium through the neighbor of Florence that serves as the team their name, and detailing how some players' prison sentences are temporarily suspended so that they may participate in the tournament), using their own footage of the games and pre-game preparations. This bit of local long-standing Florentine tradition is little known outside of Italy, taking place in the height of summer and allowed this group of students to use reporting skills in a documentary style narrative of this sport (some live during the class presentation and some recorded in the video prepared for the presentation) its history, and the tournament results.

Conclusion

At many post-secondary institutions, students typically have two questions of their teachers: what they need to do to complete the course (assignments, projects, exam dates, and the like) and the parameters for those assignments. But if we make the parameters such that creativity and originality are rewarded, then teachers become activists against a reproductionist model of education where conformity to a certain, frequently arbitrary standard (a model produced by a teacher or a model produced by another student used as an example for the rest of the class) funnels the ability of students to imagine, ideate, create, and produce deeply from their own funds of knowledge. This standard of production does not lend itself to a critical analysis because students' expectations are constantly being matched with the teacher's in hopes that their expectations match those of their instructor. In the DE model, students are encouraged to set their own goals and criteria for assessment and evaluation for themselves as well as their peers. This in turn allows them not only the freedom to establish their own parameters and criteria but allows them the freedom to, as often occurs, aim much higher than the teacher's median expectations.

Regarding this sort of assessment or parameter-setting, it is only because of students are indoctrinated to believe that only certain models of education, teaching, learning, and assessment work. On a deeper level this suggests a fundamental mistrust of students themselves. If teachers believe in the funds of knowledge of their students as a critical part of their success in becoming democratic agents of change in society then they also have to believe in democratically, evidence-based principles and methods that involve students in many if not every step of the teaching and evaluative process. Teaching and assessment can never be separated but instead must work hand in hand, symbiotically to enhance and feed off one another synergistically. Thus, if teachers allow students the freedom to discover and explore their own interest with the discipline, we can instantiate a model of deep education that assists students in creating, exploring and creating their own values together in an environment of mutual respect, collaboration and community.

References

Ahearn, L. (2001). Language and agency. *Annual Review of Anthropology, 30,* 109-137.

Ahearn, L. (2012). *Living language: An introduction to linguistic anthropology.* (1st ed.). Oxford: Wiley-Blackwell.

Amanti, C., Gonzalez, N., Moll, L., & Neff, D. (1992). Funds of knowledge for teaching: Using a qualitative approach to connect homes and classrooms. *Theory into Practice, 31(2),* 132-141.

Apple, M. W. (1982). *Education and power.* London, UK: Routledge.

Apple, M. W. (1983). *Official knowledge: Democratic education in a conservative age.* New York: Routledge.

Apple, M. W. (2013). *Can education change society?* New York: Routledge.

Ayers, W. (2012). Diving into the wreckage: Our schools, education reform, and the future society. In G. M. Boldt. (Ed.), *Challenging the politics of the teacher accountability movement: Toward a more hopeful educational future* (pp. 5-19). Retrieved from: http://bankstreet.edu/occasional-papers/issues/occasional-papers-27/introduction-27

Benson, P. (1996) Concepts of autonomy in language learning. In R. Pemberton, S. L. Edward, W. W. F. Or, & H. D. Pierson (Eds.), *Taking Control: Autonomy in Language Learning,* 27-34. Hong Kong: Hong Kong University Press.

Benson, P. (2011). *Teaching and researching autonomy in language learning.* (2nd ed.). London: Pearson Education.

Benson, P. (2012). Autonomy in Language learning, learning and life. *Synergies France 9,* 29-39. Retrieved from: http://gerflint.fr/Base/France9/benson.pdf

Benson, P. (2013). Learner autonomy. *TESOL Quarterly, 47(4),* 839-843. doi:10.1002/tesq.134.

Benson, P. & Huang, J. (2008). Autonomy in the transition from foreign language learning to foreign language teaching. *DELTA: Documentação de Estudos em Lingüística Teórica e Aplicada 24,* 421-439.

Benson, P. & Voller, P. (Eds.). (1997). *Autonomy and independence in language learning.* London: Longman.

Brown, P. S. (2011). Introducing negotiated curriculum. In K. Irie & A. Stewart (Eds.), *Realizing autonomy: Practice and reflection in language education contexts,* 49-62. New York: Palgrave Macmillan.

Büyükdumana, I. & Şirin, S. (2010). Learning portfolio (LP) to enhance constructivism and student autonomy. *Procedia Social and Behavioral Sciences, 3,* 55-61. doi:10.1016/j.sbspro.2010.07.012.

Carson, L. (2010). Language learner autonomy: Myth, magic, or miracle?. Proceedings of the international conference, 'From teaching to learning:

current trends in English Language Teaching' (pp. 77-100). South East European University, Macedonia, April 2010.

Cenoz, J., & Gorter, D. (2011). A holistic approach to multilingual education: Introduction. *Modern Language Journal, 95*(3), 339-343. doi:10.1111/j.1540-4781.2011.01204.x.

Coffey, S., & Street, B. (2008). Narrative and identity in the "Language Learning Project". *The Modern Language Journal, 92*(3), 452-464.

Cormier, D. (2008). *Community as Curriculum*. Retrieved from: http://davecormier.com/edblog/2008/06/03/rhizomatic-education-community-as-curriculum

Cullen, R., Harris, M., Hill, R. R. (2012). *The learner-centered curriculum: Design and implementation*. San Francisco: Jossey-Bass.

Dam, L. (1994). How do we recognize an autonomous classroom. In *Die Neueren Sprachen, 93*(5), 503-527.

Dam, L., (1995). *Learner autonomy 3: From theory to classroom practice*. Dublin: Authentik.

Elola, I. (2010). Collaborative writing: fostering language and writing conventions development. *Language Learning & Technology, 14*(3), 51-71.

Ferrari, L. & Zhurauskaya, D. (forthcoming). Using e-Porfolios for foreign language learning and assessment at beginner and post-beginner level. In Hernández, R. & Rankin P. (Eds.), *Third-level Education and Second Language Learning: Promoting Self-directed Learning in new Technological and Educational Contexts*. New York: Peter Lang.

Holec, H. (1979/1981). *Autonomy in foreign language learning*. Oxford: Pergamon and Strasbourg: Council of Europe.

Ikeda, D. (2010). *Soka education for the happiness of the individual*. Santa Monica: Middleway Press.

Ikeda, D. (2014). Value creation for global change: Building resilient and sustainable societies. 2014 Peace Proposal. Retrieved from: http://www.daisakuikeda.org/assets/files/peaceproposal2014.pdf.

Kumaravadivelu, B. (2006). *Understanding language teaching: From method to postmethod*. Mahwah, NJ: Lawrence Erlbaum.

Ladson-Billings, G. (1995a). But that's just good teaching! The case for culturally relevant pedagogy. *Theory into Practice, 34*(3), 159-165.

Ladson-Billings, G. (1995b). Toward a theory of culturally relevant pedagogy. *American Educational Research Journal, 32*(3), 465-491.

Lier (van), L. (1996). Interaction in the language curriculum: Awareness, autonomy and authenticity. New York: Longman.

Lier (van), L. (2010). Forward: Agency, self and identity in language learning. In B. O'Rourke & L. Carson (Eds.), *Language learner autonomy: Policy, curriculum, classroom: A festschrift in honour of David Little* (pp. ix-xviii). Oxford, UK: Peter Lang.

Little, D. (1995). Learning as dialogue: The dependence of learner autonomy on teacher autonomy. *System 23*(2), 175-181. doi:0346-251X(95)00006-2.

Little, D. (1999). Developing learner autonomy in the foreign language classroom: a social-interactive view of learning and three fundamental pedagogical principles. *Revista Canaria de Estudios Ingleses, 38*, 77-88.

Little, D. (2000). Learner autonomy and human interdependence: some theoretical and practical consequences of a social-interactive view of cognition, learning and language. In B. Sinclair, I. McGrath & T. Lamb (Eds.), *Learner autonomy, teacher autonomy: Future Directions*, 15-23. Harlow: Longman.

Little, D. (2004). Democracy, discourse and learner autonomy in the foreign language classroom. *Utbildning & Demokrati 13*(3), 105-126.

Little, D. (2007a). Language learner autonomy: Some fundamental considerations revisited. *Innovation in Language Learning and Teaching, 1*(1), 14-29.

Little, D. (2007b). Introduction: Reconstructing learner and teacher autonomy in language education. In A. Barfield & S. Brown (Eds.), *Reconstructing autonomy in language education*, 1-13. Basingstoke: Palgrave.

revisited. *Innovation in Language Learning and Teaching, 1*(1), 14-29.

Little D. (2009). Language learner autonomy and the European Language Portfolio: Two L2 English examples. *Language Teaching, 42*, 222-233. doi:10.1017/S0261444808005636.

Little, D. (2012). Two views of learner autonomy and their implications for applied linguistics research. XXXVII. FAAPI Conference, San Martin de los Andes, 20-22 September 2012.

Lüftenegger M., Schober, B., van de Schoot, R., Wagner, P., Finsterwald, M., Spiel, C. (2012). Lifelong learning as a goal: Do autonomy and self-regulation in school result in well prepared pupils? *Learning and Instruction 22*, 27-36.

doi:10.1016/j.learninstruc.2011.06.001.

Mercer, S. (2013). Working with language learner histories from three perspectives: Teachers, learners and researchers. *Studies in Second Language Learning and Teaching, 3*(2), 161-185.

Nguyen, L. T. C., & Gu, Y. (2013). Strategy-based instruction: A learner-focused approach to developing learner autonomy. *Language Teaching Research, 17*(1), 9-30. doi:10.1177/1362168812457528.

Nicolaides, C. (2008). Learner autonomy in the light of Freire [Special issue]. *DELTA: Documentação de Estudos em Lingüística Teórica e Aplicada 24*, 493-511.

Niscolescu, B. (1997, November). *The transdisciplinary evolution of the university condition for sustainable development.* Paresented at the International Congress "Universities' Responsibilities to Society,"

International Association of Universities, Bangkok, Thailand: Chulalongkorn University. 12-14 Nov. 1997.

Nunan, D. & Wong, L. L. C. (2011). The learning styles and strategies of effective language learners. *System 39*, 144-163. doi:10.1016/j.system.2011.05.004.

Ortner, S. B. (2006). *Power and projects: Reflections on agency*. In S. B. Ortner, *Anthropology and social theory: Culture, power, and the acting subject*, (pp.129-153). Durham: Duke University Press.

Reinders, H., & Balcikanli, C. (2011). Learning to foster autonomy: The role of teacher education materials. *Studies in Self-Access Learning Journal, 2*(1), 15-25.

Reinders, H., & Lamb, T. (Eds.). (2008). *Learner and teacher autonomy*. Amsterdam: John Benjamins.

Robinson, K. (2011, August 25). *Educating the heart and mind*. [Video file]. Retrieved from: https://www.youtube.com/watch?v=5MSgCut1Ils

Sameshima, P. (2009). Stop Teaching! Hosting an ethical responsibility through a pedagogy of parallax. *Journal of Curriculum & Pedagogy, 6*(1), 11-18.

Sinclair, B. (2009). The teacher as learner: Developing autonomy in an interactive learning
environment. In R. Pemberton, S. Toogood, & A. Barfield (Eds.) *Maintaining control: Autonomy and language learning*, 175-198. Hong Kong: Hong Kong University Press.

Smith, R. C. (2003a). Teacher education for teacher-learner autonomy. In J. Gollin, G. Ferguson & H. Trappes-Lomax (Eds.), *Symposium for Language Teacher Educators: Papers from Three IALS Symposia*. Edinburgh: Institute of Applied Language Studies, University of Edinburgh. Retrieved from: http://homepages.warwick.ac.uk/~elsdr/Teacher_autonomy.pdf

Smith, R. C. (2003b). Pedagogy for autonomy as (becoming-)appropriate methodology. In D. Palfreyman, & R.C. Smith (Eds), *Learner Autonomy across Cultures: Language Education Perspectives*. Basingstoke: Palgrave Macmillan.

Smith, R. C. & Erdoğan, S. (2008). Teacher-learner autonomy: Programme goals and student-teacher constructs. In Lamb, T. & Reinders, H. (Eds.), *Learner and Teacher Autonomy: Concepts, Realities and Responses*. Amsterdam: Benjamins.

Taylor, C. (1985). *Human Agency and Language: Philosophical Papers, Volume 1*. Cambridge: Cambridge University Press.

Thanasoulas, D. (2000a). What is learner autonomy and how can it be fostered?. *The Internet TESL Journal, November 2000*. Retrieved from: http://www3.telus.net/linguisticsissues/learnerautonomy.html

Tochon, F. V. (2011). Deep education: Assigning a moral role to academic work. *Educação, Sociedade & Culturas, 33*, 17-35.

Tochon, F. V. (2012). Deep education: An introduction. [PowerPoint Slides].

Tochon, F. V. (2014). *Help them learn a language deeply. Francois Victor Tochon's deep approach to world languages and cultures.* Blue Mounds, WI: Deep University Press.

Ushioda, E. (2008). Motivation and good language learners. In C. Griffiths (Ed.), *Lessons from Good Language Learners,* 19-34. Cambridge: Cambridge University Press.

Ushioda, E. (2009). A person-in-context relational view of emergent motivation, self and identity. In Z. Dörnyei & E. Ushioda (Eds.), *Motivation, language identity and the L2 self,* 215-228. Bristol, UK: Multilingual Matters.

Ushioda, E. (2011). Why autonomy? Insights from motivation theory and research. *Innovation in Language Learning and Teaching, 5*(2). 221-232. doi: 10.1080/17501229.2011.577536.

Ushioda, E., & Dörnyei, Z. (2012). Motivation. In S. Gass & A. Mackey (Eds.), *The Routledge handbook of second language acquisition,* 396-409. New York: Routledge.

Ushioda, E., Smith, R., Mann, S. & Brown, P. (2011). Promoting teacher-learner autonomy through and beyond initial language teacher education'. *Language Teaching* 44(1), 118-121.

Vieira, F. (1999). Pedagogy for autonomy: teacher development and pedagogical experimentation: an in-service teacher training project. In S. Cotterall & D. Crabbe (Eds.), *Learner Autonomy in Language Learning: Defining the Field and Effecting Change,* 153–162. Frankfurt am Main: Peter Lang.

Vieira, F. (2009). Enhancing pedagogy for autonomy through learning communities: Making our dream come true?. *Innovation in Language Learning and Teaching, 3,* 269-282.

Vieira, F. (2010). Towards teacher and learner Autonomy: Exploring a pedagogy of experience in teacher education. *Revista Canaria De Estudios Ingleses, 61,* 13-27.

Wang, Q. & Zhang, H. (2014). Promoting teacher autonomy through university-school collaborative action research. *Language Teaching Research, 18*(2) 222-241.

Yang, N. (1998). Exploring a new role for teachers: promoting learner autonomy. *System 26,* 127-135.

20.

Conclusion: An Approach to Firstness
Authority as the Problem and the Solution

Francois Victor Tochon
University of Wisconsin-Madison

> The idea of the absolutely First must be entirely separated from all conception of or reference to anything else; for what involves a second is itself a second to that second. The First must therefore be present and immediate, so as not to be second to a representation. It must be fresh and new, for if old it is second to its former state. It must be initiative, original, spontaneous, and free; otherwise it is second to a determining cause. It is also something vivid and conscious; so only it avoids being the object of some sensation. It precedes all synthesis and all differentiation; it has no unity and no parts. It cannot be articulately thought: assert it, and it has already lost its characteristic innocence; for assertion always implies a denial of something else.
> C.S. Peirce, A Guess at the Riddle, EP 1:248; CP 1.356-357, 1888

Considering recent trends in the way people are being educated around the world suggests that something has been terribly missing. This book was about this "something."

> I could have given any unknown label to the missing dimension, but chose the word "depth." Claiming that depth is the missing dimension of current education might sound like a come-back to a form of dualistic realism, in which the tension between surface and depth is exacerbated. This is not the way I see it. On the contrary, I would rather define depth as the conciliation of opposites, and a transdisciplinary layer of understanding in which opposites can abide and unite.
> (Tochon's 2016 website)

The present work was to define the missing dimension and analyze means to introduce it in forthcoming educational endeavors. Depth can't be easily reified as a form of change that could simply be brought into the current system, and that would not be our intent. Depth is not a substance, it is not a "thing." Rather it is a form of access to the higher, sounder, more meaningful dimension of what is usually being done. This makes it all the more difficult to introduce as there is not really a "deep curriculum." There is an approach to curriculum that makes the curriculum more relevant, lively, authentic, and humane. In this approach, the students are the curriculum builders.

The Core of It

The book titled "Help Them Learn a Language Deeply" emphasized that authority is depriving students from a large part of their power to learn. Authority is a difficult word, as it may imply discipline as well as its opposite, agency. Authority should be transferred to the learner if a Deep Approach is to be developed. It is good if the teacher has agency to emancipate herself from the constraints of the imposed curricula, as this form of teacher agency will help scaffold their own agency in the learners. Basically the learners should have agency as well and develop full authority on both content and process in learning settings.

This marks a revolution after so many years during which school programs have been molded under the principle of external expertise. The principles of internal authority and agency do not contradict the existence of experienced professionals who may reach a form of expertise. "The Expert Teacher" (Tochon, 1993) prefaced by late Michael Huberman demonstrated that pedagogical expertise was often ignored or despised by the powers that shape school programs. It is true that, for instance, linguists for language teaching, applied linguist and second language acquisition specialists have their word to say regarding language learning. Yet as long as the fundamental of students' agency and their authority as readers of their branch learning is not accepted by the school systems and integrated in a more flexible conception of curricula, giving rise to bottom-up agency and authority, the system may deprive students from their free will and their full power to learn. Thus freedom to learn is connected to the development of agency, to an increase in motivation that taps into intrinsic energy dynamics that stimulate the learning potential. This manifest for the students the power to learn their own way, not the prescribed way.

If we are to conceive of a more creative society, children have to be authorized to create from the start as well as when they grow along the path of their wishes and personal and interpersonal projects. It is certainly good to show them various venues through which they can and may want to develop but the choice of the curriculum, its content and process, should be the fruit of a negotiation in which the learner reaches real authority.

If educating means empowering, what is the role of authority? This is the question that Maria Betriz Greco (2007) asked in reference to the work of Jean-Joseph Jacotot (see Jacques Rancière, *The Ignorant Master*). The response is an anti-method. It indicates the limits of the teacher's action, when instruction deprives the learners from their right to learn their own way, and what they like to learn. The real issue becomes the transfer of authority. There are no teachers, there are only learners. If the conditions of learning set in our educational institutions are such that passivity and demotivation ensues, that replaces the infinite curiosity to learn that is proper to most children with dullness and a process qualified by Rancière as stultification. In The Ignorant Master, Rancière studied the libertarian approach of an 19th century teacher, Jean Joseph Jacotot. In contrast to educational spoon-feeding, Jacotot proposed not to attach too much attention to the form but insist on questions that stimulate intellectual emancipation, thinking for one-self, thinking otherwise. The focus then was not on knowledge transmission. Rather, it was placed on strengthening the will to work with one's intellect and discover new knowledge in a position of equal with the magister. Authority was then submitted to a mutation in which obedience became self-empowerment, using the power of mindful will. This opened the door to authoring one's actions. In Latin indeed, *auctoritas* comes from the verb *augere* that designate the act of augmenting the energy emerging from the source of oneself. Such growth is legitimate and does not rest on the subordination of the other.

One does not have to be an anarchist to understand the depth of this statement. School inherited from an educational concept that was anterior to its institutionalizing. In ancient times, the master-disciple relation authorized the disciple to be an equal in the process of conversational growth. When transferred into the squared walls of K-12 education, it became what John Taylor Gatto (2006) defined, in his *Underground History of American Education,* as the prison of modern schooling. Gatto's prologue adopts a view similar to Rancière's: hierarchy is a social imaginary that legitimates measures of coercion enforcing closely controlled, shallow learning:

> The shocking possibility that dumb people don't exist in sufficient numbers to warrant the millions of careers devoted to tending them will seem incredible to you. Yet that is my central proposition: the mass dumbness which justifies official schooling first had to be dreamed of; it isn't real….

And:

> Children allowed to take responsibility and given a serious part in the larger world are always superior to those who are passively schooled. (p.xv)

Unfortunately, the sense of prison persists with most systems of online education. Skinner's operant conditioning evolved into behavior analysis and its modification through conditioning results of reinforcement and punishment. Most distance education programs use behavior modification strategies in their analysis of and response to student results and the ways retributions or sanctions are imposed as forms of feedback to progress or failure. In Tochon (2015), I analyzed how an online high schooler was plunged into a state of increasing depression by the systematic application of these control strategies.

The solution proposed by Gatto (2006) is to repudiate centralization of schooling, such that schooling may be desystematized through utopian, open and flexible packages of resources from which students could create their own goals and their own curriculum. This is what we mean by Deep Education.

An Overview of the Definitions of Deep Education in the Chapters of this Book

In the Introduction to the book "Help Them Learn a Language Deeply," I referred to one core principle in Chinese educational philosophy: Education is "inexpressible".

> One teacher was once asked: "What is the first principle?" He answered: "If I were to tell you, it would become the second principle."

Linear expressible knowledge is limited to an intellectual viewpoint, it is not living knowledge with its deep pragmatic dimension. Knowledge that is standardized and replicable is not personal knowledge, which is in large part implicit, as emphasized Polanyi (1962).

This is the main reason why I did not provide a straightforward and unilateral definition of this concept that inevitably would lead to its reification, creating chains of binaries. I suggested that every teacher might develop his or her own sense of what Deep Education is. Defining an orientation is at the risk of losing its complexity. The wise shows the moon and the idiot looks at the finger, says another Chinese proverb.

Let us examine what the authors of the various chapters offered as their own definition of Deep Education. The first part of the book is an introduction to Deep Education.

In **Chapter 1**, I characterized the Deep Approach as a broad phenomenon that manifests a turning point in the way we reflect on academic disciplines. It reflects a transdisciplinary value-laden perspective. The Deep Approach is revolutionizing the ways we think about what should be accomplished in Education and Teacher Education, and how it should be done. It defines a move towards deeper conceptions of curricula and curriculum interconnectedness. The learner in this process is a creator. The student is provided agency in having the freedom to create the curriculum: the learner makes the instructional decisions and decides of a course of study. The study project become a life study project, a life project. Deep education is thus defined within the dynamics of living, not static categories.

In **Chapter 2**, Manuel Fernandez Cruz and José Gijon Puerta define depth in terms of quality and ethical responsibility. They develop a Deep Approach to professional development, overcoming usual reductive visions of training and opening it to the complexity of personal situations and social interactions. Their (auto)biographic and narrative approach allows the versatility of stories. Responsibility as a deeper form of accountability characterizes deep cognitive, social, moral and ethical development. Such emancipation which lies upon personal, intimate criteria overcomes dependence and the lack of social responsibility that situations of supervision generate. The analysis of interventions of a higher order makes it possible for teacher education to enable teachers to provisionally build and rebuild in a deliberative way the concept of curriculum, experimenting alternatives in practice. The Deep Approach of professional development establishes the conditions for innovative professional situations of genuine and singular quality. The search for quality is a crucial component of Deep Education.

In **Chapter 3**, Shirley O'Neill defines depth as root knowledge. She explores educational growth from the perspective of the semiotic tree of knowledge. Her framework for deeper learning implies a democratic environment in which the learners have much choice. Building the students' capacity and accommodating deep pedagogy principles places students in the constructivist context of project-based and problem-based learning, having the opportunity and autonomy to construct their own pathways across tailored and dynamic communities of practice.

In **Chapter 4**, Xiang Long reviews the concept and development of Liberal Education and General Education, demonstrating the enmeshing of language, culture, and content knowledge. He then explores Foreign Language General Education and Deep Education as manifested in the Deep Approach to world languages and cultures. The chapter defines the characteristics of education from a new perspective, currently emerging in China, which implies practicing languages while learning various disciplinary fields. This deeper approach to General Education may scaffold more creative and deeper forms of immersion and content-based learning. Xiang Long defines Deep Education as a cross-section of immersive experiences and General Education, on the basis of four suggestions for instructors: (a) go deep into students' feelings and thinking, (b) touch the nature of subjects and the core of the knowledge, (c) expose the internal transformation of students' learning and development, and (d) promote students' autonomous discovery and real understanding.

In **Chapter 5**, Jianfang Xiao pursues this reflection in the name of Integrated English (IE), which is also immersive and content-based. She explores IE in an international program that goes along precise rationales and several teaching principles supported by specific beliefs related to bilingual education. Language integration overcomes shallow teaching and supports deeper forms of teaching to accelerate the developments of children's intelligence, critical thinking and language competence. Language integration requires a deeper approach to foster learners' foreign language proficiency and increase their sensitivity to and understanding of other cultures, she writes. What the Deep Approach may bring to content-based instruction and integrated language is a personalization of the instructional processes in reference to a changing context. The contents and tasks are then chosen and developed by the students which makes such deep apprenticeship more relevant and meaningful, as learning becomes a form of engagement

Chapter 6 opens the second part of the book, which focuses on the theoretical aspects of Deep Education. Philip Bostic reimagines deep Soul work in Education within multicultural, community-based education spaces. He argues for a re-conceptualization of the soul coupled with a moral obligation to initiate healing work by employing a deeper approach to what it means to be human. By acknowledging the manifested soul as a political entity that is invariably interconnected and sacred, Bostic proposes a human-centered ontological and epistemic framework that foregrounds a deeper curriculum that develops ways in which we are able to see ourselves in the eyes of others, regardless of our socially-constructed identities. In this view, Deep Education characterizes the search for and manifestation of the Soul.

Chapter 7 develops the focus on professionalism further with the analysis of Family Child Care. Kate MacCrimmon turns to her experience to critically reflect on a deeper approach to Early Childhood Education. She uses auto-ethnography to reflect on the roles she performs in action. She acknowledges that by attempting to meet state requirements, she was unable to sustain high quality child care. Professional criteria should include emotion, complexity and relationships. A personalized pedagogy and professional identity is critical in family child care. It defines educational depth in a way that the imposition of and obedience to shallow standards cannot achieve. In contrast to the neoliberal definitions of quality, depth is characterized by identity work and an ethic of care.

In **Chapter 8**, Connie Lent explored the emergence of systems of narrative coherence. She analyses the creation of life stories through informal discourse analysis of written observations of children's dramatic play at 2, 3, and 4 years of age. This approach defines deep psychological development. To mediate reflection and action and generate master life-story narratives, children invest their deep identity in play, as a practiced representation of key symbols considered through the lens of life sustaining practices and Deep

Education. In this light, Deep Education defines a counter-narrative in search for deep identity and a line of work that is closely related to the exploration of the life-story, connecting the dots between experience and identity engagement.

In **Chapter 9**, Alexandra Lakind and Amos Margulies propose to overcome what they call a zombie school of thought in Early Childhood Education. Their chapter explores Freirean ideology from freedom and love to dialogue and praxis. From their perspective, the prominence of a simplistic version of developmental psychology has overshadowed what could be a deeper, critical pedagogy. Critical consciousness scaffolds an education respecting the child for who they are and not for what they will be. A deeper educational theory should validate the teachable heart and teachable mind through a unity based in plurality and diversity, not separateness. Deep education defines an ethic of freedom, a space not to 'help' children, but to love them. Depth is about asking questions, exploring experiences, making connections, and rooting ourselves in love.

After these three chapters on early childhood education, **Chapter 10** examines deep learning in Science and supports an aesthetic paradigm of Science Education. In this chapter, Merrie Koester considers the intersections of creativity, deep learning, and ways of being science teachers and learners. She defines deep teaching of science as aesthetic inquiry. Koester's sense of deep pedagogy is characterized by arts-infused teaching/learning performances that are metasemiotic, participatory, meaningful, and adaptive, rather than prescriptive. In this perspective, Deep Education characterizes the transformative nature of aesthetic inquiry.

Chapter 11 addresses the need for deep evaluation. All over the world, many educational actors are imposed a system of evaluation conditioned by standardized tests, which is at the core of neoliberal ideology. Performance testing places students, teachers, and schools in an unhealthy competition that may poison the social environment of education. Accountability measures take much time that should be devoted to learning. They eliminate the chances of success of particular social classes, and racial and ethnic groups. Shallow assessment measures create distortions in social life. The aberrant pseudo-social contract they create impacts human lives. The mental suffering engendered by standardized testing affects minority groups in particular. Standardized performance tests have become instrumental in what the *United Nations' Convention on the Prevention and Punishment of the Crime of Genocide* (1948) calls "ethnocide." Many teachers resist the culture of testing. When mechanistic and superficial evaluation becomes fundamental in schooling, then education is not anymore truly reflective, reflexive, and profound.

Performance assessment has modified spontaneous approaches to the knowledge of children, and promotes or stunts certain aspirations to steer preferred trajectories. It is a form of social manipulation. If deep learning is the goal, then deep tests should dig deep into competence and proficiency, not be the ephemeral measure of shallow rote learning. The functions of deep evaluation are the heart of teaching: (a) Individualization in the face of standardization; (b) encouragement in the face of discouragement engendered by testing; (c)dialogue in the face of administrative monologue; (d) teaching personnel in the face of public measurement.

In **Chapter 12**, Tomoko Wakana explored deep culture in the U.S. context. Intercultural understanding is often a goal and a benefit of study abroad, however defining it may be difficult. The chapter uses symbolic interactionism as a theoretical foundation for a Deep Culture Model, a theoretical foundation that was explored further in Chapter 18. The presence of fellow international students scaffolds deep culture learning, and a deeper sense of the culture of origin. Deep Education defines the search for the unconscious meanings, values, norms and hidden cultural assumptions that support the interpretation of experience as we interact with others.

Chapter 13 proposes the ultimate theorizing: Harun Serpil develops Deep Education on the foreground of Deep Symbolic Interactionism. This analytical lens for transdisciplinary education calls for a deeper, more equitable, holistic and cosmopolitan vision to improve educational phenomena. The author rejects the shallow, inequitable, self-serving and competitive view of education. Teachers often complain about unmotivated students, with no real life-purpose. Information is omnipresent, but wisdom has become rare. Deep Education is defined here as providing inquiries with holistic and humanistic tools to see the big and deep picture.

The third part of the book focuses on practice al applications of Deep Education. **Chapter 14** is written by a teacher research team in charge of the Russian Flagship course in one of the best Russian programs in America. Anya Nesterchouk, Jambul Akkaziev and Snezhana Zheltoukhova explore the development of intercultural competence at the novice level through a Deep Approach of Russian. The Deep Approach was successfully implemented in a project aiming at encouraging deep cultural understanding and developing intercultural competence. Self-directed projects were key to this development with adult L2 Russian learners. The authors posited that the Deep Approach offers an optimal framework for integrating cultural knowledge at any proficiency level and can be effectively employed by educators in a novice level classroom. So far most experiences with the Deep Approach were at the Intermediate and Advanced level. By designing individualized curricula and establishing linguistic, cultural, and personal achievement tasks within self-directed projects, the participants were in charge of their learning in a shared process of self-actualization. Creative self-actualization along the line of self- and team-determined projects thus define Deep Education in this context, as it contributes to identity-building processes.

One member of the teacher researchers above explored the role of technologies in **Chapter 15**: How could Web 2.0 be used deeply? Snezhana Zheltoukhova reviews current trends in instructional technologies that increase the productivity and autonomy of the learners. The principles of the Deep Approach are compatible with the ways new educational technologies support independent foreign language learning. Experiences of technology-enhanced Deep

Approach modules were implemented in the Russian Flagship Program. Personal learning environments may scaffold deeper learning and attune the learners with their inner life goals, real-life activities and identity building processes, which characterize Deep Education as a bottom-up methodology.

In **Chapter 16**, Mary Zuidema proposes to branch out beyond the standards. The multiliteracies framework, she notes, may help for Deep Higher Education. Communicative language teaching (CLT) and National Standards-based methods are limited if you consider 21st century approaches. In comparison, not only do multiliteracies work in practice, their uses involve translingual and transcultural applications that support a deeper approach to learning. Multileteracies practices align with many principles of Deep Education that the chapter examines one after the other. This chapter shows how Multiliteracies differ from CLT, bridge the language-literature-culture gap, and align with the teachings of the Deep Approach. Thus Deep Education would be more 'natural,' if such heavily connotated adjective can still be used in the field of second language acquisition.

Chapter 17 illustrates this aspect in an instructional unit on Africa. Mary Alice Sicard outlines the plans, procedures, strategies and results of *Projet Afrique*. This class-based project utilizes Deep Education in the French language classroom to provide holistic insights into language and culture in the Ivory Coast. French is at the service of better knowing the world and interacting genuinely on cultural contents: geography, history, art, music, politics or linguistics. Ivorians visited the students, clarifying meanings and answering their questions. Through this experience, they reached a deeper understanding of West Africa and presented their findings in French to the entire group and to the African visitors. Thus socially engaged, real life projects that target an ethic of care and social justice may characterize some of the manifestations of Deep Education.

Gizem Girgin studied in **Chapter 18** how the Deep Approach stimulates intrinsic motivation among prep school students who participated in interviews. Intrinsic motivation and identity engagement are widely regarded as pivotal for the development of proficiency. Tochon's Deep Approach is now being adapted and applied to native Turkish students in Turkey who want to learn English. It implies a paradigm shift from teacher-centered to student-centered classrooms through activities that include pair work, group work, projects and role playing. The result showed the relationship between the Deep Approach and an increase in students' motivation. For Girgin, intrinsic motivation and identity engagement are key factors defining Deep Education.

Natural settings such as a study abroad setting are propitious to deep experiences of the language and culture. In **Chapter 19**, Daniela Busciglio explored the Deep Approach in an advanced, thematic foreign language writing classroom abroad. The students used a democratically-negotiated curriculum and place-based research. Deep Education offers a consistent growth in co-constructed learner autonomy. Social agency empowers the students who pursue and design projects that are aligned with personal interests. This fosters accountability: scaffolded reflection and review before, during, and after each writing phase is associated with peer editing and self-editing evaluations. Meta-talk throughout writing and editing empowers the learners, giving them authority over their learning, further refining their language, and pragmatic and cultural competence. Within this perspective, enhancing agency and autonomy defines Deep Education.

This Conclusion, **Chapter 20**, posits authority as both the problem (when directivity imposes obedience to normative worldviews) and the solution (when agency allows learners to develop their own authorship). Deep Education may uncover something that was terribly missing. Depth can't be easily reified as a form of change that could simply be brought into the current system. Depth is not a substance, it is not a "thing." Rather it is an access to the meaningful dimension of life. It is not a matter of deep curriculum, rather it is an approach to curriculum that makes it more collaborative, relevant, lively, authentic, and humane. In this Deep Approach, the students are the curriculum builders.

Final Words on This Volume

Some nuances have not been explained in this volume. They should be clarified in these last few paragraphs. I felt necessary to protect the name Deep Education with a registered trademark. The reason is that the trademark allows us to define it as a quality label, and provide teacher training in a way that protects its deep quality. In this way, teachers who got the required training may be recognized for their deep leadership and quality in community work towards goals such as service to the world, service to Earth, deep spirit, ethic of care and respect for the learner as a human peer.

Yet I have decided not to trademark the terms "Deep Approach" such that a variety of deep understandings could be researched, studied and compared, that is why researchers may speak of Tochon's Deep Approach like one may speak of Krashen's Natural Approach, and there might be other variants. I see pros and cons with both decisions: protecting a brand with deep quality standards has the merit to maintain quality criteria across educational institutions that share the trademark. Yet in the long run it bears the risk of fossilizing the concept into rigid certification practices while the fluid emergence of bottom-up creativity should be maintained.

Not using a trademark has the value of opening the forum with people who may or may not share or even know the underlying, initial quality orientation. It may favor resilience and dissemination to a vast extent yet the concept might be diluted and soon quoted by people who did not even read the initial intent and ignore the characteristics of the approach. Therefore, in a sense this book is foundational, and it is not by chance if this initial exploration is an edited book rather than a single author's book: a variety of perspectives with their own nuances are offered, not to reify the concept too much.

To gather the conceptual threads, here are some guiding principles:

➢ The Deep Approach is non-linear, inexpressible and posits the student in a complex dynamic;
➢ It provides agency;
➢ It places the student in the situation of being the main curriculum builder;
➢ It implies transdisciplinary connections to the world and social action;
➢ It offers a value-laden approach to content.

Here is what makes this approach distinct:

- The students are in charge of their own curriculum and projects to achieve their desired expertise, using instructional agreements as thresholds to regular formative evaluations.

- The students' curriculum building is nurtured with the teacher's and the students' contents and multimedia resources organized adaptively. Multi-literacies are integrated components of the approach.

- The teacher becomes expert at scaffolding and facilitating feedback.

- Knowledge is not a 'thing' taught as an object: it is subjective and intersubjective, inseparable from identity growth. Depth is defined in opposition to the commoditization of knowledge.

- Educative projects are open and become ways of preventing knowledge sedimentation. They situate knowledge in action for a deeper purpose.

- The focus is on deep customized processing, not standardized outcomes similar for all. There is room for diversity and flexibility, and unique perspectives.

- Deep Education targets transpersonal values for a more sensible and wiser world—this way language learning becomes the means toward conflict resolution, ending war and poverty, re-greening the planet, and turning to a politic for the human.

- Yet, rather than a dualistic view, the principle of the included middle (or third space) is applied, through which two apparently opposed elements can be integrated at a deeper (still relative) level.

The instructional principles for teachers are to:

- Go by the results of motivation and identity engagement research, and provide incentives for self-directed learning and self-determination.
- Help students build their curriculum through their own thematic units. As an instructor, scaffold possibilities; make the landscape as flexible as possible for the student to choose, select, and create.
- Emphasize process rather than outcomes; refer to instructional organizers in forward planning rather than goals in a backward planning.
- Encourage individualized, peer-oriented, and small group project-based learning, focusing on cultural content and social action;
- Use deep formative feedback and empowerment evaluation. Integrate self-evaluations and peer-evaluations.
- Focus on value creation: highlight critical issues related to the respect of others, the limitations of the colonial mindset, principles of social justice, and human rights for peace building.

In sum, Deep Education is about the existence of deeper realities that may be uncovered, discovered, and symbolically deciphered from the perspective of any discipline, from an interdisciplinary cross-section, or from a higher and synergetic, transdisciplinary perspective. Deep Education however is not doctrinal as it may be interpreted in multiple ways. It may be as sound and good for the individual quest than for peer work and deep teaming. Deep Education is world-related, proactive, inquiry-based and transformative. Its teachings are unique because depth touches at singularity and quantum knowledge (Laszlo, 2016). It is connective, and it links humans in the search for deeper meanings and healthy activism towards societal fairness and better forms of justice.

It provides a new map of human existence yet is not the transmission of a pre-set normative formalism. If its core principles could be fully expressed for the linear mind, they would pertain to secondary and tertiary knowledge. Depth as a proactive concept designates an approach to what Charles S. Peirce named *Firstness*: "The First is that whose being is simply in itself, not referring to anything nor lying behind anything" (EP 1:248; CP 1.356-357, 1887-1888). Its descriptions are plural yet respect the diversity viewpoints as they circle potential realities and extend to wider and deeper horizons.

It is about the authority of creation, it suggests that life as we understand it is of symbolic nature; Its *realia* or artifacts are enmeshed in a net of meaning connections. In this respect, nature is purposeful and intelligent. The power of this understanding manifests a paradigmatic shift, a Deep Turn from a world of objects to a universe of subjects. Attuning the human mind to intelligent spaces and the acting mind reshapes the personal within the transpersonal and unfolds a cosmic vision in which consciousness is creation in the making.

Reference

Greco, M. B. (2007). Rancière et Jacotot: Une critique du concept d'autorité (Ranciere and Jacotot: Criticism of the Concept of Authority). Paris: L'Harmattan.

Gatto, J. T. (2006). *The Underground History of American Education: An Intimate Investigation Into the Prison of Modern Schooling*. New York: Oxford Village Press.

Jacotot, J.-J. (1829). Éducation universelle. Journal de l'émancipation intellectuelle (Journal for Intellectual Empowerment).

Laszlo, E. (2016). *What is Reality? The New Map of Cosmos and Consciousness*. New York: Paradigm Book/SelectBooks.

Peirce, Ch. S. (1887-1888). *A Guess at the Riddle*, EP 1:248; CP 1.356-357.

Rancière, J. (1987). The Ignorant Master.

Tochon, F. V. (2015). Mobile Experiences of an Adolescent Learning Spanish Online in a 21st Century High School. *International Journal of Pedagogies and Learning, 20*(10), 1-16.

Tochon, F. V. (2015). *Help Them Learn a Language Deeply: Tochon's Deep Approach to World Languages and Cultures*. Blue Mounds, WI: Deep University Press.

21.

Contributors

Jambul Akkaziev was born and raised in Russia's Caucasus region, in the small republic of Dagestan. He spent part of his childhood years in Siberia and his college years in Makhachkala, Dagestan, and later in Saint Petersburg. He holds two MA degrees - one in Linguistics and one in Russian History - and is currently working as an instructor in the Program in English as a Second Language at the University of Wisconsin-Madison. Over the course of his career, Jambul has taught courses in Academinc Writing and Reading, Russian Conversation and Culture, and served as a tutor in the Russian Flagship Program. He's also given presentations on the diversity of Russian culture and its peoples. He likes sharing his experiences as a foreign language learner with his students and talking with them about the places they have lived in.

Philip Bostic is a doctoral candidate in Curriculum & Instruction at the University of Wisconsin-Madison. His areas of interest are multicultural teacher education, deep education, and special education. He is a former Milwaukee high school teacher. His doctoral research concentrates on transforming educational spaces through the use of non-traditional educational curricula and classroom structures through project-based learning with the intention to re-imagine what it means to be human within historically minoritized communities. His work is based on the notion that humanity is sacred and therefore must be seen and treated as such; especially within educational learning spaces where he believes real human freedom can begin to take place for all. Contact: philipjbostic@gmail.com

Dr. Daniela F. Busciglio is an assistant professor of Italian and Second Language Acquisition at the University of Oklahoma where she teaches Italian language, literature as well as theory of second language acquisition and principles and techniques of teaching foreign language at both the undergraduate and graduate levels. She is also the section head for Italian, the Italian Language Program Director and the faculty advisor for Italian. Additionally, she serves as the World Language Education liaison to the OU College of Education and to the Oklahoma State Department of Education and she also organizes MLLL's annual graduate teaching assistant orientation and training. Over her ten-year career space, she has taught ESL/EFL, English for Academic Purposes, Italian language, literature, cinema, foreign language composition, SLA theory, and foreign language methodology. Her research interests include deep project-based language learning, foreign language program direction, and design-based qualitative research.

Manuel Fernández Cruz has a Doctorate in Sciences of Education. He has taught in non-university education and works a professor at the University of Granada since 1992. In his doctoral thesis he initiated a line of research on the (auto) biographical-narrative approach focused on teachers' professional development and he has taught postgraduate courses on this discipline in various Latin American countries. He has written around 160 scientific publications including books like "Biographical Narrative Research in Education", "Teacher Professional Development" or "Training and Development of Professional Education," among others. He has been the coordinator of the international consortium Erasmus Mundus MUNDUSFOR, is the vice president for Europe of the International Network for Language Education Policy Studies INLEPS and currently serves as the School Organization Department Head at the University of Granada. Contact: manuelfernandezcruz@gmail.com

Gizem Girgin Öztürk is an English Instructor at İstanbul Gedik University, Turkey. She was born in Istanbul, Turkey. She has been doing her M.A. in ELT. She is interested in second language learning and teaching. She has worked with Assist. Prof. Züleyha Çolak who is one of the pioneers of Tochon's Deep Approach in Turkey. Gizem taught English through Deep Approach for two years and she believes that the pedagogy of the Deep Approach enlightens her teaching. Contact: ggirginozturk@gmail.com

Merrie Koester, University of South Carolina Center for Science Education, is the director of Project Draw for Science, a collaborative action research initiative whose goal is to communicate meaning in science through drawing and visual thinking. For three decades, she had researched and developed curriculum for teaching science through the creative art and is an outspoken advocate for aesthetic

Alexandra Lakind is pursuing a joint PhD at the University of Wisconsin-Madison in the School of Education & the Nelson Institute. She is a graduate of Interlochen Arts Academy, the Royal Scottish Academy (Contemporary Performance, BA), and NYU (Educational Theater, MA). She received her teaching certification in Montessori and founded a cooperative preschool in Brooklyn, NY. Outside of her fields of study, she engages in cross-field appropriation with Science and Technology Studies, Public Humanities, and Cultural Studies. She aims to recognize and support infrastructure to provide platforms to multiple voices across categories. Through implicit and explicit, academic and performative routes, she hopes to foster supportive communities prepared to process unanswerable dilemmas together.

Amos Margulies is an 11th grade English teacher at the Community School for Social Justice, a public school in the South Bronx, and an adjunct professor at Hostos Community College, where he teaches Public Speaking, as well as cultural theory to recent immigrant high school students. Amos is currently part of TDF's Open Doors program and works with Manhattan Theater Club's playwriting program, as well as The Moth's Community Education Program. Last year, Amos was commissioned by the NYC Department of Education to write the ELL Addendum to the NYC Theater Blueprint. Amos has presented in dozens of workshops for a wide range of organizations, including TESOL International, the NYC Writing Project, the Children's First Network, the International Network for Public Schools, and the American Alliance for Theater and Education.

Anna Nesterchouk is a Faculty Assistant in the Department of English and an Instructional Lead/Curriculum Designer for the Pushkin Summer Institute at the University of Wisconsin-Madison. Anna Nesterchouk is an ESL/EFL/RFL instructor with extensive experience in language training, curriculum design, and ESL/RFL teacher training. She holds a Master of Science degree in Curriculum and Instruction with a specialization in World Language Education and a Master of Arts in Philology and Applied English Linguistics. Her B.A. is in Secondary Education: Teaching major in Foreign Language Instruction (English) and teaching minor in French. Providing students with opportunities to make lingo-cultural discoveries through a meaningful learning process regardless of the linguistic proficiency level is the essence of her pedagogy. Her professional interests include: second language acquisition, intercultural education, holistic language learning, heritage language education, Deep Approach to language learning, and world language immersion programs.

José Gijón Puerta has a Doctorate in Education. He has been a high school teacher, school principal, career counselor, adviser to the educational administration of Andalusia, and currently he is associate professor at the University of Granada. His research is focused on professionalization, teachers' training for entrepreneurship education, the use of concept maps in education and training for skills, topics on which he has conducted different research works in Spain, Latin America and the Maghreb. It is representative of the University of

Granada in the Association for Teacher Education in Europe ATEE. At present he occupies the position of Dean of the area of quality and research transfer at the Faculty of Education Sciences and also is the director of the Research Group ProfesioLab and secretary of the Journal for Educators, Teachers and Trainers JETT. Contact: josegijonpuerta@gmail.com

Harun Serpil currently works as the PA and Interpreter for the Rector of Anadolu University, Eskişehir. He earned his undergraduate degree from the Department of Education in Teaching English as a Foreign Language (TEFL) at Anadolu University in 1996, and went on to get his MA degree in TEFL from Bilkent University in 2000. He received his Ph. D. in World Language Education, Department of Curriculum & Instruction at the University of Wisconsin-Madison. He has twenty years of experience in language education; and worked at every level and stage of language teaching, testing and curriculum design. His specific academic interests include Freirean critical pedagogy, intercultural/multicultural education, culturally relevant/responsive teaching, transdisciplinary/transformative education, nature-based education, place-based education, PBL, social justice, and teacher education. Since his previous position involved teaching English to pilots, he is also interested in Aviation English and ESP. Contact: hserpil@gmail.com

François Victor Tochon is a Professor at the University of Wisconsin-Madison where he is heading World Language Education in the Department of Curriculum & Instruction, a Department ranked #1 of its specialty for 15 years in the United States. He is the designer and the Chairman of the Board of Trustees of Deep University. He has a Ph.D. in Applied Linguistics (Laval) and a Ph.D. in Educational Psychology (Ottawa), and received three Honorary Doctorates from two universities in Argentina and Peru and one international association, and an official appointment as Honorary Professor from Henan University of Technology in China. Tochon received the 2012 Award of International Excellence from the

University of Granada, Spain, and is the President of the International Network for Language Education Policy Studies. He has been awarded the 2013-2014 medal of the Council Chairperson of the Lions Club International in Taiwan, and the 2013-2014 Quest medal of the Chairperson of the Lions Club International Foundation for Service to Humanity. He is among the 1% most visited profiles of LinkedIn, and 1% most downloaded authors from Academia. International Ambassador for isIPAL, he received the 2015 Excellence in Diversity Award from the University of Wisconsin-Madison, School of Education, the 2015 International Scholar Award of Shanghai Normal University, and 2015 Eminent Scholar Award from the University of Southern Queensland, Australia. Contact: ftochon@education.wisc.edu

Jianfang Xiao is a Associate Professor and vice dean of in the School of English and Education at Guangdong University of Foreign Studies. She works on bilingual instruction in China, international language policies and EFL Teacher Development, looking for creative ways to foreign language teaching and learning. She is currently published in Chinese and English. She has published 45 papers and 10 books and textbooks. Among her books are: "The Contemporary International Bilingual Education Models" at Guangdong People's Press in 2011 and "Research on College English Teaching in a Cultural Perspective" at China Modern Economy Press in 2014. The former one received the Award of Best Works in Guangdong Provincial Social Sciences in 2013. Contact: xiao3296888@aliyun.com

Snezhana Zheltoukhova received her bachelor degree in theoretical linguistics from the Lomonosov State University in Moscow, Russia, and her masters degree in Slavic Studies from the University of Missouri-Columbia. Currently, she is pursuing a doctorate degree in Second Language Acquisition Program at University of Wisconsin-Madison. Her research interests are focused on Flagship tutoring as well as the development of intercultural competence at the novice level of linguistic proficiency. Her previous publications include a coauthored article that analyzed participant reflections in a Summer Russian Program from a sociocultural perspective. Contact: snezhana.zheltoukhova@gmail.com

Mary Zuidema received her doctorate from the University of Wisconsin-Madison in the Department of Curriculum and Instruction. She studied Spanish Linguistics and Literature at Marquette University for her Bachelor's and Master's degrees, and has taught Spanish and English as a Second Language. Her research interests include theatre and drama in education, performance-based pedagogy, differentiation, cultural consciousness development, and Teacher Education. She has worked as a supervisor and an instructor of pre-service teachers in the World Language Education program and has enjoyed performing improvisation and sketch comedy in the Chicago, IL area. She recently accepted a position as the Director of the Language Learning Center at Wittenberg University. Contact: mary.e.zuidema@gmail.com

Glossary

Academia: Cultural community of practice engaged in education and research to collaborate in the fixation of beliefs in every branch of learning. The akademeia outside Athens was Plato's famous learning center, or gymnasium.

Accuracy: Normed language production.

Achievement test: A test supposed to measure what students have learned from a program of study; evaluative part of most language programs, which attempts at matching the goals of the language course. Expression of a reductionist trend hypothesizing that achievement can be defined and measured is ways that can be generalized for all students in the same manner. Very few such tests measure deep learning; on the contrary, these tests often tend to induce shallow learning.

Active learning: process whereby learners are actively engaged in the learning process, rather than "passively" absorbing lectures. Active learning involves reading, writing, discussion, and engagement in solving problems, analysis, synthesis, and evaluation. Active learning often involves cooperative learning.

Activity Theory: A Soviet psychological framework rooted in the socio-cultural approach of Alexei Leontyev and S. L. Rubinshtein. It became one of the major theories for applied psychology, education and work psychology.

Aim and objective: An aim expresses the broad purpose of an educational unit whereas an objective states a specific goal which participants are expected to demonstrate at the completion of an instructional unit.

Alternative education: non-traditional approach to teaching and learning for students of all ages and all levels of education.

a posteriori: in retrospect, after the fact

Apprenticeship: Situated, in practice training of skilled crafts practitioners.

a priori: in principle

Assessment: Is the validation of learning activities with a logic of accountability that may, in many cases, be counterproductive and backlash in reducing the power to learn.

Assignment: Lesson, task, homework, project or other course deliverable that can be assigned to the learners to complete on their own, without instructional assistance.

Aural: Related to listening.

Authentic text: Natural or real teaching material; often this material is taken from newspapers, magazines, radio, TV or podcasts. Authentic materials are resources that have been developed specifically for native speakers. These include print, audio, and visual materials.

Autopoietic: system embedded in a dynamic of changes such as sensory-motor coupling; living element showing attributes that include responsiveness, feedback, growth, homeostatic self-regulation, energy transformation, ability to generate new forms and reproduce.

Backward design, also called **backward planning**: teacher-centered plan of a unit or lesson by identifying the intended end task or product, then working in reverse to identify the prerequisite tasks and assessment. Form of mind programming that leads to shallow, identical learning for all.

Bilingual education as various definitions:
- two languages are used for teaching;
- help is provided for children to become bilingual (such as two-way bilingual education);
- regional or native language is first used, followed by mainstreaming in classes in the national of official language;
- regional or native language is used with minimal instruction the other language.

Biliteracy: being literate in two or more languages, and considered stronger than being simply bilingual, as reading and writing are added to proficiency in listening and speaking.

Blended learning: Learning in an alternation of instructional modes, such as face-to-face teaching and online learning.

Classroom climate: Socio-affective environment created in the classroom by factors that can be physical (seats, location, postings) and psychosocial such as the interrelationship between teacher and learners, and among learners.

Classroom management: Process of organizing classroom instruction to run smoothly without disruption from students, within a shallow learning perspective based on extrinsic motivation. Includes classroom procedures, groupings, how instructions for activities are given, and management of student behavior. The most thorny aspect of teacher learning is to develop the ability to move away from classroom management based on extrinsic motivation to forms of self-management in which the learners are in charge and work on the basis of their intrinsic motivation.

Coaching: A coach is a learning facilitator who teaches and trains another person via encouragement, feedback and offer motivational support and advice.

Code-switching: Interlingual switching by bilingual speakers or intralingual switching between discourse types. Switching between subcodes in any sign system.

Communicative competence: One of the key goals of language learning, achieved through:
- how well a person has learned features and rules of the language (**grammatical competence**), which includes vocabulary, pronunciation, and sentence formation.
- how well a person speaks and is understood in social contexts (**sociolinguistic competence**), which depends on factors such as status, purpose, and expectations.
- how well a person combines grammatical forms and meanings to achieve different genres of speaking or writing (**discourse competence**).
- how well the person uses both verbal forms and non-verbal communication to compensate for lack of other competences (**strategic competence**).

Communicative Language Teaching: an approach to world language learning that emphasizes communicative competence, as a reaction away from grammar-based approaches such as the audio-lingual approach. Communicative teaching focuses on expression and understanding of functions such as requesting, describing likes and dislikes, using language appropriately in various situations, performing tasks, solving puzzles, or using language for social interaction with other people. Not incompatible with a Deep Approach if integrated with extensive reading and watching, such as reading clubs and video clubs, and intensive writing such as writing workshops.

Community of practice: Process of social learning occurring when learners or teachers who have a common interest in some discipline, topic or problem collaborate over an extended period to share plans and projects, look for solutions, and create innovations.

Comprehensible input: Language understandable to learners.

Constructivism: Constructivism views all of knowledge as constructed, because it does not reflect any external transcendent reality; it is contingent on convention, perception and social experience. An extreme expansion of social determinism, it assumes that representations of physical and biological reality, including gender and race, are socially constructed. Set of assumptions about the nature of human learning guiding active learning theories and teaching methods: constructivism values developmentally appropriate, learner-centered learning that is initiated and directed by the student.

Constructivist epistemology: A development in philosophy which criticizes essentialism, whether it is in the form of realism, rationalism, positivism or empiricism. It originated in sociology under the term social constructionism and has been given the name constructivism when referring to philosophical epistemology. Constructionism and constructivism are often used interchangeably. The common thread between various forms of constructivism is that they do not focus on an ontological reality, but on reality construction.

Controlled practice: Teacher-controlled practice of language forms.

Cooperative learning: Proposed in response to traditional curriculum-driven education. In cooperative learning environments, students interact in purposely structured heterogeneous group to support the learning of one self and others in the same group.

Cooperating teacher: Mentor teacher welcoming a student teacher in his or her class to provide the student teacher with feedback on experimental practice.

Critical pedagogy: A teaching approach which attempts to help students question and challenge domination, and the beliefs and practices that dominate. In other words, it is a theory and practice of helping students achieve critical consciousness. In this tradition the teacher works to lead students to question ideologies and practices considered oppressive (including those at school), and encourage liberatory collective and individual responses to the actual conditions of their own lives.

Critical thinking: Consists of a mental process of analyzing or evaluating information, particularly statements or propositions that people have offered as true. It forms a process of reflecting upon the meaning of statements, examining the offered evidence and reasoning, and forming judgments about the facts. Critical thinkers can gather such information from observation, experience, reasoning, and/or communication. Critical thinking has its basis in intellectual values that go beyond subject-matter divisions and which include: clarity, accuracy, precision, evidence, thoroughness and fairness.

Cultural learning: The way a group of people within a society or culture tend to learn and pass on new information. Learning styles are greatly influenced by how a culture socializes with its children and young people.

Culture: The sum of the beliefs, attitudes, behaviors, habits and customs of a group of people.

Curriculum (plural **curricula**): The set of courses and their contents offered by an institution such as a school or university. In some cases, a curriculum may be partially or entirely determined by an external body. In the United States, the basic curriculum is established by each state with the individual school districts adjusting it to their desires. A designated set of related courses focused on a field of study.

Deductive teaching: Also known as deduction, from the verb "to deduce"; a teaching technique in which the teacher presents language rules and the students then practice those rules in activities. Deductive teaching is usually based on grammar-based methodology and proceeds from generalizations about the language to specifics. (See "Inductive teaching".)

Deep Approach: Deep, reflective language learning stressing reading and writing before listening and speaking; promoting open project-based activities such team and peer work, placing the student as curriculum builders on the basic of intrinsic motivation; code-switching and scaffolding among peers is considered a natural part of deep second and third language development, which results not from automatism but from reflexive output in writing accompanied with extensive reading and listening or watching, and then in speaking.

Dialogical: in the form of dialogue, or relating to or using dialogue; of, pertaining to, or characterized by dialogue

Discourse: system of representation including a repertoire of concepts and codes for creating and maintaining worldviews within an ontological domain or discursive field.

Distance education or **distance learning**) A field of education that focuses on the pedagogy/andragogy, technology, and instructional systems design that is effectively incorporated in delivering education to students who are not physically "on site" to receive their education. Instead, teachers and students may communicate asynchronously (at times of their own choosing) by exchanging printed or electronic media, or through technology that allows them to communicate in real time (synchronously). Distance education courses that require a physical on-site presence for any reason including the taking of examinations is considered to be a hybrid or blended course or program.

Educational evaluation: Characterizing, valuing and appraising some aspect of education. No criteria can be exempt from subjectivity in the assessment process, even automated. Educational evaluation is a matter of choices on what to value and devalue, and therefore is social and political.

Educational organization: Organization for the purpose of education. This does not mean organizing the educational system as a process; it rather deals with how organizational theory applies to educating humans.

Education policy: Collection of explicit and implicit rules that govern the behavior of persons in schools. Education policy analysis is the scholarly study of education policy and common policy practices in a particular education setting.

Education reform: Policy, program, plan or movement attempting to bring about a systemic change in education theory and practice across a school system, school district(s), community, a nation, or society.

Empirical knowledge: Propositional knowledge obtained by experience or sensorial information.

Encoding: Producing text or discourse in actualizing relevant codes, foregrounding some meanings and backgrounding others.

Engagement: The sentiment a student or teacher feels or does not feel towards learning or teaching, or the educational environment.

Epistemology: Branch of philosophy that deals with the nature, form, origin and scope of knowledge. Analysis of the way of knowing, focusing on the nature and type of knowledge and how it relates to verisimilitude, truth, trustworthiness, and belief, with a concern for the justification of knowledge claims.

Experience: Perception or knowledge of, skill in or observation of things or events gained through involvement in or exposure to these things or events. Accumulation of such knowledge and understanding in terms of procedural knowledge, know-how and expertise rather than propositional knowledge.

Experiential education, learning by doing: The process of actively engaging students in an authentic experience that will have benefits and consequences. Students make discoveries and experiment with knowledge themselves instead of hearing or reading about the experiences of others. Students also reflect on their experiences, thus developing new skills, new attitudes, and new theories or ways of thinking. Experiential education is related to the constructivist learning theory.

Facilitator: A concept related to a teacher's approach to interaction with students. Particularly in communicative classrooms, teachers tend to work in partnership with students to develop their language skills. A teacher who is a facilitator tends to be more student-centered and less dominant in the classroom than in other approaches. The facilitator may also take the role of mentor or coach rather than director.

Feedback: Reporting back or giving information back, usually to the teacher; feedback can be verbal, written or nonverbal in the form of facial expressions, gestures, behaviors; teachers can use feedback to discover whether a student understands, is learning, and likes an activity.

Fluency: Natural, normal, native-like speech characterized by appropriate pauses, intonation, stress, register, word choice, interjections and interruptions.

Form-focused instruction: The teaching of specific language content (lexis, structure, phonology). See "language content".

Forward planning: A concept developed by Francois Victor Tochon that implies thematic design, the teacher plans a unit or lesson by first identifying the transdisciplinary theme and project, then identifying the tasks pertaining to each language domain or skill that can bring this experience forward.

Functional syllabus: Syllabus based on communicative acts such as making introductions, making requests, expressing opinions, requesting information, refusing, apologizing, giving advice, persuading; this type of syllabus is often used in communicative language teaching.

Genre: The category a piece of literature belongs to (ex: science fiction, biography).

Grammar translation: A method of language teaching characterized by translation and the study of grammar rules. Involves presentation of grammatical rules, vocabulary lists, and translation. Emphasizes reading rather than communicative competence.

Graphic Organizer: Visual aids which helps organize thoughts and ideas (ex: Venn Diagram, T Charts, KWL).

Guided practice: An midway stage in teaching - between controlled and free practice activities; this stage implies limited guidance from the teacher who works as a facilitator.

Heritage speaker: Student who is exposed to a language other than the official or national language at home. Some students have full oral fluency and literacy in the home language; others may have full oral fluency but their written literacy was not developed because they were schooled in English. Another group of students -- typically third- or fourth-generation -- can speak to a limited degree but cannot express themselves on a wide range of topics. Students from any of these categories may also have gaps in knowledge about their cultural heritage. Teachers who have heritage speakers of the target language in their class should assess which proficiencies need to be maintained and which need to be developed further. See also native speaker.

Heuristic teaching: helping students to learn through discovery and investigation; a method of teaching allowing pupils to learn things for themselves.

Hidden curriculum: Idea that schools do more than simply transmit knowledge written in the curricula: curricula may have invisible agendas, social implications, political underpinnings, and cultural outcomes.

Holistic: related to holism, non-binary, integrative and responding the transdisciplinary principle of the inclusive third in its relation to the whole rather than the parts of a complex system.

Home education or home schooling: An educational alternative to public or private schools, in which children learn at home and in the community, in contrast to compulsory education organized in dedicated institutions.

Homeostasis: process by which a complex system keeps balance within stable conditions of functioning whatever the conditions in its environment.

Homologous: having a related or similar position, structure

Immersion: In this model, most commonly found in elementary schools, general academic content (the primary educational goal) is taught in the target language, and language proficiency is a parallel outcome. Individual districts design their programs such that English is introduced at a given grade level, with a gradually increasing percentage of time given to English language instruction. Partial immersion programs differ in the amount of time and number of courses taught in English and in the target language.

Individualized instruction: A method of instruction in which content, instructional materials, instructional media, and pace of learning are based upon the abilities and interests of each individual learner.

Inductive teaching: Also known as induction, from the verb "to induce"; a facilitative, student-centered teaching technique where the students discover language rules through extensive use of the language and exposure to many examples. This is the preferred technique in communicative language teaching. (See " Deductive teaching".)

Informal assessment: During an informal assessment, a teacher evaluates students' progress while they are participating in a learning activity, for example, a small-group discussion. Results are typically used to make decisions about what to do next, namely, whether the students are ready to move on or whether they need more practice with the material.

Input hypothesis: Hypothesis that states that learners learn language through exposure to language that is just beyond their level of comprehension.

Interference: A phenomenon in language learning where the first language interferes with learning the target or foreign language.

Interlanguage: The language a learner uses before mastering the foreign language; it may contain features of the first language and the target language as well as non-standard features.

Interlocutor: In a conversation, this refers to the person you are speaking to.

Interpretive community: Group of people sharing the same codes.

Inquiry education: A student-centered method of education focused on asking questions. Students are encouraged to ask questions which are meaningful to them, and which do not necessarily have easy answers; teachers are encouraged to avoid speaking at all when this is possible, and in any case to avoid giving answers in favor of asking more questions.

Instructional design: The analysis of learning needs and systematic development of instruction. Instructional designers often use instructional technology as a method for developing instruction. Instructional design models typically specify a method, that if followed will facilitate the transfer of knowledge, skills and attitude to the recipient or acquirer of the instruction.

Instructional scaffolding: The provision of sufficient supports to promote learning when concepts and skills are being first introduced to students.

Integrative learning: A learning theory describing a movement toward integrated lessons helping students make connections across curricula. This higher education concept is distinct from the elementary and high school "integrated curriculum" movement.

Intrinsic motivation: Evident when people engage in an activity for its own sake, without some obvious external incentive present. A hobby is a typical example.

Knowledge transfer: In the fields of organizational development and organizational learning, is the practical problem of getting a packet of knowledge from one part of the organization to another (or all other) parts of the organization. It is considered to be more than just a communication problem.

Language education: Teaching and learning of languages, usually as foreign or world languages.

Language skills: In language teaching, this refers to the mode or manner in which language is used. Listening, speaking, reading and writing are generally called the four language skills. Speaking and writing are the productive skills, while reading and listening are the receptive skills. Often the skills are divided into sub-skills, such as discriminating sounds in connected speech, or understanding relationships within a sentence.

Learning outcome: The term may refer to course aims (intended learning outcomes) or may be roughly synonymous with educational objectives (observed learning outcomes). Usage varies between organisations.

Learning standard: Standardized Approaches to Content Development, Itemization, Publication, Assessments, Presentation, Feedback, Transmission and Runtime Packaging. There are various related and unrelated Learning Standards. Name any that apply to the specific piece of content.

Lesson plan: A teacher's detailed description of the course of instruction for an individual lesson. While there is no one way to construct a correct lesson plan, most lesson plans contain similar elements. A writing noting the method of delivery, and the specific goals and timelines associated to the delivery of lesson content. An outline or plan that guides teaching of a lesson; includes the following: pre-assessment of class; aims and objectives; warm-up and review; engagement, study, activation of language (controlled, guided and free practice); and assessment of lesson. A good lesson plan describes procedures for student motivation and practice activities, and includes alternative ideas in case the lesson is not long enough or is too difficult. It also notes materials needed.

Lifelong learning: The concept that "It's never too soon or too late for learning", a philosophy that has taken root in a whole host of different organizations. Lifelong learning sees citizens provided with learning opportunities at all ages and in numerous contexts: at work, at home and through leisure activities, not just through formal channels such as school and higher education.

Literacy: The quality of being educated and literate, and the ability to read and write with mastery over specific fields of knowledge. In modern context, the word means reading and writing in a level adequate for written communication and generally a level that enables one to successfully function at certain levels of a society. Literacy is now *deictic*, in other words sensitive to spatiotemporal changes, and is continually changing as technologies and social practices emerge while older practices fade away. Two features of contemporary literacies are: (1) the use of digital technologies for accessing, producing, interacting with and sharing meaningful content; (2) their hybrid and distributed, collaborative and participatory nature.

Mastery learning: An instructional method that presumes all children can learn if they are provided with the appropriate learning conditions. Specifically, mastery learning is a method whereby students are not advanced to a subsequent learning objective until they demonstrate proficiency with the current one.

Meta: In epistemology, which is the study of the ways of knowing, the prefix **meta-** is used to mean *about (its own category)*. For example, metadata is data about data (who has produced it, when, what format the data is in and so on). Similarly, meta-memory in psychology means an individual's intuition about whether or not they would remember something if they concentrated on recalling it. Any subject can be said to have a *meta-theory*, which is the theoretical consideration of its foundations and methods.

Metacognition: Refers to thinking, perceiving, observing, noticing, grasping one's thought process. Metacognition can be explicit, that is conscious and factual, or implicit, unconscious and procedural. The ability to think about thinking is to regulate one's own cognition and maximize one's potential to think, learn and process information.

Metalanguage: Language used to describe, analyze or explain another language. Metalanguage includes, for example, grammatical terms and the rules of syntax. The term is sometimes used to mean the language used in class to give instructions, explain things, etc. – in essence, to refer to all teacher talk that does not specifically include the "target language".

Methodology: Strictly speaking is the study and knowledge of methods; but the term is frequently used pretentiously to indicate a method or a set of methods. In other words, it is the study of techniques for problem-solving and seeking answers, as opposed to the techniques themselves.

Motivation: The driving force behind all actions of human beings and other animals. It is an internal state that activates behavior and gives it direction. Emotion is closely related to motivation, and may be regarded as the subjectively experienced component of motivational states. Paradox: Students' main motivators are factors the teacher has little control over (integrated versus instrumental motivation, which heavily influence time on task), yet motivation is critical to learning.

Native speakers: Those who speak English as their mother tongue. A native speaker considers the target language to be his or her first language. Teachers seek opportunities for students to communicate in person or through technology with native speakers. Students in foreign language classes who are first- or second-generation immigrants and who use the language extensively outside the classroom are also considered native speakers. These students typically maintain the cultural norms of their heritage in certain situations. See also heritage speaker.

Negotiation of meaning: In this process, teachers and students try to convey information to one another and reach mutual comprehension through restating, clarifying, and confirming information. The teacher may help students get started or work through a stumbling block using linguistic and other approaches.

Objective: An educational objective is a statement of a goal which successful participants are expected demonstrably to achieve before the course or unit completes. Also called lesson objectives or aims; statements of student learning outcomes based on student needs; objectives state specifically what the students will be able to do in a specified time period; objectives are measurable and therefore involve specific and discrete language skills.

Oral: Related to speaking. Oral exchange implies both speaking and listening.

Ontology: the branch of metaphysics that deals with the nature of being; the set of entities presupposed by a theory.

Paradigmatic shift: The term first used by Thomas Kuhn in his 1962 book The Structure of Scientific Revolutions to describe the process and result of a change in basic assumptions within the ruling theory of science. Don Tapscott was the first to use the term to describe information technology and business in his book of the same title. It has since become widely applied to many other realms of human experience as well.

Pastiche: a work of art that mixes styles, materials; a work of art that imitates the style of another time or artist.

Peace education: The process of acquiring the knowledge and developing the attitudes, skills, and behaviour to live in harmony with oneself and with others.Peace education is based on a philosophy that teaches nonviolence, love, compassion, trust, fairness, cooperation, respect, and a reverence for the human family and all life on our planet. It is a social practice with shared values to which anyone can make a significant contribution.

Pedagogy: The art and science of teaching children, often used, by extension, for adult education. The term comes from the Greek *paidagogos*, the slave who took little boys to and from school. "Paidia" means 'children', which is why pedagogy is normally meant for children and andragogy is meant for adults. The Latin word for pedagogy, education, is more widely used.

Peer correction or review and feedback: in writing, an activity whereby students help each other with the editing of a composition by giving each other feedback, making comments or suggestions; can be done in pairs or small groups.

Personal development (self-development or **personal growth)**: Comprises the development of the self. The term may also refer to: traditional concepts of education or training; counseling and coaching for personal transformation; New Age movement and spiritual beliefs & concepts - including "inner pathways" to solve social and psychological issues; or professional development educators treating the whole person instead of the profession only).

Praxis: the practice and practical side of a profession or field of study, as opposed to the theory

Prescriptive grammar: Grammar that is described in terms of grammar rules of what is considered the best usage, often by grammarians; prescriptive grammar may not agree with what people actually say or write.

Problem-based learning (PBL): Instructional transfer of active learning in College education, yet being adapted for use in K-12 education. The defining characteristics of PBL are: learning is driven by messy, open-ended problems; students work in small collaborative groups; and "teachers" are not required, the process uses "facilitators" of learning. Accordingly, students are encouraged to take responsibility for their group and organize and direct the learning process with support from a tutor or instructor. Advocates of PBL claim it can be used to enhance content knowledge and foster the development of communication, problem-solving, and self-directed learning skill.

Project: An extensive task purposely and collectively undertaken by group or individuals to apply knowledge and skills toward a targeted goal which will result in a product, within a certain timeframe.

Procedural knowledge or know-how: The knowledge of how to perform some **task**. Know-how is different from other kinds of knowledge such as propositional knowledge in that it can be directly applied to a task. Procedural knowledge about solving problems differs from propositional knowledge about problem solving. For example, in some legal systems, this knowledge or *know-how* has been considered the intellectual property of a company, and can be transferred when that company is purchased.

Proficiency level: Describes how well a student can use the language. Proficiency describes how well a person functions in a language. The American Council on the Teaching of Foreign Languages further defines proficiency with a set of guidelines for assessing communicative abilities. The guidelines cover how an individual performs across three criteria: function, content/context, and accuracy. When combined, these criteria determine the student's communicative ability to be Novice, Intermediate, Advanced, or Superior.

Programmed instruction: A field first studied extensively by the behaviorist B. F. Skinner. It consists of teaching through small lessons, where each lesson must be mastered in order to go on to the next. Students work through the programmed material by themselves at their own speed. After each step, they are presented with a question to test their comprehension, then are immediately shown the correct answer or given additional information.

Professionalism: More than simple vocational practice, professionalism characterizes an ethical attitude in professional problem solving, which indicates working with a conscience.

Push-down principle or principle of reduction: according to the law of least effort, cognitive responses tend to "slide" toward the lower end of the taxonomic scale. What was initially a complex problem-solving situation becomes, by force of habit, a simple regurgitation of stocked responses.

Rapport: Relationship, usually a harmonious one, established within a classroom between teacher and students and among students.

Reify: to consider or make (an abstract idea or concept) real or concrete

Rhizomatic: rhizomatous: of or relating to a thick horizontal underground stem (called a rhizome) of plants such as the mint and iris whose buds develop new roots and shoots.

Role-playing: Role-playing is an activity in which students dramatize characters or pretend that they are in new locations or situations. This activity challenges students by having them use language in new contexts.

Rote learning: A learning technique which avoids grasping the inner complexities and inferences of the subject that is being learned and instead focuses on memorizing the material so that it can be recalled by the learner exactly the way it was read or heard.

Rubric: Set of criteria and standards linked to learning objectives, used to assess students' performance, such as on a test, project, or essay. A type of assessment in which a score is derived from a list of expectations.

Schooling: Teaching and learning that takes place in formal education environments.

Self-concept or self-identity: The mental and conceptual awareness and persistent regard that sentient beings hold with regard their own being. Components of a being's self-concept include physical, psychological, and social attributes; and can be influenced by its attitudes, habits, beliefs and ideas. These components and attributes can each be condensed to the general concepts of self-image and the self-esteem.

Self-efficacy: The belief that one has the capabilities to execute the courses of actions required to manage prospective situations. Unlike efficacy, which is the power to produce an effect (in essence, competence), self-efficacy is the belief (however accurate) that one has the power to produce that effect. It is important here to understand the distinction between self-esteem and self efficacy. Self-esteem relates to a person's sense of self-worth, whereas self efficacy relates to a person's perception of their ability to reach a goal. For example, say a person is a terrible rock climber. They would likely have a poor efficacy in regard to rock climbing, but this wouldn't need to affect their self-esteem; most people don't invest much of their self-esteem in this activity.

Self-study: The content is intended to be used as a medium of study that relies on one's own self to follow through on learning tasks related to a course, module, lesson or lab medium which are all also self-contained in a unit of medium or as a file type.

Service learning: A method of teaching, learning and reflecting that combines academic classroom curriculum with meaningful youth service throughout the community. As a teaching methodology, it falls under the category of experiential education. More specifically, it integrates meaningful community service with instruction and reflection to enrich the learning experience, teach civic responsibility, encourage lifelong civic engagement, and strengthen communities.

Situated learning: Education that takes place in a setting functionally identical to that where the learning will be applied.

Skill: An ability, usually learned, to perform actions.

Social constructionism: A sociological theory of knowledge developed by Peter L. Berger and Thomas Luckman with their 1966 book, The Social Construction of Reality. The focus of social constructionism is to uncover the ways in which individuals and groups participate in the creation of their perceived reality. As an approach, it involves looking at the ways social phenomena are created, institutionalized, and made into tradition by humans. Socially constructed reality is seen as an ongoing, dynamic process; reality is re-produced by people acting on their interpretations and their knowledge of it.

Social context: Environment in which meanings are exchanged. It can be analyzed in terms of the field of discourse, tenor of discourse, and mode of discourse. The field of discourse refers to what is being discussed; the tenor of discourse refers to the participants in the exchange of meaning, including who they are and their relationships with each other (for example, teacher and students); the mode of discourse refers to what part the language is playing with what production channel (writing or speaking).

Spiraling: the process of teaching a theme or language rule to different levels of learners by creating multiple tasks that are increasingly complex. For example, a lesson on weather can be spiraled as follows: (1) Novice students can describe the weather in short formulaic sentences; (2) Intermediate students can talk about the weather and its effect on their activities, or gather information from broadcasts or newspapers; and (3) Pre-Advanced students can tell a story about a frightening weather-related event or follow a description of weather in a literary piece.

Student activism: A form of youth-led community organizing that is specifically oriented towards engaging students as activists in order to create change in the educational system.

Student-centered learning: An approach to education focusing on the needs of the students, rather than those of others involved in the educational process, such as teachers and administrators. This approach has many implications for the design of curriculum, course content, and interactivity of courses. Also called learner-centered, a way of teaching that centers on the goals, needs, interests and existing knowledge of the students. Students actively participate in such classrooms and may even be involved in setting learning outcomes. Teachers in student-centered classrooms ask students for input on their goals, needs and interests and on what they know before providing them with study topics or answers to questions (for example, grammar rules). They may also ask students to generate (help produce) materials. The teacher is seen more as a facilitator or helper than the dominant figure in the classroom.

Student teacher: Pre-service teacher having initial classroom experiences and practical training under the supervision of a cooperating teacher, or mentor teacher.

Student voice: the distinct perspectives and actions of young people throughout schools focused on education itself.

Stultify: to make useless, futile, or ineffectual, esp. by routine; to cause to appear absurd or inconsistent, to dumb down.

Syllabus: An outline or a summary of the main points of a text, lecture, or course of study.

Syntax: Sometimes called word order; how words combine to form sentences and the rules governing sentence formation.

Synthesis: Integration of two or more pre-existing elements that results in a new creation.

Task-based syllabus: A syllabus organized around a sect of real, purposeful tasks that students are expected to carry out; tasks may include telephone use, making charts or maps, following instructions, and so on; task-based learning is purposeful and a natural way to learn language.

Taxonomic sliding: see *Push-down principle*.

Taxonomy: the science or practice of classification, An educational taxonomy that classifies educational objectives into three domains: cognitive, affective, and psychomotor.

Teachable moments: Times in a language class in which the teacher realizes that a point of information not in the lesson plan will help students understand a language point; teachable moments digress for a brief time from the lesson plan and can be valuable in helping student learning and keeping students engaged.

Teacher: In education, one who teaches students, a course of study that requires planning instructional units, enabling the development of practical skills, including learning and thinking skills. There are numerous ways to teach and help students learn, often referred to as pedagogy. When deciding what teaching method to use, a teacher usually considers the students' prior knowledge, the environment, and school genres, standards and curricula set by their school district. However the teacher rarely considers the ways to free the students from the system of alienation put into place to provide more space for autonomy and deep learning.

Teacher talk: The language teachers use when teaching; involves simplifying speech for students; it may be detrimental to learning if it is childish or not close to the natural production of the target language.

Teaching: the purposeful direction and management of fruitful conditions for deep learning processes to happen.

Thematic Unit: Lessons complimenting and working together under one common topic, often cross curricular. Thematic units are designed using content as the organizing principle. Vocabulary, structures, and cultural information are included as they relate to the themes in each unit.

Whole language: A term used by reading teachers to describe an instructional philosophy which focuses on reading as an activity best taught in a broader context of meaning. Rather than focusing on reading as a mechanical skill, it is taught as an ongoing part of every student's existing language and life experience. Building on language skills each student already possesses, reading and writing are seen as a part of a broader "whole language" spectrum.

Wisdom: Intangible quality gained through experience, ability to make correct judgments and decisions, foreseeing consequences and acting to maximize beneficial results. From a complex system theory perspective, wisdom would be the attainment of homeostatic equilibrium, the balance between opposites. Wisdom is pragmatically determined by common sense, cultural, philosophical and spiritual sources.

Writing: (a) Inscribing characters on a medium, with the intention of forming words or concepts and record information in natural language or in coded form; (b) creation of materials conveyed through written language. Both activities may occur at the same time.

Workshop: Brief intensive hands-on seminar or series of meetings emphasizing interaction and exchange among a small number of participants.

DEEP UNIVERSITY PRESS
SCIENTIFIC BOARD MEMBERS

Dr. Araceli Alonso, Global Health Institute, Department of Gender and Women's Studies, University of Wisconsin-Madison, USA

Dr. Ronald C. Arnett, Chair and Professor, Department of Communication & Rhetorical Studies, Duquesne University

Dr. Gilles Baillat, Rector, ex-Director of CDIUFM Conference of French Teacher Education Directors, University of Reims, France

Dr. Niels Brouwer, Graduate School of Education, Radboud Universiteit Nijmegen, The Netherlands

Dr. Jianlin Chen, Shanghai International Studies University, China

Dr. Yuangshan Chuang, President of APAMALL, NETPAW Director, Tajen University, Taiwan, ROC

Dr. Enrique Correa Molina, Professor and Vice-Dean, Faculty of Education, University of Sherbrooke, Canada

Dr. José Correia, Dean of Education, University of Porto, Portugal

Dr. Muhammet Demirbilek, Head, Educational Science Department, Suleyman Demirel University, Isparta, Turkey

Dr. Ángel Díaz-Barriga Casales, Professor, Autonomous National University of México UNAM (Mexico)

Dr. Isabelle C. Druc, Department of Anthropology, University of Wisconsin-Madison, USA

Bertha Du-Babcock, Professor, Department of English for Business, City University of Hong Kong, Hong Kong, China

Dr. W. John Coletta , Professor, University of Wisconsin-Stevens Point, USA

Marc Durand, Professor, Faculty of Psychology and Education, University of Geneva, Switzerland

Dr. Paul Durning, Doctoral School, French National Observatory, EUSARF, University of Paris X Nanterre, Paris, France

Dr. Manuel Fernandez Cruz, Professor, University of Granada, Spain

Dr. Stephanie Fonvielle, Associate Professor, Teacher Education University Institute, University of Aix-Marseille, France

Dr. Elliot Gaines, Professor, Wright State University, President of the Semiotic Society of America, Internat. Communicology Institute

Dr. Mingle Gao, Dean, College of Education, Beijing Language and Culture University (BLCU), Beijing, China

Dr. Mercedes González Sanmamed, Professor at the University of Coruña, Spain

Dr. Gabriela Hernández Vega, Professor, University of Nariño, Colombia

Dr. Teresa Langle de Paz, Autonomous University, Feminist Research Institute Council, Complutense University of Madrid, Spain

Dr. Xiang Long, Guilin University of Electronic Technology, China

Dr. Maria Masucci, Drew University, New Jersey, USA

Dr. Liliana Morandi, Associate Professor, National University of Rio Cuarto, Cordoba, Argentina

Dr. Joëlle Morrissette, Professor, Department of Educational Psychology, Université of Montreal, Quebec, Canada

Dr. Martha Murzi Vivas, Professor, University of Los Andes, Venezuela

Dr. Thi Cuc Phuong Nguyen, Vice Rector, Hanoi University, Vietnam

Dr. Shirley O'Neill, Associate Professor, President of the International Society for leadership in Pedagogies and Learning, University of Southern Queensland, Australia

Dr. José-Luis Ortega, Professor, Foreign Language Education, Faculty of Education, University of Granada, Spain

Dr. Surendra Pathak, Head and Professor, Department of Value Education, IASE University of Gandhi Viday Mandir, India

Dr. Charls Pearson, Logic, Semiotics, Philosophy of Science, Peirce Studies, Director of Research, Semiotics Research Institute

Dr. Luis Porta Vázquez, Professor at the National University of Mar del Plata CONICET (Argentina)

Dr. Shen Qi, Associate Professor, Shanghai Foreign Studies University (SHISU), Shanghai, China

Dr. Timothy Reagan, Professor and Dean of the College of Education at Zayed University in Abu Dhabi/Dubai, Saudi Arabia

Dr. Antonia Schleicher, Professor, NARLC Director, NCTOLCTL Exec. Director, ACTFL Board, Indiana University-Bloomington, USA

Dr. Farouk Y. Seif, Exec. Director of the Semiotic Society of America, Center for Creative Change, Antioch University Seattle, Washington

Dr. Gary Shank, Professor, Educational Foundations and Leadership, Duquesne University, Pittsburgh, Pennsylvania

Dr. Kemal Silay, Professor, Flagship Program Director, Department of Central Eurasia, Indiana University-Bloomington, USA

Dr. José Tejada Fernández, Professor at the Autonomous University of Barcelona, Spain

Dr. François Victor Tochon, Professor, University of Wisconsin-Madison, President of the International Network for Language Education Policy Studies, USA

Dr. Brooke Williams Deely, Women, Culture and Society Program, Philosophy Department, University of St. Thomas, Houston

Dr. Jianfang Xiao, Associate Professor at School of English and Education, Guangdong University of Foreign Studies, China

Dr. Ronghui Zhao, Director, Institute of Linguistic Studies, Shanghai Foreign Studies University, Shanghai, China

Other referees may be contacted depending the Book Series or the nature and topic of the manuscript proposed.

Contact: publisher@deepuniversity.net

Language Education Policy Book Series

Language Education Policy (LEP) is the process through which the ideals, goals, and contents of a language policy can be realized in education practices. Language policies express ideological processes. Their analysis reveals the perceptions of realities proper to certain sociocultural contexts. LEPs further their ideologies by defining and disseminating the values of policymakers. Because Language Education Policies are related to status, ideology, and vision of what society should be and traditions of thoughts, such issues are complex, quickly evolving, submitted to trends and political views, and they need to be studied calmly. The way to approach them is to get comparative information on what has been done in many settings, which are working or not, which are their flaws and merits, and try to grasp the contextual variables that might apply in specific locations, without generalizing too fast.

Policy discourses and curricula reveal the ideological framing of the constructs that they encode and create, project, enact, and enforce aspects such as language status, power and rights through projective texts generated to forward and describe the contexts of their enactments. Policy documents are therefore socially transformative through their evaluative function that frames and guides action in order to achieve language reforms. While temperance and reflection are required to address such complex issues, because moving to fast may create trouble, nonetheless the absence of action in this domain may lead to systemic intolerance, injustice, inequity, mass discrimination and even, genocidal crimes.

http://www.deepuniversitypress.org/language-education-policy.html

Deep Language Learning Book Series

Language learning needs to be reconceptualized in two ways: first, as an expression of dynamic planning prototypes that can be activated through self-directed projects. Second, integrating structure and agency to meet deeper, humane aims. The dynamism of human exchange is meaning- producing through multiple connected intentions among language task domains.

Language-learning tasks have a cross-cultural purpose which then become meaningful within broader projects that meet higher values and aims such as deep ecology, deep culture, deep politics and deep humane economics. Applied semiotics will be a tool beyond the linguistic in favor of value-loaded projects that are chosen in order to revolutionize the current state of affairs, in increasing our sense of responsibility for our actions as humans vis-à-vis our fellow humans and our home planet. In this respect, deep instructional planning offers a grammar for action. Understanding adaptive and complex cross-cultural situations is the prime focus of such a hermeneutic inquiry.

For more, see here:

http://www.deepuniversitypress.org/deep-language-learning.html

Out of Havana:
Memoirs of Ordinary Life in Cuba

Dr. Araceli Alonso
University of Wisconsin-Madison

Out of Havana provides an uncommon ordinary woman's insight into the last half century of Cuba's tumultuous recent history. More powerfully than an academic study or historical account, it allows us intimately to grasp the enthusiasm, commitment and sense of promise that defined many average Cubans' experience of the 1959 Revolution and the first triumphant decades of the Castro regime. As the story shifts into the final decades of the last century (the 1980s Mariel Boatlift, the so-called "special period in time of peace" [from 1991 to the end of the decade], and the 1994 Balseros or Rafters Crisis), it starts gradually to reveal, with understated yet relentless eloquence, an ultimately insuperable rift between the high-flown official rhetoric of uncompromising struggle and revolutionary sacrifice and the harsh conditions and cruelly absurd situations that the protagonist, along with the majority of Cubans, begin routinely to live out. It is a rare and important document, a unique personal chronicle of an everyday Cuban reality that most Americans continue to know only fragmentarily.

Dr. Araceli Alonso is a 2013 United Nations Award Winner for her activism on women's health and women right. Associate Faculty at the University of Wisconsin-Madison in the Department of Gender and Women's Studies and in the School of Medicine and Public Health, she is the Founder and Director of the award-winning non-profit organization Health by Motorbike.

http://deepuniversitypress.org/havana.html

PERFORMING THE ART OF
LANGUAGE LEARNING
Deepening the Learning Experience through Theatre and Drama

Dr. Kelly Kingsbury Brunetto
University of Nebraska-Lincoln, USA

Truly innovative, *Performing the Art of Language Learning* delivers an exhaustive account of the role theater can and should play in second language acquisition. Kingsbury-Brunetto makes a compelling case for the integration of the performing arts within foreign language and literature departments. This will surely be an influential study for the advancement of the field.
– *Florent Masse, Director, L'Avant-Scène,
The French Theater Workshop, Princeton University, U.S.A.*

This is a well-researched and beautifully written text investigating how engagement with theater in courses designed for language acquisition and development can enhance undergraduate university students' learning. Grounded in Bakhtinian notions regarding discourse practices and Van Lier's ecological approach to second language acquisition, Professor Kingsbury Brunetto has produced a theory-rich book that also is highly readable and enjoyable. The text is methodologically rigorous and rich in detail concerning students' understandings and interactions with one another, their faculty members, the plays they enacted, and their audiences. Also included after each chapter are questions for readers' critical reflection that should produce complex discussions among readers, and especially will be helpful in graduate classes in both second language acquisition and theater.
– *Mary Louise Gomez, Professor, Languages and Literacies,
Teacher Education, University of Wisconsin-Madison, U.S.A*

I find the book very inspiring and valuable. I have been using drama and theatre in language courses for fifteen years and I still continue to expand my comprehension of their enormous potential for learning. Dr.Kingsbury Brunetto's thoroughly crafted work is a much appreciated addition to my growing understanding of the manifold processes that make the learning happen. We absolutely need research projects like this one to help drama and theatre assume a more central position in the language teaching world.
– *Barbora Müller Dočkalová, Faculty of Education, Charles University
in Prague, Czech Republic*

http://www.deepuniversitypress.org/performing.html

Science Teachers Who Draw: The *Red* Is Always There

Dr. Merrie Koester
Project Draw for Science
Center for Science Education
University of South Carolina

This book documents the ways in which science teacher researchers used drawing to construct semiotic spaces inside which students acquired significant aesthetic capital and agency. Many previously failing students brokered this new capital into improved academic achievement and a sense of felt freedom.

Science Teachers Who Draw: The Red is Always There is a book which asks, "What happens when science teachers adopt an *aesthetic* approach to inquiry, using drawing to communicate deep understanding?" This narrative inquiry was driven by quantitative studies which reveal a robust positive correlation between students' test scores in reading and science, beginning at the middle school level. When the data are disaggregated, there exists a vast achievement gap for low income and English language learners. Science teachers are faced with a semiotic nightmare. Often possessing inadequate pedagogical content knowledge themselves, science teachers must somehow symbolically *communicate* often highly abstract knowledge in ways that can be not only be decoded by their students' but later used to construct deeper, more differentiated knowledge, which can be applied to make sense of and adapt successfully to life on Planet Earth.

An invaluable resource for teachers, teacher educators, and qualitative researchers.

http://www.deepuniversitypress.org/red.html

SIGNS AND SYMBOLS IN EDUCATION
EDUCATIONAL SEMIOTICS

François Victor Tochon, Ph.D.
University of Wisconsin-Madison, USA

In this monograph on Educational Semiotics, Francois Tochon (along with a number of research colleagues) has produced a work that is truly groundbreaking on a number of fronts. First of all, in his concise but brilliant introductory comments, Tochon clearly debunks the potential notion that semiotics might provide yet another methodological tool in the toolkit of educational researchers. Drawing skillfully on the work of Peirce, Deely, Sebeok, Merrell, and others, Tochon shows us just how fundamentally different semiotic research can be when compared to the modes and techniques that have dominated educational research for many decades. That is, he points out how semiotic methods can provide the capability for both students and researchers to look at this basic and fundamental human process in inescapably transformational ways, by acknowledging and accepting that the path to knowledge is, in his words "through the fixation of belief."

But he does not stop there – instead, in four brilliantly conceived studies, he shows us how semiotic concepts in general, and semiotic mapping in particular, can allow both student teachers and researchers alike insights in these students' development of insights and concepts into the very heart of the teaching and learning process. By tackling both theoretical and practical research considerations, Tochon has provided the rest of us the beginnings of a blueprint that, if adopted, can push educational research out of (in the words of Deely) its entrenchment in the Age of Ideas into the new and exciting frontiers of the Age of Signs.

Gary Shank
Duquesne University

http://www.deepuniversity.net/book1.htm

FROM TRANSNATIONAL LANGUAGE POLICY TRANSFER TO LOCAL APPROPRIATION

The case of the National Bilingual Program in Medellín, Colombia

Dr. Jaime Usma Wilches
University of Antioquia

Drawing on the example of Medellín, Colombia, Jaime Usma's book does a magnificent work at dismantling one of the most pervasive grand narratives in globalized transnational foreign language policies: proficiency in English as one of the strongest pillars of a vibrant modern knowledge society, associated with higher economic gains for all. The author cogently demonstrates how apparently neutral and technically sound transnational and national policymaking fails to properly address structural inequality and social and economic injustice, while being creatively reenacted by local schools and actors that appropriate them according to their own goals, needs, and desires towards a more just and humane society.

—*Maria Alfredo Moreira, University of Minho, Portugal*

World wide there is a growing awareness that properly explanatory accounts of language education policy must fuse national and local perspectives, questions of structure and argument, evidence and debate and of course the various interests of the diverse players involved.

Dr Jaime Usma has made a notable contribution to this more sophisticated approach to LP with this excellent and internationally relevant analysis of Colombia's national government policy, the appropriation/adaptation of central policy in the city of Medellín and the views, experiences and accounts of teachers, officials, experts and communities and transnational agencies. In addition to its LP relevance the book has much to say about how English is constituted in an increasing number of settings globally and how claims and counterclaims about global English resonate at different levels and among different interests. All in all an excellent and worthwhile volume.

—*Joseph Lo Bianco, Professor of Language and Literacy Education, The University of Melbourne, Australia*

http://www.deepuniversitypress.org/medellin.html

Guide for Authors

What our Publishing Team can offer:

- An international editorial team, in more than 20 universities around the world.

- Dedicated and experienced topic editors who will review and provide feedback on your initial proposal.

- A specific format that will speed up the production of your book and its publication.

- Higher royalties than most publishers and a discount on batch orders.

- Global distribution and marketing through Amazon and Barnes & Noble in the U.S., UK, Australia, Europe, China, and many other countries.

- Fair recognition of your work in your area of specialization.

- Quality design. Using the latest technology, our books are produced efficiently, quickly and attractively.

- A global marketing plan, including electronic and web marketing and review mailing.

- Book Series: Archaeological Depth; Deep Activism; Deep Education; Deep Early Childhood Education; Deep Language Learning; Deep Professional Development; Deep Research Methodologies; Inclusive Education and Partnerships; Language Education Policy; Life in Signs & Symbols.

http://www.deepuniversitypress.com/universitypress.html

Contact : publisher@deepuniversity.net

Deep University Online !

For updates and more resources
Visit the Deep University Website:

www.deepuniversity.net

www.depuniversitypress.org

Contact : publisher@deepuniversity.net

❖ Online Certificate and Courses on Deep Education:
http://www.deepuniversity.net

Correspondence:

Deep University Press
10,657 Mayflower Road
Blue Mounds, WI 53517 USA

www.ingramcontent.com/pod-product-compliance
Lightning Source LLC
Chambersburg PA
CBHW031936290426
44108CB00011B/580